The Oxford Intermediate Dictionary

Compiled by
A.J. Augarde

Oxford University Press 1981

Oxford University Press, Walton Street, Oxford OX2 6DP

London   Glasgow   New York   Toronto
Delhi   Bombay   Calcutta   Madras   Karachi
Kuala Lumpur   Singapore   Hong Kong   Tokyo
Nairobi   Dar es Salaam   Cape Town   Salisbury
Melbourne   Wellington

and associate companies in
Beirut   Berlin   Ibadan   Mexico City

British Library Cataloguing in Publication Data

Augarde, Tony
 Oxford intermediate dictionary.
 1. English language – Dictionaries
 I. Title
 423   PE1625   80–41569

 ISBN 0 –19 – 910218 – X (Trade Edition)
 ISBN 0 – 19 – 910217 – 1 (School Edition)

Set in Helvetica and Ionic by
Tradespools Limited,
Frome, Somerset
and printed in
Hong Kong

Introduction

This dictionary explains the meaning of more than 12,000 words and helps you to spell and pronounce them properly.

The entries for each word are arranged in this order:

1. The word that is being explained, printed in **thick** letters.
2. In *italics*, its part of speech, which can be any of the following:

   an adjective, a word that describes a noun or adds to its meaning, such as **happy, important, old**

   an adverb, a word that tells you how, when, where, or why something happens, such as **again, here, together**

   a conjunction, a joining word, such as **and, but, whether**

   an interjection, a word used as an exclamation, such as **ah, eh, hallo**

   a noun, a word that is the name of a thing or person, such as **child, danger, tree**

   a preposition, a word put in front of a noun or pronoun to show how the noun or pronoun is connected with another word, such as **against, in, on**

   a pronoun, a word used instead of a noun, such as **it, me, they**

   a verb, a word that says what someone or something does or feels, such as **come, eat, know.**

   Where two different words are spelt the same and have the same part of speech, they are labelled as *noun*[1] and *noun*[2], *verb*[1] and *verb*[2], etc. as under **cape** and **tap.**

3. In brackets in **thick** letters, any forms of the word which are not spelt in the way you might expect:

   (*a*) for *adjectives* and *adverbs* – when the comparative and superlative are *not* made by just adding -er and -est.

   (*b*) for *nouns* – when there is a plural and it is *not* made by just adding -s.

   (*c*) for *verbs* – when the past tense and past participle are *not* made by just adding -ed.

   (*d*) for *verbs* – when the present participle is *not* made by just adding -ing.

4. If a word is difficult to say, there is help in brackets on the next line.
5. The definition, explaining what the word means. When the word means more than one thing, the different senses are numbered 1, 2, and so on. Some words are marked '*informal*' or '*slang*' to warn you that these words can only be used safely in some kinds of writing or speaking.
6. Sometimes there is a sentence or phrase in *italics*, to give you an idea of how the word can be used.
7. In **thick** letters on a new line, any common words derived from or connected with the main word.

Pronunciation

For a word which is hard to pronounce, a guide is given in brackets after '*say*' to show how it should be spoken. The syllable you *stress* in pronouncing the word is shown in **thick** letters, for example '(*say* al-**say**-shăn)'. When a guide is given to the pronunciation, the letters sound like this:

a	as in **a**nd, b**a**t, c**a**t	ŏ	as in lem**o**n, c**o**rrect, t**o**gether	
ă	as in **a**bove, **a**go, centr**a**l			
ah	as in c**al**m, f**a**ther, l**au**gh	oh	as in m**o**st, b**oa**t, g**o**	
air	as in f**air**, c**are**, th**ere**	oi	as in j**oi**n, v**oi**ce, b**oy**	
ar	as in **ar**m, b**ar**, **are**	oo	as in s**oo**n, b**oo**t, **oo**ze	
aw	as in l**aw**, p**aw**, s**aw**	oor	as in p**oor**, m**oor**, t**our**	
ay	as in pl**ay**, **a**ge, f**a**ce	or	as in f**or**, m**ore**, h**or**se	
b	as in **b**at, ha**b**it, ro**b**	ow	as in c**ow**, h**ow**, **ou**t	
ch	as in **ch**in, **ch**ur**ch**, whi**ch**	p	as in **p**en, **p**ig, hi**p**	
d	as in **d**ay, un**d**er, ha**d**	r	as in **r**ed, **r**oad, t**r**y	
e	as in b**e**d, t**e**n, **e**gg	s	as in **s**it, **s**o, ye**s**	
ĕ	as in tak**e**n, rott**e**n, sil**e**nt	sh	as in **sh**op, **sh**e, fi**sh**	
ee	as in m**ee**t, s**ee**, **ea**ch	t	as in **t**op, in**t**o, no**t**	
eer	as in b**eer**, ch**eer**, n**ear**	th	as in **th**in, me**th**od, bo**th**	
er	as in h**er**, b**ir**d, p**ur**se	*th*	as in **th**is, ei**th**er, **th**ose	
ew	as in f**ew**, d**ew**, b**eau**ty	u	as in b**u**n, c**u**p, **u**p	
ewr	as in c**ure**, p**ure**, end**ure**	ŭ	as in circ**u**s, bon**u**s, preci**ou**s	
f	as in **f**at, le**f**t, i**f**			
g	as in **g**et, wa**g**on, do**g**	uu	as in b**oo**k, l**oo**k, p**u**ll	
h	as in **h**at, **h**is, **h**ow	v	as in **v**an, ri**v**er, ha**v**e	
i	as in p**i**n, s**i**t, **i**s	w	as in **w**as, **w**ill, **w**ish	
ĭ	as in penc**i**l, bas**i**n, commun**i**ty	y	as in **y**ard, **y**es, **y**ou or when it follows a consonant = I as in cr**y**, realize	
I	as in **eye**, cr**y**, l**igh**t			
j	as in **j**am, **j**ob, en**j**oy	yoo	as in **yo**u, **u**nit, v**iew**	
k	as in **k**ing, see**k**, **c**at	yoor	as in E**u**ropean, man**ure**, d**ur**able	
l	as in **l**eg, a**l**so, wi**ll**			
m	as in **m**an, **m**e, fro**m**	yr	as in f**ire**, w**ire**, sp**ire**	
n	as in **n**ot, ha**n**d, o**n**	z	as in **z**oo, la**z**y, rai**se**	
ng	as in si**ng**, fi**ng**er, thi**ng**	zh	as in divi**s**ion, vi**s**ion, mea**s**ure	
nk	as in tha**nk**, pi**nk**, ta**nk**			
o	as in g**o**t, t**o**p, **o**n			

A consonant is sometimes doubled to make the pronunciation clearer, for example '(*say* **ass**-mă)'. The pronunciation is sometimes shown by giving a well-known word that rhymes with it.

I am grateful to the teachers and others who gave advice and help in planning this dictionary, to Mrs Anne Whear for her typing, and to Michael Grose, Alan Spooner, and Julia Swannell for their help in proof-reading.

A.J.A.

A

a *adjective* (called the *indefinite article*)
1 one; any. *Can you lend me a book?* **2** each; every. *I go there twice a month.*

abacus *noun* (**abacuses** or **abaci**)
a frame for counting with beads sliding on wires.

abandon *verb*
to give up; to leave something without intending to return. *Abandon ship!*

abbey *noun*
1 a group of buildings where monks or nuns live and work. **2** a community of monks or nuns. **3** a church which is or was part of an abbey. *Westminster Abbey.*

abbot *noun*
the head of an abbey of monks.

abbreviate *verb* (**abbreviated, abbreviating**)
to shorten something.

abbreviation *noun*
something shortened, especially a word.

ABC *noun*
the alphabet.

abdomen *noun*
1 the part of the body that contains the stomach. **2** the rear part of the body of an insect, spider, etc.
abdominal *adjective*

abide *verb* (**abode** or **abided, abiding**)
1 (*old-fashioned use*) to stay. **2** to tolerate. *I can't abide noise.* **3 abide by,** to keep a promise, etc.

able *adjective* (**abler, ablest**)
1 having the power, skill, or opportunity to do something. **2** skilful; clever.
ability *noun,* **ably** *adverb*

abnormal *adjective*
not normal; unusual.
abnormality *noun*

aboard *adverb*
on a ship or an aircraft.

abode *noun*
the place where someone lives.

abode past tense and past participle of **abide.**

abolish *verb*
to get rid of a law, custom, etc.

abolition *noun*
(*say* ab-ŏ-**lish**-ŏn)
abolishing something, especially capital punishment or slavery.
abolitionist *noun*

abominable *adjective*
1 awful; disgusting. **2 abominable snowman,** a yeti.

aborigines *plural noun*
(*say* ab-er-**ij**-in-eez)
1 the original inhabitants of a country. **2 Aborigines,** the original inhabitants of Australia.
aboriginal *adjective* and *noun*

abortion *noun*
removal of a baby from the womb before it has developed fully enough to live.

abound *verb*
to be plentiful.

about *preposition*
1 on the subject of; in connection with. *This film is about the police.* **2** all round; in various parts of. *They ran about the playground.* **3** near to; more or less. *She's about five feet tall.* **4 about to,** going to. *He was about to sing.*

about *adverb*
1 in various directions or places. *They were running about.* **2** somewhere nearby.

above *preposition*
1 higher than. **2** more than. **3 above-board,** honest.

above *adverb*
at or to a higher place.

abrasive *adjective*
that scrapes or grazes.

abreast *adverb*
1 side by side. **2** keeping up with. *We must be abreast of modern discoveries.*

abroad *adverb*
in or to another country.

abrupt *adjective*
sudden; hasty.

abscess *noun* (**abscesses**)
a collection of pus in the body.

absent *adjective*
1 not here; away. **2 absent-minded,** forgetful; not attentive.
absence *noun,* **absent-mindedly** *adverb*

absentee *noun*
someone who is not at school, work, etc.
absenteeism *noun*

absolute *adjective*
complete; not restricted.

absolutely *adverb*
1 completely. **2** (*informal*) yes; I agree.

absorb *verb*
1 to soak up. **2** to be very interesting to somebody. *This book is absorbing.*
absorbent *adjective,* **absorption** *noun*

abstract *adjective*
(*say* **ab**-strakt)
concerned with ideas, not with things.

abstract *verb*
(*say* ăb-**strakt**)
1 to take away. **2** to summarize.

abstract *noun*
(*say* **ab**-strakt)
a summary.

absurd *adjective*
ridiculous.
absurdity *noun*

abundance *noun*
plenty. *an abundance of good things.*

abundant *adjective*
plentiful.

abuse *verb* **(abused, abusing)**
(*say* ă-**bewz**)
1 to misuse. **2** to say unpleasant things about somebody.
abusive *adjective*

abuse *noun*
(*say* ă-**bewss**)
words abusing somebody or something.

academic *adjective*
1 theoretical; abstract. **2** scholarly.

academy *noun* **(academies)**
1 a college or school. **2** a society concerned with art or learning.

accelerate *verb* **(accelerated, accelerating)**
to make or become quicker.
acceleration *noun*

accelerator *noun*
a pedal that you press down to make a motor vehicle go faster.

accent *noun*
(*say* **ak**-sĕnt)
1 the way that you pronounce words. **2** accenting a word. *The accent in 'spider' is on the first syllable.* **3** a mark put over a letter to show its pronunciation. *The accent on café is an acute accent.*

accent *verb*
(*say* ăk-**sent**)
to pronounce part of a word more strongly than the other parts.

accept *verb*
to take something which is offered.
acceptance *noun*

acceptable *adjective*
worth accepting; pleasing.

access *noun* **(accesses)**
a way to reach something.

accessible *adjective*
easy to reach.
accessibility *noun*

accessory *noun* **(accessories)**
1 an extra or spare part. **2** someone who helps to commit a crime.

accident *noun*
1 an unexpected event, especially one in which someone is killed or injured. **2 by accident,** unintentionally.

accidental *adjective*
unintentional; unexpected.
accidentally *adverb*

acclaim *verb*
to welcome or applaud someone enthusiastically.
acclamation *noun*

acclimatize *verb* **(acclimatized, acclimatizing)**
to make or become used to a new climate, environment, etc.
acclimatization *noun*

accommodate *verb*
(accommodated, accommodating)
1 to provide a room or lodging for somebody.

2 to help somebody.
accommodation *noun*

accompany *verb* **(accompanied, accompanying)**
1 to go somewhere with somebody. **2** to play music that supports a singer, etc.
accompaniment *noun*, **accompanist** *noun*

accomplish *verb*
to do something successfully; to reach something.
accomplishment *noun*

accomplished *adjective*
skilful.

accord *noun*
1 agreement. **2 of your own accord,** voluntarily; without being asked or told to do something.

accord *verb*
to agree.
accordance *noun*

according *adverb*
1 according to, in the opinion of; as stated by. *According to him, we are stupid.* **2 according to,** in a way that suits. *Price the apples according to their size.*

accordingly *adverb*
1 consequently; therefore. **2** in a suitable way.

accordion *noun*
a portable musical instrument like a large concertina.
accordionist *noun*

account *noun*
1 a statement of money owed, spent, or received; a bill. **2** an arrangement to keep money in a bank, etc. **3** a description or story. **4** consideration. *Take it into account.* **5 on account of,** because of. **6 on no account,** certainly not.

account *verb*
1 to record how money has been spent. **2 account for,** to make it clear why something happens.

accountant *noun*
an expert in accounting, finance, etc.
accountancy *noun*

accumulate *verb* **(accumulated, accumulating)**
to collect; to pile up.
accumulation *noun*

accurate *adjective*
correct; exact.
accuracy *noun*

accuse *verb* **(accused, accusing)**
to say that somebody has committed a crime, etc.; to blame.
accusation *noun*

accustom *verb*
1 to make somebody used to something. **2 accustomed,** usual; normal. *I sat in my accustomed chair.*

ace *noun*
1 the card of highest or lowest value in each suit of a pack of cards. **2** a very skilful person or thing.

ache *noun*
a dull or continuous pain.

ache *verb* **(ached, aching)**
to have an ache.

address

achieve *verb* **(achieved, achieving)**
to accomplish. *She achieved her ambition.*
achievement *noun*

acid *noun*
(*in Chemistry*) a substance that contains hydrogen and neutralizes alkalis.
acidic *adjective*, **acidity** *noun*

acid *adjective*
sour. *This fruit has an acid taste.*

acknowledge *verb*
(acknowledged, acknowledging)
1 to admit that something is true. **2** to say that you have received a letter, etc. **3** to express thanks for something.
acknowledgement *noun*

acne *noun*
(*say* **ak**-ni)
red pimples on the face.

acorn *noun*
the seed of the oak-tree.

acoustic *adjective*
(*say* ă-**koo**-stik)
1 of sound or hearing. **2** (of a musical instrument) not electronic. *an acoustic guitar.*

acoustics *noun*
1 the qualities of a place which make it good or bad for sound. *This hall has bad acoustics.*
2 the science of sound.

acquaint *verb*
1 to tell somebody about something. *Acquaint him with the facts.* **2 be acquainted with,** to know somebody slightly.
acquaintance *noun*

acquire *verb* **(acquired, acquiring)**
to obtain.
acquisition *noun*

acquisitive *adjective*
keen to obtain things.

acquit *verb* **(acquitted, acquitting)**
to decide that someone is not guilty.
acquittal *noun*

acre *noun*
(*say* **ay**-ker)
a piece of land measuring 4,840 square yards.
acreage *noun*

acrobat *noun*
a performer of spectacular gymnastic feats.
acrobatic *adjective*, **acrobatics** *plural noun*

across *preposition* and *adverb*
1 from one side of a thing to the other. **2** to or on the other side of something.

act *noun*
1 an action. **2** a law passed by parliament. **3** one of the main parts of a play or opera. *An act usually includes several scenes.* **4** a short performance in a programme of entertainment. *a juggling act.* **5** a pretence. *She is only putting on an act.*

act *verb*
1 to do something. **2** to take a part in a play, film, etc. **3** to function; to have an effect.

action *noun*
1 doing something; something that has been done. **2** the part that makes a gun, musical instrument, etc. work. **3** a battle; fighting. *He*
was killed in action. **4 out of action,** not working properly. **5 take action,** to do something.

activate *verb* **(activated, activating)**
to start something working.

active *adjective*
1 doing things; taking part in activities. **2** functioning. *an active volcano.* **3** of the type of verb which affects the object. *In 'He hit me' the verb is active; in 'I was hit' the verb is passive.*

activity *noun* **(activities)**
1 an action or occupation. *outdoor activities.*
2 being active or lively.

actor *noun*
a performer in a play, film, etc.

actress *noun* **(actresses)**
a female actor.

actual *adjective*
real.
actually *adverb*

acupuncture *noun*
pricking parts of the body with needles to relieve pain or cure disease.

acute *adjective* **(acuter, acutest)**
1 sharp; strong. *acute pain.* **2 acute accent,** the mark ´ put over a letter, as in *café.* **3 acute angle,** an angle less than 90 degrees.

A.D. short for *Anno Domini,* of a year counted from the birth of Jesus Christ. *Columbus reached America in A.D. 1492.*

Adam's apple *noun*
the lump at the front of a man's neck.

adapt *verb*
to make or become suitable for a new purpose.
adaptable *adjective*, **adaptation** *noun*

adaptor *noun*
a device to connect pieces of electrical equipment.

add *verb*
1 to put one thing with another. **2 add to,** to increase. **3 add up,** to make or find a total; (*informal*) to make sense.

adder *noun*
a small poisonous snake.

addict *noun*
someone who does or uses something that he cannot give up. *a drug addict.*
addicted *adjective*, **addiction** *noun*, **addictive** *adjective*.

addition *noun*
1 the action of adding. **2** something added. **3 in addition,** also.
additional *adjective*

additive *noun*
something added to food, etc. in small amounts.

address *noun* **(addresses)**
1 the details of the place where someone lives. *My address is 29 High Street, Newtown.* **2** a speech.

address *verb*
1 to write an address on a letter, parcel, etc.
2 to make a speech, remark, etc. to somebody.

adenoids *plural noun*
spongy flesh at the back of the nose, which may hinder breathing.

adequate *adjective*
enough; suitable. *The food is not adequate.*

adhere *verb* **(adhered, adhering)**
to stick or join to something.

adhesive *adjective*
causing things to stick together.
adhesion *noun*

adhesive *noun*
a glue.

adjacent *adjective*
near or next. *Her house is adjacent to the shop.*

adjective *noun*
a word that describes a noun or adds to its meaning. (Adjectives are words like *big, honest,* and *strange*.)

adjourn *verb*
(say à-**jern**)
1 to break off a meeting, etc. until a later time. 2 to move to another place.
adjournment *noun*

adjudicate *verb* **(adjudicated, adjudicating)**
(say à-**joo**-dik-ayt)
to act as judge in a competition, etc.
adjudication *noun,* **adjudicator** *noun*

adjust *verb*
to put something into its proper position or order; to arrange.
adjuster *noun,* **adjustment** *noun*

ad-lib *adjective* and *adverb*
without any rehearsal or preparation.

administer *verb*
1 to administrate. 2 to give formally. *He administered the punishment.*

administrate *verb*
(administrated, administrating)
to manage a business, etc.; to govern.
administration *noun,* **administrative** *adjective,*
administrator *noun*

admirable *adjective*
excellent; worth admiring.
admirably *adverb*

admiral *noun*
a naval officer of high rank.

admire *verb* **(admired, admiring)**
1 to think someone or something is very good, beautiful, etc. 2 to look at something and enjoy it.
admiration *noun,* **admirer** *noun*

admit *verb* **(admitted, admitting)**
1 to let someone come in. 2 to agree or confess.
admission *noun,* **admittance** *noun*

admittedly *adverb*
as an agreed fact; without doubt.

ado *noun*
fuss; excitement.

adolescence *noun*
the time between being a child and being an adult; your teens.
adolescent *noun* and *adjective*

adopt *verb*
1 to take somebody into your family and treat him as your child. 2 to accept something.
adoption *noun,* **adoptive** *adjective*

adore *verb* **(adored, adoring)**
to love very much.
adorable *adjective,* **adoration** *noun*

adorn *verb*
to decorate.
adornment *noun*

adrenalin *noun*
a hormone that stimulates the nervous system.

adrift *adverb* and *adjective*
drifting. *The boat was adrift.*

adult *noun*
someone who is fully grown.

adultery *noun* **(adulteries)**
(say à-**dul**-ter-i)
being unfaithful to your wife or husband by having sexual intercourse with someone else.
adulterer *noun,* **adulterous** *adjective*

advance *noun*
1 a forward movement; progress. 2 a loan. 3 **in advance,** beforehand. 4 **in advance of,** before.

advance *verb* **(advanced, advancing)**
to make an advance.

advanced *adjective*
1 far on in progress, life, etc. *an advanced age.* 2 not elementary. *an examination at advanced level.*

advantage *noun*
1 something useful or helpful. 2 **take advantage of,** to use profitably or unfairly. 3 **to your advantage,** profitable or helpful to you.
advantageous *adjective*

Advent *noun*
1 the coming of Jesus Christ. 2 the period before Christmas.

adventure *noun*
1 an exciting or dangerous experience. 2 taking risks; danger. *He likes adventure.*
adventurous *adjective*

adverb *noun*
a word that tells you how, when, where, or why something happens. (Adverbs are words like *easily, outdoors,* and *soon*.)
adverbial *adjective*

adversary *noun* **(adversaries)**
an opponent or enemy.

adverse *adjective*
unfavourable; harmful. *The drug had adverse effects.*

adversity *noun* **(adversities)**
misfortune; trouble.

advertise *verb* **(advertised, advertising)**
to make something publicly known; to praise goods hoping that people will buy them.
advertisement *noun,* **advertiser** *noun*

advice *noun*
1 something said to somebody to help him decide what to do. 2 a piece of information.

advisable *adjective*
sensible; worth doing.
advisability *noun*

advise *verb* **(advised, advising)**
to give somebody advice; to recommend.
adviser *noun*, **advisory** *adjective*

advocate *noun*
(*say* ad-vŏ-kăt)
a person who speaks in favour of someone or something.

advocate *verb* **(advocated, advocating)**
(*say* ad-vŏ-kayt)
to act as an advocate for something.

aerial *adjective*
of or by the air or aircraft.

aerial *noun*
a wire, rod, etc. for receiving or transmitting radio or television waves.

aerobatics *plural noun*
spectacular feats of flying aircraft.
aerobatic *adjective*

aerodrome *noun*
an airfield.

aeronautics *plural noun*
the study of aircraft and flying.
aeronautic *adjective*, **aeronautical** *adjective*

aeroplane *noun*
a flying machine with wings.

aerosol *noun*
a device for producing a fine spray of a substance.

affair *noun*
1 a thing, a matter, or an event. **2 affairs,** business.

affect *verb*
to have an effect on; to harm. *The dampness affected her health.*

affected *adjective*
pretended; unnatural.

affection *noun*
love or liking. *I have a great affection for my nephew.*
affectionate *adjective*

afflict *verb*
to cause somebody distress.
affliction *noun*

affluent *adjective*
(*say* af-loo-ĕnt)
rich. *an affluent country.*
affluence *noun*

afford *verb*
1 to have enough money to pay for something. **2** to have enough time, etc. to do something.

afloat *adjective* and *adverb*
floating; on the sea.

afraid *adjective*
1 frightened. **2 I'm afraid,** I am sorry; I regret. *I'm afraid I've burnt the cakes.*

afresh *adverb*
again; in a new way. *We must start afresh.*

African *adjective*
of Africa.

African *noun*
a native or inhabitant of Africa.

Afrikaans *noun*
(*say* af-ri-**kahns**)
the language of Afrikaners.

Afrikaner *noun*
(*say* af-ri-**kah**-ner)
a South African of Dutch descent.

aft *adverb*
(*say* ahft)
at or towards the back of a ship or aircraft.

after *preposition*
1 later than. *Come after dinner.* **2** behind. *He came in after me.* **3** pursuing. *Run after him.* **4** in spite of. *After all I've done for him, he never thanked me.* **5** in imitation or honour of. *She was named after her aunt.*

after *adverb*
1 later. *It came a week after.* **2** behind. *Jill came tumbling after.*

after *adjective*
coming or done afterwards. *in after years.*

afternoon *noun*
the time from noon or lunchtime to evening.

afterwards *adverb*
at a later time.

again *adverb*
1 once more; another time. *Try again.* **2** as before. *You will soon be well again.* **3 again and again,** often.

against *preposition*
1 touching or hitting. *He leant against the wall.* **2** not on the side of; not in favour of. *Are you against smoking?*

age *noun*
1 how old someone or something is. **2** old age. **3** a period of history. **4** (*informal,* especially in plural) a very long time. *We've been waiting for ages.* **5 age-group,** people who are all the same age.

age *verb* **(aged, ageing)**
to make or become old.

aged *adjective*
1 (*say* ayjd) having the age of. *a girl aged 9.* **2** (*say* ay-jid) very old. *an aged man.*

agency *noun* **(agencies)**
the office or business of an agent.

agenda *noun*
(*say* ă-**jen**-dă)
a list of things to be done or discussed.

agent *noun*
1 someone who organizes things for other people. *a travel agent.* **2** a spy. *a secret agent.*

aggravate *verb* **(aggravated, aggravating)**
1 to make something worse. **2** (*informal*) to annoy.
aggravation *noun*

aggression *noun*
starting a war, attack, etc.
aggressive *adjective*, **aggressor** *noun*

agile *adjective*
moving quickly or easily.
agility *noun*

agitate *verb* **(agitated, agitating)**
1 to make someone disturbed or anxious. 2 to shake something about. 3 to campaign for something.
agitation *noun*, **agitator** *noun*

agnostic *noun*
(*say* ag-**nos**-tik)
someone who believes that nothing can be known for sure about God.

ago *adverb*
in the past. *She died long ago.*

agony *noun* **(agonies)**
severe pain or suffering.
agonizing *adjective*

agree *verb* **(agreed, agreeing)**
1 to think the same as someone else. 2 to say that you are willing. *She agreed to go with him.* 3 **agree with,** to suit or match.
agreement *noun*

agreeable *adjective*
1 willing. *We shall go if you are agreeable.* 2 pleasant. *an agreeable place.*

agriculture *noun*
farming.
agricultural *adjective*

aground *adverb*
stranded on the bottom of shallow water. *The ship ran aground.*

ah *interjection*
an exclamation of surprise, pity, admiration, etc.

ahead *adverb*
forwards; in front.

ahoy *interjection*
a shout used by seamen to attract someone's attention.

aid *noun*
1 help. 2 something that helps. *a hearing aid.* 3 money, food, etc. sent to another country to help it. *overseas aid.* 4 **in aid of,** for the purpose of; to help something.

ailment *noun*
an illness, usually a slight one.
ailing *adjective*

aim *verb*
1 to point a gun, etc. at someone or something. 2 to throw, kick, or shoot something in a particular direction. 3 to try or intend to do something.

aim *noun*
1 aiming a gun, etc. 2 purpose; intention.
aimless *adjective*, **aimlessly** *adverb*

air *noun*
1 the mixture of gases which surrounds the earth and which everyone breathes. 2 a tune; a melody. 3 an appearance or impression of something. *an air of mystery.* 4 **airs,** haughty, affected behaviour. *He puts on airs.* 5 **by air,** in an aircraft. 6 **in the air,** uncertain; spreading about. 7 **on the air,** on radio or television.

air *verb*
1 to put clothes, etc. in a warm place to finish drying. 2 to ventilate a room. 3 to express. *He aired his opinions.*

airborne *adjective*
1 flying. 2 carried by the air.

air-conditioning *noun*
a system for controlling the temperature, purity, etc. of the air in a room or building.
air-conditioned *adjective*

aircraft *noun* **(aircraft)**
1 an aeroplane or a helicopter. *Two aircraft landed together.* 2 **aircraft-carrier,** a large ship with a flat deck on which aircraft can take off and land.

Airedale *noun*
a large rough-haired terrier.

airfield *noun*
a place where aircraft can take off and land.

air force *noun*
a large group of people and aircraft organized for fighting.

airgun *noun*
a gun in which compressed air shoots the missile.

air hostess *noun*
a stewardess in an aircraft.

airline *noun*
a company that provides a regular service of aircraft.

airliner *noun*
a large aircraft for carrying passengers.

airlock *noun*
1 a compartment with airtight doors at each end. 2 a bubble of air that stops liquid flowing through a pipe.

airmail *noun*
mail carried by air.

airman *noun* **(airmen)**
1 one of the crew of an aircraft. 2 a member of an air force.

airport *noun*
an airfield, especially one for passengers and cargo.

air raid *noun*
an attack by aircraft.

airship *noun*
a large balloon with engines, designed to carry passengers or cargo.

air-strip *noun*
a strip of land prepared for aircraft to take off and land.

airtight *adjective*
not letting air get in or out.

airy *adjective* **(airier, airiest)**
1 with plenty of fresh air. 2 light as air. 3 light-hearted; insincere. *airy promises.*
airily *adverb*

aisle *noun*
(rhymes with *mile*)
1 a passage between or beside rows of seats or pews. 2 a part at the side of a church.

ajar *adverb* and *adjective*
slightly open. *Leave the door ajar.*

à la carte *adverb* and *adjective*
(*say* ah-lah-**kart**)
of a meal in a restaurant, etc.: ordered as

separate items from the menu (different from *table d'hôte*).

alarm *verb*
to make somebody frightened or anxious.

alarm *noun*
1 a warning sound or signal. 2 being alarmed. 3 an alarm-clock. **4 alarm-clock,** a clock that can be set to make a sound to wake a sleeping person.

alas *interjection*
an exclamation of sorrow.

albatross *noun* (albatrosses)
a large sea-bird with very long wings.

album *noun*
1 a book in which you can keep photographs, stamps, autographs, etc. 2 a long-playing record; a set of long-playing records.

alcohol *noun*
1 a colourless liquid made by fermenting sugar or starch. 2 an intoxicating drink containing this liquid.

alcoholic *adjective*
of or containing alcohol.

alcoholic *noun*
someone who is ill from continually drinking too much alcohol.
alcoholism *noun*

alcove *noun*
part of a room, etc. where the wall is set back from the main part.

ale *noun*
beer.

alert *adjective*
watching for something; ready to act.

alert *noun*
1 an alarm. 2 on the alert, on the look-out; watchful.

A level *noun*
the advanced level of the General Certificate of Education.

algebra *noun*
(*say* al-jib-ră)
mathematics in which letters and symbols are used to represent numbers.
algebraic *adjective*

alias *noun* (aliases)
(*say* ay-li-ăs)
a false or different name.

alias *adverb*
also named. *Robert Zimmerman, alias Bob Dylan.*

alibi *noun*
(*say* al-i-by)
1 evidence that an accused person was not present when a crime was committed. 2 (*informal*) an excuse.

alien *noun*
(*say* ay-li-ăn)
someone who is not a citizen of the country where he is living.

alien *adjective*
1 foreign. 2 alien to, contrary to; different from.

alienate *verb* (alienated, alienating)
to make somebody unfriendly. *The politician alienated his supporters.*
alienation *noun*

alight *adjective*
on fire; burning. *The bushes were alight.*

alike *adjective*
similar; like each other. *Her sisters are very much alike.*

alike *adverb*
in the same way. *He treats everybody alike.*

alimentary canal *noun*
the tube along which food passes through the body.

alimony *noun*
money paid by a man to his wife after they are separated or divorced.

alive *adjective*
1 living; existing. *Is he alive?* 2 alive to, aware of. *She is alive to the dangers.* 3 alive with, full of living or moving things.

alkali *noun*
(*say* al-kă-ly)
a substance that neutralizes acids or that combines with acids to form salts.
alkaline *adjective*

all *adverb*
adjective

all *adverb*
1 completely. *She was dressed all in white.* 2 very much. *He was all excited.* 3 to each team or competitor. *The score is four goals all.* **4 all out,** (*informal*) using all your ability. *Go all out to win.* **5 all there,** (*informal*) mentally alert; intelligent. **6 all the same,** nevertheless; making no difference.

all *noun*
1 everything. *That is all I know.* 2 everybody. *All were agreed.*

all *adjective*
the whole number or amount of. *All my books are in the desk.*

all-clear *noun*
a signal that a danger has passed.

allege *verb* (alleged, alleging)
(*say* ă-lej)
to say that someone has done something. *He alleged that I stole the ring.*
allegation *noun,* **allegedly** *adverb*

allegiance *noun*
(*say* ă-lee-jăns)
loyalty.

allegory *noun* (allegories)
a story, poem, etc. which is really about something different from what it seems to be.
allegorical *adjective*

allergic *adjective*
very sensitive to something, which may make you ill. *He is allergic to pollen, which gives him hay fever.*
allergy *noun*

alley *noun*
1 a narrow street or passage. 2 a place where you can play bowls or skittles.

alliance *noun*
a friendly connection or association between countries, etc.

alligator *noun*
a kind of crocodile.

all in *adjective*
(*informal*) exhausted. *I'm all in.*

all-in *adjective*
including or allowing everything. *an all-in price.*

allot *verb* (**allotted, allotting**)
to distribute portions, jobs, etc.

allotment *noun*
a small rented piece of ground used for growing vegetables, fruit, or flowers.

allow *verb*
1 to permit. *Smoking is not allowed.* **2** to give or provide. *She was allowed £10 for books.*
allowance *noun*

alloy *noun*
a metal formed from a mixture of metals. *Bronze is an alloy of copper and tin.*

all right *adjective*
satisfactory; in good condition.

all right *interjection*
yes; I consent. *All right, I'm coming!*

all-round *adjective*
in all respects; having all sorts of abilities. *a good all-round athlete.*
all-rounder *noun*

ally *noun* (**allies**)
(*say* **al**-I)
1 a country in alliance with another country. **2** a person who helps or co-operates with you.
allied *adjective*

almighty *adjective*
1 having complete power. **2** (*informal*) very great. *an almighty din.*

almond *noun*
(*say* **ah**-mŏnd)
an oval edible nut.

almost *adverb*
in the nearest place or condition to being something; nearly. *I am almost ready.*

aloft *adverb*
high up. *The sailors climbed aloft.*

alone *adjective*
without any other people or other things.

along *preposition* and *adverb*
1 from one end of something to the other. **2** on; onwards. *Move along, please!* **3** accompanying somebody. *I have brought my brother along.*

alongside *preposition* and *adverb*
next to something.

aloud *adverb*
in a voice that can be heard.

alp *noun*
1 a high mountain. **2 the Alps,** the high mountains in and around Switzerland.

alphabet *noun*
the letters used in a language, usually arranged in a set order.
alphabetical *adjective*, **alphabetically** *adverb*

alpine *adjective*
of alps or the Alps.

already *adverb*
by or before now. *I've already told you once.*

Alsatian *noun*
(*say* al-**say**-shăn)
a large, strong dog. *Alsatians are often used by the police.*

also *adverb*
as something or someone extra; besides; as well.

altar *noun*
the table at the end of a church, usually with a cross standing on it.

alter *verb*
to change. *Has she altered at all?*
alteration *noun*

alternate *adjective*
(*say* ol-**ter**-năt)
1 happening or coming in turns, one after the other. *alternate laughter and tears.* **2** every second one. *They work on alternate days.*
alternately *adverb*

alternate *verb* (**alternated, alternating**)
(*say* **ol**-ter-nayt)
1 to use or come alternately. **2 alternating current,** electric current that keeps reversing its direction.
alternation *noun*, **alternator** *noun*

alternative *adjective*
(*say* ol-**ter**-nă-tiv)
available instead of something else.

alternative *noun*
1 one of two or more possibilities. **2** freedom to choose.

although *conjunction*
though.

altitude *noun*
the height of something, especially above sea-level.

alto *noun*
a singer with a high voice.

altogether *adverb*
1 completely. *He is altogether wrong.* **2** on the whole. *Altogether, it wasn't a bad holiday.*

aluminium *noun*
a lightweight, silver-coloured metal.

always *adverb*
1 all the time; at all times. **2** often. *You are always crying.* **3** whatever happens. *You can always sleep on the floor.*

am 1st person present tense of **be.**

a.m. short for *ante meridiem*, before noon.

amalgamate *verb* (**amalgamated, amalgamating**)
to join together.
amalgamation *noun*

amateur *noun*
(*say* **am**-ă-ter)
someone who does something as a hobby, without being paid for it.
amateurish *adjective*

amaze *verb* (**amazed, amazing**)
to surprise somebody greatly.
amazement *noun*

ambassador *noun*
someone sent to a foreign country to represent his government.

amber *noun*
1 a hard, clear, yellowish substance used for making ornaments. 2 a yellowish colour, especially used in traffic-lights as a signal for caution.

ambiguous *adjective*
having more than one possible meaning; uncertain.
ambiguity *noun*

ambition *noun*
something you want to do very much; a strong desire to achieve something.
ambitious *adjective*

amble *verb* (ambled, ambling)
to walk slowly.

ambulance *noun*
a vehicle for carrying sick or injured people.

ambush *noun* (ambushes)
a surprise attack from a hidden place.

ambush *verb*
to attack by surprise.

amen *interjection*
a word used at the end of a prayer or hymn, meaning 'may it be so'.

amend *verb*
to change or improve something.
amendment *noun*

amenity *noun* (amenities)
a pleasant or useful feature. *The town has many amenities.*

American *adjective*
of America.

American *noun*
an American person.

amiable *adjective*
friendly; good-tempered.
amiability *noun*, **amiably** *adverb*

amicable *adjective*
friendly.
amicably *adverb*

amid or **amidst** *preposition*
in the middle of; among.

amidships *adverb*
in the middle of a ship.

amino acid *noun*
an acid found in proteins.

ammonia *noun*
a colourless gas or liquid with a strong smell.

ammunition *noun*
explosive objects used in fighting, such as bullets, shells, and grenades.

amnesty *noun* (amnesties)
pardoning offenders or letting them out of prison.

amoeba *noun*
(*say* ă-**mee**-bă)
a microscopic creature consisting of one cell.

among or **amongst** *preposition*
1 surrounded by; in. *She hid among the bushes.*
2 between. *Let's divide the money among ourselves.*

amount *noun*
a quantity.

amount *verb*
to make a total; to be equal to. *The bill amounted to £55.*

ampere *noun*
(*say* **am**-pair)
a unit of electric current.

ampersand *noun*
the sign &, which means 'and'. *The ampersand is used in the names of firms like Smith & Co.*

amphibious *adjective*
able to live or move both on land and in water.

ample *adjective* (ampler, amplest)
1 more than enough. *We had ample provisions.*
2 large. *This car has an ample boot.*
amply *adverb*

amplifier *noun*
a device, usually electronic, for making something louder.

amplify *verb* (amplified, amplifying)
1 to make something louder or stronger. 2 to give more details about something.
amplification *noun*

amputate *verb* (amputated, amputating)
to cut off a diseased leg or arm.
amputation *noun*

amuse *verb* (amused, amusing)
1 to make time pass pleasantly for someone.
2 to make somebody laugh or smile.

amusement *noun*
1 something that amuses. 2 being amused; laughing or smiling.

an *adjective* (called the *indefinite article*)
a (used instead of *a* when the next word begins with a vowel-sound or a silent h). *Take an apple. You can hire boats for one pound an hour.*

anaemia *noun*
(*say* ă-**nee**-mi-ă)
a poor condition of the blood that makes someone look pale.
anaemic *adjecive*

anaesthetic *noun*
(*say* an-iss-**thet**-ik)
a drug or gas that makes you unable to feel pain.
anaesthesia *noun*, **anaesthetist** *noun*, **anaesthetize** *verb*

anagram *noun*
a word or phrase made by rearranging the letters of another word or phrase. *'Cart-horse' is an anagram of 'orchestra'.*

analyse *verb* (analysed, analysing)
1 to examine something carefully. 2 to divide something into its parts.
analysis *noun*, **analyst** *noun*, **analytic** *adjective*, **analytical** *adjective*

anarchist *noun*
someone who thinks that governments and laws are bad and should be abolished.
anarchism *noun*

anarchy *noun*
1 lack of government or control. 2 disorder; confusion.

anatomy *noun*
the science or study of how the body is constructed.
anatomical *adjective,* **anatomist** *noun*

ancestor *noun*
anyone from whom a person is descended.
ancestral *adjective,* **ancestry** *noun*

anchor *noun*
a heavy object joined to a ship by a chain or rope and dropped to the sea-bed, etc. to stop the ship from moving.
anchorage *noun*

ancient *adjective*
1 very old. **2** of times long past. *ancient history.*

and *conjunction*
1 in addition to. *We had buns and lemonade.* **2** so that. *Work hard and you will pass.* **3** to. *Go and buy a pen.*

anemone *noun*
(*say* à-**nem**-ŏn-i)
1 a small cup-shaped flower. **2** a sea anemone.

angel *noun*
1 a messenger or attendant of God. **2** a very kind or beautiful person.
angelic *adjective,* **angelically** *adverb*

anger *noun*
strong annoyance; a feeling that you want to quarrel or fight with someone.

angle *noun*
1 the space between two lines or surfaces that meet. **2** a point of view.

angle *verb* **(angled, angling)**
1 to put something in a slanting position. **2** to present news, etc. in a particular way.

angler *noun*
someone who fishes with a fishing-rod.

Anglican *adjective*
of the Church of England.

Anglo-Saxon *noun*
an English person, especially of the time before the Norman Conquest.

angry *adjective* **(angrier, angriest)**
feeling anger.
angrily *adverb*

anguish *noun*
severe suffering; great sorrow or pain.
anguished *adjective*

angular *adjective*
1 with sharp corners. **2** bony; awkward.

animal *noun*
anything that lives and can move about. *Horses, dogs, birds, fish, bees, and men are all animals.*

animate *verb* **(animated, animating)**
1 to make something lively; to inspire. **2** to make a film by photographing a series of drawings, etc.
animation *noun,* **animator** *noun*

ankle *noun*
1 the part of the leg where it is joined to the foot. **2** **ankle sock,** a short sock just covering the ankle.

annex *verb*
(*say* à-**neks**)
1 to add something to a larger thing. **2** to seize territory.
annexation *noun*

annexe *noun*
(*say* **an**-eks)
a building added to another building.

annihilate *verb* **(annihilated, annihilating)**
(*say* à-**ny**-hil-ayt)
to destroy.
annihilation *noun*

anniversary *noun* **(anniversaries)**
a day when you remember something special that happened on the same date in a previous year.

announce *verb* **(announced, announcing)**
to make something known; to say something publicly, especially in a broadcast.
announcement *noun,* **announcer** *noun*

annoy *verb*
to give somebody a feeling of not being pleased.
annoyance *noun*

annual *adjective*
1 happening or coming every year. **2** lasting only one year or season. *annual plants.*
annually *adverb*

annual *noun*
1 a book that comes out once a year. **2** a plant that dies when winter comes.

anonymous *adjective*
1 with a name that is unknown. *an anonymous writer.* **2** by or from someone whose name is unknown. *an anonymous letter.*
anonymity *noun*

anorak *noun*
a thick, warm jacket with a hood.

another *adjective*
a different or extra. *Take another toffee.*

another *pronoun*
another person or thing.

answer *noun*
1 a reply. **2** the solution to a problem.

answer *verb*
1 to give or find an answer to. **2** to respond to a signal. *Answer the telephone.* **3** **answer back,** to reply cheekily. **4** **answer for,** to be responsible for.

ant *noun*
a tiny insect.

antagonism *noun*
being somebody's enemy; hatred.
antagonistic *adjective,* **antagonize** *verb*

Antarctic or **Antarctica** *noun*
the area round the South Pole.

ant-eater *noun*
an animal that lives by eating ants.

antelope *noun* **(antelope** or **antelopes)**
an animal like a deer, found in Africa and parts of Asia.

antenna *noun* **(antennae)**
1 a feeler on the head of an insect or crustacean. **2** (*plural* antennas) an aerial.

anthem *noun*
a religious or patriotic song, usually sung by a choir or group of people.

ant-hill *noun*
a mound of earth over an ants' nest.

anthology *noun* **(anthologies)**
a collection of poems, stories, songs, etc. in one book.

anthracite *noun*
a kind of hard coal.

anthropology *noun*
the study of human beings and their customs, beliefs, etc.
anthropological *adjective*, **anthropologist** *noun*

anti-aircraft *adjective*
used against aircraft. *anti-aircraft guns.*

antibiotic *noun*
a drug like penicillin which destroys bacteria.

anticipate *verb* **(anticipated, anticipating)**
1 to do something before the proper time. **2** to do something before someone else does it. **3** to expect.
anticipation *noun*

anticlimax *noun*
a disappointing end or result.

anticlockwise *adverb* and *adjective*
moving in the opposite direction to clockwise.

anticyclone *noun*
an area where air pressure is high, usually causing fine weather.

antidote *noun*
something which acts against the effects of a poison or disease.

antifreeze *noun*
liquid added to water to make it less likely to freeze.

antiquated *adjective*
old-fashioned.

antique *noun*
(*say* an-**teek**)
something that is valuable because it is very old.

anti-Semitic *adjective*
(*say* an-ti-sim-**it**-ik)
unfriendly or hostile to Jews.
anti-Semitism *noun*

antiseptic *noun*
a substance that kills germs.

antler *noun*
the branching horn of a deer.

anvil *noun*
a large block of iron on which a blacksmith hammers metal into shape.

anxious *adjective*
1 worried. **2** eager.
anxiety *noun*

any *adjective*
1 one or some. *Have you any wool?* **2** no matter which. *Come any day you like.* **3** every. *Any fool knows that!*

any *adverb*
at all; in some degree. *Is it any good?*

anybody *noun* and *pronoun*
anyone.

anyhow *adverb*
1 anyway. **2** (*informal*) carelessly. *He does his work anyhow.*

anyone *noun* and *pronoun*
any person.

anything *noun* and *pronoun*
any thing.

anyway *adverb*
whatever happens; whatever the situation may be.

anywhere *adverb*
in or to any place.

apart *adverb*
1 away from each other; separately. *Keep your desks apart.* **2** into pieces. *It fell apart.* **3** to one side; excluded. *Joking apart, what do you think?*

apartheid *noun*
(*say* à-**part**-hayt)
the policy in South Africa of keeping non-Europeans separate from Europeans.

apartment *noun*
a set of rooms; a flat.

apathy *noun*
not being interested in something.
apathetic *adjective*

ape *noun*
a monkey without a tail. *Gorillas, chimpanzees, and orang-utans are apes.*

aphid or **aphis** *noun*
a tiny insect that sucks sap from plants.

apiece *adverb*
to, for, or by each. *They cost five pence apiece.*

apologize *verb* **(apologized, apologizing)**
to make an apology.

apology *noun* **(apologies)**
1 saying that you are sorry for doing something wrong. **2 an apology for,** a poor specimen of something. *That was an apology for a meal.*
apologetic *adjective*, **apologetically** *adverb*

apostle *noun*
one of the twelve men sent out by Christ to preach.

apostrophe *noun*
(*say* à-**pos**-trŏ-fi)
a punctuation mark ' used to show that letters have been left out (as in *I can't*) or with *s* to show who owns something (as in *the boy's books, the boys' books*) or in the plurals of letters of the alphabet (as in *There are two l's in Bell*).

appal *verb* **(appalled, appalling)**
to shock somebody deeply. *The violence was appalling.*

apparatus *noun* **(apparatuses)**
1 equipment for a particular experiment, job, etc. **2** the equipment used for gymnastics.

apparent *adjective*
1 clear; obvious. **2** that appears to be true.
apparently *adverb*

appeal *verb*
1 to be attractive or interesting. *Football*

appeal

doesn't appeal to me. **2** to ask for something that you need. *She appealed for funds.* **3** to ask for a decision to be changed. *He appealed against the prison sentence.*

appeal *noun*
1 attraction; interest. **2** the action of appealing about a decision.

appear *verb*
1 to come into sight. **2** to seem. **3** to take part in a play, film, show, etc.

appearance *noun*
1 appearing. **2** what somebody looks like; what something seems to be.

appease *verb* **(appeased, appeasing)**
to make peace or calm, especially by giving in to demands.
appeasement *noun*

appendicitis *noun*
an inflammation or disease of the appendix.

appendix *noun* **(appendices** or **appendixes)**
1 a small tube leading off from the intestines. **2** a section added at the end of a book.

appetite *noun*
hunger; a desire to eat.
appetizer *noun,* **appetizing** *adjective*

applaud *verb*
to show that you like something, especially by clapping.
applause *noun*

apple *noun*
1 a round fruit with skin that is red, green, or yellow. **2 the apple of your eye,** somebody or something that you love.

appliance *noun*
a device. *electrical appliances.*

applicable *adjective*
suitable; relevant.

applicant *noun*
someone who applies for something.

applied *adjective*
put to practical use. *applied science.*

apply *verb* **(applied, applying)**
1 to put one thing on another. **2** to start using something. **3 apply for,** to ask for a job, etc. **4 apply to,** to concern. **5 apply yourself to,** to give all your attention to.
application *noun*

appoint *verb*
1 to choose somebody for a job. **2** to arrange officially.

appointment *noun*
1 an arrangement to meet or visit somebody. **2** choosing somebody for a job. **3** a job or position.

appreciate *verb* **(appreciated, appreciating)**
1 to enjoy or value. **2** to understand. **3** to increase in value.
appreciation *noun,* **appreciative** *adjective*

apprehension *noun*
fear; worry.
apprehensive *adjective*

apprentice *noun*
someone who is learning a trade or craft.
apprenticeship *noun*

approach *verb*
1 to come near to. **2** to go to someone with a request or offer. **3** to tackle a problem, etc.
approachable *adjective*

approach *noun* **(approaches)**
1 approaching. **2** a way or road. **3** the final part of an aircraft's flight before landing.

appropriate *adjective*
suitable.

approval *noun*
1 approving somebody or something. **2 approvals,** stamps received on approval. **3 on approval,** received by a customer to examine before he buys.

approve *verb* **(approved, approving)**
to say or think that somebody or something is good or suitable.

approximate *adjective*
not exact; nearly correct. *The approximate size of the playground is half an acre.*
approximately *adverb,* **approximation** *noun*

apricot *noun*
a juicy, orange-coloured fruit with a stone in it.

April *noun*
1 the fourth month of the year. **2 April fool,** someone who is fooled on April Fool's Day (1 April).

apron *noun*
a garment worn over the front of your body to protect your clothes.

apt *adjective*
1 likely. *He is apt to be careless.* **2** suitable. *an apt quotation.* **3** quick at learning. *an apt pupil.*

aptitude *noun*
a talent.

aquarium *noun*
a tank or building in which live fish are displayed.

aquatic *adjective*
of, on, or in water. *aquatic sports.*

aqueduct *noun*
a bridge that carries water across a valley.

Arab *noun*
a member of a Semitic people inhabiting Arabia and other parts of the Middle East and North Africa.
Arabian *adjective*

Arabic *adjective*
1 of the Arabs or their language. **2 arabic figures** or **arabic numerals,** the figures 1, 2, 3, 4, etc. (distinguished from *roman numerals*).

arable *adjective*
suitable for ploughing to grow crops on. *arable land.*

arbitrary *adjective*
(say **ar**-bit-rer-i)
random; impulsive.
arbitrarily *adverb.*

arbitration *noun*
settling a quarrel between two people or two sides
arbitrate *verb,* **arbitrator** *noun*

arc *noun*
1 a curve. 2 luminous electric current passing between two electrodes.

arcade *noun*
a covered passage or area, especially for shopping.

arch *noun* **(arches)**
a curved part that helps to support a bridge or building.

arch *verb*
to curve.

archaeology *noun*
(*say* ar-ki-**ol**-ŏ-ji)
the study of ancient remains.
archaeological *adjective,* **archaeologist** *noun*

archbishop *noun*
a chief bishop.

archer *noun*
someone who shoots with bow and arrows.
archery *noun*

architect *noun*
(*say* **ar**-ki-tekt)
someone who designs buildings.
architectural *adjective,* **architecture** *noun*

Arctic *noun*
the area round the North Pole.

are plural and 2nd person singular present tense of **be.**

area *noun*
1 part of a country, place, etc. 2 the space occupied by something. *The area of this room is 20 square metres.*

arena *noun*
(*say* ă-**ree**-nă)
1 the level space in the middle of a stadium, etc. 2 the place for a fight or contest.

aren't shortened form of *am not* or *are not.*

argue *verb* **(argued, arguing)**
1 to quarrel. 2 to give reasons for something. *She argued that housework should be shared.*

argument *noun*
1 a quarrel. 2 a reason given for something.

aria *noun*
(*say* **ah**-ri-ă)
a solo in an opera or oratorio.

arid *adjective.*
dry and barren.
aridity *noun*

arise *verb* (*past tense* **arose;** *past participle* **arisen;** *present participle* **arising**)
1 to appear; to come into existence. 2 (*old-fashioned use*) to rise; to stand up.

aristocrat *noun*
(*say* **a**-ris-tŏ-krat)
a person of high rank; a nobleman.
aristocracy *noun,* **aristocratic** *adjective*

arithmetic *noun*
the science or study of numbers; calculating with numbers.
arithmetical *adjective,* **arithmetician** *noun*

ark *noun*
the ship in which Noah and his family escaped the Flood.

arm *noun*
1 the part of the body between the shoulder and the hand. 2 a sleeve. 3 something shaped like an arm, especially the side part of a chair.
armful *noun*

arm *verb*
1 to supply with weapons. 2 to prepare for war. **3 armed forces** or **armed services,** military forces; the army, navy, and air force.

armada *noun*
(*say* ar-**mah**-dă)
a fleet of warships, especially the *Spanish Armada* which attacked England in 1588.

armadillo *noun*
a South American animal whose body is covered with a shell of bony plates.

armaments *plural noun*
weapons; military forces and their equipment.

armature *noun*
the rotating part of a dynamo which develops electric current.

armchair *noun*
a chair with arms.

armistice *noun*
an agreement to stop fighting in a war or battle.

armour *noun*
a metal covering to protect people or things in battle.
armoured *adjective*

armpit *noun*
the part underneath the top of your arm.

arms *plural noun*
1 weapons. *Lay down your arms.* 2 a coat of arms. **3 arms race,** competition between nations in building up supplies of armaments.

army *noun* **(armies)**
1 a large number of people trained to fight on land. 2 a large group. *an army of supporters.*

aroma *noun*
(*say* ă-**roh**-mă)
a smell, especially a pleasant one.
aromatic *adjective*

arose past tense of **arise.**

around *adverb* and *preposition*
round; about. *Stop running around. They stood around the pond.*

arouse *verb* **(aroused, arousing)**
to rouse.

arrange *verb* **(arranged, arranging)**
1 to organize. 2 to prepare music for a particular purpose.
arrangement *noun,* **arranger** *noun*

array *noun*
a display; a series. *An impressive array of books.*

arrest *verb*
1 to make somebody a prisoner; to seize. 2 to stop something.

arrest *noun*
1 arresting somebody or something. **2 under arrest,** seized by the police, etc.

arrive

arrive *verb* **(arrived, arriving)**
1 to reach the end of a journey; to get somewhere. 2 to come. *The great day arrived.*
arrival *noun*

arrogant *adjective*
proud; haughty.
arrogance *noun*

arrow *noun*
1 a pointed stick shot from a bow. 2 a sign used to show direction or position.

arsenal *noun*
a place where ammunition and weapons are made or stored.

arson *noun*
deliberately setting light to a house, building, etc.

art *noun*
1 producing something that is beautiful, especially by painting or drawing; things produced in this way. 2 a subject in which opinion and imagination are more important than exact measurement and calculation. *English and history are arts; chemistry and biology are sciences.* 3 a skill.

artery *noun* **(arteries)**
a tube carrying blood from the heart to parts of the body.

artful *adjective*
crafty.
artfully *adverb*

arthritis *noun*
(*say* arth-**ry**-tiss)
a disease that makes joints in the body painful and stiff.
arthritic *adjective*

article *noun*
1 a piece of writing published in a newspaper or magazine. 2 an object; a thing.

articulate *verb* **(articulated, articulating)**
(*say* ar-**tik**-yoo-layt)
1 to pronounce clearly. 2 **articulated,** with parts that are connected flexibly by joints. *an articulated lorry.*
articulation *noun*

articulate *adjective*
(*say* ar-**tik**-yoo-lăt)
able to speak clearly and fluently.

artificial *adjective*
1 not natural; made by human beings. 2 **artificial respiration,** helping somebody to start breathing properly again.
artificiality *noun,* **artificially** *adverb*

artillery *noun*
1 large guns. 2 the part of the army that uses large guns.

artist *noun*
1 someone who creates art, especially a painter. 2 an entertainer.
artistic *adjective,* **artistry** *noun*

as *conjunction*
1 when; while. *She slipped as she got off the bus.* 2 because. *Leave him here as he's grumpy.* 3 in the way that; how. *Leave it as it is.* 4 **as ... as,** in the same way; to the same extent that. *It is not as hard as you think.* 5 **as for,** with regard to. *As for you, you are a fool.* 6 **as it**

were, in some way. *She is, as it were, her own enemy.* 7 **as well,** also.

as *adverb*
equally; similarly. *This is just as easy.*

as *preposition*
in the character or role of; like. *He was dressed as a sailor.*

asbestos *noun*
a fibrous fire-proof material.

ascend *verb*
to climb; to go up.
ascent *noun*

ash *noun*[1] **(ashes)**
1 the powder that is left after something has been burned. 2 **the Ashes,** the trophy for which England and Australia play each other at cricket.
ashen *adjective,* **ashy** *adjective*

ash *noun*[2] **(ashes)**
a tree with silvery bark and winged seeds.

ashamed *adjective*
feeling shame.

ashore *adverb*
to or on the shore.

ashtray *noun*
a small bowl for cigarette ash.

Ash Wednesday *noun*
the first day of Lent.

Asian *adjective*
of Asia.
Asiatic *adjective*

aside *adverb*
to or at one side; away.

aside *noun*
something said on the stage by an actor which the other actors are supposed not to hear.

ask *verb*
1 to speak so as to find out or get something. 2 to invite. *Ask him to the party.* 3 **ask for it** or **ask for trouble,** (*informal*) to behave in such a way as to cause trouble.

asleep *adverb* and *adjective*
sleeping.

aspect *noun*
1 the appearance of somebody or something. 2 the direction a house, etc. faces. *This room has a southern aspect.* 3 one part of a problem or situation.

asphalt *noun*
(*say* **ass**-falt)
1 a sticky black substance like tar. 2 this tar mixed with gravel to surface roads, playgrounds, etc.

aspirin *noun*
a drug used to relieve pain or reduce fever.

ass *noun* **(asses)**
1 a donkey. 2 a fool.

assassin *noun*
a person who assassinates somebody.

assassinate *verb* **(assassinated, assassinating)**
to murder somebody, especially a king, politician, etc.
assassination *noun*

assault *noun*
a violent or illegal attack on someone.

assault *verb*
to make an assault on someone.

assemble *verb* (**assembled, assembling**)
to bring, put, or come together.

assembly *noun* (**assemblies**)
1 assembling. **2** a regular meeting, such as when everybody in a school meets together. **3** people who regularly meet together; a parliament. **4 assembly line,** a series of workers and machines to assemble the parts of a product.

assert *verb*
1 to declare something. **2 assert yourself,** to use firmness or authority.
assertion *noun,* **assertive** *adjective*

assess *verb*
to decide or test the value of a person or thing.
assessment *noun,* **assessor** *noun*

asset *noun*
1 something useful. **2 assets,** property.

assign *verb*
1 to give or allot. **2** to tell somebody to do a task.

assignment *noun*
something assigned, especially a task given to a journalist.

assist *verb*
to help.
assistance *noun*

assistant *noun*
1 someone who helps another person. **2** someone who serves in a shop.

associate *verb* (**associated, associating**)
(*say* à-**soh**-shi-ayt)
1 to put or go naturally or regularly together. **2** to work together.

associate *noun*
(*say* à-**soh**-shi-àt)
a colleague or companion.

association *noun*
1 an organization. **2** associating. **3 Association football,** a game between two teams of eleven players using a round ball that may usually only be handled by the goalkeepers.

assorted *adjective*
of various sorts; mixed.
assortment *noun*

assume *verb* (**assumed, assuming**)
1 to accept, without proof or question, that something is true or sure to happen. **2** to take or put on something. *He assumed an innocent look.* **3 assumed,** false. *an assumed name.*
assumption *noun*

assurance *noun*
1 being assured; a promise or guarantee. **2** life insurance.

assure *verb* (**assured, assuring**)
1 to tell somebody something positively; to promise. **2 assure yourself,** to make yourself feel certain or confident.

asterisk *noun*
a star-shaped sign * used to draw attention to something.

asteroid *noun*
one of the small planets found mainly between the orbits of Mars and Jupiter.

asthma *noun*
(*say* **ass**-mà)
a disease which makes breathing difficult.
asthmatic *adjective* and *noun*

astonish *verb*
to amaze.
astonishment *noun*

astound *verb*
to amaze or shock greatly.

astride *adverb*
with one leg on each side of something.

astrology *noun*
studying how the planets and stars may affect our lives.
astrologer *noun,* **astrological** *adjective*

astronaut *noun*
someone who travels in a spacecraft.

astronomy *noun*
studying the sun, moon, planets, and stars.
astronomer *noun,* **astronomical** *adjective*

at *preposition*
1 in a particular place, time, way, or direction. **2 at all,** in any way. **3 at it,** working at something. **4 at once,** immediately; without any delay.

ate past tense of **eat.**

atheist *noun*
someone who believes that there is no God.
atheism *noun*

athlete *noun*
someone who takes part in, or is good at, athletics.

athletic *adjective*
1 physically strong. **2** of athletics.

athletics *plural noun*
competitive sports like running and jumping.

atishoo *interjection*
the sound of a sneeze.

atlas *noun* (**atlases**)
a book of maps.

atmosphere *noun*
1 the air around the earth. **2** a feeling. *There was a happy atmosphere at the fairground.*
atmospheric *adjective*

atom *noun*
1 a tiny part of something; the smallest possible piece of a substance. *Every atom has a nucleus at its centre.* **2 atom bomb,** an atomic bomb.

atomic *adjective*
1 of atoms; nuclear. **2 atomic bomb,** a bomb that uses atomic energy. **3 atomic energy,** energy created by splitting or fusing the nuclei of some atoms.

atrocious *adjective*
(*say* à-**troh**-shùs)
awful; terrible.

attach *verb*
1 to fix or fasten. **2 attached to,** fond of.
attachment *noun*

attack

attack *noun*
1 an attempt to hurt or harm somebody or something. 2 a sudden illness or pain.

attack *verb*
to make an attack.

attain *verb*
to reach or accomplish.
attainment *noun*

attempt *verb*
to make an effort to do something.

attempt *noun*
attempting to do something.

attend *verb*
1 to give care and thought to something; to look and listen. *Why don't you attend to your teacher?* 2 to be present somewhere; to go to a meeting, place, etc. 3 to look after or serve somebody.
attendance *noun*

attendant *noun*
someone who helps or accompanies another person.

attention *noun*
1 attending to someone or something. 2 a position in which a soldier, etc. stands with feet together and arms straight downwards.

attentive *adjective*
paying attention.

attic *noun*
a room in the roof of a house.

attitude *noun*
1 the position of your body. 2 the way you think, feel, or behave.

attract *verb*
1 to get someone's attention or interest; to seem pleasant to someone. 2 to pull something by an invisible force. *Magnets attract pins.*
attraction *noun*, **attractive** *adjective*

auction *noun*
a sale when things are sold to the person who offers the most money for them.
auctioneer *noun*

audible *adjective*
loud enough to be heard.
audibility *noun*

audience *noun*
1 the people who have gathered to see or hear something. 2 a formal interview with a king, queen, etc.

audition *noun*
a test to see if a performer is suitable for a job.

auditorium *noun*
(*say* aw-dit-**or**-i-ŭm)
the part of a building where the audience sits.

August *noun*
the eighth month of the year.

aunt *noun*
your uncle's wife or the sister of your mother or father.

auntie or **aunty** *noun* (**aunties**)
(*informal*) an aunt.

au pair *noun*
(*say* oh-**pair**)
a girl or young woman from overseas who works for a time in someone's home.

au revoir *interjection*
(*say* oh-rĕ-**vwar**)
goodbye for now.

austere *adjective*
strict; without comfort or luxury.
austerity *noun*

Australian *adjective*
of Australia.

authentic *adjective*
genuine. *an authentic signature.*
authenticity *noun*

author *noun*
the writer of a book, play, poem, etc.
authorship *noun*

authority *noun* (**authorities**)
1 the right or power to give orders to other people. 2 an organization or person that can give orders to other people. 3 a very knowledgeable person; a book, etc. that gives reliable information.

authorize *verb* (**authorized, authorizing**)
to give official permission for something.

autistic *adjective*
unable to communicate with other people or respond to surroundings.

autobiography *noun* (**autobiographies**)
the story of someone's life written by himself.
autobiographical *adjective*

autograph *noun*
a person's signature.

automate *verb* (**automated, automating**)
to work by automation.

automatic *adjective*
1 working on its own; not needing continuous attention or control by human beings. 2 done without thinking.
automatically *adverb*

automation *noun*
(*say* aw-tŏm-**ay**-shŭn)
making processes automatic; using machines instead of people to do jobs.

automobile *noun*
a motor car.

autumn *noun*
the season when leaves fall off the trees, between summer and winter.
autumnal *adjective*

auxiliary *adjective*
helping; supporting.

available *adjective*
that you can get or use. *Fresh strawberries are available in June.*
availability *noun*

avalanche *noun*
(*say* **av**-ă-lahnsh)
a sudden fall of rocks or snow down the side of a mountain.

avenue *noun*
1 a wide street. 2 a road with trees along both sides.

back

average *noun*
1 the result of adding several quantities together and dividing the total by the number of quantities. *The average of 2, 4, 6, and 8 is 5.* 2 the usual or ordinary standard. *Her work is above the average.*

average *adjective*
1 worked out as an average. 2 of the usual or ordinary standard.

average *verb* (**averaged, averaging**)
to work out, produce, or amount to an average.

aviation *noun*
flying in aircraft.
aviator *noun*

avid *adjective*
eager; greedy. *He was avid for fame.*

avoid *verb*
1 to keep yourself away from someone or something. 2 to find a way of not doing something.
avoidance *noun*

await *verb*
to wait for.

awake *adjective*
not sleeping.

awake *verb* (*past tense* **awoke**; *past participle* **awoken**; *present participle* **awaking**)
to wake up.

awaken *verb*
to wake up.

award *noun*
a thing given officially to a person who has done something successful.

award *verb*
to give somebody an award.

aware *adjective*
knowing; realizing. *I was aware of his anger.*
awareness *noun*

away *adverb*
1 at or to a distance; not at the place where you usually are. 2 out of existence. *The ice-cream melted away.* 3 continuously; persistently. *He was working away at his sums.*

away *adjective*
played or gained on an opponent's ground. *an away match. an away win.*

awe *noun*
fearful or reverent wonder. *The mountains filled him with awe.*
awed *adjective*, **awe-inspiring** *adjective*, **awesome** *adjective*

awful *adjective*
1 causing fear or horror. 2 (*informal*) very bad; very great. *I've been an awful fool.*
awfully *adverb*

awhile *adverb*
for a short time.

awkward *adjective*
1 not convenient; difficult to use or deal with. 2 clumsy.

awoke past tense of **awake** *verb*.

awoken past participle of **awake** *verb*.

axe *noun*
1 a tool for chopping. 2 (*informal*) being axed. 3 **an axe to grind,** a person's particular interest in something.

axe *verb* (**axed, axing**)
(*informal*) 1 to dismiss somebody from a job. 2 to reduce expenses, wages, etc.

axis *noun* (**axes**)
1 a line through the centre of a spinning object. 2 a line dividing something in half.

axle *noun*
the rod through the centre of a wheel on which it turns.

ay or **aye** *interjection*
(*say* I)
(*old-fashioned use*) yes.

azalea *noun*
(*say* ă-**zay**-li-ă)
a flowering shrub.

azure *adjective*
sky-blue.

B

babble *verb* (**babbled, babbling**)
1 to talk in a silly or meaningless way. 2 to murmur.

baboon *noun*
a large kind of monkey.

baby *noun* (**babies**)
a very young child or animal.
babyish *adjective*

baby-sitter *noun*
someone who looks after a child while its parents are out.

bachelor *noun*
a man who is not married.

back *noun*
1 the part of something farthest from the front. 2 the part of a person's body from his shoulders to his buttocks; the similar part of an animal's body. 3 a defending player in football, hockey, etc.

back *adjective*
placed at the back. *the back row.*

back

back *adverb*
1 backwards; to the place you have come from. *Go back!* 2 to an earlier time. *Put the clock back.* 3 at a distance. *The house stands back from the road.*

back *verb*
1 to move backwards. 2 to bet on something. 3 **back out**, to withdraw from something. 4 **back up**, to give someone support or help.

backbone *noun*
the spine.

background *noun*
1 the back part of a scene, view, etc. 2 the conditions or situation underlying something. 3 a person's experience, education, etc. 4 **background music**, music used to accompany a film, etc. 5 **in the background**, not conspicuous; not obvious.

backing *noun*
1 support. 2 material that forms a support or back for something. 3 musical accompaniment.

backlash *noun* **(backlashes)**
a reaction.

backstroke *noun*
a way of swimming on your back.

backward *adjective*
1 going backwards. 2 not as clever or developed as others.

backward *adverb*
backwards.

backwards *adverb*
1 to or towards the back. 2 in reverse. *Count backwards from 10 to 1.* 3 **backwards and forwards**, in all directions.

backwater *noun*
a branch of a river that comes to a dead end.

bacon *noun*
smoked or salted meat from the back or sides of a pig.

bacteria *plural noun*
microscopic organisms. *Some bacteria cause disease.*
bacterial *adjective*

bad *adjective* **(worse, worst)**
1 not good. *The television picture is bad.* 2 serious. *a bad mistake.* 3 unhealthy; injured. *a bad leg.* 4 decayed. *This meat has gone bad.* 5 **not bad**, fairly good.

badge *noun*
something that you wear on your clothes to show people who you are, what school or club you belong to, etc.

badger *noun*
a grey animal that lives underground. *Badgers hunt for food at night.*

badger *verb*
to pester. *He badgered me for his pocket-money.*

badly *adverb*
1 in a bad way. 2 **badly off**, poor.

badminton *noun*
a game in which a lightweight object called a shuttlecock is hit to and fro across a high net.

baffle *verb* **(baffled, baffling)**
to bewilder or frustrate somebody.

bag *noun*
1 a flexible container made of paper, plastic, cloth, etc. 2 **bags**, (*informal*) plenty of something. *There's bags of room.*

bag *verb* **(bagged, bagging)**
1 to seize or catch. 2 to put into bags. 3 **bags**, (*informal*) I claim or demand.

baggage *noun*
luggage.

baggy *adjective* **(baggier, baggiest)**
hanging loosely.

bagpipes *plural noun*
a musical instrument with air squeezed out of a bag into a set of pipes.

bail *noun*[1]
money paid or promised so that an accused person will not be kept in prison before his trial.

bail *noun*[2]
one of the two small pieces of wood placed on top of the stumps in cricket.

bail *verb*
1 to scoop water out of a boat. 2 **bail out**, to bale out.
bailer *noun*

bait *noun*
food put on a hook or in a trap to catch fish or animals.

bait *verb*
1 to put bait on a hook or in a trap. 2 to torment or tease.

bake *verb* **(baked, baking)**
1 to cook in an oven. 2 to make or become very hot. 3 to make something hard by heating it.

baker *noun*
someone who makes or sells bread and cakes.
bakery *noun*

balance *noun*
1 an apparatus for weighing things, with two containers hanging from a horizontal bar. 2 steadiness; equality. 3 the difference between money paid into and money taken out of an account; an amount owed.

balance *verb* **(balanced, balancing)**
1 to make or be steady or equal. 2 **balanced diet**, the right sort and amount of food for good health.

balcony *noun* **(balconies)**
1 a platform projecting from the outside wall of a building. *A balcony usually has railings around it and can be reached from an upstairs room.* 2 the upstairs part of a cinema or theatre.

bald *adjective*
without any or much hair on your scalp.

bale *noun*
a large bundle of hay, straw, cotton, etc., usually tied up tightly.

bale *verb* **(baled, baling)**
1 to bail water out of a boat. 2 **bale out**, to jump out of an aircraft with a parachute.

barbecue

ball *noun*
1 a round object used in many games. 2 something round. *a ball of string.* 3 a grand or formal dance. 4 **ball-point** or **ball-point pen,** a pen that writes with a tiny ball round which the ink flows.

ballad *noun*
a simple song or poem, especially one that tells a story.

ballerina *noun*
(*say* ba-ler-**ee**-nă)
a female ballet-dancer.

ballet *noun*
(*say* **bal**-ay)
a stage entertainment telling a story or expressing an idea in dancing and mime.
ballet-dancer *noun*

ballistic *adjective*
1 of projectiles. 2 **ballistic missile,** a missile that is shot into the air but falls freely.

balloon *noun*
1 a round or pear-shaped bag inflated so that it can rise into the air. 2 an outline in a strip cartoon containing spoken words.

ballot *noun*
(*say* **bal**-ŏt)
1 a secret method of voting. 2 a piece of paper on which a vote is made.

balsa *noun*
a lightweight wood.

bamboo *noun*
1 a tall plant with hard hollow stems. 2 a stem of the bamboo plant.

ban *verb* **(banned, banning)**
to forbid.

banana *noun*
a tropical fruit with yellow skin.

band *noun*
1 an organized group of people. 2 a group of musicians. 3 a circular strip of something.

band *verb*
to join together in a group.

bandage *noun*
(*say* **ban**-dij)
a strip of material for binding a wound.

bandit *noun*
an outlaw.

bandstand *noun*
a platform for a band playing music outdoors.

bandwagon *noun*
1 a wagon for a band playing music in a parade. 2 **to jump** or **climb on the bandwagon,** to join in something that looks like being successful.

bandy *adjective* **(bandier, bandiest)**
having legs that curve outwards at the knee.

bang *noun*
1 a sudden loud noise. 2 a heavy blow or knock.

bang *verb*
1 to hit or shut noisily. 2 to make a loud noise.

banger *noun*
1 (*informal*) a firework that explodes. 2 (*slang*) a sausage. 3 (*slang*) a noisy old car.

banish *verb*
to punish someone by sending him away from a place.
banishment *noun*

banisters *plural noun*
a handrail with upright supports at the side of a staircase.

banjo *noun*
an instrument like a guitar with a round body.

bank *noun*
1 a business which looks after people's money. 2 a piece of raised or sloping ground. 3 the ground beside a river, canal, lake, etc. 4 a mass of clouds. 5 a row of lights, switches, etc. 6 **bank card,** a cheque card. 7 **bank holiday,** a public holiday. 8 **banknote,** a piece of paper money.

bank *verb*
1 to put money in a bank. 2 to lean over while changing direction. *The plane banked as it turned to land.* 3 **bank on,** to rely on. 4 **bank up,** to heap up; to make something higher.

bankrupt *adjective*
having no money; unable to pay your debts.
bankruptcy *noun*

banner *noun*
a large flag, piece of cloth, etc., carried on one or two poles in a procession.

banquet *noun*
(*say* **bank**-wit)
a formal feast.

baptism *noun*
baptizing.

Baptist *noun*
a Christian who believes that people should be baptized when they are old enough to understand baptism.

baptize *verb* **(baptized, baptizing)**
to receive someone into the Christian Church by sprinkling him with water, or immersing him in water, and usually giving him his Christian names.

bar *noun*
1 a long piece of hard substance. *a metal bar.* 2 a counter or room where refreshments, especially drinks, are served. 3 one of the small equal sections into which music is divided. *A waltz has three beats in a bar.*

bar *verb* **(barred, barring)**
1 to fasten with a bar. 2 to exclude.

barb *noun*
a backward-curving point on a fish-hook, spear, etc.

barbarian *noun*
an uncivilized, savage person.
barbaric *adjective,* **barbarism** *noun,* **barbarity** *noun,* **barbarous** *adjective*

barbecue *noun*
1 a place or device in which meat is cooked outdoors. 2 a party where meat is cooked outdoors.

barbed wire *noun*
wire with small spikes on it, used to make fences.

barber *noun*
a men's hairdresser.

bard *noun*
(*old-fashioned use*) a poet or minstrel.

bare *adjective* **(barer, barest)**
1 without clothing or covering. *The trees were bare.* 2 empty or almost empty. *The cupboard was bare.* 3 that is only just enough. *the bare necessities of life.*
barely *adverb*

bareback *adjective* and *adverb*
riding on a horse without a saddle.

bargain *noun*
1 an agreement to buy or sell something. 2 something bought cheaply.

bargain *verb*
1 to argue over the price of something. 2 **bargain for**, to expect. *He got more than he bargained for.*

barge *noun*
a long flat-bottomed boat used especially on canals.
bargee *noun*

barge *verb* **(barged, barging)**
1 to rush or bump heavily into. 2 **barge in**, to intrude; to interrupt rudely.

baritone *noun*
a male singer with a voice between a tenor and a bass.

bark *noun*
1 the sound made by a dog, fox, etc. 2 the outer covering of a tree's branches or trunk.

bark *verb*
1 to make the sound of a dog, fox, etc. 2 to scrape your skin accidentally on something.

barley *noun*
1 a cereal from which malt is made. 2 **barley-sugar**, a sweet made from boiled sugar.

bar mitzvah *noun*
a religious ceremony for Jewish boys of 13.

barn *noun*
1 a building on a farm where grain, etc. is stored. 2 **barn dance**, a country dance.

barnacle *noun*
a shellfish that attaches itself to rocks and the bottoms of ships.

barnyard *noun*
a farmyard.

barometer *noun*
(*say* bă-**rom**-it-er)
an instrument that measures air pressure, used in forecasting the weather.
barometric *adjective*

baron *noun*
one of the lowest rank of noblemen.
baronial *adjective*

baroness *noun* **(baronesses)**
1 a female baron. 2 a baron's wife or widow.

barrack *verb*
to jeer at somebody.

barracks *noun*
a place where soldiers live.

barrage *noun*
(*say* **ba**-rahzh)
1 heavy gunfire. 2 a dam.

barrel *noun*
1 a large cylindrical container with flat ends. 2 the metal tube of a gun, through which the shot is fired. 3 **barrel-organ**, a musical instrument which you play by turning a handle.

barren *adjective*
not producing any fruit, children, etc.

barricade *noun*
a barrier, especially one put up hastily across a street.

barricade *verb* **(barricaded, barricading)**
to block or defend with a barricade.

barrier *noun*
a fence, railing, etc. to stop people getting past; an obstacle.

barrister *noun*
a lawyer who is allowed to act as an advocate in the higher lawcourts.

barrow *noun*
1 a small cart. 2 an ancient mound of earth over a grave.

base *noun*
1 the lowest part of something; the part on which a thing stands. 2 a basis. 3 a headquarters.

base *verb* **(based, basing)**
base on or **upon**, to use something as a basis. *The story is based on actual events.*

baseball *noun*
1 an American game rather like rounders. 2 the ball used in this game.

basement *noun*
a room or rooms below ground level.

bash *verb*
(*informal*) 1 to hit hard. 2 **bash up**, to beat someone up.

bash *noun* **(bashes)**
(*informal*) 1 a hard hit. 2 an attempt. *Have a bash at it.*

bashful *adjective*
shy.

basic *adjective*
forming a base or basis; most important.
basically *adverb*

basin *noun*
1 a deep round dish. *a pudding-basin.* 2 a large container to hold water for washing in. *a wash-basin.* 3 an enclosed area of water. 4 the land drained by a river.

basis *noun* **(bases)**
something to start from or add to; the main principle or ingredient.

bask *verb*
to lie or sit comfortably warming yourself.

basket *noun*
a container, often made of woven strips of wood.
basketful *noun*

basketball *noun*
1 a game in which players try to throw a ball through a hoop fixed 10 feet above the ground. 2 the ball used in this game.

bass *adjective*
of or forming the lowest sounds in music.

bass *noun* **(basses)**
a bass singer, instrument, or part.

bassoon *noun*
a bass woodwind instrument.

bastard *noun*
1 an illegitimate person. 2 (*informal*) a person, especially an unpleasant or unfortunate person.

bat *noun*[1]
1 a wooden implement used to hit the ball in cricket, baseball, and other games. 2 **off your own bat,** without any help from other people.

bat *noun*[2]
a flying mammal that looks like a mouse with wings.

bat *verb* **(batted, batting)**
to use a bat in cricket, etc.

batch *noun* **(batches)**
a set of things.

bated *adjective*
with bated breath, anxiously; hardly daring to speak.

bath *noun*
1 washing your whole body. 2 a large container for water in which to have a bath. 3 the water used in having a bath. *Your bath is getting cold.* 4 (*usually in plural*) a swimming-bath.

bath *verb*
1 to have a bath. 2 to give someone a bath. *Bath the baby.*

bathe *verb* **(bathed, bathing)**
1 to go swimming. 2 to wash something gently.

bathe *noun*
a swim.

bathroom *noun*
a room containing a bath.

baton *noun*
a short stick, especially one used to conduct an orchestra.

batsman *noun* **(batsmen)**
someone who uses a bat in cricket, etc.

battalion *noun*
an army unit consisting of two or more companies.

batten *noun*
a strip of wood.

batter *verb*
to hit hard and often.

batter *noun*
a beaten mixture of flour, eggs, and milk, for making pancakes, etc.

battering-ram *noun*
a heavy pole used to break down gates, walls, etc.

battery *noun* **(batteries)**
1 a portable device for storing and supplying electricity. 2 a set of devices, especially a group of large guns. 3 a series of cages in which animals are kept close together on a farm. *These eggs are from battery hens.*

battle *noun*
a fight between large organized forces.

battlefield *noun*
a place where a battle is or was fought.

battlements *plural noun*
the top of a castle wall, usually indented.

battleship *noun*
a heavy warship.

bawl *verb*
to shout; to cry loudly.

bay *noun*
1 a place where the shore curves inwards. 2 an alcove or compartment. 3 the barking of a hound. 4 **at bay,** prevented from coming near someone. *Keep the enemy at bay.* 5 **bay window,** a window that sticks out from the wall of a house.

bayonet *noun*
a dagger fixed to the muzzle of a rifle.

bazaar *noun*
1 a sale to raise money for a charity, etc. 2 an oriental market.

B.B.C. short for *British Broadcasting Corporation.*

B.C. short for *before Christ,* used to show that a date is counted backwards from the birth of Jesus Christ. *Julius Caesar came to Britain in 55 B.C.*

be *verb* (*past tense* **was** or **were;** *past participle* **been;** *present participle* **being**)
1 to have a particular identity, quality, condition, etc. *She is my teacher. You are very tall.* 2 to exist. *There is a bus-stop at the corner.* 3 to become. *She wants to be a scientist.* 4 to go or come; to visit. *Has the postman been yet?* 5 used to form parts of other verbs, as in *it is coming, he was killed.*

beach *noun* **(beaches)**
part of the sea-shore.

beacon *noun*
a light used as a warning signal.

bead *noun*
1 a small perforated piece of something hard, threaded on a string or wire to make a necklace. 2 a small drop of liquid. *beads of sweat.*

beady *adjective* **(beadier, beadiest)**
like beads, especially describing eyes that are small and bright.

beagle *noun*
a small hound used for hunting hares.

beak *noun*
the hard, horny part of a bird's mouth.

beaker *noun*
1 a tall drinking-mug. 2 (*in Chemistry*) a glass container for pouring liquids.

beam *noun*
1 a long, thick bar of wood or metal. 2 a ray of light or other radiation.

beam *verb*
1 to smile radiantly. 2 to send out a beam of light, etc.

bean *noun*
1 a kind of plant with seeds growing in pods. 2 its seed or pod eaten as food.

bear *verb (past tense* **bore**; *past participle* **born** or **borne**; *present participle* **bearing**)
1 to carry or support. 2 to have or show. *The letter bore her signature.* 3 to endure or tolerate. *I can't bear this pain.* 4 to produce, especially to give birth to children. *She was born in 1950. She has borne three sons.*
bearable *adjective*

bear *noun*
a large, heavy, furry animal.

beard *noun*
hair on the lower part of a man's face.
bearded *adjective*

bearing *noun*
1 the way you behave, walk, stand, etc. 2 the direction or relative position of something. 3 **your bearings**, knowing where you are in relation to other things. *I have lost my bearings.*

beast *noun*
1 any large four-footed animal. 2 a person you dislike.
beastly *adjective*

beat *verb (past tense* **beat**; *past participle* **beaten**; *present participle* **beating**)
1 to hit someone or something often, especially with a stick. 2 to stir something briskly. 3 to shape or flatten something by beating it. 4 to make repeated movements. 5 to do better than somebody; to overcome. 6 **beat up**, to beat someone violently; to thrash.

beat *noun*
1 a regular rhythm or stroke. *the beat of your heart.* 2 a strong rhythm in pop music. *This tune has got a beat.* 3 the regular route of a policeman.

Beaufort scale *noun*
(*say* **boh**-fert skayl)
a scale for wind-speed ranging from 0 (calm) to 12 (hurricane).

beauty *noun* (**beauties**)
1 a quality that gives delight or pleasure, especially to your senses. *the beauty of the sunset.* 2 a person or thing that has beauty. 3 **beauty queen**, a woman chosen as the most beautiful in a contest.
beautiful *adjective*, **beautifully** *adverb*, **beautify** *verb*

beaver *noun*
a brown, furry, amphibious animal with strong teeth.

becalmed *adjective*
unable to sail on because the wind has dropped.

became past tense of **become**.

because *conjunction*
1 for the reason that. *We were happy because it was a holiday.* 2 **because of**, for the reason of; on account of. *He limped because of his bad leg.*

beckon *verb*
to make a sign to someone asking him to come.

become *verb (past tense* **became**; *past participle* **become**; *present participle* **becoming**)
1 to come to be; to start being. *It became darker.* 2 to be suitable for; to look attractive on someone. *That dress becomes you.* 3 **become of**, to happen to. *What will become of me?*

bed *noun*
1 something for sleeping on; a place to sleep or rest. 2 part of a garden where plants are grown. 3 the bottom of the sea or of a river. 4 a flat base; a foundation. 5 a layer of rock.

bedclothes *plural noun*
sheets, blankets, etc.

bedding *noun*
things for making a bed, such as sheets and blankets.

bedlam *noun*
uproar.

bedraggled *adjective*
(*say* bi-**drag**-úld)
very untidy; wet and dirty.

bedridden *adjective*
(*say* **bed**-rid-ên)
too ill to get out of bed.

bedroom *noun*
a room where you sleep.

bedspread *noun*
a covering put over the top of a bed.

bedstead *noun*
the framework of a bed.

bedtime *noun*
the time when you go to bed or when you ought to go to bed.

bee *noun*
1 a stinging insect that makes honey. 2 **make a bee-line for**, to go quickly towards something.

beech *noun* (**beeches**)
a tree with smooth bark and glossy leaves.

beef *noun*
the meat of an ox, bull, or cow.

beefburger *noun*
a hamburger.

beefeater *noun*
a guard at the Tower of London.

beehive *noun*
a container for bees to live in.

been past participle of **be**.

beer *noun*
an alcoholic drink made from malt and hops.
beery *adjective*

beet *noun* (**beet** or **beets**)
a plant used as a vegetable or for making sugar.

beetle *noun*
an insect with hard, shiny wing-cases.

beetroot *noun* (beetroot)
the crimson root of beet used as a vegetable.

before *adverb*
earlier; already. *Have you been here before?*

before *preposition*
1 sooner or earlier than. *the day before yesterday.* 2 in front of. *leg before wicket.*

beforehand *adverb*
earlier; before something happens.

beg *verb* (begged, begging)
1 to ask to be given money, food, etc. 2 to ask seriously or desperately. *He begged me not to tell the teacher.* 3 **I beg your pardon,** I didn't hear or understand what you said; I apologize.

began past tense of **begin.**

beggar *noun*
1 someone who lives by begging. 2 (*informal*) a person. *you lucky beggar!*

begin *verb* (*past tense* **began**; *past participle* **begun**; *present participle* **beginning**)
to start.

beginner *noun*
someone who is just starting to learn a subject.

begrudge *verb* (begrudged, begrudging)
to grudge.

begun past participle of **begin.**

behalf *noun*
1 **on my behalf,** for me. 2 **on behalf of,** for a person; done to help a person, cause, etc.

behave *verb* (behaved, behaving)
1 to act in a particular way. *They behaved very badly at the party.* 2 to show good manners. *Why can't you behave?*
behaviour *noun*

behead *verb*
to cut off someone's head.

behind *adverb*
1 at or to the back. *The others are a long way behind.* 2 staying after other people have gone. *We were left behind when the bus went.* 3 not making good progress; late. *I'm behind with my rent.*

behind *preposition*
1 at or to the back of; hidden by. *She hid behind a tree.* 2 not making such good progress as others. *He's behind the rest of the class in French.* 3 supporting. *I am behind the peace talks.* 4 **behind somebody's back,** without him knowing or approving.

behind *noun*
a person's bottom. *He kicked me on the behind.*

beige *noun* and *adjective*
(*say* bayzh)
a fawn colour.

being *noun*
1 a creature. 2 existence.

belch *verb*
1 to let wind noisily out of your stomach through your mouth. 2 to send out smoke, fire, etc.

belch *noun* (belches)
the act or sound of belching.

belfry *noun* (belfries)
a tower, or part of a tower, in which bells hang.

belief *noun*
something you believe.

believe *verb* (believed, believing)
1 to think that something is true or that someone is telling the truth. 2 **believe in,** to think that something exists or is good.
believable *adjective,* **believer** *noun*

bell *noun*
1 a device that makes a ringing sound, especially a cup-shaped metal device containing a clapper. 2 **bell-tent,** a conical tent.

bellow *verb*
to roar or shout.

bellows *plural noun*
a device for blowing air into a fire, organ-pipes, etc.

belly *noun* (bellies)
the abdomen or the stomach.

belong *verb*
1 to have a proper place. *The butter belongs in the fridge.* 2 **belong to,** to be owned by a person. *That pencil belongs to me.*

belongings *plural noun*
your possessions.

beloved *adjective*
(*say* bi-**luvd** or bi-**luv**-id)
greatly loved.

below *preposition*
lower than. *hitting below the belt.*

below *adverb*
at or to a lower place.

belt *noun*
1 a strip of material, especially one worn round the waist. 2 a long narrow area. *a belt of rain.*

bench *noun* (benches)
1 a long seat. 2 a long table for working at. 3 the seat where judges or magistrates sit.

bend *verb* (bent, bending)
1 to make or become curved or crooked. 2 to turn downwards; to stoop.

bend *noun*
1 a curve or turn. 2 a sailor's knot.

beneath *preposition* and *adverb*
under.

benefactor *noun*
someone who gives money or other help.
benefaction *noun*

benefit *noun*
1 advantage; help. 2 money paid to a poor person. 3 a game, concert, etc. to raise money for a particular person or purpose. 4 **the benefit of the doubt,** assuming that someone is innocent or correct, when you cannot be sure.
beneficial *adjective*

benevolent *adjective*
kind or helpful.
benevolence *noun*

bent

bent *adjective*
1 curved or crooked. 2 (*slang*) dishonest.
3 **bent on,** intending to do something.

bent *noun*
a liking or talent for something.

bequeath *verb*
to leave somebody something in a will.
bequest *noun*

bereaved *adjective*
left sad because someone has died.
bereavement *noun*

bereft *adjective*
deprived of something. *bereft of speech.*

beret *noun*
(*say* **bair**-ay)
a soft, round cap.

berry *noun* **(berries)**
a small, juicy fruit.

berserk *adjective*
in a frenzy.

berth *noun*
1 a sleeping-place on a ship or train. 2 a place
where a ship ties up or anchors.

beside *preposition*
1 next to; close to. *beside the seaside.* 2 having
nothing to do with. *That is beside the point.*
3 **beside yourself,** very excited or upset. *He
was beside himself with grief.*

besides *preposition*
in addition to. *Who came besides you?*

besides *adverb*
also; in addition to this. *That coat costs too
much. Besides, it's the wrong colour.*

besiege *verb* **(besieged, besieging)**
(*say* bi-**seej**)
to surround a place with troops; to attack from
all sides.

best *adjective*
1 most excellent. 2 **best man,** the bridegroom's
main helper at a wedding. 3 **best seller,** a book
that sells in very large numbers.

best *noun*
1 the best person or thing. *She was the best at
tennis.* 2 the best people or things. *These
apples are the best you can buy.* 3 victory. *We
got the best of the fight.*

best *adverb*
1 in the best way; most. 2 most usefully; most
wisely. *He is best ignored.*

bet *noun*
1 an agreement that you will pay money, etc. if
you are wrong in forecasting the result of a race,
etc. 2 the money you risk losing in a bet.

bet *verb* (*past tense* **bet;** *past participle* **bet** or
betted; *present participle* **betting**)
1 to make a bet; to risk losing money in a bet.
2 (*informal*) to be certain; to predict. *I bet I'm
right.*

betray *verb*
1 to be disloyal to a person, cause, etc. 2 to
reveal something that should have been kept
secret.
betrayal *noun*

better *adjective*
1 more excellent. 2 recovered from an illness.

better *noun*
1 a better person or thing. 2 **get the better of,** to
overcome; to get an advantage over somebody.

better *adverb*
1 in a better way. 2 more usefully; more wisely.

better *verb*
1 to improve something. 2 to do better than.

between *preposition*
1 within two or more given limits. *Call on me
between Tuesday and Friday.* 2 connecting
two or more people, places, or things. *The train
runs between London and Glasgow.* 3 shared
among. *Divide these sweets between the children.* 4 when comparing; separating. *What is
the difference between butter and margarine?*

between *adverb*
between two or more places, etc.

beware *verb*
be careful. *Beware of pickpockets.*

bewilder *verb*
to puzzle someone hopelessly.
bewilderment *noun*

bewitch *verb*
1 to put a magic spell on someone. 2 to delight
someone very much.

beyond *preposition*
1 farther than. *Don't go beyond the end of the
street.* 2 outside the range of; too difficult for.
This boat is beyond repair.

beyond *adverb*
farther on. *India and the countries beyond.*

bias *noun* **(biases)**
1 a prejudice. 2 a tendency to swerve; a slanting direction.
biased *adjective*

bib *noun*
a cloth, etc. put under a baby's chin during
meals.

Bible *noun*
the holy book of the Christian Church.
biblical *adjective*

bicycle *noun*
1 a two-wheeled vehicle driven by pedals.
2 **bicycle clip,** a clip to hold your trouser-leg
tightly round your ankle when you are cycling.
3 **bicycle pump,** a pump for inflating bicycle
tyres.

bid *noun*
1 offering an amount you will pay for something, especially at an auction. 2 an attempt.

bid *verb* **(bid, bidding)**
to make a bid.

big *adjective* **(bigger, biggest)**
1 large. 2 important. 3 elder; grown-up. *my big
sister.* 4 **big game,** large animals hunted for
sport.

bigamy *noun*
the crime of having two or more wives or
husbands at the same time.
bigamous *adjective,* **bigamist** *noun*

bike *noun*
(*informal*) a bicycle or motor-cycle.

bikini *noun*
a woman's scanty two-piece bathing costume.

bilge *noun*
1 the bottom of a ship, or the water that collects there. 2 (*slang*) nonsense.

bill *noun*
1 an account showing how much money is owing. 2 a poster. 3 a programme of entertainment. *There's a conjuror on the bill.* 4 the draft of a proposed law. 5 a bird's beak.

billiards *noun*
a game played with cues and 3 balls on a cloth-covered table.

billion *noun*
1 in Britain, a million millions (1,000,000,000,000). 2 in America, and sometimes in Britain, a thousand millions (1,000,000,000).

billow *noun*
a large wave. *the billows of the sea.*
billowy *adjective*

billy *noun* (**billies**)
a can with a lid, used by campers, etc. for making hot drinks or cooking food.

billy-goat *noun*
a male goat.

bin *noun*
a large or deep container.

binary *adjective*
involving sets of two; consisting of two parts.

bind *verb* (**bound, binding**)
1 to fasten material round something. 2 to fasten the pages of a book inside a cover. 3 to tie up or tie together. 4 to make somebody do something or promise something.

bind *noun*
(*slang*) a nuisance; a boré.

bingo *noun*
a game played with cards on which numbered squares are covered or deleted as the numbers are called out at random.

binoculars *plural noun*
a device with lenses for both eyes, for making distant objects seem nearer.

biography *noun* (**biographies**)
the story of a person's life.
biographer *noun*, **biographical** *adjective*

biology *noun*
the science or study of living things.
biological *adjective*, **biologist** *noun*

bionic *adjective*
worked by or containing electronic devices, but behaving like a living being. *They designed a bionic man.*

birch *noun* (**birches**)
1 a deciduous tree with slender branches. 2 a bundle of birch branches used for flogging people.

bird *noun*
1 a feathered animal with two wings and two legs. 2 (*slang*) a young woman. 3 (*slang*) a prison sentence. 4 **bird's-eye view**, a general view of something, especially from above.

birdseed *noun*
seeds for caged birds to eat.

birth *noun*
1 being born. 2 **birth certificate**, a document showing where and when you were born. 3 **birth control**, ways of avoiding conceiving a baby. 4 **birth rate**, the number of children born in one year for every 1000 of the population.

birthday *noun*
the anniversary of the day you were born.

birthmark *noun*
a mark which has been on your body since you were born.

birthplace *noun*
where you were born.

biscuit *noun*
a flat thin piece of crisp baked pastry.

bisect *verb*
to divide something into two equal parts.

bishop *noun*
1 an important clergyman in charge of all the churches in a city or district. 2 a chess-piece shaped rather like a mitre.

bison *noun* (**bison**)
a wild ox.

bit *noun*
1 a small piece or amount of something. 2 the part of a tool that cuts or grips. 3 the part of a horse's bridle that is put into its mouth. 4 **a bit**, slightly. *I'm a bit worried.* 5 **bit by bit**, gradually. 6 **bits and pieces**, oddments.

bit past tense of **bite.**

bitch *noun* (**bitches**)
1 a female dog, fox, or wolf. 2 (*informal*) a spiteful woman; an unpleasant thing.
bitchy *adjective*

bite *verb* (*past tense* **bit**; *past participle* **bitten**; *present participle* **biting**)
1 to cut or take with your teeth. 2 to accept bait. *The fish are biting.* 3 to penetrate; to sting or hurt. *a biting wind.* 4 **bite the dust**, to be killed.

bite *noun*
1 biting. 2 a mark or spot made by biting. *an insect bite.* 3 a snack.

bitter *adjective*
1 not sweet; tasting unpleasant. 2 resentful; envious. 3 very cold.

black *adjective*
1 of the very darkest colour, like coal or soot. 2 very dirty. 3 dismal; not hopeful. *The outlook is black.* 4 **Black**, Negro. 5 **black coffee**, coffee without milk or cream. 6 **black eye**, an eye with a bruise round it. 7 **black hole**, (*in Astronomy*) a region in space with a strong gravitational field. 8 **black ice**, thin transparent ice on roads. 9 **black market**, illegal trading.

black

black *noun*
1 black colour. **2 Black,** a Negro.

blackberry *noun* **(blackberries)**
a sweet black berry.

blackbird *noun*
a European song-bird.

blackboard *noun*
a dark board for writing on with chalk.

blacken *verb*
to make or become black.

blackleg *noun*
someone who works while other workers are on strike.

blackmail *verb*
to get money from someone by threatening to reveal something that he wants to keep secret.

blackout *noun*
1 a time when lights are obscured or turned off. 2 losing consciousness or memory for a short time.

blacksmith *noun*
someone who makes and repairs things made of iron, especially someone who makes and fits shoes for horses.

bladder *noun*
1 the bag-like part of the body in which urine collects. 2 the inflatable bag inside a football.

blade *noun*
1 the sharp part of a knife, sword, axe, etc. 2 the flat, wide part of an oar, propeller, etc. 3 a long narrow leaf. *a blade of grass.*

blame *verb* **(blamed, blaming)**
1 to say that someone or something has caused what is wrong. *My brother broke the window but Mum blamed me!* 2 **he is to blame,** he is the person who caused what is wrong.

blame *noun*
blaming. *I got the blame for what he did.*

blancmange *noun*
(*say* blā-**monj**)
a pudding like a jelly made with milk.

blank *adjective*
1 not written, drawn, or printed on. *blank paper.* 2 without interest or expression. *a blank face.* 3 **blank cartridge,** a cartridge which makes a noise but does not fire a bullet. 4 **blank verse,** poetry without rhymes.

blank *noun*
1 an empty space. 2 a blank cartridge.

blanket *noun*
a large, thick covering used especially on beds.

blare *verb* **(blared, blaring)**
to make a harsh, loud sound.

blaspheme *verb* **(blasphemed, blaspheming)**
to talk irreverently about sacred things.
blasphemous *adjective,* **blasphemy** *noun*

blast *noun*
1 a strong rush of wind or air. 2 a loud noise. *the blast of the trumpets.* 3 **blast-off,** the launching of a spacecraft.

blast *verb*
1 to blow something up with explosives. 2 (*informal*) damn.

blaze *noun*
1 a very bright flame, fire, or light. **2 blazes,** (*informal*) hell. *Go to blazes!*

blaze *verb* **(blazed, blazing)**
1 to burn or shine brightly. 2 to feel very strongly. *He was blazing with anger.* 3 **to blaze a trail,** to show the way for others to follow.

blazer *noun*
a kind of jacket, often with a badge on.

bleach *verb*
to make or become white.

bleach *noun* **(bleaches)**
a substance to make things white.

bleak *adjective*
1 bare and cold. *a bleak hillside.* 2 dreary; miserable. *The future looks bleak.*

bleary *adjective* **(blearier, bleariest)**
with eyes that do not see clearly.

bleat *noun*
the cry of a lamb, calf, etc.

bleat *verb*
to make a bleat.

bleed *verb* **(bled, bleeding)**
1 to lose blood. 2 to draw blood or fluid from.

blemish *noun* **(blemishes)**
a flaw.

blend *verb*
to mix together smoothly or easily.

bless *verb*
1 to wish or bring someone happiness. 2 to make or call a person or thing holy.

blessing *noun*
1 being blessed. 2 a short prayer. 3 something you are glad of. *It's a blessing that they are safe.*

blew past tense of **blow** *verb*

blight *noun*
1 a plant disease. 2 an evil influence.

blimey *interjection*
(*slang*) an exclamation of surprise or disgust.

blind *adjective*
1 unable to see. 2 without thought or understanding. 3 **blind alley,** a road which has one end closed.

blind *verb*
to make someone blind.

blind *noun*
1 a screen for a window. 2 a deception; something used to hide the truth.

blindfold *adjective* and *adverb*
with your eyes covered by a cloth.

blink *verb*
to shut and open your eyes quickly.

bliss *noun*
great happiness.
blissful *adjective,* **blissfully** *adverb*

blister *noun*
a swelling like a bubble on your skin.

blitz *noun* **(blitzes)**
a sudden, violent attack, especially from aircraft.

blizzard *noun*
a severe snowstorm.

bloated *adjective*
swollen; inflated.

blob *noun*
a small round mass of something. *blobs of paint.*

block *noun*
1 a solid piece of something. 2 an obstruction. 3 a large building or group of buildings. 4 (*in Australia and New Zealand*) a large plot of land. 5 **block capitals** or **block letters**, capital letters.

block *verb*
to obstruct; to stop up.
blockage *noun*

blockade *noun*
an obstruction; a kind of siege.

blond or **blonde** *adjective* **(blonder, blondest)**
fair-haired.

blonde *noun*
a fair-haired girl or woman.

blood *noun*
1 the red liquid that flows through veins and arteries. 2 your ancestors. *She has noble blood.* 3 **in cold blood**, deliberately and cruelly.

bloodhound *noun*
a large dog used to track people by their scent.

bloodshed *noun*
the killing of people.

bloodshot *adjective*
having eyes streaked with red.

bloodthirsty *adjective*
eager to kill people.

bloody *adjective* **(bloodier, bloodiest)**
1 bleeding; involving bloodshed. 2 (*slang*) damned; very great. *You're a bloody fool.* 3 **bloody-minded,** deliberately awkward or not helpful.

bloom *noun*
1 a flower. 2 **in bloom,** flowering.

blossom *noun*
1 a flower, especially on a fruit-tree. 2 a mass of flowers on a fruit-tree, etc.

blossom *verb*
1 to produce flowers. 2 to develop into something. *She blossomed out into a fine singer.*

blot *noun*
1 a spot or blob of ink. 2 a flaw or fault.

blot *verb* **(blotted, blotting)**
1 to make a blot on something. 2 to dry with blotting-paper. 3 **blot out,** to delete or obscure. 4 **blot your copybook,** to spoil your good reputation.

blotch *noun* **(blotches)**
an untidy patch of colour.
blotchy *adjective*

blotting-paper *noun*
porous paper for soaking up ink, etc.

blouse *noun*
a garment like a shirt.

blow *verb* **(past tense blew; past participle blown; present participle blowing)**
1 to move in or with a current of air. *Her hat blew off.* 2 to push air from your mouth or nose. *He blew on his tea to cool it.* 3 to make something by blowing. *Let's blow bubbles.* 4 to make a sound by blowing. *Blow the whistle.* 5 to melt with too strong an electric current. *A fuse has blown.* 6 (*informal*) to damn. *Blow you, Jack, I'm all right.* 7 **blow-lamp** or **blow-torch,** a device for directing an intense flame at something. 8 **blow up,** to inflate; to explode.

blow *noun*
1 a hard knock or hit. 2 a shock; a disaster. 3 the action of blowing.

blue *noun*
the colour of a cloudless sky.

blue *adjective* **(bluer, bluest)**
1 blue in colour. 2 miserable; depressed. 3 obscene. *blue jokes.*

bluebell *noun*
a blue wild flower.

bluebottle *noun*
a.large fly.

blueprint *noun*
a detailed plan.

blues *noun*
1 a type of song or tune that is often sad. 2 **the blues,** a very sad feeling.

bluff *verb*
to deceive someone by pretending, especially by pretending to be able to do something.

blunder *noun*
a foolish mistake.

blunt *adjective*
1 not sharp. 2 outspoken; straightforward.

blur *verb* **(blurred, blurring)**
to make or become indistinct or smeared.

blurb *noun*
a description that praises something, especially a book.

blush *verb*
to become red in the face, especially when you are embarrassed.

bluster *verb*
1 to blow in gusts. 2 to talk threateningly.
blustery *adjective*

boa or **boa constrictor** *noun*
a large South American snake that crushes its prey.

boar *noun*
1 a wild pig. 2 a male pig.

board *noun*
1 a flat piece of wood. 2 a board made for a particular purpose. *a dart-board. a notice-board.* 3 daily meals supplied in return for money or work. *board and lodging.* 4 a committee. 5 **on board,** aboard.

board *verb*
1 to go on to a ship, aircraft, etc. 2 to give or get meals and accommodation. 3 **board over** or **up,** to cover something with boards.

boarder *noun*
1 a child that lives at a boarding-school during the term. 2 a lodger.

boarding-house *noun*
a house where people lodge.

boarding-school *noun*
a school which children live in during the term.

boast *verb*
to be proud, especially in talking.
boastful *adjective,* **boastfully** *adverb*

boat *noun*
1 a device built to float and travel on water. 2 **in the same boat,** in the same situation; having the same difficulties.

boating *noun*
going out in a boat, especially a rowing-boat.

bob *verb* **(bobbed, bobbing)**
to move quickly, especially up and down.

bobble *noun*
a small round ornament, often made of wool.

bob-sled or **bob-sleigh** *noun*
a sleigh with two sets of runners.

bodice *noun*
the upper part of a woman's dress.

body *noun* **(bodies)**
1 the flesh, bones, etc. of a person or animal. 2 a corpse. 3 the main part of something. 4 a group of people, things, etc. 5 a distinct object or piece of matter. *Stars and planets are heavenly bodies.*
bodily *adjective* and *adverb*

bodyguard *noun*
a guard to protect somebody's life.

bog *noun*
1 an area of wet, spongy ground. 2 (*slang*) a lavatory.
boggy *adjective*

bogus *adjective*
not genuine; not real.

boil *verb*
1 to make or become hot enough to bubble and give off steam. 2 to cook or wash something in boiling water. 3 to be very hot.

boil *noun*
1 an inflamed spot on the skin. 2 boiling-point. *Bring the milk to the boil.*

boiler *noun*
1 a container in which water is heated or clothes are boiled. 2 **boiler suit,** overalls.

boiling-point *noun*
the temperature at which something boils.

boisterous *adjective*
noisy and lively.

bold *adjective*
1 brave; courageous. 2 impudent. 3 clear; easy to see.

bollard *noun*
1 a short, thick post on a ship, quay, etc. to which ropes are attached. 2 a short, thick post to direct or keep out traffic.

bolster *noun*
a long pillow.

bolster *verb*
bolster up, to support; to help something that is weak.

bolt *noun*
1 a sliding bar for fastening a door. 2 a thick metal pin for fastening things together. 3 a sliding bar that opens and closes the breech of a rifle. 4 a flash of lightning. 5 **a bolt from the blue,** a surprise, usually unpleasant.

bolt *verb*
1 to fasten with a bolt. 2 to swallow food quickly. 3 to run away. *The horse bolted.*

bomb *noun*
1 a device that explodes. 2 **the bomb,** an atomic bomb or hydrogen bomb.

bomb *verb*
to attack with bombs.
bomber *noun*

bombard *verb*
1 to attack with gunfire. 2 to direct a large number of questions, complaints, etc. at somebody.
bombardment *noun*

bond *noun*
1 something that binds, restrains, or unites. 2 a document stating an agreement.
bondage *noun*

bone *noun*
one of the hard pieces of a skeleton.

bonfire *noun*
an outdoor fire to burn rubbish or celebrate something.

bonnet *noun*
1 the hinged cover over a car engine. 2 a round hat usually tied under the chin.

bonus *noun* **(bonuses)**
an extra payment or benefit in addition to what you get or expect.

bony *adjective* **(bonier, boniest)**
1 thin. 2 with big bones.

boo *verb*
to show disapproval by shouting 'boo'.

booby *noun* **(boobies)**
1 a stupid or childish person. 2 **booby prize,** a prize given to someone who comes last in a contest. 3 **booby trap,** something designed to hit or injure somebody unexpectedly.

book *noun*
1 a set of sheets of paper, usually with printing or writing on, fastened together inside a cover. 2 **book-keeping,** recording details of buying, selling, etc.

book *verb*
1 to reserve a place in a theatre, hotel, train, etc. 2 to record something in a book or list.

bookcase *noun*
a piece of furniture designed to hold books.

booklet *noun*
a small book.

bookmaker *noun*
a person whose business is taking bets.

bookmark *noun*
something to mark a place in a book.

boom *verb*
1 to make a deep, hollow sound. *The guns boomed continually.* 2 to be prosperous. *Business is booming.*

boom *noun*
1 a booming sound. 2 prosperity; growth. 3 a long pole at the bottom of a sail to keep it stretched. 4 a long pole carrying a microphone, etc.

boomerang *noun*
a curved stick used in Australia as a weapon. *If it does not hit anything, a boomerang comes back to the thrower.*

boost *verb*
to increase the power, value, or reputation of a person or thing.
booster *noun*

boot *noun*
1 a shoe that covers the ankle or leg. 2 the compartment for luggage in a car. 3 **the boot is on the other foot,** the situation has been reversed.

booth *noun*
a small enclosure for telephoning, voting, etc.

border *noun*
1 a boundary. 2 an edge. 3 a flower-bed.

borderline *noun*
a boundary.

bore *verb* **(bored, boring)**
1 to drill a hole. 2 to make somebody feel tired and uninterested. *The politician bored the audience.*

bore *noun*
1 a person who bores you. 2 something uninteresting or annoying.
boredom *noun*

bore past tense of **bear** *verb*.

born or **borne** past participle of **bear** *verb*.

borough *noun*
(*say* **bu**-rŏ)
an important town or district.

borrow *verb*
to be lent something.

Borstal *noun*
a place where young offenders are sent.

bosom *noun*
a person's breast.

boss *noun* **(bosses)**
(*informal*) a person who controls a business, workers, etc.

bossy *adjective* **(bossier, bossiest)**
fond of ordering people about.

botany *noun*
the study of plants.
botanical *adjective*, **botanist** *noun*

both *adjective* and *pronoun*
the two; not only one. *Are both films good? Both are interesting.*

both *adverb*
both ... and, not only ... but also. *This house is both small and ugly.*

bother *verb*
1 to cause somebody trouble or worry. 2 to take trouble about something; to be concerned. 3 (*informal*) damn! *Oh, bother! I've forgotten my coat.*

bother *noun*
trouble or worry.

bottle *noun*
a narrow-necked container for liquids.

bottle *verb* **(bottled, bottling)**
to put something in a bottle or bottles.

bottleneck *noun*
a place where something, especially traffic, cannot flow freely.

bottom *noun*
1 the base of something. 2 the farthest part of something. *Go to the bottom of the garden.* 3 a person's buttocks.

bottomless *adjective*
1 very deep. 2 inexhaustible. *a bottomless purse.*

bough *noun*
a branch of a tree.

bought past tense and past participle of **buy** *verb*.

boulder *noun*
a large smooth stone.

bounce *verb* **(bounced, bouncing)**
1 to spring back when thrown against something. 2 to make a ball, etc. bounce. 3 to move with bounces or jumps. 4 (of a cheque) to be sent back by a bank because it is worthless.

bounce *noun*
1 the action of bouncing. 2 liveliness.
bouncy *adjective*

bouncing *adjective*
big and healthy. *a bouncing baby.*

bound past tense and past participle of **bind** *verb*.

bound *adjective*
1 **bound for,** travelling towards. *This train is bound for London.* 2 **bound to,** certain to; obliged to. *He is bound to come.* 3 **bound up with,** closely connected with. *His illness is bound up with smoking.*

bound *verb*
to leap; to run with leaps.

bound *noun*
a bounding movement.

boundary *noun* **(boundaries)**
1 a line that marks a limit. 2 a hit to the boundary of a cricket field.

bounds *plural noun*
1 a boundary. 2 **out of bounds,** where you are not allowed to go.

bouquet *noun*
(*say* boh-**kay** or boo-**kay**)
a bunch of flowers.

bout *noun*
(*say* bowt)
1 a contest at boxing or wrestling. 2 a period of illness.

boutique *noun*
(*say* boo-**teek**)
a small shop, especially one that sells fashionable clothes.

bow *noun*¹
(rhymes with *go*)
1 a knot made with loops. 2 the stick used for playing a violin, cello, etc. 3 a device for shooting arrows. 4 **bow-legged,** bandy. 5 **bow-tie,** a necktie tied in a bow.

bow *noun*²
(rhymes with *cow*)
the front part of a ship.

bow *noun*³
(rhymes with *cow*)
bowing your body. *The waiter gave a bow.*

bow *verb*
(rhymes with *cow*)
to bend your body forwards to show respect or submission. *He bowed to the Queen.*

bowels *plural noun*
the intestines.

bowl *noun*
1 a deep, round dish. 2 the rounded part of a spoon, etc. 3 a ball used in the game of bowls or bowling, in which heavy balls are rolled towards a target.

bowl *verb*
1 to send a ball towards a batsman. 2 to get a batsman out by bowling.

bowler *noun*
1 someone who bowls in cricket. 2 a hard felt hat with a rounded top.

box *noun* (boxes)
1 a container made of wood, cardboard, etc. 2 a compartment in a theatre, lawcourt, etc. *witness-box.* 3 a hut or shelter. *sentry-box.* 4 a slap on the ear. 5 an evergreen shrub. 6 **box number,** a number to show where answers should be sent to a newspaper advertisement, etc. 7 **box-office,** a place where you can book seats for a theatre, cinema, etc. 8 **the box,** (*informal*) television.

box *verb*
1 to fight with fists. 2 to put into a box. 3 **Boxing Day,** the first weekday after Christmas Day.

boxer *noun*
1 someone who boxes. 2 a dog that looks like a bulldog.

boy *noun*
1 a young male person. 2 a son. 3 **boy-friend,** a boy that a girl regularly goes out with. **boyhood** *noun*, **boyish** *adjective*

boycott *verb*
to refuse to have anything to do with. *They boycotted the buses when the fares went up.*

bra *noun*
(*informal*) a brassière.

brace *noun*
1 a device for holding something in place. 2 **braces,** straps worn over the shoulders to hold trousers up.

bracelet *noun*
an ornament worn round the wrist.

bracken *noun*
1 a large fern. 2 a mass of large ferns.

bracket *noun*
1 a mark used in pairs to enclose words or figures. *There are round brackets ( ) and square brackets [ ].* 2 a support attached to a wall, etc. *Shelves can be fixed on brackets.*

brag *verb* (bragged, bragging)
to boast.

braid *noun*
1 a plait. 2 a decorative band of cloth.

braille *noun*
a system of writing or printing which blind people can read by touch.

brain *noun*
1 the part inside the top of the head that controls the body. 2 the mind or intelligence.

brainy *adjective* (brainier, brainiest)
clever; intelligent.

brake *noun*
a device for stopping or slowing down something.

bramble *noun*
a blackberry bush or a prickly bush like it.

branch *noun* (branches)
1 a part that sticks out from the trunk of a tree. 2 part of a railway, river, road, etc. that leads off from the main part. 3 part of a large organization.

branch *verb*
1 to form a branch. 2 **branch out,** to start something new.

brand *noun*
1 a particular kind of goods. *a cheap brand of tea.* 2 a mark made by branding. *Brands are used on cattle to show who owns them.* 3 **brand-new,** completely new.

brand *verb*
to mark cattle, sheep, etc. with a hot iron.

brandish *verb*
to wave something about.

brandy *noun* (brandies)
a strong alcoholic drink.

brass *noun* (brasses)
1 an alloy made from copper and zinc. 2 wind instruments made of brass, such as trumpets and trombones. 3 **brass-rubbing,** making a picture by rubbing a piece of paper laid over a brass memorial tablet on a tomb; a picture made in this way. **brassy** *adjective*

brassière *noun*
(*say* **bras**-i-air)
a piece of underwear worn by women to support their breasts.

brave *adjective* (braver, bravest)
courageous. **bravery** *noun*

brawl *noun*
a noisy quarrel or fight.

brawn *noun*
1 muscular strength. 2 cold pork or veal pressed in a mould.

brawny *adjective* **(brawnier, brawniest)**
strong; muscular.

bray *verb*
to make a noise like a donkey.

brazen *adjective*
1 made of brass. 2 shameless. *brazen impudence.*

brazier *noun*
(*say* **bray**-zi-er)
a metal container for burning coals.

breach *noun* **(breaches)**
1 the breaking of an agreement, rule, etc. 2 a gap.

bread *noun*
1 food made by baking flour and water, usually with yeast. 2 (*slang*) money. 3 **bread-winner,** someone who earns the money for a family.

breadth *noun*
width.

break *verb* (*past tense* **broke;** *past participle* **broken;** *present participle* **breaking**)
1 to divide into two or more pieces by hitting, pressing, etc. 2 to fail to keep a promise, law, etc. 3 to change. *After a sunny week, the weather broke.* 4 to stop or end. *She broke her silence.* 5 to stop working properly. *My watch is broken.* 6 (of waves) to fall and scatter. *The waves were breaking over the rocks.* 7 to go suddenly or with force. *They broke through the enemy's defences.* 8 to get or come. *break away. break loose. break open.* 9 **break a record,** to do better than anyone has done before. 10 **break down,** to stop working properly; to collapse. 11 **break off,** to detach; to stop. 12 **break out,** to start suddenly. 13 **break the news,** to make something known. 14 **break up,** to split up; to reach the end of a school term.
breakable *adjective,* **breakage** *noun*

break *noun*
1 a broken place; a gap. 2 an escape; a sudden dash. 3 a short rest from work. 4 (*informal*) a piece of luck; a fair chance. *Give me a break.* 5 **break of day,** dawn.

breakdown *noun*
1 a collapse or failure. *a nervous breakdown.* 2 an analysis. *a breakdown of the accounts.*

breaker *noun*
a wave breaking on the shore.

breakfast *noun*
the first meal of the day.

breakneck *adjective*
dangerously fast. *He drove at breakneck speed.*

breakthrough *noun*
an important advance or achievement.

breakwater *noun*
an object built to protect a harbour or coast against heavy waves.

breast *noun*
1 one of the parts of a woman's body where milk is produced. 2 a person's or animal's chest. 3 **breast-stroke,** a way of swimming on your chest.

breath *noun*
1 the air that someone breathes. 2 **out of breath,** panting. 3 **take your breath away,** to surprise or delight you.

breathalyser *noun*
a device to measure the amount of alcohol in somebody's breath.
breathalyse *verb*

breathe *verb* **(breathed, breathing)**
1 to take air into your lungs through your nose or mouth and send it out again. 2 to speak. *Don't breathe a word of this.*

breather *noun*
a pause for rest.

breathless *adjective*
panting.

breathtaking *adjective*
surprising or delightful.

bred past tense and past participle of **breed** *verb.*

breech *noun* **(breeches)**
the part of a gun barrel where the bullets are put in.

breeches *plural noun*
(say **brich**-iz)
trousers, especially trousers that fit tightly at the knee.

breed *verb* **(bred, breeding)**
1 to produce offspring. 2 to keep animals so as to get young ones from them. 3 to bring up; to train. 4 to create. *Poverty breeds illness.*

breed *noun*
a variety of similar animals. *a breed of pigs.*

breeder *noun*
1 someone who breeds animals. 2 **breeder reactor,** a nuclear reactor that creates more radioactive material than it uses.

breeze *noun*
a gentle wind.
breezy *adjective*

breeze-block *noun*
a lightweight building-block made of cinders and cement.

Bren or **Bren gun** *noun*
a kind of machine-gun.

brethren *plural noun*
(*old-fashioned use*) brothers.

brevity *noun*
being brief or short.

brew *verb*
1 to make beer or tea. 2 to start or develop. *Trouble is brewing.*

brewery *noun* **(breweries)**
a place where beer is made.
brewer *noun*

briar *noun*
a brier.

bribe *noun*
money or a gift offered to somebody to influence him.

bribe *verb* **(bribed, bribing)**
to give someone a bribe.
bribery *noun*

brick *noun*
1 a small, hard block of baked clay, etc. used in building. 2 a rectangular block of something.

bricklayer *noun*
a workman who builds with bricks.

bride *noun*
a woman on her wedding-day.
bridal *adjective*

bridegroom *noun*
a man on his wedding-day.

bridesmaid *noun*
a girl or unmarried woman who attends the bride at a wedding.

bridge *noun*
1 a structure built over a river, railway, or road, to allow people to cross it. 2 the high platform above a ship's deck. 3 the bony upper part of the nose. 4 a card-game rather like whist.

bridle *noun*
1 the part of a horse's harness that controls its head. 2 **bridle-path** or **bridle-road**, a path suitable for horses but not vehicles.

brief *adjective*
1 lasting a short time. 2 **in brief**, in a few words.

brief *noun*
instructions and information, especially given to a barrister.

briefcase *noun*
a flat case for documents, etc.

briefs *plural noun*
very short knickers or underpants.

brier *noun*
1 a thorny bush, especially a wild rose-bush. 2 a hard root used especially for making tobacco-pipes.

brigade *noun*
1 an army unit usually consisting of three battalions. 2 a group of people in uniform. *the fire brigade.*

brigadier *noun*
an officer who commands a brigade; an officer higher than a colonel.

brigand *noun*
an outlaw.

bright *adjective*
1 giving a strong light; shining. 2 clever. 3 cheerful.

brighten *verb*
to make or become bright.

brilliant *adjective*
very bright.
brilliance *noun*

brim *noun*
1 the edge round the top of a container. 2 the projecting edge of a hat. 3 **brim-full**, completely full.

brimming *adjective*
1 full. 2 **brimming over**, overflowing.

brine *noun*
salt water.

bring *verb* **(brought, bringing)**
1 to make somebody or something come; to lead or carry here. 2 **bring about**, to cause something to happen. 3 **bring off**, to achieve something. 4 **bring round**, to make someone conscious again after fainting. 5 **bring up**, to look after and educate a child.

brink *noun*
the edge of a steep or dangerous place.

brisk *adjective*
quick and lively.

bristle *noun*
a short, stiff hair.
bristly *adjective*

British *adjective*
of Great Britain.

Briton *noun*
someone born in Great Britain.

brittle *adjective* **(brittler, brittlest)**
likely to break or snap.

broad *adjective*
1 wide. 2 complete; full. *in broad daylight.* 3 not detailed. *a broad outline.* 4 rather rude. *broad comedy.* 5 **broad bean**, a large flat bean. 6 **broad-minded**, tolerant; not easily shocked.

broadcast *noun*
a radio or television programme.

broadcast *verb* **(broadcast, broadcasting)**
to transmit or take part in a broadcast.
broadcaster *noun*

broaden *verb*
to make or become broader.

broadside *noun*
firing by all the guns on one side of a ship.

brochure *noun*
a pamphlet containing information, especially about a place.

brogue *noun*
1 a strong kind of shoe. 2 a strong accent. *He spoke with an Irish brogue.*

broil *verb*
1 to cook on a fire or grid. 2 to make or be very hot.

broke past tense of **break** *verb.*

broke *adjective*
(informal) bankrupt.

broken past participle of **break** *verb.*

broken *adjective*
1 badly spoken. *The visitor spoke in broken English.* 2 **broken home**, a home where the parents have separated.

broker *noun*
someone who buys and sells things for other people.

bronchitis *noun*
(say brong-**ky**-tiss)
a disease of the lungs.

bronze *noun*
1 an alloy of copper and tin. 2 a yellowish brown colour. 3 **Bronze Age,** the time when tools and weapons were made of bronze. 4 **bronze medal,** a medal made of bronze, usually given as the third prize.

brooch *noun* **(brooches)**
(rhymes with *coach*)
an ornament pinned on to clothes.

brood *noun*
young birds that were hatched together.

brood *verb*
1 to sit on eggs to hatch them. 2 to keep thinking about something, especially resentfully.
broody *adjective*

brook *noun*
a small stream.

broom *noun*
1 a brush with a long handle, for sweeping. 2 a shrub with yellow, white, or pink flowers.

broomstick *noun*
1 the handle of a broom. 2 a broom.

broth *noun*
a thin soup.

brother *noun*
a man or boy who has the same parents as another person.
brotherly *adjective*

brought past tense and past participle of **bring.**

brow *noun*
1 an eyebrow. 2 the forehead. 3 the top of a hill; the edge of a cliff.

brown *adjective*
1 of the colour of earth or toast. *Brown bread is often made from wholemeal flour.* 2 suntanned.

Brownie *noun*
1 a junior Guide. 2 **brownie,** (*in Australia*) sweet bread made with brown sugar and currants.

browse *verb* **(browsed, browsing)**
1 to feed on grass or leaves. 2 to read or look at something casually.

bruise *noun*
a dark mark on skin made by hitting it.

bruise *verb* **(bruised, bruising)**
to give or get a bruise.

brunette *noun*
a woman with black or dark hair.

brush *noun* **(brushes)**
1 a device for sweeping, scrubbing, painting, etc. 2 a fox's bushy tail.

brush *verb*
1 to use a brush on something. *Have you brushed your hair?* 2 to touch somebody or something gently. 3 **brush up,** to revise a subject.

Brussels sprout *noun*
a small green vegetable.

brutal *adjective*
cruel or primitive.
brutality *noun,* **brutalize** *verb,* **brutally** *adverb*

brute *noun*
1 a brutal person. 2 an animal.

bubble *noun*
1 a thin transparent ball of liquid filled wih air or gas. 2 a small ball of air in a liquid or a solid. 3 **bubble gum,** chewing-gum that you can blow up into bubbles.
bubbly *adjective*

buccaneer *noun*
a pirate.

buck *noun*
a male deer, rabbit, or hare.

buck *verb*
1 (of a horse) to jump with the back arched. 2 **buck up,** (*informal*) to hurry.

bucket *noun*
a container with a handle, for carrying liquids, etc.
bucketful *noun*

buckle *noun*
a fastener for a belt or strap.

buckle *verb* **(buckled, buckling)**
1 to fasten with a buckle. 2 to crumple. *His knees buckled.* 3 **buckle down,** to start work. *I must buckle down to this job.*

bud *noun*
a flower or leaf before it has opened.

Buddhism *noun*
(*say* **buud**-izm)
a religion that started in Asia and follows the teachings of Buddha.
Buddhist *noun*

budding *adjective*
developing. *a budding singer*

budge *verb* **(budged, budging)**
to move slightly. *This door is stuck – it won't budge.*

budgerigar *noun*
(*say* **buj**-er-i-gar)
an Australian bird often kept as a pet in a cage.

budget *noun*
1 a plan for spending money wisely. 2 the money available for a particular purpose.

budget *verb*
to plan a budget.

budgie *noun*
(*informal*) a budgerigar.

buff *adjective*
of a dull yellow colour.

buffalo *noun* **(buffalo or buffaloes)**
a bison.

buffer *noun*
something that softens a blow, especially a device on a railway engine or wagon or at the end of a railway line.

buffet *noun*
(*say* **buu**-fay)
1 a refreshment counter. 2 a meal where guests serve themselves.

bug *noun*
1 an insect. 2 (*informal*) a germ or microbe.
3 (*informal*) a secret hidden microphone.

bug *verb* (**bugged, bugging**)
1 (*informal*) to fit with a secret hidden microphone. 2 (*slang*) to annoy.

bugle *noun*
a brass instrument like a small trumpet.
bugler *noun*

build *noun*
the shape of a person's body. *of slender build.*

build *verb* (**built, building**)
1 to make something by putting parts together.
2 **build in,** to include. 3 **build up,** to accumulate or increase; to cover an area with buildings; to make stronger or more famous.

builder *noun*
someone who puts up buildings.

building *noun*
1 constructing houses, etc. 2 something built, such as a house or a block of flats. 3 **building society,** an organization that lends money to people who want to buy houses.

bulb *noun*
1 a globular device to produce electric light.
2 something that looks like an onion, planted in the ground to produce daffodils, tulips, etc.
bulbous *adjective*

bulge *noun*
a swelling.
bulgy *adjective*

bulge *verb* (**bulged, bulging**)
to swell.

bulk *noun*
1 the size of something, especially when it is large. 2 the majority. 3 **in bulk,** in large quantities.
bulky *adjective*

bull *noun*
a male ox, elephant, or whale.

bulldog *noun*
a dog with a short, thick neck.

bulldozer *noun*
a heavy vehicle used to clear or flatten land.
bulldoze *verb*

bullet *noun*
1 a small lump of metal shot from a rifle or pistol. 2 **bullet-proof,** able to stop bullets.

bulletin *noun*
an announcement of news.

bullfight *noun*
a contest between men and bulls, done as a public entertainment.
bullfighter *noun*, **bullfighting** *noun*

bullion *noun*
bars of gold or silver

bullock *noun*
a young bull.

bull's-eye *noun*
1 the centre of a target. 2 a hard peppermint sweet.

bully *verb* (**bullied, bullying**)
1 to hurt or frighten a weaker person. 2 to start play in hockey. *bully off.*

bully *noun* (**bullies**)
1 someone who bullies people. 2 starting play in hockey.

bulrush *noun* (**bulrushes**)
a tall rush with a soft, thick head.

bulwark *noun*
(*say* **buul**-werk)
1 a defence; a defending wall. 2 **bulwarks,** a ship's side above the level of the deck.

bum *noun*
(*slang*) a person's bottom.

bumble-bee *noun*
a large bee.

bump *verb*
1 to knock against something. 2 to move along with jolts. 3 **bump into,** (*informal*) to meet unexpectedly. 4 **bump off,** (*slang*) to kill.

bump *noun*
1 the action of bumping. 2 a swelling or lump.
bumpy *adjective*

bumper *noun*
1 a bar along the front or back of a motor vehicle to protect it in collisions. 2 a ball in cricket that bounces high.

bumper *adjective*
unusually large; excellent. *a bumper crop of potatoes.*

bun *noun*
1 a small cake. 2 a round bunch of hair at the back of a woman's head.

bunch *noun* (**bunches**)
a number of things joined or tied together. *a bunch of bananas.*
bunchy *adjective*

bundle *noun*
a number of things tied or wrapped together.

bundle *verb* (**bundled, bundling**)
1 to make into a bundle. 2 to put hurriedly or carelessly. *They bundled him into a taxi.*

bung *verb*
1 (*slang*) to throw. *Bung that pencil over here.*
2 **bunged up,** (*informal*) blocked.

bung *noun*
a stopper. *Put the bung in that barrel.*

bungalow *noun*
a house without any upstairs rooms.

bungle *verb* (**bungled, bungling**)
to do something unsuccessfully or clumsily.
bungler *noun*

bunk *noun*
1 a bed like a shelf, as on a ship. 2 **bunk beds,** two single beds, joined one above the other.
3 **do a bunk,** (*slang*) to run away.

bunker *noun*
1 a container for storing fuel. 2 a pit, etc. made as an obstacle on a golf-course. 3 an underground shelter.

bunny *noun* (**bunnies**)
(*informal*) a rabbit.

Bunsen burner *noun*
a device that uses gas to make a flame for scientific experiments, etc.

buoy *noun*
(*say* boi)
an anchored floating object used to mark a channel, etc.

buoyant *adjective*
1 able to float. 2 cheerful.
buoyancy *noun*

bur *noun*
part of a plant that clings to your clothes or hair.

burden *noun*
1 a heavy load. 2 something hard to put up with.
burdensome *adjective*

bureau *noun* (**bureaux**)
(*say* bewr-oh)
1 a writing-desk. 2 an office or department. *They will tell you at the Information Bureau.*

burglar *noun*
someone who breaks into a building to steal things.
burglary *noun*, **burgle** *verb*

burial *noun*
burying somebody.

burly *adjective* (**burlier, burliest**)
big and strong.
burliness *noun*

burn *verb* (**burnt** or **burned, burning**)
1 to damage or destroy something with fire or heat. 2 to be damaged or destroyed by fire or heat. 3 to be on fire. 4 to feel very hot. 5 **burn up,** to destroy by burning.

burn *noun*
1 an injury caused by burning. 2 the firing of a spacecraft's rocket.

burner *noun*
the part of a lamp or cooker that shapes the flame.

burning *adjective*
1 intense. *a burning desire.* 2 very important; hotly discussed. *a burning question.*

burp *noun*
(*informal*) a belch.

burp *verb*
(*informal*) to belch.

burrow *noun*
a hole dug by a rabbit, fox, etc.

burrow *verb*
1 to dig a burrow. 2 to dig or search deeply.

burst *verb* (**burst, bursting**)
1 to break apart. 2 to start something suddenly. *He burst out laughing and she burst into tears.* 3 to be very full, excited, etc. *bursting with energy.* 4 **burst in,** to rush in.

burst *noun*
1 bursting; a split. 2 something short and forceful. *a burst of gunfire.*

bury *verb* (**buried, burying**)
1 to put a person or thing under the ground. 2 **bury the hatchet,** to stop quarrelling or fighting.

bus *noun* (**buses**)
1 a large vehicle for passengers to travel in. 2 **bus-stop,** a place where a bus regularly stops.

bush *noun* (**bushes**)
1 a plant like a small tree with many stems or branches. 2 **the bush,** wild land, especially in Australia or Africa.
bushy *adjective*

busily *adverb*
in a busy way.

business *noun* (**businesses**)
(*say* biz-niss)
1 a person's concerns or responsibilities. *Mind your own business.* 2 an affair or subject. *I am tired of the whole business.* 3 a shop or firm. 4 buying and selling. 5 **business-like,** practical; well organized.

busker *noun*
someone who entertains in the street.

bust *noun*
1 a sculpture of a person's head and shoulders. 2 a woman's bosom.

bust *adjective*
(*informal*) 1 broken or burst. 2 bankrupt.

bustle *verb* (**bustled, bustling**)
to hurry or be very busy.

busy *adjective* (**busier, busiest**)
1 doing a lot; having much to do. 2 full of activity. *a busy street.* 3 (of a telephone line) already being used.

busybody *noun* (**busybodies**)
someone who interferes.

but *conjunction*
however; nevertheless. *I wanted to go but I couldn't.*

but *preposition*
except. *There's no one here but me.*

butane *noun*
(*say* bew-tayn)
a gas used as fuel.

butcher *noun*
1 someone who cuts up meat and sells it. 2 a cruel murderer.
butchery *noun*

butler *noun*
a senior male servant.

butt *noun*
1 the thicker end of a weapon or tool. 2 a large barrel. 3 someone who is often ridiculed.

butt *verb*
1 to hit with your head. 2 to place the edges of things together. 3 **butt in,** to interrupt or intrude.

butter *noun*
a yellow food made from cream.

buttercup *noun*
a yellow wild flower.

butter-fingers *noun*
someone who often drops things.

butterfly *noun* **(butterflies)**
1 an insect with large white or coloured wings. 2 a swimming stroke in which you raise both arms together.

butterscotch *noun* **(butterscotches)**
a kind of hard toffee.

buttocks *plural noun*
the part of the body on which a person sits.

button *noun*
1 a fastener sewn on clothes. 2 a small knob. *She pressed the button to ring the bell.*

button *verb*
to fasten with a button.

buttonhole *noun*
1 a slit for a button to pass through. 2 a flower worn on a lapel.

buttonhole *verb* **(buttonholed, buttonholing)**
to stop someone so that you can talk to him.

buttress *noun* **(buttresses)**
a support built against a wall.

buy *verb* **(bought, buying)**
1 to get something by paying for it. *I bought these sweets yesterday.* 2 *(slang)* to accept; to believe. *Nobody will buy that excuse.*
buyer *noun*

buy *noun*
a purchase.

buzz *noun* **(buzzes)**
a vibrating humming sound.

buzz *verb*
1 to make a buzz. 2 **buzz off,** *(slang)* to go away.
buzzer *noun*

buzzard *noun*
a bird of prey like a large hawk.

by *preposition*
1 near; beside. *Sit by me.* 2 through; along. *You can reach it by the path.* 3 past. *She went by the window.* 4 during. *They came by night.* 5 before. *Do your homework by tomorrow.* 6 using; by means of. *cooking by gas.* 7 according to. *Don't judge by appearances.* 8 **by the way,** incidentally; on a different subject.

by *adverb*
1 past. *I can't get by.* 2 for future use. *Put some money by for the holidays.* 3 **by and by,** soon; later on. 4 **by and large,** on the whole.

bye *noun*
a run scored in cricket when the batsman has not touched the ball.

bye-bye *interjection*
(informal) goodbye.

by-election *noun*
an election when an M.P. has died or resigned.

by-law *noun*
a law which only applies to a particular town, district, etc.

bypass *noun* **(bypasses)**
a road that takes traffic past a congested area.

by-product *noun*
something produced while something else is being made. *Tar and coke are by-products of making gas from coal.*

bystander *noun*
someone standing near but taking no part when something happens; a spectator.

C

c
1 short for **centigrade.** 2 100 in Roman numerals.

cab *noun*
1 a taxi. 2 a compartment for the driver of a lorry, bus, train, or crane.

cabaret *noun*
(*say* **kab**-à-ray)
an entertainment, especially performed in a restaurant or night-club.

cabbage *noun*
a round, green vegetable.

cabin *noun*
1 a hut or shelter. 2 a compartment in a ship, aircraft, etc. 3 a driver's cab.

cabinet *noun*
1 a cupboard with drawers or shelves. 2 the group of chief ministers who control the government. *The Prime Minister chose a new cabinet.*

cable *noun*
1 thick rope, wire, or chain. 2 a telegram sent overseas.

cackle *noun*
1 the clucking of a hen. 2 a loud, silly laugh. 3 stupid chattering.

cactus *noun* **(cacti)**
a fleshy plant that grows in hot, dry places.

caddie *noun*
someone who helps a golfer by carrying his clubs.

caddy *noun* **(caddies)**
a small container for tea-leaves from which tea is to be made.

cadet *noun*
a young person being trained for the armed forces or the police.

cadge *verb* **(cadged, cadging)**
to get something by begging for it.

café *noun*
(*say* **kaf**-ay)
a small restaurant.

cafeteria *noun*
(*say* kaf-è-**teer**-i-å)
a café where the customers serve themselves
from a counter.

caftan *noun*
a long, loose jacket or dress, with wide sleeves.

cage *noun*
a container made of bars or wires, in which
birds or animals are kept.

cagoule *noun*
a waterproof jacket.

cake *noun*
1 a baked mixture of flour, eggs, butter, etc. 2 a
flat, round lump of something. *a cake of soap.*
fish cakes.

caked *adjective*
covered with dried mud, etc.

calamine *noun*
a pink powder used to make a soothing lotion.

calamity *noun* **(calamities)**
a disaster.
calamitous *adjective*

calcium *noun*
a greyish-white element contained in teeth,
bones, and lime.

calculate *verb* **(calculated, calculating)**
1 to work out something. 2 to plan or intend
something.
calculation *noun*

calculator *noun*
a machine for doing sums.

calendar *noun*
something that shows the dates of the month or
year.

calf *noun*[1] **(calves)**
a young cow, whale, seal, etc.

calf *noun*[2] **(calves)**
the back part of the leg below the knee.

calico *noun*
cotton cloth.

call *verb*
1 to shout. 2 to tell somebody to come to you.
3 to telephone. 4 to wake somebody up. 5 to
make a visit. 6 to name somebody or something. 7 to describe as. *I call that a swindle.*
8 **call it a day,** to decide that you have done
enough work for one day, and stop working.
9 **call somebody names,** to insult him. 10 **call
up,** to make somebody join the armed forces.

call *noun*
1 a shout or cry. 2 a visit. 3 a summons or
invitation. 4 telephoning somebody.

calling *noun*
a profession or trade.

calm *adjective*
1 quiet and still. *a calm sea.* 2 not excited or
agitated. *Please keep calm.*
calmly *adverb,* **calmness** *noun*

calorie *noun*
a unit for measuring an amount of heat or the
energy produced by food.
calorific *adjective*

calves plural of **calf.**

came past tense of **come.**

camel *noun*
a large animal with a long neck and one or two
humps on its back. *Camels are used for travelling across deserts because they can go for a
long time without food or water.*

camera *noun*
a device for taking photographs, films, or television pictures.
cameraman *noun*

camouflage *noun*
(*say* **kam**-ò-flahzh)
a way of hiding things by making them look
like part of their surroundings.

camp *noun*
a place where people live in tents, huts, etc. for
a short time.

camp *verb*
to have a holiday in a camp; to make a camp.
camper *noun*

campaign *noun*
1 a series of battles in one area or with one aim.
2 a planned series of actions, especially to
arouse interest in something. *A campaign for
human rights.*

campsite *noun*
a place for camping.

can *verb*[1] (*past tense* **could**; there is no past
participle or present participle)
1 to be able to do something; to know how to
do something. *Can you lift this stone?*
2 (*informal*) to be allowed to do something. *Can I go home?*

can *verb*[2] **(canned, canning)**
1 to put in a can or cans. 2 **canned music,**
recorded music.
cannery *noun*

can *noun*
a metal container for food, drink, etc.

Canadian *adjective*
of Canada.

canal *noun*
an artificial river

canary *noun* **(canaries)**
a small yellow bird that sings.

cancel *verb* **(cancelled, cancelling)**
1 to say that something planned will not be
done or not take place. 2 to stop an order for
something. 3 to mark a stamp, ticket, etc. so
that it cannot be used again. 4 **cancel out,** to
stop the effect of one another. *The arguments
cancelled each other out.*
cancellation *noun*

cancer *noun*
1 a disease in which a harmful growth forms in
the body. 2 a harmful growth in the body.

candidate *noun*
1 someone who wants to be elected or chosen for a particular job, position, etc. 2 someone taking an examination.

candle *noun*
a stick of wax with a wick through it, giving light when burning.
candlelight *noun*

candlestick *noun*
a holder for a candle or candles.

candy *noun* **(candies)**
sweets; a sweet.

candy-floss *noun*
a fluffy mass of spun sugar.

cane *noun*
1 the stem of a reed or tall grass; a thin stick. 2 a cane used to beat somebody.

cane *verb* **(caned, caning)**
to beat somebody with a cane.

canine *adjective*
1 like a dog; of dogs. 2 **canine tooth,** a pointed tooth.

canine *noun*
1 a dog. 2 a canine tooth.

cannabis *noun*
hemp, especially smoked as a drug.

cannibal *noun*
1 a person who eats human flesh. 2 an animal that eats animals of its own kind.
cannibalism *noun*

cannon *noun* **(cannon** or **cannons)**
a large, heavy gun.

cannonball *noun*
a large ball fired from a cannon.

cannot can not. *I cannot swim.*

canoe *noun*
a narrow, lightweight boat.

canoe *verb* **(canoed, canoeing)**
to travel in a canoe.
canoeist *noun*

canopy *noun* **(canopies)**
an overhanging cover.

can't *(informal)* can not.

canteen *noun*
1 a restaurant for workers in a factory, office, etc. 2 a box containing a set of cutlery. 3 a soldier's or camper's water-flask or set of eating utensils.

canter *verb*
to go at a gentle gallop.

canvas *noun* **(canvases)**
1 strong, coarse cloth. 2 a piece of canvas for painting on; a painting.

canvass *verb*
to visit people to ask for votes, opinions, etc.

canyon *noun*
a deep valley, usually with a river running through it.

cap *noun*
1 a soft hat without a brim but often with a peak. 2 being chosen to be in a particular sports team. *He got his cap in the first eleven.*

3 a cover or top. 4 something that makes a bang when it is fired in a toy pistol.

cap *verb* **(capped, capping)**
1 to put a cap or top on something; to cover. 2 to do better than something. *Can you cap that joke?*

capable *adjective*
able to do something.
capability *noun,* **capably** *adverb*

capacity *noun* **(capacities)**
1 ability. 2 the amount that something can hold. 3 the position someone occupies. *In my capacity as your teacher.*

cape *noun*[1]
a promontory.

cape *noun*[2]
a cloak.

caper *verb*
to jump about playfully.

caper *noun*
1 capering. 2 *(slang)* an activity or adventure.

capital *adjective*
1 *(informal)* excellent. 2 **capital city,** the most important city in a country. 3 **capital letter,** a large letter of the kind used at the start of a name or a sentence. *A, B, C, etc. are capital letters.* 4 **capital punishment,** punishing criminals by killing them.

capital *noun*
1 a capital city. 2 a capital letter. 3 the top part of a pillar. 4 money or property that can be used to make more wealth.

capitalist *noun*
(*say* **kap**-it-à-list)
someone who uses his wealth to make more wealth; a very rich person.
capitalism *noun*

capsize *verb* **(capsized, capsizing)**
to overturn a boat in the water.

capsule *noun*
1 a hollow pill containing medicine. 2 a small spacecraft or pressurized cabin.

captain *noun*
1 someone in command of a ship, aircraft, sports-team, etc. 2 an officer in the army or navy.

caption *noun*
1 the words printed with a picture to describe it. 2 a heading in a newspaper or magazine.

captivating *adjective*
charming; delightful.

captive *noun*
a prisoner.

captive *adjective*
imprisoned; unable to escape.
captivity *noun*

captor *noun*
someone who has captured a person or animal.

capture *verb* **(captured, capturing)**
to catch or imprison.

car *noun*
1 a motor car. 2 a carriage. *a dining-car.*

carat *noun*
1 a measure of weight for jewels. 2 a measure of the purity of gold.

caravan *noun*
1 a covered cart or wagon used for living in, especially by gypsies or by people on holiday. 2 a company of people travelling together, especially across a desert.

carbohydrate *noun*
a compound of carbon, oxygen, and hydrogen. *Sugar and starch are carbohydrates.*

carbon *noun*
1 an element found in charcoal, graphite, diamonds, etc. 2 a carbon copy or carbon paper. 3 **carbon copy,** a copy made with carbon paper; an exact copy. 4 **carbon paper,** thin coated paper put between sheets of paper to make a copy on the bottom sheet of what is typed or written on the top sheet.

carburettor *noun*
a device for mixing fuel and air in an internal-combustion engine.

carcass *noun* **(carcasses)**
the dead body of an animal or bird.

card *noun*
1 a small, usually oblong, piece of stiff paper. 2 a playing-card. 3 cardboard. 4 **cards,** a game with playing-cards. 5 **on the cards,** likely; possible.

cardboard *noun*
thick, stiff paper.

cardigan *noun*
a knitted jacket.

cardinal *noun*
one of the leading priests in the Roman Catholic Church.

care *noun*
1 serious thought or attention; caution. *Take more care with your homework.* 2 protection; supervision. *Leave the child in my care.* 3 worry; trouble. *She was free from care.* 4 **care of,** at the address of. *Write to him care of his bank.* 5 **take care,** to be careful. 6 **take care of,** to look after; to deal with.

care *verb* **(cared, caring)**
1 to feel interested or concerned. 2 **care for,** to look after; to be fond of.

career *noun*
a job or profession; a way of earning a living or making progress.

career *verb*
to rush along wildly.

carefree *adjective*
without worries or responsibilities.

careful *adjective*
giving serious thought and attention to something; avoiding damage or danger.
carefully *adverb*

careless *adjective*
not careful.
carelessly *adverb,* **carelessness** *noun*

caress *noun*
(*say* kă-**ress**)
a gentle, loving touch.

caret *noun*
a mark (∧ or ⋏) showing where something is to be inserted in writing or printing.

caretaker *noun*
someone who looks after a school, block of flats, etc.

cargo *noun* **(cargoes)**
goods carried in a ship or aircraft.

Caribbean *adjective*
(*say* ka-ri-**bee**-ăn)
of the West Indies.

caricature *noun*
an amusing or exaggerated picture or description of someone.

carnation *noun*
a garden flower with a sweet smell.

carnival *noun*
a festival, usually with a procession in fancy dress.

carnivore *noun*
an animal that eats meat.
carnivorous *adjective*

carol *noun*
a hymn, especially a Christmas hymn.
caroller *noun,* **carolling** *noun*

carp *noun*
a freshwater fish.

carpenter *noun*
someone who makes things out of wood.
carpentry *noun*

carpet *noun*
a thick, soft covering for a floor.

carriage *noun*
1 one of the separate parts of a train where passengers sit. 2 a passenger vehicle pulled by horses. 3 carrying goods from one place to another; the cost of carrying goods.

carrier *noun*
1 someone or something that carries things. 2 **carrier-bag,** a large bag for holding shopping, etc. 3 **carrier-pigeon,** a pigeon used to carry messages.

carrot *noun*
an orange-coloured vegetable.

carry *verb* **(carried, carrying)**
1 to take something from one place to another. 2 to support the weight of something. 3 to have with you; to possess. *He is carrying a gun.* 4 to go a long distance. *Sound carries in the mountains.* 5 **carried away,** very excited. 6 **carry on,** to continue; to manage; (*informal*) to behave excitedly or strangely. 7 **carry out,** to accomplish something.

cart *noun*
1 a small vehicle for carrying loads. 2 **put the cart before the horse,** to do things in the wrong order.

cart *verb*
1 to carry in a cart. 2 (*informal*) to carry or transport something heavy or tiring. *I've been carting these books around the school.*

cart-horse *noun*
a large, heavy horse.

cartilage *noun*
(*say* **kar**-ti-lij)
tough, flexible tissue attached to a bone.

carton *noun*
a lightweight cardboard box.

cartoon *noun*
1 an amusing drawing. 2 a strip cartoon. 3 an animated film.
cartoonist *noun*

cartridge *noun*
1 the case containing the explosive for a bullet or shell. 2 a container holding film to be put into a camera, ink to be put into a pen, etc. 3 the device on a record-player that holds the stylus. 4 **cartridge paper,** strong white paper.

cartwheel *noun*
1 the wheel of a cart. 2 a somersault sideways.

carve *verb* (**carved, carving**)
1 to cut something carefully or artistically. 2 to cut meat into slices.

cascade *noun*
a waterfall.

case *noun*[1]
1 a container. 2 a suitcase.

case *noun*[2]
1 an example of something existing or happening. *four cases of chicken-pox.* 2 something investigated by the police or by a lawcourt. *a case of murder.* 3 the facts or arguments used to support something. *She made a good case for equality.* 4 the form of a word that shows how it is related to other words. Fred's *is the possessive case of* Fred. 5 **in any case,** anyway. 6 **in case,** because something may happen.

cash *noun*
1 money. 2 immediate payment for goods. *Do you want cash or hire-purchase?* 3 **cash and carry,** a place where you buy large quantities or big things that you take away with you. 4 **cash on delivery,** paying for goods when they are delivered. 5 **cash register,** a device that records and stores money received in a shop.

cash *verb*
1 to change a cheque, etc. into cash. 2 **cash in,** to take advantage.

cashier *noun*
someone in charge of the money in a bank, office, or shop.

cask *noun*
a barrel.

casket *noun*
a small box for jewellery, etc.

casserole *noun*
1 a covered dish in which food is cooked. 2 food cooked in a casserole.

cassette *noun*
1 a small sealed case containing recording tape, film, etc. 2 **cassette recorder,** a tape-recorder that uses cassettes.

cast *verb* (**cast, casting**)
1 to throw. 2 to shed or throw off. 3 to make a vote. 4 to make something of metal or plaster in a mould. 5 to choose the performers for a play, film, etc.

cast *noun*
1 a shape made by pouring liquid metal or plaster into a mould. 2 all the performers in a play, film, etc.

castanets *plural noun*
two pieces of wood, ivory, etc. held in one hand and clapped together to make a clicking sound, usually for dancing.

castaway *noun*
a shipwrecked person.

castle *noun*
1 a large, old, fortified building. 2 a piece in chess, also called a *rook.*

castor *noun*
(*say* **kah**-ster)
1 a small wheel on the leg of a table, chair, etc. 2 **castor sugar,** finely-ground white sugar.

casual *adjective*
1 not deliberate or planned. *a casual remark.* 2 informal; suitable for leisure time. *casual clothes.* 3 not permanent. *casual work.*
casually *adverb*

casualty *noun* (**casualties**)
someone killed or injured in war or in an accident.

cat *noun*
1 a small furry domestic animal. 2 a lion, tiger, leopard, etc. 3 (*informal*) a spiteful girl or woman. 4 **let the cat out of the bag,** to reveal a secret.

catalogue *noun*
a list.

catalyst *noun*
(*say* **kat**-à-list)
something that starts or speeds up a change or reaction.

catapult *noun*
a device for shooting pellets, small stones, etc.

catastrophe *noun*
(*say* kà-**tas**-trò-fi)
a great or sudden disaster.
catastrophic *adjective*

catch *verb* (**caught, catching**)
1 to get hold of somebody or something; to stop or intercept. 2 to hear or understand. 3 to be in time to get on a bus or train. 4 to get an illness. *She caught a cold.* 5 to surprise or detect somebody. *He was caught in the act.* 6 to trick somebody. 7 **catch fire,** to start burning. 8 **catch on,** (*informal*) to become popular; to understand. 9 **catch up,** to get level.

catch *noun* (**catches**)
1 catching something. 2 something caught or worth catching. 3 a trick. 4 a device for fastening a door, window, etc.

catch-phrase *noun*
a phrase that is very popular.

catchy *adjective* (**catchier, catchiest**)
easy to remember; soon becoming popular. *a catchy tune.*

category *noun* (**categories**)
a group or division of people or things.

cater *verb*
to provide food or entertainment.
caterer *noun*

caterpillar *noun*
a long, creeping creature that turns into a butterfly or moth.

cathedral *noun*
a large, important church.

Catherine-wheel *noun*
a firework that spins round.

Catholic *adjective*
1 of all Christians. *The Holy Catholic Church.* 2 Roman Catholic.

Catholic *noun*
a Roman Catholic.

catkin *noun*
a tiny flower hanging down from a willow, hazel, etc.

cattle *plural noun*
cows and bulls.

caught past tense and past participle of **catch** *verb*.

cauliflower *noun*
a cabbage with a large head of white flowers.

cause *noun*
1 what makes something happen; a reason. 2 a purpose for which people work; an organization or charity. *This collection is for a good cause.*

cause *verb* **(caused, causing)**
to make something happen.

caution *noun*
1 being careful. 2 a warning.

cautious *adjective*
careful.
cautiously *adverb*

Cavalier *noun*
a supporter of King Charles I in the English Civil War.

cavalry *noun*
soldiers who ride on horseback.

cave *noun*
a large hole in the side of a hill or cliff, or under the ground.

cave *verb* **(caved, caving)**
1 to explore caves. 2 **cave in,** to collapse.

cavern *noun*
a cave, especially a deep or dark cave.

cavity *noun* **(cavities)**
a hollow or hole.

cease *verb* **(ceased, ceasing)**
to stop.

ceaseless *adjective*
never-ending.

cedar *noun*
an evergreen tree with hard, fragrant wood.

ceiling *noun*
(*say* **see**-ling)
1 the flat surface that covers the top of a room. 2 the highest limit that something can reach.

celebrate *verb* **(celebrated, celebrating)**
1 to do something to show that a day or an event is important. 2 **celebrated,** famous.
celebration *noun*

celebrity *noun* **(celebrities)**
a famous person.

celery *noun*
a vegetable with crisp white or green stems.

cell *noun*
1 a small room, especially in a prison. 2 a microscopic part of a living creature or plant. 3 a device for producing electric current chemically.

cellar *noun*
an underground room.

cello *noun*
(*say* **chel**-oh)
a stringed instrument like a large violin, placed between the knees of the player.

celluloid *noun*
a transparent plastic.

cellulose *noun*
tissue that forms the main part of all plants and trees.

cement *noun*
1 a mixture of lime and clay used in building to make floors, join bricks together, etc. 2 a strong glue.

cemetery *noun* **(cemeteries)**
(*say* **sem**-ĕ-tri)
a place where dead people are buried.

censor *noun*
someone who looks at films, books, letters, etc. and removes anything he thinks may be harmful.
censorship *noun*

censure *noun*
criticizing or disapproving of something.

census *noun* **(censuses)**
an official count or survey of population, traffic, etc.

cent *noun*
1 a coin. *100 cents make a dollar in the United States, Canada, and Australia.* 2 a very small amount of money. *I haven't a cent.*

centenary *noun* **(centenaries)**
the hundredth anniversary of something.

centigrade *adjective*
using a scale for measuring temperature that gives 0 degrees for freezing water and 100 degrees for boiling water.

centimetre *noun*
one hundredth of a metre, about four tenths of an inch.

centipede *noun*
a long, tiny creature with many legs.

central *adjective*
1 of or at the centre. 2 most important.
centralize *verb*, **centrally** *adverb*

centre *noun*
1 the middle of something. 2 an important place; a place where particular things happen. *a shopping centre.*

centre-forward *noun*
the middle player in the front line of a team in football or hockey.

centrifugal *adjective*
1 moving away from the centre; using centrifugal force. 2 **centrifugal force,** a force that makes something revolving move out from the centre.

century *noun* **(centuries)**
1 one hundred years. 2 a hundred runs scored by one batsman in an innings at cricket.

ceramic *adjective*
of pottery.

cereal *noun*
1 a grass that produces seeds which are used as food. *Cereals include wheat, barley, oats, maize, and rye.* 2 a breakfast food made from a cereal.

ceremony *noun* **(ceremonies)**
(*say* **se**-ri-mŏn-i)
the solemn actions carried out at a wedding, funeral, or other important occasion.
ceremonial *adjective,* **ceremonious** *adjective*

certain *adjective*
1 sure; without doubt. **2 a certain person** or **thing,** someone or something that is known but not named or described. **3 for certain,** for sure. **4 make certain,** to make sure.
certainly *adverb*

certainty *noun* **(certainties)**
1 something that is sure to happen. 2 being sure.

certificate *noun*
1 an official document that can be used to prove something. *a birth certificate. a savings certificate.* **2 Certificate of Secondary Education,** an examination for pupils in secondary schools.

certify *verb* **(certified, certifying)**
to declare something officially, especially that someone is insane.

chaffinch *noun* **(chaffinches)**
a small bird.

chain *noun*
1 a row of metal rings fastened together. 2 a line of people. 3 a connected series of things. *a chain of events.* **4 chain letter,** a letter that you are asked to copy and send to several other people, who do the same. **5 chain reaction,** a series of happenings causing one another.

chair *noun*
a seat, usually with a back, for one person.

chairman *noun* **(chairmen)**
the person who is in control of a meeting.

chalet *noun*
(*say* **shal**-ay)
a small house, usually built of wood.

chalk *noun*
1 a soft white stick used for writing on blackboards, etc. 2 a kind of soft white rock.
chalky *adjective*

challenge *verb* **(challenged, challenging)**
to ask somebody to do something difficult, have a contest, etc.
challenger *noun*

challenge *noun*
challenging somebody. *I accept the challenge.*

chamber *noun*
1 (*old-fashioned use*) a room. 2 a chamber-pot. **3 chamber music,** music for a small group of players. **4 chamber-pot,** a receptacle for urine, etc., usually in a bedroom.

champagne *noun*
(*say* **sham**-payn)
a bubbly French wine.

champion *noun*
1 the best person in a sport, competition, etc. 2 someone who supports a cause by fighting, speaking, etc.

championship *noun*
a contest to decide who is the champion.

chance *noun*
1 a possibility; an opportunity. *This is your only chance.* 2 a risk. *Take a chance.* 3 the way things happen accidentally. **4 by chance,** accidentally; without being planned.

chancel *noun*
the part of a church round the altar.

chancellor *noun*
1 an important official. **2 Chancellor of the Exchequer,** the minister in charge of a country's finances.

chandelier *noun*
(*say* shan-dĕ-**leer**)
a hanging support for several lights.

change *verb* **(changed, changing)**
1 to make or become different. 2 to exchange. 3 to give coins or notes of small values in exchange for other money. *Can you change a £5 note?* 4 to go from one train, bus, etc. to another. *Change at Didcot for Oxford.*

change *noun*
1 changing. 2 the money that you get back when you give more money than is needed to pay for something. 3 a fresh set of clothes. 4 a variation in your routine. *Let's walk home for a change.*

changeable *adjective*
likely to change; often changing. *changeable weather.*

channel *noun*
1 a stretch of water joining two seas. *The English Channel is between Britain and France.* 2 a way for water to flow along. 3 the part of a river, sea, etc. that is deep enough for ships. 4 a broadcasting wavelength.

chant *noun*
a tune, especially one that is often repeated.

chant *verb*
to sing; to say or call words in a rhythm.

chaos *noun*
(*say* **kay**-oss)
complete disorder. *The room was in chaos.*
chaotic *adjective*

chap *noun*
(*informal*) a man or boy.

chapel *noun*
a place used for Christian worship; a small church or part of a church.

chapped *adjective*
with rough, cracked skin.

chapter *noun*
a section of a book.

char *verb* **(charred, charring)**
to scorch; to blacken with fire.

char *noun*
a charwoman.

character *noun*
1 a person, especially in a story or play. 2 the sort of person you are; the characteristics of a person or thing.

characteristic *noun*
something that makes a person or thing noticeable or different from others.

characteristic *adjective*
typical.

characterize *verb*
(characterized, characterizing)
1 to be a characteristic of. **2** to describe the character of.

charades *plural noun*
(*say* shă-**rahdz**)
a game in which people have to guess a word from other people's acting.

charcoal *noun*
a black substance made by burning wood slowly.

charge *noun*
1 the price asked for something. **2** rushing to attack. **3** the amount of explosive needed to fire a gun, etc. **4** electricity in something. **5** accusing somebody of a crime. **6 in charge of,** deciding what shall happen to a person or thing; controlling.

charge *verb* **(charged, charging)**
1 to ask a particular price. **2** to rush to attack someone or something. **3** to accuse somebody of committing a crime.

chariot *noun*
a horse-drawn vehicle with two wheels, used in ancient times for fighting, racing, etc.
charioteer *noun*

charisma *noun*
(*say* kă-**riz**-mă)
the quality that makes someone special, popular, influential, etc.
charismatic *adjective*

charity *noun* **(charities)**
1 giving money, help, etc. to other people. **2** an organization to help those in need.
charitable *adjective*

charm *noun*
1 attractiveness. **2** a magic spell. **3** something small worn or carried for good luck.

charm *verb*
1 to give pleasure or delight to someone; to attract. **2** to put a spell on; to bewitch.

chart *noun*
1 a large map. **2** a diagram, list, etc. giving information in an orderly way. **3 the charts,** (*informal*) a list of the records that are most popular.

charter *noun*
1 an official document giving somebody rights, etc. **2** chartering an aircraft, vehicle, etc. **3 charter flight,** a flight by a chartered aircraft.

charter *verb*
1 to hire an aircraft, vehicle, etc. **2** to give a charter to.

charwoman *noun* **(charwomen)**
a woman paid to clean a house, office, etc.
charlady *noun*

chase *verb* **(chased, chasing)**
to go quickly to try to catch up with somebody or something.

chasm *noun*
(*say* **ka**-zŭm)
a deep opening in the ground.

chassis *noun* **(chassis)**
(*say* **sha**-si)
the frame of a vehicle, etc. on which the body is put.

chat *noun*
a friendly or informal talk with someone.
chatty *adjective*

chat *verb* **(chatted, chatting)**
to have a chat.

château *noun* **(châteaux)**
(*say* **sha**-toh)
a castle or large country-house in France.

chatter *verb*
1 to talk quickly or stupidly; to talk too much. **2** to make a rattling noise.

chauffeur *noun*
(*say* **shoh**-fer)
someone paid to drive a car.

chauvinism *noun*
(*say* **shoh**-vin-izm)
1 being too proud of being a man. **2** being too patriotic.
chauvinist *noun* and *adjective*

cheap *adjective*
1 low in price; not expensive. **2** inferior.

cheat *verb*
1 to trick somebody. **2** to try to do well in an examination, game, etc. by breaking the rules.

cheat *noun*
someone who cheats.

check *verb*
1 to make sure that something is correct or in good condition. **2** to make something stop or go slower.

check *noun*
1 checking something. **2** the situation in chess when a king may be taken. **3** a pattern of squares.

checkmate *noun*
the winning situation in chess.

check-up *noun*
a careful check or examination.

Cheddar *noun*
a kind of cheese.

cheek *noun*
1 the side of the face below the eye. **2** impudence.

cheek *verb*
to be cheeky to someone.

cheeky *adjective* **(cheekier, cheekiest)**
impudent.
cheekily *adverb*, **cheekiness** *noun*

cheer *noun*
a shout of pleasure; a shout praising or encouraging somebody.

cheer *verb*
1 to give a cheer. **2** to comfort or encourage somebody. **3 cheer up,** to make or become cheerful.

cheerful *adjective*
happy; contented.

cheerio *interjection*
(*informal*) goodbye.

cheese *noun*
a solid food made from milk curds.
cheesy *adjective*

cheetah *noun*
a kind of leopard.

chef *noun*
(*say* shef)
the chief cook in a hotel or restaurant.

chemical *adjective*
of or produced by chemistry.

chemical *noun*
a substance used in or obtained by chemistry.

chemist *noun*
1 someone who makes or sells medicines. 2 an
expert in chemistry.

chemistry *noun*
1 the way that substances like elements combine and react with one another. 2 studying
these combinations, reactions, etc.

cheque *noun*
1 a written instruction to a bank to pay money
out of your account. 2 the form you write this
instruction on. 3 **cheque-book,** a number of
blank cheques fastened together. 4 **cheque
card,** a card that guarantees that your cheques
will be paid.

chequered *adjective*
marked with a pattern of squares.

cherish *verb*
1 to protect lovingly. 2 to be fond of.

cherry *noun* (**cherries**)
a small, round fruit with a stone.

chess *noun*
a game for two players with sixteen pieces each
(called **chessmen**) on a board of 64 squares
(called a **chess-board**).

chest *noun*
1 the front part of the body between the neck
and the waist. 2 a big, strong box. 3 **chest of
drawers,** a piece of furniture with drawers.
4 **get something off your chest,** (*informal*) to
say something that you are anxious to say.

chestnut *noun*
1 a tree that produces hard brown nuts. 2 the
nut of this tree. 3 an old joke or story.

chew *verb*
to grind food between your teeth.
chewy *adjective*

chewing-gum *noun*
a sticky flavoured substance for chewing.

chick *noun*
a very young bird, especially a very young
chicken.

chicken *noun*
1 a young hen. 2 a hen's flesh as food.

chicken *adjective*
(*informal*) afraid; cowardly.

chicken *verb*
chicken out, (*informal*) to stop or withdraw
because you are afraid.

chicken-pox *noun*
a disease that produces red spots on your skin.

chief *noun*
a leader; the most important person.

chief *adjective*
most important.

chiefly *adverb*
1 mainly. 2 most importantly; first of all.

chieftain *noun*
the chief of a tribe, band of robbers, etc.

chilblain *noun*
a sore, usually on a hand or foot, caused by cold
weather.

child *noun* (**children**)
1 a young person; a boy or girl. 2 someone's
son or daughter.

childhood *noun*
the time when you are a child.

childish *adjective*
1 behaving like a child. *Don't be childish!*
2 suitable for children. *a childish game.*

chill *noun*
1 coldness. 2 an illness that makes you shiver.

chill *verb*
to make something or somebody cold.

chilly *adjective* (**chillier, chilliest**)
1 slightly cold. 2 unfriendly.
chilliness *noun*

chime *noun*
a sound made by a bell.

chime *verb* (**chimed, chiming**)
to make a chime.

chimney *noun*
a tall pipe or structure that carries away smoke
from a fire.

chimney-pot *noun*
the piece of pipe at the top of a chimney.

chimney-sweep *noun*
someone who cleans the soot out of chimneys.

chimpanzee *noun*
an African ape.

chin *noun*
the part of the face under the mouth.

china *noun*
thin, delicate pottery.

Chinese *adjective*
of China.

Chinese *noun* (**Chinese**)
1 a Chinese person. 2 the Chinese language.

chink *noun*
1 a narrow opening. *He looked through a chink
in the curtains.* 2 a clinking sound. *They heard
the chink of coins.*

chip *noun*
1 a small piece of potato that is fried. 2 a small
piece of something. 3 a silicon chip. 4 a place

chip *verb* (**chipped, chipping**)
1 to knock small pieces off something. 2 to cut a potato into chips.

chirp *verb*
to make short, sharp sounds like a small bird.

chisel *noun*
a tool with a sharp end for shaping wood, stone, etc.

chisel *verb* (**chiselled, chiselling**)
1 to shape or cut with a chisel. 2 (*slang*) to swindle.
chiseller *noun*

chivalrous *adjective*
courteous; helping people.
chivalry *noun*

chlorine *noun*
a chemical used to disinfect water, etc.
chlorinate *verb*, **chlorination** *noun*

chlorophyll *noun*
the substance that makes plants green.

choc *noun*
(*informal*) chocolate.

choc-ice *noun*
an ice-cream covered with chocolate.

chocolate *noun*
1 a sweet, brown food. 2 a sweet powder used for making drinks; a drink made of it.

choice *noun*
1 choosing. 2 the power to choose between things. 3 what you have chosen.

choir *noun*
an organized group of singers, especially in a church.
choirboy *noun*

choke *verb* (**choked, choking**)
1 to stop somebody breathing properly. 2 to be unable to breathe properly. 3 to block up something.

choke *noun*
a device in a motor vehicle to control the amount of air mixed with the petrol.

cholera *noun*
(*say* kol-er-ă)
an infectious disease that is often fatal.

choose *verb* (*past tense* **chose**; *past participle* **chosen**; *present participle* **choosing**)
1 to decide to take one person or thing instead of another. 2 to make a decision about something.

chop *verb* (**chopped, chopping**)
to cut or hit something with a heavy blow.

chop *noun*
1 a chopping blow. 2 a small, thick slice of meat. 3 **the chop**, (*slang*) being dismissed or killed.

chopper *noun*
1 a small axe. 2 (*informal*) a helicopter.

choppy *adjective* (**choppier, choppiest**)
full of small waves. *a choppy sea.*

chopsticks *plural noun*
a pair of thin sticks used for eating Chinese or Japanese food.

choral *adjective*
(*say* kor-ăl)
of or for a choir or chorus.

chord *noun*
(*say* kord)
a number of musical notes sounded together.

chore *noun*
(*say* chor)
a hard job; a regular task.

chorus *noun* (**choruses**)
(*say* kor-ŭs)
1 the words repeated after every verse of a song or poem. 2 music sung by a group of people. 3 a group of people singing together.

chose, chosen, see **choose**.

christen *verb*
to baptize somebody.
christening *noun*

Christian *noun*
someone who believes in Christ.
Christianity *noun*

Christian *adjective*
1 of Christ or Christians. 2 **Christian name**, a name that someone has besides his surname.

Christmas *noun* (**Christmases**)
1 the time of celebrating Christ's birthday on 25 December or the days around it. 2 **Christmas pudding**, a rich pudding eaten at Christmas. 3 **Christmas tree**, an evergreen or artificial tree decorated at Christmas.

chromatic *adjective*
1 of colours. 2 **chromatic scale**, a scale going up or down the black and white notes of a piano.

chrome *noun*
a shiny, silvery metal.

chromium *noun*
chrome.

chromosome *noun*
the part of an animal cell that carries genes.

chronic *adjective*
1 lasting for a long time. *a chronic disease.* 2 (*informal*) very bad; severe. *chronic shortages.*
chronically *adverb*

chronicle *noun*
a record of events.

chronological *adjective*
in the order in which things happen.
chronologically *adverb*

chrysalis *noun* (**chrysalises**)
(*say* kris-ă-lis)
the cover a caterpillar makes round itself before it turns into a butterfly or moth.

chrysanthemum *noun*
a garden flower that blooms in autumn.

chubby *adjective* (**chubbier, chubbiest**)
plump.

chuck *verb*
(*informal*) to throw.

chuckle *verb* (**chuckled, chuckling**)
to laugh quietly.

chuckle *noun*
a quiet laugh.

chug *verb* (**chugged, chugging**)
to move with the sound of an engine.

chum *noun*
(*informal*) a friend.
chummy *adjective*

chunk *noun*
a thick lump.
chunky *adjective*

church *noun* (**churches**)
1 a building for Christian worship. 2 Christian worship. *Do you go to church?* 3 **Church**, a group or organization of Christians. *The Church of England.*

churchyard *noun*
the ground round a church, usually used as a graveyard.

churn *noun*
1 a large container for milk. 2 a machine for making butter.

churn *verb*
1 to make butter in a churn. 2 to stir something vigorously. 3 **churn out**, to produce large quantities of something.

chute *noun*
(*say* shoot)
a steep channel for people or things to slide down.

chutney *noun*
a strong-tasting mixture of fruit, peppers, etc., eaten with meat.

cider *noun*
an alcoholic drink made from apples.

cigar *noun*
a roll of compressed tobacco-leaves for smoking.

cigarette *noun*
a small, thin roll of shredded tobacco in thin paper for smoking.

cinder *noun*
a small piece of coal, wood, etc. partly burned.

cine camera *noun*
a camera used for taking moving pictures.

cinema *noun*
a place where people go to see films.

cinnamon *noun*
a yellowish-brown spice.

circle *noun*
1 a round, flat shape; the shape of a coin or wheel. *The edge of a circle is always the same distance from the centre.* 2 something like a circle. 3 a number of people with similar interests. 4 a balcony in a cinema or theatre.

circle *verb* (**circled, circling**)
to move in a circle; to go round something.

circuit *noun*
(*say* ser-kit)
1 a circular line or journey. 2 a race-course. 3 the path of an electric current.

circular *adjective*
like a circle; round.

circular *noun*
a letter, advertisement, etc. sent to a lot of people.

circulate *verb* (**circulated, circulating**)
1 to move around and come back to the beginning. 2 to send something to people.
circulation *noun*

circumference *noun*
the line or distance round something, especially round a circle.

circumstance *noun*
a fact, condition, event, etc. connected with someone or something.

circus *noun* (**circuses**)
an entertainment with clowns, acrobats, animals, etc., usually performed in a big tent.

cistern *noun*
a water-tank.

citizen *noun*
1 a native or inhabitant of a city or country. 2 someone who has full rights in a country.
citizenship *noun*

citrus *adjective*
of fruits like oranges, lemons, and grapefruit.

city *noun* (**cities**)
a large, important town.

civic *adjective*
of a city, citizens, or their council.

civil *adjective*
1 of citizens. 2 of the people who are not in the armed forces. 3 polite. 4 **civil rights**, the rights of citizens, especially to have freedom, equality, and the right to vote. 5 **Civil Service**, the people who administer a country's affairs.

civilian *noun*
someone who is not in the armed forces.

civilization *noun*
1 making or becoming civilized. 2 a civilized condition or society.

civilize *verb* (**civilized, civilizing**)
to improve somebody's behaviour, manners, education, etc.

clad *adjective*
clothed. *He was clad only in pyjamas.*

claim *verb*
1 to ask for something that you think belongs to you. 2 to state or assert.

claim *noun*
1 claiming. 2 something claimed, especially a piece of ground claimed or given for mining, etc.

clam *noun*
a large shellfish.

clamber *verb*
to climb something with difficulty.

clammy *adjective* (**clammier, clammiest**)
damp and cold or slimy.

clear

clamp *noun*
a device for holding things together.

clamp *verb*
1 to fix with a clamp. 2 **clamp down on,** to stop or try to stop something.

clan *noun*
a group sharing the same ancestor. *The Scottish clans include the Campbells and the MacDonalds.*

clang *verb*
to make a loud ringing sound.

clanger *noun*
(*slang*) 1 a blunder. 2 **drop a clanger,** to make a blunder.

clank *verb*
to make a loud sound like heavy pieces of metal banging together.

clap *verb* **(clapped, clapping)**
to make a noise by hitting the palms of your hands together, especially as applause.

clap *noun*
1 a sudden sharp noise. *a clap of thunder.* 2 applause.

clapper *noun*
1 the loose piece inside a bell which makes it ring when the bell is moved. 2 **like the clappers,** (*slang*) very quickly or very hard.

clarify *verb* **(clarified, clarifying)**
to make something clear.
clarification *noun*

clarinet *noun*
a woodwind instrument.
clarinettist *noun*

clarity *noun*
clearness. *Speak with clarity.*

clash *verb*
1 to make a loud sound like cymbals banging together. 2 to conflict. 3 to happen inconveniently at the same time. *I missed one of those programmes because they clashed.*

clash *noun* **(clashes)**
1 a clashing sound. 2 a conflict.

clasp *verb*
to hold somebody or something tightly.

clasp *noun*
1 a device for fastening things. 2 a grasp.

class *noun* **(classes)**
1 a group of children, students, etc. who are taught together. 2 a group of similar people, animals, or things. 3 a system of different ranks in society.

class *verb*
to classify.

classic *adjective*
generally agreed to be excellent or important.

classic *noun*
1 a classic book, film, writer, etc. 2 **classics,** Greek and Latin language or literature.

classical *adjective*
1 of Greek or Roman literature, etc. 2 serious or conventional. *classical music.*

classified *adjective*
1 put into classes or groups. 2 officially secret. 3 **classified advertisements,** small advertisements arranged in subjects.

classify *verb* **(classified, classifying)**
to put things in classes or groups.
classification *noun*

classmate *noun*
someone in the same class at school, etc.

classroom *noun*
a room where a class is taught.

clatter *noun*
a rattling or annoying noise.

clatter *verb*
to make a clatter.

clause *noun*
1 part of a contract, treaty, law, etc. 2 part of a sentence with its own verb. *There are two clauses in 'I must stay but you must go.'*

claw *noun*
one of the hard, sharp nails that some birds and other animals have on their feet

claw *verb*
to grasp or scratch with a claw or hand.

clay *noun*
a sticky kind of earth. *Clay is used for making bricks and pottery.*
clayey *adjective*

clean *adjective*
1 without any dirt or stains. 2 fresh; not yet used. *a clean page.* 3 honest; honourable. *a clean fight.* 4 not rude or obscene. *clean jokes.*
cleanliness *noun,* **cleanly** *adjective* and *adverb,* **cleanness** *noun*

clean *verb*
to make something clean.

clean *adverb*
1 (*informal*) completely. *I clean forgot.* 2 **clean-bowled,** bowled out in cricket without your bat touching the ball. 3 **clean-shaven,** without a beard or moustache.

cleaner *noun*
1 someone who cleans rooms, etc. 2 something used for cleaning. 3 **the cleaners,** a firm which cleans clothes, etc.

cleanse *verb* **(cleansed, cleansing)**
(*say* klenz)
1 to clean. 2 to make something pure.
cleanser *noun*

clear *adjective*
1 easy to understand, see, or hear. *a clear voice.* 2 free from obstacles or unwanted things. *The table is clear.*
clearly *adverb*

clear *adverb*
1 clearly. *Speak loud and clear.* 2 at a distance from something. *Stand clear of the gates.* 3 completely. *He got clear away.*

clear *verb*
1 to make or become clear. 2 to show or check that someone is innocent or reliable. 3 to jump over something without touching it. 4 **clear off,** (*informal*) to go away. 5 **clear out,** to empty or tidy; (*informal*) to go away. 6 **clear up,** to make things tidy.

clearance *noun*
1 clearing something. 2 getting rid of unwanted goods. 3 the space between two things.

clearing *noun*
an open space in a forest.

clef *noun*
a sign that shows the pitch of a stave in music.

clench *verb*
to close your teeth or fingers tightly.

clergy *plural noun*
clergymen.

clergyman *noun* **(clergymen)**
a person authorized to conduct services in a Christian church.

clerical *adjective*
1 of or done by clerks. 2 of clergymen.

clerk *noun*
(*say* klark)
someone employed to keep records and accounts, deal with papers in an office, etc.

clever *adjective*
quick to learn and understand things; skilful.

cliché *noun*
(*say* klee-shay)
a phrase or idea that is used too often.

click *noun*
a short, sharp sound. *She heard a click as someone turned on the light.*

client *noun*
someone who gets help or advice from a lawyer, architect, accountant, etc.; a customer.

cliff *noun*
a steep rock-face, especially on the coast.

climate *noun*
the normal weather in a particular area.
climatic *adjective*

climax *noun* **(climaxes)**
the most important part of a story, series of events, etc.
climactic *adjective*

climb *verb*
1 to go up or down something. 2 to grow upwards. 3 to rise. 4 **climb down**, to admit that you have been wrong.
climber *noun*

cling *verb* **(clung, clinging)**
to hold on tightly. *The child clung to its mother.*

clinic *noun*
a place where people see doctors, etc. for treatment or advice.

clink *verb*
to make a short ringing sound.

clip *noun*
a fastener for keeping things together.

clip *verb* **(clipped, clipping)**
1 to fasten with a clip. 2 to cut something with shears or scissors.
clippers *noun*

clipper *noun*
an old type of fast sailing-ship.

clipping *noun*
a piece cut off or out, especially from a newspaper or magazine.

cloak *noun*
a garment, usually without sleeves, that hangs loosely from the shoulders.

cloakroom *noun*
1 a place where you can leave coats, hats, luggage, etc. 2 a lavatory.

clock *noun*
a device that shows what the time is.

clockwise *adverb* and *adjective*
moving round a circle in the same direction as a clock's hands.

clockwork *adjective*
worked by a spring which has to be wound up.

clog *verb* **(clogged, clogging)**
to block something up.

clog *noun*
a shoe with a wooden sole.

cloister *noun*
a covered path round a courtyard or along the side of a cathedral, monastery, etc.

clone *noun*
an animal or plant made from the cells of another animal or plant.

clone *verb* **(cloned, cloning)**
to produce a clone.

close *adjective* **(closer, closest)**
(*say* klohs)
1 near. 2 careful; detailed. *with close attention.* 3 tight; with little empty space. *a close fit.* 4 in which competitors are nearly equal. *a close race.* 5 stuffy. *It's very close in this room.*
closely *adverb*, **closeness** *noun*

close *adverb* **(closer, closest)**
(*say* klohs)
closely. *Follow close behind.*

close *noun*
(*say* klohs)
1 a dead end. 2 an enclosed area, especially round a cathedral.

close *verb* **(closed, closing)**
(*say* klohz)
1 to shut. 2 to end. 3 **close in**, to get nearer or shorter.

close-up *noun*
(*say* klohs-up)
a photograph or film taken at short range.

closure *noun*
(*say* kloh-zher)
the closing of something.

clot *noun*
1 a mass of blood, cream, etc. that has nearly solidified. 2 (*informal*) a stupid person.

clot *verb* **(clotted, clotting)**
to form into clots.

cloth *noun*
1 material woven from wool, cotton, nylon, etc. 2 a piece of this material 3 a table cloth.

clothe *verb* **(clothed, clothing)**
to put clothes on.

clothes *plural noun*
1 things worn to cover your body. **2 clothes-line,** a line on which clothes are hung to dry or air. **3 clothes-peg,** a device to hold clothes on a clothes-line.

clothing *noun*
clothes.

cloud *noun*
a mass of water-vapour, smoke, dust, etc. floating in the air.
cloudless *adjective*

cloud *verb*
to fill or obscure with clouds. *The sky clouded over.*

cloudy *adjective* **(cloudier, cloudiest)**
1 full of clouds. 2 hard to see through.

clout *verb*
to hit hard.

clove *noun*
the dried bud of a tropical tree, used to flavour apple-pies, etc.

clove-hitch *noun* **(clove-hitches)**
a knot for fixing a rope to a pole, etc.

clover *noun*
a small wild plant, usually with three leaves. *A clover-leaf is like three small leaves joined together.*

clown *noun*
1 someone in a circus who makes people laugh. 2 an amusing person.

clown *verb*
to behave like a clown.

club *noun*
1 a heavy stick. 2 a stick for playing golf. 3 a group of people who meet together because they are interested in the same thing. 4 a playing-card with a black clover-leaf printed on it.

club *verb* **(clubbed, clubbing)**
1 to hit with a heavy stick. **2 club together,** to join with other people in doing something, especially raising money.

cluck *verb*
to make a noise like a hen.

clue *noun*
1 something that helps you to solve a puzzle or a mystery. **2 not have a clue,** to be ignorant or helpless.

clump *noun*
a cluster of trees.

clumsy *adjective* **(clumsier, clumsiest)**
likely to knock things over, drop things, or do something stupid.
clumsily *adverb*, **clumsiness** *noun*

clung past tense and past participle of **cling.**

cluster *noun*
a group of people or things close together.

clutch *verb*
to grasp or snatch at something.

clutch *noun*[1] **(clutches)**
1 a tight grasp. 2 a device for disconnecting the engine of a motor vehicle from its gears and wheels.

clutch *noun*[2] **(clutches)**
a set of eggs in a nest.

clutter *verb*
to make something untidy or confused.

clutter *noun*
an untidy number of things.

cm short for **centimetre** or **centimetres.**

co short for **company.**

c/o short for *care of.*

coach *noun* **(coaches)**
1 a single-decker bus used for long journeys. 2 a carriage of a railway train. 3 a carriage pulled by horses. 4 an instructor in athletics, sports, etc.

coach *verb*
to instruct or train somebody in athletics, sports, etc.

coal *noun*
a hard, black mineral used as fuel.

coarse *adjective* **(coarser, coarsest)**
not delicate or smooth; rough.

coast *noun*
the sea-shore and the land close to it.
coastal *adjective*, **coastline** *noun*

coast *verb*
to ride downhill without using power. *They stopped pedalling and coasted down the slope.*

coastguard *noun*
someone whose job is to keep watch on coasts, prevent smuggling, etc.

coat *noun*
1 a garment with sleeves, worn over other clothes. 2 a coating. *a coat of paint.* **3 coat of arms,** a design on a shield, etc. representing a family, town, etc.

coat *verb*
to cover with a coating.

coating *noun*
a covering; a layer.

coax *verb*
to persuade somebody gently or patiently.

cobalt *noun*
a silvery-white metal.

cobble *noun*
a cobble-stone.

cobbled *adjective*
paved with cobble-stones.

cobbler *noun*
1 someone who mends shoes. **2 cobblers,** *(slang)* nonsense.

cobble-stone *noun*
a smooth, round stone. *Streets used to be paved with cobble-stones.*

cobra *noun*
(say **koh**-bră)
a poisonous snake.

cobweb *noun*
a thin, sticky net spun by a spider to trap insects.

cock *noun*
a male bird, especially a male fowl.

cock *verb*
1 to make a gun ready to fire. 2 to turn something upwards or in a particular direction. *He cocked his eye at me.*

cockerel *noun*
a young male fowl.

cocker spaniel *noun*
a small spaniel.

cockle *noun*
an edible shellfish.

cockney *noun*
1 someone born in London, especially in east London. 2 a kind of English spoken by cockneys.

cockpit *noun*
the place for the pilot in an aircraft.

cockroach *noun* (cockroaches)
a dark-brown insect.

cocky *adjective* (cockier, cockiest)
(*informal*) conceited; cheeky.

cocoa *noun*
1 a hot drink that tastes of chocolate. 2 the powder from which you make this drink.

coconut *noun*
a large, round nut that grows on palm trees. *Coconuts contain a sweet white lining and a milky juice.*

cocoon *noun*
the covering round a chrysalis.

cod *noun* (cod)
a large, edible sea-fish.

code *noun*
1 a set of signs, letters, etc. for sending messages secretly or quickly. 2 a set of rules. *The Highway Code.*

coeducation *noun*
educating boys and girls together.
coeducational *adjective*

coffee *noun*
1 a hot drink made from the roasted and crushed beans of a tropical shrub. 2 the powder from which you make this drink.

coffin *noun*
the long box in which a corpse is buried or cremated.

cog *noun*
1 one of a number of projections round the edge of a wheel. 2 **cog-wheel**, a wheel with cogs.

coil *noun*
a circle or spiral of rope, wire, etc.

coil *verb*
to wind something into circles or spirals.

coin *noun*
a piece of metal money.

coin *verb*
1 to manufacture money. 2 to invent a new word.

coinage *noun*
1 coining. 2 coins; a system of money. 3 a new word.

coincide *verb* (coincided, coinciding)
to happen at the same time as something else. *The end of term coincides with my birthday.*

coincidence *noun*
two things happening accidentally at the same time; a strange happening.

coke *noun*
a solid fuel made out of coal.

colander *noun*
(*say* kul-ǎn-der)
a strainer for vegetables, etc.

cold *adjective*
1 not hot or warm. 2 not kind or emotional. 3 **cold cream**, ointment for cleaning or softening the skin. 4 **cold shoulder**, being unfriendly. 5 **cold war**, a situation where nations are enemies without actually fighting.
coldly *adverb*, **coldness** *noun*

cold *noun*
1 cold weather or temperature. 2 an illness that makes your nose run, your throat sore, etc.

cold-blooded *adjective*
1 having blood that changes temperature according to the surroundings. 2 ruthless.

collaborate *verb* (collaborated, collaborating)
to work with somebody on a job; to help.
collaboration *noun*, **collaborator** *noun*

collage *noun*
(*say* kol-ahzh or kol-**ahzh**)
a picture made by fixing small objects to a surface.

collapse *verb* (collapsed, collapsing)
1 to fall to pieces; to break. 2 to become very weak or ill.

collapsible *adjective*
that can be folded up. *a collapsible table.*

collar *noun*
1 the part of a garment that goes round your neck. 2 a band that goes round the neck of a dog, cat, horse, etc.

colleague *noun*
someone that you work with.

collect *verb*
1 to get things together from various places, especially as a hobby. *She collects stamps; I collect coins.* 2 to go and get somebody or something.
collector *noun*

collection *noun*
1 things you have collected as a hobby. 2 money given by people at a meeting, church service, etc.

collective *adjective*
including or using many or all people or things.

college *noun*
a place where people can continue learning something after they have left school.

collide *verb* (collided, colliding)
to crash into something.
collision *noun*

collie *noun*
a kind of sheep-dog.

colon *noun*
a punctuation mark (:). *Colons are often used to introduce lists like this: red, blue, green.*

colonel *noun*
(*say* **ker**-nĕl)
an army officer, usually in charge of a regiment.

colonial *adjective*
of colonies.

colony *noun* **(colonies)**
1 a country controlled by another country. 2 a group of people or animals living together.
colonist *noun*

colossal *adjective*
huge; great.

colour *noun*
1 the effect produced by rays of light of a particular wavelength. *Red, blue, and yellow are colours.* 2 the use of all colours, not just black and white. *Is this film in colour?* 3 the colour of someone's face. 4 a substance used to colour things. 5 the special flag of a ship or regiment.

colour *verb*
1 to give something a colour or colours. 2 to blush. 3 to change or exaggerate something.
colouring *noun*

colour-blind *adjective*
unable to see or distinguish between some colours.

coloured *adjective*
1 having a particular colour. 2 with a dark skin; Negro.

colourful *adjective*
full of colour; lively.

colourless *adjective*
without colour; uninteresting.

colt *noun*
a young male horse.

column *noun*
1 a pillar. 2 something long and narrow. 3 a vertical part of a page. *Newspapers are printed in columns.* 4 a regular feature in a newspaper.
columnist *noun*

coma *noun*
(*say* **koh**-mă)
an unnatural deep sleep.

comb *noun*
1 a device for making hair tidy. 2 the red, fleshy crest on a fowl's head.

comb *verb*
1 to tidy with a comb. 2 to search carefully.

combat *noun*
a fight or contest.
combatant *noun*

combination *noun*
1 combining. 2 a series of numbers or letters used to open a combination lock. 3 **combination lock,** a lock that is opened by setting a dial or dials to positions shown by numbers or letters.

combine *verb* **(combined, combining)**
(*say* kŏm-**byn**)
to join or mix together.

combine *noun*
(*say* **kom**-byn)
1 a group of people combining in business. 2 **combine harvester,** a machine that reaps and threshes grain.

combustion *noun*
the process of burning.

come *verb* (*past tense* **came;** *past participle* **come;** *present participle* **coming**)
1 to move towards a person or place. *Come here!* 2 to arrive; to reach a place. *Has that letter come yet?* 3 to become. *Dreams can come true.* 4 to occur. *It comes on the next page.* 5 to amount. *The bill came to £10.*

comedian *noun*
someone who entertains people by making them laugh.

comedy *noun* **(comedies)**
1 a play, film, etc. that makes people laugh. 2 humour.

comet *noun*
an object moving across the sky with a bright tail of light.

comfort *noun*
freedom from worry or pain.

comfort *verb*
to give somebody comfort.

comfortable *adjective*
1 pleasant to use or wear. *a comfortable chair.* 2 free from worry or pain. *The nurse made the patient comfortable.*
comfortably *adverb*

comic *adjective*
1 making people laugh. 2 **comic strip,** a series of drawings telling a comic or serial story.
comical *adjective*, **comically** *adverb*

comic *noun*
1 a paper full of comic strips. 2 a comedian.

coming *noun*
arrival. *comings and goings.*

coming *adjective*
future. *in the coming years.*

comma *noun*
a punctuation mark (,) used to mark a pause in a sentence or to separate items in a list.

command *noun*
1 telling somebody to do something. 2 authority; control. *He is in command of these soldiers.* 3 skill or ability. *She has a good command of Spanish.*

command *verb*
1 to tell somebody to do something. 2 to be in charge of.
commandant *noun*, **commander** *noun*

commandment *noun*
a sacred command, especially one of the Ten Commandments of Moses.

commando *noun*
a soldier trained for making dangerous raids.

commemorate *verb*
(commemorated, commemorating)
to be a celebration or reminder of some past event, person, etc.
commemoration *noun*, **commemorative** *adjective*

commence *verb* **(commenced, commencing)**
to begin.
commencement *noun*

commend *verb*
to praise. *He was commended for bravery.*
commendable *adjective*, **commendation** *noun*

comment *noun*
a remark or opinion.

commentary *noun* **(commentaries)**
a description of an event, especially while it is
happening.
commentate *verb*, **commentator** *noun*

commerce *noun*
trade.

commercial *adjective*
1 connected with trade. 2 profitable.
3 financed by advertisements. *commercial
radio.* 4 **commercial traveller,** someone employed to travel around and get orders for
goods from shops, etc.
commercialize *verb*, **commercially** *adverb*

commercial *noun*
an advertisement, especially on television or
radio.

commit *verb* **(committed, committing)**
1 to do something. *She committed the crime.*
2 to put a person or thing into a particular
place. *He was committed to prison.* 3 **to commit
yourself,** to promise or decide to do something.
commitment *noun*

committee *noun*
a group of people appointed to organize or
discuss something.

common *adjective*
1 ordinary; usual; occurring frequently. *The
dandelion is a common weed.* 2 of all or most
people. *It was common knowledge.* 3 shared.
Music is their common interest. 4 vulgar; rude.
5 **Common Market,** a group of European countries that trade freely together. 6 **common
sense,** normal sensible thinking or behaviour.
7 **in common,** shared by two or more people or
things.
commonly *adverb*

common *noun*
a piece of land that anyone can use.

commonplace *adjective*
ordinary; usual.

common-room *noun*
an informal room for teachers or pupils at a
school, college, etc.

commonwealth *noun*
1 a group of countries co-operating together.
2 **the Commonwealth,** an association of Britain
and various other countries, such as Canada,
Australia, and New Zealand.

commotion *noun*
an uproar.

communal *adjective*
shared by several people.

commune *noun*
a group of people sharing a home, food, etc.

communicate *verb*
(communicated, communicating)
to pass news, information, opinions, etc. to
other people.
communicative *adjective*

communication *noun*
1 communicating. 2 something communicated; a message. 3 a way of communicating.
*Communications include radio, television, and
telephones.* 4 **communication cord,** a cord or
chain inside a train that you can pull to stop
the train in an emergency.

communion *noun*
1 religious fellowship. 2 **Communion,** the
Christian ceremony in which holy bread and
wine are given to worshippers.

communism *noun*
1 a system where property is shared by the
community. 2 **Communism,** a political system
where the state controls property, production,
trade, etc.; belief in this sort of system.

Communist *noun*
someone who believes in Communism.

community *noun* **(communities)**
the people living in one area.

commuter *noun*
someone who regularly travels to work, especially by train or bus.
commute *verb*

compact *adjective*
small and neat.

compact *noun*
a small, flat container for face-powder

companion *noun*
1 a friend who is with you, or who shares
something with you. 2 a reference-book.
companionship *noun*

company *noun* **(companies)**
1 a group of people doing something together.
2 an army unit consisting of two or more
platoons. 3 having people with you. *I am
lonely: I need company.* 4 (*informal*) visitors.
We've got company.

comparable *adjective*
(*say* kom-per-å-bŭl)
similar.

comparative *noun*
the form of a word that expresses 'more'. *The
comparative of 'big' is 'bigger'; the comparative
of 'bad' is 'worse'.*

comparative *adjective*
using or connected with comparisons.
comparatively *adverb*

compare *verb* **(compared, comparing)**
1 to work out or say how things are similar.
Compare your answers. 2 **compare with,** to be
similar to; to be as good as. *Our football pitch
cannot compare with Wembley Stadium.*

comparison *noun*
the action of comparing.

compartment *noun*
a part or division of something, especially of a
railway carriage.

compass *noun* (compasses)
1 an instrument that shows you where north is. **2 compasses** or **pair of compasses,** a device for drawing circles.

compassion *noun*
pity; mercy.
compassionate *adjective*

compel *verb* (compelled, compelling)
to force somebody to do something.

compensate *verb*
(compensated, compensating)
to give somebody something to make up for a loss, injury, etc.
compensation *noun*

compère *noun*
someone who introduces the performers in a show or broadcast.

compete *verb* (competed, competing)
to take part in a competition.

competent *adjective*
able to do a particular thing. *He is not competent to teach French.*
competence *noun*

competition *noun*
a game, race, etc. in which you try to do better than other people.
competitive *adjective,* **competitor** *noun*

compile *verb* (compiled, compiling)
to collect and arrange information, quotations, etc. *She compiled an anthology of poetry.*
compilation *noun,* **compiler** *noun*

complain *verb*
to say that you are not pleased about something.

complaint *noun*
1 complaining. **2** an illness.

complement *noun*
1 the amount needed to fill or complete something. *This ship has a full complement of sailors.* **2** a word or words used after a verb to complete the meaning. *In 'She is brave' and 'He was made king', the complements are 'brave' and 'king'.*
complementary *adjective*

complete *adjective*
1 having all its parts; not lacking anything; perfect. **2** finished.
completely *adverb*

complete *verb* (completed, completing)
to make something complete.
completion *noun*

complex *adjective*
complicated.
complexity *noun*

complex *noun* (complexes)
1 a group of related things, especially a group of buildings. **2** a fixed idea or set of attitudes.

complexion *noun*
the colour or appearance of your skin, especially of your face.

complicated *adjective*
1 made of a lot of different parts. **2** difficult.

complication *noun*
1 a complicated situation or condition. **2** a difficulty, especially a new one.

compliment *noun*
words or actions that show you approve of a person or thing.
complimentary *adjective*

component *noun*
a part, especially of a vehicle.

compose *verb* (composed, composing)
1 to make or build up something. **2** to write music.
composer *noun*

composition *noun*
1 composing. **2** a piece of music. **3** an essay.

compost *noun*
manure made of decayed leaves, grass, etc.

compound *adjective*
made of two or more parts or ingredients.

compound *noun*
1 a compound substance. *Water is a compound of hydrogen and oxygen.* **2** a fenced area containing buildings.

comprehend *verb*
1 to understand. **2** to include.

comprehension *noun*
1 understanding. **2** an exercise that tests or helps your understanding of a language.

comprehensive *adjective*
1 including all or many kinds of people or things. **2 comprehensive school,** a secondary school for all or most of the children in an area.

comprehensive *noun*
a comprehensive school.

compress *verb*
1 to press or squeeze together. **2** to get something into a small space.
compression *noun,* **compressor** *noun*

comprise *verb* (comprised, comprising)
to include; to consist of.

compromise *noun*
(*say* kom-prŏ-myz)
settling a dispute by accepting less than you wanted.

compulsory *adjective*
that must be done; not voluntary.

compute *verb* (computed, computing)
to calculate.
computation *noun*

computer *noun*
a machine that quickly and automatically does calculations, solves problems, etc.

comrade *noun*
a friend or companion.
comradeship *noun*

con *verb* (conned, conning)
(*slang*) to swindle.

concave *adjective*
curved like the inside of a circle or ball.

conceal *verb*
to hide.
concealment *noun*

conceit *noun*
vanity; pride.
conceited *adjective*

conceive

conceive *verb* **(conceived, conceiving)**
1 to become pregnant. 2 to form an idea, plan, etc.
conceivable *adjective,* **conceivably** *adverb*

concentrate *verb* **(concentrated, concentrating)**
1 to give your full attention to something; to think hard about one thing. 2 to bring or come together in one place. 3 to condense a liquid, etc.

concentration *noun*
1 concentrating. 2 **concentration camp,** a place where political prisoners, etc. are confined.

concept *noun*
an idea.

conception *noun*
1 conceiving. 2 an idea.

concern *verb*
1 to be important or interesting to somebody. 2 to worry somebody. 3 to be about a particular subject. *This story concerns a shipwreck.*

concern *noun*
1 something that concerns you. 2 a business.

concerning *preposition*
on the subject of; in connection with.

concert *noun*
a musical entertainment.

concertina *noun*
a portable musical instrument that you squeeze to push air past reeds.

concerto *noun*
(*say* kŏn-**cher**-toh)
a piece of music for one instrument and an orchestra.

concise *adjective*
brief; giving a lot of information in a few words.

conclude *verb* **(concluded, concluding)**
1 to end. 2 to decide. *The jury concluded that he was not guilty.*

conclusion *noun*
1 an ending. 2 a decision. 3 **in conclusion,** lastly.

concrete *noun*
cement mixed with gravel, etc. and used in building.

concrete *adjective*
that can be touched or felt; definite.

concussion *noun*
an injury to the brain caused by a hard knock.

condemn *verb*
1 to say that you strongly disagree with something. 2 to convict or sentence a criminal. *He was condemned to death.* 3 to declare that houses, etc. are not fit to be used.
condemnation *noun*

condense *verb* **(condensed, condensing)**
1 to make liquid, etc. stronger or thicker. *condensed milk.* 2 to make something smaller or shorter. *a condensed report.* 3 to change into water or other liquid. *Steam condenses on cold windows.*
condensation *noun,* **condenser** *noun*

condition *noun*
1 the character or state of a person or thing; how someone or something is. *This bike is in good condition.* 2 being physically fit. *Get in condition.* 3 something that must happen if something else is to happen. *Learning to swim is a condition of going sailing.* 4 **on condition** or **on condition that,** only if.

condition *verb*
1 to put something into a proper condition. 2 to train or accustom.

conduct *verb*
(*say* kŏn-**dukt**)
1 to lead or guide. 2 to direct the performance of an orchestra, etc. 3 to organize or manage something. 4 to allow electricity, heat, etc. to pass along. *Copper conducts electricity well.*

conduct *noun*
(*say* **kon**-dukt)
behaviour.

conductor *noun*
1 someone who sells tickets on a bus, etc. 2 someone who conducts an orchestra, etc. 3 something that conducts electricity, heat, etc.

conductress *noun* **(conductresses)**
a female bus-conductor.

cone *noun*
1 an object which is circular at one end and pointed at the other end. 2 an ice-cream cornet. 3 the fruit of a pine, fir, or cedar.

confectioner *noun*
someone who makes or sells sweets.
confectionery *noun*

confer *verb* **(conferred, conferring)**
1 to give someone a title, honour, etc. 2 to have a discussion.

conference *noun*
a meeting for discussion.

confess *verb*
to admit that you have done something wrong.
confession *noun*

confetti *plural noun*
tiny bits of coloured paper thrown at a bride and bridegroom.

confide *verb* **(confided, confiding)**
1 to tell somebody a secret. 2 **confide in,** to talk confidentially to; to trust in.
confidant *noun*

confidence *noun*
1 trust; faith. 2 believing that you are right or that you can do something. 3 **in confidence,** as a secret. 4 **confidence trick,** swindling somebody after persuading him to trust you.

confident *adjective*
showing or feeling confidence.

confidential *adjective*
1 that should be kept secret. *This information is confidential.* 2 trusted to keep secrets. *a confidential secretary.*
confidentially *adverb*

confine *verb* **(confined, confining)**
1 to keep somebody in a place. 2 to restrict something.
confinement *noun*

confirm *verb*
1 to prove that something is true. 2 to make something definite. *Please write to confirm your booking.* 3 to make somebody a full member of the Christian Church.
confirmation *noun*

confiscate *verb* **(confiscated, confiscating)**
to take something away from somebody as a punishment.
confiscation *noun*

conflict *noun*
(*say* **kon**-flikt)
a fight, struggle, or disagreement.

conflict *verb*
(*say* kon-**flikt**)
to disagree; not to match or fit with something else. *Their ideas conflicted.*

conform *verb*
to follow accepted rules, other people's wishes, etc. *He always conforms with school rules.*
conformist *noun*, **conformity** *noun*

confront *verb*
to come or bring face to face.
confrontation *noun*

confuse *verb* **(confused, confusing)**
1 to make somebody puzzled or muddled. 2 to mistake one thing for another.
confusion *noun*

congested *adjective*
crowded; too full of something.
congestion *noun*

congratulate **(congratulated, congratulating)**
to tell somebody how pleased you are about something that has happened to him or that he has done.
congratulation *noun*

congregation *noun*
the people taking part in a church service.

congress *noun* **(congresses)**
1 a conference. 2 **Congress,** the parliament or government of the U.S.A.

conical *adjective*
shaped like a cone.

conifer *noun*
(*say* **kon**-i-fer)
an evergreen tree that bears cones.
coniferous *adjective*

conjugate *verb* **(conjugated, conjugating)**
to give the different forms of a verb.
conjugation *noun*

conjunction *noun*
a joining word. (Conjunctions are words like *and*, *but*, and *whether*.)

conjure *verb* **(conjured, conjuring)**
to perform tricks that look like magic.
conjurer *noun*

conker *noun*
1 a hard, shiny, brown nut that grows on a horse-chestnut tree. 2 **conkers,** a game played with conkers threaded on pieces of string.

connect *verb*
1 to join together. 2 to put or go naturally together.
connection *noun*, **connective** *adjective*, **connector** *noun*

conning-tower *noun*
the part on top of a submarine, containing the periscope.

conquer *verb*
to defeat; to overcome.
conqueror *noun*

conquest *noun*
conquering somebody.

conscience *noun*
(*say* kon-shĕns)
knowing what is right or wrong.

conscientious *adjective*
(*say* kon-shee-**en**-shŭs)
1 careful and honest. *conscientious work.* 2 guided by your conscience. *He was a conscientious objector to joining the army.*
conscientiously *adverb*

conscious *adjective*
(*say* **kon**-shŭs)
awake; aware of what is happening.
consciously *adverb*, **consciousness** *noun*

conscript *verb*
(*say* kŏn-**skript**)
to make somebody join the armed forces.
conscription *noun*

conscript *noun*
(*say* **kon**-skript)
a conscripted person.

consecutive *adjective*
following one after another.

consent *noun*
agreement; permission.

consent *verb*
to agree; to permit something.

consequence *noun*
1 something which happens because of an event or action. *His illness was the consequence of smoking.* 2 importance. *It is of no consequence.* 3 **consequences,** a game in which a story is constructed by two or more people.
consequently *adverb*

conservation *noun*
conserving, especially of natural surroundings.
conservationist *noun*

conservative *adjective*
1 that does not like changes; tending to conserve things. 2 **Conservative,** of Conservatives.
conservatism *noun*

conservative *noun*
1 a conservative person. 2 **Conservative,** someone who supports the Conservative Party, a political party that favours private enterprise and conserving existing institutions.

conserve *verb* **(conserved, conserving)**
to prevent something being changed or spoilt.

consider *verb*
1 to think carefully about or give attention to something. 2 to have an opinion.

considerable *adjective*
large; important.
considerably *adverb*

considerate *adjective*
kind and thoughtful.

consideration *noun*
1 being considerate. 2 careful thought or attention. 3 something that needs careful thought; a reason.

considering *preposition*
in view of; with regard to. *This car runs well, considering its age.*

consist *verb*
to be made of.

consistency *noun* **(consistencies)**
1 being consistent. 2 thickness, especially of a liquid.

consistent *adjective*
1 constant. 2 matching or agreeing with something; reasonable.
consistently *adverb*

consolation *noun*
1 comfort or sympathy given to somebody. 2 **consolation prize**, a prize given to somebody who does not win a main prize.

console *verb* **(consoled, consoling)**
to give somebody consolation.

consonant *noun*
a letter that is not a vowel. *In 'table', the consonants are t, b, and l.*

conspicuous *adjective*
noticeable; remarkable.

conspiracy *noun*
plotting to do something evil or illegal.
conspirator *noun*, **conspire** *verb*

constable *noun*
an ordinary member of the police.

constant *adjective*
1 not changing; continual. 2 faithful.
constancy *noun*, **constantly** *adverb*

constellation *noun*
a group of stars.

constipated *adjective*
unable to empty the bowels easily or regularly.
constipation *noun*

constituency *noun* **(constituencies)**
a district that elects a member of parliament.

constituent *noun*
1 a part of something. 2 someone who lives in the district of a particular member of parliament.
constituent *adjective*

constitute *verb* **(constituted, constituting)**
to form or compose something.

constitution *noun*
1 the principles or laws by which a country is governed. 2 the condition or health of someone's body.
constitutional *adjective*

construct *verb*
to build.

construction *noun*
1 building. 2 something built.

constructive *adjective*
helpful. *constructive criticism.*

consul *noun*
an official representative of one country living in another country.

consult *verb*
to go to a person, book, etc. for information, advice, etc. *Consult your dictionary for help with spelling.*
consultant *noun*, **consultation** *noun*

consume *verb* **(consumed, consuming)**
1 to eat or drink something. 2 to use up something; to destroy.

consumer *noun*
someone who buys or uses goods, services, etc.

consumption *noun*
consuming. *The consumption of beer increased.*

contact *noun*
1 touching somebody or something. 2 communication. 3 a person to communicate with. 4 **contact lens**, a small lens worn against the eyeball instead of spectacles.

contact *verb*
to get in touch with somebody.

contagious *adjective*
(say kŏn-**tay**-jŭs)
caught by contact with infected people or things. *a contagious disease.*

contain *verb*
to have something inside; to include.

container *noun*
something designed to contain things, especially a large box-shaped container for transporting goods by sea.

contaminate *verb*
(contaminated, contaminating)
to make something dirty, impure, diseased, etc.
contamination *noun*

contemplate *verb*
(contemplated, contemplating)
1 to look at something. 2 to consider something. 3 to intend or plan.
contemplation *noun*

contemporary *adjective*
1 belonging to the same period. *Dickens was contemporary with Thackeray.* 2 modern; up-to-date. *We like contemporary furniture.*

contempt *noun*
a feeling of despising somebody.
contemptible *adjective*

contemptuous *adjective*
despising somebody.

contend *verb*
1 to struggle or compete. 2 to maintain or declare.
contender *noun*

content *noun*
(say kon-tent)
the contents of something.

content *adjective*
(say kŏn-tent)
contented. *Are you content with your wages?*
contentment *noun*

contented *adjective*
(say kŏn-tent-id)
happy; satisfied.
contentedly *adverb*

contents *plural noun*
(say kon-tents)
what something contains.

conversion

contest *noun*
(*say* **kon**-test)
a competition.

contest *verb*
(*say* kŏn-**test**)
to compete; to argue about something.

contestant *noun*
(*say* kŏn-**test**-ănt)
someone in a contest.

context *noun*
the words that come before or after a particular word or phrase and help to fix its meaning.

continent *noun*
1 one of the main masses of land in the world. *The continents are Africa, Antarctica, Asia, Australia, Europe, North America, and South America.* **2 the Continent,** the mainland of Europe, not including the British Isles.
continental *adjective*

continual *adjective*
1 happening often. *his continual coughing.*
2 continuous.
continually *adverb*

continue *verb* (**continued, continuing**)
to go on doing something.
continuation *noun*

continuous *adjective*
going on all the time; without a break. *a continuous line.*
continuity *noun*, **continuously** *adverb*

contour *noun*
1 an outline. **2** a line on a map joining points that are the same height above sea-level.

contraception *noun*
a way of preventing somebody from becoming pregnant.
contraceptive *noun* and *adjective*

contract *noun*
(*say* **kon**-trakt)
a formal agreement.

contract *verb*
(*say* kŏn-**trakt**)
1 to make or become smaller. *Heated metal contracts as it cools.* **2** to make a contract. **3** to get an illness. *She contracted pneumonia.*
contraction *noun*

contradict *verb*
to say that something is not true or that someone is wrong.
contradiction *noun*, **contradictory** *adjective*

contralto *noun*
a female singer with a low voice.

contraption *noun*
a device or machine that looks strange.

contrary *adjective*
1 (*say* **kon**-trä-ri) opposite; unfavourable.
2 (*say* kŏn-**trair**-i) obstinate; awkward.

contrary *noun* (**contraries**)
(*say* **kon**-trä-ri)
1 the opposite. **2 on the contrary,** the opposite is true.

contrast *noun*
(*say* **kon**-trahst)
1 a clear difference. **2** the action of contrasting. **3** the amount of difference between colours or tones.

contrast *verb*
(*say* kŏn-**trahst**)
1 to show that two things are clearly different.
2 to be clearly different.

contribute *verb* (**contributed, contributing**)
1 to give money, help, etc. to a cause, fund, etc.
2 to write something for a magazine, newspaper, etc. **3** to help to cause something.
contribution *noun*, **contributor** *noun*

contrivance *noun*
a device.

contrive *verb* (**contrived, contriving**)
to invent; to plan cleverly.

control *verb* (**controlled, controlling**)
to be able to make somebody or something do what you want.
controller *noun*

control *noun*
1 controlling somebody or something; authority. **2** a way of controlling somebody or something. **3 control tower,** the building at an airport where people control air traffic by radio.
4 in control, controlling.

controversial *adjective*
that causes a controversy.

controversy *noun* (**controversies**)
(*say* **kon**-trŏ-ver-si or kŏn-**trov**-er-si)
a long argument or disagreement.

conundrum *noun*
a riddle.

convalescent *adjective*
recovering from an illness.
convalescence *noun*

convection *noun*
heating by air, liquid, etc. that moves.
convector *noun*

convenience *noun*
1 being convenient. **2** a public lavatory. **3 at your convenience,** as it suits you.

convenient *adjective*
easy to use or reach.
conveniently *adverb*

convent *noun*
a place where nuns live and work.

convention *noun*
an accepted way of doing things.

conventional *adjective*
1 done in the accepted way; traditional. **2** not nuclear. *conventional weapons.*
conventionally *adverb*

converge *verb* (**converged, converging**)
to come together; to approach from different directions.

conversation *noun*
talking; a talk between two or several people.
conversational *adjective*

converse *verb* (**conversed, conversing**)
(*say* kŏn-**verss**)
to talk. *They conversed in low voices.*

converse *noun*
(*say* **kon**-verss)
the opposite. *The converse is true.*

conversion *noun*
the act of converting.

convert *verb*
(*say* kŏn-**vert**)
1 to change. **2** to make somebody change his beliefs. **3** to kick a goal after scoring a try at Rugby Football.
converter *noun*, **convertible** *adjective*

convert *noun*
(*say* **kon**-vert)
someone who has changed his beliefs.

convex *adjective*
curved like the outside of a circle or ball.

convey *verb*
1 to transport. **2** to communicate a message, idea, etc.

conveyor belt *noun*
a belt, chain, etc. carrying goods in a factory, etc.

convict *noun*
(*say* **kon**-vikt)
a criminal in prison.

convict *verb*
(*say* kŏn-**vikt**)
to prove or declare that somebody is guilty of a crime.

conviction *noun*
1 being convicted of a crime. **2** being convinced of something.

convince *verb* (**convinced, convincing**)
to persuade.

convoy *noun*
a group of ships, lorries, etc. travelling together.

cook *verb*
to make food ready to eat by heating it.

cook *noun*
someone who cooks.

cooker *noun*
a device for cooking food; an oven.

cookery *noun*
the action or skill of cooking food.

cool *adjective*
1 not warm; fairly cold. **2** not emotional or excited; calm.
coolly *adverb*, **coolness** *noun*

cool *verb*
to make or become cool.
cooler *noun*

coop *noun*
a cage for poultry.

co-operate *verb* (**co-operated, co-operating**)
to work helpfully with other people.
co-operation *noun*, **co-operative** *adjective*

co-ordinate *verb* (**co-ordinated, co-ordinating**)
(*say* koh-or-din-ayt)
to get people or things working properly together.
co-ordination *noun*, **co-ordinator** *noun*

co-ordinate *noun*
(*say* koh-**or**-din-ăt)
a quantity used to fix the position of something.

coot *noun*
a water-bird with a horny white plate on its forehead.

cop *verb* (**copped, copping**)
(*slang*) to get or receive something.

cop *noun*
(*slang*) **1** a policeman. **2 not much cop**, not very good.

cope *verb* (**coped, coping**)
to deal with something successfully. *How did you cope with your homework?*

copper *noun*[1]
1 a reddish-brown metal. *Copper is used for making wire, coins, etc.* **2** a reddish-brown colour. **3** a coin made of copper or bronze. **4 copper beech**, a beech-tree with copper-coloured leaves.
coppery *adjective*

copper *noun*[2]
(*slang*) a policeman.

copulate *verb* (**copulated, copulating**)
(*say* kop-yoo-layt)
to have sexual intercourse with someone.
copulation *noun*

copy *noun* (**copies**)
1 something made to look exactly like something else. **2** something written out a second time. **3** one newspaper, magazine, book, etc. *We each have a copy of 'Alice in Wonderland'.*

copy *verb* (**copied, copying**)
1 to make a copy of something. **2** to do exactly the same as somebody else.
copier *noun*, **copyist** *noun*

coral *noun*
a hard substance built up by tiny sea-creatures. *Coral is usually red, pink, or white.*

cord *noun*
thin rope; a piece of thin rope.

cordial *adjective*
warm and friendly. *a cordial welcome.*
cordiality *noun*, **cordially** *adverb*

cordial *noun*
a sweet drink.

corduroy *noun*
(*say* **kor**-der-oi)
thick cotton cloth with raised lines across it.

core *noun*
the part in the middle of something.

cork *noun*
1 the lightweight bark of a kind of oak-tree. **2** a piece of this bark used to close a bottle.

corkscrew *noun*
1 a device for removing corks from bottles. **2** a spiral.

cormorant *noun*
a large black sea-bird.

corn *noun*[1]
grain. *a field of corn.*

corn *noun*[2]
a small, hard lump on your toe or foot.

corned *adjective*
preserved with salt. *corned beef.*

corner *noun*
1 the point where two lines, roads, or walls meet. **2** a kick from the corner of a football field; a hit from the corner of a hockey field.

cough

corner *verb*
1 to trap somebody. *The police cornered the escaped prisoner.* **2** to go round a corner. *His car cornered badly.*

cornet *noun*
1 a small edible container for ice-cream. **2** a musical instrument rather like a trumpet.

cornfield *noun*
a field where corn grows.

cornflakes *plural noun*
toasted maize flakes eaten for breakfast.

cornflour *noun*
fine flour used for making milk puddings, etc.

cornflower *noun*
a blue flower.

Cornish *adjective*
1 of Cornwall. **2 Cornish pasty,** a small pie containing meat and vegetables.

corny *adjective* **(cornier, corniest)**
(*informal*) repeated so often that people are bored. *corny jokes.*

coronation *noun*
the crowning of a king or queen.

coroner *noun*
an official who holds an inquiry into the cause of an unnatural death.

corporal *noun*
a soldier just below sergeant in rank.

corporal *adjective*
1 of the human body. **2 corporal punishment,** beating or whipping somebody.

corporation *noun*
a group of people elected to govern a town.

corps *noun* **(corps)**
(*say* kor)
1 a large unit of soldiers. **2** a special army unit. *He is in the Medical Corps.*

corpse *noun*
a dead body.

corpuscle *noun*
(*say* **kor**-pŭs-ŭl)
one of the red or white cells in the blood.

corral *noun*
(*say* kŏ-**rahl**)
an enclosure for horses, cattle, etc.

correct *adjective*
1 true; accurate; without any mistakes. *Your sums are all correct.* **2** proper. *Is that the correct way to talk to a priest?*
correctly *adverb,* **correctness** *noun*

correct *verb*
to make something correct; to mark the mistakes in something.
correction *noun*

correspond *verb*
1 to exchange letters with somebody. **2** to agree with; to match. *Your story corresponds with what I heard.*

correspondence *noun*
1 letters; writing letters. **2** similarity; agreement.

correspondent *noun*
1 someone who writes letters to you. **2** someone employed to send news or articles to a newspaper.

corridor *noun*
a long, narrow way from which doors open into rooms or compartments.

corrode *verb* **(corroded, corroding)**
to wear away by rust, chemical action, etc.
corrosion *noun,* **corrosive** *adjective*

corrugated *adjective*
shaped into folds or ridges. *corrugated iron.*

corrupt *adjective*
dishonest; wicked.
corruption *noun*

corset *noun*
a tight piece of underwear worn round the hips and waist.

cosmetics *plural noun*
substances for making the skin or hair look beautiful or different. *Lipstick and face-powder are cosmetics.*

cosmic *adjective*
(*say* **koz**-mik)
1 of the universe. **2 cosmic rays,** very strong radiation from outer space.

cosmonaut *noun*
an astronaut.

cost *noun*
1 the price of something. **2 at all costs** or **at any cost,** no matter what the cost or difficulty may be.

cost *verb* **(cost, costing)**
to have a certain price. *That book cost £5 last year.*

costly *adjective* **(costlier, costliest)**
expensive.

costume *noun*
clothes, especially for a particular purpose or of a particular period.

cosy *adjective* **(cosier, cosiest)**
warm and comfortable.

cosy *noun* **(cosies)**
a cover put over a teapot or boiled egg to keep it hot.

cot *noun*
a baby's bed with high sides.

cottage *noun*
1 a small house, especially in the country. **2 cottage pie,** minced meat covered wih mashed potato and baked.

cotton *noun*
1 a soft white substance covering the seeds of a tropical plant. **2** thread made from this substance. **3** cloth made from cotton thread.

couch *noun* **(couches)**
a long, soft seat, usually with one end raised; a sofa.

cough *verb*
(*say* kof)
1 to push air suddenly out of your lungs. **2 cough up,** (*slang*) to give somebody money, information, etc. *Where's my change? Cough it up!*

cough *noun*
(*say* kof)
1 the action or sound of coughing. **2** an illness which makes you cough frequently.

could past tense of **can** *verb*[1].

couldn't short for *could not*.

council *noun*
1 a group of people chosen or elected to organize or discuss something, especially to plan the affairs of a town; a corporation. **2** council house, a house owned and let by a council.
councillor *noun*

counsel *noun*
1 advice. **2** the barrister or barristers involved in a lawsuit.

counsel *verb* (**counselled, counselling**)
to give advice to somebody.
counsellor *noun*

count *verb*
1 to say numbers in their proper order. **2** to use numbers to find out how many people or things there are in a place. **3** to include somebody in a total. *There are 30 in the class, not counting the teacher.* **4** to have a particular value or importance. *Qualifications must count for something.* **5** count down, to make a count-down. **6** count on, to rely on.

count *noun*[1]
1 counting; a total. **2** one of the things that somebody is accused of. *He was found guilty on all counts.*

count *noun*[2]
a foreign nobleman.

count-down *noun*
counting backwards, especially before launching a rocket, etc.

countenance *noun*
someone's face; the expression on someone's face.

counter *noun*
1 a long table where customers are served in a shop, restaurant, bank, etc. **2** a small, round, flat piece of plastic, etc. used in games, especially instead of coins in gambling.

counterfeit *adjective*
(*say* kownt-er-feet)
copied so as to deceive or swindle people.
counterfeit money.

countess *noun* (**countesses**)
the wife or widow of a count or earl; a female earl.

countless *adjective*
too many to count; very many.

country *noun* (**countries**)
1 part of the world inhabited by a nation of people. **2** the people who live in a country. **3** the countryside.

countryman *noun* (**countrymen**)
1 a man who lives in the countryside. **2** someone who lives in the same country as yourself.

countryside *noun*
an area with fields, woods, villages, etc., away from towns.

county *noun* (**counties**)
one of the areas that a country is divided into. *Kent, Leicestershire, and Merseyside are counties of England.*

couple *noun*
two people or things.

couple *verb* (**coupled, coupling**)
to join things together.
coupling *noun*

coupon *noun*
a piece of paper that gives you the right to receive or do something.

courage *noun*
being courageous.

courageous *adjective*
not afraid; ready to face danger, pain, etc.

courier *noun*
(*say* koor-i-er)
someone employed to guide and help holiday-makers, especially abroad.

course *noun*
1 the direction in which something goes. *the ship's course.* **2** a series of lessons, exercises, etc. **3** part of a meal. *the meat course.* **4** a race-course. **5** a golf-course. **6** in due course, eventually; at the expected time. **7** in the course of, during. **8** of course, naturally; certainly.

court *noun*
1 the place where a king or queen lives. **2** the people who are usually at a king's or queen's court. **3** a lawcourt. **4** an enclosed place for games like tennis or netball. **5** a courtyard.

court *verb*
to try to get someone's love or support.
courtship *noun*

court-card *noun*
the king, queen, or jack in a pack of playing-cards.

courteous *adjective*
(*say* ker-ti-ùs)
polite.
courteously *adverb*, **courtesy** *noun*

court martial *noun* (**courts martial**)
1 a court for trying offenders against military law. **2** a trial in this court.

courtyard *noun*
a space surrounded by walls or buildings.

cousin *noun*
a child of your uncle or aunt.

cove *noun*
a small bay.

cover *verb*
1 to put one thing over or round another; to hide. **2** to travel a certain distance. *We covered ten miles a day.* **3** to aim a gun at or near somebody. *I've got you covered.* **4** to be enough money for something. *£2 will cover my fare.* **5** to deal with or include. *This book covers stamp-collecting.*
coverage *noun*

cover *noun*
1 something used for covering something else; a lid, wrapper, envelope, etc. **2** something that hides or shelters you.

cow *noun*
a female animal kept by farmers for its milk and beef.

coward *noun*
someone who is not brave.
cowardice *noun*, **cowardly** *adjective*

cowboy *noun*
a man who rides round looking after the cattle on a large farm in America.

cowslip *noun*
a wild plant that has yellow flowers in spring.

cox *noun* **(coxes)**
someone who steers a boat.

coxswain *noun*
(*say* **kok**-swayn or **kok**-sŭn)
a cox.

coy *adjective*
shy; pretending to be shy or modest.
coyly *adverb*, **coyness** *noun*

crab *noun*
a shellfish with ten legs.

crab-apple *noun*
a small, sour apple.

crack *noun*
1 a line on the surface of something where it has broken but not come completely apart; a narrow gap. *There's a crack in this cup.* 2 a sudden sharp noise. *the crack of a pistol shot.* 3 a sudden knock. *a crack on the head.*

crack *verb*
1 to make or get a crack. *The ceiling is cracked.* 2 to make a sudden sharp noise. 3 to tell a joke. *He cracked some old jokes.* 4 **get cracking,** (*informal*) to get busy; to start some work.

cracker *noun*
1 a paper tube which bangs when two people pull it apart. *Crackers often contain toys, paper hats, and riddles.* 2 a thin biscuit.

crackle *verb* **(crackled, crackling)**
to make small cracking sounds. *The fire crackled in the grate.*

crackling *noun*
the hard skin of roast pork.

cradle *noun*
1 a cot for a baby. 2 a supporting frame.

cradle *verb* **(cradled, cradling)**
to hold gently.

craft *noun*
1 a job which needs skill with the hands; a skill. 2 cunning; trickery. 3 a boat.

craftsman *noun* **(craftsmen)**
someone who is good at a craft.
craftsmanship *noun*

crafty *adjective* **(craftier, craftiest)**
cunning; clever.
craftily *adverb*, **craftiness** *noun*

crag *noun*
a steep piece of rough rock.
craggy *adjective*

cram *verb* **(crammed, cramming)**
1 to push a lot of things into a space. 2 to fill something very full. 3 to teach or study very hard for an examination.
crammer *noun*

cramp *noun*
pain caused by a muscle tightening suddenly.

cramp *verb*
1 to keep in a very small space. 2 to hinder somebody's freedom, growth, etc.

crane *noun*
1 a machine for lifting and moving heavy objects. 2 a large bird with long legs and neck.

crane *verb* **(craned, craning)**
to stretch your neck so that you can see something.

crane-fly *noun*
an insect with long, thin legs.

crank *noun*
1 an L-shaped rod. 2 a person with strange or fanatical ideas.
cranky *adjective*

cranny *noun* **(crannies)**
a crevice.

crash *noun* **(crashes)**
1 the loud noise of something falling or breaking. 2 a violent collision or fall.

crash *verb*
1 to make or have a crash. 2 to move with a loud noise. *The elephants crashed through the jungle.*

crash-helmet *noun*
a padded helmet worn by motor-cyclists, etc.

crash-landing *noun*
an emergency landing of an aircraft, which usually damages it.

crate *noun*
a container in which goods are transported.

crater *noun*
1 the mouth of a volcano. 2 a hole in the ground made by a bomb, etc.

crave *verb* **(craved, craving)**
to desire something strongly.

crawl *verb*
1 to move on your hands and knees. 2 to move slowly. 3 to be covered with insects, etc.

crawl *noun*
1 a crawling movement. 2 a swimming stroke with the arms hitting the water alternately.

crayon *noun*
a pencil, chalk, etc. for making coloured drawings or writing.

craze *noun*
a temporary enthusiasm for something.

crazy *adjective* **(crazier, craziest)**
1 mad. 2 **crazy paving,** paving made of odd pieces of stone fitted together.
crazily *adverb*, **craziness** *noun*

creak *noun*
a sound like the noise made by a stiff door-hinge.
creaky *adjective*

creak *verb*
to make a creak.

cream *noun*
1 the richest part of milk. 2 a yellowish-white colour. 3 a food containing or looking like cream. *chocolate cream.* 4 a substance that looks like cream. *shoe-cream.*
creamy *adjective*

crease *noun*
1 a line made in something by folding, pressing, or squashing it. 2 a line on a cricket pitch showing where a batsman should stand.

crease *verb* (**creased, creasing**)
to make a crease or creases in something.

create *verb* (**created, creating**)
to make something that no one else has made or can make.
creation *noun*, **creative** *adjective*, **creativity** *noun*

creator *noun*
1 someone who creates something. 2 the **Creator**, God.

creature *noun*
a living animal or person.

crèche *noun*
(*say* kresh)
a place where babies are looked after while their parents are busy.

credibility *noun*
1 being credible. 2 **credibility gap**, not trusting what particular people say.

credible *adjective*
that you can believe; trustworthy.
credibly *adverb*

credit *noun*
1 honour; approval. *Give her credit for her honesty.* 2 trusting somebody to pay for something later on. *Do you want cash now or can I have it on credit?* 3 an amount of money in someone's account at a bank, etc. 4 **credits** or **credit titles**, the list of people who have helped to produce a film, television programme, etc.

credit *verb*
1 to believe. 2 to enter something as a credit in an account.

creditable *adjective*
praiseworthy.
creditably *adverb*

credit card *noun*
a card allowing somebody to buy goods on credit.

creditor *noun*
someone that you owe money to.

creed *noun*
a set or statement of beliefs.

creek *noun*
1 a narrow inlet. 2 (*in Australia, New Zealand, or America*) a small stream. 3 **up the creek**, (*slang*) in trouble.

creep *verb* (**crept, creeping**)
1 to move along close to the ground. 2 to move quietly or secretly. 3 to come gradually.

creep *noun*
1 a creeping movement. 2 (*slang*) an unpleasant person, especially someone who behaves like a slave or servant to somebody. 3 **give somebody the creeps**, (*informal*) to make him feel afraid or very uncomfortable.

creeper *noun*
a plant that grows close to the ground or to walls, etc.

creepy *adjective* (**creepier, creepiest**)
that gives you the creeps; weird.

cremate *verb* (**cremated, cremating**)
to burn a corpse to ashes.
cremation *noun*

crematorium *noun* (**crematoria**)
(*say* krem-ă-**tor**-i-ŭm)
a place where corpses are cremated.

creosote *noun*
(*say* **kree**-ŏ-soht)
a brown, oily liquid used to prevent wood from rotting.

crêpe *noun*
(*say* krayp)
cloth, paper, etc. with a wrinkled surface.

crept past tense and past participle of **creep** *verb*.

crescendo *noun*
(*say* kri-**shen**-doh)
music that gets gradually louder.

crescent *noun*
1 a narrow curved shape, pointed at both ends. *The new moon is a crescent.* 2 a curved street.

cress *noun*
a green plant used in salads and sandwiches.

crest *noun*
1 a tuft of hair, feathers, or skin on an animal's head. 2 the top of a hill, wave, etc.

crevasse *noun*
a deep crack in a glacier.

crevice *noun*
a crack in rock or in a wall, etc.

crew *noun*
the people who work on a ship, aircraft, etc.

crib *noun*
1 a baby's cot. 2 a framework containing fodder for animals. 3 something cribbed. 4 a translation of a foreign book. 5 (*locally in Australia and New Zealand*) a small house. 6 (*in Australia*) a light meal; a snack.

crib *verb* (**cribbed, cribbing**)
to copy somebody else's work.

cricket *noun*[1]
a game played outdoors by two teams with a ball, two bats, and two wickets.
cricketer *noun*

cricket *noun*[2]
an insect like a grasshopper.

cried past tense and past participle of **cry** *verb*.

crime *noun*
an action that breaks the law.

criminal *noun*
someone who has committed one or more crimes.

criminal *adjective*
of crime or criminals.

crimson *adjective*
dark red.

crinkle *verb* **(crinkled, crinkling)**
to crease or wrinkle.
crinkly *adjective*

cripple *noun*
someone who cannot walk properly.

cripple *verb* **(crippled, crippling)**
1 to make somebody a cripple. **2** to damage
something seriously.

crisis *noun* **(crises)**
(*say* **kry**-sis)
an important, dangerous, or very difficult time
or situation.

crisp *adjective*
1 very dry so that it breaks easily. **2** firm and
fresh. *a very crisp apple.* **3** frosty. **4** quick and
precise. *crisp movements.*

crisp *noun*
a very thin dry slice of cold fried potato.

criss-cross *adjective* and *adverb*
with crossing lines.

critic *noun*
1 someone who gives opinions on books, plays,
films, music, etc. **2** a person who criticizes
somebody or something.

critical *adjective*
1 criticizing. **2** of critics or criticism. **3** of or at a
crisis; very serious.
critically *adverb*

criticism *noun*
(*say* **krit**-i-siz-ŭm)
what a critic says; the work of a critic.

criticize *verb* **(criticized, criticizing)**
(*say* **krit**-i-syz)
to say that somebody or something is bad,
unsatisfactory, etc.

croak *noun*
a deep, hoarse sound, like that of a frog.

crochet *noun*
(*say* **kroh**-shay)
a kind of needlework done with a hooked
needle.

crock *noun*
(*informal*) an old or worn-out person or thing.

crockery *noun*
cups, saucers, plates, etc.

crocodile *noun*
1 a large tropical reptile with a thick skin, long
tail, and huge jaws. **2 crocodile tears,** sorrow
that is not sincere.

crocus *noun* **(crocuses)**
a small spring flower. *Crocuses are yellow,
purple, or white.*

croft *noun*
a small farm in Scotland.
crofter *noun*

crook *noun*
1 someone who cheats or robs people; a
criminal. **2** a shepherd's stick with a curved
end.

crook *verb*
to bend. *She crooked her finger.*

crooked *adjective*
(*say* **kruuk**-id)
1 bent; twisted; not straight. **2** dishonest.

croon *verb*
to sing softly or sentimentally.
crooner *noun*

crop *noun*
1 something grown for food. *a good crop of
wheat.* **2** a riding-whip with a loop instead of a
lash.

crop *verb* **(cropped, cropping)**
1 to cut or bite off the top of something. *The
sheep cropped the grass.* **2** to produce a crop.
3 crop up, to happen or appear unexpectedly.

cross *noun*
1 a mark or shape like + or ×. **2** an upright post
with another post across it, used in ancient
times for crucifixions. **3 the Cross,** the cross on
which Christ was crucified, used as a symbol of
Christianity. **4** a mixture of two different
things.

cross *verb*
1 to go across something. **2** to draw one or
more lines across something. **3** to make the
sign or shape of a cross with something. *Cross
your fingers for good luck.* **4 cross out,** to draw
a line across something because it is unwanted,
wrong, etc.

cross *adjective*
1 angry; bad-tempered. **2** going from one side
to another. *cross winds.*
crossly *adverb*, **crossness** *noun*

crossbar *noun*
a horizontal bar, especially between two upright bars.

crossbow *noun*
an ancient kind of bow used for shooting
arrows, stones, etc.

cross-country *adjective*
across the countryside. *a cross-country race.*

cross-country *noun*
a race or run across the countryside.

cross-examine *verb*
(cross-examined, cross-examining)
to question somebody carefully.
cross-examination *noun*

cross-eyed *adjective*
with eyes that look or seem to look in different
directions.

crossing *noun*
a place where people can cross a road, railway,
etc.

cross-legged *adverb* and *adjective*
with legs crossed.

crossroads *noun*
a place where two or more roads cross one
another.

cross-section *noun*
1 a drawing of something as if it has been cut
through. **2** a typical sample.

crosswise *adverb* and *adjective*
with one thing crossing another.

crossword *noun*
a puzzle in which you have to guess words from
clues and write them on a chequered rectangle
or diagram.

crotchet *noun*
(*say* **kroch**-it)
a musical note equal to half a minim, written ♩.

crouch *verb*
to lower your body, with your arms and legs bent.

crow *noun*
1 a large black bird. 2 **as the crow flies,** in a straight line.

crow *verb*
1 to make a noise like a cock. 2 to boast; to be proudly triumphant.

crowbar *noun*
an iron bar used as a lever.

crowd *noun*
a large number of people in one place.

crowd *verb*
1 to make a crowd. 2 to cram; to fill uncomfortably full.

crown *noun*
1 an ornamental head-dress worn by a king or queen. 2 the king or queen. *This land belongs to the crown.* 3 the highest part of something. *the crown of the road.*

crown *verb*
1 to make somebody a king or queen. 2 to reward; to end something successfully. 3 to form or decorate the top of something.

crow's-nest *noun*
a look-out position at the top of a ship's mast.

crucial *adjective*
(*say* **kroo**-shăl)
most important.

crucifix *noun* **(crucifixes)**
a model of the Cross or of Christ on the Cross.

crucify *verb* **(crucified, crucifying)**
to execute somebody by nailing him to a cross.
crucifixion *noun*

crude *adjective* **(cruder, crudest)**
1 natural; not refined. *crude oil.* 2 rough; not finished properly. *a crude hut.* 3 vulgar; rude. *crude jokes.*

cruel *adjective* **(crueller, cruellest)**
1 pleased at, or not caring about, the pain and suffering of others. *a cruel tyrant.* 2 causing pain and suffering. *a cruel war.*
cruelly *adverb,* **cruelty** *noun*

cruise *noun*
a sailing holiday, especially visiting various places.

cruise *verb* **(cruised, cruising)**
1 to sail or travel at a slow or moderate speed. 2 to have a cruise.

cruiser *noun*
1 a fast warship. 2 a large motor-boat.

crumb *noun*
a tiny piece of bread, cake, etc.

crumble *verb* **(crumbled, crumbling)**
to break or fall into small pieces.
crumbly *adjective*

crumpet *noun*
a soft, flat cake of batter, eaten toasted with butter.

crumple *verb* **(crumpled, crumpling)**
to make or become very creased.

crunch *noun* **(crunches)**
1 the noise made by chewing hard food, walking on gravel, etc. 2 **the crunch,** (*informal*) a crucial event; a crisis.
crunchy *adjective*

crunch *verb*
to make a crunch; to chew or crush something with a crunch.

crusade *noun*
1 a military expedition made in the Middle Ages to Palestine. 2 a campaign against something that you think is bad.
crusader *noun*

crush *verb*
1 to press something so that it gets broken or harmed. 2 to defeat.

crush *noun* **(crushes)**
1 a crowd; a crowded situation. 2 a fruit-flavoured drink.

crust *noun*
the hard outside part of something, especially of a loaf.

crustacean *noun*
(*say* krus-**tay**-shăn)
a shellfish.

crutch *noun* **(crutches)**
a long walking-stick that fits under a lame person's arm.

cry *verb* **(cried, crying)**
1 to let tears fall from your eyes. 2 to shout.

cry *noun* **(cries)**
crying; a loud shout.

crypt *noun*
a room underneath a church.

crystal *noun*
1 a transparent, colourless mineral, rather like glass. 2 a small solid piece of a substance. *crystals of snow and ice.* 3 **crystal ball,** a glass ball used in crystal-gazing. 4 **crystal-gazing,** looking into a glass ball to try to see the future.
crystalline *adjective*

crystallize *verb* **(crystallized, crystallizing)**
to form into crystals.

C.S.E. short for *Certificate of Secondary Education.*

cub *noun*
1 a young lion, tiger, fox, bear, etc. 2 a junior Scout.

cubby-hole *noun*
a small compartment; a snug place.

cube *noun*
1 something that has six square sides. *Dice and sugar-lumps are cubes.* 2 the result of multiplying something by itself twice. *The cube of 3 is* $3 \times 3 \times 3 = 27$. 3 **cube root,** what gives a particular number if it is multiplied by itself twice. *The cube root of 8 is 2.*

cube *verb* **(cubed, cubing)**
to multiply a number by itself twice. *4 cubed is* $4 \times 4 \times 4 = 64$.

curse

cubic *adjective*
1 of or shaped like a cube. **2 cubic foot, cubic metre,** etc., the volume of a cube with sides that are one foot, metre, etc. long.

cubicle *noun*
a compartment of a room.

cuckoo *noun*
a bird that makes a sound like 'cuck-oo'. *Cuckoos lay their eggs in other birds' nests.*

cucumber *noun*
a long green vegetable, eaten raw.

cud *noun*
half-digested food that a cow, etc. brings back from its first stomach to chew again.

cuddle *verb* **(cuddled, cuddling)**
to put your arms closely round a person or animal that you love.
cuddly *adjective*

cue *noun*[1]
something said or done that acts as a signal for an actor, etc. to say or do something. *Your cue is: 'Here's the detective!'*

cue *noun*[2]
a long stick used to strike the ball in billiards or snooker.

cuff *noun*
1 the end of a sleeve that fits round the wrist. 2 hitting somebody with your hand.

cuff *verb*
to hit somebody with your hand.

cul-de-sac *noun*
a dead end.

culminate *verb* **(culminated, culminating)**
to reach the highest or last point.
culmination *noun*

culprit *noun*
the person who has done wrong.

cult *noun*
a religion; devotion to somebody or something.

cultivate *verb* **(cultivated, cultivating)**
1 to use land to grow crops. 2 to try to make something grow or develop. **3 cultivated,** with good manners and education.
cultivation *noun*, **cultivator** *noun*

culture *noun*
development of the mind, body, arts, music, etc.
cultural *adjective*, **cultured** *adjective*

cunning *adjective*
clever at deceiving people.

cup *noun*
1 a small container from which you drink liquid. *Cups usually have handles and are used with saucers.* 2 an ornamental cup given as a prize.

cup *verb* **(cupped, cupping)**
to put into the shape of a cup. *She cupped her hands.*

cupboard *noun*
(*say* kub-erd)
a recess or piece of furniture with a door, in which things may be stored.

cupful *noun*
as much as a cup will hold.

curate *noun*
(*say* kewr-åt)
a clergyman who helps a vicar.

curator *noun*
(*say* kewr-**ay**-ter)
someone in charge of a museum, art gallery, etc.

curb *verb*
to restrain. *Curb your impatience.*

curd *noun*
a thick substance formed when milk turns sour.

curdle *verb* **(curdled, curdling)**
1 to form into curds. **2 curdle somebody's blood,** to horrify or terrify him.

cure *verb* **(cured, curing)**
1 to get rid of somebody's illness. 2 to stop something bad. 3 to treat something so as to preserve it. *Fish can be cured in smoke.*

cure *noun*
1 something that cures a person or thing. 2 being cured.

curfew *noun*
a time or signal after which people must stay indoors until the next day.

curiosity *noun* **(curiosities)**
1 being curious. 2 something strange.

curious *adjective*
1 wanting to find out about things. 2 strange; unusual.
curiously *adverb*

curl *noun*
a curve or coil, especially of hair.

curl *verb*
1 to form into curls. **2 curl up,** to sit or lie with your knees drawn up.

curler *noun*
a device for curling the hair.

curly *adjective* **(curlier, curliest)**
full of curls; curling. *She has curly hair.*

currant *noun*
1 a small, black, dried grape. 2 a small, round, juicy berry; the bush that produces this berry.

currency *noun* **(currencies)**
1 money. *foreign currency.* 2 the general use of something. *Those words have no currency now.*

current *noun*
water, air, or electricity moving in one direction.

current *adjective*
happening or used now.
currently *adverb*

curriculum *noun* **(curricula)**
a course of study.

curry *noun* **(curries)**
food cooked with spices that make it taste hot.

curry *verb* **(curried, currying)**
1 to groom a horse. **2 curry favour,** to try to get somebody's favour or approval.

curse *noun*
1 a call or prayer for somebody to be harmed or killed. 2 something very unpleasant. 3 an angry word or words.

curse *verb* **(cursed, cursing)**
1 to make a curse; to use a curse against somebody. **2 be cursed with something,** to suffer from it.

curtain *noun*
1 a piece of cloth hung at a window or door. 2 the large cloth screen hung at the front of a stage.

curtsy *noun* **(curtsies)**
putting one foot behind the other and bending the knees. *Women and girls sometimes make curtsies to people they respect.*

curtsy *verb* **(curtsied, curtsying)**
to make a curtsy.

curvature *noun*
curving. *the curvature of the earth.*

curve *noun*
a line that bends smoothly.

curve *verb* **(curved, curving)**
to be or put in a curve. *The river curved gently.*

cushion *noun*
a bag, usually of cloth, filled with soft material so that it is comfortable to sit on or rest against.

cushion *verb*
1 to supply with cushions. *cushioned seats.*
2 to protect from shock or harm. *Savers are not cushioned against inflation.*

custard *noun*
a thick, sweet, yellow liquid eaten with puddings.

custom *noun*
1 the usual way of doing things. *It is the custom to go on holiday in the summer.* 2 regular business from customers. 3 **customs**, taxes paid on goods brought into a country; the place at a port, airport, etc. where officials examine your luggage.

customary *adjective*
usual. *It is customary to thank your host.*
customarily *adverb*

customer *noun*
someone who uses a shop, bank, business, etc.

cut *verb* **(cut, cutting)**
1 to use a knife, axe, scissors, etc. to divide, separate, or shape something. 2 to make something shorter or smaller; to remove part of something. *They are cutting all their prices.* 3 to divide a pack of playing-cards. 4 to hit a ball with a chopping movement. 5 to go sideways or across something. *The driver cut the corner.* 6 to stay away from something deliberately. *She cut her music lesson.* 7 to make a gramophone record. 8 **cut and dried**, already decided. 9 **cut a tooth**, to have a new tooth coming. 10 **cut off**, to interrupt. 11 **cut out**, to shape something by cutting; *(informal)* to stop doing something. 12 **cut short**, to stop something before it should end.

cut *noun*
1 cutting; the result of cutting. 2 a small wound. 3 *(slang)* a share. *I want a cut of the profits.*

cute *adjective* **(cuter, cutest)**
(informal) 1 clever. 2 attractive.

cutlass *noun* **(cutlasses)**
a short sword with a wide curved blade.

cutlery *noun*
knives, forks, and spoons.

cutlet *noun*
a thick slice of meat.

cut-out *noun*
something cut out of paper, cardboard, etc.

cutter *noun*
1 a person or thing that cuts. 2 a sailing-ship with one mast.

cutting *noun*
1 a steep-sided passage cut through high ground for a railway or road. 2 a clipping. 3 a piece cut off a plant to grow as a new plant.

cycle *noun*
1 a bicycle. 2 a series of events that are regularly repeated.

cycle *verb* **(cycled, cycling)**
to ride a bicycle.
cyclist *noun*

cyclone *noun*
a wind rotating round a calm central area, especially a violent wind of this kind.
cyclonic *adjective*

cygnet *noun*
(say **sig**-nit)
a young swan.

cylinder *noun*
1 an object with straight sides and circular ends. 2 part of an engine in which a piston moves.

cylindrical *adjective*
shaped like a cylinder.

cymbal *noun*
a round, concave metal plate that is hit to make a ringing sound. *Cymbals are used in all kinds of orchestras.*

cynic *noun*
(say **sin**-ik)
someone who doubts that anything can be good.
cynical *adjective*, **cynically** *adverb*, **cynicism** *noun*

cypress *noun* **(cypresses)**
an evergreen tree with dark leaves.

D

dab *noun*
a gentle touch with something soft.

dab *verb* **(dabbed, dabbing)**
to touch gently with something soft. *I dabbed my eyes with a handkerchief.*

dashboard

dabble *verb* (**dabbled, dabbling**)
1 to splash something about in water. **2** to do something as a hobby. *He is a scientist, but he dabbles in music.*

dachshund *noun*
(*say* **daks**-huund or **daks**-huunt)
a breed of dog with a long body and very short legs.

dad *noun*
(*informal*) father.

daddy *noun* (**daddies**)
(*informal*) father.

daddy-long-legs *noun* (**daddy-long-legs**)
a crane-fly.

daffodil *noun*
a yellow flower that grows from a bulb.

daft *adjective*
silly; mad.

dagger *noun*
a pointed knife with two sharp edges, used as a weapon.

dahlia *noun*
(*say* **day**-li-ǎ)
a garden plant with brightly-coloured flowers.

daily *adjective*
happening every day; done every day.

dainty *adjective* (**daintier, daintiest**)
delicate, pretty, and small.
daintily *adverb*, **daintiness** *noun*

dairy *noun* (**dairies**)
a place where milk, butter, cheese, etc. are made or sold.

daisy *noun* (**daisies**)
a small flower with white petals and a yellow centre.

dale *noun*
a valley.

Dalmatian *noun*
a large white dog with black or brown spots.

dam *noun*
a wall built to hold water back, especially across a river to make a reservoir.

dam *verb* (**dammed, damming**)
to hold water back with a dam.

damage *verb* (**damaged, damaging**)
to injure; to harm.

damage *noun*
1 injury; harm. **2 damages,** money paid to someone for an injury or loss.

Dame *noun*
1 the title of a lady who has been given the equivalent of a knighthood. **2 dame,** a comic middle-aged woman in a pantomime, usually played by a man.

damn *verb*
1 to curse; to condemn. **2 damn!,** a swear word.
damnable *adjective*, **damnation** *noun*

damned *adjective*
(*informal*) hateful; annoying.

damp *adjective*
1 slightly wet; not quite dry. **2 damp course,** a layer of material in a wall to stop dampness rising up the wall.
dampness *noun*

damson *noun*
a small purple plum.

dance *verb* (**danced, dancing**)
to move about in time to music.
dancer *noun*

dance *noun*
1 a piece of music or set of movements for dancing. **2** a party or gathering where people dance.

dandelion *noun*
a yellow wild flower with a thick stalk and jagged leaves.

dandruff *noun*
tiny white flakes of dead skin in a person's hair.

Dane *noun*
a Danish person.

danger *noun*
something that is dangerous.

dangerous *adjective*
likely to kill or harm you.

dangle *verb* (**dangled, dangling**)
to hang or swing loosely.

Danish *adjective*
of Denmark.

dappled *adjective*
marked with patches or spots of different colours. *a dappled horse.*

dare *verb* (**dared, daring**)
1 to be brave enough or rude enough to do something. *I daren't dive in. How dare you!* **2** to challenge someone to show how brave he is. *I dare you to climb that tree.*

dare-devil *noun*
a reckless or brave person.

dark *adjective*
1 with little or no light. *a dark night.* **2** not light in colour. *a dark green coat.* **3 dark-room,** a room kept dark for processing photographs.
darkly *adverb*, **darkness** *noun*

dark *noun*
1 absence of light. *Cats can see in the dark.* **2** sunset. *She went out after dark.*

darken
to make or become dark.

darling *noun*
someone who is loved very much.

darn *verb*
to mend a hole by sewing across it.

dart *noun*
an object with a sharp point, thrown at a target.

dash *noun* (**dashes**)
1 a short line (—) used in writing or printing. **2** a rush; a hurry.

dash *verb*
1 to rush. *I dashed along the road.* **2** to throw something violently; to shatter. *The ship was dashed against the rocks.*

dashboard *noun*
a panel with dials and controls in front of the driver of a car, aircraft, etc.

data

data *plural noun*
(*say* **day**-tă or **dah**-tă)
facts; information.

date *noun*
1 the day of the month, or the year, when something happens. 2 an appointment to meet someone. 3 a small, sweet, brown fruit that grows on a palm tree.

date *verb* (**dated, dating**)
1 to give a date to something. 2 to have existed from a particular time. *The church dates from 1684.* 3 to seem old-fashioned.

daughter *noun*
a girl or woman who is someone's child.

dawdle *verb* (**dawdled, dawdling**)
to walk too slowly.

dawn *noun*
the time when the sun rises.

day *noun*
1 the 24 hours between midnight and the next midnight. 2 the light part of the day. 3 **day-dream,** to have pleasant vague thoughts.

daylight *noun*
1 the light of day. 2 dawn. *We must start before daylight.*

dazed *adjective*
unable to think or see clearly.

dazzle *verb* (**dazzled, dazzling**)
to make someone dazed with bright light.

dead *adjective*
1 not alive; not lively or active. 2 complete; sure. *a dead loss.* 3 **dead end,** a street or passage with an opening at only one end. 4 **dead heat,** a race in which two or more winners finish exactly together.

deaden *verb*
to make pain, noise, etc. weaker.

deadline *noun*
a time-limit.

deadlock *noun*
a situation in which people cannot agree.

deadly *adjective* (**deadlier, deadliest**)
likely to kill.

deaf *adjective*
unable or unwilling to hear.
deafness *noun*

deafen *verb*
to be very loud. *a deafening noise.*

deal *verb* (**dealt, dealing**)
1 to hand out something. 2 to give out cards for a card-game. 3 to trade. *He deals in scrap metal.* 4 **deal with,** to be concerned with; to do something that needs doing.
dealer *noun*

deal *noun*
1 an agreement; a bargain. 2 someone's turn to deal at cards. 3 sawn fir or pine wood. 4 **a good deal** or **a great deal,** a large amount.

dean *noun*
an important clergyman in a cathedral, etc.
deanery *noun*

dear *adjective*
1 loved very much. 2 the usual way of beginning a letter. *Dear Sir. Dear John.* 3 expensive.

death *noun*
dying; the end of life.
deathly *adjective*

debate *noun*
a discussion, especially in public.

debate *verb* (**debated, debating**)
to have a debate.
debatable *adjective*

debris *noun*
(*say* **deb**-ree)
scattered fragments; wreckage.

debt *noun*
(*say* det)
something that you owe someone.

debtor *noun*
(*say* **det**-er)
someone who owes you money.

début *noun*
(*say* **day**-boo or **day**-bew)
someone's first public appearance.

decade *noun*
ten years. *The war lasted for a decade.*

decathlon *noun*
an athletic contest consisting of ten events.

decay *verb*
to go bad; to rot.

decay *noun*
decaying; the result of decaying.

deceased *adjective*
(*say* di-**seest**)
dead. *a legacy from his deceased aunt.*

deceit *noun*
(*say* di-**seet**)
deceiving someone.
deceitful *adjective*, **deceitfully** *adverb*

deceive *verb* (**deceived, deceiving**)
(*say* di-**seev**)
to make someone believe something that is not true.

December *noun*
the last month of the year.

decent *adjective*
respectable; proper; suitable.
decency *noun*, **decently** *adverb*

deception *noun*
deceiving someone.

deceptive *adjective*
misleading. *The fog was deceptive.*

decibel *noun*
a unit for measuring the loudness of sound.

decide *verb* (**decided, deciding**)
1 to make up your mind; to make a choice. 2 to settle a contest or argument.
decidedly *adverb*

deciduous *adjective*
losing its leaves in autumn. *a deciduous tree.*

decimal *adjective*
1 using tens or tenths. 2 **decimal fraction,** a fraction with tenths shown as numbers after a dot ($^3/_{10}$ is 0.3; $1\frac{1}{2}$ is 1.5). 3 **decimal point,** the dot in a decimal fraction.
decimalization *noun,* **decimalize** *verb*

decimal *noun*
a decimal fraction.

decipher *verb*
(*say* di-**sy**-fer)
1 to decode. 2 to work out the meaning of something written badly.

decision *noun*
what you have decided.

decisive *adjective*
1 that settles or ends something. *a decisive battle.* 2 determined; resolute. *a decisive person.*
decisively *adverb*

deck *noun*
1 a floor on a ship or bus. 2 **deck-chair,** a folding chair with a seat of canvas or plastic material.

declare *verb* (**declared, declaring**)
1 to say something clearly or firmly. 2 to end a cricket innings before all the batsmen are out. 3 **declare war,** to say that you have started a war against someone.
declaration *noun*

decline *verb* (**declined, declining**)
1 to refuse something. 2 to become weaker or smaller. 3 to give the grammatical cases of a word.

decode *verb* (**decoded, decoding**)
to find the meaning of something written in code.

decompose *verb* (**decomposed, decomposing**)
to decay; to rot.
decomposition *noun*

decompression *noun*
reducing the air pressure on someone who has been in compressed air.

decorate *verb* (**decorated, decorating**)
1 to make something look more beautiful or colourful. 2 to give someone a medal.
decoration *noun,* **decorative** *adjective,* **decorator** *noun*

decoy *noun*
(*say* **dee**-koi or di-**koi**)
something used to tempt a person or animal into a trap.

decrease *verb* (**decreased, decreasing**)
(*say* di-**kreess**)
to make or become smaller or fewer.

decrease *noun*
(*say* **dee**-kreess)
the amount by which something decreases.

decree *noun*
an official order or decision.

decree *verb* (**decreed, decreeing**)
to make a decree.

decrepit *adjective*
old and weak.

dedicate *verb* (**dedicated, dedicating**)
1 to devote. *She dedicated her life to nursing.* 2 to mention someone's name at the beginning of a book, etc., as a sign of friendship or thanks.
dedication *noun*

deduce *verb* (**deduced, deducing**)
to work out something by reasoning.

deduct *verb*
to subtract part of something.
deductible *adjective*

deduction *noun*
1 something deduced. 2 something deducted.

deed *noun*
1 something special that someone has done. 2 a legal document.

deep *adjective*
1 going down a long way from the top. *deep sea.* 2 wide. *a deep book-shelf.* 3 measured from top to bottom or from front to back. *a hole six feet deep.* 4 intense; strong. *deep feelings.*
deepen *verb,* **deeply** *adverb*

deer *noun* (**deer**)
a fast-running, graceful animal with four legs. *Male deer usually have antlers.*

deface *verb* (**defaced, defacing**)
to spoil the appearance of something.

defeat *verb*
to beat someone in a game or battle.

defeat *noun*
a lost game or battle.

defecate *verb* (**defecated, defecating**)
to get rid of faeces from your body.
defecation *noun*

defect *noun*
(*say* di-**fekt** or **dee**-fekt)
a flaw.
defective *adjective*

defect *verb*
(*say* di-**fekt**)
to desert a country or cause; to join the enemy.
defection *noun,* **defector** *noun*

defence *noun*
1 the action of defending. 2 something that defends.
defenceless *adjective*

defend *verb*
1 to protect, especially from attack. 2 to try to prove that a defendant is innocent.
defender *noun,* **defensible** *adjective*

defendant *noun*
a person accused of something in a law-court.

defensive *adjective*
that defends.

defer *verb* (**deferred, deferring**)
to postpone. *She deferred her departure.*
deferment *noun*

defiance *noun*
the action of defying.
defiant *adjective*

deficiency *noun* (deficiencies)
1 a shortage; a lack. 2 a weakness in the mind.
deficient *adjective*

deficit *noun*
(*say* **def**-i-sit)
the amount by which a sum of money is too small.

defile *verb* (defiled, defiling)
to make a thing dirty or impure.

define *verb* (defined, defining)
1 to explain what a word means. 2 to show clearly what something is.

definite *adjective*
fixed; certain; exact. *Choose a definite date for your holiday.*

definitely *adverb* and *interjection*
certainly.

definition *noun*
something defined, especially what a word means.

deflate *verb* (deflated, deflating)
1 to let air out of a tyre, balloon, etc. 2 to make someone less proud or confident. 3 to lower or reverse inflation.
deflation *noun*, **deflationary** *adjective*

deflect *verb*
to make something turn aside.
deflection *noun*

deformed *adjective*
not properly or naturally shaped.
deformation *noun*, **deformity** *noun*

defrost *verb*
to remove ice or frost from a refrigerator, windscreen, etc.; to thaw something out.

deft *adjective*
skilful and quick.
deftly *adverb*

defuse *verb* (defused, defusing)
1 to remove the fuse from a bomb, explosive, etc. 2 to make a situation less dangerous.

defy *verb* (defied, defying)
1 to say or show that you will not obey. 2 to challenge. 3 to prevent something being done. *The door defied all attempts to open it.*

degrade *verb* (degraded, degrading)
to humiliate; to disgrace.
degradation *noun*

degree *noun*
1 a unit for measuring temperature. *Water boils at 100 degrees centigrade, or 100°C.* 2 a unit for measuring angles. *There are 90 degrees (90°) in a right angle.* 3 extent. *to some degree.* 4 an award to someone at a university, college, etc. who has successfully finished a course. *She has a degree in English.*

dehydrated *adjective*
with all its moisture removed.
dehydration *noun*

de-ice *verb*
to remove ice from a windscreen, etc.
de-icer *noun*

deity *noun* (deities)
(*say* **dee**-i-ti or **day**-i-ti)
a god.

dejected *adjective*
sad; gloomy.
dejection *noun*

delay *verb*
to make someone or something late; to postpone.

delay *noun*
delaying. *Do it without delay.*

delegate *noun*
(*say* **del**-i-gǎt)
a representative.

delegate *verb* (delegated, delegating)
(*say* **del**-i-gayt)
to choose or send someone as a delegate.
delegation *noun*

delete *verb* (deleted, deleting)
to cross out; to erase.
deletion *noun*

deliberate *adjective*
(*say* di-**lib**-er-ǎt)
1 done on purpose. *It was a deliberate insult.* 2 slow and careful. *with deliberate movements.*
deliberately *adverb*

deliberate *verb* (deliberated, deliberating)
(*say* di-**lib**-er-ayt)
to discuss or think carefully.
deliberation *noun*

delicacy *noun* (delicacies)
1 being delicate. 2 a delicious food.

delicate *adjective*
1 fine; soft; fragile. *as delicate as a spider's web.* 2 becoming ill easily. *a delicate child.* 3 using or needing great care. *delicate peace negotiations.*
delicately *adverb*

delicatessen *noun*
a shop that mainly sells foreign foods.

delicious *adjective*
tasting or smelling very pleasant.
deliciously *adverb*

delight *verb*
to please greatly.

delight *noun*
great pleasure.
delightful *adjective*, **delightfully** *adverb*

delinquent *noun*
someone, especially a young person, who breaks the law.
delinquency *noun*

deliver *verb*
1 to bring things like milk or newspapers to someone's house. 2 to give a speech, etc. 3 to help with the birth of a baby. 4 to rescue.
deliverance *noun*, **delivery** *noun*

delphinium *noun*
a garden plant with tall, usually blue, flowers.

delta *noun*
1 the area between the branches of a river at its mouth. 2 **delta wing**, a triangular swept-back wing on an aircraft. 3 **delta-winged,** with delta wings.

deluge *noun*
1 a large flood. 2 a heavy fall of rain. 3 something coming in great numbers. *a deluge of questions.*

deluge *verb* **(deluged, deluging)**
to fall in a deluge on someone. *He was deluged with questions.*

demand *verb*
to ask for something firmly or forcefully.

demand *noun*
1 something demanded. 2 a desire to have something. *There's a great demand for old furniture.* 3 **in demand,** wanted; desired.

demerara *noun*
(*say* dem-er-**air**-ă)
light-brown cane sugar.

demist *verb*
to remove condensation from a windscreen, etc.

demo *noun*
(*informal*) a demonstration.

democracy *noun* **(democracies)**
1 government by elected representatives. 2 a country governed in this way.
democrat *noun,* **democratic** *adjective,* **democratically** *adverb*

demolish *verb*
to knock something down and break it up.
demolition *noun*

demon *noun*
1 a devil. 2 a fierce or forceful person.

demonstrate *verb*
(demonstrated, demonstrating)
1 to show. 2 to take part in a demonstration.
demonstrable *adjective,* **demonstrative** *adjective,* **demonstrator** *noun*

demonstration *noun*
1 showing how to do or work something. 2 a march, meeting, etc. to show everyone what you think about something.

den *noun*
1 a lair. 2 a place where something illegal happens. *a gambling den.* 3 a private room for study, etc.

denial *noun*
denying or refusing something.

denim *noun*
1 strong cotton cloth. 2 **denims,** trousers or overalls made of denim.

denominator *noun*
the number below the line in a fraction. *In ¼ the 4 is the denominator.*

denote *verb* **(denoted, denoting)**
to mean; to indicate.

denounce *verb* **(denounced, denouncing)**
to speak against; to accuse.
denunciation *noun*

dense *adjective* **(denser, densest)**
1 thick; packed close together. 2 (*informal*) stupid.
densely *adverb*

density *noun* **(densities)**
1 thickness. 2 (*in Physics*) the proportion of weight to volume.

dent *noun*
an impression or hollow made in a surface by hitting it.

dental *adjective*
of teeth or dentists.

dentist *noun*
a person trained to fill or remove bad teeth and fit false ones.
dentistry *noun*

denture *noun*
a set of false teeth.

deny *verb* **(denied, denying)**
to say that something is not true; to refuse.

deodorant *noun*
something that removes unwanted smells.
deodorize *verb*

depart *verb*
to go away; to leave.
departure *noun*

department *noun*
1 part of a big organization. 2 **department store,** a large shop that sells many kinds of goods.

depend *verb*
1 **depend on** or **upon,** to rely on. *He depended on them for help.* 2 **depend on** or **upon,** to be decided by something else. *Whether we can picnic depends on the weather.*
dependable *adjective*

dependant *noun*
a person who depends on another.

dependent *adjective*
depending. *He was dependent on her wages.*
dependence *noun*

depict *verb*
1 to paint or draw. 2 to describe.

deplore *verb* **(deplored, deploring)**
to be very upset or annoyed by something.
deplorable *adjective*

deport *verb*
to send somebody out of a country.
deportation *noun*

deposit *noun*
1 an amount of money paid into a bank. 2 a first payment for something. 3 a layer of solid matter in or on the earth.

depot *noun*
(*say* **dep**-oh)
a place where things are stored; a headquarters.

depress *verb*
to make somebody very sad.

depression *noun*
1 a great sadness. 2 a shallow hollow in the ground. 3 an area of low air-pressure which may bring rain.

deprive *verb* (**deprived, depriving**)
to take something away from somebody.
Women were deprived of their rights.
deprivation *noun*

depth *noun*
1 how deep something is. *the depth of the river.*
2 **in depth,** thoroughly.

deputy *noun* (**deputies**)
a substitute or chief assistant for someone.
deputize *verb*

derelict *adjective*
(*say* **de**-rě-likt)
ruined; abandoned.

derision *noun*
scorn. *They treated him with derision.*
deride *verb*, **derisive** *adjective*, **derisory** *adjective*

derive *verb* (**derived, deriving**)
to obtain a thing from another person or thing.
derivation *noun*, **derivative** *adjective* and *noun*

derrick *noun*
1 a tower that holds the drill when a well is being drilled. 2 a machine for hoisting things.

derv *noun*
diesel fuel for lorries, etc.

descant *noun*
1 a tune sung or played above another tune.
2 **descant recorder,** a high-pitched recorder.

descend *verb*
1 to go down. 2 **be descended from,** to have as your ancestor.
descendant *noun*, **descent** *noun*

describe *verb* (**described, describing**)
to say what someone or something is like.
description *noun*; **descriptive** *adjective*

desert *noun*
(*say* **dez**-ert)
1 a large area of very dry, often sandy, land.
2 **desert island,** an uninhabited island.

desert *verb*
(*say* di-**zert**)
to abandon; to leave without intending to return.
deserter *noun*, **desertion** *noun*

deserts *plural noun*
(*say* di-**zerts**)
what someone deserves. *He got his just deserts.*

deserve *verb* (**deserved, deserving**)
to have a right to; to be worthy of.
deservedly *adverb*

design *noun*
1 a plan or pattern for something. 2 the way that something is made or designed; an arrangement or pattern.

design *verb*
to draw a design; to plan a building, machine, etc.
designer *noun*

designate *verb* (**designated, designating**)
to mark or describe as something particular.
The river was designated as the boundary.

desirable *adjective*
1 worth having. *a desirable house.* 2 worth doing; advisable. *It is desirable for you to come with us.*
desirability *noun*

desire *verb* (**desired, desiring**)
to want something very much.
desirous *adjective*

desk *noun*
1 a kind of table for writing or reading at. 2 a counter behind which a receptionist, cashier, etc. sits.

desolate *adjective*
1 uninhabited. 2 sad; lonely.
desolation *noun*

despair *noun*
a feeling of hopelessness.

despatch *noun* and *verb*
dispatch.

desperate *adjective*
1 hopeless; extremely bad. *a desperate situation.* 2 violent; dangerous. *a desperate criminal.*
desperately *adverb*, **desperation** *noun*

despise *verb* (**despised, despising**)
to think someone is inferior or worthless.
despicable *adjective*

despite *preposition*
in spite of.

dessert *noun*
(*say* di-**zert**)
1 food eaten at the end of a meal. 2 **dessert-spoon,** a medium-sized spoon used for eating puddings, etc.

destination *noun*
the place you are travelling to.

destined *adjective*
intended; fated.

destiny *noun* (**destinies**)
fate. *His destiny was to die alone.*

destroy *verb*
to ruin or put an end to something.
destruction *noun*, **destructive** *adjective*

destroyer *noun*
a fast warship.

detach *verb*
to unfasten; to separate.
detachable *adjective*, **detachment** *noun*

detached *adjective*
1 separated. 2 not prejudiced; not involved.
3 **detached house,** a house not joined to another.

detail *noun*
1 a tiny part of something. 2 a small piece of information. 3 **in detail,** describing or covering each part fully.

detain *verb*
1 to keep someone waiting. 2 to keep someone at a place.

detect *verb*
to discover.
detection *noun*, **detector** *noun*

detective *noun*
a person who investigates crimes.

detention *noun*
being made to stay in a place, especially being made to stay late in school as a punishment.

deter *verb* **(deterred, deterring)**
to put someone off doing something.

detergent *noun*
a kind of washing powder or liquid.

determined *adjective*
with your mind firmly made up.
determination *noun*

deterrent *noun*
something that may deter people, especially a nuclear weapon.
deterrence *noun*

detest *verb*
to hate. *She detested noise.*
detestable *adjective*, **detestation** *noun*

detonate *verb* **(detonated, detonating)**
to set off an explosion.
detonation *noun*, **detonator** *noun*

detour *noun*
a route used instead of the normal route.

deuce *noun*
a tennis score when both sides have 40 points.

devastate *verb* **(devastated, devastating)**
to ruin or destroy; to make a place impossible to live in.
devastation *noun*

develop *verb*
1 to make or become bigger or better. **2** to treat photographic film with chemicals so that pictures can be seen.
development *noun*

device *noun*
something made for a particular purpose.

devil *noun*
an evil spirit or person.
devilish *adjective*, **devilment** *noun*, **devilry** *noun*

devise *verb* **(devised, devising)**
to invent; to plan.

devolution *noun*
giving authority to another organization or person, especially handing over responsibility for government.

devote *verb* **(devoted, devoting)**
1 to give completely. **2 devoted,** loving and loyal; very enthusiastic.
devotee *noun*, **devotion** *noun*

devour *verb*
to eat or swallow something greedily.

dew *noun*
tiny drops of water that form during the night on surfaces out of doors.
dewy *adjective*

diabetes *noun*
(*say* dy-ă-**bee**-teez)
a disease in which there is too much sugar in a person's blood.
diabetic *adjective* and *noun*

diabolical *adjective*
like a devil; of devils.

diagnose *verb* **(diagnosed, diagnosing)**
to find out what disease someone has.
diagnosis *noun*, **diagnostic** *adjective*

diagonal *noun*
a straight line joining opposite corners of a rectangle.
diagonally *adverb*

diagram *noun*
a picture or plan that explains something.

dial *noun*
a circle with numbers or letters round it. *Clocks, watches, and telephones have dials.*

dial *verb* **(dialled, dialling)**
to telephone a number by turning a telephone dial.

dialect *noun*
the way people speak in a particular district.

dialogue *noun*
a conversation.

diameter *noun*
1 the width of a circle. **2** a line drawn from one side of a circle to the other, passing through the centre.

diamond *noun*
1 a very hard jewel that looks like clear glass. **2** a shape which has four equal sides but which is not a square. **3** a playing-card with a red diamond shape on it.

diaphragm *noun*
(*say* **dy**-ă-fram)
1 the muscular part of the body between the chest and the abdomen. **2** a thin partition or membrane.

diarrhoea *noun*
(*say* dy-ă-**ree**-ă)
too frequent and too watery emptying of the bowels.

diary *noun* **(diaries)**
a book where you can write down what happens each day.

dice *noun* **(dice)**
a small cube marked with dots (1 to 6) on its sides, used in games.

dictate *verb* **(dictated, dictating)**
1 to speak or read something aloud for someone else to write down. **2** to tell somebody what to do; to give orders.
dictation *noun*

dictator *noun*
a ruler who has unlimited power.
dictatorial *adjective*, **dictatorship** *noun*

dictionary *noun* **(dictionaries)**
a book where you can find out what a word means and how to spell it. *Dictionaries usually give words in alphabetical order.*

did past tense of **do.**

didn't shortened form of *did not.*

die *verb* **(died, dying)**
to stop living; to come to an end.

diesel *noun*
1 an engine that works by burning oil. **2** fuel for this kind of engine.

diet *noun*
1 special meals that someone eats to be healthy or to lose weight. **2** the food you normally eat.

differ *verb*
1 to be different. **2** to disagree.

difference *noun*
how different something is from something else.

different *adjective*
unlike; not the same. *Her hat is different from mine.*
differently *adverb*

differential *noun*
1 a difference in wages. **2** a differential gear. **3 differential gear,** a system of gears that makes a vehicle's driving wheels revolve at different speeds when going round corners.

difficult *adjective*
not easy.
difficulty *noun*

diffuse *verb* **(diffused, diffusing)**
1 to spread something widely or thinly. *diffused lighting.* **2** to mix slowly. *diffusing gases.*
diffusion *noun*

dig *verb* **(dug, digging)**
1 to move soil; to make a hole in the ground. **2** to poke. *He dug me in the ribs.* **3** (*informal*) to understand; to like. *Do you dig classical music?*
digger *noun*

digest *verb*
to soften and change food in the stomach so that the body can absorb its goodness.
digestible *adjective*, **digestion** *noun*, **digestive** *adjective*

digit *noun*
(*say* **dij**-it)
any of the numbers from 0 to 9.

digital *adjective*
1 of or using digits. **2** of a type of clock or watch that shows the time with a row of figures, not on a dial.

dignified *adjective*
having dignity.

dignity *noun* **(dignities)**
1 a serious or noble manner. **2** a high rank.

dike *noun*
1 an embankment. **2** a ditch.

dilemma *noun*
a difficult choice.

dilute *verb* **(diluted, diluting)**
to make a liquid weaker by mixing it with water.
dilution *noun*

dim *adjective* **(dimmer, dimmest)**
not bright.
dimly *adverb*

dimension *noun*
measurement; size.
dimensional *adjective*

diminish *verb*
to make or become smaller.

dimple *noun*
a small hollow on the skin.

din *noun*
a loud noise.

dine *verb* **(dined, dining)**
to have dinner.
diner *noun*

dinghy *noun*
(*say* **ding**-i)
a small boat.

dingy *adjective*
(*say* **din**-ji)
shabby; dirty-looking.

dinner *noun*
the main meal of the day.

dinosaur *noun*
a large prehistoric animal.

dioxide *noun*
an oxide with two atoms of oxygen and one atom of another element. *carbon dioxide.*

dip *verb* **(dipped, dipping)**
to put down or go down, especially into a liquid.
dipper *noun*

dip *noun*
1 dipping. **2** a slope downward. **3** a quick swim.

diphtheria *noun*
(*say* dif-**theer**-i-ă)
a serious disease of the throat.

diploma *noun*
a certificate awarded for skill in a particular subject.

diplomacy *noun*
keeping friendly with other nations or other people.
diplomat *noun*, **diplomatic** *adjective*, **diplomatically** *adverb*

direct *adjective*
1 as straight or quick as possible. **2** straightforward; frank. **3 direct current,** electric current flowing only in one direction. **4 direct object,** the word that receives the action of a verb. *In 'she hit him', the direct object is 'him'.*
directly *adverb*, **directness** *noun*

direct *verb*
1 to show someone the way. **2** to control; to manage.
director *noun*

direction *noun*
1 the way you go to get somewhere. **2** directing something. **3 directions,** information on how to use or do something.
directional *adjective*

directory *noun* **(directories)**
a list of people with their telephone numbers, addresses, etc.

dirt *noun*
1 mud; dust; anything that is not clean. **2 dirt-track,** a racing-track made of cinders, earth, etc.

dirty *adjective* **(dirtier, dirtiest)**
1 not clean. **2** unfair; mean. *It was a dirty trick to steal my sweets.* **3** rude; obscene. *Someone has written dirty words on the wall.*
dirtily *adverb*, **dirtiness** *noun*

disinfect

disable *verb* **(disabled, disabling)**
to make someone unable to do something; to cripple.
disability *noun*

disadvantage *noun*
something that hinders you; a difficulty.
disadvantaged *adjective*

disagree *verb* **(disagreed, disagreeing)**
1 to have or express a different opinion from someone else. 2 to have a bad effect on someone. *Rich food disagrees with me.*
disagreement *noun*

disagreeable *adjective*
unpleasant.

disappear *verb*
to stop being visible; to vanish.
disappearance *noun*

disappoint *verb*
to fail to do what someone hopes for.
disappointment *noun*

disapprove *verb* **(disapproved, disapproving)**
not to approve of someone or something.
disapproval *noun*

disarm *verb*
1 to reduce the size of your army, air force, etc. 2 to take away someone's weapons.
disarmament *noun*

disaster *noun*
a very bad accident or misfortune.
disastrous *adjective*

disc *noun*
1 any round, flat object. 2 a gramophone record. 3 **disc brake,** a brake with a flat plate pressing against another plate. 4 **disc jockey,** someone who introduces and plays records. 5 **disc parking,** parking in which vehicles display a disc or card that shows when they started parking.

discard *verb*
to get rid of something.

discharge *verb* **(discharged, discharging)**
to release somebody or emit something.

disciple *noun*
a follower, especially one of Jesus's first twelve followers.

discipline *noun*
orderly and obedient behaviour.

disclose *verb* **(disclosed, disclosing)**
to reveal.
disclosure *noun*

disco *noun*
(*informal*) 1 a discotheque. 2 music of the kind played in discotheques.

discolour *verb*
to spoil or change the colour of something.

discomfort *noun*
being uncomfortable.

disconnect *verb*
to break a connection; to detach.
disconnection *noun*

discontented *adjective*
not contented; dissatisfied.

discotheque *noun*
(*say* **dis-kŏ-tek**)
1 a place or party where records are played for dancing. 2 the equipment for playing records for dancing.

discount *noun*
an amount by which a price is reduced.

discourage *verb* **(discouraged, discouraging)**
1 to take away someone's enthusiasm or confidence. *Don't get discouraged: try again.* 2 to try to persuade someone not to do something. *You should discourage him from going out in the rain.*
discouragement *noun*

discover *verb*
1 to find. 2 to find something out.
discoverer *noun,* **discovery** *noun*

discriminate *verb* **(discriminated, discriminating)**
1 to notice the differences between things; to prefer one thing to another. 2 to treat people differently or unfairly because of their race, sex, or religion.
discrimination *noun*

discus *noun* **(discuses)**
(*say* **dis-kŭss**)
a thick, heavy disc thrown in an athletic contest.

discuss *verb*
(*say* dis-**kuss**)
to talk with other people about a subject.
discussion *noun*

disease *noun*
an illness; sickness.
diseased *adjective*

disgrace *noun*
1 shame. *It's no disgrace to be poor.* 2 a person or thing that causes shame or disapproval. *The slums are a disgrace.* 3 **in disgrace,** disapproved of. *He is in disgrace for telling lies.*
disgraceful *adjective*

disgrace *verb* **(disgraced, disgracing)**
to cause disgrace to someone or something.

disguise *verb* **(disguised, disguising)**
to make someone or something look different so as to deceive people.

disguise *noun*
something used for disguising.

disgust *noun*
a strong feeling of dislike.

disgust *verb*
to cause disgust. *His manners are disgusting.*

dish *noun* **(dishes)**
1 a plate or bowl for food. 2 food served on a dish.

dishcloth *noun*
a cloth for washing or drying dishes, cups, etc.

dishonest *adjective*
not honest.
dishonesty *noun*

disinfect *verb*
to destroy germs in a thing.
disinfectant *noun*

disintegrate 76

disintegrate *verb* (disintegrated, disintegrating)
to break up into small pieces.
disintegration *noun*

dislike *noun*
a feeling of not liking somebody or something.

dislike *verb* (disliked, disliking)
not to like somebody or something.

dislocate *verb* (dislocated, dislocating)
1 to dislodge a bone from its proper place in the body. 2 to disrupt. *The fog dislocated traffic.*
dislocation *noun*

dislodge *verb* (dislodged, dislodging)
to move something from its place.

disloyal *adjective*
not loyal.

dismal *adjective*
gloomy.
dismally *adverb*

dismay *noun*
discouragement or despair.
dismayed *adjective*

dismiss *verb*
1 to send someone away, especially to stop employing him. 2 to stop considering an idea, etc. 3 to get a batsman out in cricket.
dismissal *noun*

dismount *verb*
to get off a horse or bicycle.

disobey *verb*
not to obey.
disobedience *noun*, **disobedient** *adjective*

disorder *noun*
1 confusion; disturbance. 2 an illness.
disorderly *adjective*

dispatch *noun*
a report or message.

dispatch *verb*
1 to send a person or thing off somewhere. 2 to kill.

dispense *verb* (dispensed, dispensing)
1 to distribute. 2 to prepare medicine. 3 dispense with, to do without something.

disperse *verb* (dispersed, dispersing)
to scatter. *The police dispersed the crowd.*
dispersal *noun*, **dispersion** *noun*

displace *verb* (displaced, displacing)
1 to dislodge; to move someone from his place. 2 to take the place of someone or something.

displacement *noun*
1 displacing. 2 the amount of water displaced by a ship, etc. floating in it.

display *verb*
to show; to arrange something so that it can be clearly seen.

display *noun*
1 the displaying of something; an exhibition. 2 the showing of information on a screen.

displease *verb* (displeased, displeasing)
to annoy.
displeasure *noun*

disposable *adjective*
made to be thrown away after it has been used. *a disposable towel.*

disposal *noun*
1 getting rid of something. 2 at your disposal, for you to use; ready for you.

dispose *verb* (disposed, disposing)
1 to make someone willing or ready to do something. *I am disposed to help him.* 2 dispose of, to get rid of.

disposition *noun*
a person's character or qualities.

disprove *verb* (disproved, disproving)
to prove that something is not true.

dispute *noun*
a quarrel or disagreement.

disqualify *verb* (disqualified, disqualifying)
to remove someone from a race or competition because he has broken the rules.
disqualification *noun*

disregard *verb*
to ignore. *She disregarded my objections.*

disrupt *verb*
to put into disorder. *Floods disrupted traffic.*
disruption *noun*, **disruptive** *adjective*

dissatisfied *adjective*
not satisfied.
dissatisfaction *noun*

dissect *verb*
to cut something up so as to examine it.
dissection *noun*

dissolve *verb* (dissolved, dissolving)
to mix something with a liquid so that it becomes part of the liquid.

distance *noun*
1 the amount of space between two places. 2 in the distance, far away.

distant *adjective*
1 far away. 2 not friendly or sociable.

distil *verb* (distilled, distilling)
to purify a liquid by boiling it and condensing the vapour.
distillation *noun*, **distiller** *noun*, **distillery** *noun*

distinct *adjective*
1 easily heard or seen; definite. *a distinct improvement.* 2 clearly separate or different. *A rabbit is distinct from a hare.*
distinctly *adverb*

distinction *noun*
1 a difference. 2 excellence; honour. 3 an award for excellence.

distinctive *adjective*
that distinguishes one thing from another.

distinguish *verb*
1 to mark or notice the differences between things. 2 to see or hear something clearly.

distinguished *adjective*
famous.

distort *verb*
1 to change something into an abnormal shape. *His face was distorted with anger.* 2 to change something so that it is untrue. *Newspapers sometimes distort the facts.*
distortion *noun*

distract *verb*
to take someone's attention away from something. *Don't distract me from my work.*
distraction *noun*

distress *noun*
great sorrow, pain, or trouble.

distribute *verb* **(distributed, distributing)**
1 to deal or share out. *The teacher distributed textbooks to the class.* 2 to spread or scatter around. *She distributed the seed over the soil.* 3 to sell or deliver goods to customers.
distribution *noun,* **distributive** *adjective*

distributor *noun*
1 someone who distributes goods. 2 a device that passes current to the sparking-plugs of an engine.

district *noun*
part of a town or country.

distrust *noun*
lack of trust; suspicion.
distrustful *adjective*

disturb *verb*
1 to spoil someone's peace or rest; to worry. 2 to dislodge.
disturbance *noun*

ditch *noun* **(ditches)**
a narrow trench to hold or carry away water.

ditto *noun*
the same as the thing you have just mentioned.

divan *noun*
a bed or couch without back or sides.

dive *verb* **(dived, diving)**
1 to go under water, especially head first. 2 to move down quickly.

diver *noun*
1 someone who dives. 2 someone who works under water in a special suit called a diving-suit. 3 a bird that dives.

diverse *adjective*
varied; of several different kinds.
diversify *verb,* **diversity** *noun*

divert *verb*
1 to change the direction of something. 2 to entertain or amuse.
diversion *noun*

divide *verb* **(divided, dividing)**
1 to separate or break into smaller parts; to share out. *We divided the money between us.* 2 to find out how many times one number is contained in another. *Six divided by two equals three (6÷2=3).*

dividend *noun*
a share of a business's profit.

divider *noun*
1 a partition. 2 **dividers,** a pair of compasses for measuring distances.

divine *adjective*
1 of God; coming from God. 2 like a god. 3 (*informal*) excellent; extremely beautiful.
divinely *adverb,* **divinity** *noun*

divine *verb* **(divined, divining)**
to find hidden water, metal, etc. by holding a Y-shaped stick called a divining-rod.

division *noun*
1 dividing. 2 something that divides. 3 a part of something. 4 an army unit consisting of two or more brigades.
divisible *adjective*

divorce *noun*
the legal ending of a marriage.

Diwali *noun*
(*say* di-**wah**-li)
a Hindu festival held in October or November.

D.I.Y. short for **do-it-yourself.**

dizzy *adjective* **(dizzier, dizziest)**
giddy.
dizzily *adverb,* **dizziness** *noun*

D.J. short for *disc jockey.*

do *verb* (*past tense* **did;** *past participle* **done;** *present participle* **doing**)
1 to perform an action; to carry out. *I have done my job.* 2 to deal with something; to solve a problem. *I can't do this sum.* 3 to be suitable or enough. *This room will do for two people.* 4 to manage or progress; to get on. *She is doing well at school.* 5 (*informal*) to swindle. *I'm afraid you've been done.* 6 used in questions like *do you want this?* and in statements with 'not' like *I do not want it.* 7 **could do with,** need or want. *I could do with a bath.* 8 **do away with,** to get rid of or kill. 9 **do up,** to fasten. *Do up your coat.* 10 **do without,** to manage without having something.

dock *noun*
1 a place where ships are loaded, unloaded, or repaired. 2 a place for the prisoner in a criminal court. 3 a weed with broad leaves.

dock *verb*
1 to come into a dock. 2 to join two spacecraft together in orbit.

docker *noun*
a labourer in a dockyard.

dockyard *noun*
an area with docks and equipment for building or repairing ships.

doctor *noun*
a person trained to heal sick people.

doctrine *noun*
a belief; something taught.
doctrinal *adjective*

document *noun*
something important written or printed.
documentation *noun*

documentary *noun* **(documentaries)**
a film, etc. showing real events or situations.

doddle *noun*
(*informal*) something easy to do.

dodge *verb* **(dodged, dodging)**
to move quickly to avoid someone or something.

dodge *noun*
1 a dodging movement. 2 a trick; a clever way of doing something.

dodgem *noun*
a small electrically-driven car at a fun-fair, which you have to drive around an enclosure, dodging other cars.

dodgy

dodgy *adjective*
(*informal*) awkward; tricky.

doe *noun*
a female deer, rabbit, or hare.

does 3rd singular present form of **do**. *She does what she likes.*

doesn't shortened form of *does not. He doesn't understand.*

dog *noun*
a four-legged animal that barks, often kept as a pet.

dogged *adjective*
(*say* **dog**-id)
persistent; obstinate.
doggedly *adverb*

doings *plural noun*
(*informal*) things.

do-it-yourself *adjective*
that an amateur handyman can make or use. *a do-it-yourself kit for making a dinghy.*

dole *noun*
money paid to an unemployed person.

doll *noun*
1 a toy model of a baby or person. **2 doll's house,** a tiny toy house.

dollar *noun*
a unit of money in the United States, Canada, Australia, New Zealand, and some other countries. *100 dollars is written $100.*

dolly *noun* (**dollies**)
1 (*informal*) a doll. **2 dolly mixture,** a mixture of tiny sweets.

dolphin *noun*
a sea animal like a small whale.

domain *noun*
realm.

dome *noun*
a roof shaped like the top half of a ball. *the dome of St. Paul's Cathedral.*

domestic *adjective*
1 connected with the home. *Domestic science includes things like cookery and needlework.* 2 tame. *Cats and dogs are domestic animals.*
domesticate *verb*, **domesticity** *noun*

dominant *adjective*
1 most powerful or important. 2 highest; towering.
dominance *noun*

dominate *verb* (**dominated, dominating**)
to be dominant.
domination *noun*

dominion *noun*
1 rule; authority. 2 an area ruled by a king, etc.

domino *noun* (**dominoes**)
a small, flat, oblong piece of wood or plastic with dots (1 to 6) or a blank space at each end, used in the game of dominoes.

done past participle of **do**.

donkey *noun*
an animal that looks like a small horse with long ears.

donor *noun*
someone who gives something. *a blood donor.*

don't shortened form of *do not. Don't cycle on the pavement.*

don't-know *noun*
someone who has not made up his mind about a particular question.

doodle *noun*
a drawing or scribble done absent-mindedly.

doodle *verb* (**doodled, doodling**)
to make a doodle.

doom *noun*
ruin; death; fate. *Send him to his doom.*
doomed *adjective*

door *noun*
something that opens and closes the entrance to a room, building, cupboard, etc.

doorstep *noun*
the step or piece of ground outside a door.

doorway *noun*
the opening which a door fits.

dope *noun*
(*informal*) 1 a narcotic drug. 2 information. 3 a fool.
dopey *adjective*

dormitory *noun* (**dormitories**)
1 a room designed for several people to sleep in. **2 dormitory town** or **suburb,** a place from which people regularly travel to work elsewhere.

dose *noun*
an amount of medicine taken at one time.

dossier *noun*
(*say* **dos**-i-er or **dos**-i-ay)
a set of pieces of information about a person, event, etc.

dot *noun*
a tiny spot.

dot *verb* (**dotted, dotting**)
to mark with dots.

dotty *adjective* (**dottier, dottiest**)
(*informal*) stupid or slightly mad.
dottiness *noun*

double *adjective*
1 twice as much; twice as many. *a double portion of pudding.* 2 having two of something. *a double-barrelled gun.* 3 suitable for two people. *a double bed.* **4 double bass,** a musical instrument with strings, like a large cello.
doubly *adverb*

double *verb* (**doubled, doubling**)
1 to make or become twice as big. 2 to fold something. 3 to run quickly.

double *noun*
1 two of something. 2 someone who looks exactly like someone else.

doubt *noun*
not feeling sure about something.
doubtful *adjective*, **doubtless** *adverb*

dough *noun*
1 a thick mixture of flour and water used for making bread, buns, etc. 2 (*slang*) money.
doughy *adjective*

doughnut *noun*
a round bun that has been fried and covered with sugar.

dove *noun*
1 a kind of pigeon. 2 a peaceful person.

dovetail *noun*
a wedge-shaped joint used to join two pieces of wood together.

dovetail *verb*
1 to join two pieces of wood with a dovetail. 2 to fit neatly together. *My plans dovetailed with hers.*

dowel *noun*
a headless wooden or metal pin for holding together two pieces of wood, stone, etc.

down *adverb* and *preposition*
1 to or in a lower place. *Run down the hill.* 2 along. *Go down to the shops.*

down *noun*[1]
very soft feathers or hair. *Ducks are covered with down.*
downy *adjective*

down *noun*[2]
a grass-covered hill. *The South Downs.*
downland *noun*

down *noun*[3]
have a down on somebody, to have a prejudice or grudge against him.

downfall *noun*
1 ruin; ceasing to have fortune or power. 2 a heavy fall of rain, snow, etc.

downhill *adverb*
down a slope.

downstairs *adverb* and *adjective*
to or on a lower floor.

downstream *adverb*
in the direction that a river or stream flows.

downward or **downwards** *adverb*
towards a lower place.

doze *verb* **(dozed, dozing)**
to sleep lightly.
dozy *adjective*

dozen *noun*
1 a set of twelve. 2 **dozens of,** lots of.

Dr. short for **Doctor.**

drab *adjective* **(drabber, drabbest)**
1 not colourful. *drab clothes.* 2 boring. *He lived a drab existence.*

draft *noun*
a rough sketch or plan.

draft *verb*
to make a draft.

drag *verb* **(dragged, dragging)**
1 to pull something heavy along. 2 to search a river, lake, etc. with nets and hooks.

drag *noun*
(*informal*) something that hinders or annoys you.

dragon *noun*
a fierce mythical monster.

dragonfly *noun* **(dragonflies)**
an insect with a long body and two pairs of transparent wings.

drain *noun*
a pipe, ditch, etc. for taking away water or sewage.

drain *verb*
1 to get rid of water with drains. 2 to flow or trickle away. 3 to empty liquid out of a container. *He drained his glass.* 4 to exhaust. *drained of strength.* 5 **draining-board,** a sloping surface beside a sink where washed dishes, etc. are placed.
drainage *noun*

drake *noun*
a male duck.

drama *noun*
1 a play. 2 writing or performing plays. 3 a series of exciting events.
dramatic *adjective*, **dramatically** *adverb*,
dramatics *noun*

dramatist *noun*
someone who writes plays.

dramatize *verb* **(dramatized, dramatizing)**
1 to make something into a play. 2 to exaggerate.
dramatization *noun*

drank past tense of **drink** *verb. I drank a whole bottle of lemonade.*

drape *verb* **(draped, draping)**
to hang cloth over something.

drastic *adjective*
having a strong or violent effect.
drastically *adverb*

draught *noun*
(rhymes with *craft*)
a current of usually cold air indoors.
draughty *adjective*

draughts *noun*
a game played with 24 round pieces on a chess-board.

draughtsman *noun* **(draughtsmen)**
1 someone who makes drawings. 2 a piece used in the game of draughts.

draw *verb* (*past tense* **drew**; *past participle* **drawn**; *present participle* **drawing**)
1 to make a picture, diagram, etc. with a pencil, crayon, pen, etc. *I have drawn a map of Britain.* 2 to pull. *She drew her chair up to the table.* 3 to attract. *The fair drew large crowds.* 4 to end a game or contest with the same score on both sides. *They drew 2–2 last Saturday.* 5 to come. *The ship was drawing nearer.*

draw *noun*
1 a choice made by drawing lots. 2 an attraction. 3 a drawn game.

drawback *noun*
a disadvantage.

drawbridge *noun*
a bridge that may be raised or lowered over a moat.

drawer *noun*
a sliding container in a piece of furniture.

drawing *noun*
1 something drawn with a pencil, crayon, etc.
2 **drawing-pin,** a short pin with a large flat top.
3 **drawing-room,** a sitting-room.

drawl

drawl *verb*
to speak very slowly or lazily.

dread *noun*
terror.

dread *verb*
to fear something very much.

dreadful *adjective*
awful.
dreadfully *adverb*

dreadlocks *plural noun*
hair in long ringlets worn especially by Rastafarians.

dream *noun*
1 things a person seems to see while he is asleep. 2 something imagined; an ambition or ideal.
dreamy *adjective*

dream *verb* **(dreamt** or **dreamed, dreaming)**
1 to have a dream or dreams. 2 to have an ambition. *She dreams of being a ballet dancer.* 3 to think something may happen. *I never dreamt she would leave.*

dreary *adjective* **(drearier, dreariest)**
gloomy; boring.
drearily *adverb,* **dreariness** *noun*

dredge *verb* **(dredged, dredging)**
to drag up something, especially mud from the bottom of a river or the sea.
dredger *noun*

drench *verb*
to soak. *They got drenched in the rain.*

dress *noun* **(dresses)**
1 a garment with a skirt and blouse together. 2 clothes; costume. *fancy dress.* 3 **dress rehearsal,** a rehearsal at which the cast wears its costumes.

dress *verb*
1 to put clothes on. 2 to prepare food for cooking or eating. 3 to put a bandage on a wound.

dresser *noun*
a sideboard with shelves at the top.

dressing *noun*
1 a covering for a wound; a plaster. 2 a sauce of oil, vinegar, etc. for a salad.

dressing-gown *noun*
a loose garment worn over pyjamas, etc.

drew past tense of **draw** *verb.*

dribble *verb* **(dribbled, dribbling)**
1 to let saliva trickle out of your mouth. 2 to kick a ball as you run along, so that the ball stays close to your feet

dried past tense and past participle of **dry** *verb.*

drier *noun*
something that dries hair, laundry, etc.

drift *verb*
1 to be carried gently along by water or air. 2 to move or live aimlessly.

drift *noun*
1 a drifting movement. 2 a mass of snow or sand piled up by the wind. 3 the general meaning of a speech, etc. *I don't understand your drift.*

driftwood *noun*
wood washed ashore from the sea.

drill *noun*
1 a tool for making holes. 2 repeated exercises in military training, gymnastics, etc. 3 a procedure or routine.

drill *verb*
1 to make a hole with a drill. 2 to do repeated exercises.

drink *verb* **(**past tense **drank;** past participle **drunk;** present participle **drinking)**
1 to swallow liquid. 2 to drink a lot of alcoholic drinks. *Don't drink and drive.*
drinkable *adjective,* **drinker** *noun*

drink *noun*
1 a liquid for drinking. 2 an alcoholic drink.

drip *noun*
a falling drop of liquid.

drip *verb* **(dripped, dripping)**
1 to fall in drops. 2 to let liquid fall in drops. *a dripping tap.* 3 **drip-dry clothes,** clothes that do not need ironing.

dripping *noun*
solidified fat which has come from roasting meat.

drive *verb* **(**past tense **drove;** past participle **driven;** present participle **driving)**
to make something or someone move.
driver *noun*

drive *noun*
1 a journey in a vehicle. 2 a stroke in cricket, golf, etc. 3 a road, especially leading to a large house. 4 energy; enthusiasm.

drive-in *adjective*
that you can use without getting out of your car. *a drive-in bank. a drive-in cinema.*

drizzle *noun*
gentle rain.

drone *verb* **(droned, droning)**
1 to make a low humming sound. 2 to talk in a boring voice.

drone *noun*
1 a droning sound. 2 a male bee.

droop *verb*
to hang down weakly.

drop *noun*
1 a tiny amount of liquid. 2 a fall; a decrease. *a drop in prices.*
droplet *noun*

drop *verb* **(dropped, dropping)**
1 to fall. 2 to let something fall. 3 **drop in,** to visit someone. 4 **drop out,** to stop taking part in something.

drought *noun*
(rhymes with *out*)
a long period of dry weather.

drove past tense of **drive** *verb.*

drown *verb*
1 to die or kill by suffocation under water. 2 to make so much noise that another sound cannot be heard.

drowsy *adjective* **(drowsier, drowsiest)**
sleepy.
drowsily *adverb*, **drowsiness** *noun*

drug *noun*
1 a substance that kills pain or cures a disease.
2 a substance that affects your senses or your
mind. *a drug addict.*

drug *verb* **(drugged, drugging)**
to use a drug to make someone unconscious.

drum *noun*
1 a musical instrument made of a cylinder with
a skin stretched over one end or both ends. 2 a
cylindrical container. *an oil drum.*

drum *verb* **(drummed, drumming)**
1 to play a drum or drums. 2 to tap or thump
on something. *He drummed his fingers on the
table.*
drummer *noun*

drunk *adjective*
excited, helpless, etc. through drinking too
much alcohol.

drunk *noun*
someone who is drunk.
drunkard *noun*

dry *adjective* **(drier, driest)**
1 not wet; not damp. 2 boring; dull. *a dry book.*
3 dry cleaning, a method of cleaning clothes
without using water. 4 dry dock, a dock which
can be emptied of water, for repairing ships.
5 dry ice, carbon dioxide frozen solid.
drily *adverb*, **dryness** *noun*

dry *verb* **(dried, drying)**
to make or become dry.

dual *adjective*
1 double. 2 dual carriageway, a road with four
lanes, two in each direction.

dub *verb* **(dubbed, dubbing)**
1 to make someone a knight. 2 to change or
add new sound to the sound on a film or
magnetic tape.

duchess *noun* **(duchesses)**
a duke's wife or widow.

duck *noun*
1 a web-footed bird with a flat beak. 2 a batsman's score of nought at cricket. 3 **duckbill** or
duck-billed platypus, a platypus.

duck *verb*
1 to bend down quickly to avoid something.
2 to go or push quickly under water.

duckling *noun*
a young duck.

duct *noun*
a tube or channel.

due *adjective*
1 expected. *The train is due in five minutes.*
2 owing; to be paid. *Your subscription is due.*

due *adverb*
1 directly. *The camp is due north.* 2 **due to,**
because of. *His lateness was due to an accident.*

duel *noun*
a fight between two people, especially with
pistols or swords.

duet *noun*
a piece of music for two players or two singers.

duff *noun*
a boiled pudding.

duff *adjective*
(*slang*) useless; bad. *He sold me a duff car.*

duff *verb*
duff up, (*slang*) to beat someone up.

duffle-coat *noun*
a thick overcoat with a hood.

dug past tense and past participle of **dig.**

dug-out *noun*
1 an underground shelter. 2 a canoe made by
hollowing out a tree-trunk.

duke *noun*
a very important nobleman.

dull *adjective*
1 not bright; gloomy. *a dull day.* 2 not sharp. *a
dull pain.* 3 stupid. *a dull boy.* 4 boring. *a dull
programme.*
dully *adverb*, **dullness** *noun*

duly *adverb*
rightly; as expected. *Having promised to come,
they duly arrived.*

dumb *adjective*
1 unable to speak; silent. 2 (*informal*) stupid.

dummy *noun* **(dummies)**
1 something made to look like a person or
thing; an imitation. 2 an imitation teat for a
baby to suck.

dump *noun*
1 a place where something, especially rubbish,
is left or stored. 2 (*informal*) an unpleasant
place.

dump *verb*
1 to get rid of something you don't want. 2 to
put something down carelessly.

dumpling *noun*
a lump of boiled or baked dough.

dune *noun*
a mound of loose sand shaped by the wind.

dungarees *plural noun*
overalls.

dungeon *noun*
(*say* **dun**-jŏn)
an underground prison-cell.

duplicate *noun*
(*say* **dew**-pli-kăt)
something exactly the same as something else.

duplicate *verb* **(duplicated, duplicating)**
(*say* **dew**-pli-kayt)
to make or be a duplicate.
duplication *noun*, **duplicator** *noun*

durable *adjective*
lasting; strong.
durability *noun*

duration *noun*
the time something lasts.

during *preposition*
while something else is going on.

dusk *noun*
twilight in the evening.

dust *noun*
tiny particles of dry earth or other material.

dust *verb*
1 to clear dust away. 2 to sprinkle with dust or powder.
duster *noun*

dustbin *noun*
a container for household rubbish.

dustman *noun* **(dustmen)**
a person whose job is to empty dustbins.

dustpan *noun*
a pan into which dust is brushed from the floor, etc.

dusty *adjective* **(dustier, dustiest)**
1 covered with dust. 2 like dust.

Dutch *adjective*
1 of Holland. 2 **Dutch elm disease,** a disease that kills elms.
Dutchman *noun,* **Dutchwoman** *noun*

dutiful *adjective*
doing your duty; obedient.
dutifully *adverb*

duty *noun* **(duties)**
1 what you ought to do or must do. 2 a kind of tax.

duvet *noun*
(*say* **doo**-vay)
a kind of quilt used instead of other bedclothes.

dwarf *noun*
a very small person or thing.

dwell *verb* **(dwelt, dwelling)**
1 to live somewhere. 2 **dwell on,** to think or talk about something for a long time.
dweller *noun,* **dwelling** *noun*

dwindle *verb* **(dwindled, dwindling)**
to get smaller gradually.

dye *verb* **(dyed, dyeing)**
to colour something by putting it in a special liquid.

dye *noun*
something used to dye fabrics, etc.

dying present participle of **die.**

dyke *noun*
a dike.

dynamic *adjective*
energetic; active.

dynamite *noun*
1 a powerful explosive. 2 (*informal*) something very exciting, dangerous, etc.

dynamo *noun*
a machine that makes electricity.

dynasty *noun* **(dynasties)**
(*say* **din**-ă-sti)
a succession of kings or queens of the same family.

dyslexia *noun*
(*say* dis-**leks**-i-ă)
word-blindness.

dystrophy *noun*
(*say* **dis**-trŏf-i)
a disease that weakens the muscles. *muscular dystrophy.*

E

each *adjective*
every. *Each child had a cake.*

each *pronoun*
1 every one. *Each of you may have a sweet.*
2 **each other,** said of something done together by two or more people. *We meet each other at the club.*

eager *adjective*
strongly wanting to do something; enthusiastic.
eagerly *adverb,* **eagerness** *noun*

eagle *noun*
a large bird of prey with very strong sight.

ear *noun*[1]
1 the part of the head that you hear with.
2 hearing ability. *She has a good ear for music.*

ear *noun*[2]
the cluster of seeds at the top of a stalk of corn.

eardrum *noun*
a membrane in the ear that vibrates when sound reaches it.

earl *noun*
a British nobleman.

early *adverb* and *adjective* **(earlier, earliest)**
1 before the usual or correct time. 2 near the beginning.
earliness *noun*

earmark *verb*
to decide that something shall be used for a particular purpose.

earn *verb*
to get something by working for it or as a reward.

earnest *adjective*
1 serious; determined. 2 **in earnest,** seriously.
earnestly *adverb,* **earnestness** *noun*

earnings *plural noun*
money earned.

earphone *noun*
a listening device that fits over or into the ear.

ear-ring *noun*
an ornament worn on the ear.

earth *noun*
1 the planet that we live on. 2 soil; the ground. 3 the hole where a fox or badger lives. 4 connection to the ground to complete an electric circuit. 5 **on earth**, at all. *Why on earth did you hit him?* 6 **the earth**, (*informal*) a huge amount of money. *It cost the earth.*
earthly *adjective*, **earthy** *adjective*

earthenware *noun*
crockery made of baked clay.

earthquake *noun*
a sudden violent shaking of the ground.

earthworm *noun*
a small wriggling creature that lives in the soil.

earwig *noun*
an insect with pincers at the end of its body.

ease *noun*
1 relief or freedom from difficulty or discomfort. 2 **at ease**, comfortably; (*in the army*) standing with legs apart and hands behind the back.

ease *verb* (**eased, easing**)
1 to give ease to somebody; to decrease pain, etc. 2 to make something easy. 3 to move something slowly and carefully.

easel *noun*
a stand for holding a blackboard or a painting.

easily *adverb*
1 with ease. 2 without doubt; very possibly. *He could easily be lying.*

east *noun*
the area where the sun rises.

east *adjective*
1 coming from the east. *an east wind.* 2 situated in the east. *the east coast.*
easterly *adjective*, **eastern** *adjective*

east *adverb*
towards the east.
eastward *adjective* and *adverb*, **eastwards** *adverb*

Easter *noun*
1 the day or period when the resurrection of Christ is commemorated. 2 **Easter egg**, a sweet artificial egg eaten at or near Easter.

easy *adjective* (**easier, easiest**)
1 able to be done or understood without any trouble. 2 comfortable; giving ease. *an easy chair.*
easiness *noun*

easy *adverb* (**easier, easiest**)
1 with ease; comfortably. *Take it easy.* 2 (*in the army*) standing with more freedom than 'at ease'.

eat *verb* (*past tense* **ate**; *past participle* **eaten**; *present participle* **eating**)
1 to take food into the mouth and swallow it. *Have you eaten your breakfast? I ate all mine.* 2 to use up something; to destroy.

eatable *adjective*
fit to be eaten.

eaves *plural noun*
the overhanging edges of a roof.

ebb *noun*
1 the tide when it is going out. 2 a low or weak condition. *He was at a low ebb.*

ebb *verb*
1 to go down. *The tide was ebbing.* 2 to weaken or lessen. *His strength ebbed away.*

ebony *noun* (**ebonies**)
a hard black wood. *The black keys on a piano are often made of ebony.*

eccentric *adjective*
(*say* ik-**sen**-trik)
behaving strangely.
eccentric *noun*, **eccentricity** *noun*

echo *noun* (**echoes**)
a sound that is heard again as it bounces off something.

echo *verb*
1 to make an echo. 2 to repeat a sound or saying.

éclair *noun*
(*say* ay-**klair**)
a finger-shaped cream-bun with chocolate on top.

eclipse *noun*
1 a time when the moon comes between the sun and the earth, so that all or part of the sun is hidden. 2 a time when the earth comes between the sun and the moon, so that all or part of the moon is in shadow.

ecology *noun*
(*say* ee-**kol**-ŏ-ji)
the science concerned with living creatures and plants studied in their surroundings.
ecological *adjective*, **ecologist** *noun*

economic *adjective*
(*say* eek-ŏ-**nom**-ik or ek-ŏ-**nom**-ik)
1 of economics. 2 profitable.

economical *adjective*
(*say* eek-ŏ-**nom**-ik-ăl)
careful in using money, goods, etc.; not wasteful.
economically *adverb*

economics *noun*
(*say* eek-ŏ-**nom**-iks or ek-ŏ-**nom**-iks)
the study of how money is used and how goods, etc. are made, sold, and used.

economist *noun*
(*say* i-**kon**-ŏ-mist)
an expert in economics.

economize *verb* (**economized, economizing**)
(*say* i-**kon**-ŏ-myz)
to be economical.

economy *noun* (**economies**)
(*say* i-**kon**-ŏ-mi)
1 being economical; a way of saving money. 2 managing the money, goods, etc. used by a community or household.

ecstasy *noun* (**ecstasies**)
a feeling of great delight or joy.
ecstatic *adjective*

edge *noun*
1 the part along the side or end of something. 2 the sharp part of a knife, axe, etc. 3 **on edge**, nervous; irritable.
edgy *adjective*

edge *verb* (**edged, edging**)
1 to move slowly. *She edged towards the door.* 2 to give something an edge.

edgeways *adverb*
1 with the edge outwards or forwards. **2 not get a word in edgeways,** not to be able to interrupt a talkative person.

edible *adjective*
not poisonous; eatable.

edit *verb*
1 to get a newspaper, magazine, etc. ready for publishing. 2 to put a film, tape-recording, etc. in the order you want.

edition *noun*
1 the form in which something is published. *a paperback edition.* 2 all the copies of a newspaper, book, etc. issued at the same time. *the first edition.*

editor *noun*
someone who edits, especially the main person responsible for a newspaper, magazine, etc.

editorial *adjective*
of editing or editors.

editorial *noun*
a newspaper article giving the editor's opinion on current affairs.

educate *verb* (**educated, educating**)
to give somebody knowledge or skill.
education *noun,* **educational** *adjective,* **educator** *noun*

eel *noun*
a long fish that looks like a snake.

eerie *adjective* (**eerier, eeriest**)
frighteningly strange; weird.
eerily *adverb,* **eeriness** *noun*

effect *noun*
1 something that happens because of something else. *The drink had a strange effect on Alice.* 2 a general impression. *The lights made a cheerful effect.* 3 a sound-effect.

effective *adjective*
producing an effect; impressive.
effectively *adverb,* **effectiveness** *noun*

effeminate *adjective*
(*say* i-**fem**-in-ăt)
having some of the characteristics of a woman. *an effeminate man.*

effervescent *adjective*
(*say* ef-er-**ves**-ĕnt)
fizzing. *an effervescent drink.*
effervescence *noun*

efficient *adjective*
doing work well; effective.
efficiency *noun,* **efficiently** *adverb*

effort *noun*
1 hard work; using energy. 2 an attempt.
effortless *adjective*

e.g. for example. *He teaches many subjects, e.g. chemistry and biology.*

egg *noun*
1 an oval or round object with a thin shell, laid by birds, insects, fishes, etc., in which their offspring develop. 2 a hen's or duck's egg used as food.

egg *verb*
egg on, to encourage somebody.

Egyptian *adjective*
of Egypt.

eh *interjection*
(*say* ay)
an exclamation of surprise or doubt.

eiderdown *noun*
(*say* I-der-down)
a quilt.

eight *noun*
the number 8, one more than seven.
eighth *adjective* and *noun*

eighteen *noun*
the number 18, one more than seventeen.
eighteenth *adjective* and *noun*

eighty *noun* (**eighties**)
the number 80, eight times ten.
eightieth *adjective* and *noun*

either *adjective* and *pronoun*
(*say* I-ther or **ee**-ther)
1 one of two. *Either team can win.* 2 both of two. *Put chairs at either end of the table.*

either *adverb*
also; similarly. *If you won't play, I won't either.*

either *conjunction*
either ... or, if one thing does not happen, the other must happen. *Either come in or go out.*

ejaculate *verb* (**ejaculated, ejaculating**)
(*say* i-**jak**-yoo-layt)
1 to say something suddenly. 2 to shoot liquid, especially semen, out of the body.
ejaculation *noun*

elaborate *adjective*
(*sau* i-**lab**-er-ăt)
complicated; carefully planned.

elaborate *verb* (**elaborated, elaborating**)
(*say* i-**lab**-er-ayt)
to describe or work out something in detail.
elaboration *noun*

elastic *adjective*
that goes back to its normal shape after being stretched or squeezed. *Elastic bands are made of rubber.*
elasticity *noun*

elastic *noun*
elastic material or cord. *Garters are made of elastic.*

elated *adjective*
delighted.
elation *noun*

elbow *noun*
the joint in the middle of your arm.

elder *adjective*
older. *his elder brother.*

elder *noun*
a tree with white flowers and black berries.
elderberry *noun*

elderly *adjective*
rather old.

eldest *adjective*
oldest. *my eldest sister.*

elect *verb*
to choose somebody by voting.

election *noun*
electing; a time when somebody is elected, especially to parliament.

elector *noun*
someone who votes in an election.
electoral *adjective,* **electorate** *noun*

embryo

electric *adjective*
1 of or worked by electricity. **2 electric chair,** a chair in which criminals are electrocuted.
electrical *adjective,* **electrically** *adverb*

electrician *noun*
someone whose job is to deal with electrical equipment.

electricity *noun*
a kind of energy used for lighting, heating, and making machines work.

electrify *verb* **(electrified, electrifying)**
1 to charge something with electricity. 2 to make something work with electricity. 3 to excite or startle somebody.
electrification *noun*

electrocute *verb* **(electrocuted, electrocuting)**
to kill somebody by means of electricity.
electrocution *noun*

electrode *noun*
a conductor through which electricity enters or leaves something.

electromagnet *noun*
a magnet worked by electricity.
electromagnetic *adjective*

electron *noun*
a particle of matter that carries electricity.

electronic *adjective*
of or worked by electrons.
electronically *adverb,* **electronics** *noun*

elegant *adjective*
tasteful; smart.
elegance *noun,* **elegantly** *adverb*

element *noun*
1 a substance that cannot be split up into simpler substances. *Copper, oxygen, and sulphur are elements.* 2 a part of something. 3 a principle. *Learn the elements of algebra.* 4 the wire or coil that gives out heat in an electric heater, cooker, etc. **5 the elements,** the weather, especially bad weather.

elementary *adjective*
dealing with the first or simplest stages of something; easy. *elementary arithmetic.*

elephant *noun*
a very big animal with a trunk, tusks, and large ears.

elevate *verb* **(elevated, elevating)**
to lift up; to put high up.
elevation *noun,* **elevator** *noun*

eleven *noun*
1 the number 11, one more than ten. 2 a team of eleven people in cricket, hockey, etc.
eleventh *adjective* and *noun*

elevenses *plural noun*
a snack or drink in the middle of the morning.

elf *noun* **(elves)**
a small or mischievous fairy.

eligible *adjective*
qualified or suitable for something.
eligibility *noun*

eliminate *verb* **(eliminated, eliminating)**
to get rid of somebody or something.
elimination *noun*

Elizabethan *adjective*
of the time of Queen Elizabeth I (1558-1603).

elk *noun* **(elk** or **elks)**
a large kind of deer.

ellipse *noun*
an oval.

elliptical *adjective*
1 oval-shaped. 2 with some things omitted.

elm *noun*
a tall tree with rough leaves. *Many elms have been killed by Dutch elm disease.*

elocution *noun*
speaking clearly.

elongated *adjective*
lengthened.
elongation *noun*

eloquence *noun*
speaking effectively or fluently.
eloquent *adjective*

else *adverb*
1 besides; instead. *Nobody else knows.* **2 or else,** otherwise; *(informal)* or there will be trouble. *Give me the money or else!*

elsewhere *adverb*
somewhere different.

elude *verb* **(eluded, eluding)**
to avoid being caught by somebody; to escape from somebody.
elusive *adjective*

elves plural of **elf.**

emancipate *verb* **(emancipated, emancipating)**
to set somebody free.
emancipation *noun*

embankment *noun*
a wall or mound of earth to hold back water or to support a road or railway.

embark *verb*
1 to go on board a ship. **2 embark on** or **upon,** to begin something.
embarkation *noun*

embarrass *verb*
to make somebody feel shy or awkward.
embarrassment *noun*

embassy *noun* **(embassies)**
the building where an ambassador lives and works.

embedded *adjective*
fixed firmly into something.

embers *plural noun*
small pieces of burning coal or wood in a dying fire.

emblem *noun*
a symbol. *The dove is an emblem of peace.*

embrace *verb* **(embraced, embracing)**
1 to put your arms round somebody; to hug. 2 to include.

embroider *verb*
to decorate cloth with sewn designs or pictures.
embroidery *noun*

embryo *noun*
a baby or young animal before it is born.
embryonic *adjective*

emerald *noun*
1 a green jewel. 2 a bright-green colour.

emerge *verb* **(emerged, emerging)**
to come out; to appear.
emergence *noun*

emergency *noun* **(emergencies)**
a sudden dangerous or serious event or situation.

emery-paper *noun*
a gritty paper like sandpaper.

emigrate *verb* **(emigrated, emigrating)**
to go and live in another country.
emigrant *noun*, **emigration** *noun*

eminent *adjective*
famous; outstanding.
eminence *noun*

emit *verb* **(emitted, emitting)**
to send something out. *The volcano emitted smoke and lava.*
emission *noun*

emotion *noun*
1 a strong feeling. *Fear and hate are dangerous emotions.* 2 being excited or upset. *Her voice trembled with emotion.*
emotional *adjective*, **emotionally** *adverb*

emperor *noun*
a man who rules an empire.

emphasis *noun* **(emphases)**
special importance given to something.
emphatic *adjective*, **emphatically** *adverb*

emphasize *verb* **(emphasized, emphasizing)**
to give emphasis to something.

empire *noun*
a group of countries ruled by one person.

employ *verb*
1 to pay somebody to work for you. 2 to use something.

employee *noun*
(*say* im-**ploi**-ee)
someone who is employed by somebody else.

employer *noun*
someone who employs people.

employment *noun*
1 employing or being employed. 2 a job.

empress *noun* **(empresses)**
1 a female emperor. 2 the wife of an emperor.

empties *plural noun*
empty bottles, boxes, etc.

empty *adjective* **(emptier, emptiest)**
with nothing inside or on top.
emptiness *noun*

empty *verb* **(emptied, emptying)**
to make or become empty.

emu *noun*
(*say* ee-mew)
a large Australian bird rather like an ostrich.

emulsion *noun*
1 a creamy liquid. 2 a kind of paint.

enable *verb* **(enabled, enabling)**
to make something possible for somebody. *This calculator enables you to multiply and divide.*

enamel *noun*
1 a shiny substance for coating metal, pottery, etc. 2 a hard, shiny paint. 3 the hard, shiny surface of teeth.

encamp *verb*
to settle in a camp.
encampment *noun*

enchant *verb*
1 to delight somebody. 2 to put a magic spell on somebody.
enchantment *noun*, **enchantress** *noun*

encircle *verb* **(encircled, encircling)**
to surround. *a pond encircled by trees.*

enclose *verb* **(enclosed, enclosing)**
1 to put something in a box, envelope, etc. 2 to put a fence, wall, etc. round something.
enclosure *noun*

encore *noun*
an extra item performed at a concert, show, etc. after previous items have been applauded.

encounter *verb*
to meet unexpectedly; to come across.

encourage *verb* **(encouraged, encouraging)**
to give somebody confidence or hope; to support.
encouragement *noun*

encyclopaedia *noun*
a book or set of books containing all sorts of information.
encyclopaedic *adjective*

end *noun*
1 the last part of something; the point where something stops. 2 the part that is left after something has been used. *a cigarette end.* 3 an aim or purpose. 4 **make ends meet,** to spend no more money than you earn. 5 **no end,** (*informal*) very many; a great deal. 6 **on end,** upright; continuously. *His hair stood on end. She spoke for two hours on end.*

end *verb*
to finish.

endanger *verb*
to cause danger to somebody.

endeavour *verb*
to try. *He endeavoured to please her.*

ending *noun*
the last part of something.

endless *adjective*
1 never stopping. *endless patience.* 2 with the ends joined to make a continuous strip. *an endless belt.*
endlessly *adverb*

endure *verb* **(endured, enduring)**
1 to suffer or put up with pain, suffering, etc. 2 to continue; to last.
endurance *noun*

enemy *noun* **(enemies)**
1 someone who hates you or wants to harm you. 2 **the enemy,** the nation or army that is at war with you.

energetic *adjective*
1 full of energy. 2 done with energy.
energetically *adverb*

energy *noun* **(energies)**
1 strength to do things; liveliness. 2 the ability to do work. *electrical energy*.

enforce *verb* **(enforced, enforcing)**
to make people obey a law, order, etc.
enforceable *adjective*, **enforcement** *noun*

engage *verb* **(engaged, engaging)**
1 to occupy or use. 2 to employ somebody. *He engaged a typist*. 3 to start a battle against somebody. 4 to interlock. 5 **engage in**, to take part in.

engaged *adjective*
1 having promised to marry somebody. 2 already being used. *Her telephone number is engaged*.

engagement *noun*
1 being engaged. 2 an appointment to meet somebody or do something. 3 a battle. 4 **engagement ring**, a ring that you give to somebody you have promised to marry.

engine *noun*
1 a motor. 2 a vehicle that pulls a railway train.

engineer *noun*
an expert in engineering.

engineering *noun*
designing, building, or controlling engines, machines, bridges, docks, etc.

English *adjective*
1 of England. 2 of or in the English language.
Englishman *noun*, **Englishwoman** *noun*

English *noun*
the language of England.

engrave *verb* **(engraved, engraving)**
to carve lines, words, etc. on a hard surface.
engraver *noun*

engulf *verb*
to swallow up; to swamp.

enhance *verb* **(enhanced, enhancing)**
to add to a thing's value or attractiveness.
enhancement *noun*

enjoy *verb*
to get pleasure from something.
enjoyable *adjective*, **enjoyment** *noun*

enlarge *verb* **(enlarged, enlarging)**
to make something bigger.
enlargement *noun*

enlist *verb*
to come or bring into the armed forces.
enlistment *noun*

enmity *noun* **(enmities)**
being somebody's enemy; hatred.

enormous *adjective*
huge.
enormously *adverb*

enough *adjective, noun,* and *adverb*
as much or as many as required.

enquire *verb* **(enquired, enquiring)**
to ask. *He enquired if I was well*.
enquiry *noun*

enraged *adjective*
very angry.

enrich *verb*
to make richer.
enrichment *noun*

enrol *verb* **(enrolled, enrolling)**
to make or become a member of a society, class, etc.
enrolment *noun*

ensemble *noun*
(*say* ahn-**sahmbl**)
1 a group of things that go together. 2 a group of musicians.

ensue *verb* **(ensued, ensuing)**
to happen afterwards; to follow.

ensure *verb* **(ensured, ensuring)**
to make sure.

entangle *verb* **(entangled, entangling)**
to tangle.
entanglement *noun*

enter *verb*
1 to come or go in. 2 to write something in a list, book, etc. 3 to enrol; to go in for a contest, examination, etc.

enterprise *noun*
1 being enterprising. 2 a task or project, especially one that needs courage.

enterprising *adjective*
adventurous; courageous.

entertain *verb*
1 to amuse. 2 to have people as guests and give them food and drink.
entertainer *noun*, **entertainment** *noun*

enthusiasm *noun*
a strong liking for, or interest in, somebody or something.

enthusiast *noun*
a person who has an enthusiasm for something.
enthusiastic *adjective*, **enthusiastically** *adverb*

entire *adjective*
whole. *The entire class will stay in*.
entirely *adverb*, **entirety** *noun*

entitle *verb* **(entitled, entitling)**
1 to give you a right to something. *You are entitled to three attempts at the examination*. 2 **entitled**, having the title. *a book entitled 'Animal Farm'*.

entrance *noun*
(*say* **en**-trǎns)
1 the way into a place. 2 the act of entering. *The actor made a grand entrance*.

entrance *verb* **(entranced, entrancing)**
(*say* in-**trahns**)
to enchant.

entrant *noun*
someone who goes in for a contest, examination, etc.

entreat *verb*
to ask seriously or desperately.
entreaty *noun*

entrust *verb*
to trust somebody with something; to give somebody a thing to look after. *She entrusted her necklace to me*.

entry *noun* **(entries)**
1 an entrance. **2** something written in a list, diary, etc.

envelop *verb*
(*say* en-**vel**-ŏp)
to wrap something up; to cover completely.

envelope *noun*
(*say* **en**-vĕ-lohp or **on**-vĕ-lohp)
a wrapper or covering, especially for a letter.

envious *adjective*
feeling envy.
enviously *adverb*

environment *noun*
surroundings, especially as they affect people's lives.
environmental *adjective*

envy *noun* **(envies)**
a discontented feeling you have when you want something that somebody else has got.

envy *verb* **(envied, envying)**
to feel envy about somebody.

enzyme *noun*
a chemical substance that causes changes such as digestion.

epic *noun*
1 a heroic story or poem. **2** a spectacular film.

epidemic *noun*
a disease spreading quickly through a community.

epilepsy *noun*
a nervous disorder that causes fits.
epileptic *adjective* and *noun*

epilogue *noun*
(*say* **ep**-i-log)
words written or spoken at the end of something.

episode *noun*
1 an incident in a series of events. **2** one programme in a radio or television serial.

epitaph *noun*
the words written on a tomb.

epoch *noun*
(*say* **ee**-pok)
1 an era. **2** **epoch-making,** very important.

equal *adjective*
1 the same in amount, size, value, etc. **2** be **equal to,** to be able to do. *He was equal to the task.*
equality *noun,* **equally** *adverb*

equal *noun*
a person or thing that is equal to another. *Nobody was Samson's equal.*

equal *verb* **(equalled, equalling)**
to be the same in amount, size, value, etc.

equalize *verb* **(equalized, equalizing)**
to make things equal.

equalizer *noun*
a goal, etc. that makes the score equal.

equation *noun*
(*say* i-**kway**-zhŏn)
(*in Mathematics*) a statement that two amounts are equal. *In the equation $3x+4=10$, x equals 2.*

equator *noun*
(*say* i-**kway**-ter)
an imaginary line round the earth at an equal distance from the North and South Poles.
equatorial *adjective*

equilateral *adjective*
(*say* ee-kwi-**lat**-er-ăl)
having all sides equal. *an equilateral triangle.*

equilibrium *noun*
(*say* ee-kwi-**lib**-ri-ŭm)
balance; being balanced.

equip *verb* **(equipped, equipping)**
to supply somebody or something with what is needed. *Are you equipped for mountaineering?*

equipment *noun*
the things needed for a particular purpose.

equivalent *adjective*
equal in value, importance, meaning, etc.
equivalence *noun*

er *interjection*
a sound made by somebody who hesitates while speaking.

era *noun*
(*say* **eer**-ă)
a period in history.

erase *verb* **(erased, erasing)**
1 to rub out. **2** to wipe out a recording on magnetic tape.
eraser *noun*

erect *adjective*
vertical; standing on end.

erect *verb*
1 to build. **2** to make something erect.
erection *noun*

ermine *noun*
1 a kind of weasel with brown fur in summer and white fur in winter. **2** this white fur.

erode *verb* **(eroded, eroding)**
to wear away. *Water eroded the rocks.*
erosion *noun*

errand *noun*
a short journey to take a message, fetch goods, etc.

erratic *adjective*
(*say* i-**rat**-ik)
not reliable or regular.
erratically *adverb*

error *noun*
1 a mistake. **2 in error,** by mistake; mistaken.
erroneous *adjective*

erupt *verb*
1 to burst out. **2** (*of a volcano*) to shoot out lava, etc.
eruption *noun*

escalate *verb* **(escalated, escalating)**
to get or make gradually greater or more serious. *The riots escalated into a war.*
escalation *noun*

escalator *noun*
a staircase with an endless line of steps moving up or down.

escape *verb* **(escaped, escaping)**
1 to get free; to get away. **2** to avoid something. *He escaped punishment.*

even

escape *noun*
1 escaping. 2 a way to escape from something.

escort *noun*
(*say* **ess**-kort)
1 someone who accompanies somebody, especially to protect him. 2 a group of ships, aircraft, etc. accompanying somebody or something.

escort *verb*
(*say* i-**skort**)
to act as an escort to somebody or something.

Eskimo *noun* **(Eskimos** or **Eskimo)**
one of the people who live in very cold parts of North America, Greenland, and Russia.

especially *adverb*
chiefly; more than anything else. *I like buns, especially cream buns.*

espionage *noun*
(*say* **ess**-pi-ŏn-ah*z*h)
spying. *He was accused of espionage.*

esplanade *noun*
a flat area for walking, especially by the sea.

Esq. short for **Esquire.**

Esquire *noun*
a title put after a man's name in addressing letters, etc.

essay *noun*
a short piece of writing about a particular subject.

essence *noun*
1 the most important quality or ingredient of something. 2 a concentrated liquid.

essential *adjective*
that you must have or do.
essentially *adverb*

essential *noun*
an essential thing.

establish *verb*
to start a business, government, relationship, etc.

establishment *noun*
1 establishing something. 2 a place where business is carried on; an organization. 3 **the Establishment,** people in positions of power and influence.

estate *noun*
1 an area of land with lots of houses or factories on it. 2 a large area of land belonging to one person. 3 everything that a person owns when he dies.

estate agent *noun*
someone whose business is selling or letting buildings and land.

estate car *noun*
a car with a door or doors at the back, and rear seats that can be removed or folded away.

esteem *verb*
to think that a person or thing is excellent.

estimate *noun*
(*say* **ess**-tim-ăt)
a calculation or guess about the amount or value of something.

estimate *verb* **(estimated, estimating)**
(*say* **ess**-tim-ayt)
to make an estimate.
estimation *noun*

estuary *noun* **(estuaries)**
(*say* **ess**-tew-er-i)
the mouth of a large river where it flows into the sea.

etc. short for **et cetera.**

et cetera and other similar things; and so on.

etch *verb*
to make a picture by engraving on a metal plate with an acid.
etching *noun*

eternal *adjective*
lasting for ever; not ending or changing.
eternally *adverb*, **eternity** *noun*

ether *noun*
(*say* **ee**-ther)
a colourless liquid made from alcohol, used as an anaesthetic, etc.

eucalyptus *noun* **(eucalyptuses)**
(*say* yoo-kă-**lip**-tŭs)
an evergreen tree from which an oil is obtained.

European *adjective*
of Europe.

euthanasia *noun*
(*say* yooth-ăn-**ay**-zi-ă)
causing somebody to die gently and painlessly when he is suffering from an incurable disease.

evacuate *verb* **(evacuated, evacuating)**
to move people away from a dangerous place.
evacuation *noun*, **evacuee** *noun*

evade *verb* **(evaded, evading)**
to avoid.
evasion *noun*, **evasive** *adjective*

evaluate *verb* **(evaluated, evaluating)**
to estimate the value of something.
evaluation *noun*

evangelist *noun*
someone who preaches the Christian gospel.
evangelical *adjective*, **evangelism** *noun*

evaporate *verb* **(evaporated, evaporating)**
1 to change from liquid into steam or vapour. 2 to remove moisture by heating a liquid. 3 **evaporated milk,** milk that has been thickened by evaporation.
evaporation *noun*

eve *noun*
the day or evening before an important day. *Christmas Eve.*

even *adjective*
1 equal. *Our scores were even.* 2 smooth; level. *He has an even temper.* 3 that can be divided exactly by two. *Six and fourteen are even numbers.* 4 **get even,** to take revenge on somebody. *I'll get even with him.*
evenly *adverb*, **evenness** *noun*

even *verb*
to make or become even.

even *adverb*
1 at least. *Was he even listening?* 2 remarkably enough. *She even ignored her mother.* 3 **even if,** although. 4 **even now,** at this moment. 5 **even so,** nevertheless.

evening *noun*
1 the time at the end of the day before most people go to bed. **2 evening dress,** formal clothes worn to evening parties, etc.

event *noun*
1 something that happens, especially something important. **2** an item in an athletics contest. **3 at all events** or **in any event,** anyway.

eventual *adjective*
happening at last or as a result. *Many failures preceded his eventual success.*

eventually *adverb*
finally; sooner or later.

ever *adverb*
1 at any time. *It's the best present I've ever had.* **2** always. *ever hopeful.* **3** (*informal*) at all. *Why ever didn't you tell me?* **4 ever so** or **ever such,** (*informal*) very much. *I'm ever so pleased. She's ever such a nice girl.*

evergreen *adjective*
having green leaves all through the year. *evergreen trees.*

evergreen *noun*
an evergreen tree.

everlasting *adjective*
eternal.

every *adjective*
1 all the people or things of a particular kind; each. *Every child should learn to swim.* **2 every other day, week,** etc., each alternate one; every second one.

everybody *pronoun*
everyone.

everyday *adjective*
happening or used every day; commonplace. *an everyday occurrence.*

everyone *pronoun*
every person; all people. *Everyone likes her.*

everything *pronoun*
1 all things; all. *Everything you need is here.* **2** the only or most important thing. *Beauty is not everything.*

everywhere *adverb*
in all places.

evict *verb*
to make somebody move out of a house.
eviction *noun*

evidence *noun*
1 anything that gives people reason to believe something. **2 in evidence,** clearly seen.

evident *adjective*
obvious. *It is evident that he is mad.*
evidently *adverb*

evil *adjective*
wicked; harmful.
evilly *adverb*

evil *noun*
something evil; a sin.

evolution *noun*
(*say* ee-vŏ-**loo**-shŏn)
1 gradual change into something different. **2** the development of animals and plants from earlier or simpler forms of life.
evolutionary *adjective*

evolve *verb* (**evolved, evolving**)
to develop gradually or naturally.

ewe *noun*
(*say* yoo)
a female sheep.

exact *adjective*
correct; giving all the details.
exactly *adverb,* **exactness** *noun*

exaggerate *verb* (**exaggerated, exaggerating**)
to make something seem bigger, better, worse, etc. than it really is.
exaggeration *noun*

exalt *verb*
1 to make higher or greater. **2** to praise highly.

exam *noun*
(*informal*) an examination.

examination *noun*
1 a test of somebody's knowledge or skill. **2** a close inspection of something.

examine *verb* (**examined, examining**)
to make an examination of somebody or something.
examiner *noun*

example *noun*
1 anything that shows what something is like or how it works. **2** a person or thing that you should copy or learn from. **3 for example,** as an example.

exasperate *verb* (**exasperated, exasperating**)
to make somebody very annoyed.
exasperation *noun*

excavate *verb* (**excavated, excavating**)
to make or uncover by digging.
excavation *noun,* **excavator** *noun*

exceed *verb*
1 to be greater than something else. **2** to do more than you need or ought to do.

exceedingly *adverb*
extremely; very much.

excel *verb* (**excelled, excelling**)
to be very good at something.

excellent *adjective*
very good; of the best kind.
excellence *noun*

except *preposition*
not including; apart from. *Everyone got a prize except me.*

exception *noun*
1 something that does not follow the normal rule. **2** something not included. **3** an objection to something.

exceptional *adjective*
unusual. *She has exceptional skill.*
exceptionally *adverb*

excerpt *noun*
a piece taken from a book, play, film, etc.

excess *noun* (**excesses**)
too much of something. *We have an excess of food.*

excessive *adjective*
too much or too great.
excessively *adverb*

exchange *verb* **(exchanged, exchanging)**
to give something and receive something else for it.

exchange *noun*
1 exchanging. **2** a place where shares, etc. are bought and sold. **3** a place where telephone lines are connected to each other when a call is made.

excite *verb* **(excited, exciting)**
to make somebody feel strongly; to make somebody lively, active, etc.
excitable *adjective,* **excitedly** *adverb*

excitement *noun*
1 being excited. **2** something that excites you.

exclaim *verb*
to shout or cry out.

exclamation *noun*
1 exclaiming. **2** a word or phrase that expresses surprise, pain, delight, etc. **3** **exclamation mark,** the punctuation mark ! placed after an exclamation.

exclude *verb* **(excluded, excluding)**
to shut out; to keep somebody or something out.
exclusion *noun*

exclusive *adjective*
1 that excludes. **2** not allowing many people to be involved. *an exclusive club.*
exclusively *adverb*

excrete *verb* **(excreted, excreting)**
to pass waste matter out of your body.
excrement *noun,* **excretion** *noun,* **excretory** *adjective*

excursion *noun*
a short journey made for pleasure.

excuse *noun*
(*say* iks-**kewss**)
a reason given to explain why something wrong has been done.

excuse *verb* **(excused, excusing)**
(*say* iks-**kewz**)
1 to forgive. **2** to allow somebody not to do something or leave a room, etc. *Please may I be excused from swimming?* **3** **excuse me,** a polite apology for interrupting, disagreeing, etc.
excusable *adjective,* **excusably** *adverb*

execute *verb* **(executed, executing)**
1 to kill somebody as a punishment. **2** to perform or produce something.
execution *noun,* **executioner** *noun*

executive *noun*
a senior person in a business or government organization.

exempt *adjective*
not having to do something. *Old people are sometimes exempt from paying bus fares.*
exemption *noun*

exercise *noun*
1 using your body to make it strong and healthy. **2** a piece of work done for practice. **3** **exercise book,** a book for writing in.

exercise *verb* **(exercised, exercising)**
1 to do exercises. **2** to give exercise to an animal, etc. **3** to use. *You will have to exercise patience*

exert *verb*
1 to use power, influence, etc. *He exerted all his strength to bend the bar.* **2** **exert yourself,** to make an effort.
exertion *noun*

exhale *verb* **(exhaled, exhaling)**
to breathe out.
exhalation *noun*

exhaust *noun*
1 the waste gases from an engine. **2** the pipe these gases are expelled through.

exhaust *verb*
1 to make somebody very tired. **2** to use up something completely.
exhaustion *noun*

exhibit *verb*
to display something in public.
exhibitor *noun*

exhibit *noun*
something exhibited.

exhibition *noun*
a collection of things arranged for people to look at.

exile *verb* **(exiled, exiling)**
to banish.

exile *noun*
1 a banished person. **2** having to live away from your own country. *He was in exile for ten years.*

exist *verb*
1 to be; to be real. *Do ghosts exist?* **2** to stay alive. *They existed on biscuits and water.*
existence *noun*

exit *noun*
1 the way out of a building. **2** going off the stage. *The actress made her exit.*

exit *verb*
1 to leave the stage. *Joseph exits.* **2** **exit** (*plural* **exeunt**), he or she leaves the stage. *Exit Hamlet.*

exorcize *verb* **(exorcized, exorcizing)**
to get rid of an evil spirit.
exorcism *noun,* **exorcist** *noun*

exotic *adjective*
unusual; foreign.

expand *verb*
to make or become larger.
expansion *noun*

expanse *noun*
a wide area.

expect *verb*
1 to think that something will probably happen or that someone will come. *We expected it would rain.* **2** to think that something ought to happen. *She expects us to be obedient.* **3** to be pregnant. *She is expecting.*

expectant *adjective*
1 pregnant. *an expectant mother.* **2** full of expectation or hope.
expectantly *adverb*

expectation *noun*
1 hopefully expecting something. **2** something you hope to get.

expedition *noun*
a journey made in order to do something. *a climbing expedition.*

expel *verb* **(expelled, expelling)**
1 to send or force something out. *This fan expels stale air.* **2** to make somebody leave a school, country, etc. *He was expelled for bullying.*

expenditure *noun*
spending. *We must reduce our expenditure.*

expense *noun*
1 cost; the spending of money, time, etc. **2 expenses,** money used or claimed for something particular. *travelling expenses.*

expensive *adjective*
costing a lot of money.

experience *noun*
1 what you learn from doing and seeing things. **2** something that has happened to you.

experience *verb* **(experienced, experiencing)**
to have something happen to you.

experienced *adjective*
having much experience; skilled and knowledgeable.

experiment *noun*
a test made in order to study what happens.
experimental *adjective,* **experimentally** *adverb*

experiment *verb*
to carry out experiments.
experimentation *noun,* **experimenter** *noun*

expert *adjective*
skilful; knowledgeable.

expert *noun*
an expert person.

expire *verb* **(expired, expiring)**
1 to come to an end; to stop being usable. *Your dog licence has expired.* **2** to die.
expiration *noun,* **expiry** *noun*

explain *verb*
1 to make something clear to somebody else. **2** to account for something.
explanation *noun,* **explanatory** *adjective*

explode *verb* **(exploded, exploding)**
1 to burst or suddenly release energy with a loud bang. **2** to set off a bomb. **3** to increase suddenly or quickly.

exploit *noun*
(*say* **eks**-ploit)
a brave or exciting deed.

exploit *verb*
(*say* iks-**ploit**)
1 to use or develop resources. **2** to use selfishly.
exploitation *noun*

explore *verb* **(explored, exploring)**
1 to travel through a country, etc. in order to learn about it. **2** to examine something.
exploration *noun,* **exploratory** *adjective,* **explorer** *noun*

explosion *noun*
1 the exploding of a bomb, etc. **2** a sudden or quick increase. *the population explosion.*

explosive *adjective*
likely to explode, able to cause an explosion.
explosively *adverb*

explosive *noun*
an explosive substance.

export *verb*
(*say* iks-**port**)
to send goods abroad to be sold.
exporter *noun*

export *noun*
(*say* **eks**-port)
something exported.

expose *verb* **(exposed, exposing)**
1 to reveal or uncover. **2** to let light reach a photographic film, so as to take a picture.
exposure *noun*

express *adjective*
going or sent very quickly. *an express letter*

express *noun* **(expresses)**
a fast train, stopping at few stations.

express *verb*
to put an idea or feeling into words.

expression *noun*
1 the look on a person's face. **2** a word or phrase. **3** a way of speaking, playing music, etc. that conveys feelings.
expressionless *adjective,* **expressive** *adjective*

expulsion *noun*
expelling or being expelled.

exquisite *adjective*
very delicate or beautiful.
exquisitely *adverb*

extend *verb*
1 to stretch out. **2** to make something longer or larger. **3** to offer or give. *Extend a welcome to your friends.*

extension *noun*
1 extending. **2** extent or range. **3** something added on. **4** an extra telephone in an office, house, etc.

extensive *adjective*
wide or large. *extensive gardens.*
extensively *adverb*

extent *noun*
1 the area or length of something. **2** amount or level. *To what extent are you friendly with her?*

exterior *noun*
the outside of something.

exterminate *verb* **(exterminated, exterminating)**
to destroy or kill.
extermination *noun*

external *adjective*
outside.
externally *adverb*

extinct *adjective*
1 not existing any more. *The dodo is an extinct bird.* **2** not active. *an extinct volcano.*
extinction *noun*

extinguish *verb*
to put out a fire or light.
extinguisher *noun*

extra *adjective*
more than usual; added.

extra *noun*
1 an extra person or thing. **2** somebody acting as part of the crowd in a film or play. **3** a run in cricket scored without the bat hitting the ball.

extract *noun*
(say **eks**-trakt)
1 an excerpt. **2** something obtained from something else.

extract *verb*
(say iks-**trakt**)
to remove; to take something out of something else.
extraction *noun*, **extractor** *noun*

extraordinary *adjective*
unusual; very strange.
extraordinarily *adverb*

extravagant *adjective*
spending too much; stupidly wasteful.
extravagance *noun*, **extravagantly** *adverb*

extreme *adjective*
1 very great or strong. *extreme cold.* **2** farthest away. *the extreme north.*
extremity *noun*

extreme *noun*
1 something extreme. **2** either end of something. **3 in the extreme,** extremely. **4 to extremes,** to extreme or unreasonable behaviour. *He was driven to extremes.*

extremely *adverb*
as much or as far as possible; very much.

exuberant *adjective*
very cheerful or lively.
exuberance *noun*

exult *verb*
to rejoice or triumph.
exultant *adjective,* **exultation** *noun*

eye *noun*
1 the part of the head used for seeing. **2** the small hole in a needle.

eye *verb* **(eyed, eyeing)**
to look at; to watch.

eyeball *noun*
the ball-shaped part of the eye.

eyebrow *noun*
a curved fringe of hair growing above the eye.

eyelash *noun* **(eyelashes)**
one of the short hairs that grow on an eyelid.

eyelid *noun*
the upper or lower cover of the eyeball.

eyepiece *noun*
the lens of a telescope, microscope, etc. that you put to your eye.

eyesight *noun*
the ability to see.

eyesore *noun*
something ugly to look at.

eyewitness *noun* **(eyewitnesses)**
someone who actually saw an accident, crime, etc.

F

F short for **Fahrenheit.**

fable *noun*
a story with a moral. *Many fables are about animals.*

fabric *noun*
cloth.

fabulous *adjective*
1 mythical. **2** incredibly great. **3** (*informal*) wonderful; marvellous.

face *noun*
1 the front part of the head. **2** the look on a person's face. **3** the front of something. *Put the cards face down.* **4** a surface. *A dice has six faces.* **5 face to face,** looking directly at somebody. **6 in the face of,** in spite of.
facial *adjective*

face *verb* **(faced, facing)**
1 to look in a certain direction; to have the front in a particular direction. *The church faces the school.* **2** to meet or deal with confidently or bravely. *I can't face any more quarrels.*

facet *noun*
(say **fas**-it)
one aspect of something.

facetious *adjective*
(say fă-**see**-shŭs)
trying to be funny.
facetiously *adverb*

facility *noun* **(facilities)**
(say fă-**sil**-ĭ-ti)
1 something that helps you to do things. *The youth club has facilities for dancing and sport.* **2** easiness.

fact *noun*
1 something that people know is true. **2 as a matter of fact** or **in fact,** really.

factor *noun*
1 something that helps to bring about a result or situation. *Her beauty is one factor in her popularity.* **2** a number by which a larger number can be divided exactly. *2 and 3 are factors of 6.*

factory *noun* **(factories)**
1 a large building where machines are used to make things. **2 factory farm,** a farm operated like a factory.

factual *adjective*
based on fact; real.
factually *adverb*

fad *noun*
    someone's particular like or dislike; a craze.

fade *verb* **(faded, fading)**
    1 to lose colour, freshness, or strength. **2** to disappear gradually. **3** to make a sound, etc. become gradually weaker or stronger.

faeces *plural noun*
    (*say* **fee**-seez)
    waste matter expelled from the body.

Fahrenheit *adjective*
    (*say* **fa**-rĕn-hyt)
    using a scale for measuring temperature that gives 32 degrees for freezing water and 212 degrees for boiling water.

fail *verb*
    1 to try to do something but not be able to do it. **2** to become weak or useless; to come to an end. *The crops failed.* **3** not to do something. *He failed to warn me.*

fail *noun*
    1 not being successful in an examination, etc. **2 without fail,** definitely. *I'll be there without fail.*

failing *noun*
    a fault or weakness.

failure *noun*
    1 not being successful. **2** someone or something that has failed.

faint *adjective*
    1 weak; not clear or distinct. **2** nearly unconscious; exhausted.
    faintly *adverb,* **faintness** *noun*

faint *verb*
    to become unconscious for a short time.

fair *adjective*
    1 right or just; honest. *It's not fair!* **2** light in colour. *fair hair.* **3** moderate; quite good. *a fair number.* **4** fine; favourable. *fair weather.* **5 fair copy,** a neat, correct copy.
    fairness *noun*

fair *noun*
    1 a group of outdoor entertainments like roundabouts, sideshows, and stalls. **2** an exhibition or market.

fairground *noun*
    the place where a fair is held.

fairly *adverb*
    1 honestly; justly. **2** moderately; somewhat. *It is fairly hard.*

fairy *noun* **(fairies)**
    1 a tiny imaginary creature who can do magic. **2 fairy godmother,** somebody who helps you by magic. **3 fairy story** or **fairy tale,** a story about fairies; an unbelievable story.
    fairyland *noun*

faith *noun*
    1 strong belief or trust. **2** a religion. **3 in good faith,** honestly; trustingly.
    faithless *adjective*

faithful *adjective*
    reliable; trustworthy.
    faithfully *adverb,* **faithfulness** *noun*

fake *noun*
    a copy of something made to deceive people.

fake *verb* **(faked, faking)**
    1 to make something that looks real so as to deceive people. **2** to pretend.
    faker *noun*

falcon *noun*
    a small kind of hawk.
    falconry *noun*

fall *verb* (*past tense* **fell;** *past participle* **fallen;** *present participle* **falling**)
    1 to come down; to drop down, especially suddenly. **2** to decrease. *Prices have fallen.* **3** to be captured or overthrown. *The city fell after a long siege.* **4** to die in battle. **5** to happen. *Silence fell.* **6** to become. *She has fallen ill.* **7** to come or be directed at. *His glance fell on me.* **8 fall back,** to retreat. **9 fall back on,** to use for support or in an emergency. **10 fall down,** to fail. **11 fall for,** to be attracted or convinced by. **12 fall in,** to collapse; to take your place in a military line. **13 fall out,** to quarrel; to leave your place in a military line. **14 fall through,** to fail.

fall *noun*
    1 the action of falling. **2** (*in America*) autumn. **3 falls,** a waterfall.

fallacy *noun* **(fallacies)**
    a false idea or belief.
    fallacious *adjective*

fall-out *noun*
    radioactive airborne debris from a nuclear explosion.

fallow *adjective*
    ploughed but not sown with crops. *The field was left fallow every three years.*

false *adjective* **(falser, falsest)**
    1 untrue; incorrect. **2** bogus; faked. **3** treacherous; deceitful.
    falsely *adverb,* **falseness** *noun,* **falsity** *noun*

falsehood *noun*
    a lie.

falter *verb*
    to hesitate when you move or speak.

fame *noun*
    being famous.
    famed *adjective*

familiar *adjective*
    1 well-known; often seen or experienced. *a familiar sight.* **2** knowing something well. *Are you familiar with Shakespeare's plays?* **3** very friendly.
    familiarity *noun,* **familiarly** *adverb*

family *noun* **(families)**
    1 parents and their children, sometimes including grandchildren and other relations. **2** a group of things that are alike in some way. **3 family planning,** deciding how many babies to have and when to have them; birth control. **4 family tree,** a diagram showing how people in a family are related.

famine *noun*
    a very bad shortage of food.

famished *adjective*
    very hungry.

famous *adjective*
    known to a lot of people; very well known. *a famous scientist.*

fan *noun*[1]
    a device for making the air move about, so as to cool people or things.

fan *noun*[2]
    an enthusiast. *a football fan.*

fate

fan *verb* **(fanned, fanning)**
1 to send a draught of air at something. *She fanned her face with her hand.* 2 **fan out,** to spread out.

fanatic *noun*
(*say* fă-**nat**-ik)
someone who is too enthusiastic about something.
fanatical *adjective*, **fanatically** *adverb*

fan belt *noun*
a belt driving the fan that cools a vehicle's radiator.

fanciful *adjective*
imaginary; unusual.

fancy *adjective* **(fancier, fanciest)**
1 decorated; not plain. *fancy cakes.* 2 **fancy dress,** unusual costume worn to parties, dances, etc.

fancy *verb* **(fancied, fancying)**
1 to want or desire something. *I fancied an ice-cream.* 2 to imagine or think of something. *Just fancy him riding a horse!* 3 **fancy yourself,** to be conceited.

fancy *noun* **(fancies)**
1 imagination. 2 a liking or desire for something.

fanfare *noun*
a short piece of loud music on trumpets.

fang *noun*
a long, sharp tooth.

fantastic *adjective*
1 strange; ridiculous. 2 (*informal*) marvellous; excellent.
fantastically *adverb*

fantasy *noun* **(fantasies)**
something imaginary or fantastic.

far *adverb* **(farther, farthest)**
1 a long way. *We didn't go far.* 2 much. *She's a far better singer than I am.* 3 **far and wide,** over a large area. 4 **so far,** up to now.

far *adjective* **(farther, farthest)**
1 distant; opposite. *on the far side of the river.* 2 **a far cry,** a long way; very different. 3 **Far East,** the countries of east Asia, such as China and Japan.

faraway *adjective*
distant; placed or looking a long way away.

farce *noun*
1 a ridiculous comedy. 2 ridiculous events.
farcical *adjective*

fare *noun*
the money you pay to travel on a bus, train, ship, aircraft, etc.

fare *verb* **(fared, faring)**
to get on; to progress. *How did you fare in your exam?*

farewell *interjection*
goodbye.

far-fetched *adjective*
unlikely; difficult to believe.

farm *noun*
1 an area of land where someone grows crops and keeps animals for food. 2 the buildings on a farm. 3 a farmhouse.

farm *verb*
1 to grow crops and raise animals for food. 2 to use land for growing crops.

farmer *noun*
someone who owns or looks after a farm.

farmhouse *noun*
the house where a farmer lives.

farmyard *noun*
the enclosed area around farm buildings.

farther *adverb* and *adjective*
more distant; at or to a greater distance. *She lives farther from the school than I do.*

farthest *adverb* and *adjective*
most distant; at or to the greatest distance.

farthing *noun*
a small coin that used to be worth a quarter of a penny.

fascinate *verb* **(fascinated, fascinating)**
to be very attractive or interesting to somebody.
fascination *noun*

Fascism *noun*
(*say* **fash**-iz-ŭm)
a dictatorial type of government; a belief in this type of government.
Fascist *noun* and *adjective*

fashion *noun*
1 the style of clothes or other things that most people like at a particular time. 2 a way of doing something.

fashion *verb*
to make something in a particular shape or style.

fashionable *adjective*
following the fashion; popular amongst smart people.
fashionably *adverb*

fast *adjective*
1 rapid; quick. *He's a fast runner.* 2 firmly fixed. *Make the boat fast.* 3 showing a time later than the correct time. *Your watch is fast.* 4 that does not fade. *fast colours.*

fast *adverb*
1 quickly. 2 firmly. 3 **fast asleep,** deeply asleep.

fast *verb*
to go without food.

fasten *verb*
to join one thing firmly to another.
fastener *noun*, **fastening** *noun*

fat *noun*
1 the white, greasy part of meat. 2 an oily or greasy substance used in cooking. *Butter, margarine, and lard are fats.* 3 **the fat of the land,** the best food.

fat *adjective* **(fatter, fattest)**
1 with a very thick, round body. *a fat man.* 2 thick. *a fat book.* 3 full of fat.

fatal *adjective*
that causes death or disaster. *a fatal accident.*
fatality *noun*, **fatally** *adverb*

fate *noun*
1 the power that makes things happen. 2 what will happen or has happened to somebody.

fated *adjective*
definitely going to happen.

father *noun*
a male parent.

fathom *noun*
a unit of 6 feet, used in measuring the depth of water.

fathom *verb*
to understand. *I can't fathom how you did it.*

fatigue *noun*
(*say* fă-**teeg**)
1 tiredness. **2** weakness in metals, etc. caused by repeated stress.
fatigued *adjective*

fatten *verb*
to make or become fat.

fatty *adjective* (**fattier, fattiest**)
like fat; full of fat.

fault *noun*
1 something wrong that spoils a person or thing; a flaw or mistake. **2 at fault,** wrong; responsible for a mistake.
faultless *adjective*

fault *verb*
to find faults in something.

faulty *adjective* (**faultier, faultiest**)
having a fault or faults; wrong.

fauna *noun*
(*say* **faw**-nă)
the animals of an area or period.

favour *noun*
1 something kind that you do for somebody. *Will you do me a favour?* **2** approval; goodwill. **3 in favour of,** liking or supporting somebody or something. **4 in your favour,** to your advantage.

favour *verb*
to be in favour of somebody or something.

favourable *adjective*
helpful; approving.
favourably *adverb*

favourite *adjective*
that is liked most. *my favourite book.*

favourite *noun*
a person or thing that somebody likes most.

favouritism *noun*
unfairly being kinder to one person than to others.

fawn *noun*
1 a young deer. **2** a light brown colour.

fear *noun*
1 a feeling that something unpleasant may happen to you. **2 for fear of,** because of the risk of. **3 no fear,** (*informal*) certainly not.
fearless *adjective*

fear *verb*
1 to be afraid of somebody or something. **2** to be anxious or sad about something.

fearful *adjective*
1 frightened. **2** awful.
fearfully *adverb*

feast *noun*
a large, splendid meal.

feast *verb*
1 to have a feast. **2** to give great pleasure to. *Feast your eyes on these pictures.*

feat *noun*
a brave or clever deed.

feather *noun*
one of the very light coverings that grow from a bird's skin.
feathery *adjective*

feature *noun*
1 any part of the face. **2** an important or noticeable part of something; a characteristic. **3** a long or important film, broadcast programme, or newspaper article.

feature *verb* (**featured, featuring**)
to make or be an important or noticeable part of something.

February *noun*
the second month of the year.

fed past tense and past participle of **feed** *verb*.

federal *adjective*
of a system in which several states are ruled by a central government but are responsible for some of their own internal affairs.
federation *noun*

fed up *adjective*
discontented; very annoyed.

fee *noun*
a payment, charge, or subscription.

feeble *adjective* (**feebler, feeblest**)
weak.
feebly *adverb*

feed *verb* (**fed, feeding**)
1 to give food to a person or animal. **2** to eat. **3** to supply something to a machine, etc.
feeder *noun*

feed *noun*
1 a meal. **2** food for animals.

feedback *noun*
1 something being returned to where it came from. **2** a response.

feel *verb* (**felt, feeling**)
1 to touch something to find out what it is like. **2** to experience something; to have a feeling. **3 feel like,** to want.

feeler *noun*
1 a long, thin projection on an insect's body, used for feeling. **2** a cautious question, suggestion, etc. to test people's reaction.

feeling *noun*
1 a mental or physical experience; what you feel. **2** the power to feel things. **3** sympathy or understanding. *He shows no feeling for my suffering.* **4** someone's opinion.

feet plural of **foot.**

fell *verb*
1 to cut down a tree. **2** to knock somebody down.

fell *noun*
a piece of wild, hilly country in the north of England.

fell past tense of **fall** *verb*.

fiasco

fellow *noun*
1 a friend or companion; someone who belongs to the same group. 2 (*informal*) a man or boy. *He's a good fellow.*

fellow *adjective*
of the same group, class, kind, etc. *Her fellow teachers supported her.*

fellowship *noun*
1 friendship. 2 a group of friends; a society.

felt *noun*
1 thick woollen material. 2 **felt-tip** or **felt-tipped pen,** a pen with a tip made of felt or fibre.

felt past tense and past participle of **feel.**

female *adjective*
of the sex that gives birth to offspring. *Women, girls, cows, and hens are all female.*

female *noun*
a female person or animal.

feminine *adjective*
of or like women; suitable for women.
femininity *noun*

fen *noun*
a low-lying area of marshy or flooded land.

fence *noun*
1 a barrier round a garden, field, etc. or beside a road, railway, etc. *Fences are usually made of wood or posts and wire.* 2 someone who buys stolen goods and sells them again. 3 **sit on the fence,** to avoid committing yourself to either side in a contest, argument, etc.

fence *verb* (**fenced, fencing**)
1 to put a fence round or along something. 2 to fight with thin swords as a sport.
fencer *noun*

fend *verb*
1 **fend for yourself,** to take care of yourself. 2 **fend off,** to stop something from hitting you.

fender *noun*
1 a low guard placed round a grate to stop coal from rolling into the room. 2 something hung over the side of a boat to protect it from knocks.

ferment *verb*
(*say* fer-**ment**)
to bubble and change chemically by the action of a substance like yeast.
fermentation *noun*

ferment *noun*
(*say* **fer**-ment)
1 fermenting. 2 an excited or agitated condition. *The crowd was in a ferment.*

fern *noun*
a plant with feathery leaves and no flowers.

ferocious *adjective*
fierce; savage; cruel.
ferociously *adverb,* **ferocity** *noun*

ferret *noun*
a small animal used for catching rabbits and rats.

ferret *verb*
1 to hunt with ferrets. 2 to search or rummage.

ferry *verb* (**ferried, ferrying**)
to carry people or things across a river, channel, etc.

ferry *noun* (**ferries**)
a ship or aircraft used for ferrying.

fertile *adjective*
1 producing good crops. 2 able to produce offspring.
fertility *noun*

fertilize *verb* (**fertilized, fertilizing**)
to make fertile.
fertilization *noun*

fertilizer *noun*
a substance added to the soil to make it more fertile.

fervent *adjective*
very enthusiastic; passionate.
fervently *adverb,* **fervour** *noun*

festival *noun*
a time when people arrange special celebrations, performances, etc.

festive *adjective*
of or suitable for a festival; joyful.
festivity *noun*

festoon *verb*
to decorate a place with curved chains of flowers, ribbons, etc.

fetch *verb*
1 to go and get somebody or something. 2 to be sold for a particular price. *The bookcase fetched £20.*

fête *noun*
(*say* fayt)
an outdoor entertainment with stalls and sideshows.

fetters *plural noun*
chains round a prisoner's ankles.

feud *noun*
a long-lasting quarrel or enmity.

feudal *adjective*
of the medieval system in which people could farm land in exchange for work done for the owner.
feudalism *noun*

fever *noun*
1 an unusually high body-temperature, usually with an illness. 2 excitement; agitation.
fevered *adjective,* **feverish** *adjective,* **feverishly** *adverb*

few *adjective*
not many.

few *noun*
1 a small number of people or things. 2 **a good few** or **quite a few,** a fairly large number.

fez *noun* (**fezzes**)
a round, flat-topped hat with a tassel, worn especially by Muslim men.

fiancé *noun*
(*say* fee-**ahn**-say)
a man engaged to be married.

fiancée *noun*
(*say* fee-**ahn**-say)
a woman engaged to be married.

fiasco *noun*
(*say* fi-**ass**-koh)
a complete failure.

fib *noun*
a lie, usually about something unimportant.
fibber *noun*

fibre *noun*
(*say* **fy**-ber)
1 a very thin thread. **2** a substance made up of thin threads.
fibrous *adjective*

fibreglass *noun*
material containing glass fibres, used in building, etc.

fickle *adjective*
often changing; not loyal.

fiction *noun*
1 writings about events that have not really happened; stories and novels. **2** something imagined or untrue.
fictional *adjective*, **fictitious** *adjective*

fiddle *noun*
1 a violin. **2** (*informal*) a swindle.

fiddle *verb* (**fiddled, fiddling**)
1 to play the violin. **2** to play about with something with your fingers. **3** (*informal*) to swindle; to get or change something dishonestly.
fiddler *noun*

fiddling *adjective*
(*informal*) very small; awkward to handle.
fiddly *adjective*

fidelity *noun*
(*say* fid-**el**-i-ti)
1 being faithful. **2** the exactness with which sound is reproduced.

fidget *verb*
to move about restlessly.
fidgety *adjective*

fidget *noun*
someone who fidgets.

field *noun*
1 a piece of land with crops or grass growing on it, usually surrounded by a hedge or fence. **2** an area, especially where something happens. *an important experiment in the field of science.* **3** a battlefield. **4** those taking part in a race, hunt, etc.

field *verb*
to stop or catch the ball in cricket, etc.; to be on the side not batting in cricket, etc.
fielder *noun*, **fieldsman** *noun*

fiend *noun*
(*say* feend)
a devil.
fiendish *adjective*, **fiendishly** *adverb*

fierce *adjective* (**fiercer, fiercest**)
angry and violent or cruel.
fiercely *adverb*, **fierceness** *noun*

fiery *adjective* (**fierier, fieriest**)
1 full of flames or heat. **2** very emotional; easily made angry. *He had a fiery temper.*

fiesta *noun*
(*say* fee-**est**-à)
a festival in Spain, South America, etc.

fife *noun*
a small, shrill flute.

fifteen *noun*
1 the number 15, one more than fourteen. **2** a team in Rugby Union Football.
fifteenth *adjective* and *noun*

fifth *adjective*
next after the fourth.

fifty *noun*
the number 50, five times ten.
fiftieth *adjective* and *noun*

fifty-fifty *adjective* and *adverb*
shared equally between two people or groups.

fig *noun*
a small, soft fruit full of small seeds.

fight *noun*
1 a struggle against somebody using hands, weapons, etc. **2** an attempt to overcome or destroy something. *the fight against poverty.*

fight *verb* (**fought, fighting**)
1 to have a fight. **2** to try to stop something. *They fought the fire.*
fighter *noun*

figure *noun*
1 one of the signs we use for numbers, such as 1, 2, and 3. **2** the shape of someone's body. **3** a diagram or illustration. **4** a pattern or shape. *a figure of eight.* **5** **figures,** arithmetic. *Are you good at figures?*

figure *verb* (**figured, figuring**)
1 to imagine. **2** to work out. **3** to appear or take part in something.

filament *noun*
a thread or thin wire.

file *noun*
1 a metal tool with a rough surface that is rubbed on things to make them smooth. **2** a folder, box, etc. to keep papers in. **3** a line of people one behind the other.

file *verb* (**filed, filing**)
1 to make something smooth with a file. **2** to walk one behind the other. **3** to put something in a collection of documents.

filings *plural noun*
tiny pieces of metal.

fill *verb*
1 to make or become full. **2** to put a filling in a tooth. **3** **fill in,** to complete a document; to act as a substitute. **4** **fill up,** to fill completely; to fill in a document.
filler *noun*

fill *noun*
enough to fill a person or thing. *Eat your fill.*

fillet *noun*
a piece of fish or meat without bones.

filling *noun*
something used to fill a hole or gap, especially a piece of metal put in a tooth to replace a decayed part.

filling-station *noun*
a place that sells petrol.

filly *noun* (**fillies**)
a young mare.

film *noun*
1 a moving picture that tells a story, such as those shown in cinemas. **2** a roll or piece of thin plastic, etc. put in a camera for taking photographs. **3** a very thin layer of something.
filmy *adjective*

film *verb*
to make a film of something.

filter *noun*
1 a device for removing dirt or other unwanted things from liquid, gas, etc. which passes through it. 2 a system for filtering traffic.

filter *verb*
1 to pass through a filter. 2 to move gradually. *They filtered into the hall.* 3 to move in a particular direction while other traffic is held up.

filth *noun*
disgusting dirt.
filthy *adjective*

fin *noun*
1 one of the thin, flat projections from a fish's body that helps it to swim. 2 a small projection on the outside of an aircraft, rocket, car, etc.

final *adjective*
1 coming at the end; last. 2 that puts an end to argument or doubt. *I say you must not go, and that's final!*
finality *noun,* **finally** *adverb*

final *noun*
the last of a series of contests.
finalist *noun*

finale *noun*
(*say* fin-**ah**-li)
the last part of a show, piece of music, etc.

finance *noun*
the use or management of money.
financial *adjective*

finance *verb* **(financed, financing)**
to supply money for something.
financier *noun*

finch *noun* **(finches)**
a small bird with a short, stubby beak.

find *verb* **(found, finding)**
1 to see or get something. 2 to learn or experience something. *He found that digging is hard work.* 3 **find fault,** to think or say that somebody or something is not satisfactory. 4 **find out,** to come to know something for the first time; to catch somebody doing something wrong.
finder *noun*

findings *plural noun*
things you have found out.

fine *adjective* **(finer, finest)**
1 dry and sunny; bright. *fine weather.* 2 very thin; delicate. *fine material.* 3 excellent. *a fine picture.*
finely *adverb*

fine *noun*
money which has to be paid as a punishment.

fine *verb* **(fined, fining)**
to make somebody pay a fine.

finger *noun*
1 one of the separate parts of the hand. 2 a narrow piece of something. *fish fingers.*

finger *verb*
to feel with your fingers.

fingernail *noun*
the hard covering at the end of a finger.

fingerprint *noun*
a mark made by the tip of a person's finger. *Detectives use fingerprints to identify criminals.*

finish *verb*
to come or bring to an end.

finish *noun* **(finishes)**
the end of something.

Finn *noun*
a Finnish person.

Finnish *adjective*
of Finland.

fiord *noun*
(*say* fi-**ord**)
an inlet of the sea between high cliffs. *There are many fiords in Norway.*

fir *noun*
an evergreen tree with leaves like needles.

fire *noun*
1 burning; the heat and bright light that come from burning things. 2 coal, wood, etc. burning in a grate or furnace to give heat. 3 a device using electricity, gas, etc. to give heat. *Switch on the electric fire.* 4 the shooting of guns. 5 **on fire,** burning. 6 **set fire to,** to start something burning.

fire *verb* **(fired, firing)**
1 to set fire to. 2 to bake pottery, bricks, etc. in an oven. 3 to shoot a gun. 4 to dismiss somebody from his job.

firearm *noun*
a small gun; a rifle or pistol.

fire brigade *noun*
a team of people organized to fight fires.

fire-engine *noun*
a large vehicle that carries firemen and equipment to fight fires.

fireman *noun* **(firemen)**
a member of a fire brigade.

fireplace *noun*
the part of a room where the fire and hearth are.

fireside *noun*
the part of a room near the fire.

fire station *noun*
the headquarters of a fire brigade.

firewood *noun*
wood suitable for fuel.

firework *noun*
a cardboard or paper tube containing chemicals that burn attractively or noisily.

firm *noun*
a business. *She works for a clothing firm.*

firm *adjective*
1 fixed or solid so that it will not move. 2 definite; not likely to change.
firmly *adverb,* **firmness** *noun*

first *adjective*
1 coming before all others. 2 the most important. *The First Eleven.*
firstly *adverb*

first *adverb*
before everything else.

first *noun*
1 a person or thing that is first. **2 at first,** at the beginning; to start with.

first aid *noun*
treatment given to an injured person before a doctor comes.

first-class *adjective*
excellent.

first floor *noun*
the next floor above the ground floor.

firsthand *adjective* and *adverb*
got directly from the source. *firsthand information.*

fish *noun* (**fish** or **fishes**)
an animal that always lives and breathes in the water.

fish *verb*
1 to try to catch fish. 2 to search for something; to try to get something. *He is only fishing for praise.* 3 **fish out** or **fish up,** to pull out something.

fish-cake *noun*
a small cake of mashed fish and potato.

fisherman *noun* (**fishermen**)
someone who tries to catch fish.

fishmonger *noun*
a shopkeeper who sells fish.

fishy *adjective* (**fishier, fishiest**)
1 smelling or tasting of fish. 2 (*informal*) suspicious; doubtful. *a fishy story.*

fission *noun*
(*say* fish-ŏn)
splitting something, especially splitting the nucleus of an atom.

fist *noun*
a tightly closed hand, with the fingers bent in towards the palm.

fit *adjective* (**fitter, fittest**)
1 suitable; good enough. *a meal fit for a king.* 2 healthy; strong. *Keep fit with exercises.* 3 ready; likely. *I'm fit to collapse.* 4 **see fit** or **think fit,** to decide or choose to do something.
fitness *noun*

fit *verb* (**fitted, fitting**)
1 to be the right size and shape; to be suitable. 2 to put something into place. 3 **fit in,** to be suitable or agreeable.
fitter *noun*

fit *noun*[1]
1 a sudden illness, especially one that makes you move violently or become unconscious. 2 an outburst. *a fit of rage.* 3 **by** or **in fits and starts,** not regularly; in short bursts.

fit *noun*[2]
the way something fits. *This coat is a good fit.*

fitted *adjective*
made to fit something exactly. *This room has a fitted carpet.*

fitting *adjective*
suitable; proper.

five *noun*
the number 5, one more than four.

fiver *noun*
(*informal*) a five-pound note; £5.

fives *noun*
a game in which a ball is hit with gloved hands or a bat against the walls of a court.

fix *verb*
1 to join firmly to something; to put something where it will not move. 2 to decide or settle. *We have fixed a date for the party.* 3 (*informal*) to mend. *He's fixing my bike.* 4 **fix up,** to arrange or organize.

fix *noun* (**fixes**)
1 an awkward situation. *I'm in a fix.* 2 finding the position of something.

fixture *noun*
1 something fixed in its place. 2 a sports event, race, etc. planned for a particular day.

fizz *verb*
to make a hissing, spluttering sound; to produce a lot of small bubbles.
fizzy *adjective*

flabby *adjective* (**flabbier, flabbiest**)
fat and soft; not firm.

flag *noun*[1]
1 a piece of material with a coloured pattern or shape on it, used as a sign or signal. 2 a small piece of paper that looks like a flag, especially sold in aid of charity.

flag *noun*[2]
a flagstone.

flag *verb* (**flagged, flagging**)
1 to become weak; to droop. 2 to signal with a flag or by waving.

flagpole *noun*
a pole to which a flag is attached.

flagstaff *noun*
a flagpole.

flagstone *noun*
a flat slab of paving stone.

flake *noun*
1 a very light, thin piece of something. 2 a piece of falling snow.
flaky *adjective*

flake *verb* (**flaked, flaking**)
1 to come off in flakes. 2 **flake out,** (*informal*) to faint or fall asleep.

flame *noun*
fire that is shaped like a tongue; a piece of burning gas.

flame *verb* (**flamed, flaming**)
to produce flames.

flamenco *noun*
(*say* flă-**menk**-oh)
a Spanish gypsy style of dancing or singing.

flamingo *noun*
a long-legged wading bird with pinkish feathers.

flan *noun*
a tart without any pastry on top.

flank *noun*
the side of something.

flannel *noun*
1 a piece of soft cloth used for washing yourself. *He rubbed his face with his flannel.* 2 a kind of soft material. *These trousers are made of flannel.*

flit

flap *noun*
1 a part that hangs down from one edge of something, usually to cover an opening. *Stick down the flap of the envelope.* **2** the action or sound of flapping. **3** (*slang*) a panic or fuss. *Don't get in a flap.*

flap *verb* (**flapped, flapping**)
1 to move up and down or from side to side. *The bird flapped its wings.* **2** (*slang*) to panic or fuss.

flare *noun*
1 a sudden, bright flame. **2** a bright light used as a signal. **3** a gradual widening.

flare *verb* (**flared, flaring**)
1 to burn with a sudden, bright flame. **2** to become angry suddenly. **3** to get gradually wider.

flash *noun* (**flashes**)
1 a sudden, bright burst of light. **2** a device for making a brief, bright light by which to take photographs. **3** a sudden display of anger, wit, etc. **4** a short item of news. **5 in a flash**, immediately; very quickly.

flash *verb*
1 to make a flash. **2** to appear suddenly; to move quickly. *The train flashed past.*

flashback *noun*
going back in a film or story to something that happened earlier. *The hero's childhood was shown in flashbacks.*

flashy *adjective* (**flashier, flashiest**)
gaudy.

flask *noun*
1 a bottle with a narrow neck. **2** a vacuum flask.

flat *adjective* (**flatter, flattest**)
1 with no curves or bumps; smooth and level. **2** spread out; lying at full length. *Lie flat on the ground.* **3** uninteresting; boring. *a flat voice.* **4** complete; not changing. *a flat refusal.* **5** not fizzy. *This beer is flat.* **6** below the usual musical pitch. *a tune in B flat.* **7** punctured; with no air inside. *a flat tyre.* **8** (*of feet*) without the normal arch. **9 flat out**, as fast as possible.
flatly *adverb*, **flatness** *noun*

flat *noun*
1 a set of rooms for living in, usually on one floor of a building. **2** the note below a particular musical note; the sign that indicates this.

flatten *verb*
to make or become flat.

flatter *verb*
1 to praise somebody more than he deserves. **2** to make somebody seem better or more attractive than he really is.
flatterer *noun*, **flattery** *noun*

flavour *noun*
the taste and smell of something.

flavour *verb*
to give something a flavour.
flavouring *noun*

flaw *noun*
something that makes a person or thing imperfect. *There are flaws in your argument.*
flawed *adjective*, **flawless** *adjective*

flax *noun*
a plant that produces fibres from which cloth is made and seeds from which oil is made.

flea *noun*
a small insect without wings that sucks blood.

flee *verb* (**fled, fleeing**)
to run away. *When he saw the policeman, he fled.*

fleece *noun*
the wool that covers a sheep's body.
fleecy *adjective*

fleece *verb* (**fleeced, fleecing**)
1 to shear a sheep. **2** to swindle somebody out of his money.

fleet *noun*
a number of ships, aircraft, or vehicles, owned by one country or company.

flesh *noun*
the soft substance between the skin and bones of people and animals.
fleshy *adjective*

flew past tense of **fly** *verb*.

flex *noun* (**flexes**)
flexible insulated wire for electric current.

flex *verb*
to bend your muscles, arms, etc.

flexible *adjective*
1 easy to bend. **2** easy to change or adapt.
flexibility *noun*

flick *noun*
a quick, light hit or movement.

flick *verb*
to hit or move with a flick.

flicker *verb*
to burn or shine unsteadily.

flight *noun*[1]
1 flying. **2** a journey in an aircraft, rocket, etc. **3** a group of flying birds, aircraft, etc. **4** a series of stairs. **5** the feathers or fins on a dart or arrow.

flight *noun*[2]
running away; an escape.

flimsy *adjective* (**flimsier, flimsiest**)
light and thin; fragile.

flinch *verb*
1 to quail. **2** to wince.

fling *verb* (**flung, flinging**)
to throw something violently or carelessly. *He flung his shoes under the bed.*

flint *noun*
1 a very hard kind of stone. **2** a piece of flint or hard metal used to produce sparks.
flinty *adjective*

flip *verb* (**flipped, flipping**)
to flick.

flipper *noun*
1 a limb that water-animals use for swimming. **2** a device that you wear on your feet to help you swim.

flirt *verb*
to behave lovingly towards somebody to amuse yourself.
flirtation *noun*

flit *verb* (**flitted, flitting**)
to fly or move lightly and quickly.

float

float *verb*
1 to stay or move on the surface of a liquid or in the air. 2 to make something float.

float *noun*
1 a device designed to float. 2 a vehicle used for delivering milk or for carrying a display in a parade, etc. 3 a small amount of money kept for paying small bills, giving change, etc.

flock *noun*
a group of sheep, goats, or birds.

flock *verb*
to gather or move in a large crowd.

flog *verb* **(flogged, flogging)**
1 to beat somebody severely with a whip or stick. 2 (*slang*) to sell. *He flogged me his watch.*

flood *noun*
1 a large amount of water spreading over a place that is usually dry. 2 a great amount of something. *a flood of requests.* 3 the tide when it is coming in.

flood *verb*
1 to cover with a flood. 2 to come in a flood. *Letters flooded in.*

floodlight *noun*
a lamp that makes a broad, bright beam.
floodlit *adjective*

floor *noun*
1 the part of a room that people walk on. 2 all the rooms on the same level in a building. *Her office is on the top floor.*

floor *verb*
1 to put a floor into a building. 2 to knock somebody down. 3 to baffle somebody.

floorboard *noun*
one of the boards forming the floor of a room.

flop *verb* **(flopped, flopping)**
1 to fall or sit down suddenly. 2 to flap or droop. 3 (*informal*) to be a failure.

flop *noun*
1 a flopping movement or sound. 2 (*informal*) a failure.

floppy *adjective* **(floppier, floppiest)**
hanging loosely or heavily.

flora *noun*
(*say* **flor**-ă)
the plants of a particular area or period.

floral *adjective*
of flowers.

florist *noun*
a shopkeeper who sells flowers.

flounder *verb*
to move or behave awkwardly or helplessly.

flour *noun*
a white powder made from corn and used for making bread, cakes, pastry, etc.
floury *adjective*

flourish *verb*
1 to grow or develop strongly; to be successful. 2 to wave something about.

flow *verb*
1 to move along smoothly like a river. 2 to hang loosely. *flowing hair.*

flow *noun*
1 a flowing movement or mass. 2 the tide when it is coming in. *ebb and flow.*

flower *noun*
1 the part of a plant from which seed or fruit develops. *Most flowers have coloured petals.* 2 a plant that flowers. 3 **in flower**, flowering.
flowery *adjective*

flower *verb*
to produce flowers.

flowerpot *noun*
a pot in which plants are grown.

flown *past participle of* **fly** *verb.*

flu *noun*
(*informal*) influenza.

fluctuate *verb* **(fluctuated, fluctuating)**
to rise and fall irregularly.
fluctuation *noun*

fluent *adjective*
skilful at speaking, especially at speaking a foreign language.
fluency *noun,* **fluently** *adverb*

fluff *noun*
a light, soft substance that comes off wool, hair, etc.
fluffy *adjective*

fluid *noun*
a substance that flows easily; any liquid or gas.

fluke *noun*
an unexpected piece of good luck that makes you able to do something you thought you could not do.

flung *past tense and past participle of* **fling.**

fluorescent *adjective*
creating light from radiations.
fluorescence *noun*

fluoridation *noun*
adding fluoride to drinking-water.

fluoride *noun*
a chemical that is thought to prevent tooth-decay.

flush *verb*
1 to blush. 2 to clean or remove something with a fast flow of water.

flush *adjective*
1 level; without projections. *The doors are flush with the walls.* 2 (*slang*) having plenty of money.

flustered *adjective*
nervous and confused.

flute *noun*
a musical instrument consisting of a long pipe with holes that are stopped by fingers or keys.

flutter *verb*
1 to flap wings quickly. 2 to move or flap quickly and irregularly. *The flags fluttered in the breeze.*

flutter *noun*
1 a fluttering movement. 2 a nervously excited condition. 3 (*informal*) a small bet.

fly *verb* **(past tense flew; past participle flown; present participle flying)**
1 to move through the air with wings or in an

aircraft. *I have flown from London to Paris.*
2 to wave in the air. *Flags were flying.* **3** to
make something fly. *They flew model aircraft.*
4 to move quickly. *Time flies.*

fly *noun*[1] **(flies)**
1 a small flying insect with two wings. **2** a real
or artificial fly used as bait in fishing.

fly *noun*[2] **(flies)**
the front opening of a pair of trousers.

flying saucer *noun*
a mysterious object flying through the air.

flyleaf *noun* **(flyleaves)**
a blank page at the beginning or end of a book.

flyover *noun*
a bridge that carries one road over another.

flywheel *noun*
a heavy wheel used to regulate machinery.

foal *noun*
a young horse.

foam *noun*
1 froth. **2** a spongy substance made of rubber
or plastic.
foamy *adjective*

foam *verb*
to froth.

focus *noun* **(focuses or foci)**
1 the distance at which something appears
most clear to an eye or a lens. **2** the point at
which rays, etc. meet. **3** the most important or
interesting part of something. **4 in focus,** appearing clearly. **5 out of focus,** not appearing
clearly.
focal *adjective*

focus *verb*
1 to use or adjust a lens so that objects appear
clearly. **2** to concentrate. *She focused her
attention on the problem.*

fodder *noun*
food for horses and farm animals.

foe *noun*
(*old-fashioned use*) an enemy.

foetus *noun* **(foetuses)**
(*say* **fee**-tŭs)
a developing embryo.
foetal *adjective*

fog *noun*
thick mist.
foggy *adjective*

fog-horn *noun*
a loud horn for warning ships in fog.

foil *noun*[1]
1 a very thin sheet of metal. **2** a person or thing
that makes another look better in comparison.

foil *noun*[2]
a thin sword used in fencing.

foil *verb*
to frustrate. *We foiled his evil plan.*

fold *verb*
1 to bend or move so that one part lies on
another part. **2** to blend one ingredient into
another. **3 folding,** made so that it can be
folded to take up less space. *a folding chair.*
4 fold your arms, to join your arms together in
front of your body.

fold *noun*[1]
a line where something is folded.

fold *noun*[2]
an enclosure for sheep.

folder *noun*
a folding cover for loose papers. *Keep your
homework in this folder.*

foliage *noun*
the leaves of a tree or plant.

folk *noun*
people; ordinary people, especially those who
live in the country.

follow *verb*
1 to come or go after. **2** to do a thing after
something else. **3** to take somebody or something as a guide or example. **4** to support or
take an interest in a pastime, sports team, etc.
Which football team do you follow? **5** to understand. **6** to result. **7 follow up,** to follow one
thing with another; to do more work, research,
etc. on something.
follower *noun*

following *preposition*
after; as a result of.

fond *adjective*
1 loving. *fond embraces.* **2** foolishly optimistic.
fond hopes. **3 fond of,** liking very much. *I'm
fond of trifle.*
fondly *adverb*, **fondness** *noun*

font *noun*
a basin to hold water for baptism in a church.

food *noun*
anything you eat to help you grow and be
healthy.

fool *noun*
1 a stupid or disliked person. **2** a jester or
clown. *Stop playing the fool.* **3** a pudding made
of fruit mixed with custard or cream.

fool *verb*
1 to behave like a fool. **2** to trick or deceive
somebody.

foolhardy *adjective*
reckless.
foolhardiness *noun*

foolish *adjective*
stupid.
foolishly *adverb*, **foolishness** *noun*

foolproof *adjective*
easy to use or do correctly.

foot *noun* **(feet)**
1 the lower part of a leg. **2** the lowest part of
something. *at the foot of the hill.* **3** a measure of
length, 12 inches or about 30 centimetres. **4 on
foot,** walking.

football *noun*
1 a game played by two teams which try to kick
an inflated ball into their opponents' goal.
2 the ball used in this game. **3 football pool,** a
way of gambling on the results of football
matches.
footballer *noun*

foothill *noun*
a low hill near the bottom of a mountain or
range of mountains.

foothold

foothold *noun*
a place to put your foot when climbing, etc.; a firm position.

footing *noun*
1 having your feet placed on something; what your feet are standing on. *He lost his footing and fell down.* **2** a position or status. *We are on a friendly footing with that country.*

footlights *plural noun*
a row of lights along the front of the stage in a theatre.

footnote *noun*
a note printed at the bottom of a page.

footprint *noun*
a mark made by a foot or shoe.

footsteps *plural noun*
1 the sound or marks your feet make when you walk or run. **2 follow in someone's footsteps,** to do as he did.

for *preposition*
1 intended to be received or used by. *This letter is for you.* **2** towards; in the direction of. *They set out for home.* **3** in order to have or get. *Go for a walk.* **4** as far as; as long as. *We've been waiting for hours.* **5** at the price of. *She bought it for £2.* **6** instead of; in place of. *New lamps for old!* **7** because of. *He was punished for swearing.* **8** concerning; in respect of. *She has a good ear for music.* **9** in defence or support of. *Are you for or against the government?* **10** in spite of. *For all his wealth, he is bored.* **11 for ever,** always.

for *conjunction*
because; since. *Don't go, for I have something to tell you.*

forbid *verb (past tense* **forbade;** *past participle* **forbidden;** *present participle* **forbidding)**
1 to tell somebody not to do something. **2** not to allow something.

forbidding *adjective*
looking stern or unfriendly.

force *noun*
1 strength; power. **2** an organized group of police, soldiers, etc. **3** being active or effective. *Is that law still in force?* **4 the forces,** the armed forces.

force *verb* **(forced, forcing)**
1 to use your power or strength to make somebody do something. **2** to break something open.

forceful *adjective*
using force; strong and effective.
forcefully *adverb*

forceps *noun*
(*say* for-seps)
pincers used by a dentist, surgeon, etc.

forcible *adjective*
done by force.
forcibly *adverb*

ford *noun*
a shallow place where you can wade or drive across a river.

fore *adjective*
at or towards the front.

fore *noun*
to the fore, to or at the front; prominent.

forecast *verb*
to say what you think is going to happen before it happens.

forecast *noun*
forecasting something, especially what the weather is going to be.

forefathers *plural noun*
ancestors.

forefinger *noun*
the finger next to the thumb.

foregone *adjective*
foregone conclusion, an inevitable or obvious result.

foreground *noun*
the part of a view that is nearest to you.

forehead *noun*
(*say* fo-rid or for-hed)
the part of the face above the eyebrows.

foreign *adjective*
1 of or in another country. **2** strange; unnatural. *Lying is foreign to her.*

foreigner *noun*
a person from another country.

foreman *noun* **(foremen)**
someone in charge of a group of other workers.

foremost *adjective*
most important.

foresee *verb (past tense* **foresaw;** *past participle* **foreseen;** *present participle* **foreseeing)**
to know what is going to happen before it happens; to expect. *He foresaw trouble from the prisoners.*
foreseeable *adjective,* **foresight** *noun*

forest *noun*
a lot of trees growing together.
forested *adjective,* **forester** *noun*

forestry *noun*
planting forests and looking after them.

foretell *verb* **(foretold, foretelling)**
to predict. *She foretold their defeat.*

forever *adverb*
continually. *He is forever complaining.*

forfeit *verb*
to lose or do something as a penalty.

forfeit *noun*
1 something forfeited. **2 forfeits,** a game in which people have to do ridiculous things as penalties.

forgave past tense of **forgive.**

forge *noun*
a place where metal is heated and shaped; a blacksmith's workshop.

forge *verb*[1] **(forged, forging)**
1 to shape metal by heating and hammering. **2** to copy something so as to deceive people. *These pound-notes are forged.*
forger *noun,* **forgery** *noun*

forge *verb*[2] **(forged, forging)**
forge ahead, to get ahead by making a strong effort.

foul

forget *verb* (*past tense* **forgot**; *past participle* **forgotten**; *present participle* **forgetting**)
1 to fail to remember. *I forgot my homework.*
2 to stop thinking about something. *We have forgotten our quarrels.* **3 forget yourself,** to behave rudely or thoughtlessly.

forgetful *adjective*
tending to forget things.
forgetfulness *noun*

forget-me-not *noun*
a small blue flower.

forgive *verb* (*past tense* **forgave**; *past participle* **forgiven**; *present participle* **forgiving**)
to stop being angry with somebody about something. *I forgave him when he explained.*
forgiveness *noun*

fork *noun*
1 a small device with prongs for lifting food to your mouth. **2** a large device with prongs used for digging or lifting things. **3** a place where a road, river, etc. divides into two or more parts.

fork *verb*
1 to dig or lift with a fork. **2** to divide into two or more branches. *Go left where the road forks.*
3 fork out, (*informal*) to pay out money.

fork-lift truck *noun*
a truck with two metal bars at the front for lifting and moving heavy loads.

forlorn *adjective*
unhappy; not cared for.

form *noun*
1 a class in school. **2** the shape, appearance, or condition of something. **3** the way in which something exists; a kind of thing. *Ice is a form of water.* **4** a long seat without a back. **5** a printed paper with spaces to fill in.

form *verb*
1 to shape or construct something; to create.
2 to develop. *Icicles formed.*

formal *adjective*
strictly following the accepted rules or customs; ceremonious.
formally *adverb*

formality *noun* (**formalities**)
1 formal behaviour. **2** something done to obey a rule or custom.

formation *noun*
1 the action of forming something. **2** something formed. *formations of rock.* **3** a special pattern or arrangement. *flying in formation.*

former *noun*
the former, the first of two people or things just mentioned. *Brown and Jones came in. The former looked happy.*

former *adjective*
earlier; of past times. *in former days.*
formerly *adverb*

formidable *adjective*
(*say* **for**-mid-à-bůl)
frightening; very difficult to deal with or do. *a formidable task.*
formidably *adverb*

formula *noun* (**formulas** or **formulae**)
1 a set of chemical symbols showing what a substance consists of. *H_2O is the formula for water.* **2** a rule or statement expressed in symbols or numbers. **3** a list of what is needed for making something.

formulate *verb* (**formulated, formulating**)
to express something clearly and exactly.
formulation *noun*

forsake *verb* (*past tense* **forsook**; *past participle* **forsaken**; *present participle* **forsaking**)
to abandon. *She forsook her children.*

fort *noun*
a fortified building.

forth *adverb*
forwards; onwards.

fortify *verb* (**fortified, fortifying**)
to make a place strong against attack; to strengthen.
fortification *noun*

fortnight *noun*
two weeks.
fortnightly *adverb* and *adjective*

fortress *noun* (**fortresses**)
a large fort; a fortified town.

fortunate *adjective*
lucky.
fortunately *adverb*

fortune *noun*
1 luck; chance. **2** a lot of money. **3 fortune-teller,** someone who tells you what will happen to you in the future.

forty *noun* (**forties**)
1 the number 40, four times ten. **2 forty winks,** a short sleep.
fortieth *adjective* and *noun*

forward *adjective*
1 going forwards; placed in the front. **2** having made more than normal progress; clever. **3** too eager or bold.

forward *adverb*
forwards.

forward *noun*
a player in the front line of a team at football, hockey, etc.

forwards *adverb*
to or towards the front; in the direction you are facing.

fossil *noun*
the remains of a prehistoric animal or plant that has been in the ground for a very long time and become hard like rock.
fossilized *adjective*

foster *verb*
to bring up someone else's child as if he is your own.
foster-child *noun*, **foster-mother** *noun*

fought past tense and past participle of **fight** *verb*.

foul *adjective*
1 disgusting; filthy. **2** unfair; breaking the rules. **3** colliding or entangled with something.
foully *adverb*, **foulness** *noun*

foul *noun*
an action that breaks the rules of a game.

found *verb*
1 to get something started; to establish. *She founded a hospital.* 2 to base. *This novel is founded on fact.*

found past tense and past participle of **find.**

foundation *noun*
1 the founding of something. 2 a base or basis. 3 the solid base on which a building is built.

founder *noun*
someone who founds something. *John Wesley was the founder of Methodism.*

founder *verb*
to fill with water and sink. *The ship foundered.*

foundry *noun* **(foundries)**
a place where metal or glass is made or moulded.

fountain *noun*
a device that makes water shoot up into the air.

fountain pen *noun*
a pen that can be filled with a supply of ink.

four *noun*
1 the number 4, one more than three. 2 **on all fours,** crouching on hands and knees.

fourteen *noun*
the number 14, one more than thirteen.
fourteenth *adjective* and *noun*

fourth *adjective*
next after the third.
fourthly *adverb*

fowl *noun*
a bird that is kept for its eggs or meat.

fox *noun* **(foxes)**
a wild animal that looks like a dog with a long, furry tail.
foxy *adjective*

foxglove *noun*
a tall plant with flowers like the fingers of gloves.

foyer *noun*
(*say* **foi**-ay)
the entrance hall of a cinema, theatre, hotel, etc.

fraction *noun*
1 a number that is not a whole number. $\frac{1}{2}$ *and* $^5/_3$ *are fractions.* 2 a tiny part of something.
fractional *adjective,* **fractionally** *adverb*

fracture *verb* **(fractured, fracturing)**
to break, especially to break a bone.

fracture *noun*
the fracturing of something.

fragile *adjective*
(*say* **fra**-jyl)
easy to break or damage.
fragility *noun*

fragment *noun*
1 a small piece broken off something. *a fragment of rock.* 2 a small part. *She overheard fragments of conversation.*
fragmentary *adjective,* **fragmentation** *noun,* **fragmented** *adjective*

fragrant *adjective*
(*say* **fray**-grănt)
with a sweet or pleasant smell.
fragrance *noun*

frail *adjective*
weak; fragile.
frailty *noun*

frame *noun*
1 something that fits round the outside of a picture. 2 a rigid structure that supports something. *I've broken the frame of my glasses.* 3 a human body. *He has a small frame.* 4 **frame of mind,** the way you think or feel for a while. *Wait till he's in a better frame of mind.*

frame *verb* **(framed, framing)**
1 to put a frame on or around. 2 to form or construct. *They were framing new laws.* 3 (*slang*) to make somebody seem to be guilty when he is innocent.

frame-up *noun*
(*slang*) making somebody seem to be guilty when he is innocent.

framework *noun*
1 a frame supporting something. 2 a basic plan or system.

franc *noun*
a unit of money in France, Belgium, and some other countries.

frank *adjective*
honest; making your thoughts and feelings clear to people.
frankly *adverb,* **frankness** *noun*

frank *verb*
to mark something with a postmark.

frantic *adjective*
wildly agitated or excited.
frantically *adverb*

fraud *noun*
1 a swindle; dishonesty. 2 an impostor.
fraudulent *adjective*

frayed *adjective*
worn and ragged at the edge. *Your shirt collar is frayed.*

freak *noun*
a very strange or abnormal person, animal, or thing.
freakish *adjective*

freckle *noun*
a small brown spot on the skin.
freckled *adjective*

free *adjective* **(freer, freest)**
1 able to do what you want to do or go where you want to go. 2 not costing anything. *a free ride.* 3 not having or affected by something unpleasant. *The roads are free of ice.* 4 available; not being used or occupied. *His afternoons are free.* 5 generous. *She is very free with her money.*
freely *adverb*

free *verb* **(freed, freeing)**
to make somebody or something free.

freedom *noun*
being free; independence.

free-wheel *verb*
to ride on a bicycle without pedalling.

frog

freeze *verb (past tense* **froze;** *past participle* **frozen;** *present participle* **freezing)**
1 to turn into ice; to become covered with ice. *The pond froze last night.* **2** to make or be very cold. *My hands are frozen.* **3** to keep wages, prices, etc. at a fixed level. **4** suddenly to stand completely still.

freezer *noun*
a large refrigerator for keeping food very cold. *You can keep food in freezers for months.*

freezing-point *noun*
the temperature at which a liquid freezes.

freight *noun*
(*say* frayt)
1 cargo. **2** the cost of transporting something.

freighter *noun*
a ship or aircraft carrying mainly freight.

French *adjective*
of France.
Frenchman *noun,* **Frenchwoman** *noun*

French window *noun*
a long window that serves as a door, opening on to a garden or balcony.

frenzy *noun* **(frenzies)**
wild excitement; madness.
frenzied *adjective,* **frenziedly** *adverb*

frequency *noun* **(frequencies)**
1 being frequent. **2** how often something happens. **3** the number of oscillations per second of a wave of sound, light, etc.

frequent *adjective*
(*say* **free**-kwent)
happening often.
frequently *adverb*

frequent *verb*
(*say* fri-**kwent**)
to be in or go to a place often. *They frequented the youth club.*

fresh *adjective*
1 not old, tired, or used. *fresh bread.* **2** not tinned or preserved. *fresh fruit.* **3** cool and clean. *fresh air.* **4** not salty. *fresh water.*
freshly *adverb,* **freshness** *noun*

freshen *verb*
to make or become fresh.

freshwater *adjective*
of fresh water; living in rivers or lakes. *freshwater fish.*

fret *verb* **(fretted, fretting)**
to worry or be upset about something.
fretful *adjective,* **fretfully** *adverb*

fretsaw *noun*
a very narrow saw used for making fretwork.

fretwork *noun*
cutting decorative patterns in wood; wood cut in this way.

friar *noun*
a religious man who has vowed to live a life of poverty.
friary *noun*

friction *noun*
1 the rubbing of one thing against another. **2** disagreement; quarrelling.
frictional *adjective*

Friday *noun*
the sixth day of the week.

fridge *noun*
(*informal*) a refrigerator.

friend *noun*
1 someone you like who likes you. **2** a helpful or kind person. **3 make friends,** to become somebody's friend.
friendless *adjective*

friendly *adjective* **(friendlier, friendliest)**
behaving like a friend; kind and helpful.
friendliness *noun*

friendship *noun*
being friends.

frieze *noun*
(*say* freez)
a strip of designs or pictures along the top of a wall.

frigate *noun*
a fast warship.

fright *noun*
1 sudden, great fear. **2** (*informal*) a person or thing that looks ridiculous.

frighten *verb*
to cause somebody fright or fear.

frightful *adjective*
awful.
frightfully *adverb*

frill *noun*
1 a decorative edging, usually pleated, on a dress, curtain, etc. **2** an unnecessary extra. *a simple life with no frills.*
frilled *adjective,* **frilly** *adjective*

fringe *noun*
1 a decorative edging with many threads hanging down loosely. **2** a straight line of short hair hanging down over the forehead. **3** the edge of something. *He stood on the fringe of the crowd.*
fringed *adjective*

frisk *verb*
1 to jump or run around playfully. **2** to search somebody by moving your hands over his clothes.

frisky *adjective* **(friskier, friskiest)**
playful; lively.
friskily *adverb,* **friskiness** *noun*

fritter *noun*
a slice of fruit, meat, etc. fried in batter.

fritter *verb*
to waste something gradually; to spend money or time on trivial things. *He frittered away his fortune.*

frivolous *adjective*
not behaving seriously; trivial.
frivolity *noun,* **frivolously** *adverb*

fro *adverb*
to and fro, backwards and forwards.

frock *noun*
a girl's or woman's dress.

frog *noun*
1 a small jumping animal that can live both in water and on land. **2 a frog in your throat,** hoarseness.

frogman *noun* **(frogmen)**
a swimmer equipped with flippers and breathing apparatus for swimming under water.

frolic *noun*
a lively, cheerful game or pastime.
frolicsome *adjective*

frolic *verb* **(frolicked, frolicking)**
to have frolics.

from *preposition*
1 out of. *She comes from London.* **2** measured with reference to. *We are a mile from home.* **3** starting at. *Recite the poem from the beginning.* **4** because of. *I suffer from headaches.* **5** as opposed to. *Can you tell margarine from butter?*

front *noun*
1 the part of a person or thing that faces forwards; the most important side of something. *The front of the house is blue.* **2** the part of a thing or place that is farthest forward. *Go to the front of the class.* **3** a road or promenade along the sea-shore. **4** the place where fighting is happening in a war. *More troops were moved to the front.* **5 in front,** at or near the front.
frontal *adjective*

frontier *noun*
the boundary between two countries or regions.

frost *noun*
1 powdery ice that forms on things in freezing weather. **2** weather with a temperature below freezing-point.
frosty *adjective*

frost *verb*
1 to cover with frost or frosting. **2 frosted glass,** glass that has a rough surface so that you cannot see through it.

frost-bite *noun*
harm done to the skin by very cold weather.
frost-bitten *adjective*

frosting *noun*
icing for cakes.

froth *noun*
a white mass of tiny bubbles on or in a liquid.
frothy *adjective*

froth *verb*
to form a froth.

frown *verb*
to wrinkle your forehead because you are angry or worried.

frown *noun*
a frowning movement or look.

froze past tense of **freeze.**

frozen past participle of **freeze.**

frugal *adjective*
(*say* froo-gǎl)
very economical and careful; costing little money.
frugality *noun*

fruit *noun* **(fruit** or **fruits)**
1 the seed-container that grows on a tree or plant and is often used as food. *Apples, oranges, and bananas are fruit.* **2** the result of doing something. *the fruit of his efforts.* **3 fruit salad,** a mixture of raw fruit cut up for eating.
fruity *adjective*

fruitful *adjective*
1 successful; having good results. *Their talks were fruitful.* **2** producing fruit.
fruitfully *adverb*

fruitless *adjective*
unsuccessful; having no results.
fruitlessly *adverb*

frustrate *verb* **(frustrated, frustrating)**
to prevent somebody from doing something; to disappoint.
frustration *noun*

fry *verb* **(fried, frying)**
to cook something in boiling fat.

frying-pan *noun*
1 a shallow pan in which things are fried. **2 out of the frying-pan into the fire,** from a bad situation to something worse.

fudge *noun*
a soft, sugary sweet.

fuel *noun*
something that is burnt to make heat or power. *Coal and oil are fuels.*

fuel *verb* **(fuelled, fuelling)**
to supply with fuel.

fug *noun*
(*informal*) a stuffy atmosphere in a room.
fuggy *adjective*

fugitive *noun*
(*say* few-ji-tiv)
a person who is running away from something.

fugue *noun*
(*say* fewg)
a piece of music in which themes are repeated in a pattern.

fulcrum *noun*
the point on which a lever rests.

fulfil *verb* **(fulfilled, fulfilling)**
to accomplish; to do what is required.
fulfilment *noun*

full *adjective*
1 containing as much or as many as possible. *The cinema was full.* **2** having many people or things. *full of ideas.* **3** complete. *the full story.* **4** the greatest possible. *Full speed ahead!* **5** fitting loosely; with many folds. *a full skirt.* **6 in full,** not leaving out anything. **7 to the full,** completely; thoroughly.
fullness *noun,* **fully** *adverb*

full *adverb*
completely; very. *You knew full well what I wanted.*

full moon *noun*
the moon when you can see its whole disc.

full stop *noun*
the dot used as a punctuation mark at the end of a sentence or after each letter of an abbreviation.

full-time *adjective*
of or for all the normal working hours of the day. *a full-time job.*

fumble *verb* **(fumbled, fumbling)**
to hold or handle something clumsily.

fume *verb* **(fumed, fuming)**
1 to give off fumes. **2** to be very angry.

fumes *plural noun*
strong-smelling smoke or gas.

fun *noun*
1 amusement; enjoyment. **2 make fun of,** to make people laugh at somebody; to make a person or thing seem ridiculous.

function *noun*
1 what somebody or something does or ought to do. *The function of a doctor is to cure sick people.* **2** an important event, party, etc. *The Queen attends many functions.*

function *verb*
to work properly. *These scissors won't function.*

functional *adjective*
working properly; practical.
functionally *adverb*

fund *noun*
money collected or kept for a special purpose. *They started a fund for refugees.*

fundamental *adjective*
basic.
fundamentally *adverb*

funeral *noun*
the ceremony when a corpse is buried or cremated.

fungus *noun* **(fungi)**
a plant without leaves or flowers, growing on other plants or on decayed material. *Mushrooms and toadstools are fungi.*

funk *verb*
(*informal*) to be afraid of doing something.

funnel *noun*
1 a chimney on a ship or railway-engine. **2** a tube with one very wide end to help you pour things into bottles or other containers.

funny *adjective* **(funnier, funniest)**
1 that makes you laugh or smile. *a funny joke.* **2** strange; odd. *a funny smell.*
funnily *adverb,* **funniness** *noun*

fur *noun*
1 the soft hair that covers some animals. **2** animal skin with the fur on it, used for clothing; fabric that looks like animal fur.

furious *adjective*
very angry or agitated; raging.
furiously *adverb*

furl *verb*
to roll up and fasten a sail, flag, or umbrella.

furlong *noun*
one eighth of a mile, 220 yards or about 201 metres.

furnace *noun*
a device in which great heat can be produced for making glass, heating metals, etc.

furnish *verb*
to provide furniture for a place.

furniture *noun*
tables, chairs, beds, cupboards, and other movable things that you need inside a house, school, office, etc.

furrow *noun*
1 a long cut in the ground made by a plough. 2 a deep wrinkle on the skin.

furry *adjective* **(furrier, furriest)**
like fur; covered with fur.

further *adverb* and *adjective*
1 farther. *I can't walk any further.* **2** more. *We need further information.*

further *verb*
to help something progress. *We furthered the cause of peace.*

further education *noun*
education for people above school age.

furthermore *adverb*
also; moreover.

furthest *adverb* and *adjective*
farthest.

fury *noun* **(furies)**
wild anger or agitation; a rage.

fuse *noun*[1]
a safety device containing a short piece of wire that melts if too much electricity passes through it.

fuse *noun*[2]
a device for setting off an explosive.

fuse *verb* **(fused, fusing)**
1 to stop working because a fuse has melted. *The lights have fused.* **2** to blend together, especially through melting.

fuselage *noun*
(*say* **few**-zěl-ah*zh*)
the body of an aircraft. *Wings and tail are fitted to the fuselage.*

fusion *noun*
(*say* **few**-*zh*ŏn)
1 the action of blending or uniting. **2** the uniting of atomic nuclei, usually releasing energy.

fuss *noun* **(fusses)**
1 unnecessary excitement or worry about something unimportant. **2 make a fuss of,** to treat somebody with much kindness and attention.

fuss *verb*
to cause a fuss.

fussy *adjective* **(fussier, fussiest)**
1 fussing; inclined to make a fuss. **2** full of unnecessary details or decorations.
fussily *adverb,* **fussiness** *noun*

futile *adjective*
(*say* **few**-tyl)
useless; having no result.
futility *noun*

future *noun*
1 the time that will come. **2** what is going to happen in the time that will come. **3 in future,** from now onwards.

fuzzy *adjective* **(fuzzier, fuzziest)**
1 blurred; not clear. **2** fluffy.
fuzzily *adverb,* **fuzziness** *noun*

G

g. short for **gram.**

gabble *verb* (**gabbled, gabbling**)
to talk so quickly that it is difficult for people to understand what you are saying.

gable *noun*
the three-sided part of a wall between two sloping roofs.
gabled *adjective*

gadget *noun*
(*say* **gaj**-it)
a small, useful device. *a gadget for opening tins.*
gadgetry *noun*

gag *verb* (**gagged, gagging**)
to put something over somebody's mouth so that he cannot speak.

gag *noun*
1 something used to gag somebody. **2** a joke.

gaiety *noun*
being cheerful; amusement.

gaily *adverb*
in a cheerful way.

gain *verb*
1 to get something that you did not have before. **2** **gain on** or **gain upon,** to come closer to somebody or something you are chasing.

gain *noun*
something gained; profit.

gala *noun*
(*say* **gah**-lă)
a festival; a series of sports contests, especially at swimming.

galaxy *noun* (**galaxies**)
(*say* **gal**-ăk-si)
a very large group of stars. *You can see three galaxies without a telescope.*
galactic *adjective*

gale *noun*
a very strong wind.

gallant *adjective*
1 brave. **2** chivalrous.
gallantly *adverb*, **gallantry** *noun*

galleon *noun*
a large Spanish sailing-ship used from the 15th to the 17th century.

gallery *noun* (**galleries**)
1 a platform projecting from the inside wall of a building. **2** the highest balcony in a cinema or theatre. **3** a long room or passage. **4** a building or room where works of art are displayed.

galley *noun*
1 an ancient type of long ship propelled by oars. **2** the kitchen in a ship.

gallon *noun*
a measure of liquid, 8 pints or about 4½ litres.

gallop *noun*
1 the fastest pace a horse can go. **2** a fast ride on a horse.

gallop *verb*
to go at a gallop. *The cowboys galloped away.*

gallows *noun*
a framework on which criminals are hanged.

Gallup poll *noun*
questioning a number of people so as to estimate what most people think about something.

galvanize *verb* (**galvanized, galvanizing**)
1 to coat iron with zinc to protect it from rust. **2** to stimulate or shock somebody into doing something.

gamble *verb* (**gambled, gambling**)
1 to play a game for money. **2** to take great risks.
gambler *noun*

game *noun*
1 something that you can play, usually with rules. *Football, chess, and ludo are games.* **2** one section of a long game like tennis or whist. *In tennis, you must win at least 6 games to win a set.* **3** a trick or scheme. **4** wild animals or birds hunted for sport or food. *Some people shoot game-birds like pheasants or partridges.* **5 the game is up,** a swindle or secret has been revealed.

game *adjective*
1 able and willing to do something. *He's game for all kinds of tricks.* **2** brave.
gamely *adverb*

gamekeeper *noun*
someone who protects game-birds and animals, especially from poachers.

gammon *noun*
a kind of ham or thick bacon.

gander *noun*
a male goose.

gang *noun*
1 a group of people who do things together. **2** a group of gangsters.

gangplank *noun*
a plank for walking on to or off a ship.

gangster *noun*
a violent criminal.

gangway *noun*
1 a gap left for people to move along between rows of seats or through a crowd. **2** a gangplank or other structure for getting on or off a ship.

gaol *noun*
(*say* jayl)
a prison.
gaoler *noun*

gaol *verb*
to put somebody in prison.

gap *noun*
an opening or break in something; an interval.

gape *verb* (**gaped, gaping**)
1 to open your mouth wide. **2** to stare in amazement.

gender

garage *noun*
(*say* **ga**-rah*z*h or **ga**-rij)
1 a building in which motor vehicles are kept or repaired. **2** a filling-station.

garbage *noun*
rubbish.

garden *noun*
1 a piece of ground where flowers, fruit, or vegetables are grown. **2 garden plant,** a plant of the sort grown in gardens, not wild.
gardener *noun,* **gardening** *noun*

gargle *verb* **(gargled, gargling)**
to wash your throat by moving liquid around inside it.

garland *noun*
a decorative wreath of flowers.

garlic *noun*
a plant rather like an onion, used for flavouring.

garment *noun*
something you wear; a piece of clothing.

garnish *verb*
to decorate food.

garrison *noun*
troops stationed in a town or fort to defend it.

garter *noun*
a band of elastic to hold up a sock or stocking.

gas *noun* **(gases)**
1 a substance like air. *Oxygen and hydrogen are gases.* **2** an inflammable gas used for heating or cooking. *Gas is used for gas cookers and gas fires.* **3 gas ring,** a hollow perforated ring from which gas flows for cooking on.
gaseous *adjective*

gas *verb* **(gassed, gassing)**
to overcome or harm somebody with a poisonous gas.

gash *noun* **(gashes)**
a long, deep cut or wound.

gasket *noun*
a flat ring or strip of soft material for sealing a joint between metal surfaces.

gasometer *noun*
(*say* gas-**om**-it-er)
a large, round tank in which gas is stored.

gasp *verb*
to breathe quickly and noisily when you are tired, ill, or astonished; to speak in a breathless way.

gastric *adjective*
of the stomach.

gasworks *noun*
a place where gas is made for heating and cooking.

gate *noun*
1 something that opens and closes the entrance to a garden, field, etc. **2** a barrier used to control the flow of water. *a lock-gate.* **3** the number of people attending a football-match, etc.

gateway *noun*
1 an opening containing a gate. **2** a way to reach something. *the gateway to success.*

gather *verb*
1 to come or bring together; to collect or pick. **2** to understand, decide, or learn. *I gather that you are on holiday.* **3 gather speed,** to get faster gradually.

gathering *noun*
an assembly or meeting of people; a party.

gaudy *adjective* **(gaudier, gaudiest)**
too showy and bright.

gauge *noun*
(*say* gayj)
1 the normal measurement of something. **2** the distance between a pair of railway lines. **3** a measuring instrument.

gauge *verb* **(gauged, gauging)**
1 to measure. **2** to estimate; to judge.

gaunt *adjective*
1 (*of a person*) lean and haggard. **2** (*of a place*) grim and desolate.

gauntlet *noun*
a glove with a wide covering for the wrist.

gauze *noun*
thin, net-like material of wire, silk, cotton, etc.

gave past tense of **give.**

gay *adjective*
1 cheerful. **2** brightly coloured. **3** (*informal*) homosexual.

gaze *verb* **(gazed, gazing)**
to look at something for a long time. *He gazed at the sunset.*

gaze *noun*
a long, steady look.

gazelle *noun*
a small antelope.

gazump *verb*
(*informal*) to raise the price of a house after accepting an offer from somebody.

G.C.E. short for *General Certificate of Education.*

gear *noun*
1 equipment; clothes. *mountaineering gear.* **2** a set of toothed wheels working together in a machine, especially those transmitting power from an engine to the wheels of a vehicle. **3 in gear,** with the gears connected. **4 out of gear,** with the gears not connected.

gee *interjection*
1 a command to a horse to go on or go faster. **2** an exclamation of surprise, disappointment, etc.

geese plural of **goose.**

Geiger counter *noun*
a device that detects and measures radioactivity.

gelatine *noun*
a transparent, tasteless substance used to make jellies, etc.
gelatinous *adjective*

gem *noun*
1 a jewel. **2** a very valuable or beautiful thing.

gender *noun*
(*say* **jen**-der)
the group in which a noun or pronoun is classed in some languages. *The genders in French are masculine and feminine.*

gene *noun*
(*say* jeen)
one of the factors that controls heredity in the body.

general *adjective*
1 of or concerning all or most people or things. *general knowledge.* **2** not detailed; not specialized. *a general education.* **3 General Certificate of Education,** an examination for pupils in secondary schools. **4 general election,** electing members of parliament for the whole country. **5 in general,** usually.

general *noun*
a high-ranking army officer.

generalize *verb* **(generalized, generalizing)**
to talk about general things, not particular things; to state principles.
generalization *noun*

generally *adverb*
usually.

generate *verb* **(generated, generating)**
to produce or create something. *Electricity is generated in a power-station.*
generator *noun*

generation *noun*
1 generating something. **2** a single stage in a family. *Three generations were included: grandparents, parents, and children.* **3** all the people born about the same time. *His generation grew up during the war.* **4 generation gap,** parents and children failing to understand or communicate with each other.

generous *adjective*
ready to give or share what you have.
generosity *noun,* **generously** *adverb*

genetic *adjective*
(*say* ji-**net**-ik)
of genes.
genetically *adverb*

genitals *plural noun*
the parts of the body used for sexual activities.

genius *noun* **(geniuses)**
an unusually clever person.

gent *noun*
1 (*slang*) a gentleman; a man. **2 the Gents,** (*informal*) a lavatory for men.

gentle *adjective* **(gentler, gentlest)**
kind and quiet; not rough or severe.
gentleness *noun,* **gently** *adverb*

gentleman *noun* **(gentlemen)**
1 a man. *Good evening, ladies and gentlemen!* **2** a well-mannered or honest man. *He's a real gentleman.*
gentlemanly *adverb*

genuine *adjective*
real; not faked or pretending. *Is that diamond genuine?*
genuinely *adverb*

genus *noun* **(genera)**
(*say* **jee**-nŭs)
a group of similar animals or plants. *Lions and tigers belong to the same genus.*

geography *noun*
the science or study of the world and its climate, peoples, and products.
geographer *noun,* **geographical** *adjective,* **geographically** *adverb*

geology *noun*
(*say* ji-**ol**-ŏ-ji)
the science or study of the earth's crust, its rocks, etc.
geological *adjective,* **geologically** *adverb,* **geologist** *noun*

geometry *noun*
the science or study of lines, angles, surfaces, and solids.
geometric *adjective,* **geometrical** *adjective,* **geometrically** *adverb*

geranium *noun*
(*say* jĕ-**ray**-ni-ŭm)
a plant with red, pink, or white flowers that is often grown in a pot.

gerbil *noun*
(*say* **jer**-bil)
a small, brown animal with long back legs. *Gerbils are often kept as pets.*

germ *noun*
a tiny living thing, especially one that causes a disease.

German *adjective*
of Germany.

germinate *verb* **(germinated, germinating)**
to start growing and developing.
germination *noun*

gesture *noun*
(*say* **jes**-cher)
a movement or action which expresses what you feel.

get *verb* **(got, getting)**
1 to become. *Are you getting angry?* **2** to obtain or receive something. *I got a new bike yesterday.* **3** to reach a place. *We'll get there by midnight.* **4** to put or move. *I can't get my shoe on.* **5** to prepare. *Shall I get the tea?* **6** to persuade or order. *Get him to wash up.* **7** (*informal*) to understand. *Do you get what I mean?* **8 get by,** to manage. **9 get off,** to stop riding on a bus, horse, etc.; to avoid being punished. **10 get on,** to start riding on a bus, horse, etc.; to make progress; to be friendly with somebody. **11 get on with,** to work at something. **12 get out of,** to avoid something. **13 get over,** to recover from an illness, shock, etc. **14 get your own back,** to have your revenge. **15 have got to,** must.

getaway *noun*
an escape.

geyser *noun*
(*say* **gee**-zer or **gy**-zer)
a natural spring that shoots up columns of hot water.

ghastly *adjective* **(ghastlier, ghastliest)**
horrible; awful.

ghetto *noun*
(*say* **get**-oh)
an area of a city inhabited by a group of people who are discriminated against.

ghost *noun*
the spirit of a dead person seen by a living person.
ghostly *adjective*

gleam

giant *noun*
a huge man.
giantess *noun*

giant *adjective*
huge.

giddy *adjective* **(giddier, giddiest)**
having or causing the feeling that everything is
turning round in circles.
giddily *adverb*, **giddiness** *noun*

gift *noun*
1 a present. 2 a talent. *She has a gift for music.*

gifted *adjective*
talented.

gig *noun*
(*informal*) an occasion when a musician or band
plays rock music, jazz, etc. in public.

gigantic *adjective*
huge.
gigantically *adverb*

giggle *verb* **(giggled, giggling)**
to laugh in a silly way.

giggle *noun*
1 a silly laugh. 2 (*informal*) something amusing; a joke. *We did it for a giggle.*

gild *verb* **(gilded** or **gilt, gilding)**
to cover something with a thin layer of gold
paint or gold.

gill *noun*
one of the parts on a fish's side that it breathes
through.

gimmick *noun*
something unusual done or used to attract
people's attention. *The comedian's funny hat
was a gimmick.*
gimmicky *adjective*

gin *noun*
a colourless alcoholic drink.

ginger *noun*
1 a flavouring that makes food taste hot. 2 a
reddish yellow colour. 3 liveliness; energy.
gingery *adjective*

gingerbread *noun*
a cake or biscuit flavoured with ginger.

gingerly *adverb*
cautiously.

gipsy *noun* **(gipsies)**
a gypsy.

giraffe *noun*
a tall African animal with a very long neck.

girder *noun*
a metal beam supporting part of a building or
bridge.

girdle *noun*
1 a belt. 2 a corset.

girl *noun*
1 a young female person. 2 a daughter. 3 **girl-
friend,** a girl that a boy regularly goes out with.
girlhood *noun*, **girlish** *adjective*

girth *noun*
1 the measurement round something. 2 a band
fastened round a horse's belly to keep its saddle
in place.

give *verb* (*past tense* **gave**; *past participle* **given**;
present participle **giving**)
1 to let somebody have something. *She has
given me a sweet.* 2 to make; to do something
suddenly. *He gave a laugh.* 3 to present or
perform. *They gave a concert.* 4 to bend or go
downwards; to collapse. *Will this branch give if
I sit on it?* 5 **give away,** to sacrifice something;
to reveal a secret. 6 **give in,** to surrender. 7 **give
off,** to emit. 8 **give out,** to hand out; to become
worn out. 9 **give up,** to stop doing or trying
something; to surrender. 10 **give way,** to collapse; to let somebody go before you.
giver *noun*

given *adjective*
1 definite; stated; agreed. *Meet at a given time.*
2 **given to,** tending to; having a particular
habit. *He is given to boasting.*

glacial *adjective*
(*say* **glay**-shăl)
of ice; icy.

glacier *noun*
(*say* **glas**-i-er)
a river of ice moving slowly along a valley.

glad *adjective* **(gladder, gladdest)**
1 pleased; happy. 2 **glad of,** grateful for;
pleased with.
gladden *verb*, **gladly** *adverb*, **gladness** *noun*

glamour *noun*
attractiveness; beauty.
glamorize *verb*, **glamorous** *adjective*

glance *verb* **(glanced, glancing)**
1 to look at something briefly. 2 to hit and slide
off something. *The ball glanced off his bat.*

glance *noun*
a brief look.

gland *noun*
an organ of the body that separates some
substances from the blood.
glandular *adjective*

glare *verb* **(glared, glaring)**
1 to shine with a very bright or dazzling light.
2 to look angrily at somebody.

glare *noun*
1 very strong light. 2 an angry stare.

glass *noun* **(glasses)**
1 a hard, brittle substance which is usually
transparent. *Glass is used for making windows,
mirrors, dishes, etc.* 2 a cup made of glass,
usually without a handle. 3 a mirror. 4 a lens or
telescope. 5 **glasses,** spectacles; binoculars.
glassful *noun*

glassy *adjective* **(glassier, glassiest)**
1 like glass. 2 dull; lifeless; without expression.
a glassy stare.

glaze *verb* **(glazed, glazing)**
1 to fit or cover with glass. 2 to give a shiny
surface to pottery, etc. 3 to become glassy.

glazier *noun*
someone who fits glass into window-frames.

gleam *noun*
1 a beam of soft light, especially one that
comes and goes. 2 a small amount. *a gleam of
hope.*

gleam *verb*
to shine with gleams.

glee *noun*
delight; joy.
gleeful *adjective*, **gleefully** *adverb*

glen *noun*
a narrow valley, especially in Scotland.

glide *verb* (**glided, gliding**)
1 to fly or move smoothly. 2 to fly without using an engine.

glider *noun*
an aircraft that does not use an engine.

glimmer *noun*
a faint gleam.

glimmer *verb*
to gleam faintly.

glimpse *verb* (**glimpsed, glimpsing**)
to see something briefly.

glimpse *noun*
seeing something briefly.

glint *verb*
to flash or sparkle.

glisten *verb*
to shine like something wet or polished.

glitter *verb*
to sparkle.

global *adjective*
of the whole world.
globally *adverb*

globe *noun*
1 something shaped like a ball. 2 a ball with a map of the whole world on it. 3 **the globe**, the world.

globular *adjective*
shaped like a globe.

gloom *noun*
a gloomy condition or feeling.

gloomy *adjective* (**gloomier, gloomiest**)
1 almost dark; not lighted. 2 depressed; sad.
gloomily *adverb*, **gloominess** *noun*

glorify *verb* (**glorified, glorifying**)
1 to praise highly. 2 to make something seem splendid.
glorification *noun*

glorious *adjective*
having glory.
gloriously *adverb*

glory *noun* (**glories**)
1 fame and honour; praise. 2 splendour; beauty.

gloss *noun* (**glosses**)
1 the shine on a smooth surface. 2 a paint that gives surfaces a gloss.
glossy *adjective*

glossary *noun* (**glossaries**)
a list of words with their meanings explained. *Your French book has a glossary at the back.*

glove *noun*
a covering for the hand.

glow *noun*
1 brightness and warmth without flames. 2 a cheerful or excited condition. *a glow of enthusiasm.*

glow *verb*
to make or have a glow.

glower *verb*
to scowl.

glow-worm *noun*
an insect whose tail gives out a green light.

glucose *noun*
a type of sugar.

glue *noun*
a thick liquid for sticking things together.
gluey *adjective*

glue *verb* (**glued, gluing**)
to stick with glue.

glum *adjective* (**glummer, glummest**)
depressed; sad.
glumly *adverb*

glutton *noun*
someone who eats too much.
gluttonous *adjective*, **gluttony** *noun*

gnarled *adjective*
(*say* narld)
twisted and knobbly, like an old tree.

gnash *verb*
(*say* nash)
to strike your teeth together.

gnat *noun*
(*say* nat)
a tiny fly that bites.

gnaw *verb*
(*say* naw)
to keep biting something that is hard. *The dog gnawed the bone.*

gnome *noun*
(*say* nohm)
a kind of dwarf in fairy-tales that usually lives underground.

go *verb* (*past tense* **went**; *past participle* **gone**; *present participle* **going**)
1 to move in any direction. *Where are you going?* 2 to leave; to set out. *We shall go in a minute.* 3 to lead; to extend. *This road goes to Bristol.* 4 to become. *The milk went sour.* 5 to work properly. *My watch isn't going.* 6 to have a proper place; to belong. *Plates go on that shelf.* 7 to happen or proceed. *The show went well.* 8 to make a particular movement or sound. *The gun went bang.* 9 to be finished or lost. *My money has gone.* 10 to be sold. *The house went very cheaply.* 11 **go back on**, not to keep a promise. 12 **go in for**, to do or take part in something. 13 **go off**, to explode; to become stale; to stop liking somebody or something. 14 **go on**, to happen; to do something more than once. 15 **go one better**, to do better than somebody else. 16 **go out**, to leave a house, home, etc.; to go to entertainments; to stop burning or shining.

go *noun* (**goes**)
1 a turn or try. *May I have a go?* 2 (*informal*) a success. *They made a go of it.* 3 (*informal*) energy; liveliness. *She's full of go.* 4 **on the go**, active; always working or moving.

goal *noun*
1 the two posts that the ball must go between to score a point in football, hockey, etc. 2 a point scored in football, hockey, netball, etc. 3 an objective.

goalie *noun*
(*informal*) a goalkeeper.

goalkeeper *noun*
the player in football, hockey, etc. who stands in the goal and guards it.

goat *noun*
1 an animal with horns, kept for its milk and meat. 2 **to get somebody's goat,** (*informal*) to annoy him.

gob *noun*
1 (*slang*) your mouth. 2 **gob-stopper,** a large sweet for sucking.

gobble *verb* **(gobbled, gobbling)**
to eat something quickly and greedily.

goblin *noun*
an evil or mischievous fairy.

god *noun*
1 someone or something that is worshipped. 2 **God,** the creator of the Universe in Christian, Jewish, and Muslim belief.
goddess *noun,* **godless** *adjective,* **godlike** *adjective,* **godly** *adjective*

godparent *noun*
someone who promises, when a child is baptized, to see that it is brought up as a Christian.
godchild *noun,* **god-daughter** *noun,* **godfather** *noun,* **godmother** *noun,* **godson** *noun*

goggles *plural noun*
large spectacles to protect the eyes from wind, water, dust, etc.

going *noun*
1 the condition of the ground for walking, riding, etc. 2 speed of working or moving. *It was good going to get there by noon.* 3 departure. *comings and goings.*

going *adjective*
1 working well; prosperous. *a going concern.* 2 existing. *the going rate.* 3 **going to,** ready or likely to do something.

go-kart *noun*
a tiny racing-car.
go-karting *noun*

gold *noun*
1 a precious yellow metal. 2 a bright yellow colour. 3 **gold medal,** a golden medal awarded as the first prize.

golden *adjective*
1 made of gold. 2 coloured like gold. 3 precious; important. *a golden opportunity.* 4 **golden wedding,** the 50th anniversary of a wedding.

gold-field *noun*
an area where gold is found or mined.

goldfinch *noun* **(goldfinches)**
a brightly-coloured bird with yellow feathers in its wings.

goldfish *noun* **(goldfish)**
a small red or orange fish, often kept as a pet.

golf *noun*
an outdoor game played by hitting a small white ball with a club into a series of small holes.
golfer *noun,* **golfing** *noun*

golf-course *noun*
an area of land where golf is played.

gondola *noun*
(*say* **gon**-dŏl-ă)
a boat with high pointed ends, used on the canals in Venice.
gondolier *noun*

gone past participle of **go** *verb.*

gong *noun*
a large metal disc that makes an echoing sound when it is hit.

goo *noun*
something sticky or sloppy.
gooey *adjective*

good *adjective* **(better, best)**
1 of the kind that people like, want, or praise. *a good book.* 2 kind. *It was good of you to help us.* 3 well-behaved. *Be a good boy.* 4 healthy; giving benefit. *Exercise is good for you.* 5 thorough; large enough. *Have a good drink.* 6 quite large; considerable. *It's a good distance to the station.* 7 useful; suitable. *This desk is good enough for me.* 8 **as good as,** nearly. 9 **good evening,** a polite way of greeting somebody in the evening. 10 **good morning,** a polite way of greeting somebody in the morning. 11 **good night,** a polite way of saying goodbye to somebody at night.

good *noun*
1 something good or right. *Do good to others.* 2 benefit; profit. *I'm telling you for your own good.* 3 **for good,** for ever. 4 **no good,** useless.

goodbye *interjection*
a word you use when you leave somebody or at the end of a telephone-call.

Good Friday *noun*
the Friday before Easter, commemorating the Crucifixion.

good-looking *adjective*
attractive; handsome.

good-natured *adjective*
kind.
good-naturedly *adverb*

goodness *noun*
1 being good. 2 the good part of something. 3 **goodness gracious, goodness me,** or **my goodness,** ways of expressing surprise.

goods *plural noun*
1 things that are bought and sold. 2 things that are carried on trains, lorries, etc.

goodwill *noun*
being friendly; approval.

goose *noun* **(geese)**
a large bird that is kept for its meat and eggs. *Geese have webbed feet.*

gooseberry *noun* **(gooseberries)**
a small green fruit that grows on a prickly bush.

gore *verb* **(gored, goring)**
to wound with a horn or tusk. *The bull gored the matador.*

gorge *noun*
a narrow valley with steep sides.

gorgeous *adjective*
magnificent; beautiful.
gorgeously *adverb*

gorilla *noun*
a large, strong African ape.

gorse *noun*
a prickly bush with small yellow flowers.

gosh *interjection*
(*slang*) an exclamation of surprise.

gosling *noun*
a young goose.

go-slow *noun*
a way of protesting by deliberately working slowly.

gospel *noun*
1 the teachings of Jesus Christ. 2 **the Gospels,** the first four books of the New Testament. 3 something that you can safely believe. *You can take what I say as gospel.*

gossip *verb*
1 to talk a lot about other people. 2 to talk a lot in a friendly way.

gossip *noun*
1 gossiping. 2 someone who likes gossiping.

got past tense and past participle of **get.**

Gothic *adjective*
of the style of building common from the 12th to the 16th century, with pointed arches and much carving.

gouge *verb* **(gouged, gouging)**
(*say* gowj)
to press or scoop out something.

gourd *noun*
1 the hard-skinned fruit of a climbing plant. 2 this fruit hollowed out to make a bowl or container.

govern *verb*
to be in charge of a country or organization.
governor *noun*

government *noun*
the group of people who govern a country.
governmental *adjective*

gown *noun*
a loose, flowing garment, especially for a woman.
gowned *adjective*

grab *verb* **(grabbed, grabbing)**
to take hold of something suddenly, firmly, or greedily.

grace *noun*
1 beauty, especially in movement. 2 goodwill; favour. 3 a short prayer before or after a meal.

graceful *adjective*
beautiful, especially in movement.
gracefully *adverb*, **gracefulness** *noun*

gracious *adjective*
1 kind; pleasant to other people. 2 merciful. 3 used as an exclamation of surprise. *Good gracious! Gracious me!*
graciously *adverb*

grade *noun*
1 a step in a scale of quality, value, or rank; a standard. *Coal is sold in grades: Grade A coal is the best.* 2 **make the grade,** (*informal*) to reach the proper standard.

grade *verb* **(graded, grading)**
to sort or divide into grades.

gradient *noun*
(*say* **gray**-di-ĕnt)
1 a slope. 2 the amount that a road or railway slopes.

gradual *adjective*
happening slowly but steadily.
gradually *adverb*

graduate *noun*
(*say* **grad**-yoo-ăt)
someone who has been to a university or college and got a degree.

graduate *verb* **(graduated, graduating)**
(*say* **grad**-yoo-ayt)
1 to get a university degree. 2 to divide something into graded sections; to mark something with degrees. *a graduated measuring-jug.*
graduation *noun*

graffiti *plural noun*
(*say* gră-**fee**-tee)
words or drawings scribbled on a wall.

grain *noun*
1 cereals when they are growing or after they have been harvested. 2 the seed of a cereal; a small, hard seed or piece. 3 the pattern of lines on a piece of wood.
grainy *adjective*

gram *noun*
a unit of weight in the metric system, a thousandth of a kilogram.

grammar *noun*
1 the rules for using words. 2 a book that gives the rules for using words. 3 **grammar school,** a kind of secondary school.

grammatical *adjective*
of grammar.
grammatically *adverb*

gramophone *noun*
1 a machine for reproducing sound from recorded discs. 2 **gramophone record,** a disc used on a gramophone.

grand *adjective*
1 great; splendid. 2 complete. *the grand total.* 3 **grand piano,** a large piano with horizontal strings.
grandly *adverb*

grandad *noun*
(*informal*) grandfather.

grandchild *noun* **(grandchildren)**
a child of your son or daughter.
granddaughter *noun*, **grandson** *noun*

grandeur *noun*
greatness; splendour.

grandfather *noun*
1 the father of your mother or father. 2 **grandfather clock,** a clock in a tall wooden case.

grandma *noun*
(*informal*) grandmother.

grandmother *noun*
the mother of your mother or father.

grandpa *noun*
(*informal*) grandfather.

greenery

grandparent *noun*
a grandmother or grandfather.

grandstand *noun*
a structure with rows of seats for spectators at a race-course or sports ground.

granite *noun*
a very hard kind of rock.

granny *noun* **(grannies)**
(*informal*) grandmother.

granny-knot *noun*
a reef-knot with the strings crossed the wrong way.

grant *verb*
1 to give or allow somebody what he has asked for. **2 take for granted,** to assume that something is true or will always be available.

granulated *adjective*
in white grains. *granulated sugar.*

grape *noun*
a small green or purple fruit that grows in bunches.

grapefruit *noun* **(grapefruit)**
a large, round, yellow citrus fruit with a soft, juicy pulp.

graph *noun*
1 a diagram that shows how two amounts are related. **2 graph paper,** paper covered with small squares, used for making graphs.

graphic *adjective*
1 short and lively. *a graphic account of the race.* **2** of drawing or painting. *a graphic artist.*
graphically *adverb*

graphite *noun*
a soft kind of carbon used for the lead in pencils, for lubricating, etc.

grapple *verb* **(grappled, grappling)**
1 to struggle or wrestle. **2** to hold something firmly. **3 grapple with,** to try to deal with a problem, etc.

grasp *verb*
1 to hold tightly. **2** to understand.

grasp *noun*
the power to grasp things; a firm hold.

grasping *adjective*
greedy for money or possessions.

grass *noun* **(grasses)**
1 a green plant with thin stalks. **2** ground covered with grass.
grassy *adjective*

grasshopper *noun*
a jumping insect that makes a shrill noise.

grass snake *noun*
a small, harmless snake.

grate *noun*
1 a metal framework that keeps fuel in the fireplace. **2** a fireplace.

grate *verb* **(grated, grating)**
1 to shred something into small pieces. *grated cheese.* **2** to make an unpleasant noise by rubbing something. *The chalk grated on the blackboard.*

grateful *adjective*
feeling glad that someone has done something for you. *I am grateful for your help.*
gratefully *adverb*

grating *noun*
a framework of metal bars placed across an opening.

gratitude *noun*
being grateful.

grave *noun*
the place where a corpse is buried.

grave *adjective* **(graver, gravest)**
serious; solemn; important. *grave news.*
gravely *adverb*

gravel *noun*
small stones mixed with coarse sand. *Gravel is often used to make paths.*
gravelled *adjective*, **gravelly** *adjective*

gravestone *noun*
a stone monument over a grave.

graveyard *noun*
a place where corpses are buried.

gravity *noun*
1 the force that pulls everything towards the earth. **2** seriousness.
gravitation *noun*, **gravitational** *adjective*

gravy *noun*
a hot brown liquid that is poured over meat before it is eaten.

graze *verb* **(grazed, grazing)**
1 to eat grass as it grows. *The cows were grazing in the field.* **2** to hurt your skin by rubbing against something; to scrape something as you pass it. *I grazed my arm on the wall.*

grease *noun*
thick fat or oil.
greasy *adjective*

great *adjective*
1 very large. **2** very important; extremely clever or talented. *a great composer.* **3** (*informal*) very good. *It's great to see you again.* **4** older by one generation. *Your great-grandfather is the grandfather of one of your parents.*
greatly *adverb*, **greatness** *noun*

Grecian *adjective*
of Greece.

greed *noun*
being greedy.

greedy *adjective* **(greedier, greediest)**
wanting more food or money than you need.
greedily *adverb*, **greediness** *noun*

Greek *adjective*
of Greece.

green *adjective*
of the colour of grass, leaves, etc.

green *noun*
1 green colour. **2** an area of grass, especially in the middle of a village or used for a particular game. *the village green. a putting-green.*

greenery *noun*
green leaves or plants.

greengage *noun*
a green kind of plum.

greengrocer *noun*
someone who keeps a shop that sells fruit and vegetables.
greengrocery *noun*

greenhouse *noun*
a glass building where plants are grown.

greenish *adjective*
rather green.

greens *plural noun*
green vegetables, such as cabbage and spinach.

greet *verb*
to welcome; to receive. *The singer was greeted with applause.*

greeting *noun*
1 words or actions used to greet somebody. 2 **greetings**, good wishes.

grenade *noun*
a small bomb usually thrown by hand.

grew past tense of **grow.**

grey *adjective*
of the colour between black and white, like ashes or lead.

greyhound *noun*
a fast, slender dog used in racing.

grid *noun*
a framework or pattern of bars or lines crossing each other.

grief *noun*
1 deep sadness. 2 **come to grief**, to have an accident or misfortune.

grievance *noun*
something that you are discontented about.

grieve *verb* **(grieved, grieving)**
1 to feel very sad. 2 to make somebody feel very sad.

grievous *adjective*
that causes grief; serious.
grievously *adverb*

grill *verb*
1 to cook something over or under a flame or heated element. 2 to question somebody closely and severely. *He was grilled by the police.*

grill *noun*
1 a device for grilling food. 2 grilled food. 3 a grating.

grim *adjective* **(grimmer, grimmest)**
stern; severe; frightening; unpleasant.
grimly *adverb*, **grimness** *noun*

grimace *noun*
a strange or twisted expression on the face.

grime *noun*
dirt.
grimy *adjective*

grin *noun*
a smile showing your teeth.

grin *verb* **(grinned, grinning)**
1 to make a grin. 2 **grin and bear it**, to endure something without complaining.

grind *verb* **(ground, grinding)**
1 to crush something into tiny pieces. *The wheat was ground into flour.* 2 to sharpen or polish something by rubbing it on a rough surface. 3 to move with a harsh grating noise. *The bus ground to a halt.*
grinder *noun*

grindstone *noun*
1 a rough revolving stone used for grinding things. 2 **keep your nose to the grindstone**, to make you work hard without stopping.

grip *verb* **(gripped, gripping)**
1 to hold tightly. 2 to keep somebody's attention. *a gripping story.*

grip *noun*
1 a grasp. 2 a handle.

grisly *adjective* **(grislier, grisliest)**
horrible.

gristle *noun*
the tough, rubbery part of meat.
gristly *adjective*

grit *noun*
1 tiny pieces of stone or sand. 2 courage; endurance.
gritty *adjective*

grit *verb* **(gritted, gritting)**
1 to clench your teeth. 2 to put grit on a road or path.

grizzly bear *noun*
a large, fierce bear of North America.

groan *verb*
to make a long, deep sound of pain or distress.

groan *noun*
a groaning sound.

grocer *noun*
someone who keeps a shop that sells food, drink, and other goods for the house.

grocery *noun* **(groceries)**
1 a grocer's shop. 2 **groceries**, goods sold by a grocer.

groom *noun*
1 someone whose job is to look after horses. 2 a bridegroom.

groom *verb*
1 to clean and brush a horse or other animal. 2 to make neat and trim.

groove *noun*
a long narrow cut in the surface of something. *Records have grooves in them.*

grope *verb* **(groped, groping)**
to feel about for something you cannot see.

gross *adjective*
1 fat and ugly. 2 with bad manners; vulgar. 3 very bad or shocking. *gross stupidity.* 4 total; without anything deducted. *gross income.*
grossly *adverb*, **grossness** *noun*

gross *noun* **(gross)**
144; twelve dozen of something.

grotesque *adjective*
(*say* groh-**tesk**)
very strange; ridiculous.
grotesquely *adverb*

ground *noun*
1 the earth. 2 a sports field. 3 **grounds,** reasons. *Have you any grounds for suspicion?* 4 **the grounds,** the gardens of a large house.

ground past tense and past participle of **grind.**

grounded *adjective*
prevented from flying. *The aircraft were grounded because of fog.*

ground floor *noun*
in a building, the floor that is level with the ground.

groundsheet *noun*
a piece of waterproof material for spreading on the ground.

groundsman *noun* (groundsmen)
someone whose job is to look after a sports ground.

group *noun*
a number of people, animals, or things that belong together in some way.

group *verb*
to make a group.

grouse *verb* (groused, grousing)
to complain.
grouser *noun*

grouse *noun* (grouse)
a large bird with feathered feet.

grove *noun*
a group of trees; a small wood.

grow *verb* (*past tense* **grew**; *past participle* **grown**; *present participle* **growing**)
1 to become bigger. *He has grown a lot.* 2 to develop. *The seeds are growing.* 3 to plant something in the ground and look after it. *She grows lovely roses.* 4 to become. *He grew rich.* 5 **grow on,** to become more attractive or more natural to somebody. *This music grows on you.* 6 **grow out of,** to get too big or too old for something. 7 **grow up,** to develop; to become an adult.
grower *noun*

growl *noun*
a deep, rough sound.

growl *verb*
to make a growl. *Angry dogs growl.*

grown-up *noun*
an adult.

growth *noun*
1 growing; development. 2 something that has grown.

grub *noun*
1 a tiny creature that will become an insect. 2 (*slang*) food.

grubby *adjective* (grubbier, grubbiest)
rather dirty.

grudge *noun*
a dislike of somebody because you think he has harmed you or because you are jealous.

grudge *verb* (grudged, grudging)
to resent letting somebody have something.
grudgingly *adverb*

gruelling *adjective*
exhausting. *a gruelling race.*

gruesome *adjective*
horrible.

gruff *adjective*
with a rough, unfriendly voice or manner.
gruffly *adverb*

grumble *verb* (grumbled, grumbling)
1 to complain continually or with a bad temper. 2 to growl quietly.
grumbler *noun*

grumpy *adjective* (grumpier, grumpiest)
bad-tempered.
grumpily *adverb,* **grumpiness** *noun*

grunt *verb*
to make the sound a pig makes.

grunt *noun*
a grunting sound.

guarantee *noun*
a promise to do something, especially to repair something if it goes wrong.

guarantee *verb* (guaranteed, guaranteeing)
to give a guarantee.

guard *verb*
1 to protect. 2 to prevent somebody from escaping. 3 **guard against,** to be careful to prevent something.

guard *noun*
1 guarding; protection. 2 someone who guards a person or place. 3 a group of soldiers or policemen acting as a guard. 4 the person in charge of a railway train. 5 a protecting device. 6 **on guard,** guarding.

guardian *noun*
1 someone who guards. 2 someone who is legally in charge of a child whose parents cannot look after him.
guardianship *noun*

guerrilla *noun*
(*say* gĕ-**ril**-ă)
someone who fights by means of ambushes and surprise attacks.

guess *noun* (guesses)
an opinion or answer that you give about something you are not sure of.
guesswork *noun*

guess *verb*
to make a guess.

guest *noun*
(*say* gest)
1 a person who is invited to visit or stay at somebody's house. 2 someone staying at a hotel. 3 someone taking part in a show which he does not usually appear in.

guide *noun*
1 someone who shows people the way, helps them, or points out interesting sights. 2 a book that tells you about a place. 3 **Guide,** a member of the Girl Guides Association, an organization for girls.

guide *verb* (guided, guiding)
1 to act as a guide to somebody. 2 **guided missile,** a missile that is controlled while it is in flight.

guild *noun*
(*say* gild)
a society of people with similar skills or interests.

guillotine *noun*
(*say* gil-ŏ-teen)
1 a device used in France for cutting off people's heads. **2** a device with a sharp blade for cutting paper.

guilt *noun*
1 the fact that you have done something wrong. **2** a feeling that you have done something wrong.
guilty *adjective*

guinea *noun*
21 shillings or £1.05.

guinea-pig *noun*
1 a small furry animal without a tail. *Guinea-pigs are often kept as pets.* **2** a person who is used in an experiment. *In testing the drug, they used him as a guinea-pig.*

guitar *noun*
a musical instrument with strings that you pluck.
guitarist *noun*

gulf *noun*
1 a large bay. *The Gulf of Mexico.* **2** a wide gap; a great difference.

gull *noun*
a seagull.

gullet *noun*
the tube from the throat to the stomach.

gully *noun* (**gullies**)
a narrow channel that carries water.

gulp *verb*
1 to swallow quickly or greedily. **2** to make a loud swallowing noise; to gasp.

gum *noun*[1]
the fleshy part of the mouth that holds the teeth.

gum *noun*[2]
1 a sticky substance used as glue. **2** chewing-gum.
gummy *adjective*

gum *verb* (**gummed, gumming**)
to cover or stick with gum.

gum-tree *noun*
1 a eucalyptus tree. **2 up a gum-tree,** (*slang*) in great difficulties.

gun *noun*
1 a weapon that fires shells or bullets from a metal tube. **2** a starting-pistol. **3** a device that forces a substance out of a tube. *grease-gun.*
gunfire *noun*, **gunshot** *noun*

gunboat *noun*
a small warship.

gunman *noun* (**gunmen**)
a criminal with a gun.

gunner *noun*
someone who works with a gun.
gunnery *noun*

gunpowder *noun*
an explosive.

gurgle *verb* (**gurgled, gurgling**)
to make a bubbling sound. *The water gurgled as it flowed out of the bath.*

gush *verb*
1 to flow quickly. **2** to talk too enthusiastically or emotionally.

gust *noun*
a sudden rush of wind, rain, smoke, etc.
gusty *adjective*

gut *verb* (**gutted, gutting**)
1 to remove the guts from a dead fish or other animal. **2** to remove or destroy the inside of something. *The factory was gutted by fire.*

guts *plural noun*
1 the digestive system; the insides of a person or thing. **2** (*informal*) courage.

gutter *noun*
a long, narrow channel at the side of a street or along the edge of a roof, to carry away rain-water.

guy *noun*[1]
1 a figure in the form of Guy Fawkes, burnt on or near 5 November in memory of the Gun-powder Plot. **2** (*informal*) a man.

guy or **guy-rope** *noun*[2]
a rope used to hold something in place. *Slacken the guy-ropes of your tent at night.*

guzzle *verb* (**guzzled, guzzling**)
to eat or drink greedily.
guzzler *noun*

gym *noun*
(*say* jim)
(*informal*) **1** a gymnasium. **2** gymnastics.

gymkhana *noun*
(*say* jim-**kah**-nă)
a series of horse-riding contests.

gymnasium *noun*
a place designed for gymnastics.

gymnastics *plural noun*
exercises for strengthening your body.
gymnast *noun*

gypsy *noun* (**gypsies**)
one of a race of people who live in caravans and often wander from place to place.

gyroscope *noun*
a device that keeps steady because of a heavy wheel spinning inside it.
gyroscopic *adjective*

H

habit *noun*
something that you do without thinking, because you have done it so often.
habitual *adjective*, **habitually** *adverb*

habitat *noun*
where an animal or plant lives naturally.

hack *verb*
to chop or cut roughly.

hacksaw *noun*
a saw for cutting metal.

had past tense and past participle of **have.**

haddock *noun* **(haddock)**
a sea-fish that can be eaten.

hadn't short for *had not.*

hag *noun*
an ugly old woman.

haggard *adjective*
looking ill or very tired.

haggis *noun* **(haggises)**
a Scottish food made from parts of a sheep.

haggle *verb* **(haggled, haggling)**
to argue about a price or agreement.

haiku *noun* **(haiku)**
(*say* hy-koo)
a short poem, usually with three lines.

hail *noun*
frozen drops of rain.
hailstone *noun*, **hailstorm** *noun*

hail *verb*[1]
(*of hail*) to fall. *It is hailing.*

hail *verb*[2]
to call out to somebody. *She hailed the captain.*

hair *noun*
1 a soft covering that grows on the heads and bodies of people and animals. *Her hair is black.* **2** one of the threads that makes up this soft covering. *I found a hair in the soup.* **3 in your hair,** annoying you. **4 keep your hair on,** (*informal*) do not lose your temper.
hairbrush *noun*, **haircut** *noun*

hairdresser *noun*
someone whose job is to cut people's hair and arrange it in particular ways.

hairpin *noun*
1 a pin for keeping your hair in place. **2 hairpin bend,** a very sharp bend in a road.

hair-raising *adjective*
terrifying.

hairy *adjective* **(hairier, hairiest)**
1 with a lot of hair. *a hairy man.* **2** (*slang*) hair-raising; difficult. *a hairy situation.*

hake *noun* **(hake)**
a sea-fish that can be eaten.

half *noun* **(halves)**
one of the two equal parts that something is or can be divided into. *Two halves make a whole.*

half *adverb*
1 partly; not completely. *This meat is only half cooked.* **2 not half,** (*slang*) very much. *Was she cross? Not half!*

half-hearted *adjective*
not very enthusiastic.
half-heartedly *adverb*

half-life *noun* **(half-lives)**
the time it takes for radioactivity to fall to half the original amount.

halfpenny *noun* **(halfpennies** or **halfpence)**
(*say* hayp-ni)
a coin worth half a penny.

half-term *noun*
a short holiday in the middle of a term.

half-time *noun*
the time half-way through a game.

half-way *adverb* and *adjective*
at a point half the distance or amount between two places or times.

halibut *noun* **(halibut)**
a large flat fish that can be eaten.

hall *noun*
1 the first room or passage inside the front door of a house. **2** a very large room for meetings, concerts, etc. *the school hall.* **3** a large, important building or house. *the Town Hall.*

hallo *interjection*
a word used to greet somebody or to attract their attention.

Hallowe'en *noun*
31 October, when some people think that magic things happen.

hallucination *noun*
thinking that you can see or hear something that is not really there.

halo *noun* **(haloes)**
a circle of light, especially shown round the head of a saint in a picture.

halt *verb*[1]
to stop.

halt *verb*[2]
to walk or speak hesitantly. *a halting speech.*

halter *noun*
a rope or strap put round a horse's head so that it can be controlled.

halve *verb* **(halved, halving)**
1 to divide something into halves. **2** to reduce something to half its size.

halves plural of **half** *noun.*

ham *noun*
1 meat from a pig's leg. **2** (*slang*) an actor or performer who is not very good. **3** (*slang*) someone who sends and receives radio messages as a hobby.

hamburger *noun*
1 a fried flat cake of minced beef. **2** a bread-roll containing this.

hammer *noun*
a heavy tool used for hitting nails, breaking rocks, etc.

hammer *verb*
1 to hit with a hammer. 2 to knock loudly. *He hammered on the door.* 3 (*informal*) to treat roughly; to defeat.

hammock *noun*
a bed made of a strong net or piece of cloth hung up above the ground or floor.

hamper *noun*
a big basket with a lid, often used to carry food or picnic things.

hamper *verb*
to hinder.

hamster *noun*
a small animal with brown fur. *Hamsters are often kept as pets.*

hand *noun*
1 the part of the body at the lower end of the arm. 2 a pointer on a clock or dial. 3 a worker. 4 one of a ship's crew. *All hands on deck!* 5 the cards held by one player in a card-game. 6 side or direction. *on the other hand.* 7 **at first hand,** directly from the person concerned. 8 **at hand,** near. 9 **by hand,** using your hand or hands. 10 **hands down,** winning easily or completely. 11 **in hand,** in your possession; being dealt with. 12 **on hand,** available. 13 **out of hand,** out of control.

hand *verb*
to give or pass something to somebody.

handbag *noun*
a woman's bag to hold her money and personal items.

handbook *noun*
a book that gives useful facts about something.

handcuffs *plural noun*
a pair of metal rings used for locking a person's wrists together.

handful *noun*
1 what you can carry in one hand. 2 a small number of people or things. 3 (*informal*) a troublesome person, especially a child.

handicap *noun*
a disadvantage.

handicapped *adjective*
1 suffering from a disadvantage. 2 disabled.

handicraft *noun*
artistic work done with the hands. *Handicrafts include needlework, woodwork, and pottery.*

handiwork *noun*
1 something done or made by the hands. 2 **your handiwork,** something you have done.

handkerchief *noun*
(*say* hang-ker-cheef)
a square piece of material for wiping the nose.

handle *noun*
the part of a thing by which you can hold or control it.

handle *verb* (**handled, handling**)
1 to touch or feel something with your hands. 2 to manage or deal with something.
handler *noun*

handlebars *plural noun*
the bar that steers a bicycle, with a handle at each end.

handrail *noun*
a rail for holding on to.

handsome *adjective* (**handsomer, handsomest**)
1 attractive; good-looking. *a handsome man.* 2 generous. *a handsome gift.*
handsomely *adverb*

handstand *noun*
balancing on your hands with your feet in the air.

handwriting *noun*
writing done by hand.
handwritten *adjective*

handy *adjective* (**handier, handiest**)
convenient; useful.

handyman *noun* (**handymen**)
someone who does small jobs or repairs.

hang *verb* (**hung, hanging**)
1 to fix the top part of something to a hook, nail, etc. 2 to stick wallpaper to a wall. 3 to float in the air. 4 (in this sense, the past tense and past participle are **hanged**) to kill someone by hanging him from a rope that tightens around his neck. 5 **hang about** or **hang around,** to loiter; to wait. 6 **hang on,** to hold tightly; (*informal*) to wait. 7 **hang out,** (*slang*) to live in a place. 8 **hang up,** to end a telephone conversation; to cause someone delay or difficulty.

hangar *noun*
a large shed where aircraft are kept.

hanger *noun*
a device on which to hang things. *a coat-hanger.*

hang-glider *noun*
a device on which a person can glide through the air.
hang-gliding *noun*

hangman *noun* (**hangmen**)
a man whose job is to hang people condemned to death.

hangover *noun*
an unpleasant feeling after drinking too much alcohol.

hang-up *noun*
(*informal*) a difficulty; something that makes you unhappy or frustrated.

hank *noun*
a coil or piece of wool, thread, etc.

hanky *noun* (**hankies**)
(*informal*) a handkerchief.

haphazard *adjective*
(*say* hap-**haz**-erd)
accidental; done or chosen at random.
haphazardly *adverb*

happen *verb*
1 to take place; to occur. 2 **happen to,** to do something by chance. *I happened to see the jewels.*

happening *noun*
something that happens; an unusual event.

happy *adjective* (**happier, happiest**)
pleased; glad; contented; enjoying yourself.
happily *adverb,* **happiness** *noun*

hasty

harass *verb*
(*say* **ha**-rås)
to annoy or trouble somebody often.
harassment *noun*

harbour *noun*
a place where ships can shelter or unload.

harbour *verb*
to give shelter to somebody; to hide a criminal, etc.

hard *adjective*
1 firm; solid; not soft. *hard ground.* **2** difficult. *hard sums.* **3** severe; harsh. *a hard frost.* **4** energetic; using great effort. *a hard worker.* **5 hard of hearing,** slightly deaf. **6 hard shoulder,** a piece of road beside a motorway where motorists can park in emergencies. **7 hard up,** short of money. **8 hard water,** water containing minerals that prevent soap from making much lather.
hardness *noun*

hard *adverb*
1 with great effort. *Work hard.* **2** with difficulty. *hard-earned money.* **3** so as to be hard. *The ground froze hard.*

hardboard *noun*
stiff board made of compressed wood-pulp.

hard-boiled *adjective*
1 boiled until it is hard. *a hard-boiled egg.* **2** harsh; not sympathetic. *a hard-boiled salesman.*

harden *verb*
to make or become hard.
hardener *noun*

hardly *adverb*
only just; only with difficulty. *She was hardly able to walk.*

hardship *noun*
something that causes suffering or discomfort.

hardware *noun*
1 metal implements and tools; machinery. **2** the machinery of a computer.

hardwood *noun*
hard, heavy wood from deciduous trees.

hardy *adjective* (**hardier, hardiest**)
1 strong; able to endure cold or hardships. **2** able to grow outdoors all the year round. *hardy plants.*

hare *noun*
an animal like a large rabbit. *Hares can run very fast.*

hark *verb*
1 to listen. **2 hark back,** to return to an earlier subject.

harm *verb*
to hurt or damage.

harm *noun*
injury; damage.
harmful *adjective*

harmless *adjective*
not dangerous or offensive.
harmlessly *adverb*

harmonica *noun*
a mouth-organ.

harmonium *noun*
a small organ with bellows that you work with your feet.

harmonize *verb* (**harmonized, harmonizing**)
to produce harmony.
harmonization *noun*

harmony *noun* (**harmonies**)
1 a pleasant combination of musical notes. **2** agreement; friendship.
harmonic *adjective,* **harmonically** *adverb,* **harmonious** *adjective,* **harmoniously** *adverb*

harness *noun* (**harnesses**)
the straps put over a horse's head and round its neck to control it.

harness *verb*
1 to put a harness on a horse. **2** to use something to produce power, etc. *They harnessed the river to make electricity.*

harp *noun*
a musical instrument made of strings stretched across a frame and plucked by the fingers.
harpist *noun*

harp *verb*
to keep on talking about something in a boring way. *He keeps harping on his misfortunes.*

harpoon *noun*
a spear attached to a rope, fired from a gun to catch whales and other large sea-animals.

harpsichord *noun*
a musical instrument like a piano but with the strings plucked and not struck.

harrow *noun*
a heavy device pulled over the ground to break up the soil.

harsh *adjective*
rough and unpleasant; cruel.
harshly *adverb,* **harshness** *noun*

harvest *noun*
1 the time when farmers gather in the corn, fruit, or vegetables they have grown. **2** the crop that is gathered in. **3 harvest festival,** a celebration of the harvest.

harvest *verb*
to gather in the crops.
harvester *noun*

has 3rd person singular of **have.**

hash *noun* (**hashes**)
1 a mixture of small pieces of meat and vegetables, usually fried. **2** (*informal*) a mess. *You made a hash of that job.*

hasn't short for *has not.*

hassle *noun*
(*informal*) a difficulty; a disagreement.

haste *noun*
a hurry.

hasten *verb*
to hurry.

hasty *adjective* (**hastier, hastiest**)
hurried; done too quickly.
hastily *adverb,* **hastiness** *noun*

hat *noun*
1 a covering for your head. **2 hat trick,** getting three goals, wickets, victories, etc. one after the other. **3 under your hat,** secret. *Keep it under your hat.*

hatch *noun* **(hatches)**
an opening in a floor, wall, or door, usually with a covering.

hatch *verb*
1 to break out of an egg. *These chicks hatched this morning.* 2 to keep an egg warm until a baby bird is born. 3 to plan. *They were hatching a plot.*

hatchback *noun*
a car with a sloping back hinged at the top.

hatchet *noun*
a small axe.

hate *verb* **(hated, hating)**
to dislike very much.

hate *noun*
1 hatred. 2 (*informal*) someone or something that you hate.

hateful *adjective*
hated; very nasty.
hatefully *adverb*

hatred *noun*
(*say* **hay**-trid)
a great dislike.

haughty *adjective* **(haughtier, haughtiest)**
(*say* **haw**-ti)
too proud of yourself; having contempt for other people.
haughtily *adverb,* **haughtiness** *noun*

haul *verb*
to pull with all your strength.

haunt *verb*
1 to visit a place often. 2 (*of ghosts*) to appear often in a place or to a person. 3 to stay in your mind. *The memory haunts me.*

have *verb* **(had, having)**
1 to own; to possess. *We haven't any money.* 2 to contain. *This tin had sweets in it.* 3 to enjoy. *We had a good party.* 4 to experience or suffer. *She has had an accident.* 5 to be forced to do something. *We had to wash up.* 6 to get something done. *I'm having my watch mended.* 7 to receive; to get. *I had a letter from her.* 8 forming the past tenses of verbs. *She has gone. I have counted. We had eaten them.* 9 **have somebody on,** (*informal*) to fool him.

haven *noun*
(*say* **hay**-věn)
1 a harbour. 2 a safe place.

haven't short for *have not.*

haversack *noun*
a bag carried on your back.

hawk *noun*
1 a bird of prey with very strong eyesight. 2 a warlike person.

hawk *verb*
to go round selling things.
hawker *noun*

hawthorn *noun*
a thorny tree with small red berries.

hay *noun*
1 dried grass for feeding to animals. **2 hay fever,** irritation of the nose, throat, and eyes caused by pollen or dust.

haymaking *noun*
spreading grass to dry after mowing it.
haymaker *noun*

haystack *noun*
a large, neat pile of stored hay.

hazard *noun*
a danger; a risk.
hazardous *adjective*

haze *noun*
thin mist.

hazel *noun*
1 a small nut-tree. 2 a nut from this tree. 3 a light brown colour.

hazy *adjective* **(hazier, haziest)**
1 misty. 2 obscure; uncertain.
hazily *adverb,* **haziness** *noun*

H-bomb *noun*
a hydrogen bomb.

he *pronoun*
the male person or animal being talked about.

he *noun*
1 a male animal. *This cat is a he.* 2 (*informal*) a game in which people chase one another.

head *noun*
1 the part of the body containing the brains, eyes, and mouth. 2 brains; intelligence. *Use your head!* 3 a talent or ability. *He has a head for sums.* 4 the side of a coin on which someone's head is shown. 5 a person. *It costs £1 per head.* 6 the top or front of something. *a pin-head.* 7 the chief; the person in charge of something. *She's the head of this school.* 8 a crisis. *Things came to a head.* 9 **above your head** or **over your head,** too difficult for you. 10 **keep your head,** to stay calm.

head *verb*
1 to be at the top or front of something. 2 to hit a ball with your head. 3 to move in a particular direction. *They headed for the coast.* 4 **head off,** to get in front of somebody.

headache *noun*
1 a pain in the head that goes on hurting. 2 (*informal*) a problem or difficulty.

head-dress *noun* **(head-dresses)**
a decorative covering for the head.

header *noun*
1 heading the ball in football. 2 a dive head-first.

head-first *adverb*
with your head at the front. *I dived in head-first.*

heading *noun*
a word or words at the top of a piece of printing or writing.

headland *noun*
a promontory.

headlight *noun*
a strong light at the front of a car, railway engine, etc.

headline *noun*
1 a heading in a newspaper. 2 **the headlines,** the main points of the news.

headlong *adverb and adjective*
1 falling head-first. 2 in a hasty or thoughtless way.

headmaster *noun*
the man in charge of a school.

headmistress *noun* (**headmistresses**)
the woman in charge of a school.

head-on *adverb and adjective*
with the front parts colliding. *a head-on collision.*

headphone *noun*
a listening device that fits over the top of your head.

headquarters *noun*
the place from which an organization is controlled.

headway *noun*
progress. *They made no headway.*

heal *verb*
to make or become healthy; to cure.
healer *noun*

health *noun*
1 the condition of a person's body or mind. *His health is bad.* 2 being healthy. *in sickness and in health.*

healthy *adjective* (**healthier, healthiest**)
1 free from illness; having good health. 2 producing good health. *Fresh air is healthy.*
healthily *adverb,* **healthiness** *noun*

heap *noun*
1 a pile, especially an untidy pile. 2 **heaps,** (*informal*) a large amount. *We've got heaps of time.*

heap *verb*
1 to make into a heap. 2 to put on large amounts. *She heaped his plate with food.*

hear *verb* (**heard, hearing**)
1 to take in sounds through the ears. 2 to receive news or information. 3 **hear! hear!,** I agree.

hearing *noun*
1 the ability to hear. 2 a chance to be heard; a trial in court. 3 **hearing-aid,** a device to help deaf people to hear.

hearse *noun*
a vehicle for taking the coffin to a funeral.

heart *noun*
1 the part of the body that makes the blood circulate. 2 your feelings or emotions; sympathy. 3 courage or enthusiasm. 4 the middle or most important part of something. 5 a curved shape representing a heart; a playing-card with this shape on it. 6 **break somebody's heart,** to make him very unhappy. 7 **by heart,** memorized. 8 **heart attack** or **heart failure,** a time when the heart stops working properly.

hearth *noun*
the floor of or near a fireplace.

heartless *adjective*
cruel.

hearty *adjective* (**heartier, heartiest**)
1 strong; vigorous. 2 enthusiastic; sincere. *Hearty congratulations!*
heartily *adverb,* **heartiness** *noun*

heat *noun*
1 being hot; great warmth. 2 a race or contest to decide who will take part in the final. 3 **heat wave,** a long period of hot weather.

heat *verb*
to make or become hot.
heater *noun*

heath *noun*
wild, flat land often covered with heather or bushes.

heathen *noun*
someone who does not believe in one of the world's chief religions.

heather *noun*
a low bush with small purple, pink, or white flowers.

heave *verb* (**heaved** or, in senses 3 and 4, **hove, heaving**)
1 to lift or move something heavy. 2 (*informal*) to throw. 3 **heave in sight,** to appear. 4 **heave to,** to stop without anchoring or mooring. *The ship hove to.*

heaven *noun*
1 the place where God and angels are thought to live. 2 a very pleasant place or condition. 3 **good heavens!** or **heavens!,** an exclamation of surprise. 4 **the heavens,** the sky.

heavenly *adjective*
1 in the sky. *heavenly bodies.* 2 (*informal*) very nice. *This cake is heavenly.*

heavy *adjective* (**heavier, heaviest**)
1 weighing a lot; hard to lift or carry. 2 strong; important; severe. *heavy rain.* 3 hard; difficult. *heavy work.* 4 unhappy. *with a heavy heart.*
heavily *adverb,* **heaviness** *noun*

heavyweight *noun*
1 a heavy person. 2 a boxer or wrestler of the heaviest weight.

hectare *noun*
(*say* hek-tar)
a unit of area equal to 10,000 square metres or nearly 2½ acres.

hectic *adjective*
very active or excited.

hedge *noun*
a row of bushes forming a barrier.

hedge *verb* (**hedged, hedging**)
1 to make or trim a hedge. 2 to surround something with a hedge. 3 to avoid being too definite.

hedgehog *noun*
a small animal covered with prickles.

hedgerow *noun*
a hedge.

heed *verb*
to pay attention to.

heed *noun*
attention given to something.
heedless *adjective*

heel

heel *noun*
1 the back part of the foot. 2 the part of a sock, shoe, etc. round or under the heel. 3 **take to your heels**, to run away.

heel *verb*[1]
1 to mend the heel of a shoe. 2 to kick a ball with your heel.

heel *verb*[2]
to lean over to one side.

hefty *adjective* (**heftier, heftiest**)
big and strong.

heifer *noun*
(*say* **hef**-er)
a young cow.

height *noun*
1 how high somebody or something is. 2 a high place. 3 the highest or most important part of something.

heighten *verb*
to make or become higher; to increase.

heir *noun*
(*say* air)
someone who inherits something.
heiress *noun*

held past tense and past participle of **hold** *verb*.

helicopter *noun*
a kind of aircraft with a large horizontal propeller. *Helicopters can rise straight up into the air.*

helium *noun*
(*say* **hee**-li-ŭm)
a light, colourless gas that does not burn.

hell *noun*
1 a place where people are thought to be punished after they die. 2 a very unpleasant place or condition. 3 **hell!**, an exclamation of anger. 4 **hell for leather**, at great speed.
hellish *adjective*

he'll short for *he will*.

hello *interjection*
hallo.

helm *noun*
the handle or wheel used to steer a ship.
helmsman *noun*

helmet *noun*
a strong covering to protect your head.

help *verb*
1 to do something useful for somebody. 2 to avoid. *I can't help coughing.* 3 to serve food, etc. to somebody.
helper *noun*, **helpful** *adjective*, **helpfully** *adverb*

help *noun*
1 helping somebody. 2 someone who helps, especially with housework.

helping *noun*
a portion of food.

helpless *adjective*
not able to do things or look after yourself.
helplessly *adverb*, **helplessness** *noun*

helter-skelter *noun*
a spiral slide at a fair.

hem *noun*
the edge of a piece of cloth that is folded over and sewn down.

hem *verb* (**hemmed, hemming**)
1 to put a hem on something. 2 **hem in**, to surround; to restrict somebody's movements.

hemisphere *noun*
half a sphere; half the globe.

hemp *noun*
1 a plant that produces coarse fibres from which cloth and ropes are made. 2 a drug made from this plant.

hen *noun*
1 the ordinary female fowl kept on farms, etc. 2 any female bird.

hence *adverb*
1 henceforth. 2 therefore.

henceforth *adverb*
from now on; from this time.

her *pronoun*
a word used for *she*, usually when it is the object of a sentence. *I can see her. It's her all right.*

her *adjective*
of her; belonging to her. *That is her book.*

herald *noun*
1 someone who used to make announcements or carry messages for a king or queen. 2 a person or thing that heralds something.

herald *verb*
to say that someone or something is coming.

heraldry *noun*
the study of coats of arms.
heraldic *adjective*

herb *noun*
a plant used for flavouring or for making medicines.
herbal *adjective*

herd *noun*
1 a group of cattle that feed together. 2 a mass of people; a mob.

herd *verb*
to gather or move in a herd.

here *adverb*
1 in or to this place. 2 **here and there**, in or to various places.

heredity *noun*
(*say* hi-**red**-i-ti)
inheriting characteristics from your parents or ancestors.
hereditary *adjective*

heritage *noun*
what you have inherited.

hermit *noun*
someone who lives alone and keeps away from everyone else.
hermitage *noun*

hero *noun* (**heroes**)
1 a man or boy who has done something very brave. 2 the most important man or boy in a story, play, etc.
heroic *adjective*, **heroically** *adverb*, **heroism** *noun*

heroin *noun*
a very strong drug.

heroine *noun*
1 a woman or girl who has done something very brave. 2 the most important woman or girl in a story, play, etc.

heron *noun*
a wading bird with long legs and a long neck.

herring *noun* **(herring** or **herrings)**
a sea-fish that can be eaten.

hers *pronoun*
of her; belonging to her. *Those books are hers.*

herself *pronoun*
1 her and nobody else. *She hurt herself. She ought to be ashamed of herself.* 2 **by herself**, on her own; alone.

hesitant *adjective*
hesitating.
hesitantly *adverb*

hesitate *verb* **(hesitated, hesitating)**
to be slow or uncertain in speaking, moving, etc.
hesitation *noun*

hew *verb* (*past tense* **hewed;** *past participle* **hewed** or **hewn;** *present participle* **hewing**)
to cut or carve.

hexagon *noun*
a shape with six sides.
hexagonal *adjective*

hey *interjection*
an exclamation used to express surprise or to call somebody's attention.

hi *interjection*
an exclamation used to call somebody's attention or to greet somebody.

hibernate *verb* **(hibernated, hibernating)**
(*say* hy-ber-nayt)
to sleep for a long time during cold weather. *Bats, tortoises, and hedgehogs all hibernate.*
hibernation *noun*

hiccup *noun*
a high gulping sound made when your breath is briefly interrupted.

hide *verb* (*past tense* **hid;** *past participle* **hidden** or **hid;** *present participle* **hiding**)
1 to get into a place where you cannot be seen. *I hid behind a tree.* 2 to keep somebody or something from being seen. *The gold was hidden in a cave.* 3 to keep something secret. *Are you hiding the truth from me?*

hide-and-seek *noun*
a game in which one person looks for others who are hiding.

hideous *adjective*
very ugly or unpleasant.
hideously *adverb*

hide-out *noun*
a place where somebody hides.

hiding *noun*[1]
1 being hidden. *She went into hiding.* 2 **hiding-place,** a place where someone or something is hidden.

hiding *noun*[2]
a thrashing; a beating. *Give him a good hiding.*

hieroglyphics *plural noun*
(*say* hyr-ŏ-glif-iks)
pictures used especially in ancient Egypt to represent words.

hi-fi *noun*
(*informal*) 1 high fidelity. 2 equipment that gives high fidelity.

higgledy-piggledy *adverb* and *adjective*
in disorder; completely mixed up.

high *adjective*
1 reaching a long way up. *a high building.* 2 far above the ground or above sea-level. *high flying.* 3 measuring from top to bottom. *two metres high.* 4 very important; chief. *the high road.* 5 very large; greater than normal. *high prices.* 6 lively; happy. *in high spirits.* 7 going bad. *This meat is high.* 8 (*slang*) intoxicated; affected by drugs. 9 **high jump,** an athletic contest of jumping over a horizontal bar. 10 **high time,** when you should do something at once. *It's high time you started work.*

higher education *noun*
education at a university, polytechnic, or college.

high explosive *noun*
a very strong explosive.

high fidelity *noun*
reproducing sound with very little distortion.

highland *adjective*
of or in the highlands.

highlands *plural noun*
mountainous country, especially in Scotland.
highlander *noun*

highlight *noun*
the most interesting part of something.

highly *adverb*
1 extremely. *highly amusing.* 2 favourably. *He thinks highly of her.*

Highness *noun*
a title for a prince or princess. *His Royal Highness, Prince Charles.*

high-rise *adjective*
with many storeys. *high-rise blocks of flats.*

high school *noun*
a secondary school.

high tea *noun*
a meal in the early evening.

highway *noun*
1 an important road or route. 2 **Highway Code,** a set of rules for people using roads.

highwayman *noun* **(highwaymen)**
a man who robbed travellers on highways in former times.

hijack *verb*
to seize control of an aircraft or vehicle during a journey.
hijacker *noun*

hike *noun*
a long walk in the country.

hike *verb* **(hiked, hiking)**
to go for a hike.
hiker *noun*

hilarious *adjective*
very funny or merry.
hilariously *adverb,* **hilarity** *noun*

hill *noun*
a piece of ground that is higher than the ground around it.
hillside *noun,* **hilly** *adjective*

hilt *noun*
1 the handle of a sword or dagger. 2 **to the hilt,** completely.

him *pronoun*
a word used for *he,* usually when it is the object of a sentence. *I'll tell him. Is that him?*

himself *pronoun*
1 him and nobody else. *He hurt himself. He ought to be ashamed of himself.* 2 **by himself,** on his own; alone.

hind *adjective*
(*say* hynd)
at the back. *the hind legs of a donkey.*

hind *noun*
(*say* hynd)
a female deer.

hinder *verb*
(*say* hin-der)
to get in someone's way; to make it difficult for a person to do something.
hindrance *noun*

Hindu *noun*
someone who believes in Hinduism, one of the religions of India.

hinge *noun*
a joining device on which a door, gate, or lid swings when it opens.

hinge *verb* (**hinged, hinging**)
1 to fix with a hinge. 2 **hinge on,** to depend on.

hint *noun*
1 a slight indication or suggestion. *Give me a hint of what you want.* 2 a useful idea. *household hints.*

hip *noun*[1]
the bony part at the side of the body between the waist and the thigh.

hip *noun*[2]
the fruit of the wild rose.

hip *interjection*
part of a cheer. *Hip, hip, hooray!*

hippo *noun*
(*informal*) a hippopotamus.

hippopotamus *noun* (**hippopotamuses**)
a very large African animal that lives near water.

hire *verb* (**hired, hiring**)
to pay to get the use of something.

hire-purchase *noun*
buying something by paying in instalments.

his *adjective*
of him; belonging to him.

hiss *verb*
to make a sound like an *s. The snakes were hissing.*

historian *noun*
someone who writes or studies history.

historic *adjective*
famous or important in history.

history *noun* (**histories**)
1 what happened in the past. 2 studying what happened in the past. 3 a description of important events.
historical *adjective,* **historically** *adverb*

hit *verb* (**hit, hitting**)
1 to come against somebody or something with force; to knock or strike. 2 to have a bad effect on somebody or something. *Famine hit the poor countries.* 3 to reach. *I can't hit that high note.*

hit *noun*
1 hitting; a knock or stroke. 2 a shot that hits the target. 3 a success, especially a successful song or gramophone record.

hitch *verb*
1 to pull something up quickly or with a jerk. 2 to fasten with a loop, hook, etc. 3 (*informal*) to hitch-hike.

hitch *noun* (**hitches**)
1 a hitching movement. 2 a knot. 3 a slight difficulty or delay.

hitch-hike *verb* (**hitch-hiked, hitch-hiking**)
to travel by getting lifts in other people's vehicles.
hitch-hiker *noun*

hither *adverb*
1 to or towards this place. 2 **hither and thither,** · in various directions.

hitherto *adverb*
up to now.

hive *noun*
1 a beehive. 2 a very busy place.

H.M.S. short for *His* or *Her Majesty's Ship.*

ho *interjection*
an exclamation of triumph, surprise, etc.

hoard *noun*
a secret store of money, treasure, food, etc.

hoard *verb*
to store things away, especially like a miser.
hoarder *noun*

hoarding *noun*
a tall fence covered with advertisements.

hoar-frost *noun*
white frost.

hoarse *adjective* (**hoarser, hoarsest**)
with a rough or croaking voice. *He was hoarse from shouting.*
hoarsely *adverb,* **hoarseness** *noun*

hoax *verb*
to deceive somebody as a joke.

hobble *verb* (**hobbled, hobbling**)
to walk with difficulty; to limp.

hobby *noun* (**hobbies**)
something that you do for pleasure in your spare time. *Gardening and stamp-collecting are popular hobbies.*

hockey *noun*
an outdoor game played by two teams with curved sticks and a small hard ball.

honour

hoe *noun*
a tool for scraping up weeds.

hoe *verb* **(hoed, hoeing)**
to scrape or dig with a hoe.

hog *noun*
1 a male pig. **2** a greedy person. **3 go the whole hog,** (*informal*) to do something completely or thoroughly.

hog *verb* **(hogged, hogging)**
to take more than your fair share of something.

Hogmanay *noun*
New Year's Eve in Scotland.

hoist *verb*
to lift up, especially using ropes or pulleys.

hold *verb* **(held, holding)**
1 to have something in your hands. **2** to have; to possess or keep. *She holds the high-jump record.* **3** to keep steady; to stop somebody or something moving. *They held the thief until help arrived.* **4** to contain. *This jug holds a litre.* **5** to support. *This plank won't hold my weight.* **6** to stay unbroken; to continue. *Will this good weather hold?* **7** to believe; to value. *She held it dear.* **8** to stop. *Hold everything!* **9 hold it,** (*informal*) stop; wait a minute. **10 hold on,** to keep holding something; (*informal*) to wait. **11 hold out,** to last or continue. **12 hold your tongue,** (*informal*) stop talking. **13 hold up,** to hinder; to rob somebody with threats or force.

hold *noun*
1 holding something; a grasp. **2** something to hold on to. **3** the part of a ship where cargo is stored. **4 get hold of,** to grasp; to get; to make contact with somebody.

holdall *noun*
a large portable bag or case.

holder *noun*
a person or thing that holds something. *the holder of this job. a cigarette-holder.*

hold-up *noun*
1 a delay. **2** a robbery with threats or force.

hole *noun*
1 a gap or opening made in something. **2** a burrow.
holey *adjective*

holiday *noun*
1 a day or time when you do not go to work or school; a time when you go away to enjoy yourself. **2 on holiday,** having a holiday.

holidaymaker *noun*
someone who is on holiday.

hollow *adjective*
with an empty space inside; not solid.

hollow *verb*
to make something hollow.

hollow *noun*
1 a hollow place; a hole. **2** a small valley.

holly *noun* **(hollies)**
an evergreen bush with shiny, prickly leaves. *Holly often has red berries in winter.*

holocaust *noun*
(*say* hol-ŏ-kawst)
an immense destruction, especially by fire. *the nuclear holocaust.*

holster *noun*
a leather case for a pistol, usually attached to a belt.

holy *adjective* **(holier, holiest)**
of God; religious; revered.
holiness *noun*

home *noun*
1 the place where you live. **2** the place where you were born or where you feel you belong. **3** a place where people are looked after. *an old people's home.* **4** the place that you try to reach in a game. **5 feel at home,** to feel comfortable and happy. **6 home economics,** studying how to run a house and look after a family.
homeless *adjective*

home *adverb*
1 to or at home. *Go home! Is she home yet?* **2** to the place aimed at. *Push the bolt home.* **3 bring something home to somebody,** to make him realize it.

homely *adjective* **(homelier, homeliest)**
simple; ordinary. *a homely meal.*
homeliness *noun*

home-made *adjective*
made at home; not bought from a shop.

homesick *adjective*
sad because you are away from home.
homesickness *noun*

homestead *noun*
a farmhouse, usually with the land around it.

homeward or **homewards** *adverb*
towards home.

homework *noun*
school work that a pupil has to do at home.

homing *adjective*
trained to fly home. *a homing pigeon.*

homosexual *adjective*
(*say* hoh-mŏ-**seks**-yoo-ăl or hom-ŏ-**seks**-yoo-ăl)
loving or attracted to people of your own sex.
homosexual *noun*

honest *adjective*
not stealing, cheating, or telling lies; fair; truthful.
honestly *adverb*, **honesty** *noun*

honey *noun*
a sweet, sticky food made by bees.

honeycomb *noun*
a wax structure made by bees to hold their honey and eggs.

honeymoon *noun*
a holiday spent together by a newly-married couple.

honeysuckle *noun*
a climbing plant with fragrant yellow or pink flowers.

honk *noun*
a loud sound like the one made by a car-horn or a wild goose.

honour *noun*
1 great respect for somebody. **2** something given to a deserving person. **3** an honourable reputation. **4** a person or thing that brings honour.

honour *verb*
1 to feel or show honour for somebody. 2 to acknowledge; to accept and pay a cheque, bill, etc.

honourable *adjective*
honest or loyal.
honourably *adverb*

hood *noun*
1 a covering of soft material for the head and neck. 2 a folding roof or cover.
hooded *adjective*

hoof *noun*
the horny part of the foot of a horse, ox, or deer. *You could hear the horses' hoofs.*

hook *noun*
a piece of bent or curved metal for hanging things on or catching hold of something.
hooked *adjective*

hook *verb*
1 to catch with a hook. 2 to fasten with or on a hook.

hooligan *noun*
a rough, noisy person.

hoop *noun*
a large ring made of metal or wood.

hoop-la *noun*
a game in which you try to throw hoops around objects.

hooray *interjection*
hurrah.

hoot *noun*
1 a sound like the one made by an owl or a train-whistle. 2 a jeer. 3 **doesn't care a hoot** or **two hoots,** (*informal*) doesn't care at all.

hoot *verb*
to make a hoot.
hooter *noun*

hop *verb* **(hopped, hopping)**
1 to jump on one foot. 2 to move in jumps. 3 (*informal*) to move quickly. *Here's the car—hop in!* 4 **hop it,** (*slang*) go away. 5 **hopping mad,** (*informal*) very angry.

hop *noun*[1]
a hopping movement.

hop *noun*[2]
a climbing plant used to give beer its flavour.

hope *noun*
1 wanting something that you think will happen. 2 a person or thing that gives you hope.

hope *verb* **(hoped, hoping)**
to have hope; to expect.

hopeful *adjective*
1 feeling hope. 2 likely to be good or successful.
hopefully *adverb*

hopeless *adjective*
1 without hope. 2 very bad at something. *I'm hopeless at cricket.*
hopelessly *adverb*, **hopelessness** *noun*

hopscotch *noun*
a game in which you hop into squares drawn on the ground.

horde *noun*
a large crowd; a gang.

horizon *noun*
(*say* hŏ-**ry**-zŏn)
the line where the sky and the land or sea seem to meet.

horizontal *adjective*
(*say* ho-ri-**zon**-tǎl)
level; flat; going from left to right.
horizontally *adverb*

hormone *noun*
a substance that stimulates part of the body. *Hormones are produced naturally in the body or made artificially.*

horn *noun*
1 a kind of pointed bone that grows on the heads of bulls, cows, rams, etc. 2 a brass musical instrument that you blow. 3 a device for making a warning sound.
horny *adjective*

hornet *noun*
a large kind of wasp.

hornpipe *noun*
a lively sailors' dance.

horoscope *noun*
a forecast of future events by an astrologer.

horrible *adjective*
horrifying; nasty.
horribly *adverb*

horrid *adjective*
horrible.
horridly *adverb*

horrific *adjective*
horrifying.
horrifically *adverb*

horrify *verb* **(horrified, horrifying)**
to cause horror in somebody.

horror *noun*
1 great fear, dislike, or shock. 2 a horrifying person or thing.

horse *noun*
1 a four-legged animal used for riding, pulling carts, etc. 2 a framework to hang clothes on to dry. 3 a structure to jump over in gymnastics. 4 **on horseback,** mounted on a horse.

horse-chestnut *noun*
1 a large tree with conical clusters of blossom, producing dark brown nuts. 2 a conker.

horseman *noun* **(horsemen)**
a man who rides a horse, especially skilfully.
horsemanship *noun*, **horsewoman** *noun*

horsepower *noun* **(horsepower)**
1 a unit for measuring the power of an engine. 2 the power of an engine.

horseshoe *noun*
a U-shaped piece of metal nailed to a horse's hoof.

hose *noun*
1 a long flexible tube for carrying water or sending water at something in a stream or spray. 2 stockings and socks.

hospitable *adjective*
welcoming; liking to give hospitality.
hospitably *adverb*

hospital *noun*
a place where sick or injured people are looked after.

hospitality *noun*
welcoming people and giving them food and entertainment.

host *noun*[1]
someone who has guests and looks after them.
hostess *noun*

host *noun*[2]
a large crowd. *a host of people.*

hostage *noun*
somebody that you hold as a prisoner or threaten with death until you get what you want.

hostel *noun*
a lodging-house for travellers, students, etc.

hostile *adjective*
being an enemy; unfriendly.
hostility *noun*

hot *adjective* **(hotter, hottest)**
1 very warm; with a high temperature. **2** having a burning taste like pepper or mustard. **3** excited; angry. *a hot temper.* **4 hot air,** (*informal*) nonsense; boastful words. **5 hot line,** a direct telephone line by which important people can communicate with each other. **6 hot water,** (*informal*) trouble.
hotly *adverb*

hot *verb* **(hotted, hotting)**
hot up, (*informal*) to make or become hotter or more exciting.

hot cross bun *noun*
a spicy bun with a cross marked on it, eaten at Easter

hot dog *noun*
a hot sausage in a bread-roll.

hotel *noun*
a building where people pay to have meals and stay for the night.

hot-house *noun*
a heated greenhouse.

hotpot *noun*
a stew.

hot-water bottle *noun*
a container that you fill with hot water to make a bed warm.

hound *noun*
a dog used for hunting or racing.

hound *verb*
to chase; to harass.

hour *noun*
1 sixty minutes. **2** a particular time. *Why are you up at this hour?*

hour-glass *noun* **(hour-glasses)**
an old-fashioned device for telling the time, with sand running from one glass container into another.

hourly *adjective* and *adverb*
every hour; done once an hour.

house *noun*
(*say* howss)
1 a building where people live, usually designed for one family. **2** a building used for a special purpose. *the opera house.* **3** a building

for a government assembly; the assembly itself. *The Houses of Parliament consist of the House of Commons and the House of Lords.* **4** one of the divisions of a school for sports competitions, etc.

house *verb* **(housed, housing)**
(*say* howz)
to provide a house or room for somebody or something.

houseboat *noun*
a boat that you can live in.

household *noun*
all the people who live together in the same house.

householder *noun*
someone who owns or rents a house.

housekeeper *noun*
a woman employed to look after a household.

housekeeping *noun*
1 looking after a household. **2** the money for a household's food and other necessities.

house-proud *adjective*
very careful to keep a house clean and tidy.

house-trained *adjective*
trained to be clean in the house. *This dog is not house-trained.*

house-warming *noun*
a party to celebrate moving to a new home.

housewife *noun* **(housewives)**
a woman who does the housekeeping for her family.

housework *noun*
the work like cooking and cleaning that has to be done in a house.

housing *noun*
1 accommodation; houses. **2** a cover or guard for a piece of machinery. **3 housing estate,** a group of houses planned and built together.

hove see **heave.**

hover *verb*
1 to stay in one place in the air. **2** to wait near somebody or something; to loiter.

hovercraft *noun*
a vehicle that travels just above the surface of water or land, supported by a strong current of air.

how *adverb*
1 in what way. *How did you do it?* **2** to what extent. *How sure are you?* **3** in what condition. *How are you?* **4 how about,** would you like? *How about a game of football?* **5 how do you do?,** something said when you meet somebody. **6 how many,** what total. **7 how much,** what amount; what price. **8 how's that?,** the way to ask a cricket umpire if a batsman is out.

however *adverb*
in whatever way; to whatever extent. *You will never catch him, however hard you try.*

however *conjunction*
nevertheless; and yet. *It was snowing; however, he went out.*

howl *verb*
to make a long, loud cry like an animal in pain.

howl *noun*
a howling sound.

howler *noun*
a silly mistake.

h.p. short for **hire-purchase.**

H.Q. short for **headquarters.**

hub *noun*
the centre of a wheel.

huddle *verb* **(huddled, huddling)**
to crowd together with other people for warmth, comfort, etc.

hue *noun*[1]
a colour.

hue *noun*[2]
hue and cry, widespread alarm or protest.

huff *noun*
an annoyed or offended mood. *She's in a huff.*

hug *noun*
clasping somebody tightly in your arms, usually lovingly.

hug *verb* **(hugged, hugging)**
1 to give somebody a hug. **2** to keep close to something. *The ship hugged the shore.*

huge *adjective* **(huger, hugest)**
extremely large.
hugely *adverb*

huh *interjection*
an exclamation of contempt or questioning.

hulk *noun*
1 an old decaying ship. **2** a large, clumsy person or thing.
hulking *adjective*

hull *noun*
the main part or framework of a ship.

hullabaloo *noun*
an uproar.

hullo *interjection*
hallo.

hum *verb* **(hummed, humming)**
1 to sing a tune with your lips closed. **2** to make a low, continuous sound like a bee.

hum *noun*
a humming sound.

human *noun*
any man, woman, or child.

human *adjective*
of humans; that is a human.

humane *adjective*
(*say* hew-**mayn**)
kind; merciful.
humanely *adverb*

humanitarian *adjective*
(*say* hew-man-i-**tair**-i-ăn)
concerned with helping humanity and relieving suffering.

humanity *noun* **(humanities)**
1 mankind. **2** being human. **3** being humane; kind-heartedness. **4 humanities,** arts subjects, not sciences.

humble *adjective* **(humbler, humblest)**
modest; not proud.
humbly *adverb*

humbug *noun*
1 nonsense; deceitful talk or behaviour. **2** a hard peppermint sweet.

humid *adjective*
(*say* **hew**-mid)
damp; moist.
humidity *noun*

humiliate *verb* **(humiliated, humiliating)**
to lower somebody's pride or dignity.
humiliation *noun*

humility *noun*
being humble.

humming-bird *noun*
a small bird that makes a humming sound with its wings.

humour *noun*
1 being amusing; what makes people laugh. **2** being able to enjoy comical things. *He has no sense of humour.* **3** a mood. *Keep him in a good humour.*
humorist *noun*, **humorous** *adjective*

humour *verb*
to please somebody by doing what he wants.

hump *noun*
a round lump, especially one on a person's or camel's back.
humpback *noun*, **humpbacked** *adjective*

hump *verb*
1 to form a hump. **2** to carry something on your back.

humus *noun*
(*say* **hew**-mŭs)
rich earth made by decayed plants.

hunch *noun* **(hunches)**
1 a hump. **2** a feeling that you can guess what will happen. *I have a hunch that she won't come.*

hunch *verb*
to form into a hump. *He hunched his shoulders.*

hunchback *noun*
a person with a hump on his back.
hunchbacked *adjective*

hundred *noun*
1 the number 100, ten times ten. **2 hundreds and thousands,** tiny coloured decorations for a cake.
hundredth *adjective*

hundredweight *noun*
a unit of weight equal to 112 pounds or just over 50 kilograms.

hung past tense and past participle of **hang.**

hunger *noun*
1 feeling that you want to eat; a need for food. **2 hunger strike,** refusing to eat as a way of making a protest.

hungry *adjective* **(hungrier, hungriest)**
feeling hunger.
hungrily *adverb*

hunk *noun*
a chunk.

hunt *verb*
1 to go after a wild animal because you want to kill it. **2** to search for something.
hunter *noun*, **huntsman** *noun*

hunt noun
1 hunting, especially for foxes. 2 a group of people who go hunting.

hurdle noun
1 a frame that you jump over in hurdling. 2 an obstacle or difficulty.

hurdling noun
racing in which you run and jump over obstacles.
hurdler noun

hurl verb
to throw something as far as you can.

hurrah or **hurray** interjection
a shout of joy or approval; a cheer.

hurricane noun
a storm with a very strong wind.

hurry verb (hurried, hurrying)
1 to move quickly; to do something quickly.
2 to try to make somebody be quick.
hurriedly adverb

hurry noun
1 hurrying. 2 in a hurry, hurrying; impatient.

hurt verb (hurt, hurting)
to cause pain or harm to a person or animal.

hurtle verb (hurtled, hurtling)
to move very quickly. The train hurtled along.

husband noun
the man that a woman has married.

hush verb
1 to make or become silent. 2 hush up, to prevent people knowing about something.

husk noun
the dry covering of a seed.

husky adjective (huskier, huskiest)
1 hoarse. 2 big and strong.
huskily adverb, **huskiness** noun

husky noun (huskies)
a dog used by Eskimos.

hustle verb (hustled, hustling)
1 to hurry. 2 to jostle.

hut noun
a small house or shelter.

hutch noun (hutches)
a box or cage for a pet rabbit, etc.

hyacinth noun
a fragrant flower that grows from a bulb.

hybrid noun
an animal or plant that combines two different species. A mule is a hybrid of a donkey and a mare.

hydrangea noun
(say hy-**drayn**-jă)
a shrub with large pink, blue, or white flowers.

hydrant noun
an outdoor water-tap.

hydraulic adjective
worked by the force of water or other liquid. hydraulic brakes.
hydraulically adverb

hydrochloric acid noun
a colourless acid containing hydrogen and chlorine.

hydroelectric adjective
using water-power to make electricity.

hydrofoil noun
a boat designed to skim over the surface of the water.

hydrogen noun
1 a very light gas without colour, taste, or smell. 2 hydrogen bomb, a very powerful bomb using energy from the fusion of hydrogen nuclei.

hyena noun
(say hy-**ee**-nă)
a wild animal that looks like a wolf and makes a shrieking howl.

hygiene noun
(say hy-jeen)
keeping clean and healthy.
hygienic adjective, **hygienically** adverb

hymn noun
a religious song, usually praising God.
hymn-book noun

hypermarket noun
a very large supermarket, usually outside a town.

hyphen noun
a short dash used to join words or parts of words together. There is a hyphen in the word 'hymn-book' but not in 'hydrogen bomb'.
hyphenated adjective, **hyphenation** noun

hypnosis noun
(say hip-**noh**-sis)
a condition like a deep sleep in which someone's actions may be controlled by someone else.

hypnotism noun
(say hip-nŏ-tizm)
producing hypnosis.
hypnotic adjective, **hypnotist** noun, **hypnotize** verb

hypocrite noun
(say **hip**-ŏ-krit)
someone who pretends to be more virtuous than he really is.
hypocrisy noun, **hypocritical** adjective

hypodermic adjective
(say hy-pŏ-**der**-mik)
injecting something under the skin. a hypodermic syringe.

hypotenuse noun
(say hy-**pot**-i-newz)
the side opposite the right angle in a right-angled triangle.

hypothesis noun (hypotheses)
(say hy-**poth**-i-sis)
a suggestion that tries to explain something.
hypothetical adjective

hysteria noun
wild, uncontrollable excitement or emotion.
hysterical adjective, **hysterically** adverb, **hysterics** plural noun

I

I *pronoun*
a word used by somebody to refer to himself.

ice *noun*
1 frozen water. 2 an ice-cream.

ice *verb* (**iced, icing**)
1 to make or become icy. 2 to put icing on a cake.

iceberg *noun*
a large mass of ice floating in the sea.

ice-breaker *noun*
a ship with strong bows for breaking through ice.

ice-cream *noun*
a sweet, creamy, frozen food; a portion of this.

ice-hockey *noun*
a game like hockey played on ice by skaters.

ice-lolly *noun* (**ice-lollies**)
a piece of flavoured ice or ice-cream on a small stick.

icicle *noun*
a thin, pointed piece of ice hanging down.

icing *noun*
a sugary substance for decorating cakes.

icy *adjective* (**icier, iciest**)
like ice; very cold.
icily *adverb*

I'd short for *I had, I should,* or *I would.*

idea *noun*
something you have thought of; a plan.

ideal *adjective*
perfect.
ideally *adverb*

ideal *noun*
something that you think is perfect or worth trying to be like.

identical *adjective*
exactly the same.
identically *adverb*

identify *verb* (**identified, identifying**)
1 to discover who somebody is or what something is. 2 **identify with,** to think that you share another person's feelings, another group's beliefs, etc.
identification *noun*

identikit *noun*
a picture of someone built up from descriptions of him.

identity *noun* (**identities**)
who somebody is. *He revealed his identity by signing his name.*

idiom *noun*
(*say* id-i-ŏm)
a phrase that means something different from the meanings of the words it is composed of. *'Jump the gun' and 'on your last legs'* are idioms.
idiomatic *adjective,* **idiomatically** *adverb*

idiot *noun*
1 someone who is mentally deficient. 2 a very stupid person.
idiocy *noun,* **idiotic** *adjective,* **idiotically** *adverb*

idle *adjective* (**idler, idlest**)
1 doing nothing; lazy. 2 useless; with no particular purpose. *idle gossip.*
idly *adverb*

idol *noun*
a person or thing that people worship or treat as if it were a god.
idolatry *noun,* **idolize** *verb*

i.e. short for the Latin *id est,* which means 'that is'. *He teaches two subjects, i.e. French and German.*

if *conjunction*
1 supposing that; on condition that. *You can have this book if you pay me.* 2 although; even though. *I'll finish this job if it kills me!* 3 whenever. *I get a headache if I don't wear my glasses.* 4 whether. *Tell me if you're hungry.* 5 **if only,** I wish. *If only I were rich!*

igloo *noun*
an Eskimo's round house made of blocks of hard snow.

igneous *adjective*
(*say* ig-ni-ŭs)
formed by volcanic action. *igneous rocks.*

ignite *verb* (**ignited, igniting**)
to set light to; to set on fire.

ignition *noun*
1 igniting. 2 starting the fuel in an engine burning so as to drive a vehicle or machine.

ignorant *adjective*
not knowing about something or many things.
ignorance *noun,* **ignorantly** *adverb*

ignore *verb* (**ignored, ignoring**)
to take no notice of somebody or something.

ill *adjective*
1 not well; in bad health. 2 bad; harmful. *There were no ill effects.*

ill *adverb*
badly. *She was ill-treated.*

I'll short for *I shall* or *I will.*

illegal *adjective*
not legal; against the law.
illegally *adverb*

illegible *adjective*
(*say* i-lej-i-bŭl)
not clear enough to read.
illegibly *adverb*

illegitimate *adjective*
(*say* il-i-jit-i-măt)
not legitimate.

illiterate *adjective*
(*say* i-lit-er-ăt)
unable to read or write.
illiteracy *noun*

illness *noun* **(illnesses)**
being ill; something that makes people ill.

illogical *adjective*
not logical.
illogically *adverb*

illuminate *verb* **(illuminated, illuminating)**
1 to light something up; to decorate streets, etc. with lights. **2** to clarify or explain something.
illumination *noun*

illusion *noun*
an imaginary thing; something that you wrongly think you see.

illustrate *verb* **(illustrated, illustrating)**
1 to show something by pictures, examples, etc. **2** to put illustrations in a book.
illustrative *adjective*, **illustrator** *noun*

illustration *noun*
1 a picture in a book. **2** illustrating something. **3** an example that explains something.

illustrious *adjective*
(*say* i-**lus**-tri-ùs)
famous.

I'm short for *I am*.

image *noun*
1 a picture or statue of a person or thing. **2** what you see in a mirror, through a lens, etc. **3** a person who looks very much like another. **4** the way that people think of a person or thing.

imaginary *adjective*
not real; imagined.

imagination *noun*
being able to imagine things.
imaginative *adjective*

imagine *verb* **(imagined, imagining)**
to make pictures in your mind of things and people that you cannot see.
imaginable *adjective*

imbecile *noun*
(*say* **im**-bi-seel)
an idiot.

imitate *verb* **(imitated, imitating)**
to copy.
imitation *noun*, **imitator** *noun*

immature *adjective*
not mature.
immaturity *noun*

immediate *adjective*
1 happening or done without any delay. **2** nearest. *our immediate neighbours.*

immediately *adverb*
without any delay; at once.

immense *adjective*
huge.
immensely *adverb*, **immensity** *noun*

immerse *verb* **(immersed, immersing)**
1 to put something completely into a liquid. **2 be immersed in something,** to be very interested or involved.

immersion *noun*
1 immersing; being immersed. **2 immersion heater,** a device that heats water with an electric element immersed in the water.

immigrant *noun*
someone who has immigrated.

immigrate *verb* **(immigrated, immigrating)**
to come into a country to live there.
immigration *noun*

immobile *adjective*
not moving.
immobility *noun*

immobilize *verb* **(immobilized, immobilizing)**
to stop something moving or working.

immoral *adjective*
not moral; wicked.
immorality *noun*

immortal *adjective*
living for ever; never dying.
immortality *noun*

immune *adjective*
safe from danger or attack, especially from disease.
immunity *noun*

immunize *verb* **(immunized, immunizing)**
to make somebody immune.
immunization *noun*

imp *noun*
1 a small devil. **2** a naughty child.
impish *adjective*

impact *noun*
1 a collision; the force of a collision. **2** a strong influence or effect.

impair *verb*
to harm or weaken. *The wound impaired his health.*
impairment *noun*

impale *verb* **(impaled, impaling)**
to fix on to a sharp object; to pierce.

impartial *adjective*
not favouring one side more than the other; fair.
impartiality *noun*, **impartially** *adverb*

impassable *adjective*
that you cannot get past or through.

impatient *adjective*
not patient; in a hurry.
impatience *noun*, **impatiently** *adverb*

imperative *noun*
a command; the form of a verb that expresses a command.

imperceptible *adjective*
difficult or impossible to see.
imperceptibly *adverb*

imperfect *adjective*
not perfect; not complete.
imperfection *noun*, **imperfectly** *adverb*

imperial *adjective*
of an empire or its rulers.

impersonal *adjective*
1 not affected by personal feelings; showing no emotion. **2** not referring to a particular person.
impersonally *adverb*

impersonate *verb*
(impersonated, impersonating)
to pretend to be somebody else.
impersonation *noun*, **impersonator** *noun*

impertinent *adjective*
impudent.
impertinence *noun*

implement *noun*
(*say* im-pli-měnt)
a tool; a device for working with.

implement *verb*
(*say* im-pli-ment)
to put a plan, idea, etc. into action.

implore *verb* (**implored, imploring**)
to beg somebody to do something.

imply *verb* (**implied, implying**)
to suggest something without actually saying
it. *His silence implies that he agrees with us.*
implication *noun*

impolite *adjective*
not polite.

import *verb*
(*say* im-**port**)
to bring in goods from another country.
importer *noun*

import *noun*
(*say* im-port)
1 something imported. **2** the meaning of something.

important *adjective*
1 worth considering seriously; having a great
effect. *an important decision.* **2** powerful or
influential. *an important politician.*
importance *noun*, **importantly** *adverb*

impose *verb* (**imposed, imposing**)
1 to inflict. **2** to charge a tax. **3 impose on
somebody,** to take unfair advantage of him.

imposing *adjective*
looking important; impressive.

imposition *noun*
something imposed, especially as a punishment.

impossible *adjective*
1 not possible. **2** (*informal*) very annoying. *He
is impossible!*
impossibility *noun*, **impossibly** *adverb*

impostor *noun*
someone who is not what he pretends to be.

impress *verb*
1 to make somebody think you are very good at
something. **2 impress on,** to remind somebody
strongly about something.

impression *noun*
1 a vague idea. **2** an effect on your mind or
feelings. **3** an imitation of a person or a sound.

impressive *adjective*
impressing; having a strong effect.
impressively *adverb*

imprison *verb*
to put somebody in prison.
imprisonment *noun*

improbable *adjective*
unlikely.
improbability *noun*, **improbably** *adverb*

impromptu *adjective* and *adverb*
(*say* im-**promp**-tew)
done without any rehearsal or preparation.

improper *adjective*
1 not proper; wrong. **2** obscene.
improperly *adverb*, **impropriety** *noun*

improve *verb* (**improved, improving**)
to make or become better.
improvement *noun*

improvise *verb* (**improvised, improvising**)
1 to do something impromptu, especially to
play music without rehearsing. **2** to make
something quickly with what is available.
improvisation *noun*

impudent *adjective*
not respectful; rude.
impudence *noun*

impulse *noun*
1 a sudden desire to do something. **2** a push;
driving force. **3** (*in Physics*) a force acting for a
very short time.
impulsive *adjective*, **impulsively** *adverb*

impure *adjective*
not pure.
impurity *noun*

in *preposition*
1 at; inside. *in London.* **2** during. *in winter.*
3 into. *She has fallen in the water.* **4** arranged
as; consisting of. *a serial in four parts.* **5 in all,**
altogether.

in *adverb*
1 inwards; inside. *Get in.* **2** at home; indoors.
Is anybody in? **3** batting. *Which team is in?*
4 in for, likely to get. *You're in for a shock.* **5 in
on,** taking part in something. *I want to be in
on this game.*

inability *noun*
being unable to do something.

inaccessible *adjective*
that you cannot reach.

inaccurate *adjective*
not accurate.
inaccuracy *noun*, **inaccurately** *adverb*

inactive *adjective*
not active.
inaction *noun*, **inactivity** *noun*

inadequate *adjective*
not enough.
inadequacy *noun*, **inadequately** *adverb*

inanimate *adjective*
(*say* in-**an**-im-ăt)
not living or moving.

inappropriate *adjective*
not appropriate.
inappropriately *adverb*

inattention *noun*
not being attentive; not listening.
inattentive *adjective*

inaudible *adjective*
that you cannot hear.
inaudibility *noun*, **inaudibly** *adverb*

incapable *adjective*
unable to do something. *He is incapable of
work.*

incarnate *adjective*
having a human body. *a devil incarnate.*
incarnation *noun*

incendiary *adjective*
that starts a fire. *an incendiary bomb.*

incense *noun*
(*say* **in**-sens)
a substance that makes a spicy smell when it is burnt.

incense *verb* (**incensed, incensing**)
(*say* in-**sens**)
to make somebody very angry.

incentive *noun*
an encouragement to do something, especially to work harder.

incessant *adjective*
continual; not stopping.
incessantly *adverb*

inch *noun* (**inches**)
1 a measure of length, one-twelfth of a foot or about 2½ centimetres. **2 within an inch of his life,** so that he almost died.

incident *noun*
an event.

incidental *adjective*
1 not important. **2 incidental music,** background music.
incidentally *adverb*

incinerator *noun*
a device in which rubbish is burnt.

inclination *noun*
a tendency.

incline *verb* (**inclined, inclining**)
(*say* in-**klyn**)
1 to lean or bend. **2 be inclined,** to have a tendency to do something.

incline *noun*
(*say* in-klyn)
a slope.

include *verb* (**included, including**)
to make or consider something as part of a group of other things.
inclusion *noun*

inclusive *adjective*
including everything; including all the things mentioned. *Stay from Monday to Thursday inclusive.*

income *noun*
1 the money that you get regularly. **2 income tax,** tax charged on your income.

incompetent *adjective*
unable to do a job properly.
incompetence *noun*, **incompetently** *adverb*

incomplete *adjective*
not complete.
incompletely *adverb*

incomprehensible *adjective*
that you cannot understand.

incongruous *adjective*
(*say* in-**kong**-roo-ŭs)
not suitable or harmonious; out of place.
incongruity *noun*, **incongruously** *adverb*

inconsiderate *adjective*
not considerate.
inconsiderately *adverb*

inconsistent *adjective*
not consistent.
inconsistency *noun*, **inconsistently** *adverb*

inconspicuous *adjective*
not conspicuous.
inconspicuously *adverb*

inconvenient *adjective*
not convenient; awkward.
inconvenience *noun*, **inconveniently** *adverb*

incorporate *verb* (**incorporated, incorporating**)
to include.
incorporation *noun*

incorrect *adjective*
not correct; wrong.
incorrectly *adverb*

increase *verb* (**increased, increasing**)
(*say* in-**kreess**)
to make or become bigger.
increasingly *adverb*

increase *noun*
(*say* **in**-kreess)
increasing; the amount by which something increases.

incredible *adjective*
unbelievable.
incredibly *adverb*

incredulous *adjective*
not believing somebody.
incredulity *noun*, **incredulously** *adverb*

incubate *verb* (**incubated, incubating**)
to hatch eggs by keeping them warm.
incubation *noun*, **incubator** *noun*

indebted *adjective*
owing something to somebody.

indecent *adjective*
not decent; obscene.
indecency *noun*, **indecently** *adverb*

indeed *adverb*
really; truly; admittedly. *He was very wet indeed.*

indefinite *adjective*
1 not definite; vague. **2 indefinite article,** the word 'a' or 'an'.

indefinitely *adverb*
for an indefinite or unlimited time.

indelible *adjective*
impossible to rub out or remove.
indelibly *adverb*

indent *verb*
1 to make notches or recesses in something. **2** to print or write the beginning of a line farther to the right than usual.
indentation *noun*

independent *adjective*
not controlled or influenced by any other person or thing.
independence *noun*, **independently** *adverb*

index *noun* (**indexes**)
1 a list of names, subjects, titles, etc., especially at the end of a book. **2** a number showing how prices or wages have changed. **3 index finger,** the forefinger.

Indian *adjective*
1 of India. 2 of American Indians. 3 **Indian summer,** a warm period in late autumn.

Indian *noun*
1 an inhabitant or native of India. 2 one of the original inhabitants of North America.

indicate *verb* (**indicated, indicating**)
1 to point out or show something. 2 to be a sign of something.
indication *noun,* **indicator** *noun*

indifferent *adjective*
1 not caring about something; not interested. 2 not very good; ordinary. *an indifferent cricketer.*
indifference *noun,* **indifferently** *adverb*

indigestible *adjective*
not easy to digest.

indigestion *noun*
pain caused by difficulty in digesting food.

indignant *adjective*
angry at something that seems unfair or wicked.
indignantly *adverb,* **indignation** *noun*

indigo *noun*
a deep blue colour.

indirect *adjective*
not direct.
indirectly *adverb*

indispensable *adjective*
essential.

indistinct *adjective*
not clear.
indistinctly *adverb*

indistinguishable *adjective*
impossible to distinguish.

individual *adjective*
1 of or for one person. 2 single; separate.
individually *adverb*

individual *noun*
one person.

individuality *noun*
the things that make one person or thing different from another.

indivisible *adjective*
that you cannot divide or separate.
indivisibly *adverb*

indoctrinate *verb* (**indoctrinated, indoctrinating**)
to fill somebody's mind with particular ideas or beliefs.
indoctrination *noun*

indoor *adjective*
placed or done indoors. *indoor sports.*

indoors *adverb*
inside a building.

induce *verb* (**induced, inducing**)
1 to persuade. 2 to start the birth of a baby artificially.
inducement *noun*

indulge *verb* (**indulged, indulging**)
1 to let somebody have or do what he wants. 2 **indulge in,** to have something that you like to eat, drink, etc.
indulgence *noun,* **indulgent** *adjective*

industrial *adjective*
1 of or in industry. 2 **industrial action,** ways for workers to protest, such as striking or working to rule. 3 **Industrial Revolution,** the expansion of industry using machines in the early 19th century.
industrialist *noun,* **industrially** *adverb*

industrialize *verb* (**industrialized, industrializing**)
to increase or develop the industry in a country.
industrialization *noun*

industrious *adjective*
working hard.
industriously *adverb*

industry *noun* (**industries**)
1 making things in factories; making goods to sell. 2 being industrious.

ineffective *adjective*
not effective; inefficient.
ineffectively *adverb*

ineffectual *adjective*
ineffective; not confident or convincing.
ineffectually *adverb*

inefficient *adjective*
not efficient.
inefficiency *noun,* **inefficiently** *adverb*

inequality *noun* (**inequalities**)
not being equal.

inert *adjective*
not moving or reacting.

inertia *noun*
(*say* in-er-shă)
1 being inert. 2 the condition that makes things keep moving or stay where they are.

inevitable *adjective*
unavoidable.
inevitability *noun,* **inevitably** *adverb*

inexhaustible *adjective*
that you cannot use up completely; never-ending.

inexpensive *adjective*
not expensive; cheap.
inexpensively *adverb*

inexperience *noun*
not having experience.
inexperienced *adjective*

inexplicable *adjective*
impossible to explain.
inexplicably *adverb*

infallible *adjective*
never wrong; never-failing.
infallibility *noun,* **infallibly** *adverb*

infamous *adjective*
(*say* in-fă-mŭs)
wicked; thought to be wicked.
infamy *noun*

infant *noun*
a baby or young child.
infancy *noun*

infantile *adjective*
1 of or like infants; childish. 2 **infantile paralysis,** poliomyelitis.

infantry *noun*
soldiers trained to fight on foot.
infantryman *noun*

infect *verb*
to give somebody a disease.

infection *noun*
1 infecting. **2** an infectious disease.

infectious *adjective*
that can spread from one person to another. *an infectious disease.*

infer *verb* **(inferred, inferring)**
to reach an opinion from something that is implied; to guess. *He inferred from her silence that she agreed.*
inference *noun*

inferior *adjective*
less good or important; low or lower in position, quality, etc.
inferiority *noun*

inferior *noun*
a person who is inferior to another.

infernal *adjective*
1 like or of hell. **2** *(informal)* awful; very annoying. *an infernal nuisance.*
infernally *adverb*

inferno *noun*
(say in-**fer**-noh)
a terrifying fire.

infested *adjective*
full of troublesome things like insects, rats, etc.

infiltrate *verb* **(infiltrated, infiltrating)**
to get into a place or organization without being noticed.
infiltration *noun*, **infiltrator** *noun*

infinite *adjective*
(say in-**fin**-it)
endless; too large to be measured or imagined.
infinitely *adverb*

infinitive *noun*
(say in-**fin**-i-tiv)
the form of a verb that does not change to indicate a particular tense, etc. *The infinitive usually occurs with 'to', as in 'to go'.*

infinity *noun* **(infinities)**
(say in-**fin**-i-ti)
an infinite number or distance.

infirm *adjective*
weak; ill.
infirmity *noun*

inflame *verb* **(inflamed, inflaming)**
to make fiery, angry, or red.
inflammation *noun*, **inflammatory** *adjective*

inflammable *adjective*
that can be set alight.

inflate *verb* **(inflated, inflating)**
1 to fill something with air or gas. **2** to raise or expand too much; to make somebody too proud.
inflatable *adjective*

inflation *noun*
1 inflating. **2** a general rise in prices.
inflationary *adjective*

inflect *verb*
1 to change a word to make it fit with other words. *'Sing' is inflected to 'sang' in the past tense.* **2** to change the sound of your voice when speaking.
inflexion *noun*

inflexible *adjective*
that you cannot bend or change.
inflexibility *noun*, **inflexibly** *adverb*

inflict *verb*
to make somebody suffer something. *She inflicted a severe blow on him.*

influence *noun*
the power to affect somebody or something.
influential *adjective*

influence *verb* **(influenced, influencing)**
to have influence on somebody or something; to affect.

influenza *noun*
(say in-floo-**en**-ză)
an infectious disease that causes fever, catarrh, and pain.

inform *verb*
1 to tell somebody something. **2 inform against** or **on**, to tell the police about somebody.

informal *adjective*
not formal; relaxed. *Words in this dictionary are marked 'informal' if you would use them when you are talking but not when you are writing formally.*
informality *noun*, **informally** *adverb*

informant *noun*
a person who tells you something.

information *noun*
facts; knowledge; what someone tells you.

informative *adjective*
(say in-**form**-ă-tiv)
containing a lot of helpful information.

informed *adjective*
knowing about something.

informer *noun*
a person who informs on somebody else.

infrequent *adjective*
not frequent.
infrequency *noun*, **infrequently** *adverb*

infuriate *verb* **(infuriated, infuriating)**
to make somebody very angry.

ingenious *adjective*
clever, especially at thinking of new ways to do things.
ingeniously *adverb*, **ingenuity** *noun*

ingot *noun*
a lump of metal after it has been cast, usually shaped like a brick.

ingrained *adjective*
deep in the surface of something. *ingrained dirt.*

ingredient *noun*
(say in-**greed**-i-ent)
one of the parts of a mixture; one of the things used in a recipe.

inhabit *verb*
to live in a place.
inhabitable *adjective*, **inhabitant** *noun*

inhale *verb* (inhaled, inhaling)
to breathe in.
inhaler *noun*

inherent *adjective*
(*say* in-**heer**-ĕnt)
naturally or permanently part of something.
inherently *adverb*

inherit *verb*
1 to receive money, property, a title, etc. when
its previous owner dies. 2 to get certain qualities from your parents or predecessors.
inheritance *noun*, **inheritor** *noun*

inhospitable *adjective*
(*say* in-**hos**-pit-ă-bŭl)
not hospitable; unfriendly to visitors.

inhuman *adjective*
cruel; without pity or kindness.
inhumanity *noun*

initial *noun*
the first letter of a word or name, especially of
someone's Christian names. *Shaw's initials are
G.B., standing for George Bernard.*

initial *adjective*
first; of the beginning. *the initial stages of the
work.*
initially *adverb*

initiate *verb* (initiated, initiating)
(*say* in-**ish**-i-ayt)
1 to start something. 2 to admit somebody as a
member of a society or group, often with special
ceremonies.
initiation *noun*

initiative *noun*
(*say* in-**ish**-ă-tiv)
1 the action that starts something. *He took the
initiative in making peace.* 2 ability or power to
start things or to get them done on your own.

inject *verb*
to put a medicine or drug through somebody's
skin into their body using a hollow needle.
injection *noun*

injure *verb* (injured, injuring)
to harm or hurt somebody.
injurious *adjective*, **injury** *noun*

injustice *noun*
unjust action or treatment.

ink *noun*
a black or coloured liquid used for writing and
printing.
inky *adjective*

inkling *noun*
a slight idea or suspicion.

inland *adverb*
in or to a place away from the coast.

inlet *noun*
a strip of water reaching into the land from a
sea, river, or lake.

inn *noun*
a hotel or public house, especially in the
country.
innkeeper *noun*

inner *adjective*
1 inside; nearest the centre. 2 **inner tube**, the
inflatable tube inside a tyre.
innermost *adjective*

innings *noun* (innings)
the time when a cricket team or player is
batting.

innocent *adjective*
1 not guilty or wicked. 2 harmless.
innocence *noun*, **innocently** *adverb*

innocuous *adjective*
harmless.

innovation *noun*
1 inventing or using new things. 2 something
new that you have just invented or started
using.
innovative *adjective*, **innovator** *noun*

innumerable *adjective*
too many to be counted.

inoculate *verb* (inoculated, inoculating)
to inject somebody to protect him from a
disease.
inoculation *noun*

in-patient *noun*
someone who stays at a hospital for treatment.

input *noun*
what you put into something.

inquest *noun*
an inquiry to decide why somebody died.

inquire *verb* (inquired, inquiring)
to ask; to make an inquiry.

inquiry *noun* (inquiries)
an official investigation.

inquisitive *adjective*
always asking questions, especially about other
people's business; always trying to look at
things.
inquisitively *adverb*

insane *adjective* (insaner, insanest)
mad.
insanely *adverb*, **insanity** *noun*

insanitary *adjective*
not clean or healthy.

inscribe *verb* (inscribed, inscribing)
to write or carve something.
inscription *noun*

insect *noun*
a small animal with six legs and no backbone.
Flies, ants, butterflies, and bees are insects.

insecticide *noun*
a poison for killing unwanted insects.

insecure *adjective*
1 not secure or safe. 2 not feeling safe or confident.
insecurely *adverb*, **insecurity** *noun*

insensitive *adjective*
not sensitive.
insensitively *adverb*, **insensitivity** *noun*

inseparable *adjective*
that cannot be separated; very friendly.
inseparably *adverb*

insert *verb*
to put a thing into something else.
insertion *noun*

inside *noun*
1 the middle or centre of something; the part nearest to the middle. 2 (*informal*) your stomach or abdomen. 3 **inside out,** with the inside turned so that it faces outwards.

inside *adjective*
placed in or coming from the inside; in or nearest to the middle. *an inside page.*

inside *preposition*
on or to the inside of something. *It's inside that box.*

inside *adverb*
on or to the inside; indoors. *Come inside.*

insight *noun*
being able to see the truth about things; understanding.

insignificant *adjective*
not important or influential.
insignificance *noun*

insincere *adjective*
not sincere.
insincerely *adverb*, **insincerity** *noun*

insist *verb*
to be very firm in asking or saying something. *He insisted that he was innocent.*
insistence *noun*, **insistent** *adjective*

insolent *adjective*
very impudent; insulting.
insolence *noun*

insoluble *adjective*
1 impossible to solve. *an insoluble problem.* 2 impossible to dissolve.
insolubility *noun*

insomnia *noun*
(*say* in-**som**-ni-à)
not being able to sleep.

inspect *verb*
to look carefully at people or things; to supervise.
inspection *noun*

inspector *noun*
1 someone employed to inspect. 2 an officer in the police.

inspire *verb* (**inspired, inspiring**)
to fill somebody with good or useful thoughts or feelings. *The applause inspired her with confidence.*
inspiration *noun*

install *verb*
1 to put something in position and ready to use. *They installed central heating.* 2 to put somebody into an important position with a ceremony. *He was installed as pope.*
installation *noun*

instalment *noun*
one of the parts in which something is given or paid for gradually. *He is paying for his bike in monthly instalments.*

instance *noun*
an example. *for instance.*

instant *adjective*
1 happening immediately. *instant success.* 2 that can be made very quickly. *instant coffee.*

instant *noun*
1 a moment. *I don't believe it for an instant.* 2 an exact time. *Come here this instant!*

instantaneous *adjective*
immediate.
instantaneously *adverb*

instantly *adverb*
immediately.

instead *adverb*
in place of something else; as a substitute. *There were no potatoes, so we had bread instead.*

instep *noun*
the top of the foot between the toes and the ankle.

instinct *noun*
a natural tendency to do or feel something. *Spiders spin webs by instinct.*
instinctive *adjective*, **instinctively** *adverb*

institute *noun*
1 a society or organization. 2 a building used by a society.

institute *verb* (**instituted, instituting**)
to establish; to start.

institution *noun*
1 an institute. 2 a habit or custom; a well-known person or thing.

instruct *verb*
1 to educate. 2 to inform. 3 to tell somebody what to do.
instruction *noun*, **instructional** *adjective*, **instructive** *adjective*, **instructor** *noun*, **instructress** *noun*

instrument *noun*
1 a device for making musical sounds. 2 an implement for delicate or scientific work.

instrumental *adjective*
1 of or using musical instruments. 2 serving to do something. *She was instrumental in getting him a job.*

instrumentation *noun*
the use or arrangement of instruments.

insufficient *adjective*
not enough.
insufficiently *adverb*

insulate *verb* (**insulated, insulating**)
to cover something so as to stop the movement of heat, cold, electricity, etc.
insulation *noun*, **insulator** *noun*

insult *verb*
(*say* in-**sult**)
to speak or behave in a way that hurts somebody's feelings or pride.

insult *noun*
(*say* **in**-sult)
an insulting remark or action.

insurance *noun*
an agreement to pay regular sums of money to a firm which, in return, will compensate you if you suffer a loss, injury, etc.

insure *verb* (**insured, insuring**)
to protect yourself or your goods with insurance.

intact *adjective*
not damaged; complete.

intake *noun*
1 taking something in. 2 the number of people or things taken in. *The school had a high intake of pupils.*

integer *noun*
(*say* in-ti-jer)
a whole number.

integral *adjective*
(*say* in-ti-grăl)
1 that is an essential part of something. 2 whole; complete.
integrally *adverb*

integrate *verb* (**integrated, integrating**)
(*say* in-ti-grayt)
1 to make parts into a whole; to connect together. 2 to join together into a single community; to get people of different races to live happily together.
integration *noun*

integrity *noun*
(*say* in-**teg**-ri-ti)
honesty.

intellect *noun*
the ability to think.

intellectual *adjective*
1 of or using the intellect. 2 with a good intellect; keen to study and learn.
intellectually *adverb*

intellectual *noun*
an intellectual person.

intelligence *noun*
1 being intelligent. 2 information, especially of military value; the people who collect and study this information.

intelligent *adjective*
good at thinking and learning.
intelligently *adverb*

intelligible *adjective*
that you can understand.
intelligibility *noun*, **intelligibly** *adverb*

intend *verb*
to have in mind what you plan to do; to plan. *She was intending to go swimming.*

intense *adjective* (**intenser, intensest**)
very strong or great. *intense heat.*
intensely *adverb*

intensify *verb* (**intensified, intensifying**)
to make or become more intense.
intensification *noun*

intensity *noun* (**intensities**)
how strong or great something is.

intensive *adjective*
concentrated; thorough; using a lot of effort.
intensively *adverb*

intent *adjective*
1 eager; very interested. 2 **intent on,** eager for; intending to do something.
intently *adverb*

intent *noun*
intention. *with good intent.*

intention *noun*
what you intend; a plan.

intentional *adjective*
deliberate; intended.
intentionally *adverb*

interact *verb*
to have an effect on one another.
interaction *noun*

intercept *verb*
to stop or catch a person or thing going from one place to another.
interception *noun*, **interceptor** *noun*

interchange *verb* (**interchanged, interchanging**)
1 to put two things in each other's place. 2 to give and receive something; to exchange.
interchangeable *adjective*, **interchangeably** *adverb*

interchange *noun*
1 interchanging. 2 a place where you can move from one motorway, etc. to another.

intercom *noun*
(*informal*) a device for communicating by radio, telephone, etc.

intercourse *noun*
1 communication or dealings between people. 2 sexual intercourse.

interest *verb*
to make somebody want to look, listen, help with something, etc.

interest *noun*
1 being interested; curiosity. 2 a thing that interests somebody. 3 money paid regularly in return for money loaned or deposited.

interfere *verb* (**interfered, interfering**)
1 to take part in something that has nothing to do with you. 2 to get in the way.
interference *noun*

interior *noun*
the inside of something.

interjection *noun*
an exclamation. *Interjections are words like 'ah' and 'oh'.*

interlock *verb*
to fit into one another. *The gear-wheels interlocked.*

interlude *noun*
1 an interval. 2 music played during an interval.

intermediate *adjective*
coming between two things in place, order, time, etc.

interminable *adjective*
(*say* in-ter-min-ă-bŭl)
endless; seeming to go on for ever.
interminably *adverb*

intermission *noun*
an interval in a play, film, etc.

intermittent *adjective*
happening at intervals.
intermittently *adverb*

intern *verb*
to imprison somebody in a special camp or building, usually in wartime.
internee *noun*, **internment** *noun*

internal *adjective*
1 of or in the inside of something. 2 **internal-combustion engine**, an engine that makes power by burning fuel inside the engine. *Cars have internal-combustion engines.*
internally *adverb*

international *adjective*
of, in, or concerning more than one country. *Interpol is an international police organization.*
internationally *adverb*

interplanetary *adjective*
between planets. *interplanetary travel.*

interpret *verb*
1 to explain what something means. 2 to translate from one language into another.
interpretation *noun*, **interpreter** *noun*

interrogate *verb* (**interrogated, interrogating**)
to question somebody closely.
interrogation *noun*, **interrogator** *noun*

interrupt *verb*
to stop somebody talking or something going on.
interruption *noun*

intersect *verb*
to cross or divide something. *intersecting lines.*
intersection *noun*

interstellar *adjective*
between the stars.

interval *noun*
1 a time between two events or between two parts of a play, film, etc. 2 a space between two things. 3 **at intervals**, with some time or distance between each one; not continuously.

intervene *verb* (**intervened, intervening**)
1 to come between two events. *in the intervening years.* 2 to interrupt an argument, fight, etc. and try to stop it or change its result.
intervention *noun*

interview *noun*
a meeting with somebody to ask him questions or to discuss something.

interview *verb*
to have an interview with somebody.
interviewer *noun*

intestine *noun* or **intestines** *plural noun*
the long tube along which food passes from the stomach.
intestinal *adjective*

intimate *adjective*
(*say* **in**-tim-ăt)
1 very friendly. 2 private; personal. *intimate thoughts.* 3 detailed; close. *intimate knowledge.*
intimacy *noun*, **intimately** *adverb*

intimate *verb* (**intimated, intimating**)
(*say* **in**-tim-ayt)
to tell or hint.
intimation *noun*

intimidate *verb* (**intimidated, intimidating**)
to frighten somebody so as to make him do something.
intimidation *noun*

into *preposition*
1 to the inside of; to a place inside. *Go into the house.* 2 to a particular condition, situation, job, etc. *He got into trouble. She got into acting.* 3 saying how many times one number is included in another. *3 into 12 goes 4.*

intolerable *adjective*
unbearable. *intolerable noise.*
intolerably *adverb*

intolerant *adjective*
not tolerant.
intolerance *noun*, **intolerantly** *adverb*

intonation *noun*
the pitch or tone of a voice or musical instrument.

intoxicate *verb* (**intoxicated, intoxicating**)
1 to make somebody drunk. 2 to make somebody very excited.
intoxication *noun*

intransitive *adjective*
used without a direct object. *'Giggle' and 'tingle' are intransitive verbs.*
intransitively *adverb*

intrepid *adjective*
brave; fearless.
intrepidly *adverb*

intricate *adjective*
complicated.
intricacy *noun*, **intricately** *adverb*

intrigue *verb* (**intrigued, intriguing**)
(*say* in-**treeg**)
1 to interest somebody very much. 2 to make secret plans.

introduce *verb* (**introduced, introducing**)
1 to make somebody known to other people. 2 to announce a broadcast, speaker, etc. 3 to start something being used or considered.

introduction *noun*
1 introducing somebody or something. 2 a piece at the beginning of a book, speech, etc.
introductory *adjective*

intrude *verb* (**intruded, intruding**)
to come in where you are not wanted; to interfere.
intrusion *noun*, **intrusive** *adjective*

intruder *noun*
1 someone who intrudes. 2 a burglar.

intuition *noun*
(*say* in-tew-**ish**-ŏn)
the power to know or understand things without having to think hard.
intuitive *adjective*

inundate *verb* (**inundated, inundating**)
to flood.
inundation *noun*

invade *verb* (**invaded, invading**)
to attack and enter a country, place, etc.
invader *noun*

invalid *noun*
(*say* **in**-vă-leed)
someone who is ill or weakened by a long illness.

invalid *adjective*
(*say* in-**val**-id)
not valid. *This passport is invalid.*

invaluable *adjective*
very valuable.

invariable *adjective*
that never changes.

invariably *adverb*
always.

invasion *noun*
invading or being invaded.

invent *verb*
to be the first person to make or think of a particular thing.
invention *noun*, **inventive** *adjective*, **inventor** *noun*

inverse *adjective*
reversed; opposite.
inversely *adverb*

invert *verb*
1 to turn something upside down. **2 inverted commas**, punctuation marks, "" or '', put before or after spoken words.
inversion *noun*

invertebrate *noun*
(*say* in-**vert**-i-brăt)
an animal without a backbone.

invest *verb*
1 to use money so as to earn interest or make a profit. **2** to give somebody an honour, medal, etc.
investment *noun*, **investor** *noun*

investigate *verb* (**investigated, investigating**)
to find out as much as you can about something, especially about a crime.
investigation *noun*, **investigator** *noun*

invigilate *verb* (**invigilated, invigilating**)
to supervise candidates at an examination.
invigilation *noun*, **invigilator** *noun*

invigorate *verb* (**invigorated, invigorating**)
to give somebody vigour or courage.

invincible *adjective*
that cannot be defeated.
invincibly *adverb*

invisible *adjective*
that you cannot see.
invisibility *noun*, **invisibly** *adverb*

invite *verb* (**invited, inviting**)
to ask somebody politely to do something, especially to come to a party, etc.
invitation *noun*

inviting *adjective*
attractive; tempting.
invitingly *adverb*

invoice *noun*
a list of goods sent or work done, with the prices charged.

involuntary *adjective*
not deliberate; unintentional.
involuntarily *adverb*

involve *verb* (**involved, involving**)
1 to mean; to result in. *The job involved great effort.* **2** to affect; to make somebody part of something. *We are involved in charity work.* **3** involved, complicated.
involvement *noun*

inward *adjective*
1 on the inside. **2** going or facing inwards.
inwardly *adverb*

inward *adverb*
inwards.

inwards *adverb*
towards the inside.

iodine *noun*
(*say* I-ŏ-deen or I-ŏ-dyn)
a chemical used as an antiseptic.

ion *noun*
(*say* I-ŏn)
an electrically-charged particle.

IOU *noun*
(*say* I-oh-yoo)
a piece of paper on which you write that you owe somebody money.

iris *noun* (**irises**)
1 the coloured part of the eyeball. **2** a flower with long, pointed leaves.

Irish *adjective*
of Ireland.
Irishman *noun*, **Irishwoman** *noun*

iron *noun*
1 a strong, heavy metal. **2** a device that is heated for smoothing clothes or cloth. **3** a tool made of iron. *a branding-iron.* **4 Iron Curtain**, the frontier dividing Russia and associated countries from the other countries of the world. **5 irons**, fetters.

iron *verb*
to smooth clothes or cloth with an iron.

ironic *adjective*
(*say* I-ron-ik)
using irony; full of irony.
ironical *adjective*, **ironically** *adverb*

ironing-board *noun*
a folding table on which clothes are ironed.

ironmonger *noun*
someone who keeps a shop that sells tools, nails, and other metal things.
ironmongery *noun*

irony *noun* (**ironies**)
(*say* I-rŏn-i)
1 saying the opposite of what you mean so as to emphasize it. *You use irony if you say 'What a lovely day' when it is pouring with rain.* **2** an unexpected or strange event or situation.

irrational *adjective*
not rational.
irrationality *noun*, **irrationally** *adverb*

irregular *adjective*
1 not regular; not usual. **2** against the rules.
irregularity *noun*, **irregularly** *adverb*

irrelevant *adjective*
(*say* i-rel-i-vănt)
not relevant.
irrelevance *noun*, **irrelevantly** *adverb*

irresistible *adjective*
that you cannot resist; very attractive.
irresistibly *adverb*

irresponsible *adjective*
not trustworthy or sensible.
irresponsibility *noun*, **irresponsibly** *adverb*

irreverent *adjective*
not reverent; not respectful.
irreverence *noun*, **irreverently** *adverb*

irrigate *verb* **(irrigated, irrigating)**
to supply land with water so that crops can grow.
irrigation *noun*

irritable *adjective*
easily annoyed; bad-tempered.
irritability *noun*, **irritably** *adverb*

irritate *verb* **(irritated, irritating)**
1 to annoy somebody. **2** to make part of your body itch or feel sore.
irritant *noun*, **irritation** *noun*

is 3rd person singular present tense of **be**.

Islam *noun*
(*say* **iz**-lahm)
the religion of Muslims.
Islamic *adjective*

island *noun*
a piece of land surrounded by water.
islander *noun*

isle *noun*
an island.

isn't short for *is not*.

isobar *noun*
(*say* **I**-sō-bar)
a line on a map connecting places that have the same atmospheric pressure.

isolate *verb* **(isolated, isolating)**
to separate; to put somebody or something apart from others.
isolation *noun*

isosceles *adjective*
(*say* I-**sos**-i-leez)
(*of a triangle*) with two sides equal.

isotope *noun*
(*say* **I**-sō-tohp)
a form of an element that is different from other forms in nuclear properties but not chemical properties.

Israeli *adjective*
(*say* iz-**ray**-li)
of Israel.

issue *verb* **(issued, issuing)**
1 to send or give out; to supply. *They issued blankets to the refugees.* **2** to publish; to put into circulation. *The dictionary was issued in parts.* **3** to come out. *Smoke was issuing from the chimney.*

issue *noun*
1 issuing something. *the issue of passports.*

2 something issued. *a Christmas issue of stamps.* **3** a magazine or newspaper brought out at a particular time. *Tuesday's issue of The Guardian.* **4** a subject for discussion or concern. *What are the real issues?* **5** a result. *Await the issue.*

isthmus *noun* **(isthmuses)**
(*say* **iss**-mŭs)
a narrow strip of land connecting two larger pieces of land.

it *pronoun*
1 the thing being talked about. **2** the player in a game who has to catch other people.

Italian *adjective*
of Italy.

italic *adjective*
(*say* it-**al**-ik)
printed sloping *like this*.
italicize *verb*

italics *plural noun*
(*say* it-**al**-iks)
italic letters.

itch *noun* **(itches)**
1 a tickling feeling in your skin that makes you want to scratch it. **2** a longing to do something. *He has an itch to go to America.*
itchy *adjective*

itch *verb*
to have an itch.

item *noun*
one thing in a list or group of things, especially a piece of news.

itinerary *noun* **(itineraries)**
(*say* I-**tin**-er-er-i)
a list of places to be visited on a journey; a route.

it'll short for *it will*.

its *pronoun*
of it; belonging to it. *The cat hurt its paw.*

it's short for *it is*. *Can you see if it's raining?*

itself *pronoun*
1 it and nothing else. **2** **by itself,** on its own; alone.

ITV short for *Independent Television*.

ivory *noun* **(ivories)**
1 the hard creamy-white substance that forms elephants' tusks. **2** a creamy-white colour. **3 ivories,** (*slang*) the keys of a piano.

ivy *noun* **(ivies)**
a climbing evergreen plant with shiny leaves.

J

jab *verb* **(jabbed, jabbing)**
to poke; to stab or pierce.

jab *noun*
1 a jabbing movement. **2** (*informal*) an injection.

jabber *verb*
to speak quickly and not clearly; to chatter.

jack *noun*
1 a device for lifting something heavy off the ground. **2** a playing-card with a picture of a knave on it. **3** a small white ball that you aim at in the game of bowls.

jack *verb*
1 to lift something with a jack. **2** jack in, (*slang*) to give up or abandon something.

jackal *noun*
a wild animal rather like a dog.

jackass *noun* (jackasses)
1 a male donkey. **2** a stupid person. **3** laughing jackass, a kookaburra.

jackdaw *noun*
a bird like a small crow. *Jackdaws sometimes steal bright things and hide them.*

jacket *noun*
1 a coat which covers the top half of the body. **2** a cover for a book, water-heater, etc. **3** the skin of a potato that is baked without being peeled.

jack-in-the-box *noun* (jack-in-the-boxes)
a toy figure that springs out of a box when you lift the lid.

jackpot *noun*
an amount of prize-money that increases until someone wins it.

jade *noun*
a green stone which is carved to make ornaments.

jaded *adjective*
tired and bored; weary.

jagged *adjective*
(*say* jag-id)
uneven and sharp.

jaguar *noun*
a large, fierce animal rather like a leopard.

jail *noun*
a prison.
jailer *noun*

Jain *noun*
(rhymes with *mine*)
a believer in an Indian religion rather like Buddhism.

jam *noun*
1 a sweet food made of fruit boiled with sugar until it is thick. **2** a lot of people, cars, logs, etc. crowded together so that it is difficult to move. *a traffic jam.* **3** (*informal*) a difficult situation. *He's in a jam.* **4** (*informal*) something very easy. *Doing this job is money for jam.*

jam *verb* (jammed, jamming)
1 to make or become fixed and difficult to move. *The door has jammed.* **2** to squeeze or wedge. *I jammed my fingers in the door.*

jamboree *noun*
1 a large party or celebration. **2** a large gathering of Scouts.

jammy *adjective*
1 smeared or sticky with jam. **2** (*informal*) very easy or lucky.

jangle *verb* (jangled, jangling)
to make a harsh ringing sound.

January *noun*
the first month of the year.

Japanese *adjective*
of Japan.

jar *noun*
a container made of glass or earthenware.

jar *verb* (jarred, jarring)
1 to make a harsh sound or jolt. **2** to have an unpleasant effect on your feelings.

jaundice *noun*
a disease that makes your skin yellow.

jaunt *noun*
a short pleasure-trip.

jaunty *adjective* (jauntier, jauntiest)
lively and cheerful.
jauntily *adverb,* **jauntiness** *noun*

javelin *noun*
a light spear.

jaw *noun*
1 the lower part of the face. **2** one of the two bones that hold the teeth.

jay *noun*
a noisy, brightly-coloured bird.

jazz *noun*
a kind of music with strong rhythm, often improvised.
jazzy *adjective*

jealous *adjective*
unhappy or resentful because you feel that somebody rivals you or is better or luckier than you.
jealously *adverb,* **jealousy** *noun*

jeans *plural noun*
trousers made of strong, usually blue, cloth.

Jeep *noun*
a small, sturdy motor car used especially on rough ground.

jeer *verb*
to laugh or shout at somebody rudely or scornfully.

jelly *noun* (jellies)
1 a soft, sweet food that melts in your mouth. **2** any soft, slippery substance.
jellied *adjective*

jellyfish *noun* (jellyfish)
a sea animal with a body like jelly.

jerk *verb*
to make a sudden sharp movement.

jerk *noun*
1 a jerking movement. **2** (*slang*) a fool.
jerkily *adverb,* **jerkiness** *noun,* **jerky** *adjective*

jersey *noun*
a pullover with sleeves.

jest *noun*
1 a joke. **2** in jest, joking; not seriously.

jester *noun*
a professional entertainer at a king's court in the Middle Ages.

jet *noun*[1]
1 a stream of liquid, gas, flame, etc. forced out of a narrow opening. 2 a narrow opening from which a jet comes out. *a gas-jet.* 3 a jet aircraft. 4 **jet aircraft**, an aircraft with jet engines. 5 **jet engine**, an engine that sends out a jet of hot gas at the back.
jet-propelled *adjective*, **jet-propulsion** *noun*

jet *noun*[2]
1 a hard black mineral. 2 a deep glossy black colour.

jet *verb* **(jetted, jetting)**
1 to come or send out in a strong stream. 2 (*informal*) to travel in a jet aircraft.

jetty *noun* **(jetties)**
a small landing-stage.

Jew *noun*
1 a member of the race of people descended from the ancient tribes of Israel. 2 someone who believes in Judaism.
Jewess *noun*, **Jewish** *adjective*

jewel *noun*
a precious stone; an ornament.
jewelled *adjective*

jeweller *noun*
someone who sells or makes jewellery.

jewellery *noun*
jewels or ornaments that you wear.

jib *noun*
1 a triangular sail stretching forward from the mast. 2 the projecting arm of a crane.

jig *noun*
1 a lively dance. 2 a device that holds something in place while you work on it with tools.

jig *verb* **(jigged, jigging)**
1 to dance a jig. 2 to move up and down quickly and jerkily.

jigsaw *noun*
1 a saw that can cut curved shapes. 2 a jigsaw puzzle. 3 **jigsaw puzzle**, a puzzle made of shapes that you fit together to make a picture.

jingle *verb* **(jingled, jingling)**
to make a tinkling or clinking sound.

jingle *noun*
1 a jingling sound. 2 a verse or group of words with repetitive sounds. 3 a simple song used in a broadcast commercial.

job *noun*
1 work that someone does regularly to earn a living. *He got a job as a postman.* 2 a particular task. *We shall have tea when we finish this job.* 3 (*informal*) a difficult task. *You'll have a job to lift that box.* 4 (*informal*) a situation; a state of affairs. *It's a good job you're here.* 5 **just the job**, (*informal*) exactly what you want.

jockey *noun*
someone who rides horses in races.

jodhpurs *plural noun*
(*say* **jod**-perz)
trousers for horse-riding, fitting closely from the knee to the ankle.

jog *verb* **(jogged, jogging)**
1 to run slowly, especially for exercise. 2 to give something a slight knock or push. 3 **jog somebody's memory**, to help him remember something.
jogger *noun*

jogtrot *noun*
a slow trot.

join *verb*
1 to put or come together; to fasten or unite. 2 to become a member of an organization, group, etc. 3 **join in**, to take part in something.

join *noun*
a place where things join.

joiner *noun*
someone whose job is to make furniture and other things out of wood.
joinery *noun*

joint *noun*
1 a join. 2 the place where two bones fit together. 3 a large piece of meat.

joint *adjective*
shared or done by two or more people, countries, etc.
jointly *adverb*

joist *noun*
a long beam supporting a floor or ceiling.

joke *noun*
1 something said or done to make people laugh. 2 a trick. 3 **no joke**, something serious.

joke *verb* **(joked, joking)**
to make jokes.
jokingly *adverb*

joker *noun*
1 someone who jokes. 2 a playing-card with a picture of a jester on it, used in some games as the highest trump. 3 (*slang*) a person; a fool.

jolly *adjective* **(jollier, jolliest)**
happy; cheerful.
jollity *noun*

jolly *adverb*
(*informal*) very. *That film was jolly good!*

jolt *verb*
to jerk; to move jerkily.

jolt *noun*
1 a jolting movement. 2 a surprise or shock.

jostle *verb* **(jostled, jostling)**
to push roughly.

jot *verb* **(jotted, jotting)**
to write something quickly.

jotter *noun*
a notebook.

journal *noun*
1 a newspaper or magazine. 2 a diary.

journalist *noun*
someone who writes for a newspaper or magazine.
journalism *noun*, **journalistic** *adjective*

journey *noun*
1 going from one place to another. 2 the distance you travel or the time you take to travel somewhere. *a day's journey.*

journey *verb*
to make a journey.

joust

joust *verb*
to fight on horseback with lances. *Jousting was popular in the Middle Ages.*

jovial *adjective*
cheerful; good-humoured.
joviality *noun,* **jovially** *adverb*

joy *noun*
1 great happiness. **2** (*informal*) success or satisfaction. *I tried to claim my money back but I got no joy.*

joyful *adjective*
very happy.
joyfully *adverb*

joyous *adjective*
joyful.
joyously *adverb*

joy-ride *noun*
(*informal*) a ride in a motor car, usually without its owner's permission.

jubilant *adjective*
(*say* **joo**-bil-ǎnt)
rejoicing; joyful.
jubilantly *adverb,* **jubilation** *noun*

jubilee *noun*
(*say* **joo**-bil-i)
a special anniversary. *A silver jubilee is the 25th anniversary; a golden jubilee is the 50th anniversary; and a diamond jubilee is the 60th anniversary.*

Judaism *noun*
(*say* **joo**-day-izm)
the religion of the Jewish people.

judge *noun*
1 someone appointed to hear cases in a law-court and decide what should be done. **2** someone appointed to decide who has won a contest or competition. **3** someone who is good at forming opinions or making decisions about things. *She's a good judge of character.*

judge *verb* **(judged, judging)**
1 to act as judge for a case or contest. **2** to estimate or guess; to form an opinion about something.

judgement *noun*
1 judging. **2** the decision made in a lawcourt. **3** ability to judge wisely. **4** someone's opinion. **5** something considered as a punishment from God. *Your failure is a judgement on you!*

judicial *adjective*
(*say* joo-**dish**-ǎl)
of lawcourts, judges, or judgements.
judicially *adverb*

judicious *adjective*
(*say* joo-**dish**-ūs)
having or showing good sense.
judiciously *adverb*

judo *noun*
(*say* **joo**-doh)
a Japanese method of wrestling and self-defence.

jug *noun*
a container for liquids, with a handle and lip.

juggernaut *noun*
a huge lorry.

juggle *verb* **(juggled, juggling)**
to keep a number of objects moving in the air without dropping any.
juggler *noun*

juice *noun*
the liquid from fruit, vegetables, or other food.
juicy *adjective*

juke-box *noun* **(juke-boxes)**
a machine that plays a record when you put a coin in.

July *noun*
the seventh month of the year.

jumble *verb* **(jumbled, jumbling)**
to mix things up in confusion.

jumble *noun*
1 a confused mixture; a muddle. **2 jumble sale,** a sale of second-hand goods to raise money for charity, etc.

jumbo jet *noun*
a huge jet aircraft.

jump *verb*
1 to move up suddenly from the ground into the air. **2** to go over something by jumping. *The horse jumped the fence.* **3** to move quickly or suddenly. *He jumped out of his seat.* **4 jump at,** (*informal*) to accept something eagerly. **5 jump the gun,** to start before you should. **6 jump the queue,** not to wait for your proper turn.

jump *noun*
1 a jumping movement. **2** an obstacle to jump over.

jumper *noun*
1 a person or animal that jumps. **2** a jersey.

jumpy *adjective* **(jumpier, jumpiest)**
nervous.

junction *noun*
a place where roads or railway lines join.

June *noun*
the sixth month of the year.

jungle *noun*
a thick, tangled forest, especially in a hot country.
jungly *adjective*

junior *adjective*
1 younger. **2** for young children. *a junior school.* **3** lower in rank or importance.

junior *noun*
a junior person.

junk *noun*[1]
rubbish; things that are worth little or nothing.

junk *noun*[2]
a Chinese sailing-boat.

junket *noun*
1 a sweet, runny food made from milk. **2** a party, celebration, or outing.

kettle

jury *noun* **(juries)**
a group of people appointed to make a decision about a case in a lawcourt. *There are usually 12 people in a jury.*
juror *noun,* **juryman** *noun,* **jurywoman** *noun*

just *adjective*
1 fair; right; giving proper consideration to everybody. **2** deserved. *He got his just reward.*
justly *adverb*

just *adverb*
1 exactly. *It's just what I wanted.* **2** only; simply. *I just wanted another cake.* **3** hardly; barely; by only a short distance. *just below the belt.* **4** near this moment. *She has just gone.*

justice *noun*
1 fairness; being just. **2** the law. **3 do justice to something,** to be fair to it; to show or use it in the best way possible.

justify *verb* **(justified, justifying)**
to show that something is fair, reasonable, or acceptable.
justifiable *adjective,* **justifiably** *adverb,*
justification *noun*

jut *verb* **(jutted, jutting)**
to stick out.

juvenile *adjective*
(*say* **joo**-vi-nyl)
1 of or for young people. **2 juvenile delinquent,** a young person who breaks the law.

K

kaleidoscope *noun*
(*say* kăl-l-dŏs-kohp)
a tube that you look through to see brightly-coloured patterns which change as you turn the end of the tube.
kaleidoscopic *adjective*

kangaroo *noun*
an Australian animal that jumps on its strong hind legs. *Female kangaroos have pouches in which they carry their babies.*

karate *noun*
(*say* kă-**rah**-ti)
a Japanese method of self-defence using the hands, arms, and feet.

kayak *noun*
(*say* **ky**-ak)
a canoe with a covering over the top.

keel *noun*
1 the long piece of wood or metal along the bottom of a boat. **2 on an even keel,** steady or steadily.

keel *verb*
to tilt or overturn. *The ship keeled over.*

keen *adjective*
1 enthusiastic; very interested. *She is keen on swimming.* **2** sharp. *a keen knife.* **3** very cold. *a keen wind.*
keenly *adverb,* **keenness** *noun*

keep *verb* **(kept, keeping)**
1 to have something and not get rid of it. **2** to stay; to remain. *Keep still!* **3** to make somebody or something stay in the same position or condition. *The fire kept us warm.* **4** to stay in good condition. *Will the milk keep until tomorrow?* **5** to prevent. *How can we keep the teacher from knowing?* **6** to do something continually. *She kept laughing.* **7** to be faithful to something; not to break something. *He kept his* promise. **8** to look after; to give a home and food to people or animals. *They keep chickens.* **9 keep up,** to make the same progress as others; to continue something.

keep *noun*
1 the food or money that you need to live. *She earns her keep.* **2** a strong tower in a castle. **3 for keeps,** (*informal*) to keep; permanently. *Is this football mine for keeps?*

keeper *noun*
someone who looks after an animal, place, building, etc. *a lighthouse-keeper. the park-keeper.*

keeping *noun*
1 care; looking after something. *in safe keeping.* **2 in keeping with,** agreeing with; suiting.

keg *noun*
a small barrel.

kennel *noun*
a small hut for a dog.

kept past tense and past participle of **keep** *verb.*

kerb *noun*
the edge of a pavement.
kerbstone *noun*

kernel *noun*
the eatable part in the middle of a nut.

kestrel *noun*
a kind of falcon.

ketchup *noun*
a thick sauce made from tomatoes.

kettle *noun*
1 a metal container with a spout and handle, used for boiling water in. **2 a pretty kettle of fish,** a strange or difficult situation.

kettledrum *noun*
a drum made of skin stretched over a metal hemisphere.

key *noun*
1 a piece of metal shaped so that it opens a lock. 2 a device for winding up a clockwork train, clock, etc. 3 a small lever that you press with your finger. *Typewriters and pianos have keys.* 4 a scale of musical notes related to each other. *the key of C major.* 5 a thing that explains or solves something. *the key to the mystery.*

keyboard *noun*
the set of keys on a piano, typewriter, etc.

keyhole *noun*
the hole through which a key is put into a lock.

keynote *noun*
1 the note on which a key in music is based. *The keynote of C major is C.* 2 the main idea in something said, written, or done.

kg. short for **kilogram.**

khaki *noun*
(*say* **kah**-ki)
a dull yellowish brown colour.

kibbutz *noun* (**kibbutzim**)
a commune in Israel, especially for farming.

kick *verb*
1 to hit somebody or something with your foot. 2 to move your legs about vigorously. 3 (*of a gun*) to recoil when it is fired. 4 **kick off,** to start a football match; (*informal*) to start doing something. 5 **kick out,** to get rid of; to dismiss. 6 **kick up,** (*informal*) to make a noise or fuss.

kick *noun*
1 a kicking movement. 2 the recoiling movement of a gun. 3 (*informal*) a thrill; a bit of excitement or pleasure. 4 (*informal*) an interest or activity. *He's on a health kick.*

kick-off *noun*
the start of a football match.

kid *noun*
1 a young goat. 2 (*informal*) a child.

kid *verb* (**kidded, kidding**)
(*informal*) to deceive or tease.

kidnap *verb* (**kidnapped, kidnapping**)
to take somebody away and keep him prisoner until you get what you want.
kidnapper *noun*

kidney *noun*
1 one of two organs in the body that remove unwanted substances from the blood and excrete them in urine. 2 **kidney machine,** a machine that does what the kidneys should do, used by someone with kidney disease.

kill *verb*
1 to make somebody or something die. 2 to destroy; to put an end to something.
killer *noun*

kiln *noun*
an oven for hardening or drying pottery, bricks, hops, etc.

kilo *noun*
a kilogram.

kilogram *noun*
a unit of weight equal to 1,000 grams or about 2⅕ pounds.

kilometre *noun*
(*say* **kil**-ŏ-meet-er or kil-**om**-it-er)
a unit of length equal to 1,000 metres or about ⅗ of a mile.

kilowatt *noun*
a unit of electrical power equal to 1,000 watts.

kilt *noun*
a kind of pleated skirt worn especially by Scotsmen.
kilted *adjective*

kin *noun*
1 your family or relatives. 2 **next of kin,** your closest relative.

kind *noun*
1 a type or sort of something. *What kind of food do you like?* 2 **kind of,** (*informal*) vague or vaguely. *I kind of hoped you would come.*

kind *adjective*
ready to help and love other people; friendly.
kind-hearted *adjective*, **kindness** *noun*

kindergarten *noun*
(*say* **kin**-der-gar-tĕn)
a school or class for very young children.

kindle *verb* (**kindled, kindling**)
1 to set light to something. 2 to start burning.

kindling *noun*
small pieces of wood for lighting fires.

kindly *adverb*
1 in a kind way. 2 please. *Kindly close the door.*

kindly *adjective* (**kindlier, kindliest**)
kind. *She gave a kindly smile.*
kindliness *noun*

kinetic *adjective*
(*say* kin-**et**-ik)
of or produced by movement. *kinetic energy.*

king *noun*
1 a man who has been crowned as the ruler of a country. 2 a piece in chess. 3 a playing-card with a picture of a king on it.
kingly *adjective*

kingdom *noun*
a country that is ruled by a king or queen.

kingfisher *noun*
a brightly-coloured bird that lives near water and catches fish.

kink *noun*
1 a short twist in a rope, wire, piece of hair, etc. 2 something peculiar or eccentric.
kinky *adjective*

kiosk *noun*
(*say* **kee**-osk)
1 a telephone box. 2 a small hut or stall where newspapers, sweets, tobacco, etc. are sold.

kipper *noun*
a smoked herring.

kiss *noun* (**kisses**)
touching somebody with your lips as a sign of affection.

kiss *verb*
to give somebody a kiss.

kit *noun*
1 equipment; clothes. 2 a set of parts sold to be fitted together.

kitchen *noun*
a room where food is prepared and cooked.

kite *noun*
a light frame covered with cloth, paper, etc. and flown in the wind at the end of a long piece of string.

kitten *noun*
a very young cat.
kittenish *adjective*

kitty *noun*[1] **(kitties)**
1 an amount of money that you can win in a game. 2 a fund.

kitty *noun*[2] **(kitties)**
(informal) a kitten.

kiwi *noun*
(say **kee**-wee)
a New Zealand bird that cannot fly.

knack *noun*
a special skill.

knapsack *noun*
a bag carried on the back by hikers, soldiers, etc.

knave *noun*
1 *(old-fashioned use)* a dishonest man. 2 the jack in a pack of playing-cards.
knavery *noun,* **knavish** *adjective*

knead *verb*
to press and stretch something soft, especially dough, with your hands.

knee *noun*
the joint in the middle of the leg.

kneecap *noun*
the bony part at the front of the knee.

kneel *verb* **(knelt, kneeling)**
to be or get into a position on your knees.

knew past tense of **know.**

knickers *plural noun*
underpants worn by women or girls.

knife *noun* **(knives)**
a cutting instrument made of a short blade set in a handle.

knife *verb* **(knifed, knifing)**
to stab somebody with a knife.

knight *noun*
1 a man who has been given the honour that lets him put 'Sir' before his name. 2 a piece in chess, with a horse's head.
knighthood *noun*

knit *verb* **(knitted** or **knit, knitting)**
to make something by looping together woollen or other yarn, using long needles or a machine.
knitter *noun,* **knitting-needle** *noun*

knives plural of **knife** *noun.*

knob *noun*
1 the round handle of a door, drawer, etc. 2 a lump or swelling. 3 a control to adjust a radio or television set, etc.
knobbly *adjective,* **knobby** *adjective*

knock *verb*
1 to hit something hard or by accident.
2 *(informal)* to criticize something unfavourably. 3 **knock off,** *(informal)* to stop working; to deduct something from a price; to steal something. 4 **knock out,** to hit somebody so as to make him unconscious.

knock *noun*
the act or sound of knocking.

knocker *noun*
a device for knocking on a door.

knock-out *noun*
1 knocking somebody out. 2 a contest in which competitors have to drop out one by one. 3 *(slang)* an excellent person or thing.

knot *noun*
1 a place where pieces of string, rope, ribbon, etc. are tied together. 2 a tangle; a lump. 3 a round spot on a piece of wood where there was a branch. 4 a cluster of people or things. 5 a unit for measuring the speed of ships and aircraft. *One knot equals 2,025 yards (or 1,852 metres) per hour.*

knot *verb* **(knotted, knotting)**
to make a knot in something.

knotty *adjective* **(knottier, knottiest)**
1 full of knots. 2 difficult; puzzling. *a knotty problem.*

know *verb* (*past tense* **knew;** *past participle* **known;** *present participle* **knowing**)
1 to have something in your mind that you have learnt or discovered. *I knew she was honest.* 2 to recognize or be familiar with a person or place. *I have known him for years.*

know-all *noun*
someone who thinks he knows everything.

know-how *noun*
skill; ability for a particular job.

knowing *adjective*
showing that you know something; cunning. *He gave me a knowing look.*

knowingly *adverb*
1 in a knowing way. 2 deliberately.

knowledge *noun*
(say **nol**-ij)
what someone or everybody knows.

knowledgeable *adjective*
(say **nol**-ij-ă-bŭl)
having much knowledge; clever.
knowledgeably *adverb*

knuckle *noun*
one of the places where your fingers bend.

koala *noun*
(say koh-**ah**-lă)
a furry Australian animal that looks like a small bear. *Koalas climb trees.*

kookaburra *noun*
(say kuuk-ă-bu-ră)
a large Australian kingfisher that makes a laughing or shrieking noise.

kraal *noun*
(say krahl)
a South African village surrounded by a fence.

kung fu *noun*
(say kuung-**foo**)
a Chinese method of self-defence rather like karate.

L

L short for **learner.**

label *noun*
a piece of paper, cloth, etc. fixed on or beside something to show what it is, whose it is, how much it costs, or where it is going.

label *verb* **(labelled, labelling)**
to put a label on something.

laboratory *noun* **(laboratories)**
(*say* lă-**bo**-ră-ter-i)
a room or building where scientific work is done.

laborious *adjective*
needing a lot of effort; very hard.
laboriously *adverb*

labour *noun*
1 hard work. **2** the contractions of the womb when a baby is born. **3 Labour,** those who support the Labour Party, a political party representing socialist ideas.

labourer *noun*
someone who does hard manual work, especially out of doors.

Labrador *noun*
a large black or light-brown dog.

laburnum *noun*
a tree with hanging yellow flowers.

labyrinth *noun*
a complicated and confusing path, road, etc.

lace *noun*
1 thin material with decorative patterns of holes in it. **2** a piece of thin cord used to tie up a shoe, football, etc.
lacy *adjective*

lack *noun*
being without something. *There was a lack of water for the crops.*

lack *verb*
to be without something. *He lacks intelligence.*

lacquer *noun*
a kind of varnish.

lacrosse *noun*
a game like hockey but using a stick with a net on it to catch and throw the ball.

lad *noun*
a boy; a youth.

ladder *noun*
1 a device to help you climb up or down something, made of upright pieces of wood, metal, or rope with cross-pieces called rungs. **2** a vertical flaw in a stocking.

laden *adjective*
carrying a heavy load.

ladle *noun*
a large, deep spoon used for serving soup or other liquids.

lady *noun* **(ladies)**
1 a polite name for a woman. **2 Lady,** the title of a noblewoman. **3 the Ladies,** a lavatory for women.
ladylike *adjective,* **ladyship** *noun*

ladybird *noun*
a small flying beetle, usually red with black spots.

lag *verb*[1] **(lagged, lagging)**
to fall behind because you are going too slowly. *He's lagging behind again.*

lag *verb*[2] **(lagged, lagging)**
to wrap pipes, boilers, etc. with insulating material to keep them warm.

lager *noun*
(*say* **lah**-ger)
a light kind of beer.

lagoon *noun*
1 a lake separated from the sea by sandbanks or reefs. **2** (*in Australia and New Zealand*) a pond, often a stagnant pond.

laid past tense and past participle of **lay** *verb*.

lain past participle of **lie** *verb*[1].

lair *noun*
the place where a wild animal lives.

lake *noun*
a large area of water surrounded by land.

lamb *noun*
1 a young sheep. **2** the meat from young sheep.

lame *adjective* **(lamer, lamest)**
1 unable to walk properly. **2** weak; not convincing. *a lame excuse.*
lamely *adverb,* **lameness** *noun*

lament *verb*
to express grief about something.
lamentable *adjective,* **lamentably** *adverb,*
lamentation *noun*

laminated *adjective*
made of layers joined together.

lamp *noun*
a device for producing light from electricity, gas, or oil.
lampshade *noun*

lamp-post *noun*
a tall post in a street, etc., with a lamp at the top.

lance *noun*
a long spear.

lance-corporal *noun*
a soldier who ranks between a corporal and a private.

land *noun*
1 a country. **2** all the dry parts of the world's surface. **3** the ground used for farming, building, etc.

land *verb*
1 to bring or arrive in a ship or aircraft. 2 to reach the ground after jumping or falling. 3 to get or bring to a particular place or situation. *They landed in gaol.*

landing *noun*
the floor at the top of a flight of stairs.

landing-stage *noun*
a platform on which people and goods are landed from a ship.

landing-strip *noun*
an air-strip.

landlady *noun* **(landladies)**
1 a woman who lets rooms to lodgers. 2 a female landlord.

landlord *noun*
1 someone who rents a house or land to somebody else. 2 someone who looks after a public house.

landmark *noun*
an object in a landscape easily seen from a distance.

landowner *noun*
someone who owns a large amount of land.

landscape *noun*
1 a view or picture of the countryside. 2 **landscape gardening,** laying out a large garden so that it looks beautiful.

landslide *noun*
1 earth or rocks sliding down the side of a hill. 2 a great victory for one side in an election.

lane *noun*
1 a narrow road, especially in the country. 2 a strip of road for a single line of traffic. 3 a strip of track or water for one runner or swimmer in a race.

language *noun*
1 words spoken or written. 2 the words used in a particular country or by a particular group of people. 3 a system of signs or symbols to convey information. *a computer language.* 4 **language laboratory,** a room equipped with devices to help you learn languages.

lanky *adjective* **(lankier, lankiest)**
awkwardly tall and thin.
lankiness *noun*

lantern *noun*
a transparent box for holding a light and shielding it from the wind.

lap *noun*
1 the part from the waist to the knees of a person sitting down. 2 going round a racecourse once. *The 800 metres race consisted of 2 laps.*

lap *verb* **(lapped, lapping)**
1 to drink with the tongue. *The cat lapped up the milk.* 2 to make a gentle splash. *Small waves were lapping against the rocks.*

lapel *noun*
(*say* lă-**pel**)
the flap on either of the front edges of a coat.

lapse *noun*
1 a slight mistake or fault. 2 the passing of time.

lapwing *noun*
a peewit.

larch *noun* **(larches)**
a deciduous tree that bears small cones.

lard *noun*
white fat from pigs, used in cooking.

larder *noun*
a cupboard or small room where food is kept.

large *adjective* **(larger, largest)**
more than the ordinary or average size; big.
largeness *noun*

largely *adverb*
mainly; mostly.

lark *noun*[1]
a skylark.

lark *noun*[2]
(*informal*) something amusing; a bit of fun. *They only did it for a lark.*

larva *noun* **(larvae)**
an insect in the first stage of its life, after it comes out of the egg.

laser *noun*
(*say* **lay**-zer)
a device that makes a very strong narrow beam of light.

lash *noun* **(lashes)**
1 a stroke with a whip. 2 the cord of a whip. 3 an eyelash.

lash *verb*
1 to strike with or like a whip. *Rain lashed against the window.* 2 to tie something tightly. *They lashed it to the mast.*

lass *noun* **(lasses)**
a girl.

lasso *noun*
(*say* la-**soo**)
a rope with a movable noose at the end. *Cowboys use lassos for catching cattle.*

last *adjective*
1 coming after all the others; final. *the last bus.* 2 most recent; the latest. *last night.* 3 **at last,** finally; at the end. 4 **the last straw,** a final or added thing that makes something unbearable.
lastly *adverb*

last *verb*
to continue; to go on being used.

latch *noun* **(latches)**
a fastener on a gate or door.

late *adjective* **(later, latest)**
1 coming after the proper or expected time. 2 near the end of a period of time. 3 recent. *the latest news.* 4 no longer alive. *the late king.*
lateness *noun*

lately *adverb*
recently.

latent *adjective*
(*say* **lay**-těnt)
existing but not yet active, developed, or visible.

lateral *adjective*
1 of, at, or from the sides of something. 2 **lateral thinking,** thinking of unusual ways to solve problems or achieve things.

lathe *noun*
(*say* layth)
a machine for holding and turning pieces of wood or metal while you shape them.

lather *noun*
a mass of froth.

Latin *noun*
the language of the ancient Romans.

latitude *noun*
1 how far a place is from the Equator, measured in degrees. 2 freedom.

latter *noun*
the latter, the second of two people or things just mentioned. *Brown and Jones came in. The latter looked sad.*

latter *adjective*
later; recent.
latterly *adverb*

lattice *noun*
a criss-cross framework.

laugh *verb*
to make sounds that show you are happy or think something is very funny.

laugh *noun*
1 an act or sound of laughing. 2 (*informal*) something that makes you laugh.

laughable *adjective*
that deserves to be laughed at.

laughter *noun*
laughing. *They heard laughter.*

launch *verb*
1 to send a ship into the water. 2 to send a rocket into space. 3 to start something new. 4 **launching pad** or **launch pad**, a platform or place from which rockets are launched.

launch *noun* (**launches**)
1 a large motor-boat. 2 the launching of a ship or rocket.

launder *verb*
to clean and press clothes.

launderette *noun*
a shop with washing-machines that people pay to use.

laundry *noun* (**laundries**)
1 clothes to be washed. 2 a place where clothes are sent or taken to be laundered.

laurel *noun*
an evergreen bush with smooth, shiny leaves.

lav *noun*
(*informal*) a lavatory.

lava *noun*
molten rock that flows from a volcano, or the solid rock formed when it cools.

lavatory *noun* (**lavatories**)
a place where the body can get rid of its waste.

lavender *noun*
1 a bush with pale purple flowers that smell very sweet. 2 a pale purple colour.

lavish *adjective*
generous; plentiful.

law *noun*
1 a rule or set of rules that everyone must keep.
2 something that always happens. *the law of gravity*. 3 **-in-law**, used to distinguish somebody who became your relative by marriage. *Your brother-in-law is the brother of your wife or husband.*

lawcourt *noun*
a place where people decide whether someone has broken the law.

lawful *adjective*
allowed or accepted by the law.
lawfully *adverb*

lawless *adjective*
not obeying the law; without laws.
lawlessly *adverb*, **lawlessness** *noun*

lawn *noun*
an area of mown grass in a garden.

lawn-mower *noun*
a machine with revolving blades for cutting grass.

lawsuit *noun*
a dispute, claim, etc. considered in a lawcourt.

lawyer *noun*
an expert on law; someone whose job is to help people with lawsuits.

laxative *noun*
a medicine that stimulates the bowels to empty.

lay *verb* (**laid, laying**)
1 to put something down in a particular place or in a particular way. 2 to arrange things, especially for a meal. *He laid the table.* 3 to produce an egg. 4 **lay off**, to stop employing somebody for a while; (*informal*) to stop doing something. 5 **lay on**, to supply or provide. 6 **lay out**, to arrange or prepare; to knock somebody unconscious.

lay past tense of **lie** *verb*[1].

lay-by *noun*
1 a place where vehicles can stop beside a main road. 2 (*in Australia and New Zealand*) the action of reserving goods by paying for them in instalments.

layer *noun*
something flat that lies on or under something else. *The cake had a layer of icing on top and a layer of jam inside.*

layout *noun*
the arrangement or design of something.

laze *verb* (**lazed, lazing**)
to spend time in a lazy way.

lazy *adjective* (**lazier, laziest**)
not wanting to work; doing little work.
lazily *adverb*, **laziness** *noun*

lb. short for *pound* or *pounds* in weight. *I bought 5 lb. of potatoes.*

l.b.w. short for *leg before wicket.*

lead *verb* (**led, leading**)
(*say* leed)
1 to guide a person or animal, especially by going in front. 2 to be in charge of something. 3 to be winning in a race or contest. 4 to go; to be a way to. *This road leads to the beach.* 5 to play the first card in a card game. 6 **lead to**, to result in.

lead *noun*[1]
(*say* leed)
1 leading; guidance. *Give us a lead.* **2** a leading place or position. *She took the lead.* **3** a leash. **4** an electric wire. *Don't trip over that lead.*

lead *noun*[2]
(*say* led)
1 a soft, heavy, grey metal. **2** the writing substance in the middle of a pencil.

leader *noun*
someone who leads; a chief.
leadership *noun*

leaf *noun* **(leaves)**
1 one of the usually green and flat growths on trees and plants. **2** a page of a book. **3** a very thin sheet of metal. *gold leaf.* **4** a flap that makes a table larger.
leafless *adjective*, **leafy** *adjective*

leaflet *noun*
a piece of paper printed with information, instructions, etc.

league *noun*
(*say* leeg)
1 a group of teams that play matches against each other. **2** **in league with**, working or plotting together.

leak *noun*
1 a hole, crack, etc. through which liquid or gas escapes. **2** the revealing of some secret information.
leaky *adjective*

leak *verb*
to get out or let out through a leak.
leakage *noun*

lean *verb* **(leant or leaned, leaning)**
1 to bend your body towards or over something. **2** to put or be in a sloping position. **3** to rest against something.

lean *adjective*
1 without fat. *lean meat.* **2** thin. *a lean person.*

leaning *noun*
a tendency.

lean-to *noun*
a building or shed with its roof leaning against the side of a larger building.

leap *noun*
1 a vigorous jump. **2** a sudden increase or advance.

leap *verb* **(leapt or leaped, leaping)**
to make a leap.

leap-frog *noun*
a game in which each player jumps with legs apart over the bended backs of the others.

leap year *noun*
a year when February has twenty-nine days. *It is usually a leap year when you can divide the date by 4, as in 1940 and 1984.*

learn *verb* **(learnt or learned, learning)**
to find out about something; to get knowledge or skill.

learned *adjective*
(*say* **lern**-id)
clever; knowledgeable.

learner *noun*
someone who is learning something, especially how to drive a car.

learning *noun*
knowledge.

lease *noun*
an agreement to let somebody pay to use a building or land for a fixed period.

leash *noun* **(leashes)**
a strap or cord for leading a dog.

least *adjective*
1 smallest; less than all the others. *the least expensive bike.* **2** **at least,** not less than what is mentioned; anyway.

least *noun*
the smallest amount.

leather *noun*
a strong material made from animal skins.
leathery *adjective*

leave *verb* **(left, leaving)**
1 to go away from a person, place, or group. **2** to let something stay where it is or remain as it is. *I've left my book at home.* **3** to give something as a legacy. *He left me £100 in his will.* **4** **left over,** remaining when other things have been used.

leave *noun*
1 permission. **2** permission to be away from work; the time when you are allowed to be away from work; holiday.

leaves plural of **leaf.**

lectern *noun*
a stand to hold a Bible or other large book from which you read.

lecture *noun*
1 a talk about a subject to an audience or a class. **2** a speech telling somebody off.

lecture *verb* **(lectured, lecturing)**
to give a lecture.
lecturer *noun*

led past tense and past participle of **lead** *verb*.

ledge *noun*
a narrow shelf.

ledger *noun*
a book in which financial accounts are kept.

lee *noun*
the sheltered side of something, away from the wind.
leeward *adjective* and *adverb*

leek *noun*
a white vegetable like an onion with broad leaves.

leer *verb*
to look unpleasantly or evilly at somebody.

left *adjective*
1 on or near the left hand. **2** in favour of political reforms.

left *noun*
the left side. *In Britain, we drive on the left of the road.*

left past tense and past participle of **leave** *verb*.

left hand *noun*
the hand that most people use less than the other, on the same side of the body as the heart. *When they eat, most people hold the fork in their left hand and the knife in their right hand.* **left-hand** *adjective*

left-handed *adjective*
using the left hand more than the right hand.

left-overs *plural noun*
food not eaten by the end of a meal.

leg *noun*
1 one of the parts of a human's or animal's body on which it stands, walks, and runs. 2 the part of a garment that covers a leg. 3 one of the supports of a chair or other piece of furniture. 4 one part of a journey, championship, etc. 5 **leg before wicket**, when a batsman in cricket is out because of obstructing the ball with his body. 6 **on your last legs**, exhausted.

legacy *noun* **(legacies)**
something given to somebody in a will.

legal *adjective*
1 lawful. 2 of the law or lawyers. **legality** *noun*, **legally** *adverb*

legalize *verb* **(legalized, legalizing)**
to make something lawful.

legend *noun*
(*say* **lej**-ĕnd)
an old story handed down from the past. **legendary** *adjective*

legible *adjective*
clear enough to read. *Your writing is hardly legible.* **legibility** *noun*, **legibly** *adverb*

legion *noun*
1 a division of the ancient Roman army. 2 a group of soldiers or former soldiers.

legislate *verb* **(legislated, legislating)**
to make laws. **legislation** *noun*, **legislator** *noun*

legitimate *adjective*
(*say* li-**jit**-i-măt)
1 lawful. 2 born when your parents are married to each other. *a legitimate child.* **legitimacy** *noun*, **legitimately** *adverb*

leisure *noun*
1 a time that is free from work, when you can do what you like. 2 **at leisure**, having leisure; not hurried. **leisurely** *adjective* and *adverb*

lemon *noun*
1 a yellow fruit with a sour taste. 2 a pale yellow colour. 3 **lemon cheese** or **lemon curd**, a creamy jam made with lemons.

lemonade *noun*
a drink with a flavour of lemons.

lend *verb* **(lent, lending)**
1 to let somebody have something of yours for a short time. *She lent me her bike yesterday.* 2 **lend a hand**, to help somebody.

length *noun*
1 how long something is. 2 a piece of rope, wire, cloth, etc. 3 **at length**, finally.

lengthen *verb*
to make or become longer.

lengthways or **lengthwise** *adverb*
from end to end; along the longest part of something.

lengthy *adjective* **(lengthier, lengthiest)**
long; too long. *a lengthy speech.*

lenient *adjective*
(*say* **lee**-ni-ĕnt)
merciful; not severe. **lenience** *noun*, **leniently** *adverb*

lens *noun* **(lenses)**
a curved piece of glass or plastic used to focus things.

lent past tense and past participle of **lend.**

Lent *noun*
the period of about six weeks before Easter.

lentil *noun*
a small bean.

leopard *noun*
(*say* **lep**-erd)
a large spotted wild animal.

leotard *noun*
(*say* **lee**-ŏ-tard)
a close-fitting garment worn by acrobats and dancers.

leper *noun*
someone who has leprosy.

leprosy *noun*
a skin disease that makes parts of the body waste away. **leprous** *adjective*

less *adjective* **(lesser, least)**
smaller; not so much. *Eat less meat.*

less *adverb*
1 to a smaller extent. *It is less important.* 2 **no less than**, at least.

less *preposition*
minus; deducting. *She earned £100, less tax.*

lessen *verb*
to make or become less.

lesson *noun*
1 the time when someone is teaching you. 2 something that you have to learn. 3 a passage from the Bible read aloud in church.

lest *conjunction*
so that something should not happen; to prevent something. *He ran away lest he should be seen.*

let *verb* **(let, letting)**
1 to allow somebody to do something. 2 to allow something to happen. 3 to allow somebody to use a house, building, etc. in return for payment. 4 to leave. *Let it alone.* 5 **let down**, to deflate; to disappoint somebody. 6 **let off**, to explode; to excuse somebody from a punishment or duty. 7 **let's**, (*informal*) shall we; I suggest.

lethal *adjective*
deadly. *a lethal gas.* **lethally** *adverb*

letter *noun*
1 one of the symbols used for writing words, such as a, b, or c. 2 a written message sent to another person.

letter-box *noun* (letter-boxes)
a box or slot into which letters are delivered or posted.

lettering *noun*
letters drawn or painted.

lettuce *noun*
a green vegetable used in salads.

leukaemia *noun*
(*say* lew-kee-mi-ă)
a disease in which there are too many white corpuscles in the blood.

level *adjective*
1 flat; horizontal. *level ground.* 2 equal; alongside a person or thing. *He was level with the others.* 3 **level crossing,** a place where a road crosses a railway at the same level.

level *verb* (levelled, levelling)
1 to make something level. 2 to aim a gun.

level *noun*
1 height. *eye level.* 2 a device that shows if something is level. 3 a level surface. 4 the standard or position of something. 5 **on the level,** (*informal*) honest.

lever *noun*
a bar that is pushed or pulled to lift something heavy, force something open, or make a machine work.
leverage *noun*

liable *adjective*
1 likely to do or get something. 2 responsible for something.
liability *noun*

liar *noun*
someone who tells lies.

liberal *adjective*
1 generous; ample. 2 not strict; tolerant. 3 **Liberal,** a supporter of the Liberal Party, a political party that favours moderate reforms.
liberality *noun*, **liberally** *adverb*

liberate *verb* (liberated, liberating)
to set somebody free, especially from oppression.
liberation *noun*

liberty *noun* (liberties)
1 freedom. 2 **take liberties,** to behave too freely or informally.

librarian *noun*
someone who looks after or works in a library.
librarianship *noun*

library *noun* (libraries)
a place where books are kept for people to use or borrow.

lice plural of **louse.**

licence *noun*
an official document allowing somebody to do, use, or own something. *a dog licence.*

license *verb* (licensed, licensing)
to give a licence to somebody; to permit. *We are licensed to sell alcoholic drinks.*
licensee *noun*

lichen *noun*
(*say* ly-kĕn)
a dry-looking plant that grows on rocks, walls, trees, etc.

lick *verb*
1 to move your tongue over something. 2 (*informal*) to defeat; to beat.

lick *noun*
1 the act of licking. 2 (*informal*) a fast speed.

lid *noun*
1 a cover for a box, pot, etc. 2 an eyelid.

lie *verb*[1] (*past tense* **lay;** *past participle* **lain;** *present participle* **lying**)
1 to be, put, or get in a flat position, especially to rest with your body flat as it is in bed. *He lay on the grass. The cat has lain here all night.* 2 to stay; to be. *The castle was lying in ruins. The valley lay before us.* 3 **lie low,** to keep yourself hidden.

lie *verb*[2] (lied, lying)
to say something that is not true.

lie *noun*
something that is deliberately untrue.

lieutenant *noun*
(*say* lef-ten-ănt)
an officer in the army or navy.

life *noun* (lives)
1 the time between birth and death. 2 being alive. 3 living things. *Is there life on Mars?* 4 liveliness. *full of life.* 5 a biography.

lifebelt *noun*
a circle of material that will float, used to support someone's body in water.

lifeboat *noun*
a boat for rescuing people at sea.

life-guard *noun*
someone whose job is to rescue swimmers who are in difficulty.

life insurance *noun*
insurance to compensate for a person's death.

life-jacket *noun*
a jacket of material that will float, used to support someone's body in water.

lifeless *adjective*
1 without life. 2 unconscious.

lifelike *adjective*
looking exactly like a real person or thing.

lifelong *adjective*
lasting throughout someone's life; lasting a very long time.

lifetime *noun*
the time for which someone is alive.

lift *verb*
1 to pick up; to raise. 2 to rise. 3 (*informal*) to steal.

lift *noun*
1 the act of lifting. 2 a device for taking people or goods up and down inside a building. 3 a ride in somebody else's car, lorry, etc.

lift-off *noun*
the vertical take-off of a rocket.

light *noun*
1 what makes things visible, the opposite of darkness. *There was not enough light to see the garden.* 2 something that provides light or a flame, especially an electric lamp. *Switch on the light.*

light *adjective*[1]
1 full of light; not dark. 2 pale. *light blue.*

light *adjective*[2]
1 not heavy; weighing little. 2 not large; not strong. *a light wind.* 3 not serious or profound. *light music.*
lightly *adverb*

light *verb* **(lit or lighted, lighting)**
1 to start something burning. *Have you lit the fire? I lit it just now. a lighted torch.* 2 to begin to burn. *The fire won't light.* 3 to give light to something. *The tower was lit by floodlights.* 4 **light up,** to make or become light or bright; to turn lights on, especially at dusk.

lighten *verb*
to make or become lighter.

lighter *noun*
a device for lighting something like a cigarette or a fire.

light-hearted *adjective*
cheerful; free from worry; not serious.
light-heartedly *adverb*, **light-heartedness** *noun*

lighthouse *noun*
a tower with a bright light at the top to warn ships that there are rocks or other dangers nearby.

lighting *noun*
lamps, or the light they provide.

lightning *noun*
1 a flash of bright light in the sky during a thunderstorm. 2 **lightning-conductor,** a metal wire or rod fixed on a building to divert lightning into the earth.

lightship *noun*
an anchored ship with a bright light on it to warn ships that there are rocks or other dangers nearby.

lightweight *adjective*
not weighing much; less than average weight.

light-year *noun*
the distance that light travels in one year (about 6 million million miles).

like *verb* **(liked, liking)**
1 to think someone or something is pleasant or satisfactory. 2 **should like** or **would like,** to want. *I should like to see him.*
likeable *adjective*

like *preposition*
1 resembling; similar to; in the manner of. *He cried like a baby.* 2 such as. *We need things like knives and forks.* 3 typical of. *It was like her to forgive him.* 4 **like anything** or **like mad,** (*informal*) very much; vigorously.

like *adjective*
similar. *They are as like as two peas.*

likely *adjective* **(likelier, likeliest)**
1 probable; expected to happen or to be true, useful, etc. 2 **not likely!,** (*informal*) that is impossible; I refuse.

likeness *noun* **(likenesses)**
a resemblance.

likewise *adverb*
similarly.

lilac *noun*
1 a bush with fragrant purple or white flowers. 2 a pale purple colour.

lily *noun* **(lilies)**
a garden flower grown from a bulb.

limb *noun*
a leg, arm, or wing.

lime *noun*[1]
a white, chalky powder used in making cement or as a fertiliser.

lime *noun*[2]
a green fruit rather like a lemon.
lime-juice *noun*

lime *noun*[3]
a tree with yellow blossom.

limelight *noun*
great publicity.

limerick *noun*
(say **lim-er-ik**)
a comical poem of five lines.

limestone *noun*
rock from which lime is made.

limit *noun*
a line or point that you cannot or should not pass; an edge of something.
limitless *adjective*

limit *verb*
to restrict.
limitation *noun*

limited *adjective*
1 restricted; small. 2 that is a *limited company* or *limited liability company,* a business company whose members are responsible for only some of its debts. *'Ltd.' after the name of a business shows that it is a limited company.*

limp *verb*
to walk with difficulty because something is wrong with your leg or foot.

limp *noun*
a limping movement.

limp *adjective*
not stiff or firm; without strength.

limpet *noun*
a small shellfish that attaches itself firmly to rocks.

line *noun*
1 a long, thin mark. 2 a row or series of people or things. 3 a length of rope, string, wire, etc. 4 a railway; a length of railway track. 5 a system of ships, aircraft, buses, etc. 6 a way of working, behaving, etc. 7 **in line,** forming a straight line; conforming.

line *verb* **(lined, lining)**
1 to mark something with lines. 2 to form into lines. 3 to make an edge or border for something.

linen *noun*
1 cloth made from flax, used to make sheets, table-cloths, handkerchiefs, etc. 2 things made of this cloth; clothes.

liner *noun*
a large ship or aircraft, usually carrying passengers.

linesman *noun* (linesmen)
an official in football, tennis, etc. who decides whether the ball has crossed a line.

linger *verb*
to be slow to leave; to stay somewhere for a long time.

lingerie *noun*
(*say* **lan**-zher-ee)
women's underclothes.

linguist *noun*
an expert in languages.
linguistic *adjective*, **linguistics** *noun*

lining *noun*
a layer covering the inside of something.

link *noun*
1 one of the rings in a chain. 2 a connection.

link *verb*
to join things together; to connect.

lino *noun*
(*say* **ly**-noh)
linoleum.

linoleum *noun*
(*say* lin-**oh**-li-ŭm)
a stiff, shiny covering for the floor.

lint *noun*
a soft material for covering wounds.

lion *noun*
a large, strong, light-brown wild animal found in Africa and India.

lioness *noun*
a female lion.

lip *noun*
1 one of the two edges of the mouth. 2 the edge of something hollow such as a cup or a crater. 3 a projecting part at the top of a jug, saucepan, etc. to help pouring.

lipstick *noun*
a stick of a substance for colouring the lips.

liquid *noun*
a substance that can flow like water or oil.

liquor *noun*
(*say* **lik**-er)
alcoholic drink.

liquorice *noun*
(*say* **lik**-er-iss)
a soft black sweet with a strong taste.

lisp *verb*
to pronounce *s* as *th*. '*I'll thcream,*' lisped *Violet Elizabeth.*

list *noun*
a number of things or names written down or printed one after another.

list *verb*[1]
to make a list of things.

list *verb*[2]
to lean over to one side in the water. *The ship was listing badly.*

listen *verb*
to pay attention in order to hear something.
listener *noun*

listless *adjective*
too tired to be active or enthusiastic.
listlessly *adverb*, **listlessness** *noun*

lit past tense and past participle of **light** *verb*.

literacy *noun*
(*say* **lit**-er-ă-si)
the ability to read and write.

literal *adjective*
meaning exactly what it says; precise.
literally *adverb*

literary *adjective*
(*say* **lit**-er-er-i)
of or interested in literature.

literate *adjective*
(*say* **lit**-er-ăt)
able to read and write.

literature *noun*
1 books or writings, especially those considered to have been written well. 2 printed material about a subject. *Get some literature about coach-tours.*

litmus *noun*
a blue substance used to show whether something is an acid or an alkali.
litmus-paper *noun*

litre *noun*
(*say* **lee**-ter)
a measure of liquid, about 1¾ pints.

litter *verb*
to make a place untidy with litter

litter *noun*[1]
rubbish or untidy things left lying about.

litter *noun*[2]
all the young animals born to the same mother at one time.

little *adjective* (less or littler, least or littlest)
1 small. *a little boy.* 2 not much. *We have little time.* 3 a small amount of something. *Have a little sugar.* 4 **little by little,** gradually.

live *verb* (lived, living)
(rhymes with *give*)
1 to be alive. 2 to have your home in a particular place. *She is living in Glasgow.* 3 to pass your life in a certain way. *He lived as a hermit.* 4 **live on,** to use something as food; to depend upon.

live *adjective*
(rhymes with *hive*)
1 alive. 2 carrying electricity. 3 broadcast while it is actually happening. 4 recorded with an audience present.

livelihood *noun*
(*say* **lyv**-li-huud)
the way in which you earn a living.

lively *adjective* (livelier, liveliest)
full of energy or cheerfulness.
liveliness *noun*

liver *noun*
1 the organ in the body that purifies the blood. 2 the liver of some animals, used as food.

lives plural of **life**.

livestock *noun*
farm animals.

living *noun*
the way that you live or keep alive; enough money for a normal life. *He earned a living as a salesman.*

living-room *noun*
a sitting-room; a room for general use during the day.

lizard *noun*
a four-legged reptile with scaly skin.

llama *noun*
(*say* **lah**-mă)
a South American animal with woolly fur.

load *noun*
1 something to be carried. 2 the quantity that can be carried. 3 (*informal*) a large amount. *It's a load of nonsense.*

load *verb*
1 to put a load on something. 2 to put a weight into a thing. *loaded dice.* 3 to give somebody large amounts of something. *They loaded him with gifts.* 4 to put a bullet or shell into a gun. 5 to put a film into a camera.

loaf *noun* (**loaves**)
bread in the shape it was baked in.

loaf *verb*
to loiter; to waste time.
loafer *noun*

loam *noun*
rich, fertile soil.
loamy *adjective*

loan *noun*
something that has been lent to somebody.

loan *verb*
to lend.

loath *adjective*
(rhymes with *both*)
unwilling. *I was loath to go.*

loathe *verb* (**loathed, loathing**)
(rhymes with *clothe*)
to hate. *She loathed bad manners.*
loathsome *adjective*

loaves plural of **loaf** *noun*.

lob *verb* (**lobbed, lobbing**)
to throw or hit something high up into the air.

lobby *noun* (**lobbies**)
an entrance-hall.

lobe *noun*
the rounded part at the bottom of an ear.

lobster *noun*
a large shellfish with eight legs and two claws.

lobster-pot *noun*
a basket for catching lobsters.

local *adjective*
1 of or belonging to a particular place or district. *local government.* 2 affecting a particular area. *a local anaesthetic.*
locally *adverb*

local *noun*
(*informal*) 1 someone who lives in a particular district. 2 a public house near a person's home.

locality *noun* (**localities**)
a district; a location.

locate *verb* (**located, locating**)
1 to discover where something is. *I have located the fault.* 2 **located**, situated. *The cinema is located in the High Street.*

location *noun*
1 the place where something is. 2 **on location**, filmed in natural surroundings, not in a studio.

loch *noun*
a lake in Scotland.

lock *noun*
1 a fastening that is opened with a key. 2 part of a canal or river between gates where boats are raised or lowered to a different level. 3 the distance that a vehicle's front wheels can turn. 4 a piece of hair. 5 **lock, stock, and barrel,** completely.

lock *verb*
1 to fasten or secure with a lock. 2 to become fixed in one place; to jam.

locker *noun*
a small cupboard.

locomotive *noun*
a railway engine.

locust *noun*
an insect that flies in large swarms which eat all the plants in an area.

lodge *noun*
1 a small house. 2 a room or small house at the entrance to a large house, college, etc.

lodge *verb* (**lodged, lodging**)
1 to stay somewhere as a lodger. 2 to give someone a place to sleep. 3 to become fixed. *The ball lodged in the branches.* 4 **lodge a complaint,** to make a formal complaint.
lodging-house *noun*, **lodgings** plural *noun*

lodger *noun*
someone who pays to live in someone else's house.

loft *noun*
the room or space under the roof of a house.

lofty *adjective* (**loftier, loftiest**)
1 tall. 2 noble; proud.
loftily *adverb*, **loftiness** *noun*

log *noun*[1]
1 a large piece of a tree that has fallen or been cut down. 2 a detailed record kept of a ship's voyage, aircraft's flight, etc.

log *noun*[2]
a logarithm.

logarithm *noun*
one of a series of numbers set out in tables, used to help you do arithmetic.

log-book *noun*
1 a book in which a log of a ship's voyage, etc. is kept. 2 a booklet or card listing details of a motor-vehicle.

lot

logic *noun*
reasoning.
logical *adjective*, **logically** *adverb*

loiter *verb*
to stand about with nothing to do.
loiterer *noun*

loll *verb*
to sit or lie in an untidy, lazy way.

lollipop *noun*
1 a sweet on the end of a stick. 2 **lollipop lady** or **lollipop man**, (*informal*) an official who uses a circular sign on a stick to signal traffic to stop so that children can cross the road.

lolly *noun* (**lollies**)
1 (*informal*) an ice-lolly. 2 (*informal*) a lollipop. 3 (*slang*) money.

lone *adjective*
solitary. *a lone rider.*

lonely *adjective* (**lonelier, loneliest**)
1 unhappy because you are on your own. 2 far from other inhabited places; not often used or visited. *a lonely village.*
loneliness *noun*

long *adjective*
1 measuring a lot from one end to the other. *a long river.* 2 taking a lot of time. *a long holiday.* 3 from one end to the other. *A cricket pitch is 22 yards long.* 4 **long division,** dividing one number by another and writing down all your calculations. 5 **long jump,** an athletic contest of jumping as far as you can with one leap. 6 **long wave,** a radio wave of more than 1,000 metres wavelength.

long *adverb*
1 for a long time. *Have you been waiting long?* 2 at a long time in the past. *They left long ago.* 3 **as long as** or **so long as,** provided that; on condition that.

long *verb*
long for, to want something very much.

longitude *noun*
(*say* lonj-i-tewd)
the distance east or west, measured in degrees, from the Greenwich meridian.
longitudinal *adjective*

long-playing *adjective*
(*of a record*) that plays for about 20 minutes on each side.
long-player *noun*

loo *noun*
(*informal*) a lavatory.

look *verb*
1 to use your eyes; to turn your eyes towards something. 2 to face in a particular direction. 3 to seem; to appear. *You look sad.* 4 **look after,** to protect; to attend to somebody's needs. 5 **look down on,** to despise. 6 **look for,** to try to find something. 7 **look forward to,** to wait for something eagerly or expectantly. 8 **look out,** to be careful. 9 **look up to,** to admire or respect.

look *noun*
1 the act of looking. 2 appearance; what something seems to be.

looking-glass *noun* (**looking-glasses**)
a mirror made of glass.

look-out *noun*
1 a place from which you watch for something. 2 someone whose job is to keep watch. 3 watching; being watchful. 4 (*informal*) something you can expect or hope for.

loom *noun*
a machine for weaving cloth.

loom *verb*
to appear large and threatening. *An iceberg loomed up through the fog.*

loop *noun*
the shape made by a curve crossing itself; a piece of string, ribbon, wire, etc. made into this shape.

loop *verb*
to make into a loop.

loophole *noun*
1 a narrow opening. 2 a way of avoiding a law, rule, etc.

loose *adjective* (**looser, loosest**)
1 not tight; not firm. *a loose tooth.* 2 not tied up or shut in. *The dog got loose.* 3 **at a loose end,** with nothing to do.
loosely *adverb*, **looseness** *noun*

loose *verb* (**loosed, loosing**)
to make something loose; to untie or release.

loose-leaf *adjective*
with each leaf or page removable. *a loose-leaf folder.*

loosen *verb*
to make or become loose.

loot *noun*
stolen things.

loot *verb*
to rob a place or an enemy, especially in a time of war or disorder.
looter *noun*

lopsided *adjective*
with one side lower than the other; uneven.

lord *noun*
1 a nobleman, especially one who is allowed to use the title 'Lord' in front of his name. 2 **Lord Mayor,** the mayor of a large city. 3 **Our Lord,** Jesus Christ. 4 **the Lord,** God.
lordly *adjective*, **lordship** *noun*

lorry *noun* (**lorries**)
a large motor-vehicle for carrying goods.

lose *verb* (**lost, losing**)
1 to be without something you once had, especially because you cannot find it. *I've lost my hat.* 2 to be beaten in a contest or game. *We lost last Friday's match.* 3 to become slow. *My watch loses two minutes every day.* 4 **be lost** or **lose your way,** not to know where you are. 5 **get lost!,** (*slang*) go away!
loser *noun*

loss *noun* (**losses**)
1 losing something. 2 something you have lost. 3 **at a loss,** puzzled; unable to do something.

lot *noun*
1 something for sale at an auction. 2 **a lot** or **lots,** a large amount; plenty. 3 **draw lots,** to choose one person or thing from a group by a method that depends on chance. 4 **the lot,** everything.

lotion *noun*
a liquid that is put on the skin.

lottery *noun* **(lotteries)**
a way of raising money by selling numbered tickets and giving prizes to people who have the winning tickets.

lotto *noun*
a game like bingo.

loud *adjective*
1 noisy; easily heard. 2 bright; gaudy. *loud colours.*
loudly *adverb,* **loudness** *noun*

loudspeaker *noun*
a device that changes electrical impulses into sound.

lounge *noun*
a sitting-room.

lounge *verb* **(lounged, lounging)**
to sit or stand lazily.

louse *noun* **(lice)**
1 a small insect that lives on animals or plants. 2 *(slang)* a hateful person.

lousy *adjective* **(lousier, lousiest)**
1 full of lice. 2 *(slang)* very bad. 3 **lousy with,** *(slang)* having many or much of something.

lout *noun*
a bad-mannered or clumsy man.
loutish *adjective*

love *verb* **(loved, loving)**
to like somebody or something very much.
lovable *adjective,* **lover** *noun,* **lovingly** *adverb*

love *noun*
1 a loving feeling; great affection or kindness. 2 sexual feelings between people. 3 a sweetheart. 4 in games, a score of nothing. 5 **in love,** feeling strong love for another person.

lovely *adjective* **(lovelier, loveliest)**
1 beautiful. 2 *(informal)* very pleasant or enjoyable.
loveliness *noun*

low *adjective*
not high.
lowness *noun*

low *verb*
to moo like a cow.

lower *verb*
to make or become less, or less high; to bring down. *He lowered the flag.*

lowland *adjective*
of or in the lowlands.

lowlands *plural noun*
1 low country. 2 the south of Scotland.
lowlander *noun*

lowly *adjective* **(lowlier, lowliest)**
humble.
lowliness *noun*

loyal *adjective*
always true to your friends; faithful.
loyally *adverb,* **loyalty** *noun*

lozenge *noun*
a small sweet tablet, especially one that contains medicine.

L.P. *noun*
a long-playing record.

LSD *noun*
a strong drug that produces hallucinations.

L-shaped *adjective*
shaped like the letter L. *an L-shaped room.*

Ltd. short for **limited.**

lubricate *verb* **(lubricated, lubricating)**
to put oil or grease on something so that it moves smoothly.
lubricant *noun,* **lubrication** *noun*

lucid *adjective*
(*say* **loo**-sid)
clear; easy to understand.
lucidity *noun,* **lucidly** *adverb*

luck *noun*
1 the way things happen that have not been planned. 2 good things happening to you.

lucky *adjective* **(luckier, luckiest)**
1 having or bringing good luck. 2 **lucky dip,** a box or tub containing articles of various values, from which you pick one at random.
luckily *adverb*

ludicrous *adjective*
(*say* **loo**-dik-rŭs)
ridiculous.
ludicrously *adverb*

ludo *noun*
a game played with dice and counters on a board.

lug *verb* **(lugged, lugging)**
to drag. *She lugged the case up the stairs.*

luggage *noun*
suitcases, bags, boxes, etc. taken with you on a journey.

lukewarm *adjective*
slightly warm.

lull *verb*
to soothe or calm; to send somebody to sleep.

lull *noun*
a short period of quiet or rest.

lullaby *noun* **(lullabies)**
a song that is sung to send a baby to sleep.

lumbago *noun*
(*say* lum-**bay**-goh)
pain in the lower part of the back.

lumber *noun*
1 rough timber. 2 junk; old unwanted furniture or other things.

lumber *verb*
1 to move along clumsily or noisily. *The elephants lumbered past.* 2 to fill a place with junk. 3 *(informal)* to leave somebody with a problem, unpleasant job, etc.

lumberjack *noun*
someone whose job is to cut down trees or transport them.

luminous *adjective*
(*say* loo-min-ŭs)
that shines or glows in the dark.
luminosity *noun*

lump *noun*
1 a solid piece of something. *a lump of sugar.*
2 a swelling.
lumpy *adjective*

lump *verb*¹
to put or deal with things together.

lump *verb*²
lump it, (*informal*) to put up with something you do not like. *You'll have to like it or lump it.*

lunacy *noun* (**lunacies**)
(*say* loo-nă-see)
madness.

lunar *adjective*
1 of the moon. **2 lunar month,** the period between new moons; four weeks.

lunatic *noun*
(*say* loo-nă-tik)
a mad person.

lunch *noun* (**lunches**)
1 a meal that you eat in the middle of the day.
2 a snack.
lunchtime *noun*

luncheon *noun*
1 lunch. **2 luncheon meat,** cold meat ready to eat, made from pressed pork or ham.

lung *noun*
one of the two parts inside the body used for breathing.

lunge *verb* (**lunged, lunging**)
to thrust or move forward suddenly.

lupin *noun*
a garden plant with tall spikes of flowers.

lurch *verb*
to stagger; to lean suddenly to one side.

lurch *noun* (**lurches**)
1 a lurching movement. **2 leave somebody in**

the lurch, to desert somebody, leaving him in difficulties.

lure *verb* (**lured, luring**)
to tempt a person or animal into a trap; to attract.

lurk *verb*
to wait where you cannot be seen.

luscious *adjective*
1 delicious. **2** (*informal*) very attractive.

lush *adjective*
1 growing abundantly. *lush grass.* **2** luxurious. *lush furniture.*
lushly *adverb,* **lushness** *noun*

lust *noun*
powerful desire.
lustful *adjective*

lustre *noun*
(*say* lus-ter)
brightness; brilliance.
lustrous *adjective*

lute *noun*
an old-fashioned musical instrument rather like a guitar.

luxury *noun* (**luxuries**)
1 something expensive that you enjoy but do not really need. **2** having many luxuries.
luxurious *adjective*

lying present participle of **lie** *verb*¹ and *verb*².

lynch *verb*
to execute somebody without a proper trial. *The mob lynched the cowboy.*

lyre *noun*
1 an ancient musical instrument like a small harp. **2 lyre-bird,** an Australian bird, of which the male has a fan-shaped tail.

lyric *noun*
(*say* li-rik)
1 a short poem expressing feelings and emotions. **2** lyric or **lyrics,** the words of a song.
lyrical *adjective*

M

m. short for *metres, miles,* or *millions.*

ma *noun*
(*informal*) mother.

mac *noun*
(*informal*) a mackintosh.

macaroni *noun*
flour paste made into tubes.

machine *noun*
something with several parts that work together to do a job. *a washing-machine.*

machine-gun *noun*
a gun that can keep firing bullets quickly one after another.

machinery *noun*
1 machines. **2** mechanism. **3** a system for doing something.

mackerel *noun* (**mackerel**)
an edible sea-fish.

mackintosh *noun* (**mackintoshes**)
a raincoat.

mad *adjective* (**madder, maddest**)
1 having something wrong with your mind; not sane or sensible. **2** very keen. *He's mad about football.* **3** (*informal*) very excited or annoyed. **4 like mad,** (*informal*) with great speed, energy, enthusiasm, etc.
madly *adverb,* **madman** *noun,* **madness** *noun*

madam *noun*
a word sometimes used when speaking politely to a woman, instead of her name. *'Can I help you, madam?' said the shopkeeper.*

madden *verb*
to make somebody mad or angry.

made past tense and past participle of **make** *verb*.

magazine *noun*
1 a paper-covered publication that comes out regularly. 2 the part of a gun that holds the cartridges. 3 a store for ammunition, explosives, etc. 4 a device that holds film for a camera or slides for a slide-projector.

maggot *noun*
the larva of some kinds of fly.

magic *noun*
the power to do wonderful things or clever tricks that people cannot usually do.
magical *adjective*, **magically** *adverb*, **magician** *noun*

magistrate *noun*
a judge in a local court.

magma *noun*
a molten substance beneath the earth's crust.

magnesium *noun*
a silvery-white metal that makes a very bright flame when it burns.

magnet *noun*
a piece of metal that can attract iron or steel and that points north and south when it is hung in the air.
magnetism *noun*

magnetic *adjective*
1 having or using the powers of a magnet. 2 **magnetic tape**, a plastic strip coated with a magnetic substance for recording sound.
magnetically *adverb*

magnetize *verb* (**magnetized, magnetizing**)
1 to make something into a magnet. 2 to attract like a magnet.

magnificent *adjective*
looking grand or important; excellent.
magnificence *noun*, **magnificently** *adverb*

magnify *verb* (**magnified, magnifying**)
to make something look bigger than it really is.
magnification *noun*, **magnifier** *noun*, **magnifying glass** *noun*

magnitude *noun*
how large or important something is.

magnolia *noun*
a tree with large white flowers.

magpie *noun*
a black and white bird. *Magpies sometimes steal bright things and hide them.*

mahogany *noun*
(*say* mă-**hog**-ă-ni)
a reddish-brown wood.

maid *noun*
1 a female servant. 2 (*old-fashioned use*) a girl.

maiden *noun*
(*old-fashioned use*) a girl.

maiden *adjective*
1 not married. *a maiden aunt.* 2 **maiden name**, a woman's name before she got married. 3 **maiden over**, a cricket over in which no runs are scored. 4 **maiden voyage**, a ship's first voyage.

mail *noun*[1]
1 letters, parcels, etc. sent by post. 2 **mail order**, ordering goods to be sent by post.

mail *noun*[2]
armour made of metal rings joined together.

mail *verb*
to send something by post.

maim *verb*
to injure somebody so that part of his body is useless.

main *adjective*
most important; largest.

main or **mains** *noun*
the main pipe or cable in a system carrying water, gas, or electricity to a building.

mainland *noun*
the main part of a country, not the islands around it.

mainly *adverb*
most importantly; almost completely; usually.

maintain *verb*
1 to keep something in good condition. 2 to have or state a belief. 3 to provide money for somebody.
maintenance *noun*

maisonette *noun*
a small flat or house.

maize *noun*
a tall kind of corn with large seeds.

majestic *adjective*
imposing; dignified.
majestically *adverb*

majesty *noun* (**majesties**)
1 being majestic. 2 the title used in speaking about or to a king or queen. *Her Majesty the Queen. Yes, Your Majesty.*

major *adjective*
1 more important; main. *major roads.* 2 of the musical scale that has a semitone between the 3rd and 4th notes and between the 7th and 8th notes.

major *noun*
an army officer higher than captain.

majority *noun* (**majorities**)
(*say* mă-**jo**-ri-ti)
1 the greater part of a group of people or things. *The majority of the class wanted a quiz.* 2 the difference between a larger and a smaller number of votes. *She had a majority of 25 over her opponent.*

make *verb* (**made, making**)
1 to get something new, usually by putting things together. *They are making a raft out of logs.* 2 to cause something to happen. *The bang made him jump.* 3 to get or earn. *She makes £5,000 a year.* 4 to score. *He has made 20 runs so far.* 5 to reach. *The swimmer just made the*

shore. **6** to estimate or reckon. *What do you make the time?* **7** to equal; to amount to. *4 and 6 makes 10.* **8** to give. *Make me an offer.* **9** to tidy or arrange for use. *Make the beds.* **10** to make something successful or happy. *Her visit made my day.* **11 make do,** to manage with something that is not what you really want. **12 make for,** to go towards. **13 make off,** to leave quickly. **14 make out,** to manage to see, hear, or understand something; to pretend. **15 make up,** to build or put together; to invent a story, etc.; to compensate for something; to put on make-up. **16 make up your mind,** to decide.

make *noun*
1 how something is made. **2** a brand of goods; something made by a particular firm. *What make of car is that?*

make-believe *noun*
pretending; imagining things.

maker *noun*
the person or firm that has made something.

makeshift *adjective*
used because you have nothing better. *a makeshift table.*

make-up *noun*
1 cosmetics. **2** a person's character.

malaria *noun*
(*say* mă-**lair**-i-ă)
a feverish disease spread by mosquitoes.

male *adjective*
of the sex that does not give birth to offspring.

male *noun*
a male person or animal.

malevolent *adjective*
(*say* mă-**lev**-ŏ-lĕnt)
intending to harm other people.
malevolence *noun,* **malevolently** *adverb*

malice *noun*
a desire to harm other people.
malicious *adjective,* **maliciously** *adverb*

mallet *noun*
a large hammer, usually made of wood.

malnutrition *noun*
not having enough food to eat.
malnourished *adjective*

malt *noun*
dried barley used in brewing, making vinegar, etc.
malted *adjective*

mammal *noun*
any animal of which the female can feed her babies with her own milk.
mammalian *adjective*

mammoth *noun*
an extinct kind of hairy elephant.

mammoth *adjective*
huge.

man *noun* **(men)**
1 a grown-up male human being. **2** a person. **3** mankind. **4** one of the pieces used in a board-game like chess or draughts.

man *verb* **(manned, manning)**
to supply with people to work something. *Man the pumps!*

manage *verb* **(managed, managing)**
1 to be able to do something difficult. **2** to be in charge of a shop, factory, etc.
manageable *adjective,* **management** *noun,* **manager** *noun,* **manageress** *noun,* **managerial** *adjective*

mane *noun*
the long hair along the back of the neck of a horse or lion.

manger *noun*
(*say* **mayn**-jer)
a trough for animals to feed from.

mangle *noun*
a wringer.

mangle *verb* **(mangled, mangling)**
1 to crush or cut up something roughly. **2** to squeeze wet clothes in a wringer.

manhole *noun*
a hole, usually with a cover, through which a workman can get into a sewer, boiler, etc. to inspect or repair it.

mania *noun*
violent madness.
maniac *noun,* **manic** *adjective*

manifesto *noun*
a statement of a group's or person's policy or principles.

manipulate *verb* **(manipulated, manipulating)**
to handle or arrange something cleverly or cunningly.
manipulation *noun,* **manipulator** *noun*

mankind *noun*
all the people in the world.

manly *adjective* **(manlier, manliest)**
strong or brave; suitable for a man.
manliness *noun*

manner *noun*
1 the way that something happens or is done. **2 manners,** how you behave with other people; behaving politely.

manœuvre *noun*
(*say* mă-**noo**-ver)
a movement or action done to deceive or beat somebody; a difficult or skilful action.

manœuvre *verb* **(manœuvred, manœuvring)**
to make a manœuvre.
manœuvrable *adjective*

manor *noun*
a large, important house in the country.

mansion *noun*
a large, impressive house.

manslaughter *noun*
(*say* **man**-slaw-ter)
killing somebody without meaning to do so.

mantelpiece *noun*
a shelf above a fireplace.

mantle *noun*
a cloak.

manual *adjective*
done with the hands. *manual work.*
manually *adverb*

manual *noun*
a handbook.

manufacture *verb*
(manufactured, manufacturing)
to make things with machines.
manufacturer *noun*

manure *noun*
fertilizer, especially made from animal waste.

manuscript *noun*
something written or typed but not printed.

Manx *adjective*
1 of the Isle of Man. 2 **Manx cat,** a breed of cat without a tail.

many *adjective* **(more, most)**
large in number.

many *noun*
a large number of people or things.

Maori *noun*
(*say* **mow**-ri)
one of the aboriginal people of New Zealand.

map *noun*
1 a diagram of part or all of the earth's surface, showing towns, mountains, rivers, etc. 2 **on the map,** famous or important.

map *verb* **(mapped, mapping)**
1 to make a map of an area. 2 **map out,** to arrange or organize something.

maple *noun*
a tree with broad leaves.

mar *verb* **(marred, marring)**
to spoil. *The rain marred our display.*

marathon *noun*
a long-distance race for runners. *The marathon is usually 26 miles long.*

marauder *noun*
someone who raids and plunders.
marauding *adjective*

marble *noun*
1 a small glass ball used in games. 2 a hard kind of limestone that is polished and used for building or sculpture.

March *noun*[1]
the third month of the year.

march *noun*[2] **(marches)**
1 the action of marching. 2 a piece of music suitable for marching.

march *verb*
1 to walk like soldiers, with regular steps. 2 to make somebody walk somewhere.
marcher *noun*

mare *noun*
a female horse or donkey.

margarine *noun*
(*say* mar-jă-**reen**)
a substance that looks like butter, made from animal or vegetable fats.

marge *noun*
(*say* marj)
(*informal*) margarine.

margin *noun*
1 the empty space between the edge of a page and the writing or pictures. 2 the small difference between two scores, prices, etc. *She won by a narrow margin.*
marginal *adjective,* **marginally** *adverb*

marigold *noun*
a yellow or orange garden-flower.

marijuana *noun*
(*say* ma-ri-**hwah**-nă)
a drug made from hemp.

marina *noun*
(*say* mă-**ree**-nă)
a harbour for yachts, motor-boats, etc.

marine *adjective*
(*say* mă-**reen**)
of or concerned with the sea.

marine *noun*
(*say* mă-**reen**)
a soldier trained to serve on land and sea.

mariner *noun*
a sailor.

marionette *noun*
a puppet worked by strings or wires.

mark *noun*[1]
1 a spot, dot, line, stain, etc. on something. 2 a number, letter, etc. put on a piece of work to show how good it is. 3 a distinguishing feature of something. 4 the place from which you start a race.

mark *noun*[2]
a German unit of money.

mark *verb*
1 to put a mark on something. 2 to give a mark to a piece of work; to correct. 3 to pay attention to something. *Mark my words!* 4 **mark time,** to march on one spot, without moving forward; to wait.

market *noun*
1 a place where things are bought and sold, usually from stalls in the open air. 2 a situation in which goods can be sold. 3 **on the market,** available to buy.

market *verb*
to sell.
marketable *adjective*

marksman *noun* **(marksmen)**
an expert in shooting at a target.
marksmanship *noun*

marmalade *noun*
jam made from oranges or lemons.

maroon *verb*
to abandon somebody in a deserted place.

maroon *adjective*
brownish or dark red.

marquee *noun*
(*say* mar-**kee**)
a very large tent.

marriage *noun*
1 the state of being married. 2 a wedding.

marrow *noun*
1 a large gourd eaten as a vegetable. 2 the soft substance inside bones.

marry *verb* **(married, marrying)**
1 to become the husband or wife of somebody. 2 to make two people into husband and wife.

marsh *noun* **(marshes)**
a low-lying area of very wet ground.
marshy *adjective*

marshal *noun*
1 an official who supervises a contest, ceremony, etc. 2 a high-ranking officer. *Field Marshal*. 3 an official in the U.S.A. like a sheriff.

marshmallow *noun*
a soft, spongy sweet.

marsupial *noun*
(*say* mar-**soo**-pi-ăl)
an animal such as a kangaroo or wallaby. *Female marsupials have a pouch for carrying their babies.*

martial *adjective*
1 of or like war. 2 **martial law**, government by the armed forces.

martin *noun*
a bird rather like a swallow.

martyr *noun*
(*say* **mar**-ter)
someone who is killed or suffers because of his beliefs.
martyrdom *noun*

marvel *noun*
a wonderful thing.

marvel *verb* (**marvelled, marvelling**)
to be filled with wonder or astonishment.

marvellous *adjective*
excellent.
marvellously *adverb*

Marxism *noun*
the Communist ideas of the German writer Karl Marx (1818–83).
Marxist *noun* and *adjective*

marzipan *noun*
a soft, sweet food made from almonds and sugar.

mascot *noun*
a person, animal, or object that is believed to bring good luck.

masculine *adjective*
of, like, or suitable for men.
masculinity *noun*

mash *verb*
to crush something into a soft mass. *mashed potato.*

mash *noun*
(*informal*) mashed potatoes.

mask *noun*
a covering worn over the face to disguise or protect it.

mask *verb*
1 to cover your face with a mask. 2 to hide something.

mason *noun*
1 someone who builds or works with stone. 2 **Mason,** a member of a secret society.

masonry *noun*
the stone parts of a building.

mass *noun*[1] (**masses**)
1 a large amount. *masses of flowers.* 2 a lump; a heap. 3 **mass production,** producing goods in large quantities.

mass *noun*[2] (**masses**)
the Communion service in a Roman Catholic church.

massacre *verb* (**massacred, massacring**)
(*say* **mas**-ă-ker)
to kill a large number of people.

massage *verb* (**massaged, massaging**)
(*say* **mas**-ah*zh*)
to rub and press the body to make it less stiff or less painful.
masseur *noun*, **masseuse** *noun*

massive *adjective*
huge; large and heavy.
massively *adverb*

mast *noun*
a tall pole that holds up a ship's sail, a flag, or an aerial.

master *noun*
1 a man who teaches in a school. 2 someone who is in charge of something. 3 a great artist, composer, sportsman, etc. 4 something from which copies are made. 5 **Master,** a word used before a boy's name when addressing a letter to him.

master *verb*
1 to learn a subject or skill. 2 to defeat.

masterly *adjective*
very clever.

master-mind *noun*
1 a very clever person. 2 someone who organizes a scheme, crime, etc.

masterpiece *noun*
1 an excellent piece of work. 2 someone's best piece of work.

mastery *noun*
1 complete control of something. 2 thorough knowledge or skill.

mastodon *noun*
a large extinct animal rather like an elephant.

masturbate *verb* (**masturbated, masturbating**)
to excite yourself by fingering your genitals.
masturbation *noun*

mat *noun*
1 a small carpet. 2 a small piece of material put on a table to protect the surface from hot or wet cups or plates.

matador *noun*
someone who fights and kills the bull in a bull-fight.

match *noun*[1] (**matches**)
a small, thin stick that gives a flame when rubbed on something rough.
matchbox *noun*, **matchstick** *noun*

match *noun*[2] (**matches**)
1 a game or contest between two teams or players. 2 one person or thing that matches another. 3 a marriage.

match *verb*
1 to be equal or similar to another person or thing. 2 to put somebody in competition with somebody else.

mate *noun*[1]
1 a friend or companion. 2 one of a mated pair. 3 one of the officers on a ship.

mate *noun*[2]
a situation in chess when you cannot stop the king being taken.

mate *verb* **(mated, mating)**
to come or put together so as to have offspring.

material *noun*
1 anything used for making something else.
2 cloth.

maternal *adjective*
of a mother or mothers; motherly.
maternally *adverb*

maternity *noun*
having a baby.

mathematician *noun*
(*say* math-ĕm-ă-**tish**-ăn)
an expert in mathematics.

mathematics *noun*
the study of numbers, measurements, and shapes.
mathematical *adjective*, **mathematically** *adverb*

maths *noun*
(*informal*) mathematics.

matinée *noun*
(*say* **mat**-in-ay)
an afternoon performance at a theatre or cinema.

matrimony *noun*
(*say* **mat**-ri-mŏn-i)
marriage.
matrimonial *adjective*

matt *adjective*
not shiny. *matt paint.*

matted *adjective*
tangled. *matted hair.*

matter *noun*
1 something you need to think about or do. *a serious matter.* 2 a substance. *colouring matter.* 3 **a matter of fact,** something true. 4 **no matter,** it does not matter. 5 **what's the matter?,** what is wrong?

matter *verb*
to be important.

matting *noun*
mats; rough material for covering a floor.

mattress *noun* **(mattresses)**
a large, flat bag filled with soft or springy material and used on or as a bed.

mature *adjective*
fully grown or developed; grown-up.
maturely *adverb*, **maturity** *noun*

mauve *adjective*
(*say* mohv)
pale purple.

maximum *noun* **(maxima)**
the greatest possible number or amount. *10 out of 10 is the maximum.*

maximum *adjective*
greatest. *maximum speed.*

may *verb* (*past tense* **might**)
1 to be allowed to. *May I have a sweet?* 2 will possibly; has possibly. *He may come tomorrow. He might have missed the train.*

May *noun*[1]
1 the fifth month of the year. 2 **May Day,** 1 May.

may *noun*[2]
hawthorn blossom.

maybe *adverb*
perhaps.

mayday *noun*
an international radio-signal calling for help.

mayonnaise *noun*
(*say* may-ŏn-**ayz**)
a creamy sauce made from eggs, oil, vinegar, etc.

mayor *noun*
the person in charge of the council in a town or city.
mayoral *adjective*, **mayoress** *noun*

maypole *noun*
a decorated pole round which people dance on May Day.

maze *noun*
a complicated and puzzling network of paths or lines to follow.

me *pronoun*
the person who is speaking or writing.

meadow *noun*
a field of grass.

meagre *adjective*
(*say* **meeg**-er)
scanty; not sufficient.

meal *noun*
a time when food is eaten; the food eaten at breakfast, lunch, tea, dinner, or supper.
mealtime *noun*

mean *verb* **(meant, meaning)**
1 to try to convey something; to indicate; to be the same as something. '*Maybe*' means '*perhaps*'. 2 to intend. *I meant to tell him, but I forgot.*

mean *adjective*[1]
1 not generous; selfish. *a mean man.* 2 unkind; spiteful. *a mean trick.*
meanly *adverb*, **meanness** *noun*

mean *adjective*[2]
average. *the mean temperature.*

meander *verb*
(*say* mee-**an**-der)
to wander; to take a winding course. *The river meandered across the plain.*

meaning *noun*
what something means.
meaningful *adjective*, **meaningless** *adjective*

means *noun*
1 a way of doing something; a method. 2 money; resources. 3 **by all means,** certainly. 4 **by means of,** using; with. 5 **by no means,** not at all.

meantime *noun*
in the meantime, meanwhile.

meantime *adverb*
meanwhile.

meanwhile *adverb*
at the same time.

measles *noun*
an infectious disease that causes small red spots on the skin.

men

measly *adjective* **(measlier, measliest)**
(*informal*) very small or poor. *What a measly ice-cream!*

measure *verb* **(measured, measuring)**
1 to find out how big something is. 2 to be a certain size. 3 **measure out**, to mark or give a particular amount.
measurable *adjective*, **measurement** *noun*

measure *noun*
1 a unit used for measuring. 2 a device used for measuring. 3 the size of something. 4 something done for a particular purpose; a law.

meat *noun*
animal flesh used as food.
meaty *adjective*

mechanic *noun*
someone who makes, uses, or mends machines.

mechanical *adjective*
1 of, like, or done by machines. 2 automatic; done without thought.
mechanically *adverb*

mechanics *noun*
1 the study of force and movement. 2 the study or use of machines.

mechanism *noun*
the moving parts of a machine; the way a machine works.

medal *noun*
a piece of metal shaped like a coin, star, or cross, given to somebody for being brave or for achieving something.

medallist *noun*
someone who has won a medal.

meddle *verb* **(meddled, meddling)**
to interfere.
meddler *noun*, **meddlesome** *adjective*

media *plural noun*
(*say* **meed**-i-ă)
1 plural of **medium** *noun*. 2 **the media**, things like broadcasting and newspapers which convey information and ideas to the public. *The media are very influential.*

medical *adjective*
connected with the treatment of disease.
medically *adverb*

medicine *noun*
1 a substance, usually swallowed, used to try to cure a disease. 2 the treatment of disease.
medicinal *adjective*

medieval *adjective*
(*say* med-i-**ee**-văl)
of the Middle Ages.

mediocre *adjective*
(*say* meed-i-**oh**-ker)
not very good.
mediocrity *noun*

meditate *verb* **(meditated, meditating)**
to think deeply and seriously.
meditation *noun*, **meditative** *adjective*

Mediterranean *adjective*
of or like the Mediterranean Sea or the countries round it. *a Mediterranean climate.*

medium *adjective*
1 average; of middle size. 2 **medium wave**, a radio wave with a wavelength between 100 and 1,000 metres.

medium *noun* **(mediums or media)**
1 a thing in which something exists, moves, or is expressed. *Newspapers and television are media for advertising.* 2 someone who claims to communicate with the dead. *He visited several mediums.*

meek *adjective*
humble; quiet and obedient.
meekly *adverb*, **meekness** *noun*

meet *verb* **(met, meeting)**
1 to come together from different places; to come face to face. *I met her at the station.* 2 to pay a bill, solve a problem, etc.

meet *noun*
a gathering of riders and hounds for a hunt.

meeting *noun*
a time when people come together for a discussion, contest, etc.

megaphone *noun*
a funnel-shaped device for amplifying somebody's voice.

melancholy *adjective*
sad; gloomy.

mellow *adjective*
not harsh; sweet; friendly.

melodious *adjective*
sounding sweet; pleasant to hear.

melodrama *noun*
a play full of excitement and emotion.
melodramatic *adjective*

melody *noun* **(melodies)**
a tune, especially a pleasing tune.
melodic *adjective*

melon *noun*
a large, round, juicy fruit with yellow or green skin.

melt *verb*
1 to make or become liquid by heating. 2 to go away or disappear slowly.

member *noun*
someone who belongs to a society or group.
membership *noun*

membrane *noun*
a thin skin or covering.

memorable *adjective*
worth remembering; easy to remember.
memorably *adverb*

memorial *noun*
something to remind people of a person or an event. *a war memorial.*

memorize *verb* **(memorized, memorizing)**
to put something into your memory so that you do not forget it.

memory *noun* **(memories)**
1 the ability to remember things. 2 something that you remember. 3 the part of a computer where information is stored. 4 **in memory of**, as a memorial to a person or an event.

men plural of **man** *noun*.

menace *verb* **(menaced, menacing)**
to threaten somebody with harm or danger.
menacingly *adverb*

menace *noun*
1 something menacing. **2** an annoying person
or thing.

menagerie *noun*
(*say* min-**aj**-er-i)
a small zoo.

mend *verb*
to make a damaged thing as useful as it was
before.
mender *noun*

mending *noun*
clothes, etc. to be mended.

menstruate *verb* **(menstruated, menstruating)**
to bleed from the womb about once a month, as
normally happens to women until they are
middle-aged.
menstrual *adjective*, **menstruation** *noun*

mental *adjective*
1 of or in the mind. **2** (*informal*) mad.
mentally *adverb*

mention *verb*
to speak about somebody or something, especially when you are talking about something
else.

menu *noun*
(*say* **men**-yoo)
a list of the food that is available in a restaurant
or served at a meal.

mercenary *adjective*
working only for money or some other reward.

mercenary *noun* **(mercenaries)**
a soldier paid to fight for a foreign country.

merchandise *noun*
goods for buying and selling.

merchant *noun*
1 someone involved in trade. **2 merchant navy,**
the merchant ships of a country. **3 merchant
ship,** a ship carrying merchandise.

merciful *adjective*
kind to someone instead of punishing him.
mercifully *adverb*

merciless *adjective*
not at all merciful; cruel.
mercilessly *adverb*

mercury *noun*
a heavy, silvery metal that is usually liquid.
Some thermometers contain mercury.

mercy *noun* **(mercies)**
1 being merciful. **2** something to be thankful
for. *Thank God for small mercies.*

mere *adjective*
1 not more than; no better than. *He's a mere
child.* **2 the merest,** a very small. *the merest
trace of colour.*

merely *adverb*
only; simply. *She was merely joking.*

merge *verb* **(merged, merging)**
to combine.

merger *noun*
making two businesses or companies into one.

meridian *noun*
(*say* mer-**rid**-i-ăn)
a line on a map or globe from one pole to the
other. *The Greenwich meridian passes through
Greenwich.*

meringue *noun*
(*say* mer-**rang**)
a crisp cake made from the whites of eggs
mixed with sugar and baked.

merit *noun*
1 something that deserves praise. **2 merits,** the
qualities of a person or thing. *Judge it on its
merits.*
meritorious *adjective*

merit *verb*
to deserve. *He merits a reward.*

mermaid *noun*
a mythical creature that looks like a woman
but has a fish's tail instead of legs.

merry *adjective* **(merrier, merriest)**
happy; cheerful.
merrily *adverb*, **merriment** *noun*

merry-go-round *noun*
a revolving machine on which people, especially children, ride for amusement.

mesh *noun* **(meshes)**
1 one of the spaces in a net, sieve, or other criss-
cross structure. **2** material made like a net; a
network. *wire mesh.*

mess *noun* **(messes)**
1 an untidy or dirty condition or thing. **2** a
difficult or confused situation. *He made a mess
of the job.* **3** a place where soldiers or sailors eat
their meals.

mess *verb*
1 mess about, to behave stupidly or idly.
2 mess up, to make a mess of something.

message *noun*
a question or piece of information sent from one
person to another.

messenger *noun*
someone who carries a message.

Messiah *noun*
(*say* mi-**sy**-ă)
1 the person that the Jews expected to come
and set them free. **2** Jesus Christ.

messy *adjective* **(messier, messiest)**
1 untidy or dirty. **2** difficult or complicated.
messily *adverb*, **messiness** *noun*

met past tense and past participle of **meet** *verb.*

metal *noun*
a hard substance that melts when it is hot.
Iron, steel, gold, and tin are all metals.
metallic *adjective*

metallurgy *noun*
(*say* mi-**tal**-er-ji)
the study of metals; the craft of making and
using metals.
metallurgical *adjective*, **metallurgist** *noun*

metamorphic *adjective*
(*say* met-ă-**mor**-fik)
formed or changed by heat or pressure.
metamorphic rocks.

metaphor *noun*
(*say* **met**-ă-fer)
using a word or words to suggest something different from the literal meaning. *'Food for thought' and 'heart of stone' are metaphors.*
metaphorical *adjective*, **metaphorically** *adverb*

meteor *noun*
(*say* **meet**-i-er)
a piece of rock or metal that moves through space and burns up when it gets near the earth.
meteoric *adjective*

meteorite *noun*
(*say* **meet**-i-er-ryt)
a meteor that has landed on the earth.

meteorology *noun*
(*say* meet-i-er-**ol**-ŏ-ji)
the study of the weather.
meteorological *adjective*, **meteorologist** *noun*

meter *noun*
a machine for measuring something, especially for measuring how much of something has been used. *a gas meter.*

method *noun*
1 a way of doing something. **2** methodical behaviour.

methodical *adjective*
(*say* mi-**thod**-i-kăl)
done carefully; well organized.
methodically *adverb*

Methodist *noun*
someone who believes in Methodism, a Christian religious movement started by John and Charles Wesley in the 18th century.

meths *noun*
(*informal*) methylated spirit.

methylated spirit or **spirits** *noun*
a liquid fuel made from alcohol.

meticulous *adjective*
working very carefully or precisely.
meticulously *adverb*

metre *noun*
(*say* **meet**-er)
1 the main unit of length in the metric system, equal to about 39½ inches. **2** a particular type of rhythm in poetry.

metric *adjective*
1 of or in the metric system. **2** of poetic metre. **3 metric system,** a measuring system based on decimal units. *In the metric system, the metre is the unit of length, the kilogram is the unit of weight, and the litre is the unit of capacity.*
metrically *adverb*

metricate *verb* (**metricated, metricating**)
to change to the metric system.
metrication *noun*

metronome *noun*
(*say* **met**-rŏ-nohm)
a device that makes a regular clicking noise to help you keep in time when practising music.

mew *verb*
to make a sound like a cat.

miaow *verb*
(*say* mee-**ow**)
to mew.

mice plural of **mouse.**

microbe *noun*
(*say* **my**-krohb)
a microscopic creature.

microfilm *noun*
film on which something is photographed in a miniature size.

microphone *noun*
an electrical device that picks up sound waves for amplifying, broadcasting, or recording.

micro-processor *noun*
a silicon chip.

microscope *noun*
(*say* **my**-krŏ-skohp)
a device with lenses that magnify tiny objects.

microscopic *adjective*
(*say* my-krŏ-**skop**-ik)
1 too small to be seen without a microscope; tiny. **2** of the microscope.

mid *adjective*
in the middle of. *The holiday is from mid-July to mid-August.*

midday *noun*
noon.

middle *noun*
1 the place or part of something that is at the same distance from all its sides or edges or from both its ends. **2** someone's waist.

middle *adjective*
1 placed in the middle. **2 middle age,** the time between youth and old age. **3 Middle Ages,** the period in history from about A.D. 1100 to about 1500. **4 middle class,** the class of people between the upper class and the working class. **5 Middle East,** the countries roughly between Libya and India. **6 middle school,** a school for children aged from about 9 to 13.

middle-aged *adjective*
of or in middle age.

midge *noun*
a small insect like a gnat.

midget *noun*
an unusually short person.

midland *adjective*
of the Midlands.

Midlands *plural noun*
the middle part of England.

midnight *noun*
twelve o'clock at night.

midst *noun*
the middle of something.

midsummer *noun*
the middle of summer, which is the end of June in the northern hemisphere.

midway *adverb*
half-way.

midwife *noun* (**midwives**)
someone trained to help when a baby is being born.
midwifery *noun*

might past tense of **may** *verb*.

might *noun*
strength; great power.

mighty *adjective* **(mightier, mightiest)**
very strong or powerful.
mightily *adverb,* **mightiness** *noun*

migraine *noun*
(*say* **mee**-grayn)
a severe kind of headache.

migrant *noun*
(*say* **my**-gr ănt)
a migrating person or animal.

migrate *verb* **(migrated, migrating)**
(*say* my-**grayt**)
to go to live in another country. *The birds migrated every autumn.*
migration *noun,* **migratory** *adjective*

mike *noun*
(*informal*) a microphone.

mild *adjective*
gentle.
mildly *adverb,* **mildness** *noun*

mile *noun*
a measure of distance, equal to 1,760 yards or about 1⅗ kilometres.

mileage *noun*
the number of miles travelled.

milestone *noun*
1 a stone of a kind that used to be placed beside a road to mark the distance between towns. **2** an important event.

militant *adjective*
prepared or wanting to fight or be aggressive.
militancy *noun*

militarism *noun*
belief in, or use of, military methods.
militarist *noun,* **militaristic** *adjective*

military *adjective*
of soldiers or the armed forces.

milk *noun*
1 a white liquid that female mammals produce in their bodies to feed to their babies. *People drink milk from cows and goats.* **2 milk pudding,** a pudding made with milk.

milk *verb*
to get the milk from a cow or other animal.

milkman *noun* **(milkmen)**
a man who delivers milk to people's houses.

milky *adjective* **(milkier, milkiest)**
like milk; white.

mill *noun*
1 a building with machinery for grinding corn to make flour. **2** a factory. *a paper-mill.* **3** a grinding machine. *a coffee-mill.*

mill *verb*
1 to grind corn into flour. **2** to move in a confused crowd. *The animals were milling about.*
miller *noun*

millet *noun*
a kind of cereal with tiny seeds.

milligram *noun*
one thousandth of a gram.

millimetre *noun*
one thousandth of a metre.

million *noun*
the number 1,000,000; a thousand thousands.
millionth *adjective*

millionaire *noun*
an extremely rich person.

milometer *noun*
(*say* my-**lom**-it-er)
a device for measuring how far a vehicle has travelled.

mime *verb* **(mimed, miming)**
to tell somebody something, act a story, or pretend to do something by using actions, not words.

mimic *verb* **(mimicked, mimicking)**
to imitate somebody, especially so as to make fun of him.
mimicry *noun*

mince *verb* **(minced, mincing)**
to cut food into very small pieces.
mincer *noun*

mince *noun*
1 minced meat. **2 mince pie,** a pie containing mincemeat.

mincemeat *noun*
a sweet mixture of currants, raisins, chopped apple, etc. used in pies.

mind *noun*
1 the power to think, feel, understand, and remember; your thoughts and feelings. **2** someone's opinion. *Have you changed your mind?* **3 mind's eye,** imagination.

mind *verb*
1 to look after. *He was minding the baby.* **2** to be careful of; to watch out for. *Mind the doors!* **3** to be sad or upset about something; to object to something. *I don't mind missing the party.*

mine *adjective* and *pronoun*
belonging to me. *That book is mine.*

mine *noun*
1 a place where coal, metal, jewels, etc. are dug out of the ground. **2** an explosive hidden under the ground or in the sea to destroy people and things that come close to it.

mine *verb* **(mined, mining)**
1 to dig something from a mine. **2** to lay explosive mines in a place.

miner *noun*
someone who works in a mine.

mineral *noun*
1 a hard substance that can be dug out of the ground. *Iron-ore and coal are minerals.* **2** a cold fizzy drink.

mingle *verb* **(mingled, mingling)**
to mix or blend.

mingy *adjective* **(mingier, mingiest)**
(*say* **min**-ji)
(*informal*) mean; stingy.

miniature *adjective*
(*say* **min**-i-cher)
tiny; copying something on a very small scale.

minibus *noun* **(minibuses)**
a vehicle like a small bus with seats for several people.

minim *noun*
a musical note equal to half a semibreve, written *d*.

minimum *noun* **(minima)**
the smallest possible amount or number. *The teacher wants a minimum of noise.*
minimal *adjective,* **minimize** *verb*

minister *noun*
1 someone in charge of a government department. *The Minister of Health decided to close the hospital.* **2** a clergyman.

ministry *noun* **(ministries)**
1 a government department. **2** the work of a clergyman.

mink *noun*
1 a small animal rather like a stoat. **2** this animal's valuable brown fur.

minnow *noun*
a tiny freshwater fish.

minor *adjective*
1 less important; not very important. *a minor operation.* **2** of the musical scale that has a semitone between the 2nd and 3rd notes.

minority *noun* **(minorities)**
(*say* myn-**o**-ri-ti)
1 the smaller part of a group of people or things. **2** a small group that is different from others.

minstrel *noun*
a wandering musician in the Middle Ages.

mint *noun*[1]
1 a green plant with fragrant leaves used for flavouring. **2** a sweet flavoured with peppermint. **3 mint sauce,** chopped mint-leaves in vinegar, used as a sauce on roast lamb.

mint *noun*[2]
a place where coins are made.

mint *adjective*
unused and clean. *a mint stamp.*

minus *preposition*
reduced by subtracting; less. *Eight minus two equals six (8 − 2 = 6).*

minute *noun*
(*say* **min**-it)
1 one sixtieth of an hour. **2** (*informal*) a short time. *I'll be ready in a minute!* **3 minutes,** a summary of what has been said at a meeting.

minute *adjective*
(*say* my-**newt**)
1 tiny. *a minute insect.* **2** very detailed. *a minute examination.*
minutely *adverb*

miracle *noun*
a wonderful or magical happening that is unexpected.
miraculous *adjective,* **miraculously** *adverb*

mirage *noun*
(*say* **mi**-rahzh)
something that a person imagines he sees but which is not there at all. *The lake he thought he saw in the desert was a mirage.*

mirror *noun*
a glass or metal device or surface that reflects things clearly.

mirth *noun*
laughter; cheerfulness.

misbehave *verb* **(misbehaved, misbehaving)**
to behave badly or naughtily.
misbehaviour *noun*

miscarriage *noun*
the birth of a baby too early, so that it dies.

miscellaneous *adjective*
(*say* mis-**êl**-**ay**-ni-ûs)
of various kinds.
miscellany *noun*

mischief *noun*
naughty or troublesome behaviour.
mischievous *adjective*

miser *noun*
someone who hoards money and spends as little as he can.
miserly *adjective*

miserable *adjective*
unhappy; wretched.
miserably *adverb*

misery *noun* **(miseries)**
1 unhappiness; suffering. **2** (*informal*) someone who is miserable or always complaining.

misfit *noun*
1 someone who does not fit in well with other people or with his surroundings. **2** a garment that does not fit.

misfortune *noun*
1 an unlucky event; an accident. **2** bad luck.

mishap *noun*
(*say* **mis**-hap)
an unfortunate accident.

mislay *verb* **(mislaid, mislaying)**
to lose something for a short time.

mislead *verb* **(misled, misleading)**
to give somebody a wrong idea or impression; to deceive. *I was misled into thinking he was reliable.*

misprint *noun*
a mistake in printing.

miss *verb*
1 to fail to hit, reach, catch, see, hear, or find something. **2** to be sad because someone or something is not with you. *I missed my mother when she was in hospital.* **3** to notice that something has gone.

miss *noun*[1] **(misses)**
1 missing something. *Was that shot a hit or a miss?* **2** (*informal*) an unsuccessful gramophone record or tune.

Miss *noun*[2] **(Misses)**
a word used before the name of a girl or unmarried woman when speaking or writing politely to or about her. *Dear Miss Jones.*

missal *noun*
a Roman Catholic prayer-book.

missile *noun*
a weapon fired or thrown at a target.

missing *adjective*
lost; not in the proper place.

mission *noun*
1 an important job that someone is sent to do or that someone feels he must do. 2 a place or building where missionaries work.

missionary *noun* **(missionaries)**
someone who goes to another country to spread his religion.

mist *noun*
1 damp cloudy air like a thin fog. 2 condensed water-vapour on a window, mirror, etc.

mistake *noun*
1 something wrong; an incorrect action or idea. 2 **by mistake,** by being careless, forgetful, etc.

mistake *verb (past tense* **mistook;** *past participle* **mistaken;** *present participle* **mistaking)**
to misunderstand; to choose or identify wrongly.

mistaken *adjective*
incorrect; wrong.
mistakenly *adverb*

mister *noun*
1 Mr. 2 *(informal)* sir. *Can you tell me the time, mister?*

mistletoe *noun*
a plant with green leaves and white berries in winter. *People kiss each other under the mistletoe that is used as a Christmas decoration.*

mistreat *verb*
to treat somebody badly or unfairly.
mistreatment *noun*

mistress *noun* **(mistresses)**
1 a woman who teaches in a school. 2 a woman in charge of something. 3 the woman who owns a dog or other animal. 4 a woman that a man loves, even though he is married to somebody else.

mistrust *verb*
not to trust somebody or something.

misty *adjective* **(mistier, mistiest)**
1 full of mist. 2 not clear.
mistily *adverb,* **mistiness** *noun*

misunderstand *verb*
(misunderstood, misunderstanding)
to get a wrong idea or impression of something. *You misunderstood what I said.*

misuse *verb* **(misused, misusing)**
(say mis-**yooz**)
to use something wrongly; to treat something badly.

misuse *noun*
(say mis-**yooss**)
misusing something.

mite *noun*
1 a tiny insect found in food. 2 a small child.

mitre *noun*
(say **my**-ter)
1 the tall, tapering hat worn by a bishop. 2 a joint of two tapering pieces of wood, cloth, etc.

mitten *noun*
a glove without separate parts for the fingers.

mix *verb*
1 to stir or shake different things together to make one thing; to combine. 2 to get together with other people. 3 **mix up,** to confuse.
mixer *noun*

mixed *adjective*
for or containing various kinds of people or things, especially males and females (*a mixed school*) or people of different races or religions (*a mixed marriage*).

mixture *noun*
something made of different things mixed together.

mm. short for *millimetre* or *millimetres.*

moan *noun*
1 a long low sound, usually of suffering. 2 a grumble.

moan *verb*
to make a moan.

moat *noun*
a deep ditch round a castle, usually full of water.

mob *noun*
1 a dangerous crowd of people. 2 (*in Australia and New Zealand*) a flock of sheep, herd of cattle, group of kangaroos, etc.

mob *verb* **(mobbed, mobbing)**
to crowd round somebody.

mobile *adjective*
that can or does move. *a mobile shop.*
mobility *noun*

mobile *noun*
something decorative made to be hung from a ceiling, etc. so that it moves about in the air.

mobilize *verb* **(mobilized, mobilizing)**
to assemble people or things ready for a particular purpose, especially for war.
mobilization *noun*

moccasin *noun*
(say **mok**-ă-sin)
a soft leather shoe like those worn by North American Indians.

mock *adjective*
not real; imitation. *mock cream.*

mock *verb*
to make fun of somebody or something.
mockery *noun*

mock-up *noun*
a model of something. *They made a mock-up of the rocket.*

mode *noun*
1 the way that something is done. 2 what is fashionable.

model *noun*
1 a small copy of an object. *He makes models of aircraft.* 2 a particular version or design of something. *We saw the new models at the motor show.* 3 someone who poses for an artist or photographer. 4 someone whose job is to display clothes by wearing them. 5 an excellent person or thing.

model *verb* **(modelled, modelling)**
1 to make a model of something. 2 to make something by following a pattern. 3 to work as an artist's model or a fashion model.

moderate *adjective*
(say **mod**-er-ăt)
that is not too little and not too much; medium.
moderately *adverb,* **moderation** *noun*

moderate *verb* (moderated, moderating)
(*say* mod-er-ayt)
to make something less strong or severe.

modern *adjective*
of the kind that is normal now. *a modern house.*
modernity *noun*

modernize *verb* (modernized, modernizing)
to make something modern; to change something to suit modern tastes.
modernization *noun*

modest *adjective*
1 not thinking too much of how good you are.
2 moderate. *Their needs were modest.*
modestly *adverb*, **modesty** *noun*

modify *verb* (modified, modifying)
to change something slightly.
modification *noun*

module *noun*
(*say* mod-yool)
1 an independent part of a spacecraft, building, etc. **2** a unit used in measuring.

moist *adjective*
damp.
moisture *noun*

moisten *verb*
(*say* moi-sĕn)
to make or become moist.

molar *noun*
(*say* moh-ler)
one of the wide teeth at the back of the mouth.

mole *noun*
1 a small, grey, furry animal that digs holes under the ground. **2** a small dark spot on someone's skin.

molecule *noun*
(*say* mol-i-kewl)
the smallest part into which you can divide a substance without changing its chemical nature; a group of atoms.
molecular *adjective*

molehill *noun*
1 a small pile of earth thrown up by a mole.
2 make a mountain out of a molehill, to give something too much importance.

mollusc *noun*
an animal with a soft body and usually a hard shell. *Snails, slugs, and oysters are molluscs.*

molten *adjective*
melted.

moment *noun*
1 a very short period of time. *Wait a moment.*
2 a particular time. *He arrived at the last moment.* **3 at the moment,** now.

momentary *adjective*
(*say* moh-mĕn-ter-i)
lasting for only a moment.
momentarily *adverb*

momentous *adjective*
(*say* moh-**ment**-ŭs)
very important.

momentum *noun*
(*say* moh-**ment**-ŭm)
movement; the amount or force of movement.

monarch *noun*
a king, queen, emperor, or empress.
monarchy *noun*

monastery *noun* (monasteries)
(*say* mon-ă-ster-i)
a building where monks live and work.
monastic *adjective*

Monday *noun*
the second day of the week.

money *noun*
1 coins and notes used by people to buy things.
2 money for jam or **money for old rope,** (*informal*) profit easily made.

Mongol *noun*[1]
a Mongolian person.

mongol *noun*[2]
someone born with a condition that limits his mental development.

Mongolian *adjective*
of Mongolia.

mongoose *noun*
a small animal rather like a stoat, that can kill snakes.

mongrel *noun*
(*say* **mung**-rĕl)
a dog of mixed breeds.

monitor *noun*
1 a pupil who is given a special job to do at school. **2** a device used for checking how something is working.

monk *noun*
a member of a religious community of men.

monkey *noun*
1 an animal rather like man, with long arms and a tail. **2** a mischievous person.

monologue *noun*
(*say* **mon**-ŏ-log)
a long speech by one person or performer.

monopoly *noun* (monopolies)
doing all the business, trade, etc. in one thing; controlling the supply of something. *The government has a monopoly in supplying electricity.*
monopolize *verb*

monorail *noun*
a railway that uses only one rail.

monotonous *adjective*
(*say* mŏn-**ot**-ŏn-ŭs)
boring because it does not change. *monotonous work.*
monotonously *adverb*, **monotony** *noun*

monsoon *noun*
a strong wind in and around the Indian Ocean, bringing heavy rain in summer.

monster *noun*
a large, frightening creature.

monster *adjective*
huge.

monstrous *adjective*
1 like a monster; huge. **2** very shocking or cruel.
monstrosity *noun*

month *noun*
one of the twelve parts into which a year is divided.

monthly *adjective*
happening every month; done every month.

monument *noun*
a statue, building, column, etc. put up as a memorial of some person or event.

monumental *adjective*
1 of or for a monument. 2 great; huge. *a monumental achievement.*

moo *verb*
to make the sound of a cow.

mood *noun*
the way someone feels. *She's in a good mood.*

moody *adjective* (**moodier, moodiest**)
gloomy; likely to become bad-tempered suddenly.
moodily *adverb*, **moodiness** *noun*

moon *noun*
the satellite of the earth that shines in the sky at night.
moonless *adjective*, **moonlight** *noun*, **moonlit** *adjective*

moor *noun*
an area of rough, windy land with bushes but no trees.

moor *verb*
to tie up a boat; to secure something.
moorings *plural noun*

moorhen *noun*
a small water-bird.

moose *noun* (**moose**)
a North American elk.

mop *noun*
a piece of soft material on the end of a stick, used for cleaning floors or dishes.

mop *verb* (**mopped, mopping**)
1 to clean with a mop. 2 **mop up**, to clear away the remains of something.

mope *verb* (**moped, moping**)
to be sad.

moped *noun*
(*say* **moh**-ped)
a small motor-cycle.

moral *adjective*
1 virtuous. 2 connected with right and wrong.
morality *noun*, **morally** *adverb*

moral *noun*
1 a lesson taught by a story or event. 2 **morals**, standards of behaviour; virtuousness.

morale *noun*
(*say* mŏ-**rahl**)
confidence or courage.

more *adjective*
larger in number or amount.

more *noun*
a larger number or amount. *I want more.*

more *adverb*
1 again. *I'll tell you once more.* 2 to a greater extent. *You must work more.* 3 **more or less**, about; approximately.

moreover *adverb*
also; in addition.

Mormon *noun*
a member of a Christian religious group founded in the U.S.A.

morning *noun*
the part of the day before noon or before lunchtime.

moron *noun*
1 a person with very poor mental abilities. 2 (*informal*) a stupid person.
moronic *adjective*

morphine *noun*
(*say* **mor**-feen)
a drug made from opium, used to relieve pain.

morris dance *noun*
a traditional English folk-dance by people in costume with ribbons and bells.

Morse code *noun*
a code using dots and dashes to represent letters and numbers. *Radio operators often use Morse code to send messages.*

morsel *noun*
a small piece of food.

mortal *adjective*
1 that can die. *All men are mortal.* 2 that causes death. *a mortal wound.*
mortality *noun*, **mortally** *adverb*

mortar *noun*
a mixture of sand, cement, and water used in building to stick bricks together.

mortgage *noun*
(*say* **mor**-gij)
an agreement to borrow money to buy a house.

mortuary *noun* (**mortuaries**)
a place where dead bodies are kept before they are buried.

mosaic *noun*
(*say* mŏ-**zay**-ik)
a picture or design made from small coloured pieces of glass, stone, paper, etc.

Moslem *noun*
(*say* **moz**-lĕm)
a Muslim.

mosque *noun*
(*say* mosk)
a building where Muslims worship.

mosquito *noun* (**mosquitoes**)
(*say* mos-**kee**-toh)
an insect that sucks blood. *Mosquitoes spread malaria.*

moss *noun* (**mosses**)
a plant that grows in damp places and has no flower.
mossy *adjective*

most *adjective*
largest in number or amount.

most *noun*
the largest number or amount.

most *adverb*
1 more than any other. *I liked that teacher most.* 2 very; extremely. *It was most amusing.*

mostly *adverb*
mainly.

M.O.T. or **M.O.T. test** *noun*
(*informal*) a compulsory annual test of vehicles that are more than a certain age.

motel *noun*
(*say* moh-**tel**)
a hotel for motorists.

moth *noun*
an insect rather like a butterfly that usually flies around at night.

mother *noun*
1 a female parent. **2 Mothering Sunday** or **Mother's Day,** the fourth Sunday in Lent, when people often give presents to their mothers.
motherhood *noun*, **motherless** *adjective*

motherly *adjective*
kind or tender like a mother.

motion *noun*
movement.
motionless *adjective*

motive *noun*
what makes a person do something.

motor *noun*
a machine that provides power.

motor bike *noun*
(*informal*) a motor cycle.

motor boat *noun*
a boat driven by a motor.

motor car *noun*
a motor vehicle large enough to carry several people.

motor cycle *noun*
a motor vehicle with two wheels.
motor-cyclist *noun*

motorist *noun*
someone who drives a motor car, especially for pleasure.

motor vehicle *noun*
a vehicle driven by a motor, for use on roads.

motorway *noun*
a wide road for fast long-distance traffic.

mottled *adjective*
marked with spots or patches of colour.

motto *noun* (**mottoes**)
1 a short saying used as a guide for behaviour. *His motto was 'I serve'.* **2** a short verse, riddle, etc. found inside a cracker.

mould *noun*[1]
a container for making things like jelly or plaster set in the shape that is wanted.

mould *noun*[2]
a furry growth that appears on some moist surfaces, especially on something decaying. *There is mould on this cheese.*
mouldy *adjective*

mould *verb*
to make something have a particular shape or character.

moult *verb*
(*say* mohlt)
to lose feathers or hair. *Our cat is moulting.*

mound *noun*
a pile of earth, stones, etc.; a small hill.

mount *verb*
1 to get on to a horse or bicycle so that you can ride it. **2** to rise. **3** to put something firmly in place for use or display. *Mount your photos in an album.*

mount *noun*
1 a mountain. *Mount Everest.* **2** something in or on which an object is mounted. **3** an animal on which you are riding.

mountain *noun*
a very high hill.
mountainous *adjective*

mountaineer *noun*
someone who climbs mountains.
mountaineering *noun*

mourn *verb*
to be sad, especially because someone has died.
mourner *noun*

mournful *adjective*
sad.
mournfully *adverb*

mouse *noun* (**mice**)
a small animal with a long tail and a pointed nose.
mousetrap *noun*, **mousy** *adjective*

mousse *noun*
(*say* mooss)
a sweet flavoured pudding made with cream and served cold.

moustache *noun*
(*say* mŭs-**tahsh**)
hair growing above a man's upper lip.

mouth *noun*
1 the part of the face that opens for eating and speaking. **2** the place where a river enters the sea. **3** an opening or outlet.
mouthful *noun*

mouth-organ *noun*
a musical instrument played by blowing and sucking.

mouthpiece *noun*
the part of a musical instrument or other device that you put to your mouth.

movable *adjective*
that can be moved.

move *verb* (**moved, moving**)
1 to take or go from one place to another. **2** to affect somebody's emotions. *Their story moved us deeply.* **3 moving picture,** a series of photographs shown in quick succession to give the appearance of movement. **4 moving staircase,** an escalator.

move *noun*
1 a movement. **2** somebody's turn in a game. **3 get a move on,** (*informal*) to hurry up. **4 on the move,** moving; making progress.

movement *noun*
1 the action of moving or being moved. **2** a group of people working for a particular cause. **3** one of the main parts of a piece of music. *a symphony in four movements.*

movie *noun*
a moving picture; a film.

mow *verb* (*past tense* **mowed**; *past participle* **mown**; *present participle* **mowing**)
1 to cut grass. **2 mow down**, to knock down or kill in large numbers.
mower *noun*

M.P. short for *Member of Parliament*.

m.p.h. short for *miles per hour*.

Mr. *noun* (**Messrs.**)
(*say* **mis**-ter)
a word used before the name of a man when speaking or writing politely to or about him.

Mrs. *noun* (**Mrs.** or **Mesdames**)
(*say* **mis**-iz)
a word used before the name of a married woman when speaking or writing politely to or about her.

Ms. *noun*
(*say* miz)
a word used before the name of a woman when speaking or writing to or about her.

much *adjective*
existing in a large amount. *much work*.

much *noun*
a large amount of something.

much *adverb*
1 greatly; considerably. *much to my surprise*. **2** about; approximately. *It's much the same*.

muck *noun*
1 dirt; filth. **2** a mess. *You have made a muck of it.*
mucky *adjective*

muck *verb*
(*informal*) **1 muck about** or **muck around**, to mess about. **2 muck up**, to mess up.

mud *noun*
wet, soft earth.
muddy *adjective*

muddle *verb* (**muddled**, **muddling**)
to mix things up; to confuse.
muddler *noun*

muddle *noun*
a confusion or mess.

mudguard *noun*
a device to stop mud and water being thrown up by the wheels of a vehicle.

muesli *noun*
(*say* **mooz**-li)
a food made of cereals, nuts, dried fruit, etc.

muffle *verb* (**muffled**, **muffling**)
1 to cover or wrap something up to protect it or keep it warm. **2** to deaden the sound of something. *a muffled scream*.

mug *noun*
1 a large cup, usually used without a saucer. **2** (*slang*) a fool; someone who is easily cheated. **3** (*slang*) a person's face.

mug *verb* (**mugged**, **mugging**)
to attack and rob somebody in the street.
mugger *noun*

muggy *adjective* (**muggier**, **muggiest**)
unpleasantly warm and damp. *muggy weather*.

mule *noun*
an animal that is a hybrid of a donkey and a mare.

multiple *adjective*
having or involving many parts or elements.

multiple *noun*
a number that contains an exact amount of another number. *30 and 50 are multiples of 10.*

multiply *verb* (**multiplied**, **multiplying**)
1 to take a number a given quantity of times. *Five multiplied by four equals twenty* ($5 \times 4 = 20$). **2** to increase quickly. *The rabbits were multiplying.*
multiplication *noun*

multiracial *adjective*
(*say* mul-ti-**ray**-shăl)
consisting of people of many different races. *a multiracial society.*

multitude *noun*
a very large number of people or things.
multitudinous *adjective*

mum *noun*
(*informal*) mother.

mumble *verb* (**mumbled**, **mumbling**)
to speak so that you are not easy to hear.
mumbler *noun*

mummy *noun*[1] (**mummies**)
a corpse preserved for burial as was the custom in ancient Egypt.
mummify *verb*

mummy *noun*[2] (**mummies**)
(*informal*) mother.

mumps *noun*
an infectious disease that makes your neck swell up.

munch *verb*
to chew noisily.

municipal *adjective*
(*say* mew-**nis**-i-păl)
of a town or city.

mural *noun*
a picture painted on a wall.

murder *verb*
to kill somebody deliberately.
murderer *noun*, **murderess** *noun*

murder *noun*
1 the murdering of somebody. **2** (*informal*) something very difficult or unpleasant.
murderous *adjective*

murky *adjective* (**murkier**, **murkiest**)
dark and gloomy.

murmur *noun*
a low continuous sound; softly spoken words.

murmur *verb*
to make a murmur.

muscle *noun*
one of the parts inside the body that cause movement.
muscular *adjective*

museum *noun*
a place where interesting objects, especially old things, are displayed for people to see.

mushroom *noun*
an edible fungus with a dome-shaped top.
mushroom *verb*
to grow or appear suddenly. *Blocks of flats mushroomed in the city.*
music *noun*
1 pleasant or interesting sounds made by instruments or by the voice. 2 printed or written instructions for making music. 3 **music centre,** a radio, record-player, and cassette recorder combined in one cabinet.
musical *adjective*
1 of or for music. *musical instruments.* 2 good at music; interested in music. *Are you musical?*
musically *adverb*
musical *noun*
a play or film containing a lot of music.
musician *noun*
a musical person; someone who plays a musical instrument.
musket *noun*
an old type of rifle.
musketeer *noun*
Muslim *noun*
(*say* **muuz**-lim)
someone who follows the religious teachings of Muhammad.
muslin *noun*
thin, fine cotton cloth.
mussel *noun*
a black shellfish, often found sticking to rocks.
must *verb*
1 to have to; to be forced or obliged to do something. *I must go home soon.* 2 to be sure to; to be definitely. *You must be joking!*
mustard *noun*
1 a yellow paste or powder used to give food a hot taste. 2 **mustard and cress,** small green plants eaten in salads.
muster *verb*
to assemble or gather together.
musty *adjective* (**mustier, mustiest**)
smelling or tasting mouldy or stale.
mustiness *noun*
mutation *noun*
a change in the form or shape of something.
mute *adjective*
unable to speak; silent.
muted *adjective,* **mutely** *adverb*

mute *noun*
1 a mute person. 2 **a** device fitted to a musical instrument to make it quieter.
mutilate *verb* (**mutilated, mutilating**)
to damage something by breaking or cutting off part of it.
mutilation *noun*
mutineer *noun*
(*say* mew-tin-**eer**)
someone who mutinies.
mutiny *noun* (**mutinies**)
(*say* **mew**-tin-i)
a rebellion by sailors or soldiers against their officers.
mutinous *adjective,* **mutinously** *adverb*
mutiny *verb* (**mutinied, mutinying**)
(*say* **mew**-tin-i)
to take part in a mutiny.
mutter *verb*
to murmur or grumble.
mutton *noun*
meat from a sheep.
mutual *adjective*
(*say* **mew**-tew-ăl)
exchanged equally; shared. *mutual help.*
mutually *adverb*
muzzle *noun*
1 an animal's nose and mouth. 2 a cover put over an animal's nose and mouth so that it cannot bite. 3 the open end of a gun.
my *adjective*
of me; belonging to me.
myself *pronoun*
1 me and nobody else. *I'm ashamed of myself.* 2 **by myself,** on my own; alone.
mystery *noun* (**mysteries**)
something strange or puzzling.
mysterious *adjective,* **mysteriously** *adverb*
mystify *verb* (**mystified, mystifying**)
to puzzle or bewilder somebody.
mystification *noun*
myth *noun*
1 a legend. 2 an untrue story or belief.
mythological *adjective,* **mythology** *noun*
mythical *adjective*
imaginary; of the sort you find in myths. *mythical beasts.*
myxomatosis *noun*
(*say* miks-ŏ-mă-**toh**-sis)
a disease that kills rabbits.

N

nab *verb* (**nabbed, nabbing**)
(*informal*) to catch; to grab.

nag *verb* (**nagged, nagging**)
to keep telling somebody that you are not pleased with him.

nag *noun*
(*informal*) a horse.

nail *noun*
1 the hard covering on the end of a finger or toe. 2 a small, sharp piece of metal used to fix pieces of wood together.

naïve *adjective*
(*say* nah-**eev**)
not experienced; innocent.
naïvely *adverb*, **naïvety** *noun*

naked *adjective*
(*say* **nay**-kid)
1 nude; without any covering. **2 the naked eye,**
the eye when it is not helped by a telescope,
microscope, etc.
nakedly *adverb*, **nakedness** *noun*

name *noun*
what you call a person or thing.
nameless *adjective*

name *verb* (**named, naming**)
1 to give somebody or something a name. 2 to
mention a name.

namely *adverb*
that is to say. *Only one boy was absent, namely
Harry Smith.*

nanny *noun* (**nannies**)
(*informal*) 1 a nursemaid. 2 a grandmother.

nanny-goat *noun*
a female goat.

nap *noun*
a short sleep.

napalm *noun*
(*say* **nay**-pahm)
a substance made of petrol, used in some kinds
of bomb.

napkin *noun*
1 a serviette. 2 a nappy.

nappy *noun* (**nappies**)
a piece of cloth put round a baby's bottom.

narcissus *noun* (**narcissi**)
(*say* nar-**sis**-ŭs)
a garden flower like a daffodil.

narcotic *noun*
(*say* nar-**kot**-ik)
a drug that makes you sleepy or unconscious.

narrate *verb* (**narrated, narrating**)
to tell a story; to give an account of something.
narration *noun*, **narrative** *noun*, **narrator** *noun*

narrow *adjective*
1 not wide. 2 with only a small margin of
safety. *a narrow escape.*
narrowly *adverb*

narrow-minded *adjective*
not liking or understanding other people's
ideas.

nasturtium *noun*
(*say* nă-**ster**-shŭm)
a garden flower with round leaves.

nasty *adjective* (**nastier, nastiest**)
not pleasant; unkind.
nastily *adverb*, **nastiness** *noun*

nation *noun*
1 a large number of people who live in the same
part of the world and have the same language,
customs, etc. 2 a country and the people who
live there.
national *adjective*, **nationally** *adverb*

nationalist *noun*
someone who is very patriotic; someone who
wants his nation to be independent
nationalism *noun*, **nationalistic** *adjective*

nationality *noun* (**nationalities**)
the nation someone belongs to. *What is his
nationality?*

nationalize *verb* (**nationalized, nationalizing**)
to put something under government control.
nationalization *noun*

native *noun*
1 someone born in a particular place. *He is a
native of Sweden.* 2 one of the original inhabitants of a country. *Settlers traded with the
natives.*

native *adjective*
1 natural; belonging to somebody from his
birth. *native ability.* 2 of the country where you
were born. *my native language.* 3 of natives.
native customs.

nativity *noun* (**nativities**)
(*say* nă-**tiv**-i-ti)
1 somebody's birth. **2 the Nativity,** the birth of
Jesus.

natural *adjective*
1 made or done by nature, not by people or
machines. 2 normal; not surprising. 3 of a musical note that is not sharp or flat. **4 natural
history,** the study of plants and animals.
naturally *adverb*

natural *noun*
1 a natural note in music; a sign (♮) that shows
a note is natural. 2 someone who is naturally
good at something.

naturalist *noun*
someone who studies natural history.

naturalize *verb* (**naturalized, naturalizing**)
1 to make somebody a full citizen of a country.
2 to make something fit into a place where it is
not normally found.
naturalization *noun*

nature *noun*
1 everything in the universe that was not made
by people. 2 the qualities or characteristics of a
person or thing. *She has a loving nature.* 3 a
kind or sort of thing. *He likes things of that
nature.* **4 nature trail,** a path in the country
where you can walk and see things connected
with natural history.

naughty *adjective* (**naughtier, naughtiest**)
not behaving as you should; disobedient or
rude.
naughtily *adverb*, **naughtiness** *noun*

nautical *adjective*
connected with ships or sailors.

naval *adjective*
of the navy.

nave *noun*
the main central part of a church.

navel *noun*
1 the dimple at the front of your stomach where
the umbilical cord was detached. **2 navel** or
navel orange, a large orange without pips.

navigate *verb* (**navigated, navigating**)
1 to steer a ship on the sea, up a river, etc. 2 to
make sure that an aircraft or vehicle is going in
the right direction.
navigable *adjective*, **navigation** *noun*,
navigator *noun*

navy *noun* **(navies)**
1 a fleet of ships and the people trained to use them. 2 **navy** or **navy blue**, dark blue.

Nazi *noun*
(*say* **nah**-tsi)
a member of the German National Socialist Party in Hitler's time, with Fascist beliefs.
Nazism *noun*

near *adverb* and *adjective*
not far away. *The end is near.*
nearness *noun*

near *preposition*
not far away from something. *She lives near the town.*

near *verb*
to come near to something. *They were nearing the harbour.*

nearby *adverb* and *adjective*
near. *She lives nearby.*

nearly *adverb*
1 almost. *It was nearly midnight.* 2 closely. *nearly related.* 3 **not nearly**, far from; not at all. *There is not nearly enough food.*

neat *adjective*
1 tidy; simple and pleasant to look at. 2 skilfully done.
neatly *adverb*, **neatness** *noun*

necessary *adjective*
needed very much; essential; unavoidable.
necessarily *adverb*, **necessity** *noun*

neck *noun*
1 the part of the body that joins the head to the shoulders. 2 a narrow part of something, especially of a bottle.

necklace *noun*
an ornament worn round the neck.

necktie *noun*
a thin strip of material tied round the collar of a shirt.

nectar *noun*
a sweet liquid collected by bees from flowers.

need *verb*
1 to be without something that you should have. 2 to have to do something. *I needed to get a haircut.*

need *noun*
1 something that you need. 2 a situation in which something is necessary. *There is no need to cry.* 3 **in need**, needing money, help, comfort, etc.
needless *adjective*, **needlessly** *adverb*

needle *noun*
1 a very thin, pointed piece of metal used for sewing. 2 something long, thin, and sharp. *a knitting-needle.* 3 the pointer of a meter or compass.

needlework *noun*
sewing or embroidery.

needy *adjective* **(needier, neediest)**
very poor.

negative *adjective*
1 that says 'no'. *a negative answer.* 2 not definite; not positive. 3 less than nought. 4 of the kind of electric charge carried by electrons.
negatively *adverb*

negative *noun*
1 something negative. 2 a photograph or film from which prints are made.

neglect *verb*
not to look after or attend to something; to fail to do something. *He neglected his homework.*
neglectful *adjective*

negligible *adjective*
(*say* **neg**-lij-i-bŭl)
not big enough or important enough to bother about.

negotiate *verb* **(negotiated, negotiating)**
(*say* nig-**oh**-shi-ayt)
1 to try to reach agreement about something by discussion. 2 to get over or through an obstacle or difficulty.
negotiation *noun*, **negotiator** *noun*

Negro *noun* **(Negroes)**
a person with very dark skin.
Negress *noun*

neigh *verb*
to make a high-pitched cry like a horse.

neighbour *noun*
someone who lives next door or near to you.
neighbouring *adjective*, **neighbourly** *adjective*

neighbourhood *noun*
the surrounding district.

neither *adjective* and *pronoun*
(*say* **ny**-ther or **nee**-ther)
not either. *Neither of them likes cabbage.*

neither *conjunction*
neither...nor, not one thing or the other. *I neither know nor care.*

neon *noun*
(*say* **nee**-on)
a gas that glows when electricity passes through it. *Neon lights use neon in a glass tube.*

nephew *noun*
the son of a brother or sister.

nerve *noun*
1 one of the fibres inside the body that carry messages to and from the brain, so that the body can feel and move. 2 courage; calmness in a dangerous situation. *Don't lose your nerve.* 3 (*informal*) impudence. *He had the nerve to ask for more.* 4 **get on somebody's nerves**, to annoy him. 5 **nerves**, nervousness.

nervous *adjective*
1 easily upset or agitated; timid. 2 of the nerves.
nervously *adverb*, **nervousness** *noun*

nest *noun*
1 the place where a bird lays its eggs. 2 a warm place where some small animals keep their babies.

nest *verb*
to make or have a nest. *Birds were nesting in the roof.*

nestle *verb* **(nestled, nestling)**
to curl up comfortably.

net *noun*
1 something made of pieces of thread, cord, wire, etc. joined together in a criss-cross pattern with holes between. 2 material of this kind.

net *adjective*
that is left when nothing else is to be taken away. *After tax was deducted, his net pay was £80 a week.*

netball *noun*
a game in which two teams try to throw a ball through a high net hanging from a ring.

nettle *noun*
a wild plant with leaves that sting.

network *noun*
1 a criss-cross arrangement. 2 a system with many connections or parts. *a television network.*

neuter *adjective*
(*say* **new**-ter)
not masculine or feminine.

neutral *adjective*
(*say* **new**-trăl)
1 not supporting either side in a war or quarrel. 2 not distinct or distinctive. *neutral colours.* 3 of gears that are not connected to the driving parts of an engine.
neutrality *noun*, **neutrally** *adverb*

neutralize *verb* (**neutralized, neutralizing**)
to make something neutral or ineffective.

neutron *noun*
1 a particle with no electric charge. 2 **neutron bomb**, a nuclear bomb that kills people but does little damage to buildings.

never *adverb*
1 at no time; not ever; not at all. 2 **the never-never**, (*informal*) hire-purchase.

nevertheless *conjunction* and *adverb*
in spite of this; although that is a fact.

new *adjective*
1 not old; just bought, made, received, etc. 2 different; unfamiliar. 3 **new moon,** the moon when it appears as a thin crescent.
newly *adverb*, **newness** *noun*

newcomer *noun*
someone who has recently arrived in a place.

news *noun*
1 information about recent events. 2 a broadcast report about recent events.

newsagent *noun*
a shopkeeper who sells newspapers and magazines.

newspaper *noun*
a daily or weekly publication of large sheets of printed paper folded together, containing news reports, articles, advertisements, etc.

newt *noun*
a small animal rather like a lizard, that lives near or in water.

next *adjective*
1 the nearest; following immediately after. 2 **next door,** in the house on one side of yours.

next *adverb*
in the nearest place; at the nearest time. *What comes next?*

nib *noun*
the pointed metal part at the end of a pen that uses ink.

nibble *verb* (**nibbled, nibbling**)
to take tiny bites at something.

nice *adjective* (**nicer, nicest**)
1 pleasant; friendly; kind. 2 delicate; precise.
nicely *adverb*, **niceness** *noun*

nick *noun*
1 a notch. 2 (*slang*) a prison or police-station. *in the nick.* 3 (*slang*) the condition of something. *in good nick.* 4 **in the nick of time,** only just in time.

nick *verb*
1 to make a notch in something. 2 (*slang*) to steal.

nickel *noun*
1 a silvery-white metal. 2 in America, a 5-cent coin.

nickname *noun*
a name given to someone instead of his real name. *William Cody's nickname was Buffalo Bill.*

nicotine *noun*
(*say* **nik**-ŏ-teen)
a poisonous substance found in tobacco.

niece *noun*
the daughter of a brother or sister.

night *noun*
the time when it is dark, between sunset and sunrise.
night-time *noun*

night-club *noun*
a club or restaurant where there is entertainment at night.

nightfall *noun*
dusk.

nightingale *noun*
a small, brown bird that sings sweetly.

nightly *adjective*
happening every night.

nightmare *noun*
a frightening dream.
nightmarish *adjective*

nil *noun*
nothing. *Our team's score was nil.*

nimble *adjective* (**nimbler, nimblest**)
agile.
nimbly *adverb*

nine *noun*
the number 9, one more than eight.
ninth *adjective* and *noun*

nineteen *noun*
the number 19, one more than eighteen.
nineteenth *adjective* and *noun*

ninety *noun* (**nineties**)
the number 90, nine times ten.
ninetieth *adjective* and *noun*

nip *verb* (**nipped, nipping**)
1 to pinch or bite quickly. 2 (*informal*) to go quickly.

nip *noun*
1 a quick pinch or bite. 2 a cold feeling. *There's a nip in the air.*

nipple *noun*
the small part that sticks out at the front of a person's breast.

nippy *adjective* (**nippier, nippiest**)
(*informal*) 1 cold. 2 quick.

nit *noun*
1 a parasitic insect or its egg. 2 (*slang*) a stupid person. 3 **nit-picking**, finding tiny faults or making trivial criticisms.

nitric *adjective*
(*say* **ny**-trik)
1 of nitrogen; containing nitrogen. 2 **nitric acid**, a very strong colourless acid.

nitrogen *noun*
(*say* **ny**-trŏ-jĕn)
a gas that makes up about four-fifths of the air we breathe.

nitwit *noun*
(*informal*) a stupid person.
nitwitted *adjective*

no *adjective and adverb*
not any. *She had no money.*

no *interjection*
a word used to deny or refuse something.

noble *adjective* (**nobler, noblest**)
1 of high rank; aristocratic. 2 virtuous and generous. *a noble king.* 3 stately; impressive. *a noble building.*
nobility *noun*, **nobly** *adverb*

noble *noun*
a nobleman.

nobleman *noun* (**noblemen**)
a man of high rank.
noblewoman *noun*

nobody *pronoun*
no person; not anyone. *Nobody knows.*

nobody *noun* (**nobodies**)
an unimportant person. *He's a nobody.*

nocturnal *adjective*
(*say* nok-**ter**-năl)
active at night; of or in the night.

nod *verb* (**nodded, nodding**)
1 to move your head up and down as a way of agreeing with somebody or as a greeting. 2 to be drowsy.

noise *noun*
a loud sound, especially one that is unpleasant or unwanted.
noiseless *adjective*, **noiselessly** *adverb*

noisy *adjective* (**noisier, noisiest**)
making a lot of noise.
noisily *adverb*, **noisiness** *noun*

nomad *noun*
(*say* **noh**-mad)
someone who wanders about with a tribe, usually looking for pasture for his animals.
nomadic *adjective*

no-man's-land *noun*
unoccupied land, especially between two armies at war.

nominate *verb* (**nominated, nominating**)
to propose that somebody should be a candidate in an election.
nomination *noun*

none *pronoun*
not any; not one. *None of us went.*

none *adverb*
not at all. *He's none too bright.*

nonetheless *conjunction and adverb*
nevertheless.

non-fiction *noun*
writings that are not fiction; books about real things and true events.

nonsense *noun*
1 something that does not mean anything. 2 absurd or stupid ideas or behaviour.
nonsensical *adjective*

non-stop *adjective*
that does not stop.

noon *noun*
twelve o'clock in the middle of the day.

no one *pronoun*
no person; not anyone.

noose *noun*
a loop in a rope that gets smaller when the rope is pulled.

nor *conjunction*
and not. *He cannot do it; nor can I.*

normal *adjective*
1 usual; typical. *It's normal to take a holiday.* 2 sane. *He's not normal.*
normality *noun*, **normally** *adverb*

north *noun*
the direction to the left of a person facing the east.

north *adjective*
1 coming from the north. 2 situated in the north. 3 **north country**, the northern part of England.
northerly *adjective*, **northern** *adjective*, **northerner** *noun*

north *adverb*
towards the north.
northward *adjective* and *adverb*, **northwards** *adverb*

Norwegian *adjective*
(*say* nor-**wee**-jăn)
of Norway.

nose *noun*
1 the part of the face that is used for breathing and smelling. 2 the front part of something.

nose *verb* (**nosed, nosing**)
1 to push the nose near or into something; to pry. 2 to go forward cautiously. *The ship nosed through the ice.*

nosey *adjective* (**nosier, nosiest**)
(*informal*) inquisitive.
nosily *adverb*, **nosiness** *noun*

nostalgia *noun*
(*say* nos-**tal**-jă)
remembering or longing for the past.
nostalgic *adjective*

nostril *noun*
one of the two openings in the nose.

not *adverb*
a word used to change the meaning of something to its opposite.

notable *adjective*
remarkable; famous.
notably *adverb*

notch *noun* **(notches)**
a small cut or mark, usually shaped like a V.

note *noun*
1 something written down as a reminder or help. **2** a short letter. **3** a single sound in music. **4** a sound or quality that indicates something. *a note of optimism.* **5** a bank-note. *a five-pound note.* **6** notice. *Take note of what I say.*

note *verb* **(noted, noting)**
1 to make a note of something. **2** to notice or pay attention.

notebook *noun*
a book in which you note things.

nothing *noun*
not anything.

notice *noun*
1 something written or printed and displayed for people to see. **2** attention. *It escaped my notice.* **3** a warning that something is going to happen.

notice *verb* **(noticed, noticing)**
to see; to become aware of something.
noticeable *adjective*, **noticeably** *adverb*

notion *noun*
an idea, especially a vague idea.

notorious *adjective*
(*say* noh-**tor**-i-ŭs)
well-known for doing something bad.
notoriety *noun*, **notoriously** *adverb*

nougat *noun*
(*say* **noo**-gah)
a chewy sweet made from nuts, sugar, etc.

nought *noun*
(*say* nawt)
1 the figure 0. **2** nothing.

noun *noun*
a word that is the name of a thing or a person. (Nouns are words like *cat, courage, Diana, England,* and *tent.*)

nourish *verb*
to feed somebody enough good food to keep him alive and well.
nourishment *noun*

novel *adjective*
unusual. *a novel idea.*
novelty *noun*

novel *noun*
a story that fills a whole book.

novelist *noun*
(*say* **nov**-ĕl-ist)
someone who writes novels.

November *noun*
the eleventh month of the year.

novice *noun*
a beginner; someone inexperienced.

now *adverb*
1 at this time. **2** by this time. **3 for now,** until a later time. *Goodbye for now.* **4 now and again** or **now and then,** occasionally; sometimes.

now *conjunction*
since; as. *I do remember, now you mention it.*

now *noun*
this moment. *I haven't seen him up to now.*

nowadays *adverb*
at the present time.

nowhere *adverb*
not anywhere; in or to no place.

nozzle *noun*
the part at the end of a hose or pipe from which something flows.

nuclear *adjective*
(*say* **new**-kli-er)
1 of a nucleus. **2** of or using the energy that is created by reactions in the nuclei of atoms.

nucleus *noun* **(nuclei)**
(*say* **new**-kli-ŭs)
the part in the centre of something, round which other things are grouped; the central part of an atom or cell.

nude *adjective*
not wearing any clothes.
nudism *noun*, **nudist** *noun*, **nudity** *noun*

nudge *verb* **(nudged, nudging)**
to touch or push somebody with your elbow.

nugget *noun*
a lump of gold.

nuisance *noun*
a person or thing that annoys you.

numb *adjective*
unable to feel or move.
numbly *adverb*, **numbness** *noun*

number *noun*
1 a numeral. **2** a quantity of something. **3** one issue of a magazine or newspaper. **4** a song or piece of music.

number *verb*
1 to count. **2** to amount to. *The crowd numbered 10,000.* **3** to mark with numbers.

numeral *noun*
a figure or word that tells you how many there are.

numerical *adjective*
of numbers.
numerically *adverb*

numerous *adjective*
many. *The birds were numerous.*

nun *noun*
a member of a religious community of women.
nunnery *noun*

nurse *noun*
someone whose job is to look after people who are ill or hurt.

nurse *verb* **(nursed, nursing)**
1 to look after somebody who is ill. **2** to hold carefully in your arms. **3** to feed a baby.

nursemaid *noun*
a woman whose job is to look after small children.

nursery *noun* **(nurseries)**
1 a place where very young children are looked after or play. **2** a place where young plants are grown and usually sold. **3 nursery rhyme,** a simple rhyme or song that young children like.

nursing home *noun*
a small or private hospital.

nurture *verb* **(nurtured, nurturing)**
to train or educate a child, etc.

nut *noun*
1 a fruit with a hard shell. **2** a kernel. **3** a hollow piece of metal for screwing on to a bolt. **4** (*slang*) someone's head. **5** (*slang*) a mad or eccentric person.
nutty *adjective*

nutmeg *noun*
a hard seed that is made into a powder and used as a spice.

nutrient *noun*
(*say* **new**-tri-ènt)
something nourishing.

nutrition *noun*
(*say* new-**trish**-ŏn)
nourishment; the study of what nourishes people.
nutritional *adjective*

nutritious *adjective*
(*say* new-**trish**-ŭs)
nourishing. *a nutritious meal.*

nutshell *noun*
1 the shell of a nut. **2 in a nutshell,** briefly.

nuzzle *verb* **(nuzzled, nuzzling)**
to rub gently against something with the nose.

nylon *noun*
a lightweight synthetic cloth or fibre.

nymph *noun*
a mythical goddess or girl living in rivers, trees, etc.

O

oak *noun*
a large tree with seeds called acorns.

oar *noun*
a pole with a flat part at one end, used for rowing a boat.
oarsman *noun*

oasis *noun* **(oases)**
(*say* oh-**ay**-sis)
a place with water and trees in a desert.

oath *noun*
1 a solemn promise. **2** a swear-word.

oatmeal *noun*
a substance made by grinding oats.

oats *plural noun*
a cereal used to make food for humans and animals. *Porridge is made from oats.*

obedient *adjective*
obeying; willing to obey.
obedience *noun*, **obediently** *adverb*

obey *verb*
to do what you are told to do.

obituary *noun* **(obituaries)**
(*say* ŏ-**bit**-yoo-er-i)
a report that someone has died, usually with a short biography.

object *noun*
(*say* **ob**-jikt)
1 something that can be seen or touched. **2** the purpose of something. **3** (*in grammar*) something towards which the action of a verb is directed. *'Him' is the object in 'I hit him'.*

object *verb*
(*say* ŏb-**jekt**)
to say that you do not like or agree with something. *She objected to my speech.*
objection *noun*, **objector** *noun*

objectionable *adjective*
unpleasant; not liked.

objective *noun*
what you are trying to reach or do; an aim.

obligation *noun*
a duty.
obligatory *adjective*

oblige *verb* **(obliged, obliging)**
1 to help and please someone. **2 obliged to,** forced to do something.

oblique *adjective*
(*say* ŏ-**bleek**)
slanting; not straight or direct.
obliquely *adverb*

oblong *noun*
a rectangle that is longer than it is wide.

oboe *noun*
(*say* **oh**-boh)
a high-pitched woodwind instrument.

obscene *adjective* **(obscener, obscenest)**
(*say* ŏb-**seen**)
not decent or modest; very offensive.
obscenely *adverb*, **obscenity** *noun*

obscure *adjective* **(obscurer, obscurest)**
1 not clear. **2** not famous.
obscurely *adverb*, **obscurity** *noun*

observance *noun*
obeying a law; keeping a custom.

observant *adjective*
quick at noticing things.
observantly *adverb*

observation *noun*
1 observing; watching. **2** a remark.

observatory *noun* **(observatories)**
(*say* ŏb-**zerv**-ă-ter-i)
a building equipped with telescopes for observing the stars, planets, etc.

observe *verb* **(observed, observing)**
1 to watch. **2** to notice. **3** to obey a law or keep a custom. **4** to make a remark.
observer *noun*

obsess *verb*
to upset somebody by always being in his mind.
obsession *noun*

obsolete *adjective*
not used any more; out of date.

obstacle *noun*
something that hinders you.

obstinate *adjective*
not ready to change your ideas or ways, even though they may be wrong.
obstinacy *noun*, **obstinately** *adverb*

obstruct *verb*
to stop something from getting past; to hinder.
obstruction *noun*, **obstructive** *adjective*

obtain *verb*
to buy, take, or be given something.
obtainable *adjective*

obtuse *adjective*
1 stupid. **2 obtuse angle,** an angle between 90 and 180 degrees.

obvious *adjective*
very easy to see or understand.
obviously *adverb*

occasion *noun*
the time when something happens; a special event.

occasional *adjective*
happening at intervals.
occasionally *adverb*

occupant *noun*
someone who occupies a place.

occupation *noun*
1 a job or hobby. **2** the occupying of territory.

occupy *verb* **(occupied, occupying)**
1 to live in a place. **2** to fill a space or position. **3** to capture territory in a war. **4** to keep somebody busy and interested.

occur *verb* **(occurred, occurring)**
1 to happen; to take place. **2** to be found; to exist. **3** to come into your mind. *An idea occurred to me.*
occurrence *noun*

ocean *noun*
1 the sea. **2** a large sea. *The Pacific Ocean.*

o'clock *adverb*
by the clock. *Lunch is at one o'clock.*

octagon *noun*
a shape with eight sides.
octagonal *adjective*

octave *noun*
the distance between one musical note and the next note of the same name above or below it; these two notes played together.

October *noun*
the tenth month of the year.

octopus *noun* **(octopuses)**
a sea creature with eight arms which are called 'tentacles'.

odd *adjective*
1 strange. **2** not an even number. *Five and nine are odd numbers.* **3** left over; spare. *I've got an odd sock.* **4** of various kinds; occasional. *odd jobs.*
oddity *noun*, **oddly** *adverb*, **oddness** *noun*

oddments *plural noun*
small things of various kinds.

odds *plural noun*
1 the chances that something will happen; the proportion of money that you will win if a bet is successful. *When the odds are 10 to 1, you will win £10 if you bet £1.* **2 odds and ends,** oddments.

odour *noun*
a smell.
odorous *adjective*

oesophagus *noun*
(oesophagi or **oesophaguses)**
(*say* ee-**sof**-ă-gŭs)
the gullet.

of *preposition*
1 belonging to; coming from. *a native of Italy.* **2** away from. *two miles north of the town.* **3** about; concerning. *news of peace.* **4** made from. *built of stone.*

off *adverb*
1 not on; away. *His hat blew off.* **2** not working or happening. *The heating is off.* **3** behind or at the side of a stage. *There were noises off.*

off *preposition*
1 not on; away or down from. *He fell off his chair.* **2** not taking or wanting. *She is off her food.*

offend *verb*
1 to hurt somebody's feelings; to be unpleasant to somebody. **2** to break a law; to do wrong.
offence *noun*, **offender** *noun*

offensive *adjective*
1 that offends somebody. **2** used for attacking; aggressive.
offensively *adverb*

offer *verb*
1 to hold out something so that someone can take it if he wants it. **2** to say that you are willing to do something. **3** to say what you are willing to give for something.

offer *noun*
offering; an amount offered.

office *noun*
1 a room or building where people do typing, accounts, business, etc. **2** a government department. *The Foreign and Commonwealth Office.* **3** an important job or position.

officer *noun*
1 someone who is in charge of other people, especially in the armed forces; an official. **2** a policeman.

official *adjective*
1 done or said by someone with authority. **2** connected with a job of authority or trust.
officially *adverb*

official *noun*
someone who does an official job.

officious *adjective*
(*say* ŏ-**fish**-ŭs)
too ready to order people about.
officiously *adverb*

offspring *noun* (**offspring**)
a child or young animal.

often *adverb*
many times; in many cases.

ogre *noun*
a cruel giant.
ogress *noun*

oh *interjection*
a cry of surprise, pain, delight, etc.

ohm *noun*
(rhymes with *home*)
a unit of electrical resistance.

oil *noun*
1 a thick, slippery liquid that does not mix with water. 2 a kind of petroleum used as fuel.
oil-well *noun*, **oily** *adjective*

oil *verb*
to put oil on something to make it work smoothly.

oil-colour *noun*
paint made with oil.

oilfield *noun*
an area where oil is found under the ground or under the sea.

oil-painting *noun*
1 a painting done with oil-colours. 2 **no oil-painting,** ugly. *She is no oil-painting.*

ointment *noun*
a cream for putting on sore skin and cuts.

O.K. *adverb* and *adjective*
(*informal*) all right.

old *adjective*
1 not new; born or made a long time ago. 2 of a particular age. *I'm ten years old.*

old age *noun*
1 the time when a person is more than about 60 years old. 2 **old-age pension,** a pension paid to an old person. 3 **old-age pensioner,** someone who gets an old-age pension; an old person.

old-fashioned *adjective*
of the kind that was usual a long time ago.

O level *noun*
the ordinary level in the G.C.E. examination.

olive *noun*
1 an evergreen tree with a small, bitter fruit. 2 the fruit of the olive-tree. 3 **olive-branch,** something that shows you want to make peace.

Olympic *adjective*
(*say* ŏ-**lim**-pik)
of the Olympic Games or the Olympics, a series of international sports contests held every four years in different countries.

ombudsman *noun* (**ombudsmen**)
(*say* **om**-bŭdz-măn)
an official who investigates people's complaints against government departments.

omelette *noun*
(*say* **om**-lit)
eggs beaten together and fried, often with a filling or flavouring.

omen *noun*
a sign that something is going to happen.

ominous *adjective*
threatening; suggesting that trouble is coming.
ominously *adverb*

omit *verb* (**omitted, omitting**)
1 to miss something out. 2 to fail to do something.
omission *noun*

on *preposition*
1 at or over the top or surface of something. *Sit on the floor.* 2 at the time of. *on my birthday.* 3 about; concerning. *a talk on butterflies.* 4 towards; near. *They advanced on the town.*

on *adverb*
1 so as to be on something. *Put your hat on.* 2 forwards. *Move on.* 3 working; in action. *Is the heater on?* 4 **on to,** to a position on something.

once *adverb*
at one time; ever.

once *conjunction*
as soon as. *We can get out once I open this door.*

one *noun*
1 a person on his own; a thing on its own. *One of my friends is ill.* 2 the number 1, representing a person or thing alone. *One and one make two.* 3 **one another,** each other.

oneself *pronoun*
one's own self; yourself. *One should not always think of oneself.*

one-way *adjective*
where traffic may only go in one direction. *a one-way street.*

ongoing *adjective*
continuing to exist; making progress.

onion *noun*
a round vegetable with a strong flavour. *Onions make you cry when you peel them.*

onlooker *noun*
a spectator.

only *adjective*
1 being the one person or thing of a kind. *He's the only person we can trust.* 2 **only child,** a child who has no brothers or sisters.

only *adverb*
1 no more than. *There are only three cakes.* 2 **not only...but also,** both...and. *He not only thanked me but also paid me.* 3 **only too,** extremely. *I'm only too happy to help.*

only *conjunction*
but then; however. *I want to come, only I'm busy that night.*

onto *preposition*
on to.

onward or **onwards** *adverb*
forwards.

ooze *verb* (**oozed, oozing**)
to flow out slowly, especially through a narrow opening. *Blood oozed from his wound.*

opaque

opaque *adjective*
(*say* ŏ-**payk**)
not transparent or translucent.

open *adjective*
1 not shut. *an open door.* 2 not enclosed. *open land.* 3 not folded; spread out. *with open arms.* 4 honest; not secret or secretive. *open government.* 5 not settled or finished. *an open question.* 6 **in the open air,** not inside a house or building.

open *verb*
1 to make or become open. 2 to start.
opener *noun*

opening *noun*
1 a space or gap in something. 2 the beginning of something. 3 an opportunity.

openly *adverb*
without secrecy.

opera *noun*
a play in which all or most of the words are sung.
operatic *adjective*

operate *verb* **(operated, operating)**
1 to make something work. 2 to work; to be in action. 3 to do a surgical operation on somebody.

operation *noun*
1 operating; working. 2 something done by a surgeon to somebody to deal with a disease or injury. 3 a planned military activity.

operator *noun*
someone who works something, especially a telephone switchboard.

opinion *noun*
1 what you think of something; a belief. 2 **opinion poll,** an estimate of what people think, made by questioning a sample of them.

opium *noun*
a drug made from poppies, used as a sedative and anaesthetic.

opponent *noun*
someone who is against you in a contest, war, or argument.

opportunity *noun* **(opportunities)**
a time when you can do something that you cannot do at other times.

oppose *verb* **(opposed, opposing)**
to be against somebody or something.

opposite *adjective*
1 completely different. *They went in opposite directions.* 2 facing; on the other side. *She lives on the opposite side of the road to me.*

opposite *noun*
something opposite. *'Happy' is the opposite of 'sad'.*

opposition *noun*
1 opposing something; resistance. 2 **the Opposition,** the political party or parties in parliament that oppose the government.

oppress *verb*
1 to govern or treat somebody cruelly or unjustly. 2 to weigh somebody down with worry or sadness.
oppression *noun,* **oppressive** *adjective,* **oppressor** *noun*

opt *verb*
1 to choose. 2 **opt out,** to decide not to join in.

optical *adjective*
1 of sight; of the eyes. 2 **optical illusion,** something you think you see that is not really there.
optically *adverb*

optician *noun*
(*say* op-**tish**-ăn)
someone who tests your eyesight and supplies spectacles.

optimism *noun*
expecting that things will turn out right.
optimist *noun,* **optimistic** *adjective*

option *noun*
a choice; something chosen.

optional *adjective*
that you can choose; not compulsory.
optionally *adverb*

opulent *adjective*
(*say* **op**-yoo-lĕnt)
rich; luxurious.
opulence *noun,* **opulently** *adverb*

or *conjunction*
a word used to show that there is a choice or alternative. *Do you want a bun or a biscuit?*

oral *adjective*
spoken; using the mouth.
orally *adverb*

orange *noun*
1 a round, juicy fruit with thick reddish-yellow peel. 2 a reddish-yellow colour.

orangeade *noun*
a drink with a flavour of oranges.

orang-utan *noun*
(*say* or-ang-**oo**-tan or or-ang-ŭ-**tan**)
a large kind of ape.

orator *noun*
(*say* **o**-ră-ter)
someone who makes speeches.
oration *noun,* **oratorical** *adjective,* **oratory** *noun*

oratorio *noun*
(*say* o-ră-**tor**-i-oh)
a piece of music for voices and orchestra, usually on a religious subject.

orbit *noun*
the path taken by something moving round a planet or other body in space.
orbital *adjective*

orbit *verb*
to move in an orbit round something. *The satellite orbited the earth.*

orchard *noun*
a place where a lot of fruit trees grow.

orchestra *noun*
a large group of people playing musical instruments together.
orchestral *adjective*

orchid *noun*
(*say* **or**-kid)
a brightly-coloured flower.

ordeal *noun*
something very hard to endure

order *noun*
1 a command. 2 a request for something to be supplied. 3 obedience; good behaviour. 4 tidiness; neatness. 5 the way something is arranged; condition. 6 a kind or sort of thing. 7 **in order that,** so that. 8 **in order to,** so as to; for the purpose of.

order *verb*
1 to tell somebody to do something. 2 to ask for something to be supplied to you. 3 **order about,** to keep giving somebody commands.

orderly *adjective*
1 arranged tidily or well; methodical. 2 well-behaved; obedient.
orderliness *noun*

ordinary *adjective*
1 normal; not special in any way. 2 **ordinary level,** the basic standard in the G.C.E. examination.
ordinarily *adverb*

ore *noun*
rock with metal in it. *iron ore.*

organ *noun*
1 a large musical instrument with one or more keyboards. 2 a part of the body with a particular function. *the digestive organs.*

organism *noun*
a living animal or plant.

organist *noun*
someone who plays the organ.

organization *noun*
1 an organized group of people. 2 the organizing of something.

organize *verb* (organized, organizing)
1 to get people together to do something. 2 to plan something. *She organized the picnic.* 3 to put something in order.
organizer *noun*

orgasm *noun*
(*say* **or**-gazm)
the climax of sexual excitement.

oriental *adjective*
of the countries east of the Mediterranean, especially China and Japan.

orienteering *noun*
(*say* or-i-en-**teer**-ing)
the sport of finding your way across rough country with a map and compass.

origami *noun*
(*say* o-ri-**gah**-mi)
folding pieces of paper to make decorative shapes.

origin *noun*
the start of something; the point where something began.

original *adjective*
1 existing from the start; earliest. *the original inhabitants.* 2 new; not a copy or an imitation. *an original design.* 3 producing new ideas. *an original thinker.*
originality *noun,* **originally** *adverb*

originate *verb* (originated, originating)
to start; to create.
origination *noun,* **originator** *noun*

ornament *noun*
a thing put in or on something to make it look pretty; a decoration.
ornamental *adjective,* **ornamentation** *noun*

ornithology *noun*
(*say* or-ni-**thol**-ŏ-ji)
the scientific study of birds.
ornithological *adjective,* **ornithologist** *noun*

orphan *noun*
a child whose parents are dead.

orphanage *noun*
a home for orphans.

orthodox *adjective*
1 having correct or generally accepted beliefs. 2 **Orthodox Church,** the Christian Churches of Eastern Europe.
orthodoxy *noun*

oscillate *verb* (oscillated, oscillating)
to move to and fro.
oscillation *noun*

ostrich *noun* (ostriches)
a large, long-legged bird that can run fast but cannot fly.

other *adjective*
1 not the same as this. *The other pudding was better.* 2 **the other day** or **the other week,** a few days or weeks ago.

otherwise *adverb*
1 if you do not; if things happen differently. *Write it down, otherwise you'll forget it.* 2 in other ways. *It rained a lot but otherwise the holiday was good.*

otter *noun*
a furry, long-tailed animal that lives near water.

ouch *interjection*
a cry of pain.

ought *verb*
should; must; to have a duty to. *You ought to stop fighting.*

ounce *noun*
a unit of weight equal to $\frac{1}{16}$ of a pound or about 28 grams.

our *adjective*
belonging to us. *our house.*

ours *pronoun*
belonging to us. *This house is ours.*

ourselves *pronoun*
us and nobody else. *We washed ourselves.*

out *adverb*
1 not in; away from a place. 2 not burning. *The fire is out.* 3 loudly. *She cried out.* 4 **out for** or **out to,** wanting; seeking. 5 **out of,** from; without. 6 **out of date,** old-fashioned; not used any more. 7 **out of doors,** in the open air. 8 **out of the way,** unusual.

out-and-out *adjective*
complete; thorough.

outback *noun*
the remote inland areas of Australia.

outboard motor *noun*
a motor fitted to the outside of a boat's stern.

outbreak *noun*
the sudden start of a disease, war, anger, etc.

outburst *noun*
the bursting out of steam, laughter, anger, etc.

outcast *noun*
someone who has been rejected by his family, friends, or society.

outcome *noun*
the result of something.

outdoor *adjective*
done or used outdoors. *outdoor clothes.*

outdoors *adverb*
in the open air. *It is cold outdoors.*

outer *adjective*
1 nearer the outside; external. 2 **outer space,** the universe beyond the earth's atmosphere.

outfit *noun*
1 clothes that are worn together. 2 a set of things needed for doing something.

outgrow *verb (past tense* **outgrew;** *past participle* **outgrown;** *present participle* **outgrowing)**
1 to grow out of clothes, habits, etc. 2 to grow faster or taller than somebody else.

outhouse *noun*
a small building attached to or near a larger building.

outing *noun*
a journey for pleasure.

outlaw *noun*
a lawless person; a robber, especially one who roams about.

outlet *noun*
a way for something to come out; a way to get rid of something.

outline *noun*
1 the line round the outside of something; a line that shows the shape of a thing. 2 a summary.

outline *verb* **(outlined, outlining)**
1 to make an outline of something. 2 to summarize or describe something.

outlook *noun*
1 a view. 2 the way that someone regards things. 3 future prospects.

outlying *adjective*
far from a town or city; distant.

outnumber *verb*
to be more numerous than something else.

out-patient *noun*
someone who visits a hospital for treatment but does not stay there.

outpost *noun*
a distant settlement.

output *noun*
the amount produced.

outrage *noun*
something very shocking or cruel.
outrageous *adjective*

outright *adverb*
completely; not gradually.

outset *noun*
the beginning of something.

outside *noun*
the surface or edges of a thing; the part farthest from the middle.

outside *adjective*
1 placed in or coming from the outside. 2 **outside broadcast,** a broadcast that is not made from a studio.

outside *preposition*
on or to the outside of something. *The milk is outside the door.*

outside *adverb*
on or to the outside; outdoors. *Come outside.*

outsider *noun*
1 someone who is not a member of a particular group of people. 2 a horse or person unlikely to win a race or contest.

outskirts *plural noun*
the parts on the outside of an area; suburbs.

outspoken *adjective*
speaking frankly; not tactful.

outstanding *adjective*
1 extremely good or distinguished. *an outstanding athlete.* 2 not yet dealt with. *outstanding debts.*

outward *adjective*
1 going outwards. 2 on the outside.
outwardly *adverb*

outwards *adverb*
towards the outside.

outwit *verb* **(outwitted, outwitting)**
to get the better of somebody by being clever.

oval *adjective*
shaped like an egg or a number 0.

oval *noun*
an oval shape.

ovary *noun* **(ovaries)**
part of a female body where egg-cells are produced.

oven *noun*
a closed space in which things are cooked or heated.

over *adverb*
1 finished. *Playtime is over.* 2 left; remaining. 3 into 7 goes 2 and 1 over. 3 sideways; into a different position. *He fell over.* 4 through; thoroughly. *Think it over.* 5 too much. *Don't get over-excited.* 6 all **over,** everywhere; finished. 7 **over and over,** repeatedly; many times.

over *preposition*
1 above; covering. *I knocked his hat over his eyes.* 2 across. *They ran over the road.* 3 more than. *There are over 20,000 kinds of insect in Britain.*

over *noun*
in cricket, a series of balls bowled by one person. *There are usually 6 balls in an over.*

overall *adjective and adverb*
including everything.

overalls *plural noun*
a garment worn over other clothes to protect them.

overboard *adverb*
over the side of a boat into the water. *She jumped overboard.*

overcoat *noun*
a warm outdoor coat.

overcome *verb* (*past tense* **overcame;** *past participle* **overcome;** *present participle* **overcoming**)
1 to gain a victory over somebody; to defeat. **2** to make somebody helpless. *She was overcome by the fumes.*

overdo *verb* (*past tense* **overdid;** *past participle* **overdone;** *present participle* **overdoing**)
1 to do something too much. **2** to cook food for too long.

overdose *noun*
too large a dose of a drug or medicine.

overflow *verb*
to flow over its edges or banks. *The river overflowed.*

overgrown *adjective*
covered with weeds or unwanted plants.

overhaul *verb*
1 to examine something thoroughly and repair it if necessary. **2** to overtake.

overhead *adjective* and *adverb*
above your head; in the sky.

overheads *plural noun*
the expenses of running a business.

overhear *verb* (**overheard, overhearing**)
to hear something accidentally.

overland *adjective* and *adverb*
over the land, not by sea.

overlap *verb* (**overlapped, overlapping**)
to lie across part of something. *The tiles overlapped.*

overlook *verb*
1 not to notice something. **2** not to punish an offence. **3** to have a view over something.

overnight *adverb* and *adjective*
for a whole night; during the night.

overpower *verb*
1 to overcome. **2 overpowering,** very strong.

overrun *verb* (*past tense* **overran;** *past participle* **overrun;** *present participle* **overrunning**)
1 to spread harmfully over an area. *The place is overrun with mice.* **2** to go on longer than it should. *The broadcast overran by ten minutes.*

overseas *adverb*
abroad. *They travelled overseas.*

oversight *noun*
a mistake made by not noticing something.

overtake *verb* (*past tense* **overtook;** *past participle* **overtaken;** *present participle* **overtaking**)
to pass a moving vehicle or person.

overthrow *verb* (*past tense* **overthrew;** *past participle* **overthrown;** *present participle* **overthrowing**)
to make something fall or fail; to defeat.

overtime *noun*
time spent working outside the normal hours.

overture *noun*
1 a piece of music played at the start of a concert, opera, ballet, etc. **2 overtures,** a friendly attempt to start a discussion with somebody.

overturn *verb*
1 to make something turn or fall over. **2** to turn over. *The car overturned.*

overwhelm *verb*
to overcome; to weigh down or bury under a huge mass of something.

overwork *verb*
1 to work too hard. **2** to use something too much. *an overworked word.*

ovum *noun* (**ova**)
(*say* **oh**-vŭm)
a female cell that can develop into offspring.

owe *verb* (**owed, owing**)
1 to have a duty to pay or give something to someone, especially money that you have borrowed. *I owed her a pound.* **2** to have something because of somebody else. *They owed their lives to the pilot's skill.* **3 owing to,** because of.

owl *noun*
a bird of prey with large eyes. *Owls usually fly at night.*

own *adjective*
1 belonging to yourself. **2 get your own back,** (*informal*) to get revenge. **3 on your own,** by yourself; alone.

own *verb*
1 to have something that belongs to you. **2 own up,** (*informal*) to confess or admit.

owner *noun*
the person who owns something.
ownership *noun*

ox *noun* (**oxen**)
a large animal kept for its meat and for pulling carts.

oxide *noun*
a compound of oxygen and another element.
oxidation *noun,* **oxidize** *verb*

oxygen *noun*
one of the gases in the air that people need to stay alive.

oyster *noun*
a shellfish whose shell sometimes contains a pearl.

oz. short for *ounce* or *ounces.*

P

pa *noun*
(*informal*) father.

pace *noun*
1 one step in walking or marching. **2** speed. *She ran at a fast pace.*

pace *verb* (**paced, pacing**)
1 to walk with slow or regular steps. **2 pace off** or **pace out,** to measure a distance in paces.

pacemaker *noun*
1 someone who sets the speed for somebody else in a race. **2** a device to keep the heart beating.

pacifist *noun*
(*say* **pas**-i-fist)
someone who believes that war is always wrong.
pacifism *noun*

pacify *verb* (**pacified, pacifying**)
(*say* **pas**-i-fy)
to make peaceful or calm.
pacification *noun*

pack *noun*
1 a bundle or collection of things. **2** a set of playing-cards. **3** a haversack. **4** a group of hounds, wolves, or other animals. **5** a group of people, especially a group of Brownies or Cubs.

pack *verb*
1 to put things into a suitcase, bag, box, etc. in order to move them or store them. **2** to fill a place. *The hall was packed.*
packer *noun*

package *noun*
1 a parcel or packet. **2** a package deal. **3 package deal,** a number of things offered or accepted together. **4 package holiday** or **package tour,** a holiday with everything arranged by travel agents.

packet *noun*
a small parcel.

pad *noun*
1 a piece of padding. **2** a device to protect the leg in cricket or other games. **3** a flat surface from which helicopters, spacecraft, etc. take off. **4** a number of sheets of paper joined together along one edge so that you can tear off a sheet when you need it.

pad *verb*[1] (**padded, padding**)
1 to put a pad on or in something. **2 pad out,** to make a book, essay, etc. longer, usually when it is not necessary.

pad *verb*[2] (**padded, padding**)
to walk softly.

padding *noun*
1 soft material used to protect or shape something. **2** something used to pad a thing out.

paddle *verb* (**paddled, paddling**)
1 to walk about in shallow water. **2** to move a boat along with a paddle.

paddle *noun*
1 a time spent paddling. **2** a short oar.

paddock *noun*
1 a small field or enclosure for horses. **2** (*in Australia and New Zealand*) a field of any size.

paddy *noun* (**paddies**)
a field where rice is grown.

padlock *noun*
a lock with a metal loop that you can fix on something.

page *noun*[1]
a piece of paper that is part of a book, magazine, etc.; one side of this piece of paper.

page *noun*[2]
a boy who acts as a servant or attendant.

pageant *noun*
(*say* **paj**-ĕnt)
1 a play or entertainment about historical events and people. **2** a procession of people in costume.
pageantry *noun*

pagoda *noun*
(*say* pă-**goh**-dă)
a tall religious building in the Far East.

paid past tense and past participle of **pay** *verb.*

pail *noun*
a bucket.

pain *noun*
1 an unpleasant feeling caused when part of your body is injured or diseased. **2 pains,** careful effort or trouble. *He took pains to do the job properly.*
painless *adjective*

painful *adjective*
that causes pain.
painfully *adverb*

painstaking *adjective*
making a careful effort.

paint *noun*
a substance put on something to colour or cover it.
paintbox *noun,* **paintbrush** *noun*

paint *verb*
1 to put paint on something. **2** to make a picture with paints.

painter *noun*[1]
someone who paints.

painter *noun*[2]
a rope used to tie up a boat.

painting *noun*
1 a painted picture. *These paintings are by Degas.* **2** using paints to make a picture. *She likes painting.*

pair *noun*
1 two things or people that go together or are the same kind. *a pair of shoes.* **2** something made of two joined parts. *a pair of scissors.*

pal *noun*
(*informal*) a friend.

palace *noun*
a mansion where a king or queen or other important person lives.

palate *noun*
(*say* **pal**-ăt)
1 the roof of the mouth. 2 a person's sense of taste.

pale *adjective* **(paler, palest)**
1 almost white. *a pale face.* 2 not bright in colour; faint. *a pale blue sky.*
palely *adverb*, **paleness** *noun*

palette *noun*
(*say* **pal**-it)
a board on which an artist mixes his colours.

paling *noun*
a wooden fence.

pallid *adjective*
pale, especially because of illness.
pallor *noun*

palm *noun*
1 the inner part of the hand, between the fingers and the wrist. 2 a tropical tree with large leaves and no branches. 3 **Palm Sunday**, the Sunday before Easter.

palmist *noun*
someone who tells your fortune by looking at your hand.
palmistry *noun*

pampas *noun*
1 the grassy plains of South America. 2 **pampas-grass**, a tall spiky plant with feathery flowers.

pamper *verb*
to be too kind or indulgent towards a person or animal.

pamphlet *noun*
a thin book with a cover of paper or thin cardboard.

pan *noun*
a pot or dish with a flat base.

pancake *noun*
a thin flat cake of fried batter

panda *noun*
1 a large, furry, black-and-white animal found in China. 2 **panda car**, a police patrol-car.

pandemonium *noun*
uproar.

pane *noun*
a sheet of glass in a window.

panel *noun*
1 a long, flat piece of wood, metal, etc. that is part of a door, wall, or piece of furniture. 2 a group of people appointed to discuss or decide something.

pang *noun*
a sudden feeling of guilt, sadness, or other emotion.

panic *noun*
sudden uncontrollable fear.
panicky *adjective*

panic *verb* **(panicked, panicking)**
to be filled with panic.

pannier *noun*
a bag or basket hung on one side of a bicycle or horse.

panorama *noun*
a view or picture of a wide area.
panoramic *adjective*

pansy *noun* **(pansies)**
a small, brightly-coloured garden-flower.

pant *verb*
to take short, quick breaths, usually after running or working hard.

panther *noun*
a leopard.

panties *plural noun*
(*informal*) short knickers or underpants.

pantomime *noun*
a Christmas entertainment based on a fairy-tale.

pantry *noun* **(pantries)**
a larder.

pants *plural noun*
(*informal*) 1 underpants. 2 trousers.

paper *noun*
1 a thin substance used for writing or printing on, wrapping up things, etc. 2 a newspaper. 3 a document.

paper *verb*
to stick wallpaper on a wall or ceiling.

paperback *noun*
a book with thin flexible covers.

papier maché *noun*
(*say* pap-yay **mash**-ay)
paper made into pulp and used to make models, ornaments, etc.

papyrus *noun* **(papyri)**
(*say* pă-**py**-rŭs)
1 a kind of paper made of reeds, used in ancient Egypt. 2 something written on a piece of this paper.

parable *noun*
a story told to teach people something, especially one of the stories told by Jesus.

parachute *noun*
an umbrella-shaped device on which people or things can float slowly down to the ground from an aircraft.
parachuting *noun*, **parachutist** *noun*

parade *noun*
1 a procession that displays people or things. 2 an assembly of troops for inspection, drill, etc.

parade *verb* **(paraded, parading)**
1 to move in a parade. 2 to assemble for a parade.

paradise *noun*
1 heaven; a heavenly place. 2 the Garden of Eden.

paradox *noun* **(paradoxes)**
(*say* **pa**-ră-doks)
something that seems strange or senseless but which contains a truth. *'More haste, less speed' is a paradox.*
paradoxical *adjective*, **paradoxically** *adverb*

paraffin *noun*
an oil used as fuel.

paragraph *noun*
a division of a piece of writing, starting on a new line. *Paragraphs usually contain several sentences.*

parallel *adjective*
of lines that are the same distance apart for their whole length. *Railway lines are parallel.*

parallelogram *noun*
a four-sided figure with its opposite sides parallel to each other.

paralyse *verb* (**paralysed, paralysing**)
to affect somebody with paralysis; to make something unable to move.

paralysis *noun*
(*say* pă-**ral**-i-sis)
being unable to move or feel anything.
paralytic *adjective*

parapet *noun*
a low wall along the edge of a balcony, bridge, roof, etc.

paraphernalia *noun*
(*say* pa-ră-fer-**nay**-li-ă)
numerous pieces of equipment, small possessions, etc.

paraphrase *verb* (**paraphrased, paraphrasing**)
to give the meaning of a piece of writing in other words.

parasite *noun*
an animal or plant that lives in or on another, from which it gets its food.
parasitic *adjective*

parasol *noun*
a lightweight umbrella used to shade yourself from the sun.

paratroops *plural noun*
troops using parachutes.
paratrooper *noun*

parcel *noun*
something wrapped up to be posted or carried.

parched *adjective*
very dry or thirsty.

parchment *noun*
a heavy, paper-like substance made from animal skins, used for writing on.

pardon *verb*
1 to forgive or excuse someone. 2 **pardon me,** I beg your pardon.
pardonable *adjective*, **pardonably** *adverb*

pardon *noun*
1 forgiveness. 2 used as an exclamation to mean 'pardon me'.

parent *noun*
a father or mother.
parentage *noun*, **parental** *adjective*,
parenthood *noun*

parenthesis *noun* (**parentheses**)
(*say* pă-**ren**-thi-sis)
1 something extra inserted in a sentence between brackets or dashes. 2 one of a pair of brackets used in the middle of a sentence.

parish *noun* (**parishes**)
a district that has its own church.
parishioner *noun*

park *noun*
1 a large garden for public use. 2 a place where vehicles may be parked.

park *verb*
to leave a vehicle somewhere for a time.

parka *noun*
a warm jacket with a hood attached.

parking-meter *noun*
a device that shows how long a vehicle has been parked in a street. *When you park your car, you put a coin in the parking-meter.*

parliament *noun*
the assembly that makes a country's laws.
parliamentary *adjective*

parlour *noun*
a sitting-room.

parody *noun* (**parodies**)
a play, poem, etc. that makes fun of people or things by imitating them.

parole *noun*
(*say* pă-**rohl**)
letting a convict out of prison before his sentence is finished, on condition that he behaves well. *He was on parole.*

parrot *noun*
a brightly-coloured bird that can learn to repeat things said to it.

parsley *noun*
a green plant used to flavour and decorate food.

parsnip *noun*
a pale-yellow vegetable.

parson *noun*
a clergyman.
parsonage *noun*

part *noun*
1 anything that belongs to something bigger; a piece. 2 the character played by an actor or actress; the words spoken by a character in a play. 3 **part of speech,** one of the groups into which words can be divided, such as nouns, adjectives, verbs, etc.

part *verb*
1 to separate. 2 to divide hair so that it goes in two different directions. 3 **part with,** to give away or get rid of something.

part-exchange *noun*
giving something you own as well as some money to get something else.

partial *adjective*
1 of a part; not complete. *a partial eclipse.* 2 **partial to,** fond of.
partially *adverb*

participate *verb* (**participated, participating**)
to take part or have a share in something.
participant *noun*, **participation** *noun*

patch

participle *noun*
a word formed from a verb and used as part of the verb or as an adjective. *Participles are words like going, gone, sailed, and sailing.*

particle *noun*
a tiny piece. *particles of dust.*

particular *adjective*
1 only this one and no other; special; individual. **2** fussy; hard to please. **3 in particular,** especially; chiefly.
particularly *adverb*

particular *noun*
a detail; a single fact.

parting *noun*
1 leaving; separation. **2** the line where your hair is parted.

partition *noun*
1 a thin dividing wall. **2** dividing something into parts.

partly *adverb*
not completely; somewhat.

partner *noun*
one of a pair of people who do something together, especially in business, dancing, or playing a game.
partnership *noun*

partridge *noun*
a game-bird with brown feathers.

part-time *adjective* and *adverb*
working for only some of the normal hours.
part-timer *noun*

party *noun* **(parties)**
1 a time when people get together to enjoy themselves. *my birthday party.* **2** a group of people working or travelling together. *a search party.* **3** an organised group of people with similar political beliefs. *The Labour Party.* **4** a person who is involved in an action or legal case. *the guilty party.*

pass *verb*
1 to go by. **2** to move or go. *They passed over the bridge.* **3** to give something to somebody; to hand over. *Please pass the salt.* **4** to be successful in an examination. **5** to spend time. **6** to disappear. **7** to approve or accept. *The law was passed.*
passable *adjective*

pass *noun* **(passes)**
1 passing something. **2** a permit to go in or out of a place. **3** a narrow way between hills.

passage *noun*
1 a corridor. **2** a way through something. *The police forced a passage through the crowd.* **3** a journey by sea or air. **4** a section of a piece of writing or music. **5** passing. *the passage of time.*
passageway *noun*

passenger *noun*
someone who is driven in a car, train, aircraft, etc.

passer-by *noun* **(passers-by)**
someone who happens to be going past.

passion *noun*
1 strong emotion. **2** great enthusiasm. **3 the Passion,** Christ's suffering on the Cross.
passionate *adjective*, **passionately** *adverb*

passive *adjective*
1 not active; not resisting or fighting. **2** describing the type of verb which affects the subject, not the object. *The verb is passive in 'She was hit on the head'.*
passively *adverb*

Passover *noun*
a Jewish religious festival.

passport *noun*
an official document that you must have if you want to travel abroad.

password *noun*
a secret word or phrase used to distinguish friends from enemies.

past *noun*
the time before now.

past *adjective*
1 of the past. **2 past participle,** a word used after *has, have, was, were,* etc. to describe an action that happened in the past. *'Done', 'overtaken', and 'written' are past participles.*

past *preposition*
1 beyond. *Go past the school.* **2** after. *It is past midnight.* **3 past it,** (*slang*) too old to be able to do something.

paste *noun*
a soft and moist or gluey substance.

paste *verb* **(pasted, pasting)**
to stick with paste.

pastel *noun*
1 a crayon like chalk. **2** a light, delicate colour.

pasteurize *verb* **(pasteurized, pasteurizing)**
(*say* **pahs**-cher-ryz)
to purify milk by heating it.
pasteurization *noun*

pastille *noun*
a small flavoured sweet.

pastime *noun*
something done to pass time pleasantly.

pastry *noun* **(pastries)**
1 a mixture of flour, fat, and water rolled flat and baked. **2** something made of pastry.

pasture *noun*
land covered with grass that cattle, sheep, or horses can eat.

pasty *noun* **(pasties)**
(*say* **pas**-ti)
a small pie. *I had meat pasty and chips.*

pasty *adjective* **(pastier, pastiest)**
(*say* **pay**-sti)
pale or white. *a pasty face.*

pat *verb* **(patted, patting)**
to tap gently with the open hand or with something flat.

pat *noun*
1 a patting movement or sound. **2** a small piece of butter. **3 a pat on the back,** congratulations or praise.

patch *noun* **(patches)**
1 a piece of material put over a hole or damaged place. **2** an area that is different from its surroundings. **3** a small area of land. **4** a small piece of something.

patch *verb*
1 to put a patch on something. **2 patch up**, to repair something roughly; to settle a quarrel.

patchwork *noun*
joining small pieces of different cloth together. *a bedspread made of patchwork.*

patchy *adjective* (**patchier, patchiest**)
occurring in patches; uneven.

patent *noun*
(*say* **pat**-ĕnt or **pay**-tĕnt)
official authority to make something you have invented and to stop other people copying it.

patent *adjective*
(*say* **pay**-tĕnt)
1 protected by a patent. 2 obvious. **3 patent leather**, glossy leather.

patent *verb*
to get a patent for something.

path *noun*
1 a narrow way to walk or ride along. 2 the line along which something moves.

pathetic *adjective*
1 sad; pitiful. *The orphan looked pathetic.* 2 sadly or comically inadequate or useless. *He made a pathetic attempt to climb the tree.*
pathetically *adverb*

patience *noun*
(*say* **pay**-shĕns)
1 being patient. 2 a card-game for one person.

patient *adjective*
(*say* **pay**-shĕnt)
1 able to wait for a long time without getting angry. 2 able to bear pain or trouble.
patiently *adverb*

patient *noun*
(*say* **pay**-shĕnt)
someone who is ill or who is getting treatment from a doctor or dentist.

patio *noun*
(*say* **pat**-i-oh)
a paved area next to a house.

patriot *noun*
(*say* **pay**-tri-ŏt or **pat**-ri-ŏt)
someone who loves his country and supports it loyally.
patriotic *adjective*, **patriotism** *noun*

patrol *verb* (**patrolled, patrolling**)
to move around a place or a thing so as to guard it and see that all is well.

patrol *noun*
1 a patrolling group of people, ships, aircraft, etc. 2 a group of Scouts or Guides. **3 on patrol**, patrolling. **4 patrol-car**, a car in which police, etc. patrol an area.
patrolman *noun*

patron *noun*
(*say* **pay**-trŏn)
1 someone who supports a person or cause with money or encouragement. **2 patron saint**, a saint who is thought to protect a particular place, person, etc.
patronage *noun*

patter *noun*
1 a series of light, tapping sounds. 2 the quick talk of a comedian, conjuror, salesman, etc.

pattern *noun*
1 a decorative group of lines or shapes. 2 a thing that you copy in order to make something. *a dress pattern.*

pause *noun*
a very short stop.

pause *verb* (**paused, pausing**)
to make a pause.

pave *verb* (**paved, paving**)
1 to make a hard surface for a road, path, etc. **2 pave the way**, to prepare for something.

pavement *noun*
a paved path along the side of a street.

pavilion *noun*
a building at a sports ground for the use of players or spectators.

paw *noun*
an animal's foot.

paw *verb*
to touch with a paw or hand.

pawn *noun*
1 one of the least valuable pieces in chess. 2 a person who is controlled by somebody else.

pawn *verb*
to leave something with a pawnbroker so as to borrow money from him. *I pawned my watch.*

pawnbroker *noun*
a shopkeeper who lends money to people in return for objects that they leave with him.

pay *verb* (**paid, paying**)
1 to give money in return for something. *Have you paid for your lunch?* 2 to be profitable. *It pays to advertise.* 3 to give or make. *He paid me a compliment.* 4 to suffer for something you have done. *I'll make you pay for this!* **5 pay back**, to pay money that you owe; to get revenge on someone.

pay *noun*
wages. *Have you had your pay?*

payment *noun*
1 the action of paying. 2 money paid.

P.E. short for *physical education.*

pea *noun*
a tiny, round, green vegetable that grows inside a pod.

peace *noun*
1 a time when there is no war, violence, or disorder. 2 quietness; calm.
peaceable *adjective*, **peaceably** *adverb*

peaceful *adjective*
1 having peace. *a peaceful country.* 2 liking or working for peace. *a peaceful man.*
peacefully *adverb*

peach *noun* (**peaches**)
a round, soft, juicy fruit with a large stone.

peacock *noun*
a large bird with a long, brightly-coloured tail that it can spread out like a fan.

peak *noun*
1 the top of a mountain. 2 the highest or best point of something. *He is at the peak of his career.* 3 the part of a cap that sticks out in front.
peaked *adjective*

penetrate

peal *verb*
to make a loud ringing sound.

peal *noun*
a pealing sound.

peanut *noun*
1 a small, round nut that grows in a pod in the ground. **2 peanut butter,** roasted peanuts crushed into a paste.

pear *noun*
a juicy fruit that gets narrower near the stalk.

pearl *noun*
1 a small, shiny, white ball found in the shells of some oysters and used as a jewel. **2 pearl barley,** grains of barley made small by grinding.
pearly *adjective*

peasant *noun*
someone who works on a farm.
peasantry *noun*

peat *noun*
rotted plant material that can be dug out of the ground and used as fuel or fertilizer.

pebble *noun*
a small round stone.
pebbly *adjective*

peck *verb*
to bite or eat something with the beak. *The hens were pecking at the corn.*

peculiar *adjective*
1 strange; unusual. **2 peculiar to,** restricted to. *This custom is peculiar to this tribe.*
peculiarity *noun,* **peculiarly** *adverb*

pedal *noun*
part of a machine worked by a person's foot. *A bicycle has two pedals.*

pedal *verb* **(pedalled, pedalling)**
to use a pedal; to move something by using pedals.

peddle *verb* **(peddled, peddling)**
to sell things as a pedlar.

pedestal *noun*
1 the base that supports a statue, pillar, etc. **2 put somebody on a pedestal,** to admire or worship him.

pedestrian *noun*
someone who is walking.

pedigree *noun*
a list of a person's or animal's ancestors, especially to show how purely an animal has been bred.

pedlar *noun*
someone who goes from house to house selling small things.

peel *noun*
the skin of some fruit and vegetables.

peel *verb*
1 to remove the peel or covering from something. 2 to lose a covering or skin.

peep *verb*
1 to look quickly or secretly. 2 to look through a narrow opening. 3 to show slightly or briefly. *The moon peeped out through the clouds.*
peep-hole *noun*

peer *verb*
to look at something closely or with difficulty.

peer *noun*
a nobleman.
peeress *noun*

peewit *noun*
a kind of plover.

peg *noun*
1 a clip or pin for fixing things in place or for hanging things on. 2 a clothes-peg.

peg *verb* **(pegged, pegging)**
1 to fix something with pegs. 2 to keep at a fixed amount. *The government pegged wages.* **3 peg out,** *(informal)* to die.

peg-board *noun*
a board with holes in, where things can be hung.

Pekingese or **Pekinese** *noun* **(Pekingese** or **Pekinese)**
(say peek-i-**neez)**
a small kind of dog with short legs and long silky hair.

pelican *noun*
a large bird with a pouch in its long beak for storing fish.

pellet *noun*
a tiny ball of metal, food, wet paper, etc.

pelt *verb*
1 to throw a lot of things at somebody. 2 to move very quickly. 3 to rain very hard.

pelt *noun*
an animal skin, especially with the fur or hair on it.

pen *noun*[1]
1 a device with a metal point for writing with ink. **2 pen-friend,** someone that you write to regularly but do not meet.

pen *noun*[2]
an enclosure for cattle or other animals.

penalize *verb* **(penalized, penalizing)**
1 to punish. 2 to give a penalty against someone in a game.

penalty *noun* **(penalties)**
1 a punishment. 2 an advantage given to one side in a game when a member of the other side breaks a rule. 3 a goal scored as the result of a penalty.

pence *plural noun*
pennies. *These sweets cost 50 pence.*

pencil *noun*
a device for drawing or writing, made of a thin stick of lead or coloured chalk enclosed in a cylinder of wood or metal.

pencil *verb* **(pencilled, pencilling)**
to draw or write with a pencil.

pendant *noun*
an ornament hung round the neck on a long chain or string.

pendulum *noun*
a rod with a weight on the end so that it swings to and fro. *Some clocks are worked by pendulums.*

penetrate *verb* **(penetrated, penetrating)**
to make or find a way through or into something.
penetration *noun*

penguin *noun*
an Antarctic sea-bird that cannot fly but uses its wings as flippers for swimming.

penicillin *noun*
an antibiotic obtained from fungi.

peninsula *noun*
a long piece of land that is almost surrounded by water.
peninsular *adjective*

penis *noun* **(penises)**
the part of the body with which a male urinates or has sexual intercourse.

penitence *noun*
regret that you have done wrong.
penitent *adjective*

penknife *noun* **(penknives)**
a small folding knife.

pennant *noun*
a triangular or tapering flag.

penniless *adjective*
bankrupt; very poor.

penny *noun* **(pennies** or **pence)**
a British coin worth a hundredth of a pound. *Before 1971, there were 240 pennies in a pound.*

pension *noun*
regular payments made to somebody who has retired.

pensioner *noun*
someone who receives a pension; an old person.

pentagon *noun*
1 a shape with five sides. **2 the Pentagon,** the leaders of the American armed forces, named after their five-sided headquarters near Washington.

peony *noun* **(peonies)**
(*say* **pee**-ŏ-ni)
a large garden-flower.

people *plural noun*
1 men, women, and children. **2** the natives or inhabitants of a country.

pepper *noun*
1 a hot-tasting powder used to flavour food. **2** a bright green or red vegetable.
peppery *adjective*

peppermint *noun*
1 a kind of mint used for flavouring. **2** a sweet flavoured with this mint.

per *preposition*
1 for each; in each. *The charge is £2 per person.* **2 per cent,** for or in every hundred. *A pay-rise from £100 to £110 is a 10 per cent (10%) increase.*

perceive *verb* **(perceived, perceiving)**
to notice.
perceptible *adjective*, **perceptibly** *adverb*, **perception** *noun*

percentage *noun*
the proportion out of every hundred of something. *Out of £80 he spent £20, a percentage of 25.*

perceptive *adjective*
quick to notice things.

perch *noun*[1] **(perches)**
a place where a bird sits or rests.

perch *noun*[2] **(perch)**
an edible freshwater fish.

perch *verb*
to sit or stand on the edge of something or on something small.

percolator *noun*
a device for making coffee.

percussion *noun*
musical instruments played by hitting or shaking. *Drums, cymbals, and tambourines are percussion instruments.*
percussive *adjective*

perennial *adjective*
1 lasting or recurring for many years. *a perennial problem.* **2** flowering for many years. *perennial plants.*
perennially *adverb*

perfect *adjective*
(*say* **pur**-fikt)
1 so good that it cannot be made any better; without any faults. **2** complete. *a perfect stranger.*
perfection *noun*, **perfectly** *adverb*

perfect *verb*
(*say* per-**fekt**)
to make something perfect.

perforate *verb* **(perforated, perforating)**
to make tiny holes in something, especially so that it can be torn easily.
perforation *noun*

perform *verb*
1 to do something in front of an audience. *They performed 'Macbeth' in the school hall.* **2** to do something you have to do or ought to do. *The surgeon performed the operation.*
performance *noun*, **performer** *noun*

perfume *noun*
1 a liquid with a very sweet smell. **2** a sweet smell.

perhaps *adverb*
it may be; possibly.

peril *noun*
danger. *She was in great peril.*
perilous *adjective*, **perilously** *adverb*

perimeter *noun*
(*say* per-**im**-it-er)
the distance round the edge of something; a boundary.

period *noun*
1 a length of time. **2** the time when a woman or girl menstruates.
periodic *adjective*, **periodically** *adverb*

periodical *noun*
a magazine published regularly.

periscope *noun*
a device using mirrors to let you see something on a higher level than where you are.

perish *verb*
1 to die. **2** to rot. *The tyres have perished.* **3** (*informal*) to make somebody very cold. *I'm perished.*
perishable *adjective*

permanent *adjective*
1 lasting for ever or for a very long time. **2 permanent wave,** long-lasting waves made in hair.
permanence *noun*, **permanently** *adverb*

permission *noun*
permitting something; a statement that something is permitted.

permissive *adjective*
letting people do what they wish; tolerant.
permissively *adverb*, **permissiveness** *noun*

permit *verb* **(permitted, permitting)**
(*say* per-**mit**)
to say that somebody may do something; to let somebody do something.
permissible *adjective*

permit *noun*
(*say* **per**-mit)
a written or printed statement that something is permitted.

perpendicular *adjective*
upright; at a right angle to the base or to another line.

perpetual *adjective*
continual; permanent.
perpetually *adverb*, **perpetuate** *verb*

perplex *verb*
to bewilder; to puzzle somebody.
perplexity *noun*

persecute *verb* **(persecuted, persecuting)**
to be continually cruel to somebody, especially because you disagree with his beliefs.
persecution *noun*, **persecutor** *noun*

persevere *verb* **(persevered, persevering)**
to go on despite difficulties.
perseverance *noun*

persist *verb*
to keep on doing something; to persevere.
persistence *noun*, **persistent** *adjective*,
persistently *adverb*

person *noun*
a man, woman, or child.

personal *adjective*
belonging to, done by, or concerning a particular person; private.
personally *adverb*

personality *noun* **(personalities)**
1 a person's character or qualities. *She has a friendly personality.* 2 a well-known person. *television personalities.*

personnel *noun*
(*say* per-sŏn-**el**)
the people employed in a particular place.

perspective *noun*
1 the impression of depth and space in a picture or scene. 2 **in perspective**, having a balanced view of things.

perspire *verb* **(perspired, perspiring)**
to give off moisture through the pores of your skin.
perspiration *noun*

persuade *verb* **(persuaded, persuading)**
to get somebody to agree with something.
persuasion *noun*, **persuasive** *adjective*

perverse *adjective*
(*say* per-**vers**)
obstinately being unreasonable or wicked.
perversely *adverb*, **perversity** *noun*

pervert *verb*
(*say* per-**vert**)
1 to make something go wrong. 2 to make somebody behave wickedly or abnormally.
perversion *noun*

pervert *noun*
(*say* **per**-vert)
someone who behaves wickedly or abnormally.

pessimism *noun*
expecting that things will not happen as you want.
pessimist *noun*, **pessimistic** *adjective*

pest *noun*
a destructive or annoying animal or person.

pester *verb*
to annoy somebody with frequent questions, requests, etc.

pet *noun*
1 a tame animal kept for companionship and amusement. 2 a person treated as a favourite. *teacher's pet.*

petal *noun*
one of the separate coloured parts of a flower. *Daisies have a lot of white petals.*

petition *noun*
a written request for something, usually signed by a large number of people.

petrify *verb* **(petrified, petrifying)**
to paralyse somebody with terror, surprise, etc.

petrol *noun*
1 a liquid made from petroleum, used to drive the engines of cars, aircraft, etc. 2 **petrol pump**, a device for putting petrol into the tank of a motor vehicle. 3 **petrol station**, a place where petrol is supplied.

petroleum *noun*
(*say* pi-**troh**-li-ŭm)
an oil found underground that is refined to make petrol and paraffin.

petticoat *noun*
a woman's garment worn under a skirt or dress.

petty *adjective* **(pettier, pettiest)**
small and unimportant; trivial. *petty regulations.*
pettily *adverb*, **pettiness** *noun*

pew *noun*
one of the long wooden seats in a church.

pewter *noun*
a grey alloy of tin and lead.

phase *noun*
a stage in the progress or development of something.

phase *verb* **(phased, phasing)**
1 to carry out something in stages. *a phased withdrawal.* 2 **phase in**, to start something gradually. 3 **phase out**, to stop something gradually.

pheasant *noun*
(*say* **fez**-ănt)
a game-bird with a long tail.

phenomenal *adjective*
(*say* fin-**om**-in-ăl)
amazing.
phenomenally *adverb*

phenomenon *noun* **(phenomena)**
an event or fact, especially one that is remarkable or unusual. *We observed some strange phenomena.*

philately *noun*
(*say* fil-**at**-ĕl-i)
collecting postage stamps. *My hobby is philately.*
philatelic *adjective*, **philatelist** *noun*

philosophical *adjective*
1 of philosophy. **2** not upset by suffering, misfortune, etc. *He was philosophical about his illness.*
philosophically *adverb*

philosophy *noun* **(philosophies)**
(*say* fil-**os**-ŏ-fi)
1 the study of truths about life, morals, etc. **2** a way of thinking; a system of beliefs.
philosopher *noun*

phobia *noun*
(*say* **foh**-bi-ă)
a great or abnormal fear of something.

phoenix *noun* **(phoenixes)**
(*say* **fee**-niks)
a mythical bird that was said to burn itself to death on a fire and be born again from the ashes.

phone *noun*
a telephone.

phone *verb* **(phoned, phoning)**
to telephone.

phone-in *noun*
a broadcast programme in which listeners or viewers telephone the studio and take part in the programme.

phosphorescent *adjective*
luminous.
phosphorescence *noun*

phosphorus *noun*
a yellowish element that glows in the dark.
phosphoric *adjective*

photo *noun*
a photograph.

photocopy *noun* **(photocopies)**
a copy of a document, page, etc. made by photography.

photoelectric *adjective*
1 of or using the electrical effects of light. **2 photoelectric cell,** an electronic device that emits electricity when light falls on it.

photo-finish *noun* **(photo-finishes)**
a very close finish of a race, photographed so that the winner can be decided.

photograph *noun*
a picture made on film using a camera.
photographic *adjective*, **photography** *noun*

photograph *verb*
to take a photograph of somebody or something.
photographer *noun*

photosynthesis *noun*
the process by which plants use sunlight to turn carbon dioxide and water into complex substances, giving off oxygen.

phrase *noun*
1 a small group of words. **2** a short part of a tune.

phrase *verb* **(phrased, phrasing)**
to put something into words.

physical *adjective*
1 of or concerned with the body. **2** of things that you can touch or see. **3 physical education** or **physical training,** gymnastics or other exercises done to keep healthy.
physically *adverb*

physician *noun*
a doctor.

physics *noun*
the study of energy, movement, heat, light, sound, etc.
physicist *noun*

physiology *noun*
(*say* fiz-i-**ol**-ŏ-ji)
the study of the bodies of people and other living things.
physiological *adjective*, **physiologist** *noun*

pianist *noun*
someone who plays the piano.

piano *noun*
a large musical instrument with a keyboard.

piccolo *noun*
a small flute.

pick *verb*
1 to choose. *Pick somebody to dance with.* **2** to take something from where it is. *She picked some flowers.* **3** to steal from someone's pocket. **4** to open a lock without using a key. **5** to pull bits off or out of something. **6 pick holes in,** to find faults in something. **7 pick on,** to keep criticizing or bothering a particular person. **8 pick up,** to take something upwards from where it is; to collect a thing; to take somebody with you in a vehicle; to manage to hear something.

pick *noun*[1]
1 a choice. **2** the best part of something.

pick *noun*[2]
a pickaxe.

pickaxe *noun*
a heavy pointed tool with a long handle, for breaking up hard ground, concrete, etc.

picket *noun*
a group of strikers who try to persuade other people not to work.

picket *verb*
to act as a picket during a strike.

pickle *noun*
1 a strong-tasting food made of pickled vegetables, etc. **2** (*informal*) a naughty or playful child. **3** (*informal*) a difficulty.

pickle *verb* **(pickled, pickling)**
to preserve something in vinegar or salt water.

pickpocket *noun*
someone who steals from people's pockets.

pick-up *noun*
1 the part of a record-player holding the stylus. **2** an open truck for carrying small loads.

picnic *noun*
a meal eaten in the open air away from home.

picnic *verb* **(picknicked, picknicking)**
to have a picnic.
picnicker *noun*

pictorial *adjective*
with or using pictures.
pictorially *adverb*

picture *noun*
1 a painting, drawing, or photograph. **2** a film at the cinema. **3 in the picture,** knowing the facts about something.

picture *verb* **(pictured, picturing)**
1 to show in a picture. **2** to imagine.

picturesque *adjective*
(*say* pik-cher-**esk**)
attractive or charming; vivid.

pie *noun*
meat or fruit covered with pastry and baked.

piece *noun*
1 a part of something; a bit. **2** something written, composed, etc. *a piece of music.* **3** one of the objects used on a board to play a game. *a chess-piece.* **4 in one piece,** not broken. **5 piece by piece,** gradually; one part at a time.

piece *verb* **(pieced, piecing)**
to join pieces together to make something. *The detective pieced together what had really happened.*

piecemeal *adverb*
piece by piece.

pier *noun*
1 a long structure built out into the sea for people to walk on. **2** a pillar supporting a bridge.

pierce *verb* **(pierced, piercing)**
1 to make a hole through something; to penetrate. **2 piercing,** very strong or very loud.

pig *noun*
1 a fat animal with short legs and a blunt snout, kept by farmers for its meat. **2** (*informal*) someone who is greedy, dirty, or unpleasant.
piggy *adjective* and *noun*

pigeon *noun*
1 a bird that can be taught to fly home from far away. **2** (*informal*) somebody's business or responsibility. *That's his pigeon.*

pigeon-hole *noun*
a small compartment where you can put papers, letters, etc.

piggy-back *noun*
a ride on somebody's back.

pig-headed *adjective*
obstinate.

piglet *noun*
a young pig.

pigment *noun*
a substance that colours something.

pigmy *noun* **(pigmies)**
a pygmy.

pigsty *noun* **(pigsties)**
a building for pigs.

pigtail *noun*
a single plait of hair at the back of the head.

pike *noun*
1 a large freshwater fish. **2** a heavy spear.

pilchard *noun*
a small sea-fish.

pile *noun*[1]
1 a number of things on top of one another. **2** (*informal*) a large amount of something, especially money.

pile *noun*[2]
a heavy beam driven vertically into the ground to support something.

pile *verb* **(piled, piling)**
1 to put things on top of one another. **2 pile up,** to become numerous. *Jobs were piling up.*

pilfer *verb*
to steal small things.

pilgrim *noun*
someone who goes on a pilgrimage.

pilgrimage *noun*
a journey to a holy place.

pill *noun*
1 a small pellet of medicine. **2 the pill,** a pill taken to prevent pregnancy.

pillar *noun*
a tall stone or wooden post.

pillar-box *noun* **(pillar-boxes)**
a post-box standing in a street.

pillion *noun*
the seat on a motor cycle behind the driver's seat.

pillow *noun*
a cushion for a person to rest his head on, especially in bed.

pillowcase *noun*
a cover made of cotton, linen, etc. for a pillow.

pilot *noun*
1 someone who drives an aircraft. **2** someone who helps to steer a ship through narrow or dangerous places.

pilot *verb*
to be a pilot of an aircraft or ship.

pimple *noun*
a small, round swelling on the skin.
pimply *adjective*

pin *noun*
1 a short piece of metal with a sharp point and a rounded head, used to fasten pieces of paper, cloth, etc. together. **2** a pointed device for fixing or marking something. **3 pins and needles,** a tingling feeling.

pin *verb* **(pinned, pinning)**
1 to fasten with a pin. **2** to keep a person or thing in one place. *He was pinned under the wreckage.*

pinafore *noun*
1 an apron. **2 pinafore dress,** a dress without collar or sleeves.

pincer *noun*
1 the claw of a shellfish such as the lobster. **2 pincers,** a tool for gripping and pulling things.

pinch *verb*
1 to squeeze something tightly between two things, especially between your finger and thumb. 2 (*informal*) to steal.

pinch *noun* (pinches)
1 a pinching movement. 2 the amount you can pick up between the tips of your finger and thumb. *a pinch of salt.* 3 at a pinch, if it is necessary.

pincushion *noun*
a small pad in which needles and pins are stuck to keep them ready for use.

pine *noun*
an evergreen tree with leaves shaped like needles.

pine *verb* (pined, pining)
1 to long for somebody or something. 2 to become weak or ill through sorrow or yearning.

pineapple *noun*
a large tropical fruit with prickly leaves and skin.

ping-pong *noun*
table-tennis.

pink *adjective*
pale red.

pink *noun*
a fragrant garden-flower.

pint *noun*
an eighth of a gallon.

pioneer *noun*
one of the first people to go to a place, do something, investigate a subject, etc.

pious *adjective*
very religious.
piously *adverb*

pip *noun*
1 a seed of an apple, orange, pear, etc. 2 one of the spots on playing-cards, dice, or dominoes. 3 a short, high-pitched sound. *She heard the 6 pips of the time-signal on the radio.*

pipe *noun*
1 a tube for carrying water, gas, etc. from one place to another. 2 a short tube with a small bowl at one end, used to smoke tobacco. 3 a tubular musical instrument. 4 the pipes, bagpipes.

pipe *verb* (piped, piping)
1 to send something along pipes or wires. 2 to play on a pipe or the bagpipes. 3 pipe down, (*informal*) be quiet. 4 piping hot, very hot.

pipeline *noun*
a pipe for carrying oil, water, etc. a long distance.

piper *noun*
someone who plays a pipe or the bagpipes.

pirate *noun*
a sailor who attacks and robs other ships.
piracy *noun*, **piratical** *adjective*

pistil *noun*
the part of a flower that produces the seed.

pistol *noun*
a small gun for use with one hand.

piston *noun*
a disc that moves up and down inside a cylinder in an engine, pump, etc.

pit *noun*
1 a deep hole or depression. 2 a coal-mine. 3 the part of a race-course where racing-cars are refuelled, repaired, etc.

pit *verb* (pitted, pitting)
1 to make deep holes or depressions in something. *The ground was pitted with craters.* 2 to put somebody in competition with somebody else. *He was pitted against their strongest fighter.*

pitch *noun*[1] (pitches)
1 a piece of ground marked out for cricket, football, or another game. 2 the height of a voice or musical note. 3 intensity; strength. *Excitement was at a high pitch.*

pitch *noun*[2]
1 a black, sticky substance like tar. 2 pitch-black or pitch-dark, very black or dark; with no light at all.

pitch *verb*
1 to throw. 2 to put up a tent. 3 to fall heavily. 4 to move up and down on a rough sea. 5 to set something at a particular height. 6 pitched battle, a battle between troops in prepared positions. 7 pitch in, to start working or eating vigorously.

pitcher *noun*
a large jug, usually with two handles.

pitchfork *noun*
a large fork with two prongs for lifting hay.

pitfall *noun*
an unsuspected danger or difficulty.

pitiful *adjective*
1 causing pity. *a pitiful sight.* 2 inadequate; arousing contempt. *a pitiful attempt to make us laugh.*
pitifully *adverb*

pitiless *adjective*
having or showing no pity.
pitilessly *adverb*

pity *noun* (pities)
1 the feeling of being sorry that someone is in pain or trouble. *I feel pity for these invalids.* 2 something that you are sorry about. *It's a pity you can't meet me.* 3 take pity on, to help somebody in trouble.

pity *verb* (pitied, pitying)
to feel pity for someone.

pivot *noun*
a point on which something turns or balances.

pixie or **pixy** *noun* (pixies)
a small fairy.

pizza *noun*
(*say* **peets**-ă)
a layer of dough covered with cheese, vegetables, etc. and baked.

pizzicato *adverb* and *adjective*
(*say* pits-i-**kah**-toh)
plucking the strings of a musical instrument.

placard *noun*
a poster; a notice.

platoon

place *noun*
1 a particular part of space, especially where something belongs; a position or area. 2 a seat. *Save me a place.* 3 **from place to place,** from one place to another; travelling around. 4 **in place,** in the proper position. 5 **in place of,** instead of. 6 **out of place,** not in the proper position; unsuitable. 7 **take place,** to happen.

place *verb* **(placed, placing)**
to put something in a particular place.

placid *adjective*
calm; peaceful.
placidity *noun*, **placidly** *adverb*

plague *noun*
1 a dangerous illness that spreads very quickly. 2 a large number of pests. *a plague of locusts.*

plague *verb* **(plagued, plaguing)**
to pester or annoy. *They were plagued with enquiries.*

plaice *noun*
a flat, edible sea-fish.

plaid *noun*
(*say* plad)
cloth with a tartan or chequered pattern.

plain *adjective*
1 not decorated. 2 not pretty. 3 easy to understand or see. 4 frank; straightforward. 5 **plain clothes,** civilian clothes worn instead of a uniform.
plainly *adverb*, **plainness** *noun*

plain *noun*
a large area of flat country.

plaintiff *noun*
a person who brings a complaint against somebody else to a lawcourt.

plaintive *adjective*
that sounds sad. *a plaintive cry for help.*
plaintively *adverb*

plait *noun*
(*say* plat)
a length of hair, rope, etc. with several strands twisted together.

plait *verb*
(*say* plat)
to make into a plait.

plan *noun*
1 a way of doing something, thought out in advance. 2 a drawing showing what something should look like. 3 a map of a town or district.

plan *verb* **(planned, planning)**
to make a plan for something.
planner *noun*

plane *noun*[1]
1 an aeroplane. 2 a tool for making wood smooth. 3 a flat surface.

plane *noun*[2]
a tree with wide leaves.

plane *verb* **(planed, planing)**
to smooth wood with a plane.

planet *noun*
a heavenly body that orbits round the sun. *The main planets are Mercury, Venus, Earth, Mars, Jupiter, Saturn, Uranus, Neptune, and Pluto.*
planetary *adjective*

plank *noun*
a long, flat piece of wood.

plankton *noun*
tiny creatures that float in the sea, lakes, etc.

plant *noun*
1 something that grows out of the ground. *Flowers, bushes, trees, and vegetables are plants.* 2 a factory or its equipment.

plant *verb*
1 to put something in the ground to grow. 2 to put something firmly in place. 3 to hide something where it will be found, usually to cause somebody trouble.
planter *noun*

plantation *noun*
an area of land where tobacco, tea, etc. is planted.

plaque *noun*
(*say* plak or plahk)
1 a metal or porcelain plate fixed on a wall as a memorial or an ornament. 2 a filmy substance on teeth.

plasma *noun*
(*say* **plaz**-mǎ)
the colourless liquid part of blood which carries the corpuscles.

plaster *noun*
1 a small adhesive covering for a wound. 2 a mixture of lime, sand, water, etc. used to cover walls and ceilings. 3 plaster of Paris. 4 **plaster of Paris,** a white paste used for making moulds and casts.

plaster *verb*
1 to cover a surface with plaster. 2 to cover something thickly. 3 **plastered,** (*informal*) drunk.
plasterer *noun*

plastic *noun*
a strong, light, synthetic substance that can be moulded into different shapes.

plastic *adjective*
1 made of plastic. *a plastic bag.* 2 **plastic surgery,** surgery to replace deformed or injured parts of the body.

Plasticine *noun*
a soft, coloured, plastic substance used for making models.

plate *noun*
1 a dish that is flat or almost flat. 2 a flat sheet of metal, glass, etc. 3 an illustration on a separate page in a book.
plateful *noun*

plate *verb* **(plated, plating)**
to coat metal with a thin layer of gold, silver, tin, etc.

plateau *noun* **(plateaux)**
(*say* **plat**-oh)
a flat area of high land.

platform *noun*
1 the raised area along the side of the line at a railway station. 2 a small stage in a hall. 3 the policy of a political party.

platinum *noun*
a silver-coloured metal that does not tarnish.

platoon *noun*
a small unit of soldiers.

platypus *noun* **(platypuses)**
an Australian animal with a beak and feet like those of a duck.

play *verb*
1 to take part in a game or other amusement. 2 to make music or sound with a musical instrument, record-player, etc. 3 to perform a part in a play or film. 4 **play about, play around,** or **play up,** to be naughty.
player *noun*

play *noun*
1 a story acted on a stage or broadcast on radio or television. 2 playing; having fun.

playback *noun*
playing something that has been recorded.

playful *adjective*
wanting to play; full of fun; not serious.
playfully *adverb*, **playfulness** *noun*

playground *noun*
a place out of doors where children can play.

play-group *noun*
a group of young children who play together regularly, supervised by adults.

playing-card *noun*
one of a set of cards used for playing games.

playmate *noun*
somebody that you play games with.

playtime *noun*
the time when schoolchildren may go out to play.

playwright *noun*
a dramatist.

plea *noun*
1 a request or appeal. 2 an excuse.

plead *verb*
1 to make a plea. 2 **plead guilty,** to admit that you are guilty.

pleasant *adjective*
that pleases you; that you like.
pleasantly *adverb*

please *verb* **(pleased, pleasing)**
1 to make someone happy or satisfied. *Nothing pleases him.* 2 used when you want to make a request polite. *Shut the door, please. Please may I have a slice of cake?* 3 to wish; to think fit. *Do as you please.*

pleasure *noun*
1 being pleased; something that pleases you. 2 **with pleasure,** gladly; willingly.
pleasurable *adjective*

pleat *noun*
a fold made in the cloth of a garment.
pleated *adjective*

pledge *noun*
a solemn promise.

plentiful *adjective*
large in amount.
plentifully *adverb*

plenty *noun*
1 a lot of something. 2 more than enough.

pliable *adjective*
easy to bend or influence.
pliant *adjective*

pliers *plural noun*
a tool for gripping something or for breaking wire.

plight *noun*
a difficult situation.

plimsoll *noun*
a canvas shoe with a rubber sole.

plod *verb* **(plodded, plodding)**
1 to walk slowly and heavily. 2 to work slowly but steadily.
plodder *noun*

plop *noun*
the sound of something dropping into water.

plot *noun*
1 a secret plan. 2 what happens in a story, play, film, etc. 3 a piece of ground for a house or garden.

plot *verb* **(plotted, plotting)**
to make a secret plan.
plotter *noun*

plough *noun*
(*say* plow)
a device used on farms for turning over the soil.

plough *verb*
(*say* plow)
1 to turn over soil with a plough. 2 to go through something with difficulty. *He ploughed through the book.*
ploughman *noun*

plover *noun*
(*say* **pluv**-er)
a long-legged wading bird.

pluck *verb*
1 to pull the feathers off a bird. 2 to pick a flower or fruit. 3 to pull something up or out. 4 to pull a string and let it go again. 5 **pluck up courage,** to overcome your fear.

pluck *noun*
bravery.
pluckily *adverb*, **plucky** *adjective*

plug *noun*
1 something used to stop up a hole. 2 the part by which an electric wire is fitted into a socket. 3 (*informal*) a piece of publicity for something.

plug *verb* **(plugged, plugging)**
1 to stop up a hole. 2 (*informal*) to publicize something. 3 **plug in,** to put an electric plug into a socket.

plum *noun*
a soft, juicy fruit with a stone in the middle.

plumage *noun*
(*say* **ploo**-mij)
feathers.

plumb *verb*
1 to measure how deep something is. 2 to reach the bottom of something.

plumber *noun*
someone who fits and mends water-pipes in a building.

plumbing *noun*
1 the work of a plumber. 2 the water-pipes and water-tanks in a building.

plume *noun*
a large feather.
plumed *adjective*

plump *adjective*
slightly fat; rounded.

plump *verb*
plump for, to choose.

plunder *verb*
to loot.
plunderer *noun*

plunge *verb* **(plunged, plunging)**
1 to jump or put suddenly into water. **2** to thrust.

plural *noun*
the form of a word that refers to more than one person or thing. *'Buns', 'children', 'mice', and 'teeth' are plurals.*

plural *adjective*
of the plural; referring to more than one.

plus *preposition*
with the next number added. *2 plus 2 equals 4 (2+2=4).*

plutonium *noun*
(*say* ploo-**toh**-ni-um)
a radioactive element used in nuclear weapons and reactors.

plywood *noun*
wood made from thin sheets of wood glued together.

p.m. short for Latin *post meridiem* which means 'after midday'.

pneumatic *adjective*
(*say* new-**mat**-ik)
1 filled with air. *pneumatic tyres.* **2** using compressed air. *pneumatic drill.*

pneumonia *noun*
(*say* new-**moh**-ni-ă)
a lung disease.

poach *verb*
1 to cook an egg in or over boiling water without its shell. **2** to hunt animals illegally on someone else's land.
poacher *noun*

pocket *noun*
1 part of a garment shaped like a small bag, for keeping things in. **2 your pocket,** what you can afford.
pocketful *noun*

pocket *adjective*
small enough to carry in your pocket. *a pocket calculator.*

pocket-money *noun*
a small amount of money given to a child to spend as he likes.

pod *noun*
a long seed-container on a pea or bean plant.

podgy *adjective* **(podgier, podgiest)**
short and fat.

poem *noun*
a piece of poetry.

poet *noun*
someone who writes poetry.

poetry *noun*
writing arranged in short lines, usually with a particular rhythm.
poetic *adjective*, **poetical** *adjective*

point *noun*
1 the sharp end of something. *Don't hold that knife by the point.* **2** a dot or mark. *the decimal point.* **3** a particular place or time. *She gave up at this point.* **4** a detail; a characteristic. *He has some good points.* **5** purpose; value. *There's no point in hurrying.* **6 point of view,** how you see things or think of things. **7 points,** a device for changing a railway train from one track to another. **8 the point,** the essential thing. *Come to the point.*

point *verb*
1 to show where something is, especially by holding out your finger towards it. **2** to aim something. *She pointed the gun at him.* **3 point out,** to show or explain something.

pointed *adjective*
1 with a point at the end. *a pointed stick.* **2** clearly directed at somebody or his behaviour. *a pointed remark.*
pointedly *adverb*

pointer *noun*
1 a stick, rod, mark, etc. used to point at something. **2** a dog that points with its muzzle at birds it scents. **3** an indication or hint.

pointless *adjective*
with no purpose or meaning.
pointlessly *adverb*

point-to-point *noun*
a horse-race or series of horse-races on a course marked only at certain places.

poise *noun*
1 balance. **2** a dignified, self-confident appearance.

poise *verb* **(poised, poising)**
to balance.

poison *noun*
a substance that can kill or harm you.
poisonous *adjective*

poison *verb*
1 to give poison to somebody. **2** to put poison in something.
poisoner *noun*

poke *verb* **(poked, poking)**
1 to prod. **2 poke out,** to stick out.

poker *noun*
1 a metal rod for poking a fire. **2** a card-game in which the players bet on who has the best cards.

polar *adjective*
of or near the North or South Pole.

polar bear *noun*
a white Arctic bear.

Pole *noun*[1]
a Polish person.

pole *noun*[2]
1 a long, round piece of wood or metal. **2 up the pole,** (*slang*) mad; in difficulties.

pole *noun*[3]
1 the **North Pole** or the **South Pole,** one of the two points on the earth's surface farthest away from the equator. **2** one end of a magnet.

pole-vault *noun*
a jump over a high bar done with the help of a long pole.

police *noun*
the people whose job is to catch criminals and make sure that the law is kept.
policeman *noun*, **policewoman** *noun*

policy *noun* **(policies)**
the aims and ideals of a person or group; a plan of action.

polio *noun*
(*say* **poh**-li-oh)
(*informal*) poliomyelitis.

poliomyelitis *noun*
(*say* poh-li-oh-my-il-l-tis)
a paralysing disease.

Polish *adjective*
(*say* **poh**-lish)
of Poland.

polish *verb*
(*say* **pol**-ish)
1 to make a surface shiny or smooth. **2 polish off**, (*informal*) to finish something quickly.

polish *noun* **(polishes)**
(*say* **pol**-ish)
1 a substance used in polishing. **2** a shine.

polished *adjective*
elegant; refined.

polite *adjective* **(politer, politest)**
having good manners; respectful and thoughtful towards other people.
politely *adverb*, **politeness** *noun*

political *adjective*
connected with the governing of a country.
politically *adverb*

politician *noun*
someone involved or interested in politics.

politics *noun*
political matters.

polka *noun*
1 a lively dance. **2 polka dots**, an even pattern of round dots on cloth.

poll *noun*
1 voting at an election. **2** an opinion poll.

pollen *noun*
the yellow powder found inside flowers.

pollute *verb* **(polluted, polluting)**
to make a place or thing dirty or impure.
pollution *noun*

polo *noun*
1 a game rather like hockey, with players on horseback using mallets with long handles. **2 polo-neck**, a high, round, turned-over collar.

poltergeist *noun*
(*say* **pol**-ter-gyst)
a mischievous, destructive ghost.

polygon *noun*
a figure or shape with many sides. *Hexagons and octagons are polygons.*

polystyrene *noun*
(*say* pol-i-**sty**-reen)
a kind of plastic used for insulating, packing, etc.

polytechnic *noun*
(*say* pol-i-**tek**-nik)
a college for higher education, especially in technical or professional subjects.

polythene *noun*
(*say* **pol**-i-theen)
a lightweight plastic used to make bags, wrappings, etc.

pomp *noun*
splendid, dignified display or ceremony.

pompous *adjective*
thinking too much of your own importance.
pomposity *noun*, **pompously** *adverb*

poncho *noun*
a piece of cloth with a hole in the middle for the head, worn as a cloak.

pond *noun*
a small lake.

ponder *verb*
to think seriously about something.

ponderous *adjective*
1 heavy. **2** not fluent; not easy to read or listen to. *He writes in a ponderous style.*
ponderously *adverb*

pontoon *noun*
1 a boat or float supporting a bridge over a river. **2** a card-game in which players try to get cards whose value totals 21; a score of 21 with two cards in this game.

pony *noun* **(ponies)**
a small horse.

pony-tail *noun*
a bunch of long hair tied at the back of the head.

pony-trekking *noun*
travelling across country on ponies for pleasure.

poodle *noun*
a dog with long, curly hair.

pool *noun*[1]
1 a pond. **2** a puddle. **3** a swimming-pool.

pool *noun*[2]
1 a fund of money. **2** a group of things shared by several people. **3 the pools**, football pools.

poor *adjective*
1 having very little money. *a poor family.* **2** bad; inadequate. *poor work.* **3** unfortunate. *Poor fellow!*

poorly *adverb*
in a poor way. *poorly dressed.*

poorly *adjective*
unwell. *I feel poorly.*

pop *noun*[1]
1 a small explosive sound. **2** a fizzy drink.

pop *noun*[2]
modern popular music.

pop *verb* **(popped, popping)**
1 to make a small explosive sound. **2** (*informal*) to go or put quickly. *She popped it in the oven.*

popcorn *noun*
maize heated to make fluffy balls.

Pope *noun*
the leader of the Roman Catholic Church.

poplar *noun*
a tall, straight tree.

poppy *noun* **(poppies)**
a red flower.

popular *adjective*
liked by a lot of people.
popularity *noun,* **popularize** *verb,* **popularly** *adverb*

populated *adjective*
inhabited. *The land is thinly populated.*

population *noun*
the people who live in a particular place.

populous *adjective*
inhabited by a lot of people.

porcelain *noun*
(*say* por-sĕl-in)
a fine kind of china.

porch *noun* **(porches)**
a small roofed area outside the door of a building.

porcupine *noun*
a small animal covered with long prickles.

pore *noun*
a tiny opening in the skin through which sweat passes.

pore *verb* **(pored, poring)**
pore over, to study something closely.

pork *noun*
meat from a pig.

pornography *noun*
(*say* por-**nog**-ră-fi)
obscene pictures, writings, etc.
pornographer *noun,* **pornographic** *adjective*

porous *adjective*
that allows liquid or air to pass through. *Sandy soil is porous.*

porpoise *noun*
(*say* por-pŭs)
a sea-animal like a small whale.

porridge *noun*
oatmeal boiled in water to make a thick edible paste.

port *noun*[1]
1 a harbour. **2** a city or town with a harbour. **3** the left side of a ship or aircraft when you are facing forward.

port *noun*[2]
a strong red Portuguese wine.

portable *adjective*
that you can carry. *a portable tape-recorder.*

portcullis *noun* **(portcullises)**
a grating that can be lowered to block the gateway to a castle.

porter *noun*[1]
someone whose job is to carry other people's luggage at railway stations, hotels, etc.

porter *noun*[2]
someone whose job is to look after the entrance to a building.

porthole *noun*
a small round window in the side of a ship or aircraft.

portion *noun*
a part or share given to somebody.

portly *adjective* **(portlier, portliest)**
stout; fat.
portliness *noun*

portrait *noun*
a picture of a person.

portray *verb*
1 to make a portrait of somebody. **2** to describe or show. *The play portrays the king as a kind man.*
portrayal *noun*

Portuguese *adjective*
of Portugal.

pose *noun*
1 a position in which someone can paint a picture or take a photograph of you. **2** a pretence; unnatural behaviour to impress people.

pose *verb* **(posed, posing)**
1 to take up a pose. **2** to put into a pose. **3** to pretend. **4** to present a question or problem.

poser *noun*
1 a puzzling question or problem. **2** someone who poses.

posh *adjective*
(*informal*) very smart; high-class.

position *noun*
1 the place where something is or should be. **2** the way in which someone or something is placed or arranged. *in a sitting position.* **3** a situation or condition. *I am in no position to help you.* **4** a regular job.

positive *adjective*
1 sure; definite. *I am positive that my book was in my desk.* **2** that says 'yes'. *a positive answer.* **3** more than nought. **4** of the kind of electric charge that lacks electrons.
positively *adverb*

posse *noun*
(*say* **poss**-i)
a group that helps a sheriff.

possess *verb*
1 to own something. **2 possessed,** mad; controlled by an evil spirit.
possessor *noun*

possession *noun*
1 something that you own. **2** possessing; being possessed.

possessive *adjective*
1 wanting to get and keep things for yourself. **2** showing that somebody owns something. *'His' and 'yours' are possessive pronouns.*

possible *adjective*
1 able to exist, happen, be done, or be used. **2 as possible,** as can happen; as can be done. *Come as quickly as possible.*
possibility *noun*

possibly *adverb*
1 in any way. **2** perhaps.

post *noun*[1]
1 an upright piece of wood, concrete, metal, etc., usually fixed in the ground. **2** the post marking the start or finish of a race. *He was left at the post.*

post *noun*²
1 the conveying of letters, parcels, etc. 2 letters, parcels, etc. carried by post; mail. 3 a collection or delivery of mail.

post *noun*³
1 a regular job. 2 the place where a sentry stands. 3 a place occupied by soldiers, traders, etc.

post *verb*¹
1 to send a letter, parcel, or card to somebody. 2 to put a letter, card, etc. into a post-box.

post *verb*²
to put up a notice, poster, etc.

postage *noun*
1 the cost of sending something by post. 2 **postage stamp**, a small piece of paper that you must stick on a letter, parcel, etc. before it is posted.

postal *adjective*
1 of or by the post. 2 **postal order**, a document bought from a post office, used for sending money by post.

post-box *noun* (post-boxes)
a box into which you place letters to be sent by post.

postcard *noun*
a piece of card that you can write a message on and post.

postcode *noun*
a group of letters and numbers included in an address to help sorting. *My postcode is OX2 7SA.*

poster *noun*
a large notice for everyone to read.

postman *noun* (postmen)
someone who delivers letters, parcels, etc.

postmark *noun*
an official mark stamped on something sent by post.

post-mortem *noun*
an examination of a dead person to find out why he died.

post office *noun*
a place where you can buy stamps, postal orders, etc., send telegrams, post letters, etc.

postpone *verb* (postponed, postponing)
to decide that something will happen later than you originally intended.
postponement *noun*

postscript *noun*
something extra added at the end of a letter or book.

posture *noun*
the way that somebody stands, sits, or walks.

pot *noun*
1 a round container. 2 a chamber-pot. 3 **go to pot,** (*slang*) to be ruined. 4 **pots,** (*slang*) lots of something. *He's got pots of money.*

pot *verb* (potted, potting)
1 to put something into a pot. 2 **potted,** (*informal*) shortened. *a potted version.*

potato *noun* (potatoes)
a vegetable that grows underground.

potent *adjective*
powerful.
potency *noun,* **potently** *adverb*

potential *adjective*
capable of happening or being used sometime in the future.
potentiality *noun,* **potentially** *adverb*

potential *noun*
ability, especially ability to do something in the future.

pot-hole *noun*
1 a deep natural hole in the ground. 2 a hole in a road.

pot-holing *noun*
exploring underground pot-holes.
pot-holer *noun*

potion *noun*
(*say* poh-shŏn)
a drink containing medicine, poison, or something magical.

potter *verb*
to work in a leisurely or casual way.

potter *noun*
someone who makes pottery.

pottery *noun* (potteries)
1 pots, cups, plates, etc. made of baked clay. 2 a place where a potter works.

potty *adjective* (pottier, pottiest)
(*slang*) 1 mad. 2 trivial; unimportant.

potty *noun* (potties)
(*informal*) a child's chamber-pot.

pouch *noun* (pouches)
1 a small bag. 2 a kind of pocket that some animals have in their skin. *Kangaroos keep their babies in pouches.*

pouffe *noun*
(*say* poof)
a large firm cushion.

poultry *noun*
birds kept for their eggs and meat. *Chickens, geese, and turkeys are poultry.*

pounce *verb* (pounced, pouncing)
to jump on somebody or something suddenly.

pound *noun*
1 a unit of money, equal to 100 pence. 2 a unit of weight, equal to 16 ounces or about 454 grams.

pound *verb*
to hit something often, especially so as to crush it; to thump.

pour *verb*
1 to make a liquid flow out of a container. 2 to flow. 3 to rain heavily. *It was pouring.* 4 to come or go in large amounts. *Letters poured in.*

pout *verb*
to stick out your lips when you are not pleased.

poverty *noun*
being poor.

powder *noun*
1 tiny pieces of something dry, like flour or dust. 2 a cosmetic or scented powder.
powdery *adjective*

pregnant

powder *verb*
1 to make into powder. 2 to put powder on your face, etc.

power *noun*
1 strength; great force, energy, or might. 2 ability; authority. 3 a powerful country. 4 electricity or other energy.
powered *adjective*, **powerless** *adjective*

powerful *adjective*
very strong or important.
powerfully *adverb*

powerhouse *noun*
a power-station.

power-station *noun*
a building where electricity is produced.

practicable *adjective*
possible to do or use.

practical *adjective*
1 able to do useful things; able to make things. *He is very practical.* 2 likely to be useful. *a practical idea.* 3 concerned with doing or making things. *She has had practical experience.* 4 **practical joke,** an amusing trick played on somebody.

practically *adverb*
1 in a practical way. 2 almost.

practice *noun*
1 practising. *Have you done your piano practice?* 2 actually doing something rather than thinking or talking about it. *It works well in practice.* 3 the business of a doctor or lawyer.

practise *verb* **(practised, practising)**
1 to do something repeatedly so as to get better at it. 2 to do something, especially regularly. *He practises what he preaches.* 3 to work as a doctor, lawyer, etc.

prairie *noun*
a large area of flat grass-covered land in North America.

praise *verb* **(praised, praising)**
to say that somebody or something is very good.

praise *noun*
words that praise somebody or something.

pram *noun*
a small vehicle with four wheels, to carry a baby.

prance *verb* **(pranced, prancing)**
to jump about in a lively or happy way.

prank *noun*
a practical joke.

prawn *noun*
an edible shellfish like a large shrimp.

pray *verb*
1 to talk to God. 2 to ask earnestly for something.

prayer *noun*
praying; what you say when you pray.

preach *verb*
to give a religious or moral talk.
preacher *noun*

precarious *adjective*
(*say* pri-**kair**-i-ŭs)
not secure or safe.
precariously *adverb*

precaution *noun*
something done to prevent future trouble or danger.

precede *verb* **(preceded, preceding)**
to come or go in front of somebody or something.
precedence *noun*

precinct *noun*
(*say* **pree**-sinkt)
1 part of a town where traffic is not allowed. *a pedestrian precinct.* 2 the area round a cathedral.

precious *adjective*
very valuable.

precipice *noun*
the steep face of a mountain, cliff, etc.

précis *noun* **(précis)**
(*say* **pray**-see)
a summary of a piece of writing.

precise *adjective*
exact; clearly stated.
precisely *adverb*, **precision** *noun*

predator *noun*
(*say* **pred**-ă-ter)
an animal that hunts other animals.
predatory *adjective*

predecessor *noun*
(*say* **pree**-di-ses-er)
1 an ancestor. 2 someone who did the job that you do now.

predict *verb*
to say what is going to happen before it happens.
predictable *adjective*, **prediction** *noun*

predominate *verb* **(predominated, predominating)**
to be largest or most important.
predominance *noun*, **predominant** *adjective*

preface *noun*
(*say* **pref**-ăss)
an introduction at the beginning of a book.

prefect *noun*
a school pupil who is given certain duties to perform.

prefer *verb* **(preferred, preferring)**
to like one person or thing more than another.
preference *noun*

preferable *adjective*
(*say* **pref**-er-ă-bŭl)
preferred; that you want or like more.
preferably *adverb*

prefix *noun* **(prefixes)**
a word or syllable joined to the front of a word to change or add to its meaning, as in *dis*order, *out*stretched, and *un*happy.

pregnant *adjective*
having an unborn baby growing inside your body.
pregnancy *noun*

prehistoric *adjective*
of a very long time ago, before written records were kept.
prehistory *noun*

prejudice *noun*
1 a fixed opinion which is formed without examining the facts fairly. 2 behaviour or unfair treatment that results from a prejudice.
prejudiced *adjective*

preliminary *adjective*
preceding or preparing for something.

prelude *noun*
(*say* prel-yood)
1 a thing that introduces or leads up to something else. 2 a short piece of music.

premier *noun*
(*say* prem-i-er)
a prime minister.

première *noun*
(*say* prem-yair)
the first public performance of a play or showing of a film.

premises *plural noun*
1 a building with its land. 2 **on the premises,** in a particular building.

premium *noun*
(*say* pree-mi-ŭm)
1 an amount paid regularly to an insurance company. 2 **at a premium,** above the normal price; valued highly. 3 **premium bond,** a savings certificate that gives you a chance to win a prize of money.

preoccupied *adjective*
with your thoughts completely occupied by something.
preoccupation *noun*

prep *noun*
(*informal*) 1 homework. 2 **prep school,** a preparatory school.

preparation *noun*
1 the action of preparing. 2 a thing done to prepare for something. 3 homework.

preparatory *adjective*
(*say* pri-pa-rǎ-ter-i)
1 preparing for something. 2 **preparatory school,** a school that prepares pupils for a higher school.

prepare *verb* (**prepared, preparing**)
1 to get ready. 2 **be prepared,** to be ready or willing to do something.

preposition *noun*
a word put in front of a noun or pronoun to show how the noun or pronoun is connected with another word. *In the sentence 'I stayed at the seaside from Monday to Friday with my friends', 'at', 'from', 'to', and 'with' are prepositions.*

prescribe *verb* (**prescribed, prescribing**)
1 to give somebody a prescription for a particular medicine. 2 to say what must be done.

prescription *noun*
a doctor's order for a medicine to be prepared.

presence *noun*
1 being at a place. *Your presence is expected.* 2 **in the presence of somebody,** where he is.

present *adjective*
(*say* prez-ĕnt)
1 in a particular place; here. *Nobody else was present.* 2 existing now. *the present King.* 3 **present participle,** a word used after *am, are, is,* etc. to describe an action that is happening now, or used after *was, were,* etc. to describe an action that went on for some time in the past. *In 'I am looking' and 'you were sleeping', 'looking' and 'sleeping' are present participles.*

present *noun*[1]
(*say* prez-ĕnt)
the time now. *Our teacher is away at present.*

present *noun*[2]
(*say* prez-ĕnt)
something that you give to somebody.

present *verb*
(*say* pri-zent)
1 to give something to somebody, especially with a ceremony. 2 to put on a play or other entertainment. 3 to show.
presentation *noun,* **presenter** *noun*

presently *adverb*
soon. *I shall be with you presently.*

preserve *verb* (**preserved, preserving**)
to keep something safe or in good condition.
preservation *noun,* **preservative** *noun*

preside *verb* (**presided, presiding**)
(*say* pri-zyd)
to be in charge of a meeting, council, etc. *The mayor presided over the council.*

president *noun*
1 the person in charge of a society, business, etc. 2 the head of a republic. *Roosevelt and Kennedy were American Presidents.*
presidency *noun,* **presidential** *adjective*

press *verb*
1 to push hard on something; to squeeze. 2 to make something flat and smooth. 3 to urge or demand. 4 to be urgent.

press *noun* (**presses**)
1 the action of pressing. 2 a device for pressing things. 3 a device or firm that does printing. 4 newspapers; journalists. 5 **press conference,** an interview with a group of journalists.

pressure *noun*
1 continuous pressing. 2 the force with which something presses. 3 an influence that persuades or forces you to do something.

pressurize *verb* (**pressurized, pressurizing**)
1 to keep a place, vehicle, etc. at the same air-pressure all the time. *This aircraft is pressurized.* 2 to try to force somebody to do something.

prestige *noun*
(*say* pres-teezh)
good reputation; honour that comes from being successful, rich, etc.
prestigious *adjective*

presumably *adverb*
probably; according to what you may presume.

presume *verb* (**presumed, presuming**)
1 to suppose. *I presumed that he was dead.* 2 to dare. *I wouldn't presume to advise you.*
presumption *noun*

presumptuous *adjective*
too bold or confident.

pretend *verb*
1 to behave as if something untrue or imaginary is true. 2 to claim.
pretence *noun*, **pretender** *noun*

pretty *adjective* (**prettier, prettiest**)
pleasant to look at or hear; attractive.
prettily *adverb*, **prettiness** *noun*

pretty *adverb*
(*informal*) quite; moderately. *It's pretty cold outside.*

prevail *verb*
1 to be most frequent or general. *The prevailing wind in Britain comes from the south-west.* 2 to be victorious.
prevalent *adjective*

prevent *verb*
to stop something from happening; to make something impossible.
prevention *noun*, **preventive** *adjective*

preview *noun*
a showing of a film, play, etc. before it is shown to the public.

previous *adjective*
coming before this; preceding. *the previous week.*
previously *adverb*

prey *noun*
(*say* pray)
1 an animal hunted and eaten by another animal. **2 bird of prey,** a bird that lives by killing and eating other animals.

prey *verb*
(*say* pray)
prey on, to hunt and kill for food; to make somebody anxious or nervous.

price *noun*
1 the amount of money for which something is sold. 2 what you have to give or do to get something. *What is the price of peace?* **3 at any price,** at any cost.

price *verb* (**priced, pricing**)
to decide the price of something.

priceless *adjective*
1 very valuable. 2 (*informal*) very amusing.

prick *verb*
1 to make a tiny hole in something. 2 to hurt somebody with a pin, needle, etc. **3 prick up your ears,** to start listening suddenly.

prickle *noun*
a thin, sharp thing like a thorn.
prickly *adjective*

pride *noun*
1 being proud. 2 something that makes you feel proud. 3 a group of lions.

priest *noun*
1 a clergyman. 2 someone who conducts religious ceremonies; a religious leader.
priestess *noun*, **priesthood** *noun*

prig *noun*
a self-righteous person.
priggish *adjective*

prim *adjective* (**primmer, primmest**)
not liking anything rough or rude.
primly *adverb*, **primness** *noun*

primary *adjective*
1 first; most important. **2 primary colours,** the colours from which all other colours can be made by mixing: red, yellow, and blue for paint, and red, green, and violet for light. **3 primary school,** a school for young children.
primarily *adverb*

prime *adjective*
1 chief; most important. *the prime cause.* 2 excellent. *prime beef.* **3 prime number,** a number that can only be divided exactly by 1 or by itself. *2, 3, 5, 7, 11, and 37 are prime numbers.*

prime *noun*
the best part of a person's life. *He was in the prime of life.*

prime *verb* (**primed, priming**)
1 to get something ready for use. 2 to put a first coat of paint on something.

prime minister *noun*
the leader of a government.

primer *noun*
1 paint used to prime a surface. 2 an elementary textbook.

primeval *adjective*
(*say* pry-**mee**-văl)
of the earliest times of the world; ancient.

primitive *adjective*
of or at an early stage of development or civilization; not complicated or sophisticated.

primrose *noun*
a pale yellow flower that comes out in spring.

prince *noun*
1 the son of a king or queen. 2 a man or boy in a royal family.
princely *adjective*

princess *noun* (**princesses**)
1 the daughter of a king or queen. 2 a woman or girl in a royal family. 3 the wife of a prince.

principal *adjective*
chief; most important. *the principal cities of Britain.*
principally *adverb*

principal *noun*
the head of a college or school.

principle *noun*
1 a general truth, belief, or rule. *He taught me the principles of geometry.* **2 in principle,** in general, not in details.

print *verb*
1 to put words or pictures on paper with a machine. 2 to write with letters that are not joined together. 3 to make a print of a photograph. **4 printed circuit,** an electric circuit made by pressing thin metal strips on to a board.
printer *noun*

print *noun*
1 printed words or pictures. 2 a mark made by something pressing on a surface. *Her thumb left a print on the glass.* 3 a photograph made by shining light through a negative on to sensitive paper.

print-out *noun*
sheets of printed paper produced by a computer.

priority *noun* **(priorities)**
(*say* pry-o-ri-ti)
1 something that is more urgent or important than other things. **2** the right to be considered before other things.

prise *verb* **(prised, prising)**
to force something open. *They prised the box open.*

prism *noun*
a piece of glass that breaks up light into the colours of the rainbow.
prismatic *adjective*

prison *noun*
a place where criminals are kept as a punishment.
prisoner *noun*

private *adjective*
1 belonging to or used by a particular person or people. *a private road.* **2** confidential. *a private letter.* **3** secluded. *a private place for a bathe.*
privacy *noun*, **privately** *adverb*

private *noun*
1 a soldier of the lowest rank. **2** **in private,** in secret; where only particular people can see, hear, or take part.

privet *noun*
an evergreen shrub often used to make hedges.

privilege *noun*
a special advantage for one person or group of people.
privileged *adjective*

prize *noun*
1 something won in a game, competition, etc.; an award. **2** something captured from an enemy.

prize *verb* **(prized, prizing)**
to value something highly. *She prizes her garden more than anything else.*

pro *noun*
(*informal*) a professional.

probable *adjective*
likely to be true; likely to happen.
probability *noun*, **probably** *adverb*

probation *noun*
1 testing a person's character or abilities. **2** **on probation,** being supervised by a probation officer. **3** **probation officer,** an official who supervises the behaviour of a convicted criminal who is not in prison.
probationary *adjective*

probe *noun*
1 a long, thin device used to explore wounds, etc. **2** an investigation.

probe *verb* **(probed, probing)**
1 to explore with a probe. **2** to investigate something.

problem *noun*
something difficult to answer, understand, or overcome.

procedure *noun*
an orderly way of doing something.

proceed *verb*
(*say* prō-**seed**)
to go on; to continue.

proceedings *plural noun*
1 things that happen. **2** a lawsuit.

proceeds *plural noun*
(*say* proh-seedz)
the money made from a sale, show, etc.

process *noun* **(processes)**
a series of actions for doing something or manufacturing something.

process *verb*
to use a process to change or deal with something. *processed cheese.*

procession *noun*
a number of people, vehicles, etc. moving steadily forwards.

proclaim *verb*
to announce officially or publicly.
proclamation *noun*

prod *verb* **(prodded, prodding)**
to push hard with a stick, finger, etc.

prodigal *adjective*
wasteful; extravagant.
prodigality *noun*, **prodigally** *adverb*

produce *verb* **(produced, producing)**
(*say* prō-**dewss**)
1 to make or create something. **2** to bring something out so that it can be seen. **3** to organize the performance of a play, making of a film, etc.
producer *noun*

produce *noun*
(*say* prod-yewss)
things produced, especially by farming.

product *noun*
1 something produced. *the products of this factory.* **2** the result of multiplying two numbers.

production *noun*
1 the action of producing. **2** a thing or amount produced.

productive *adjective*
producing a lot of things; useful.
productivity *noun*

profession *noun*
an occupation for which you need special knowledge and training. *The professions include being a doctor, nurse, clergyman, or lawyer.*

professional *adjective*
1 of or belonging to a profession. **2** doing a regular job for money. *a professional footballer.*
professionally *adverb*

professional *noun*
someone doing a regular job for money.

professor *noun*
a senior teacher in a university.
professorial *adjective*

proficient *adjective*
(*say* prō-**fish**-ĕnt)
skilled; doing something properly.
proficiency *noun*, **proficiently** *adverb*

profile *noun*
1 a side view of someone's face. **2** a short description of a person's life or character.

profit *noun*
1 the extra money got by selling something for more than it cost to buy or make. 2 an advantage or benefit.

profit *verb*
to get a profit.
profitable *adjective*, **profitably** *adverb*

profound *adjective*
1 very deep. 2 showing or needing great knowledge or thought.
profoundly *adverb*, **profundity** *noun*

profuse *adjective*
(*say* prŏ-**fewss**)
plentiful.
profusely *adverb*, **profusion** *noun*

program *noun*
a coded series of actions for a computer to carry out.

program *verb* (**programmed, programming**)
to prepare or control a computer by means of a program.
programmer *noun*

programme *noun*
1 a show, play, talk, etc. on radio or television. 2 a list of an organized series of events; a leaflet or pamphlet giving details of an entertainment, contest, etc.

progress *noun*
(*say* proh-gress)
1 forward movement; an advance. 2 a development or improvement.

progress *verb*
(*say* prŏ-**gress**)
to make progress.
progression *noun*, **progressive** *adjective*

prohibit *verb*
to forbid. *Smoking is prohibited.*
prohibition *noun*

project *noun*
(*say* **proj**-ekt)
1 the task of finding out as much as you can about something and writing about it. 2 a plan.

project *verb*
(*say* prŏ-**jekt**)
1 to stick out. 2 to show a picture on a screen.
projection *noun*

projector *noun*
a machine for showing films or photographs on a screen.
projectionist *noun*

prologue *noun*
(*say* **proh**-log)
an introduction or preface.

prolong *verb*
to make something last longer.

promenade *noun*
(*say* prom-ĕn-**ahd**)
1 a place suitable for walking, especially beside the sea-shore. 2 a leisurely walk. 3 **promenade concert,** a concert where some of the audience stand or walk about.

prominent *adjective*
1 sticking out. 2 important.
prominence *noun*, **prominently** *adverb*

promise *noun*
1 saying that you will definitely do or not do something. 2 an indication of future success or good results. *She shows promise.*

promise *verb* (**promised, promising**)
1 to make a promise. 2 **promising,** likely to be good or successful. *a promising pupil.*

promontory *noun* (**promontories**)
(*say* **prom**-ŏn-ter-i)
a piece of high land sticking out into the sea.

promote *verb* (**promoted, promoting**)
1 to move somebody to a higher rank or position. 2 to help the progress or sale of something. 3 to organize a public entertainment.
promoter *noun*, **promotion** *noun*

prompt *adjective*
without delay. *a prompt reply.*
promptly *adverb*, **promptness** *noun*

prompt *verb*
1 to cause or encourage somebody to do something. 2 to remind an actor of his words when he forgets them.
prompter *noun*

prone *adjective*
1 lying face downwards. 2 **prone to,** likely to do or suffer something. *He is prone to jealousy.*

prong *noun*
one of the pointed spikes at the end of a fork.

pronoun *noun*
a word used instead of a noun. (Pronouns are words like *he, her, it, them,* and *those.*)

pronounce *verb* (**pronounced, pronouncing**)
1 to say a sound or word in a particular way. *'Too' and 'two' are pronounced the same.* 2 to declare formally. *I now pronounce you man and wife.* 3 **pronounced,** obvious; definite.
pronouncement *noun*

pronunciation *noun*
(*say* prŏ-nun-si-**ay**-shŏn)
how you pronounce something.

proof *noun*
1 a fact which shows that something is true. 2 a printed copy of something made for checking before other copies are printed.

proof *adjective*
giving protection against something. *a bullet-proof jacket.*

prop *noun*
a support, especially made of· a long piece of wood or metal.

prop *verb* (**propped, propping**)
to support something by leaning it on something else. *The ladder was propped up against the wall.*

propaganda *noun*
publicity intended to make people believe something.

propel *verb* (**propelled, propelling**)
1 to move something forward. 2 **propelling pencil,** a pencil with a lead that can be moved in and out.
propellant *noun*

propeller *noun*
a device with blades that spin round to drive an aircraft or ship.

proper *adjective*
1 suitable; right. *Is that screwdriver the proper size?* 2 respectable. *prim and proper.* 3 (*informal*) complete; great. *He's in a proper mess.* 4 **proper noun,** the name of one person or thing. *'Mary' and 'London' are proper nouns.*
properly *adverb*

property *noun* **(properties)**
1 things that belong to someone. 2 buildings or land belonging to someone. 3 a characteristic or quality. *the chemical properties of iron.*

prophecy *noun* **(prophecies)**
(*say* prof-i-si)
something predicted.

prophesy *verb* **(prophesied, prophesying)**
(*say* prof-i-sy)
to predict. *She prophesied a war.*

prophet *noun*
1 someone who makes prophecies. 2 a great religious teacher.
prophetic *adjective*

proportion *noun*
1 a fraction; a share. 2 a ratio. 3 the correct relationship between the size, amount, or importance of two things. 4 **proportions,** size; importance. *a ship of large proportions.*
proportional *adjective,* **proportionally** *adverb,* **proportionate** *adjective*

propose *verb* **(proposed, proposing)**
1 to suggest an idea or plan. 2 to ask somebody to marry you.
proposal *noun*

proprietor *noun*
(*say* prŏ-**pry**-ĕt-er)
the owner of a shop or business.

propulsion *noun*
propelling something.

prose *noun*
writing that is not in verse.

prosecute *verb* **(prosecuted, prosecuting)**
to make somebody go to court to be tried for a crime.
prosecution *noun,* **prosecutor** *noun*

prospect *noun*
(*say* pros-pekt)
1 a possibility; a hope. *no prospects of success.* 2 a wide view.

prospect *verb*
(*say* prŏ-**spekt**)
to search for gold or some other mineral.
prospector *noun*

prosper *verb*
to be successful; to do well.

prosperous *adjective*
successful; rich.
prosperity *noun*

prostitute *noun*
a woman who has sexual intercourse with men for payment.

protect *verb*
to keep somebody or something safe.
protection *noun,* **protective** *adjective,* **protector** *noun*

protein *noun*
(*say* proh-teen)
a substance in food that is necessary for good health.

protest *noun*
(*say* proh-test)
something you say or do because you disagree with what somebody else is saying or doing.

protest *verb*
(*say* prŏ-**test**)
to make a protest.
protester *noun*

Protestant *noun*
(*say* prot-is-tănt)
a Christian who does not belong to the Roman Catholic or Orthodox Churches.

protoplasm *noun*
(*say* proh-tŏ-plazm)
a colourless substance of which animal and vegetable cells are made.

prototype *noun*
(*say* proh-tŏ-typ)
the first example of something, used as a model for the manufacture of others.

protractor *noun*
a device for measuring angles.

protrude *verb* **(protruded, protruding)**
to stick out.
protrusion *noun*

proud *adjective*
1 very pleased with yourself or with someone else who has done well. *I am proud of my sister.* 2 too satisfied because of who you are or what you have done. *He's too proud to talk to us.*
proudly *adverb*

prove *verb* **(proved, proving)**
1 to show that something is true. 2 to turn out to be. *My pen proved to be useless.*

proverb *noun*
a short, well-known saying that states a truth. *'A stitch in time saves nine'* and *'Many hands make light work'* are proverbs.
proverbial *adjective*

provide *verb* **(provided, providing)**
1 to supply something. 2 to prepare for something. 3 **provided** or **providing,** on condition; on condition that. *You can come with us providing that you pay for yourself.*

province *noun*
1 a part of a country. 2 **the provinces,** the part of a country outside the capital.
provincial *adjective*

provision *noun*
1 providing something. *the provision of free meals for old people.* 2 a statement in a document. *the provisions of the treaty.* 3 **provisions,** supplies of food and drink.

provoke *verb* **(provoked, provoking)**
to make somebody angry; to arouse or stimulate.
provocation *noun,* **provocative** *adjective*

prow *noun*
the front end of a ship.

prowl *verb*
to move quietly or cautiously.
prowler *noun*

prudent *adjective*
(*say* proo-dĕnt)
careful; not reckless.
prudence *noun*, **prudently** *adverb*

prune *noun*
a dried plum.

prune *verb* (**pruned, pruning**)
to cut off unwanted parts of a tree, bush, etc.

pry *verb* (**pried, prying**)
to look or ask inquisitively. *She pried into our business.*

P.S. short for **postscript.**

psalm *noun*
(*say* sahm)
a religious song, especially one of those in the Book of Psalms in the Bible.
psalmist *noun*

pseudonym *noun*
(*say* s'**yoo**-dŏn-im)
a false name used by an author.

psychiatrist *noun*
(*say* sy-**ky**-ă-trist)
a person trained to cure mental illness.
psychiatric *adjective*, **psychiatry** *noun*

psychic *adjective*
(*say* **sy**-kik)
1 supernatural. **2** having or using telepathy or supernatural powers.

psychologist *noun*
(*say* sy-**kol**-ŏ-jist)
someone who studies how the mind works.
psychological *adjective*, **psychology** *noun*

P.T. short for *physical training.*

pub *noun*
(*informal*) a public house.

puberty *noun*
(*say* **pew**-ber-ti)
the time when a young person starts to become an adult.

public *adjective*
1 belonging or open to everyone; used or known by everyone. **2 public house,** a building where alcoholic drinks are served to the public. **3 public school,** a secondary school that charges fees; in Scotland, the United States, etc.: a school run by the state or by the local authority.
publicly *adverb*

public *noun*
1 all the people; everyone. **2 in public,** openly; where anyone can see, hear, or take part.

publication *noun*
1 publishing something. **2** something that is published.

publicity *noun*
information or activity to make people interested in somebody or something; advertising.

publicize *verb* (**publicized, publicizing**)
(*say* **pub**-li-syz)
to give publicity to something.

publish *verb*
1 to print and sell something. **2** to announce something in public.
publisher *noun*

puck *noun*
the hard rubber disc used in ice-hockey.

pucker *verb*
to wrinkle.

pudding *noun*
1 a food made in a soft mass, especially with a mixture of flour and other ingredients. **2** the sweet course of a meal.

puddle *noun*
a small pool, usually of rain-water.

puff *noun*
1 a small amount of breath, wind, smoke, steam, etc. **2** a soft pad for putting powder on the skin. **3** a small cake filled with cream.

puff *verb*
1 to blow out puffs of smoke, steam, etc. **2** to breathe with difficulty. **3** to inflate or swell something. *He puffed out his chest.*

puffin *noun*
a sea-bird with a large striped beak.

pull *verb*
1 to get hold of something and make it come towards you or follow behind you. **2** to move. *The train pulled into the station.* **3 pull a face,** to make a strange face. **4 pull off,** to achieve something. **5 pull somebody's leg,** to play a trick on somebody; to tease. **6 pull through,** to recover from an illness. **7 pull yourself together,** to become calm or sensible.

pulley *noun*
a wheel with a rope round it, used for lifting heavy things.

pullover *noun*
a knitted garment for the top half of the body.

pulp *noun*
a soft, wet mass of something, especially for making paper.

pulp *verb*
to make something into pulp.

pulpit *noun*
a small enclosed platform where the preacher stands in a church.

pulse *noun*
1 a throbbing in the arteries that shows how fast the heart is beating. **2** a regular throb.

pumice *noun*
(*say* **pum**-iss)
a kind of porous stone rubbed on things to clean or polish them.

pump *noun*
1 a device that pushes air or liquid into or out of something, or along pipes. **2** a lightweight shoe.

pump *verb*
1 to move air or liquid with a pump. **2 pump up,** to inflate something.

pumpkin *noun*
a very large, round fruit with a hard yellow skin.

pun *noun*
a joke made by using words that sound similar. *The teacher made a pun by saying that he would write it on the board if we were bored.*
punning *noun*

punch *verb*
1 to hit somebody with your fist. **2** to make a hole in something.

punch *noun*[1] **(punches)**
1 a hit with the fist. **2** a device for making holes in paper, metal, or other substances. **3** force or vigour. **4 punch line,** words that give the climax of a joke or story. **5 punch-up,** (*informal*) a fight.

punch *noun*[2]
a hot alcoholic drink.

punctual *adjective*
exactly on time; not arriving late.
punctuality *noun,* **punctually** *adverb*

punctuate *verb* **(punctuated, punctuating)**
to put punctuation in a piece of writing.

punctuation *noun*
marks such as commas, full stops, and brackets put into a piece of writing to make it easy to read.

puncture *noun*
a hole in a tyre.

punish *verb*
to make somebody suffer because he has done wrong.
punishment *noun*

punk *noun*
1 (*slang*) a rough, dirty, or worthless person. **2** someone who likes punk rock. **3 punk rock,** a kind of loud, simple rock music.

punt *noun*
a flat-bottomed boat.

punt *verb*
to use a pole to push a boat along.

puny *adjective* **(punier, puniest)**
(*say* **pew**-ni)
small and weak.

pup *noun*
a puppy.

pupa *noun* **(pupae)**
(*say* **pew**-pă)
a chrysalis.

pupil *noun*
1 someone who is being taught by a teacher. **2** the opening in the centre of the eye.

puppet *noun*
a kind of doll that can be made to move by fitting it over your hand or by working it with strings or wires.

puppy *noun* **(puppies)**
a young dog.

purchase *verb* **(purchased, purchasing)**
to buy.
purchaser *noun*

purchase *noun*
1 something you have bought. **2** the action of buying something. **3** a firm hold or grip.

pure *adjective* **(purer, purest)**
not mixed with anything else; clean or clear.
purely *adverb,* **purity** *noun*

purge *verb* **(purged, purging)**
to get rid of unwanted people or things.

purify *verb* **(purified, purifying)**
to make something pure.
purification *noun,* **purifier** *noun*

Puritan *noun*
1 a Protestant in the 16th or 17th century who wanted simpler religious ceremonies and strictly moral behaviour. **2 puritan,** a person with very strict morals.
puritanical *adjective*

purple *adjective*
deep reddish-blue.

purpose *noun*
1 what you intend to do; a plan or aim. **2 on purpose,** intentionally; not by chance.
purposeful *adjective,* **purposeless** *adjective*

purposely *adverb*
on purpose.

purr *verb*
to make a gentle murmuring sound like a cat when it is pleased.

purse *noun*
a small bag to hold money.

pursue *verb* **(pursued, pursuing)**
1 to chase. **2** to continue with; to work at. *She pursued her studies at college.*
pursuer *noun*

pursuit *noun*
1 the action of chasing. **2** something you spend time doing; a regular activity.

push *verb*
1 to use force to move something away from you; to press. **2 push off,** (*slang*) to go away.

push *noun* **(pushes)**
1 a pushing movement. **2 at a push,** in a crisis; if necessary. **3 the push,** (*informal*) dismissal from a job.

push-chair *noun*
a folding chair on wheels, in which a child can be pushed along.

puss or **pussy** *noun* **(pusses** or **pussies)**
(*informal*) a cat.

put *verb* **(put, putting)**
1 to move something into a place. **2** to cause someone or something to be in a particular condition. *Put the light out.* **3** to express something in words. *She put it tactfully.* **4 put off,** to postpone; to stop someone wanting something. **5 put out,** to stop a fire burning, light shining, etc. **6 put up,** to raise; to give someone a place to sleep. **7 put up with,** to tolerate.

putt *verb*
to hit a golf-ball gently towards the hole.
putter *noun,* **putting-green** *noun*

putty *noun*
a soft paste that sets hard, used especially for fitting windows in their frames.

puzzle *noun*
1 a difficult question; a problem. **2** a game where you have to solve a problem or do something difficult.

puzzle *verb* **(puzzled, puzzling)**
1 to give someone a problem. 2 to think deeply about something.

pygmy *noun* **(pygmies)**
(*say* **pig**-mi)
a very small person.

pyjamas *plural noun*
a loose jacket and trousers worn in bed.

pylon *noun*
a metal tower that supports electric cables.

pyramid *noun*
1 a structure with a square base and four sloping sides coming to a point. 2 an ancient Egyptian monument shaped like this.
pyramidal *adjective*

python *noun*
a large snake that crushes its prey.

Q

quack *noun*
the sound made by a duck.

quad *noun*
(*informal*) 1 a quadrangle. 2 a quadruplet.

quadrangle *noun*
a rectangular courtyard.

quadrilateral *noun*
a four-sided figure.

quadruple *adjective*
1 having four parts. 2 multiplied by four.

quadruplet *noun*
one of four children born to the same mother at one time.

quail *noun*
a bird that looks like a small partridge.

quail *verb*
to feel or show fear.

quaint *adjective*
attractive in an unusual or old-fashioned way.

quake *verb* **(quaked, quaking)**
to tremble; to shake.

Quaker *noun*
a member of a religious group founded by George Fox in the 17th century.

qualify *verb* **(qualified, qualifying)**
1 to be or make suitable for a job. 2 to moderate a statement, etc.
qualification *noun*

quality *noun* **(qualities)**
1 how good or bad something is. 2 a characteristic.

quantity *noun* **(quantities)**
how much there is of something; how many things there are of one sort.

quarantine *noun*
(*say* **kwo**-răn-teen)
a period when a person or animal is isolated to prevent a disease from spreading.

quarrel *noun*
a strong or angry argument.
quarrelsome *adjective*

quarrel *verb* **(quarrelled, quarrelling)**
to have a quarrel with someone.

quarry *noun* **(quarries)**
1 a place where stone, slate, etc. is dug out of the ground. 2 an animal that is being hunted.

quart *noun*
a quarter of a gallon.

quarter *noun*
1 one of four equal parts into which something is divided or can be divided. 2 three months. 3 **at close quarters**, close together. *They fought at close quarters.* 4 **quarters**, lodgings.

quartet *noun*
(*say* kwor-**tet**)
1 a group of four musicians. 2 a piece of music for four musicians.

quartz *noun*
(*say* kworts)
a hard mineral.

quaver *verb*
to tremble.

quaver *noun*
1 a trembling sound. 2 a musical note equal to half a crotchet, written ♪

quay *noun*
(*say* kee)
a harbour wall or pier where ships tie up.

queen *noun*
1 a woman who is the crowned ruler of a country. 2 a king's wife. 3 a female bee that produces eggs. 4 an important piece in chess. 5 a playing-card with a picture of a queen on it. 6 **queen mother**, a king's widow who is the mother of the present king or queen.

queer *adjective*
1 strange. 2 ill. *I feel queer.* 3 (*slang*) homosexual.

quench *verb*
1 to satisfy your thirst. 2 to put out a fire.

query *noun* **(queries)**
(*say* **kweer**-i)
1 a question. 2 a question mark.

quest *noun*
a search. *the quest for gold.*

question *noun*
1 something you ask. *I cannot answer your question.* **2** a problem; a subject. *Parliament debated the question of immigration.* **3 in question,** that is being discussed. **4 out of the question,** impossible. **5 question mark,** the punctuation mark put at the end of a question.

question *verb*
1 to ask someone questions. **2** to be doubtful about something.
questionable *adjective*, **questioner** *noun*

questionnaire *noun*
(*say* kwes-chŏn-**air**)
a list of questions.

queue *noun*
(*say* kew)
a line of people or vehicles waiting for something.

queue *verb* (**queued, queueing** or **queuing**)
(*say* kew)
to wait in a queue.

quick *adjective*
1 rapid. **2** done in a short time. **3** lively; clever. *quick-witted.* **4** (*old-fashioned use*) alive. *the quick and the dead.*
quicken *verb*

quicksand *noun*
loose, wet sand that can quickly swallow up people, animals, etc.

quid *noun* (**quid**)
(*slang*) a pound (£1).

quiet *adjective*
1 silent. **2** not loud. *a quiet voice.* **3** without much movement. *a quiet sea.*

quieten *verb*
to make or become quiet.

quill *noun*
a large feather; a pen made from a large feather.

quilt *noun*
a thick, soft cover for a bed.

quintet *noun*
1 a group of five musicians. **2** a piece of music for five musicians.

quit *verb* (**quitted** or **quit, quitting**)
1 to leave or abandon. **2** (*informal*) to stop doing something.
quitter *noun*

quite *adverb*
1 completely; truly. *I am quite all right.* **2** somewhat; rather. *He's quite a good swimmer.*

quiver *verb*
to tremble.

quiver *noun*
a container for arrows.

quiz *noun* (**quizzes**)
a series of questions, especially as an entertainment or competition.

quoit *noun*
(*say* koit)
a ring thrown at a peg in the game of *quoits.*

quota *noun*
(*say* **kwoh**-tă)
1 a share. **2** a limited amount.

quotation *noun*
1 the action of quoting. **2** something quoted. **3 quotation marks,** inverted commas.

quote *verb* (**quoted, quoting**)
to repeat words that were first spoken or written by someone else.

quotient *noun*
(*say* **kwoh**-shĕnt)
the result of dividing one number by another.

R

rabbi *noun*
(*say* **rab**-I)
a Jewish religious leader.

rabbit *noun*
a furry animal with long ears. *Rabbits live in burrows.*

rabid *adjective*
(*say* **rab**-id)
1 furious; violent. **2** affected with rabies.
rabidly *adverb*

rabies *noun*
(*say* **ray**-beez)
a disease that makes dogs go mad.

race *noun*[1]
a competition to be the first to reach a particular place.

race *noun*[2]
1 a group of people with the same ancestors, characteristics, or skin-colour. **2 race relations,** relationships, especially good ones, between people of different races.
racial *adjective*

race *verb* (**raced, racing**)
1 to have a race against someone. **2** to move very fast.
racer *noun*

race-course *noun*
a place for horse-races.

racialism *noun*
(*say* **ray**-shăl-izm)
1 believing that your own race of people is better than others. **2** hostility between different races of people.
racialist *noun* and *adjective*

rally

racism *noun*
(*say* **ray**-sizm)
racialism.
racist *noun* and *adjective*

rack *noun*
1 a framework used as a shelf or container. 2 an ancient device for torturing people by stretching them.

racket *noun*[1]
a bat used in tennis, badminton, etc., made of strings stretched across a wooden or metal frame.

racket *noun*[2]
1 a loud noise. 2 a swindle.

radar *noun*
(*say* **ray**-dar)
a system that shows on a screen the position of objects which you cannot see because of darkness, fog, distance, etc.

radiant *adjective*
1 bright; shining. 2 looking very happy.
radiance *noun*, **radiantly** *adverb*

radiate *verb* (**radiated, radiating**)
1 to give out heat, light, or other energy. 2 to be arranged like the spokes of a wheel.

radiation *noun*
1 heat, light, or other energy given out by something. 2 radioactivity.

radiator *noun*
1 a device that gives out heat, especially a metal container through which steam or hot water flows. 2 the device that cools the engine of a vehicle.

radical *adjective*
1 basic; sweeping. *radical changes.* 2 favouring reforms in society or politics. *a radical politician.*
radical *noun*, **radically** *adverb*

radio *noun*
1 an apparatus for receiving broadcast sound programmes. 2 sending or receiving sound by means of electrical waves.

radioactive *adjective*
giving out atomic energy.
radioactivity *noun*

radish *noun* (**radishes**)
a small, hard, round, red vegetable, eaten raw in salads.

radium *noun*
a radioactive element.

radius *noun* (**radii**)
1 a straight line from the centre of a circle to the circumference. 2 the distance between the centre and the circumference of a circle.

raffia *noun*
soft straw used to weave mats, baskets, etc.

raffle *noun*
a way of raising money by selling numbered tickets which may win prizes.

raft *noun*
a floating platform of logs, barrels, etc. fastened together.

rafter *noun*
one of the long, sloping pieces of wood that hold up a roof.

rag *noun*
1 a torn or old piece of cloth. 2 a piece of ragtime music.

rage *noun*
1 great or violent anger. 2 **all the rage,** (*informal*) very fashionable or popular.

rage *verb* (**raged, raging**)
1 to be very angry. 2 to be violent or noisy.

ragged *adjective*
(*say* **rag**-id)
1 torn or frayed. *ragged clothes.* 2 wearing torn or old clothes. *a ragged man.* 3 not smooth. *a ragged performance.*

ragtime *noun*
an old-fashioned kind of jazzy music.

raid *noun*
a sudden attack.

raid *verb*
to attack suddenly.
raider *noun*

rail *noun*
1 a bar or rod. *a towel-rail.* 2 a long metal bar that is part of a railway track. 3 **by rail,** on a train.

railings *plural noun*
a fence made of metal bars.

railway *noun*
1 the parallel metal bars that trains travel on. 2 a system of transport using rails.

rain *noun*
drops of water that fall from the sky.
raindrop *noun*, **rainy** *adjective*

rain *verb*
1 to come or send down like rain. 2 **it is raining,** rain is falling.

rainbow *noun*
a curved band of colours seen in the sky when the sun shines through rain. *The colours in a rainbow are red, orange, yellow, green, blue, indigo, and violet.*

raincoat *noun*
a waterproof coat.

rainfall *noun*
the amount of rain that falls in a particular place or time.

raise *verb* (**raised, raising**)
1 to move something to a higher place or upright position. 2 to manage to get the money or people needed for something. 3 to bring up young children or animals. 4 to make or cause. *He raised a laugh with his joke.* 5 to end a siege.

raisin *noun*
a dried grape.

rake *noun*
a gardening tool with a row of short spikes fixed to a long handle.

rake *verb* (**raked, raking**)
1 to move or smooth with a rake. 2 to search. 3 **rake in,** (*informal*) to make money or profit.

rally *noun* (**rallies**)
1 a large meeting. 2 a competition to test skill in driving. *The Monte Carlo Rally.* 3 a series of strokes in tennis, etc. before a point is scored. 4 a recovery.

rally *verb* **(rallied, rallying)**
1 to bring or come together for a united effort. **2** to revive; to recover.

ram *noun*
1 a male sheep. **2** a device for battering or hitting something.

ram *verb* **(rammed, ramming)**
to push one thing hard against another.

Ramadan *noun*
(*say* ram-ă-**dan**)
the ninth month of the Muslim year, when Muslims fast during the daytime.

ramble *noun*
a long walk in the country.

ramble *verb* **(rambled, rambling)**
1 to go for a ramble; to wander. **2** not to keep to a subject.
rambler *noun*

ramp *noun*
a slope between two levels.

rampage *verb* **(rampaged, rampaging)**
(*say* ram-**payj**)
to rush about wildly or destructively.

ran past tense of **run** *verb*.

ranch *noun* **(ranches)**
a large cattle-farm in America.
rancher *noun*

random *noun*
at random, by chance; without any choice, purpose, or plan. *In bingo, the numbers are picked at random.*

random *adjective*
done or taken at random. *a random sample.*

rang past tense of **ring** *verb*.

range *noun*
1 a line or series of things. *a range of mountains.* **2** the limits between which things exist; a number of things. *a wide range of goods.* **3** the distance that a gun can shoot, an aircraft can fly, etc. **4** a place with targets for shooting-practice. **5** a large area of land. **6** a kitchen fireplace with ovens.

range *verb* **(ranged, ranging)**
1 to exist between two limits; to extend. *Prices ranged from £1 to £50.* **2** to arrange. **3** to wander; to move over a wide area.

ranger *noun*
1 someone who looks after a park, forest, etc. **2** a mounted policeman in a remote area. **3 Ranger,** a senior Guide.

rank *noun*
1 a line of people or things. *a taxi-rank.* **2** a position in a series of people or things, especially in society or in the armed forces. *He was promoted to the rank of captain.*

ransack *verb*
to search thoroughly, leaving things untidy.

ransom *noun*
1 money paid so that a prisoner can be set free. **2 hold to ransom,** to keep somebody a prisoner and demand a ransom.

rap *verb* **(rapped, rapping)**
1 to knock quickly and loudly. **2** (*slang*) to talk.

rap *noun*
1 a rapping movement or sound. **2** (*slang*) a talk. **3 the rap,** (*slang*) the blame for something.

rapid *adjective*
moving or working at speed.
rapidity *noun*, **rapidly** *adverb*

rapids *plural noun*
part of a river where the water flows very quickly.

rare *adjective* **(rarer, rarest)**
unusual; not often found or experienced. *She died of a rare disease.*
rarely *adverb*, **rarity** *noun*

rascal *noun*
a dishonest or mischievous person.

rash *adjective*
recklessly hasty.

rash *noun* **(rashes)**
a red patch or red spots on the skin.

rasher *noun*
a slice of bacon.

raspberry *noun* **(raspberries)**
a small, soft, red fruit.

Rastafarian *noun*
(*say* ras-tă-**fair**-i-ăn)
a member of a religious group that started in Jamaica.

rat *noun*
1 an animal like a large mouse. **2** a nasty or treacherous person. **3 rat-race,** a continuous competition for success in your career, business, etc.

rate *noun*
1 speed. *The train moved at a great rate.* **2** cost; charge. *What is the rate for a letter to Italy?* **3** quality; standard. *first-rate. second-rate.* **4 at any rate,** anyway. **5 at this rate** or **at that rate,** if this is typical or true. **6 rates,** a tax paid by householders to the local council.

rate *verb* **(rated, rating)**
to value something; to regard as. *He rated me among his friends.*

rather *adverb*
1 slightly; somewhat. *It was rather dark.* **2** preferably; more willingly. *I would rather not come.* **3** more truly. *He lay down, or rather fell, on the bed.* **4** (*informal*) definitely. '*Do you want to come to my party?*' '*Rather!*'

ratio *noun*
(*say* **ray**-shi-oh)
the relationship between two numbers; how often one number goes into another. *The ratio between 6 and 24 is 4.*

ration *noun*
(*say* **rash**-ŏn)
an amount allowed to one person. *You have had your ration of sweets for today.*

ration *verb*
(*say* **rash**-ŏn)
to share something out in fixed amounts.

rational *adjective*
(*say* **rash**-ŏn ăl)
reasonable; sane.
rationalize *verb*, **rationally** *adverb*

rebound

rattle *verb* **(rattled, rattling)**
1 to make a series of short, sharp, hard sounds.
2 *(informal)* to make someone flustered.

rattle *noun*
1 a rattling noise. 2 a baby's toy that rattles.

rattlesnake *noun*
a poisonous American snake that makes a rattling noise with its tail.

rave *verb* **(raved, raving)**
to talk or behave madly or very enthusiastically.

raven *noun*
a large black bird.

ravenous *adjective*
(*say* rav-ĕn-ŭs)
very hungry.
ravenously *adverb*

ravine *noun*
(*say* ră-**veen**)
a very deep, narrow gorge.

raw *adjective*
1 not cooked. *a raw steak.* 2 in the natural state; not processed. *raw materials.* 3 without experience. *raw recruits.* 4 with the skin removed. *a raw wound.* 5 cold and damp. *a raw wind.* 6 **raw deal,** *(informal)* unfair treatment.

ray *noun*
a thin line of light, heat, or other energy.

razor *noun*
a device with a very sharp blade, especially one used for shaving.

reach *verb*
1 to get to a place or thing. 2 to stretch out your hand to get or touch something.

reach *noun* **(reaches)**
1 the distance you can reach with your hand. 2 a distance that you can easily travel. *My uncle lives within reach of the sea.* 3 a straight stretch of a river or canal.

react *verb*
to have a reaction.

reaction *noun*
an action or feeling caused by another person or thing.

reactor *noun*
an apparatus for producing nuclear power.

read *verb* **(read, reading)**
to look at something written and printed, and understand it or say it aloud. *Have you read this book? I read it last year.*
readable *adjective*

reader *noun*
1 someone who reads. 2 a book that helps you learn to read.

readily *adverb*
1 willingly. 2 quickly; without any difficulty.

reading *noun*
1 the action of reading a book, magazine, etc. 2 an amount shown on a measuring instrument. *Check the barometer readings every day.*

ready *adjective* **(readier, readiest)**
1 able or willing to do something or to be used at once; prepared. 2 quick. *ready answers.* 3 **at the ready,** ready for use or action.
readiness *noun*

real *adjective*
1 existing; true; not imaginary. 2 genuine; not a copy.

realism *noun*
seeing or showing things as they really are.
realist *noun*, **realistic** *adjective*, **realistically** *adverb*

reality *noun* **(realities)**
what is real; something real.

realize *verb* **(realized, realizing)**
to understand something clearly; to accept something as true.
realization *noun*

really *adverb*
truly; certainly; in fact.

realm *noun*
(*say* relm)
1 a kingdom. 2 an area of knowledge, interest, activity, etc.

reap *verb*
to cut down and gather corn when it is ripe.
reaper *noun*

reappear *verb*
to appear again.
reappearance *noun*

rear *adjective*
placed at the back.

rear *noun*
1 the back of something. 2 a person's buttocks.

rear *verb*
1 to bring up young children or animals. 2 to rise up on the hind legs. *The horse reared up in fright.*

rearrange *verb* **(rearranged, rearranging)**
to arrange something differently.
rearrangement *noun*

reason *noun*
1 a cause for something; an explanation. 2 reasoning; common sense. *Listen to reason.*

reason *verb*
to use reasoning.

reasonable *adjective*
1 sensible; logical. 2 fair; moderate. *reasonable prices.*
reasonableness *noun*, **reasonably** *adverb*

reasoning *noun*
thinking in an orderly way.

reassure *verb* **(reassured, reassuring)**
to remove somebody's doubts or fears.
reassurance *noun*

rebel *verb* **(rebelled, rebelling)**
(*say* ri-**bel**)
to refuse to obey somebody in authority, especially the government.
rebellion *noun*, **rebellious** *adjective*

rebel *noun*
(*say* **reb**-ĕl)
someone who rebels.

rebound *verb*
to bounce back after hitting something.

rebuild *verb* **(rebuilt, rebuilding)**
to build again; to put something together again.

recall *verb*
1 to ask somebody to come back. 2 to remember.

recapture *verb* **(recaptured, recapturing)**
to capture something or someone again.

recede *verb* **(receded, receding)**
to go back. *The floods receded.*

receipt *noun*
(*say* ri-**seet**)
1 a written statement that money has been received. 2 receiving something.

receive *verb* **(received, receiving)**
1 to get something that is given or sent to you. 2 to welcome somebody.

receiver *noun*
1 someone who receives something. 2 someone who buys and sells stolen goods. 3 an official who takes charge of a bankrupt's property. 4 a radio or television set. 5 the part of a telephone that you hold to your ear.

recent *adjective*
made or happening a short time ago.
recently *adverb*

receptacle *noun*
something for holding what is put into it; a container.

reception *noun*
1 the way that someone or something is received. 2 a formal party. *a wedding reception.* 3 a place in a hotel, office, etc. where visitors are welcomed, registered, etc. 4 **reception-room**, a sitting-room.

receptionist *noun*
someone employed at the reception of a hotel, office, etc.

recess *noun* **(recesses)**
1 an alcove. 2 a time when work or business is stopped for a while.

recipe *noun*
(*say* **ress**-i-pi)
instructions for preparing or cooking food.

reciprocal *adjective*
(*say* ri-**sip**-rŏ-kăl)
given and received; mutual. *reciprocal help.*

recital *noun*
(*say* ri-**sy**-tăl)
a concert by a small number of performers.

recite *verb* **(recited, reciting)**
to say something aloud that you have learnt.
recitation *noun*

reckless *adjective*
doing things without thinking or caring about them.
recklessly *adverb*, **recklessness** *noun*

reckon *verb*
1 to calculate; to count. 2 to have an opinion; to think.

reclaim *verb*
1 to make something usable again. *reclaimed land.* 2 to claim or get something back.
reclamation *noun*

recline *verb* **(reclined, reclining)**
to lean or lie back.

recognize *verb* **(recognized, recognizing)**
1 to know who somebody is because you have seen him before; to realize that you know something you have seen before. 2 to accept; to agree with something.
recognition *noun*, **recognizable** *adjective*

recoil *verb*
to move backwards suddenly; to spring back.

recollect *verb*
to remember.
recollection *noun*

recommend *verb*
to suggest or praise somebody or something, especially for doing a job.
recommendation *noun*

reconcile *verb* **(reconciled, reconciling)**
1 to restore peace or friendship. 2 to persuade somebody to put up with something. *He became reconciled to wearing glasses.*
reconciliation *noun*

record *noun*
(*say* **rek**-ord)
1 a flat, round piece of plastic that makes music or other sounds when it is played on a record-player. 2 the best performance in a sport or most remarkable event of its kind. *She broke the record for swimming 100 metres.* 3 a description of things that have happened.

record *verb*
(*say* ri-**kord**)
1 to put music or other sounds on a tape or disc. 2 to describe things that have happened.

recorder *noun*
1 a tape-recorder. 2 a wooden musical instrument played by blowing into one end. 3 someone who records something.

record-player *noun*
a device for reproducing sound from records.

recover *verb*
1 to get better after being ill. 2 to get something back that you had lost.
recovery *noun*

recreation *noun*
1 games, hobbies, and other enjoyable pastimes done in your spare time. 2 **recreation ground,** a public playground for children.
recreational *adjective*

recruit *noun*
someone who has just joined the armed forces or a business, society, etc.

rectangle *noun*
a shape with four straight sides and four right angles.
rectangular *adjective*

recur *verb* **(recurred, recurring)**
1 to happen again. 2 **recurring decimal,** a decimal in which the same numbers are repeated indefinitely.
recurrence *noun*, **recurrent** *adjective*

recycle *verb* **(recycled, recycling)**
to treat waste material so that it can be used again. *Waste paper can be recycled to make cardboard.*

red *adjective* **(redder, reddest)**
1 of the colour of blood. 2 of Communists; favouring Communism. 3 **red herring,** a thing that misleads somebody or diverts his attention. 4 **red tape,** excessive rules and forms in official business.
redden *verb,* **reddish** *adjective*

red *noun*
1 red colour. 2 a Communist. 3 **in the red,** in debt.

redeem *verb*
1 to save somebody from sin, faults, etc. 2 to get something back by paying for it.
redeemer *noun,* **redemption** *noun*

red-handed *adjective*
while committing a crime. *He was caught red-handed.*

Red Indian *noun*
an American Indian.

reduce *verb* **(reduced, reducing)**
1 to make something smaller or less. 2 to force into a situation. *She was reduced to borrowing the money.*
reduction *noun*

redundant *adjective*
not needed, especially for a particular job.
redundancy *noun*

reed *noun*
1 a plant that grows in or near water. 2 a thin strip that vibrates to make the sound in a clarinet, saxophone, oboe, etc.
reedy *adjective*

reef *noun*
a line of rocks near the surface of the sea.

reef-knot *noun*
a symmetrical double knot.

reek *verb*
to have a strong, unpleasant smell.

reel *noun*
1 a spool. 2 a lively Scottish dance.

reel *verb*
1 to stagger; to be dizzy. 2 **reel off,** to say something quickly.

refer *verb* **(referred, referring)**
1 to pass a question, problem, etc. to somebody else. 2 **refer to,** to mention; to look in a book, etc. for information; to be connected with.

referee *noun*
someone who makes sure that people keep to the rules of a game.

referee *verb* **(refereed, refereeing)**
to act as a referee.

reference *noun*
1 a mention of something. 2 a place in a book, file, etc. where information can be found. 3 a testimonial. 4 **in** or **with reference to,** concerning; in connection with. 5 **reference book,** a book that gives information.

referendum *noun*
(*say* ref-er-**en**-dùm)
a vote on a particular question by all the people in a country.

refill *noun*
a thing used to replace something that has been used up. *My lighter needs a refill.*

refine *verb* **(refined, refining)**
1 to purify. 2 **refined,** cultured; with good manners.
refinement *noun,* **refinery** *noun*

reflect *verb*
1 to send back light from a shiny surface. 2 to show a picture of something, as in a mirror. 3 to ponder.
reflection *noun,* **reflective** *adjective,* **reflector** *noun*

reflex *noun* **(reflexes)**
(*say* **ree**-fleks)
a movement or action done without any conscious thought.

reflexive *adjective*
(*say* ri-**flek**-siv)
referring to an action that affects the subject of the sentence. *In 'He washed himself', the verb is reflexive.*

reform *verb*
to improve a person or thing by getting rid of faults.
reformer *noun*

refrain *verb*
to keep yourself from doing something. *Please refrain from talking.*

refrain *noun*
the chorus of a song.

refresh *verb*
to make a tired person feel fresh and strong again; to give something new strength.

refreshments *plural noun*
drinks and snacks.

refrigerate *verb* **(refrigerated, refrigerating)**
to freeze something so as to preserve it.
refrigeration *noun*

refrigerator *noun*
a metal cupboard in which food is kept cold and fresh.

refuel *verb* **(refuelled, refuelling)**
to supply a ship, aircraft, etc. with fuel.

refuge *noun*
a place where you are safe from pursuit or danger.

refugee *noun*
(*say* ref-yoo-**jee**)
someone who has had to leave his home or country because of war, persecution, disaster, etc.

refund *verb*
(*say* ri-**fund**)
to pay money back.

refund *noun*
(*say* **ree**-fund)
money paid back. *I want a refund for this bad fruit that I bought.*

refuse *verb* **(refused, refusing)**
(*say* ri-**fewz**)
to say that you will not do or accept something. *She refuses to help.*
refusal *noun*

refuse *noun*
(*say* **ref**-yooss)
rubbish. *Dustmen collect the refuse.*

regain *verb*
1 to get something back. 2 to reach a place again.

regard *verb*
1 to look at. 2 to think of someone or something in a certain way.

regard *noun*
1 a gaze. 2 consideration; respect. 3 **regards**, kind wishes. 4 **with regard to,** concerning.

regarding *preposition*
concerning.

regardless *adjective*
paying no attention to something. *Get it, regardless of the cost.*

regatta *noun*
(*say* ri-**gat**-ă)
a meeting for boat or yacht races.

reggae *noun*
(*say* **reg**-ay)
a West Indian style of music with a strong beat.

regiment *noun*
an army unit consisting of two or more battalions.
regimental *adjective*

region *noun*
a part of a country; a part of the world.
regional *adjective*

register *noun*
a book in which information is recorded, especially of attendance at a school.

register *verb*
1 to list in a register; to record information officially. *Is this car registered?* 2 to indicate; to show. *The thermometer registered 100°.* 3 to pay extra for a letter or parcel to be sent with special care.
registration *noun*

regret *noun*
the feeling of being sorry or sad about something.
regretful *adjective*, **regretfully** *adverb*

regret *verb* (**regretted, regretting**)
to feel regret about something.
regrettable *adjective*, **regrettably** *adverb*

regular *adjective*
1 always happening at certain times. *regular meals.* 2 even; symmetrical. *regular teeth.* 3 normal; correct. *the regular procedure.* 4 of a country's permanent armed forces. *a regular soldier.*
regularity *noun*, **regularly** *adverb*

regulate *verb* (**regulated, regulating**)
to adjust or control.
regulator *noun*

regulation *noun*
1 the regulating of something. 2 a rule or law.

rehearse *verb* (**rehearsed, rehearsing**)
to practise something before it is performed in front of an audience.
rehearsal *noun*

reign *verb*
to be king or queen; to rule.

reign *noun*
the time when someone is king or queen.

rein *noun*
a strap used to guide a horse.

reindeer *noun* (**reindeer**)
a kind of deer that lives in cold countries.

reinforce *verb* (**reinforced, reinforcing**)
1 to strengthen. 2 **reinforced concrete**, concrete with metal bars or wires embedded in it.

reinforcement *noun*
1 something that reinforces. 2 **reinforcements**, extra troops, ships, etc. sent to strengthen a force.

reject *verb*
(*say* ri-**jekt**)
to refuse to accept a person or thing; to get rid of. *She rejected my offer of help.*
rejection *noun*

reject *noun*
(*say* **ree**-jekt)
a rejected person or thing.

rejoice *verb* (**rejoiced, rejoicing**)
to be very happy.

relate *verb* (**related, relating**)
1 to connect or compare one thing with another. 2 to narrate. 3 **related**, belonging to the same family.

relation *noun*
1 a relative. 2 the way that one thing is related to another.

relationship *noun*
how people or things are related; how people get on with one another.

relative *noun*
someone in your family.

relative *adjective*
comparative; connected with something.
relatively *adverb*

relax *verb*
to become less stiff or less strict; to rest.
relaxation *noun*

relay *verb*
to pass on a message or broadcast.

relay *noun*
1 one of a series of groups. *The firemen worked in relays.* 2 a relay race. 3 a device for relaying a broadcast. 4 **relay race**, a race between two teams in which each competitor covers part of the distance.

release *verb* (**released, releasing**)
1 to set free; to unfasten. 2 to emit. 3 to make a film, record, etc. available to the public.

release *noun*
1 being released. 2 something released. 3 a device that unfastens something.

relegate *verb* (**relegated, relegating**)
(*say* **rel**-i-gayt)
to put a team into a lower division of a league.
relegation *noun*

relent *verb*
to be less angry or more merciful than you were going to be.

relentless *adjective*
1 pitiless 2 that you cannot stop.
relentlessly *adverb*

relevant *adjective*
(*say* **rel**-i-vănt)
connected with what is being discussed or dealt with. *His ideas are not relevant to our difficulties.*
relevance *noun,* **relevantly** *adverb*

reliable *adjective*
that you can trust or depend on.
reliability *noun,* **reliably** *adverb*

relic *noun*
something that has survived from an ancient time.

relief *noun*
1 the ending or lessening of pain, trouble, boredom, etc. 2 something that causes relief. 3 a person or thing that takes over or helps with a job. 4 a method of making a map, design, etc. that stands out from a flat surface. *A relief map shows hills and valleys by shading or moulding.*

relieve *verb* (**relieved, relieving**)
1 to give relief to someone or something. 2 **relieve someone of something,** to take it from him. *He relieved me of my watch.*

religion *noun*
what people believe about God or gods, and how they worship.
religious *adjective,* **religiously** *adverb*

reluctant *adjective*
not wanting to do something; not keen.
reluctance *noun,* **reluctantly** *adverb*

rely *verb* (**relied, relying**)
rely on or **upon,** to trust someone or something to help or support you.
reliance *noun,* **reliant** *adjective*

remain *verb*
1 to continue in the same place or condition. 2 to be left over.
remainder *noun*

remains *plural noun*
1 something left over. 2 ruins; relics. 3 a corpse.

remark *verb*
to say something that you have thought or noticed.

remark *noun*
something said.

remarkable *adjective*
so unusual that you notice or remember it.
remarkably *adverb*

remedial *adjective*
(*say* ri-**mee**-di-ăl)
helping to cure an illness or deficiency.

remedy *noun* (**remedies**)
a cure; a medicine.

remember *verb*
to keep something in your mind; to bring something into your mind when you want to.
remembrance *noun*

remind *verb*
to help or make someone remember something.
reminder *noun*

reminisce *verb* (**reminisced, reminiscing**)
(*say* rem-in-**iss**)
to think or talk about things you remember.
reminiscence *noun,* **reminiscent** *adjective*

remnant *noun*
a small piece of something left over.

remorse *noun*
deep regret for having done wrong.
remorseful *adjective,* **remorseless** *adjective*

remote *adjective* (**remoter, remotest**)
1 far away. 2 unlikely; slight. *a remote chance.* 3 **remote control,** controlling something from a distance, usually by means of radio or electricity.
remotely *adverb,* **remoteness** *noun*

removal *noun*
removing or moving something, especially moving furniture from one house to another.

remove *verb* (**removed, removing**)
to take something away or off.

render *verb*
1 to put somebody in a particular condition. *She was rendered speechless by the shock.* 2 to give or perform something. *a reward for services rendered.*

rendezvous *noun* (**rendezvous**)
(*say* **ron**-day-voo)
a meeting with somebody; a place or appointment to meet somebody.

renew *verb*
to make something as it was before or replace it with something new.
renewal *noun*

renown *noun*
fame. *a man of great renown.*
renowned *adjective*

rent *noun*[1]
a regular payment for the use of something, especially a house, that belongs to another person.

rent *noun*[2]
a torn place in a piece of cloth.

rent *verb*
to pay rent for something.

repair *verb*
to mend.

repair *noun*
1 repairing something. 2 condition. *His car is in good repair.*

repay *verb* (**repaid, repaying**)
to pay back. *She has repaid her debt.*
repayment *noun*

repeat *verb*
to say or do the same thing again.
repeatedly *adverb,* **repetition** *noun,* **repetitive** *adjective*

repeat *noun*
something that is repeated, especially a radio or television programme.

repel *verb* (**repelled, repelling**)
1 to repulse. 2 to disgust somebody.
repellent *adjective*

repent *verb*
to be sorry for what you have done.
repentance *noun,* **repentant** *adjective*

replace *verb* (**replaced, replacing**)
1 to put something back in its place. **2** to take the place of another person or thing. **3** to put a new thing in the place of an old one.
replacement *noun*

replay *noun*
1 a football match played again after a draw. **2** a repeat of a recording.

replica *noun*
(*say* **rep**-lik-à)
an exact copy.

reply *noun* (**replies**)
something said or written to deal with a question, letter, etc.; an answer.

reply *verb* (**replied, replying**)
to give a reply; to answer.

report *verb*
1 to describe something that has happened or something you have studied. **2** to make a complaint or accusation against somebody. **3** to go to somebody and say that you are ready for work.

report *noun*
1 a description or account of something. **2** a regular statement of how someone has worked or behaved, especially at school. **3** an explosive sound.

reporter *noun*
someone whose job is to collect news for a newspaper, radio, television, etc.

represent *verb*
1 to be a picture, model, or symbol of something or somebody. **2** to be an example of something. **3** to help somebody by speaking or acting for him.
representation *noun,* **representative** *noun*

repress *verb*
to keep something down or under; to prevent somebody or something from being free.
repression *noun,* **repressive** *adjective*

reprieve *noun*
(*say* ri-**preev**)
postponing or cancelling a punishment, especially the death penalty.

reprimand *verb*
to tell somebody off.

reprisal *noun*
(*say* ri-**pry**-zàl)
an act of revenge.

reproach *verb*
to tell somebody off; to find fault with somebody.

reproduce *verb* (**reproduced, reproducing**)
1 to make something be heard or seen again. *Sound can be reproduced by discs or magnetic tapes.* **2** to copy something. **3** to have babies.
reproduction *noun,* **reproductive** *adjective*

reptile *noun*
an animal that creeps or crawls. *Snakes, lizards, crocodiles, and tortoises are reptiles.*
reptilian *adjective*

republic *noun*
a country ruled by an elected president and government.
republican *adjective* and *noun*

repulse *verb* (**repulsed, repulsing**)
to drive or force somebody or something away.

repulsive *adjective*
disgusting.
repulsion *noun*

reputation *noun*
what people think about a person or thing. *He has a reputation for being honest.*

request *verb*
to ask politely for something.

request *noun*
1 the action of asking for something. **2** what someone asks for.

require *verb* (**required, requiring**)
1 to need or want. *We require some paper.* **2** to make somebody do something. *Drivers are required to license their cars.*
requirement *noun*

reread *verb* (**reread, rereading**)
to read something again.

rescue *verb* (**rescued, rescuing**)
to save somebody from danger, capture, etc.
rescuer *noun*

research *noun* (**researches**)
careful study or investigation.
researcher *noun*

resemblance *noun*
being similar. *There is a resemblance between the brothers.*

resemble *verb* (**resembled, resembling**)
to look or sound like another person or thing.

resent *verb*
to feel indignant or angry about something.
resentful *adjective,* **resentment** *noun*

reservation *noun*
1 reserving something. **2** something reserved. **3** an area of land kept for a special purpose. **4** a limit on how much you agree with something.

reserve *verb* (**reserved, reserving**)
1 to keep or order something for a particular person or for a special use. **2** **reserved,** shy; not sociable.

reserve *noun*
1 a person or thing kept ready to be used if necessary. **2** an area of land kept for a special purpose. *This island is a nature reserve.*

reservoir *noun*
(*say* **rez**-er-vwar)
a place, especially an artificial lake, where water is stored.

reside *verb* (**resided, residing**)
to live in a particular place.
resident *noun*

residence *noun*
where somebody lives.
residential *adjective*

resign *verb*
1 to give up your job or position. **2** **resign yourself to something,** to accept it without complaining or arguing.
resignation *noun*

resin *noun*
(*say* **rez**-in)
a sticky substance that comes from plants or is
made artificially.
resinous *adjective*

resist *verb*
to try to stop somebody or something; to fight.
resistance *noun*, **resistant** *adjective*

resolute *adjective*
(*say* **rez**-ŏ-loot)
determined; firm.
resolutely *adverb*

resolution *noun*
1 being resolute. 2 something resolved.

resolve *verb* (**resolved, resolving**)
1 to make a decision. 2 to overcome disagree-
ments, doubts, etc.

resort *noun*
1 a place where people go for holidays. 2 **the
last resort,** the last thing you can try.

resound *verb*
to fill a place with sound; to echo.

resource *noun*
something that can be used. *The land is rich in
natural resources.*

respect *noun*
1 admiration for somebody's good qualities,
achievement, etc. 2 consideration; concern.
Have respect for people's feelings. 3 a detail or
aspect. *In this respect, he is like his sister.*
4 **with respect to,** concerning.

respect *verb*
to have respect for somebody.

respectable *adjective*
1 having good manners, character, social
position, etc. 2 of a good size or standard. *He
earns a respectable amount.*
respectability *noun*, **respectably** *adverb*

respectful *adjective*
showing respect; polite.
respectfully *adverb*

respecting *preposition*
concerning.

respective *adjective*
of or for each individual. *We went to our
respective rooms.*
respectively *adverb*

respiration *noun*
breathing.
respirator *noun*, **respiratory** *adjective*

respond *verb*
1 to reply. 2 to react.

response *noun*
1 a reply. 2 a reaction.

responsible *adjective*
1 looking after something and likely to take the
blame if anything goes wrong. 2 trustworthy.
3 important. *a responsible job.* 4 causing something. *His carelessness was responsible for
their deaths.*
responsibility *noun*, **responsibly** *adverb*

rest *noun*¹
1 a time of sleep, relaxation, freedom from
work, etc. 2 a support. *an arm-rest.*
restful *adjective*

rest *noun*²
the part that is left; the others. *I shall go; the
rest can stay here.*

rest *verb*
1 to have a rest. 2 to support or be supported.

restaurant *noun*
a place where you can buy a meal and eat it.

restless *adjective*
unable to rest or keep still.
restlessly *adverb*, **restlessness** *noun*

restore *verb* (**restored, restoring**)
to put something back as it was; to repair.
restoration *noun*

restrain *verb*
to hold someone or something back; to keep
under control.
restraint *noun*

restrict *verb*
to keep a person or thing within certain limits.
restriction *noun*, **restrictive** *adjective*

result *noun*
1 a thing that happens because something else
has happened. 2 the score or situation at the
end of a game, competition, race, etc. 3 the
answer to a sum or problem.

result *verb*
to happen as a result; to have a particular
result. *The game resulted in a draw.*
resultant *adjective*

resume *verb* (**resumed, resuming**)
to start again after stopping for a while.
resumption *noun*

retail *verb*
to sell goods to the public.
retailer *noun*

retain *verb*
1 to keep something. 2 to hold something in
place.

retina *noun*
(*say* **ret**-in-ă)
a layer at the back of the eyeball that is
sensitive to light.

retire *verb* (**retired, retiring**)
1 to give up work, usually because you are
getting old. 2 to retreat; to withdraw. 3 to go to
bed. 4 **retiring,** shy.
retirement *noun*

retort *verb*
to reply quickly or angrily.

retrace *verb* (**retraced, retracing**)
to go back over something.

retreat *verb*
to go back so as to avoid death or danger.

retrieve *verb* (**retrieved, retrieving**)
to get something back; to find.
retrievable *adjective*, **retrieval** *noun*

retriever *noun*
a dog that can find and bring back birds and
other animals that have been shot.

return *verb*
1 to come or go back to a place. 2 to give or send something back.
returnable *adjective*

return *noun*
1 returning. 2 something returned. 3 profit. *He gets a good return on his savings.* 4 a return ticket. 5 **return game** or **return match,** a second game between two teams. 6 **return ticket,** a ticket for a journey to a place and back again.

reunion *noun*
a meeting of people who have not met for some time.

rev *verb* (revved, revving)
(*informal*) to make an engine run quickly.

rev *noun*
(*informal*) a revolution of an engine.

Rev. short for **Reverend.**

reveal *verb*
to let something be seen or known.
revelation *noun*

revenge *noun*
the action of harming somebody because he has harmed you or your friends.

revenue *noun*
(*say* rev-ĕn-yoo)
income.

revere *verb* (revered, revering)
(*say* ri-**veer**)
to respect deeply or religiously.
reverence *noun*, **reverent** *adjective*

Reverend *noun*
the title of a clergyman. *The Reverend John Smith.*

reverse *noun*
1 the opposite way or side. 2 reverse gear. 3 **in reverse,** going in the opposite direction. 4 **reverse gear,** the gear used to drive backwards.

reverse *verb* (reversed, reversing)
1 to turn something round. 2 to go backwards in a vehicle.
reversal *noun*, **reversible** *adjective*

review *noun*
1 an inspection or survey. 2 a published description and opinion of a book, film, play, etc.

review *verb*
to make a review of something.
reviewer *noun*

revise *verb* (revised, revising)
1 to get ready for an examination, etc. by studying work that you have already done. 2 to correct or change something.
revision *noun*

revive *verb* (revived, reviving)
1 to bring or come back to life or strength. 2 to start using or performing something again.
revival *noun*

revolt *verb*
1 to rebel. 2 to disgust or horrify somebody.

revolution *noun*
1 a rebellion that overthrows the government. 2 a complete change. 3 one turn of a wheel, engine, etc.

revolutionary *adjective*
of or involving a revolution.

revolutionize *verb*
(revolutionized, revolutionizing)
to change something completely.

revolve *verb* (revolved, revolving)
to go round in a circle.

revolver *noun*
a pistol that can be fired several times without having to be loaded again.

reward *noun*
something given to a person because he has done something, behaved well, etc.

reward *verb*
to give somebody a reward.

rewrite *verb* (*past tense* **rewrote;** *past participle* **rewritten;** *present participle* **rewriting**)
to write something again or differently.

rheumatism *noun*
(*say* **roo**-mă-tizm)
a disease that causes pain and stiffness in joints and muscles.
rheumatic *adjective*

rhinoceros *noun* (**rhinoceroses** or **rhinoceros**)
(*say* ry-**nos**-er-ŏs)
a large, heavy animal with either one or two horns on its nose.

rhododendron *noun*
(*say* roh-dŏ-**den**-drŏn)
an evergreen shrub with large flowers.

rhubarb *noun*
a plant with pink or green stalks used as fruit.

rhyme *noun*
1 similar sounds in the endings of words, as in *bat* and *mat, batter* and *matter.* 2 a short rhyming poem.

rhyme *verb* (rhymed, rhyming)
to have rhymes, especially at the ends of lines. *This verse doesn't rhyme.*

rhythm *noun*
a regular pattern of beats, sounds, or movements. *Most poetry and music has rhythm.*
rhythmic *adjective*, **rhythmical** *adjective*,
rhythmically *adverb*

rib *noun*
one of the curved bones above the waist.

ribbon *noun*
a strip of nylon, silk, or other material. *Her hair was tied up with a ribbon.*

rice *noun*
white seeds that are used as food.

rich *adjective*
1 having a lot of money or property. 2 full of goodness, quality, strength, etc. 3 costly; luxurious.
richly *adverb*, **richness** *noun*

riches *plural noun*
wealth.

rick *noun*
a large, neat stack of hay or straw.

rickety *adjective*
unsteady; likely to fall down.

rickshaw *noun*
a two-wheeled carriage pulled by one or more people. *Rickshaws are used in the Far East.*

ricochet *verb*
(*say* rik-ŏ-shay)
to bounce off something. *The bullets ricocheted off the wall.*

rid *verb* (**rid, ridding**)
1 to make a person or place free from something unwanted. *He rid the town of rats.* 2 **get rid of**, to cause to go away; to get free of. *I wish I could get rid of these spots.*

riddle *noun*
a puzzling question, especially as a joke. *Here is a riddle. Why was the farmer cross? Because someone trod on his corn.*

ride *verb* (*past tense* **rode;** *past participle* **ridden;** *present participle* **riding**)
1 to sit on a horse, bicycle, etc. and be carried along on it. *I have never ridden a pony.* 2 to travel in a car, bus, train, etc. *We rode to the seaside in a coach.*
rider *noun*

ride *noun*
a journey on a horse, bicycle, etc. or in a vehicle.

ridge *noun*
a long, narrow part of something higher than the rest of it. *There are special tiles for the ridge of a roof.*

ridicule *verb* (**ridiculed, ridiculing**)
to make fun of somebody or something.

ridiculous *adjective*
so silly as to make people laugh.
ridiculously *adverb*

rifle *noun*
a long gun that you hold against your shoulder when you fire it. *Rifles have grooved barrels and they fire bullets.*

rift *noun*
1 a crack or split. 2 a disagreement between friends.

rig *verb* (**rigged, rigging**)
1 to provide a ship with rigging, sails, etc. 2 **rig out**, to provide somebody with clothes, equipment, etc. 3 **rig up**, to make something quickly.

rig *noun*
1 a framework to support the equipment for drilling an oil-well. 2 the way a ship's masts and sails are arranged.

rigging *noun*
the ropes that support a ship's masts and sails.

right *adjective*
1 on the side opposite the left. 2 correct. *Is this sum right?* 3 fair; virtuous. *Is it right to cheat?* 4 Conservative; not in favour of political reforms.
rightly *adverb*, **rightness** *noun*

right *noun*
1 the side opposite the left. *In France, cars drive on the right.* 2 what is fair or just; something that people ought to be allowed. *They protested for their rights.*

right *adverb*
1 on or towards the right-hand side. *Turn right.* 2 completely. *Turn right round.* 3 exactly. *She stood right in the middle.* 4 straight; directly. *Go right ahead.* 5 **right away**, immediately.

right *verb*
to make something right or upright. *They righted the boat.*

right angle *noun*
an angle of 90 degrees. *The angles in a square are right angles.*

righteous *adjective*
virtuous; obeying the law.
righteously *adverb*, **righteousness** *noun*

rightful *adjective*
deserved; proper. *his rightful place.*
rightfully *adverb*

right hand *noun*
the hand that most people use more than the other.
right-hand *adjective*

right-handed *adjective*
using the right hand more than the left hand.

rigid *adjective*
(*say* rij-id)
1 firm; stiff. *a rigid support.* 2 strict; harsh. *rigid rules.*
rigidity *noun*, **rigidly** *adverb*

rim *noun*
the outer edge of a wheel or other round object.

rind *noun*
the skin on bacon, cheese, or fruit.

ring *noun*
1 a circle. 2 a thin circular piece of metal worn on a finger. 3 the space where a circus performs. 4 the place where a boxing-match or other contest is held.

ring *verb*[1] (*past tense* **rang;** *past participle* **rung;** *present participle* **ringing**)
1 to cause a bell to sound. *Have you rung the bell?* 2 to make a clear, musical sound like a bell. 3 to telephone. *She rang her brother last night.*

ring *verb*[2]
to put a ring round something.

ringleader *noun*
someone who leads other people in rebellion, mischief, crime, etc.

ring-master *noun*
the person who is in charge of what happens in the circus ring.

ring-road *noun*
a road that encircles a town.

rink *noun*
a place made for skating.

rinse *verb* (**rinsed, rinsing**)
to wash something in clean water.

riot *noun*
wild or violent behaviour by a crowd of people.
riotous *adjective*

rip *verb* (**ripped, ripping**)
1 to tear roughly. 2 **rip off**, (*slang*) to swindle.

rip *noun*
1 a torn place. 2 **rip-off,** (*slang*) a swindle.

rip-cord *noun*
the cord that you pull to open a parachute.

ripe *adjective* **(riper, ripest)**
ready to be harvested or eaten.
ripeness *noun*

ripen *verb*
to make or become ripe.

ripple *noun*
a small wave on the surface of water.

ripple *verb* **(rippled, rippling)**
to form ripples.

rise *verb* (*past tense* **rose**; *past participle* **risen**;
present participle **rising**)
1 to go upwards. *Prices have risen.* 2 to get up.
They all rose as she came in. 3 to rebel. *They
rose against the government.*

rise *noun*
1 the action of rising; an upward movement.
2 an increase, especially in wages. 3 an upward
slope. 4 **give rise to,** to cause.

risk *noun*
a chance of danger or loss.
risky *adjective*

risk *verb*
to take the chance of damaging or losing something.

rissole *noun*
a fried cake of minced meat.

rite *noun*
a ceremony.

ritual *noun*
a regular ceremony or series of actions.
ritualistic *adjective*, **ritually** *adverb*

rival *noun*
a person or thing that competes with another,
or tries to do the same thing.
rivalry *noun*

rival *verb* **(rivalled, rivalling)**
to be a rival of somebody or something.

river *noun*
water flowing in one direction along a channel.

rivet *noun*
a strong bolt for holding pieces of metal together.

rivet *verb*
1 to fasten something with rivets. 2 to fix. *She
stood riveted to the spot.* 3 to fascinate. *The
concert was riveting.*
riveter *noun*

road *noun*
a level way with a hard surface made for traffic
to go along.
roadside *noun*, **roadway** *noun*

roam *verb*
to wander. *They roamed about the world.*

roar *noun*
a loud, deep sound of the kind that a lion
makes.

roar *verb*
1 to make a roar. 2 **a roaring trade,** brisk selling
of something.

roast *verb*
1 to cook something in an oven or over a fire.
2 to make or be very hot.

rob *verb* **(robbed, robbing)**
to steal something from somebody. *He robbed
me of my watch.*
robber *noun*, **robbery** *noun*

robe *noun*
a long, loose garment.

robin *noun*
a small brown bird with a red chest.

robot *noun*
(*say* **roh**-bot)
a machine that can move and behave in some
ways like a person.

rock *noun*[1]
1 a large stone. 2 a large mass of stone. 3 a
hard sweet usually shaped like a stick and sold
at the seaside. 4 **rock plant,** a plant suitable for
a rockery.
rocky *adjective*

rock *noun*[2]
1 a rocking movement. 2 rock music. 3 **rock
music,** popular music with a heavy beat.

rock *verb*
to move gently backwards and forwards or from
side to side.

rocker *noun*
1 something that rocks. 2 a rocking-chair.
3 one of the curved bars that supports a
rocking-chair. 4 **off your rocker,** (*slang*) mad.

rockery *noun* **(rockeries)**
part of a garden where flowers grow between
rocks.

rocket *noun*
1 a firework that shoots high into the air. 2 a
tubular device shot into the air by hot gases,
especially as a spacecraft or missile.
rocketry *noun*

rocking-chair *noun*
a chair which can be rocked by the person
sitting in it.

rod *noun*
a long, thin stick or bar, especially one with a
line attached for fishing.

rode past tense of **ride** *verb*.

rodent *noun*
an animal that has large front teeth for gnawing
things. *Rats, mice, and squirrels are rodents.*

rodeo *noun*
(*say* roh-**day**-oh *or* **roh**-di-oh)
a display or contest of cowboys' skill in riding,
controlling cattle, etc.

rogue *noun*
a rascal.
roguery *noun*, **roguish** *adjective*

role *noun*
a performer's part in a play, film, etc.

roll *verb*
1 to move along by turning over and over, like a
ball or wheel. 2 to form something into the
shape of a cylinder or ball. 3 to flatten something by rolling a rounded object over it. 4 to
sway from side to side. 5 to make a long
vibrating sound.

roll *noun*
1 a cylinder made by rolling something up. 2 a very small loaf of bread shaped like a bun. 3 a list of names. 4 a long vibrating sound. *a roll on the drums.*

roller *noun*
1 something that rolls. 2 a long sea-wave.

roller-skate *noun*
a device with wheels that you can fit under your shoe, making you able to move quickly and smoothly over the ground.
roller-skating *noun*

rolling-pin *noun*
a heavy cylinder rolled over pastry to flatten it.

Roman *noun*
an inhabitant of Rome.

Roman *adjective*
1 of Rome. 2 **Roman candle,** a firework that sends out coloured balls of flame. 3 **Roman Catholic,** a member of the Church that has the Pope as its head. 4 **Roman numerals,** letters that represent numbers. *In Roman numerals, I=1, V=5, X=10, etc.*

romance *noun*
1 experiences, feelings, stories, etc. connected with love. 2 a love-story.

romantic *adjective*
1 of or like romance. 2 emotional or imaginative; imaginary.
romantically *adverb*

romp *verb*
to play in a lively way.

rompers *plural noun*
a young child's garment that covers most of the body.

roof *noun*
1 the part that covers the top of a building, shelter, or vehicle. 2 the upper part of the mouth.

rook *noun*
1 a black bird that looks like a crow. 2 a piece in chess shaped like a castle.

room *noun*
1 a part of a building with its own walls and ceiling. 2 enough space for somebody or something. *Is there room for me?*
roomful *noun*

roomy *adjective* (**roomier, roomiest**)
with plenty of room or space.

roost *noun*
the place where a bird rests.

rooster *noun*
a cockerel.

root *noun*
1 the part of a plant that grows under the ground. 2 a source or basis of something. *Money is the root of all evil.* 3 a number in relation to the number it produces when multiplied by itself. *9 is the root, or square root, of 81.* 4 **take root,** to grow roots; to become established.

root *verb*
1 to take root. 2 to fix somebody in a particular spot. 3 **root out,** to get rid of something.

rope *noun*
1 threads or strands twisted together. 2 **show somebody the ropes,** to show him how to do something.

rose *noun*
a sweet-smelling flower with a thorny stem.

rose past tense of **rise** *verb.*

rosette *noun*
a large circular badge.

rosy *adjective* (**rosier, rosiest**)
1 pink. 2 hopeful; cheerful.

rot *verb* (**rotted, rotting**)
to go soft or bad so that it is useless; to decay. *This wood has rotted.*

rot *noun*
1 decay. 2 (*informal*) nonsense.

rotate *verb* (**rotated, rotating**)
1 to go round like a wheel. 2 to arrange or happen in a series.
rotary *adjective,* **rotation** *noun*

rotor *noun*
something that rotates, especially the large horizontal propeller of a helicopter.

rotten *adjective*
1 rotted. *rotten fruit.* 2 (*informal*) nasty; very bad. *rotten weather.*
rottenness *noun*

rough *adjective*
1 not smooth; uneven. *a rough surface.* 2 not gentle. *a rough boy.* 3 not exact; done quickly. *a rough guess.*
roughly *adverb,* **roughness** *noun*

roughen *verb*
to make or become rough.

round *adjective*
1 shaped like a circle or ball. 2 full; complete. *a round dozen.* 3 that returns to where it started. *a round trip.*

round *adverb*
1 in a circle or curve; by a longer route. *Go round to the back of the house.* 2 in all or various directions. *Hand the cakes round.* 3 in a new direction. *Turn your chair round.* 4 to someone's house, office, etc. *Come round at lunchtime.*

round *preposition*
1 on all sides of something. *a fence round the field.* 2 in a curve or circle about something. *The earth moves round the sun.* 3 to all or various parts of something. *Show them round the house.* 4 **round the bend** or **round the twist,** (*slang*) mad.

round *noun*
1 a whole slice of bread; a sandwich made from two whole slices of bread. 2 a series of visits or calls made by a doctor, postman, etc. 3 one stage in a competition. *The winners go on to the next round.* 4 a shot or series of shots from a gun; a piece of ammunition. 5 a song in which people sing the same words but start at different times.

round *verb*
1 to make or become round. 2 to travel round. 3 **round off,** to finish something. 4 **round up,** to gather people, cattle, etc. together.

roundabout *noun*
1 a road junction where traffic has to go round a circle. 2 a merry-go-round.

rounders *noun*
a game in which players try to hit a ball and run round a circuit.

Roundhead *noun*
an opponent of King Charles I in the English Civil War.

rouse *verb* (roused, rousing)
to make somebody awake, active, or excited.

rout *verb*
(*say* rowt)
to defeat and chase away an enemy.

route *noun*
(*say* root)
the way you have to go to get to a place.

routine *noun*
(*say* roo-**teen**)
a regular way of doing things.

rove *verb* (roved, roving)
to wander; to travel.
rover *noun*

row *noun*[1]
(rhymes with *go*)
a line of people or things.

row *noun*[2]
(rhymes with *cow*)
1 a great noise or disturbance. 2 a quarrel; a noisy argument or scolding.

row *verb*
(rhymes with *go*)
to use oars to make a boat move.
rower *noun*, **rowing-boat** *noun*

rowdy *adjective* (rowdier, rowdiest)
noisy and disorderly.
rowdily *adverb*, **rowdiness** *noun*, **rowdyism** *noun*

rowlock *noun*
(*say* **rol**-ŏk)
a device on the side of a boat to hold an oar in place.

royal *adjective*
of or connected with a king or queen.
royally *adverb*, **royalty** *noun*

rub *verb* (rubbed, rubbing)
1 to move something backwards and forwards while pressing it on something else. *He rubbed his hands together.* 2 **rub off** or **rub out,** to make something disappear by rubbing it.

rubber *noun*
1 a strong elastic substance used for making tyres, balls, hoses, etc. 2 a piece of rubber for rubbing out pencil marks.
rubbery *adjective*

rubbish *noun*
1 things that are not wanted or needed. 2 nonsense.

rubble *noun*
broken pieces of brick or stone.

ruby *noun* (rubies)
a red jewel.

rucksack *noun*
a haversack.

rudder *noun*
a flat, hinged device at the back of a ship or aircraft, used for steering.

ruddy *adjective* (ruddier, ruddiest)
1 red and healthy-looking. *a ruddy face.* 2 (*informal*) bloody. *a ruddy nuisance.*

rude *adjective* (ruder, rudest)
1 not polite. 2 obscene; indecent. 3 roughly made; simple.
rudely *adverb*, **rudeness** *noun*

ruffian *noun*
a violent, cruel man.

ruffle *verb* (ruffled, ruffling)
to disturb the smoothness of something or the calmness of someone. *The bird ruffled its feathers.*

rug *noun*
1 a thick mat for the floor. 2 a thick blanket.

Rugby or **Rugby football** *noun*
a kind of football game using an oval ball that the players are allowed to touch. *There are 13 players on each side in Rugby League but 15 in Rugby Union.*

rugged *adjective*
(*say* **rug**-id)
1 rough; uneven. *a rugged face.* 2 rocky. *a rugged coast.*

rugger *noun*
(*informal*) Rugby football.

ruin *verb*
to spoil something completely; to destroy.

ruin *noun*
1 a building that has fallen down. 2 the action of ruining; destruction.
ruinous *adjective*

rule *noun*
1 something that people have to obey; a way that people must behave. 2 ruling or being ruled. 3 **as a rule,** usually.

rule *verb* (ruled, ruling)
1 to govern; to reign. 2 to make a decision. *The referee ruled that it was a foul.* 3 to draw a straight line with a ruler or some other straight edge.

ruler *noun*
1 someone who governs. 2 a strip of wood, plastic, or metal with straight edges, used for measuring and drawing straight lines.

rum *noun*
a strong alcoholic drink made from sugar or molasses.

rumble *verb* (rumbled, rumbling)
to make a deep, heavy sound like thunder.

rummage *verb* (rummaged, rummaging)
to turn things over or move them about while looking for something. *She rummaged in the wardrobe.*

rummy *noun*
a card-game in which players try to form sequences or sets of cards.

rumour *noun*
something that a lot of people are saying, although it may not be true.

rump *noun*
the hind part of an animal.

run *verb (past tense* **ran;** *past participle* **run;** *present participle* **running)**
1 to use your legs to move quickly. **2** to go or travel; to flow. *Tears ran down his cheeks.* **3** to produce a flow of liquid. *Your nose is running.* **4** to work or function. *The engine was running smoothly.* **5** to manage or organize. *She runs a grocery shop.* **6 run a risk,** to take a chance. **7 run away,** to leave a place quickly or secretly. **8 run out,** to have used up your stock of something. *We have run out of sugar.* **9 run over,** to knock somebody down with your car, bicycle, etc.

run *noun*
1 a time spent running. *Go for a run.* **2** a point scored in cricket or baseball. **3** a ladder in a stocking or other garment. **4** a continuous series of events. *She had a run of good luck.* **5** an enclosure for animals. *a chicken run.* **6 on the run,** running away.

runaway *noun*
someone who has run away.

rung *noun*
one of the short crossbars on a ladder.

rung past participle of **ring** *verb*[1].

runner *noun*
1 a person or animal that runs, especially in a race. **2** the part of a sledge that slides along the ground. **3 runner bean,** a kind of climbing bean. **4 runner-up,** someone who comes second in a race or competition.

runny *adjective* **(runnier, runniest)**
flowing or moving like liquid.

runway *noun*
an air-strip.

rural *adjective*
of or like the countryside.

rush *verb*
1 to hurry. **2** to attack or capture by rushing.

rush *noun*[1] **(rushes)**
1 a hurry. **2** a sudden movement of people to a gold-field. **3 rush-hour,** the time when traffic is busiest.

rush *noun*[2] **(rushes)**
a plant with a thin stem that grows in wet or marshy places.

rusk *noun*
a kind of biscuit for babies to chew.

Russian *adjective*
of Russia.

rust *noun*
a red or brown substance formed on metal as it corrodes; the process of forming this.
rusty *adjective*

rust *verb*
to make or become rusty.

rustic *adjective*
rural.

rustle *verb* **(rustled, rustling)**
1 to make a gentle sound like dry leaves being blown by the wind. **2** to steal horses or cattle. **3 rustle up,** (*informal*) to get together or provide a meal, helpers, etc.
rustler *noun*

rut *noun*
1 a deep groove in the ground made by wheels. **2** a boring habit or way of life. *We are getting into a rut.*
rutted *adjective*

ruthless *adjective*
pitiless; merciless; cruel.
ruthlessly *adverb,* **ruthlessness** *noun*

rye *noun*
a cereal used to make bread, biscuits, etc.

S

Sabbath *noun*
a weekly day for rest and prayer, Saturday for Jews, Sunday for Christians.

sabotage *noun*
(*say* **sab**-ŏ-tah*zh*)
deliberate damage or disruption to hinder an enemy, employer, etc.
saboteur *noun*

sac *noun*
part of an animal or plant that is shaped like a bag.

saccharin *noun*
(*say* **sak**-ă-rin)
a sweet substance used as a substitute for sugar.

sack *noun*
1 a large bag made of strong material. **2 the sack,** being dismissed from a job. *They gave me the sack.*

sack *verb*
to dismiss someone from a job.

sacred *adjective*
holy.

sacrifice *noun*
1 giving or doing something that you think will please a god. **2** giving up a thing that you value so that something good may happen. **3** something sacrificed.
sacrificial *adjective*

sacrifice *verb* **(sacrificed, sacrificing)**
to give something as a sacrifice.

sad *adjective* (**sadder, saddest**)
unhappy.
sadly *adverb*, **sadness** *noun*

sadden *verb*
to make someone sad.

saddle *noun*
1 a seat designed to be put on the back of a horse or other animal. 2 the seat of a bicycle.

saddle *verb* (**saddled, saddling**)
to put a saddle on a horse.

sadist *noun*
(*say* **say**-dist)
someone who likes hurting other people.
sadism *noun*, **sadistic** *adjective*

safari *noun*
(*say* så-**far**-i)
1 an expedition to see or hunt wild animals.
2 **safari park**, a park where wild animals are kept to be seen by visitors.

safe *adjective* (**safer, safest**)
free from danger; not dangerous; protected.
safely *adverb*

safe *noun*
a strong cupboard or box in which valuables can be locked safely.

safeguard *noun*
a protection.

safety *noun*
1 being safe; protection. 2 **safety-belt**, a belt to hold somebody securely in a seat. 3 **safety-pin**, a curved pin made with a clip to protect the point.

sag *verb* (**sagged, sagging**)
to go down in the middle because something heavy is pressing on it. *The chair sagged under his weight.*

sago *noun*
a starchy white food used in puddings.

said past tense and past participle of **say**.

sail *noun*
1 a large piece of strong cloth attached to a mast to make a boat move. 2 a short voyage.
3 an arm of a windmill.

sail *verb*
1 to travel in a ship. 2 to start a voyage. *We sail at noon.* 3 to control a boat. 4 to be moved along by means of a sail or sails. *This boat sails beautifully.*

sailor *noun*
someone who sails; a member of a ship's crew.

saint *noun*
a holy or very good person.
saintly *adjective*

sake *noun*
for the sake of, because of; so as to help or please a person, get a thing, etc. *Do it for my sake or for my father's sake.*

salad *noun*
1 a mixture of vegetables eaten raw or cold. 2 **salad cream,** a creamy sauce like mayonnaise.

salary *noun* (**salaries**)
a regular wage, usually paid every month.

sale *noun*
1 the selling of something. 2 a time when things are sold at reduced prices. 3 **for sale** or **on sale,** that can be bought.

salesman *noun* (**salesmen**)
someone whose job is to sell things.
salesmanship *noun*

saliva *noun*
(*say* så-**ly**-vå)
the natural liquid in a person's mouth.

salmon *noun* (**salmon**)
a large edible fish with pink flesh.

saloon *noun*
1 a motor car with a hard roof. 2 a room where people can sit, drink, etc.

salt *noun*
1 the white substance that gives sea-water its taste and is used for flavouring food. 2 a small pot for salt.
salty *adjective*

salt *verb*
to use salt to flavour or preserve food.

salute *verb* (**saluted, saluting**)
1 to raise your hand to your forehead as a sign of respect or greeting. 2 to greet somebody politely.

salute *noun*
1 the act of saluting. 2 the firing of guns as a sign of respect for someone.

salvage *verb* (**salvaged, salvaging**)
to save or rescue something, especially a damaged ship, so that it can be used again.

salvage *noun*
1 the salvaging of something. 2 something salvaged.

salvation *noun*
saving someone or something.

same *adjective*
not different. *We are the same age.*

sample *noun*
a small amount that shows what something is like. *They are giving away samples of cheese.*

sample *verb* (**sampled, sampling**)
to take a sample of something; to try part of something. *She sampled the cake.*

sanctuary *noun* (**sanctuaries**)
a safe place. *a bird sanctuary.*

sand *noun*
1 the tiny grains of rock that you find on beaches and in deserts. 2 **sands,** a sandy area.

sand *verb*
to smooth or polish with sandpaper or some other rough material.
sander *noun*

sandal *noun*
a lightweight shoe with straps that go round the foot.

sandbag *noun*
a bag filled with sand, used as a defence.

sandpaper *noun*
strong paper with sand glued to it, rubbed on rough surfaces to make them smooth.

sandstone *noun*
rock made of compressed sand.

sandwich *noun* **(sandwiches)**
two slices of bread and butter with jam, meat, cheese, etc. between them.

sandy *adjective* **(sandier, sandiest)**
1 made of sand; covered with sand. 2 yellowish-red. *sandy hair.*

sane *adjective* **(saner, sanest)**
not mad; with a healthy mind.
sanely *adverb*, **sanity** *noun*

sang past tense of **sing**.

sanitary *adjective*
1 free from germs and dirt. 2 **sanitary towel**, an absorbent pad used during menstruation.

sanitation *noun*
devices or arrangements for drainage and the disposal of sewage.

sank past tense of **sink** *verb*.

sap *noun*
the liquid inside a plant.

sap *verb* **(sapped, sapping)**
to weaken somebody's strength or energy.

sapling *noun*
a young tree.

sapphire *noun*
a bright-blue jewel.

sarcastic *adjective*
saying amusing or bitter things that hurt someone's feelings.
sarcasm *noun*, **sarcastically** *adverb*

sardine *noun*
a small sea-fish, usually sold in tins.

sari *noun*
(*say* **sar**-i)
a long length of cloth worn as a dress, especially by Indian women and girls.

sash *noun* **(sashes)**
1 a strip of cloth worn round the waist or over one shoulder. 2 **sash window**, a window that slides up and down.

sat past tense and past participle of **sit**.

satchel *noun*
a bag worn over the shoulder or on the back, especially for carrying books to and from school.

satellite *noun*
a small planet, spacecraft, etc. that moves in an orbit round a planet.

satin *noun*
smooth cloth that is very shiny on one side.

satire *noun*
using humour or exaggeration to make fun of someone or something; a play, poem, etc. that does this.
satirical *adjective*, **satirist** *noun*, **satirize** *verb*

satisfaction *noun*
being satisfied; something that satisfies you.

satisfactory *adjective*
good enough; sufficient.
satisfactorily *adverb*

satisfy *verb* **(satisfied, satisfying)**
1 to give someone what he needs or wants. 2 to convince. *I am satisfied that you have done your best.*

saturate *verb* **(saturated, saturating)**
1 to soak. 2 to make something take in as much as possible of a substance.
saturation *noun*

Saturday *noun*
the seventh day of the week.

sauce *noun*
1 a thick liquid used to flavour food. 2 (*informal*) impudence; being cheeky.
saucy *adjective*

saucepan *noun*
a metal cooking-pan with a handle.

saucer *noun*
a small curved plate on which a cup is put.

sauna *noun*
(*say* **saw**-nă or **sow**-nă)
a place where you can have a bath in steam. *a sauna bath.*

saunter *verb*
to walk in a leisurely way.

sausage *noun*
1 a tube of skin or plastic stuffed with minced meat and other ingredients. 2 **sausage-meat**, minced meat of the kind used in sausages. 3 **sausage roll**, sausage-meat in a small, short roll of pastry.

savage *adjective*
wild and fierce; cruel.
savagely *adverb*, **savagery** *noun*

savage *noun*
a primitive or savage person.

savannah *noun*
(*say* să-**van**-ă)
a grassy plain in a hot country, with no trees.

save *verb* **(saved, saving)**
1 to free a person or thing from danger. 2 to keep something, especially money, so that it can be used later. 3 to stop a ball going into your goal.
saver *noun*

savings *plural noun*
1 money saved. 2 **savings certificate**, a document that you can buy at a post office to give you interest on money you save.

saviour *noun*
1 a person who saves somebody. 2 **our Saviour** or **the Saviour**, Jesus Christ.

savoury *adjective*
tasty but not sweet.

saw *noun*
a tool with sharp teeth for cutting wood, metal, etc.

saw *verb* (*past tense* **sawed**; *past participle* **sawn** or **sawed**; *present participle* **sawing**)
to cut something with a saw. *Have you sawn that plank yet? I sawed it in half yesterday.*

saw past tense of **see**.

sawdust *noun*
powder that comes from wood when it is cut with a saw.

saxophone *noun*
a musical wind instrument with a reed in the mouthpiece.

say *verb* **(said, saying)**
1 to make words with your voice. **2** to give an opinion.

saying *noun*
a well-known phrase; a proverb.

scab *noun*
1 a hard crust that forms over a cut or graze. **2** (*informal*) a blackleg.

scabbard *noun*
a cover for the blade of a sword or dagger.

scaffold *noun*
1 a platform on which criminals are executed. **2** a scaffolding.

scaffolding *noun*
a structure of poles and planks for workmen to stand on, especially when building or repairing a house; the poles used to build this structure.

scald *verb*
1 to burn yourself with very hot liquid. **2** to clean something with boiling water.

scale *noun*¹
1 a series of units, steps, or marks for measuring something. *This ruler has one scale in centimetres and another in inches.* **2** a series of musical notes going up or down in a fixed pattern. **3** proportion; ratio. *The scale of this map is one inch to the mile.* **4** the relative size or importance of something. *They were building houses on a large scale.*

scale *noun*²
one of the thin overlapping parts on the outside of fish, snakes, etc.
scaly *adjective*

scale *verb* **(scaled, scaling)**
to climb up something.

scales *plural noun*
a weighing-machine. *bathroom scales.*

scalp *noun*
the skin on top of the head.

scalp *verb*
to cut off someone's scalp.

scamper *verb*
to run quickly. *The rabbits scampered for safety.*

scampi *plural noun*
large edible prawns.

scan *verb* **(scanned, scanning)**
1 to look at every part of something. **2** to glance at something. **3** to analyse the rhythm of a line of poetry; to have a poetic rhythm. *This line doesn't scan.* **4** to sweep a radar or electronic beam over an area in search of something.
scanner *noun*

scandal *noun*
1 a disgraceful action. **2** gossip that damages someone's reputation.
scandalous *adjective*

Scandinavian *adjective*
of Scandinavia. *The Scandinavian countries are Norway, Sweden, Denmark, and Finland.*

scanty *adjective* **(scantier, scantiest)**
hardly big enough; small.
scantily *adverb*

scapegoat *noun*
someone who is blamed or punished for other people's mistakes, sins, etc.

scar *noun*
the mark left on the skin by a cut or burn after it has healed.

scar *verb* **(scarred, scarring)**
to make a scar or scars on skin.

scarce *adjective* **(scarcer, scarcest)**
1 not available in sufficient amounts; not seen or found very often. *Wheat was scarce because of the bad harvest.* **2 make yourself scarce,** to go away or keep out of the way.
scarcity *noun*

scarcely *adverb*
hardly.

scare *verb* **(scared, scaring)**
to frighten.
scary *adjective*

scarecrow *noun*
a figure of a man dressed in old clothes, set up to frighten birds away from crops.

scarf *noun* **(scarves)**
a strip of material worn round the neck or head.

scarlet *adjective*
1 bright red. **2 scarlet fever,** an infectious disease which produces a scarlet rash.

scatter *verb*
1 to throw things in various directions. **2** to move quickly in various directions.

scene *noun*
1 the place where something happens. *the scene of the crime.* **2** part of a play or film. **3** a view. **4** a place represented on the stage by scenery; scenery. **5** an angry or noisy outburst. *She made a scene about the money.*

scenery *noun*
1 the natural features of an area. *They admired the scenery.* **2** painted screens, curtains, etc. put on a stage to make it look like another place.

scent *noun*
(*say* sent)
1 a perfume. **2** an animal's smell, that other animals can use to find him.
scented *adjective*

sceptical *adjective*
(*say* **skep**-tik-ǎl)
not inclined to believe things.
sceptic *noun*, **sceptically** *adverb*, **scepticism** *noun*

schedule *noun*
(*say* **shed**-yool)
1 a list of details, things to be done, etc. **2 on schedule,** on time; punctual.

scheme *noun*
a plan or plot.

scheme *verb* **(schemed, scheming)**
to plot.
schemer *noun*

scrappy

scholar *noun*
1 someone who studies a lot or knows much.
2 someone who has a scholarship.
scholarly *adjective*

scholarship *noun*
1 money given to someone to help pay for his
education. 2 the knowledge or methods of
scholars.

school *noun*
1 a place where children are educated. 2 the
children who go to a school. *The whole school
had a holiday.* 3 the time when children are
taught at school. *School begins at 9 o'clock.*
schoolboy *noun,* **schoolchild** *noun,* **schoolgirl**
noun, **schoolmaster** *noun,* **schoolmistress**
noun, **schoolroom** *noun,* **schoolteacher** *noun*

schooner *noun*
(*say* skoo-ner)
a sailing-ship with at least two masts.

science *noun*
1 studying things and testing ideas about how
they work or are made; knowledge gained in
this way. 2 **science fiction,** stories about the
future.
scientific *noun,* **scientifically** *adverb*

scientist *noun*
an expert in science; someone who studies
science.

scissors *plural noun*
a cutting device made of two movable blades
joined together.

scoff *verb*
to make fun of somebody; to jeer.

scold *verb*
to tell somebody off angrily or noisily.

scone *noun*
(*say* skon or skohn)
a small bun, usually eaten with butter.

scoop *noun*
1 a deep spoon for serving ice-cream, mashed
potato, etc. 2 a deep shovel. 3 (*informal*) an
important piece of news published by only one
newspaper.

scoop *verb*
to lift or dig with a scoop.

scooter *noun*
1 a kind of motor cycle with a small engine and
small wheels. 2 a toy with two wheels and a
narrow platform that you ride on.

scope *noun*
1 opportunity; possibility. *Her job gives her
scope for development.* 2 the range of something. *Hockey is outside the scope of the sports
that we can do.*

scorch *verb*
1 to make something go brown by heating or
burning it. *He scorched the shirt he was ironing.* 2 (*slang*) to travel very fast. 3 **scorch-
ing,** (*informal*) very hot.

score *noun*
1 the number of points or goals made in a
game. 2 twenty. *He reached the age of four-
score.*

score *verb* (**scored, scoring**)
1 to get a goal or point in a game. 2 to keep a
count of the score in a game. 3 to scratch a
surface.
scorer *noun*

scorn *noun*
treating a person or thing as worthless or
laughable.
scornful *adjective,* **scornfully** *adverb*

scorpion *noun*
a kind of spider with a poisonous sting in its
tail.

Scot *noun*
a person from Scotland.
Scotsman *noun*

Scotch *adjective*
1 Scottish. 2 **Scotch terrier,** a small terrier with
rough hair.

Scottie *noun*
(*informal*) a Scotch terrier.

Scottish *adjective*
of Scotland.

scoundrel *noun*
a wicked person; a rascal.

scour *verb*
1 to rub something until it is clean and bright.
2 to search an area thoroughly.

scout *noun*
1 someone sent out to collect information, spy
on an enemy, etc. 2 **Scout,** a member of the
Scout Association, an organization mainly for
boys.

scowl *verb*
to look bad-tempered.

scramble *verb* (**scrambled, scrambling**)
1 to move quickly and awkwardly; to struggle.
2 to cook eggs by mixing them up and heating
them in a pan.

scramble *noun*
1 the action of scrambling. 2 a motor-cycle
race across rough country.

scrap *noun*[1]
1 a small piece of something. *a scrap of cloth.*
2 rubbish, especially unwanted metal. 3 **scrap-
book,** a book in which you stick newspaper
cuttings, souvenirs, etc.

scrap *noun*[2]
(*informal*) a fight.

scrap *verb* (**scrapped, scrapping**)
to get rid of something you do not want.

scrape *verb* (**scraped, scraping**)
1 to rub with something rough, hard, or sharp.
He was scraping the frying-pan. 2 to move
along or get past, touching or almost touching
something. *The car scraped past.* 3 to use
effort or care to get something. *They scraped
together enough money for a holiday.*
scraper *noun*

scrape *noun*
1 a scraping movement or sound. 2 a mark
made by scraping. 3 an awkward situation
caused by foolishness.

scrappy *adjective* (**scrappier, scrappiest**)
made of scraps or bits; not complete.

scratch *verb*
1 to damage a surface by rubbing something sharp over it. 2 to rub the skin with fingernails or claws because it itches.

scratch *noun* (**scratches**)
1 a mark made by scratching. 2 the action of scratching. 3 **start from scratch,** to begin at the very beginning. 4 **up to scratch,** up to the proper standard.
scratchy *adjective*

scrawl *verb*
to scribble, especially big letters or marks.

scream *noun*
1 a loud cry of pain, fear, etc. 2 (*informal*) something very amusing.

scream *verb*
to make a scream.

screech *verb*
to make a harsh, high-pitched sound. *The brakes screeched as the car turned the corner.*

screen *noun*
1 a flat surface on which films or television programmes are shown. 2 a movable wall or covered framework used to hide an object, divide a room, etc. 3 something that gives shelter or protection. *a smoke-screen.*

screen *verb*
1 to show a film or television programme. 2 to hide, divide, etc. with a screen.

screw *noun*
1 a nail with a spiral thread. 2 a twisting movement. 3 a propeller.

screw *verb*
1 to fix with screws. 2 to twist.

screwdriver *noun*
a tool for turning a screw.

scribble *verb* (**scribbled, scribbling**)
1 to write untidily or carelessly. 2 to make meaningless marks.
scribbler *noun*

script *noun*
1 the words of a play or broadcast. 2 handwriting; something handwritten.

scripture *noun*
a sacred book, especially the Bible.

scroll *noun*
a roll of paper or parchment with writing on it.

scrotum *noun*
(*say* skroh-tŭm)
the pouch of skin behind the penis, containing the testicles.

scrounge *verb* (**scrounged, scrounging**)
(*informal*) to get something without paying for it. *He scrounged a meal from us.*
scrounger *noun*

scrub *verb* (**scrubbed, scrubbing**)
1 to rub something with a hard brush. *He scrubbed the floor.* 2 (*slang*) to cancel something. *We'll have to scrub the show.*

scrub *noun*[1]
the action of scrubbing.

scrub *noun*[2]
low trees and bushes, or land covered with them.

scrum or **scrummage** *noun*
a group of players from each side in Rugby football pushing against each other and trying to heel the ball which is thrown between them.

scrutinize *verb* (**scrutinized, scrutinizing**)
to examine or look at something closely.
scrutiny *noun*

scuffle *noun*
a confused struggle or fight.

scull *noun*
a small or lightweight oar.

scullery *noun* (**sculleries**)
a small room where the washing-up is done.

sculptor *noun*
someone who makes sculptures.

sculpture *noun*
1 something carved or shaped out of stone, clay, metal, etc. 2 the art or work of a sculptor.

scum *noun*
1 froth or dirt on the top of a liquid. 2 worthless people.

scurry *verb* (**scurried, scurrying**)
to run with short steps; to hurry.

scurvy *noun*
a disease caused by lack of fresh fruit and vegetables.

scuttle *noun*
a bucket or container for coal in a house.

scuttle *verb*[1] (**scuttled, scuttling**)
to sink your own ship deliberately.

scuttle *verb*[2] (**scuttled, scuttling**)
to scurry.

scythe *noun*
a tool with a long curved blade for cutting grass or corn.

sea *noun*
1 the salt water that covers most of the earth's surface. 2 a very large area of water. *the Mediterranean Sea.* 3 a large area of something. *a sea of faces.* 4 **at sea,** on the sea; bewildered. 5 **sea anemone,** a sea creature with short tentacles round its mouth.

sea-bird *noun*
a bird that lives close to the sea.

seafaring *adjective* and *noun*
travelling or working on the sea.
seafarer *noun*

seafood *noun*
fish or shellfish from the sea eaten as food.

seagull *noun*
a sea-bird with long wings.

sea-horse *noun*
a small fish with a head rather like a horse's head.

seal *noun*[1]
a sea-animal that eats fish.

seal *noun*[2]
1 a design pressed into wax, lead, etc. 2 something designed to close an opening. 3 a small decorative sticker.

seal *verb*
to close something by sticking two parts together; to close tightly. *She sealed the envelope.*

sediment

sea-level *noun*
the level of the sea halfway between high and low tide.

sea-lion *noun*
a large kind of seal.

seam *noun*
1 the line where two edges of cloth, wood, etc. join together. 2 a layer of coal in the ground.

seaman *noun* **(seamen)**
a sailor.
seamanship *noun*

seaplane *noun*
an aeroplane that can land on water.

seaport *noun*
a port on the sea-coast.

search *verb*
1 to look very carefully for something. 2 to examine a person, place, etc. thoroughly. 3 **searching,** thorough.
searcher *noun*

search *noun* **(searches)**
1 a very careful look for somebody or something. 2 **search-party,** a group of people making a search.

searchlight *noun*
a light with a strong beam that can be turned in any direction.

sea-shore *noun*
the land close to the sea, especially the part between high and low water marks.

sea-sick *adjective*
sick because of the movement of a ship.
sea-sickness *noun*

seaside *noun*
a place, town, etc. by the sea.

season *noun*
1 one of the four main parts of the year. *The seasons are spring, summer, autumn, and winter.* 2 a period when something happens. *the football season.* 3 (*informal*) a season-ticket. 4 **season-ticket,** a ticket that can be used as often as you like throughout a period of time.
seasonal *adjective*

season *verb*
to put salt, pepper, etc. on food to flavour it.
seasoning *noun*

seat *noun*
1 something for sitting on. 2 **seat-belt,** a safety-belt.

seat *verb*
1 to have seats for a particular number of people. *The theatre seats 3,000.* 2 **seat yourself,** to sit down.

seaweed *noun*
plants that grow in the sea.

secateurs *plural noun*
(*say* sek-à-**terz**)
clippers held in the hand for pruning plants.

secluded *adjective*
isolated; not crowded. *a secluded beach.*
seclusion *noun*

second *adjective*
1 next after the first. 2 **second nature,** habitual or automatic behaviour. *Lying is second nature to him.*
secondly *adverb*

second *noun*
1 a person or thing that is second. 2 someone who helps a fighter in a boxing-match, duel, etc. 3 something that is not of the best quality. 4 a very short period of time. *60 seconds = 1 minute.*

second *verb*
1 to act as a second to a fighter. 2 to support a proposal, motion, etc.

secondary *adjective*
1 coming second; not original or essential. *of secondary importance.* 2 of or for the education of children more than about 11 years old. *a secondary school.*

second-hand *adjective* and *adverb*
1 bought or used after someone else has used it. *a second-hand car.* 2 that sells used goods. *a second-hand shop.*

secret *adjective*
1 that must not be told or shown to other people. 2 that is not known by everybody. 3 **secret agent,** a spy.
secrecy *noun,* **secretly** *adverb*

secret *noun*
1 something secret. 2 **in secret,** secretly.

secretary *noun* **(secretaries)**
(*say* **sek**-rĕ-tri)
someone whose job is to type letters, answer the telephone, and make business arrangements for a person, organization, etc.
secretarial *adjective*

secrete *verb* **(secreted, secreting)**
(*say* si-**kreet**)
1 to hide something. 2 to form a substance in the body. *Saliva is secreted in the mouth.*
secretion *noun*

secretive *adjective*
(*say* **seek**-rĭt-iv)
liking or trying to keep things secret.
secretively *adverb,* **secretiveness** *noun*

sect *noun*
a group of people who have different opinions, beliefs, etc. from the majority of people.

section *noun*
a part of something.
sectional *adjective*

sector *noun*
part of an area.

secure *adjective* **(securer, securest)**
safe; firm; tightly shut or fixed.
securely *adverb,* **security** *noun*

secure *verb* **(secured, securing)**
1 to make something secure. 2 to get hold of something. *She secured two tickets for the show.*

sedate *adjective*
(*say* si-**dayt**)
calm and dignified.
sedately *adverb*

sedative *noun*
(*say* **sed**-à-tiv)
a medicine that makes somebody calm.
sedation *noun*

sediment *noun*
solid matter that floats in liquid or sinks to the bottom of it.

sedimentary

sedimentary *adjective*
(*say* sed-i-**ment**-er-i)
formed from particles that have settled on a surface. *sedimentary rocks.*

see *verb* (*past tense* **saw**; *past participle* **seen**; *present participle* **seeing**)
1 to use your eyes to get to know things, recognize people, etc. *Have you seen my brother?* **2** to meet or visit somebody. *See me in my office.* **3** to understand. *She saw what I meant.* **4** to imagine. *Can you see yourself as a teacher?* **5** to experience. *The old man had seen five reigns.* **6** to attend to; to make sure. *See that the windows are shut.* **7** to escort; to lead. *I'll see you to the door.* **8 see through,** not to be deceived by something; to continue with something until it is finished. **9 see to,** to attend to something.

seed *noun*
a tiny part of a plant that can grow in the ground to make a new plant.

seedling *noun*
a very young plant.

seek *verb* (**sought, seeking**)
1 to try to find a person or thing. *We sought him everywhere.* **2** to try to get something. *She is seeking fame.*

seem *verb*
to give the impression of being something. *He seems clever but he is a fool.*
seemingly *adverb*

seen past participle of **see.**

seep *verb*
to ooze through or out of something.
seepage *noun*

see-saw *noun*
a plank balanced in the middle so that people can sit at each end and make it go up and down.

seethe *verb* (**seethed, seething**)
1 to boil or bubble. **2** to be very angry or excited. *She seethed with anger.*

segment *noun*
a section; a part cut off something.
segmented *adjective*

segregate *verb* (**segregated, segregating**)
(*say* **seg**-ri-gayt)
to separate people of different races, religions, etc.; to isolate.
segregation *noun*

seize *verb* (**seized, seizing**)
(*say* seez)
1 to take hold of somebody or something suddenly or eagerly. **2 seize up,** to become jammed or stuck.
seizure *noun*

seldom *adverb*
not often. *I seldom cry.*

select *verb*
to choose a person or thing.
selection *noun*, **selective** *adjective*, **selector** *noun*

select *adjective*
small and carefully chosen; exclusive. *a select group of friends.*

self *noun* (**selves**)
a person as an individual; a person's particular nature, interests, etc. *He always puts self first.*

self-centred *adjective*
selfish.

self-confidence *noun*
confidence in your own abilities.
self-confident *adjective*

self-conscious *adjective*
embarrassed or shy because you are wondering what other people are thinking of you.
self-consciously *adverb*, **self-consciousness** *noun*

self-contained *adjective*
having all the necessary facilities; not sharing rooms with other people. *a self-contained flat.*

self-control *noun*
the ability to control your own behaviour or feelings.
self-controlled *adjective*

self-defence *noun*
a way of defending yourself.

selfish *adjective*
only interested in yourself and what you want. *The selfish boy ate all the sweets.*
selfishly *adverb*, **selfishness** *noun*

self-raising *adjective*
(*of flour*) that makes cakes rise as they are cooking.

self-respect *noun*
the feeling that you are behaving, thinking, etc. in the proper way.

self-righteous *adjective*
convinced that you are better than other people; thinking too much of your own good qualities.

self-service *adjective*
where customers help themselves and pay a cashier for what they have taken. *a self-service shop.*

self-sufficient *adjective*
providing for all your own needs without help from others.
self-sufficiency *noun*

sell *verb* (**sold, selling**)
1 to give goods or property in exchange for money. *I sold my bike yesterday.* **2 sell out,** to sell all your stock of something; (*informal*) to betray somebody.

Sellotape *noun*
sticky tape that is usually transparent.

semaphore *noun*
a system of signalling with the arms, usually holding flags.

semen *noun*
(*say* **see**-men)
white liquid produced by males when they are sexually excited.

semibreve *noun*
(*say* **sem**-i-breev)
the longest musical note normally used, written o.

semicircle *noun*
half a circle.
semicircular *adjective*

semicolon *noun*
a punctuation-mark (;).

semi-detached *adjective*
joined to the side of one other house. *a semi-detached house.*

semi-final *noun*
a match played to decide who will take part in the final.
semi-finalist *noun*

semitone *noun*
half a tone in music.

semolina *noun*
a milk pudding made with grains of wheat.

Senate *noun*
(*say* **sen**-ăt)
1 the upper house of parliament in France, the United States, and some other countries. 2 the highest council in ancient Rome.
senator *noun*

send *verb* (**sent, sending**)
1 to make a person or thing go somewhere. *Have you sent her a card? I sent one last week.* 2 **send for,** to ask for somebody or something to come to you. 3 **send up,** (*informal*) to make fun of.

senior *adjective*
1 older. 2 more important.
seniority *noun*

senior *noun*
someone who is older or more important than you are.

sensation *noun*
1 a feeling. *a sensation of warmth.* 2 a very exciting event or situation. *The news caused a great sensation.*
sensational *adjective*, **sensationally** *adverb*

sense *noun*
1 the ability to see, hear, smell, touch, or taste. 2 the ability to feel or appreciate something; awareness. *a sense of humour.* 3 the power to think, make wise decisions, etc. *He hasn't got the sense to come in out of the rain.* 4 meaning. '*Reach' has several senses.* 5 **make sense,** to have a meaning; to be reasonable. 6 **senses,** sanity. *He is out of his senses.*

sense *verb* (**sensed, sensing**)
1 to feel; to be vaguely aware of something. *I sensed that she did not like me.* 2 to detect something. *This device senses radioactivity.*
sensor *noun*

senseless *adjective*
1 stupid; not sensible. 2 unconscious.

sensible *adjective*
1 wise; having or showing common sense. 2 practical, not fashionable. *sensible shoes.*
sensibly *adverb*

sensitive *adjective*
1 easily hurt or affected. *sensitive skin.* 2 easily offended. *She is very sensitive about her height.* 3 affected by light. *sensitive photographic paper.*
sensitively *adverb*, **sensitivity** *noun*, **sensitize** *verb*

sent past tense and past participle of **send.**

sentence *noun*
1 a group of words that belong together, starting with a capital letter and ending with a full stop, a question mark, or an exclamation mark. 2 the punishment announced to a criminal in a lawcourt.

sentence *verb* (**sentenced, sentencing**)
to give someone a sentence in a lawcourt. *The judge sentenced him to a year in prison.*

sentiment *noun*
1 a feeling; an emotion. 2 sentimental behaviour.

sentimental *adjective*
arousing or showing emotion, especially weak or foolish emotion. *That love-story is too sentimental.*
sentimentality *noun*, **sentimentally** *adverb*

sentinel *noun*
a sentry.

sentry *noun* (**sentries**)
1 a soldier guarding something. 2 **sentry-box,** a tall narrow hut to shelter a sentry.

separate *adjective*
(*say* **sep**-er-ăt)
not joined to anything; on its own.
separately *adverb*

separate *verb* (**separated, separating**)
(*say* **sep**-er-ayt)
1 to make or become separate; to divide. 2 to stop living together as a married couple.
separable *adjective*, **separation** *noun*

September *noun*
the ninth month of the year.

septic *adjective*
infected with germs.

sequel *noun*
(*say* **see**-kwĕl)
1 a book, film, etc. that continues the story of an earlier one. 2 something that results from an earlier event.

sequence *noun*
(*say* **see**-kwĕnss)
a series; the order in which things happen.

sequin *noun*
(*say* **see**-kwin)
one of the tiny bright discs sewn on clothes to decorate them.

serene *adjective*
calm; peaceful.
serenely *adverb*, **serenity** *noun*

sergeant *noun*
(*say* **sar**-jĕnt)
a soldier or policeman who is in charge of other soldiers or policemen.

sergeant-major *noun*
a soldier who is one rank higher than a sergeant.

serial *noun*
a story, film, etc. that is presented in separate parts.

series *noun* (**series**)
a number of things following each other or connected with each other.

serious *adjective*
1 not funny or trivial. *a serious talk.* 2 thoughtful; solemn. *His face was serious.* 3 very bad. *a serious accident.*
seriously *adverb*, **seriousness** *noun*

sermon *noun*
a talk given by a preacher.

serpent *noun*
a snake.

servant *noun*
a person whose job is to work in someone else's house.

serve *verb* **(served, serving)**
1 to work for somebody or something. 2 to sell things to people in a shop. 3 to give food to people at a meal. 4 to be suitable for some purpose. 5 (*in tennis*) to start play by hitting the ball towards your opponent. 6 **it serves you right,** you deserve it.

serve *noun*
the action of serving in tennis.

service *noun*
1 working for somebody or something. 2 something that helps people, supplies what they want, etc. *There is a good bus service.* 3 a gathering to worship God; a religious ceremony. *a church service.* 4 providing people with goods, food, etc. *quick service.* 5 a set of plates, crockery, etc. for a meal. *a dinner service.* 6 the servicing of a vehicle, machine, etc. 7 (*in tennis*) a serve. 8 **services,** the armed forces. 9 **service station,** a place beside the road where petrol is sold.

service *verb* **(serviced, servicing)**
to repair or maintain a vehicle, machine, etc.

serviette *noun*
a piece of cloth or paper used to keep your clothes or hands clean at a meal.

session *noun*
1 a time spent doing one thing. 2 a meeting.

set *verb* **(set, setting)**
1 to put or place. *Set the vase on the table.* 2 to fix or prepare. *Have you set the alarm?* 3 to become solid or hard. *The jelly has set.* 4 to go down towards the horizon. *The sun was setting.* 5 to start. *The news set me thinking.* 6 to give somebody a task, problem, etc. *Has the teacher set your homework?* 7 **set about,** to start doing something; (*informal*) to attack somebody. 8 **set off,** to begin a journey; to start something happening. 9 **set out,** to begin a journey; to display or declare something. 10 **set sail,** to start a voyage. 11 **set up,** to place in position; to establish.

set *noun*
1 a group of people or things that belong together. 2 an apparatus for receiving radio or television programmes. 3 the scenery on a stage. 4 one of the main sections of a tennis-match.

set-square *noun*
a triangular device with one of the angles a right angle, used for drawing and measuring angles.

settee *noun*
a sofa.

setting *noun*
1 the surroundings of something. 2 a set of cutlery or crockery for one person.

settle *verb* **(settled, settling)**
1 to decide or solve something. *That settles the problem.* 2 to make or become comfortable, calm, etc. *He settled down in the armchair.* 3 to

go and live somewhere. *They settled in Canada.* 4 to sink; to come to rest on something. *The dust was settling on the books.* 5 to pay a bill or debt. *She settled the bill.*
settlement *noun,* **settler** *noun*

set-up *noun*
(*informal*) the way that something is organized or arranged.

seven *noun*
the number 7, one more than six.
seventh *adjective* and *noun*

seventeen *noun*
the number 17, one more than sixteen.
seventeenth *adjective* and *noun*

seventy *noun* **(seventies)**
the number 70, seven times ten.
seventieth *adjective* and *noun*

sever *verb*
to cut or break.

several *adjective*
more than two but not a lot.

severe *adjective* **(severer, severest)**
1 strict; not gentle or kind. *Their teacher was severe.* 2 very bad; violent. *a severe cold.*
severely *adverb,* **severity** *noun*

sew *verb* (*past tense* **sewed;** *past participle* **sewn** or **sewed;** *present participle* **sewing**)
1 to use a needle and cotton to join pieces of cloth, etc. together. 2 to work with a needle and thread.

sewage *noun*
(*say* **soo**-ij)
waste matter carried away in drains.

sewer *noun*
(*say* **soo**-er)
a drain that carries sewage away.

sewing-maching *noun*
a machine for sewing things.

sex *noun* **(sexes)**
1 one of the two groups, male or female, that people and animals belong to. 2 the instinct that causes members of the two sexes to be attracted to one another. 3 sexual intercourse.

sexism *noun*
discrimination against people of a particular sex, especially against women.
sexist *noun* and *adjective*

sextet *noun*
1 a group of six musicians. 2 a piece of music for six musicians.

sexual *adjective*
1 of sex or the sexes. 2 **sexual intercourse,** the coming together of two people to make love, usually by the male putting his penis into the female's vagina.
sexuality *noun,* **sexually** *adverb*

sexy *adjective* **(sexier, sexiest)**
(*informal*) 1 attractive to people of the opposite sex. 2 concerned with sex.

shabby *adjective* **(shabbier, shabbiest)**
1 very old and worn. *shabby clothes.* 2 mean; unfair. *a shabby trick.*
shabbily *adverb,* **shabbiness** *noun*

shack *noun*
a roughly-built hut.

shade *noun*
1 an area sheltered from bright light. 2 a device that decreases or shuts out bright light. 3 a colour; how light or dark a colour is. 4 a slight difference. *This word has several shades of meaning.*

shade *verb* (**shaded, shading**)
1 to shelter something from bright light. 2 to make part of a drawing darker than the rest.

shadow *noun*
1 the dark shape that falls on a surface when something is between it and the light. 2 an area of shade.
shadowy *adjective*

shadow *verb*
1 to cast a shadow on something. 2 to follow somebody secretly.

shady *adjective* (**shadier, shadiest**)
1 that gives shade. *a shady tree.* 2 situated in the shade. *a shady spot.* 3 not completely honest. *a shady deal.*

shaft *noun*
1 a thin pole or rod. *the shaft of an arrow.* 2 a deep, narrow hole; a vertical space. *a mine shaft.* 3 a ray of light.

shaggy *adjective* (**shaggier, shaggiest**)
1 with long, untidy hair. 2 **shaggy-dog story,** a very long and usually boring story or joke.

shake *verb* (*past tense* **shook;** *past participle* **shaken;** *present participle* **shaking**)
1 to move quickly up and down or from side to side. *Have you shaken the bottle?* 2 to shock or upset. *The news shook her.* 3 to tremble. *His voice was shaking.* 4 **shake hands,** to clasp somebody's right hand when you meet or part, or as a sign that you agree.

shake *noun*
1 the action of shaking. 2 (*in America or New Zealand*) an earthquake. 3 (*informal*) a moment. *I'll be there in two shakes.*

shaky *adjective* (**shakier, shakiest**)
rickety; that shakes.
shakily *adverb,* **shakiness** *noun*

shall *verb* (*past tense* **should**)
used with other verbs to refer to the future. *We shall arrive tomorrow. We told them we should arrive the next day.*

shallow *adjective*
not deep. *shallow water.*

sham *noun*
something that is not genuine; a pretence.

shamble *verb* (**shambled, shambling**)
to walk or run in a lazy or awkward way.

shambles *noun*
a scene of great disorder or bloodshed.

shame *noun*
1 a feeling of great sorrow or guilt because you have done wrong. 2 something that you regret.
shameful *adjective,* **shamefully** *adverb,* **shameless** *adjective,* **shamelessly** *adverb*

shampoo *noun*
liquid soap for washing hair.

shamrock *noun*
a small plant rather like clover.

shandy *noun* (**shandies**)
a mixture of beer with lemonade or some other soft drink.

shan't short for *shall not.*

shanty *noun*[1] (**shanties**)
a sailor's traditional song.

shanty *noun*[2] (**shanties**)
a shack.

shape *noun*
1 the outline of something; the way that something looks. *Books are rectangular in shape.* 2 the proper form or condition of something. *Get it into shape.*
shapeless *adjective*

shape *verb* (**shaped, shaping**)
to make something into a particular shape.

shapely *adjective* (**shapelier, shapeliest**)
having an attractive shape.

share *noun*
1 one of the parts into which something is divided between several people or things. 2 one of the parts into which a company's capital is divided, paid by someone who then receives a share of the profits.

share *verb* (**shared, sharing**)
1 to divide something between several people or things. *She shared out the toffees.* 2 to use something else that someone is also using. *May I share your book?*

shark *noun*
a large sea-fish with sharp teeth.

sharp *adjective*
1 with an edge or point that can cut or make holes. *a sharp knife.* 2 quick to learn or notice things. *sharp eyes.* 3 sudden; severe. *a sharp bend in the road.* 4 slightly sour. *This stewed apple tastes sharp.* 5 above the usual musical pitch. *F sharp is a semitone above F.*
sharply *adverb,* **sharpness** *noun*

sharp *adverb*
1 sharply. *Turn sharp right.* 2 punctually; exactly. *at six o'clock sharp.*

sharp *noun*
the note above a particular musical note; the sign that indicates this.

sharpen *verb*
to make something sharper. *She sharpened her pencil.*
sharpener *noun*

shatter *verb*
1 to break suddenly into tiny pieces. 2 to destroy. *Our hopes were shattered.* 3 to make somebody very weak or upset. *We were shattered by the news.*

shave *verb* (**shaved, shaving**)
1 to cut hair from the surface of the skin with a razor. 2 to cut or scrape a thin slice off something.
shaver *noun*

shave *noun*
1 the act of shaving the face. 2 **close shave,** (*informal*) a narrow escape.

shavings *plural noun*
thin strips shaved off a piece of wood.

shawl *noun*
a piece of cloth or knitted material worn round the shoulders or head, or wrapped round a baby.

she *pronoun*
the female person or animal being talked about.

sheaf *noun* **(sheaves)**
a bundle of corn stalks tied together after reaping.

shear *verb* (*past tense* **sheared;** *past participle* **shorn** or **sheared;** *present participle* **shearing**)
1 to cut the wool off a sheep. 2 **shear off,** to break off.
shearer *noun*

shears *plural noun*
a tool like a very large pair of scissors for trimming bushes, shearing sheep, etc.

sheath *noun*
1 a scabbard 2 a cover that fits something closely.

sheathe *verb* **(sheathed, sheathing)**
1 to put a sword into its sheath. 2 to put a protective covering on something.

shed *noun* ·
a simply-made building used for storing things, sheltering animals, etc.; a hut.

shed *verb* **(shed, shedding)**
to let something fall or flow. *The caterpillar has shed its skin. We shed tears.*

sheen *noun*
a shine on a surface.

sheep *noun* **(sheep)**
a timid animal kept by farmers for its wool and meat. *They had twenty sheep.*

sheep-dog *noun*
a dog trained to guard and herd sheep.

sheepish *adjective*
shy; embarrassed.
sheepishly *adverb*

sheer *adjective*
1 complete; thorough. *sheer stupidity.* 2 perpendicular; vertical. *a sheer drop.* 3 very thin; transparent. *sheer stockings.*

sheer *verb*
to move sharply away from somebody or something.

sheet *noun*
1 a large piece of lightweight cloth put on a bed. 2 a whole flat piece of paper, glass, or metal. 3 a wide area of water, snow, flame, etc.

shelf *noun* **(shelves)**
1 a board fixed to a wall or fitted in a piece of furniture so that books, ornaments, etc. may be put on it. 2 a flat, level surface that sticks out like a shelf.

shell *noun*
1 the hard cover round or over a nut, egg, snail, tortoise, etc. 2 a very large bullet. 3 the walls or framework of a building, ship, etc.

shell *verb*
1 to take something out of its shell. 2 to fire very large bullets at something. 3 **shell out,** (*slang*) to pay money for something.

shellfish *noun* **(shellfish)**
a sea-animal that has a shell.

shelter *noun*
1 a place that protects people from rain, wind, danger, etc. 2 protection.

shelter *verb*
1 to protect or cover. *The hill shelters the house from the wind.* 2 to find a shelter. *They sheltered under the trees.*

shelve *verb* **(shelved, shelving)**
1 to put something on a shelf or shelves. 2 to reject or postpone a plan, etc. 3 to slope.

shepherd *noun*
1 someone whose job is to look after sheep. 2 **shepherd's pie,** cottage pie.

sherbet *noun*
a fizzy sweet powder or drink.

sheriff *noun*
1 (*in Britain*) the chief officer in a county or district. 2 (*in America*) the chief officer who enforces the law in a county.

sherry *noun* **(sherries)**
a kind of strong wine.

shield *noun*
1 a large piece of metal, wood, etc. used to protect the body. *Soldiers used to hold shields in front of them when they were fighting.* 2 a protection.

shield *verb*
to protect. *I was shielded from the wind.*

shift *noun*
1 a change of position, condition, etc. 2 a group of workers who start work as another group finishes; the time when they work. *the nightshift.* 3 a woman's dress that hangs straight down from the shoulders.

shift *verb*
1 to move or change. 2 to manage to do something; to make a living. *Shift for yourself.*

shilling *noun*
a British coin that used to be worth a twentieth of a pound.

shimmer *verb*
to shine with a quivering light. *The sea shimmered in the sunlight.*

shin *noun*
the front of the leg between the knee and the ankle.

shine *verb* (**shone** or in 'polish' sense **shined, shining**)
1 to give out or reflect light; to be bright. 2 to polish. *Have you shined your shoes?* 3 to be excellent. *He does not shine in maths.*

shine *noun*
brightness; polish
shiny *adjective*

shingle *noun*
pebbles on a beach.

ship *noun*
a large boat, especially one that goes to sea.

ship *verb* **(shipped, shipping)**
to send something on a ship.

shipping *noun*
ships. *Britain's shipping.*

shipwreck *noun*
the wrecking of a ship.
shipwrecked *adjective*

shipyard *noun*
a dockyard.

shire *noun*
1 a county. **2 shire-horse,** a large, heavy kind
of horse.

shirk *verb*
to avoid doing something that you ought to do.

shirt *noun*
1 a garment worn on the top half of the body.
*Most shirts have sleeves, a collar, and buttons
down the front.* **2 in your shirt-sleeves,** not
wearing a jacket over your shirt.

shiver *verb*
to tremble with cold or fear.
shivery *adjective*

shoal *noun*[1]
a large number of fish swimming together.

shoal *noun*[2]
a shallow place.

shock *noun*
1 a sudden unpleasant surprise. 2 a violent
knock or jolt. 3 an effect caused by electric
current passing through the body.

shock *verb*
1 to give someone a shock. 2 to fill someone
with disgust or outrage.

shoddy *adjective* **(shoddier, shoddiest)**
of poor quality. *shoddy work.*

shoe *noun*
1 a strong covering for the foot. 2 a horseshoe.
3 in somebody's shoes, in his situation. **4 on a
shoe-string,** with only a small amount of
money.
shoelace *noun,* **shoemaker** *noun*

shone past tense and past participle of **shine**
verb.

shook past tense of **shake** *verb.*

shoot *verb* **(shot, shooting)**
1 to fire a gun, missile, etc. 2 to hurt or kill by
shooting. *He has shot many lions.* 3 to move or
send very quickly. *The car shot past.* 4 to kick
or hit a ball at a goal. 5 to film or photograph
something. *The film was shot in Africa.* **6 shooting star,** a meteor.

shoot *noun*
a young branch or growth of a plant.

shop *noun*
1 a building where people buy things. 2 a workshop. **3 shop steward,** a trade-union official
who represents his fellow-workers.

shop *verb* **(shopped, shopping)**
to go and buy things at shops.
shopper *noun*

shopkeeper *noun*
someone who owns or looks after a shop.

shoplifter *noun*
someone who steals from shops.
shoplifting *noun*

shopping *noun*
1 buying things at shops. *I like shopping.*
2 what somebody has bought. *Will you carry
my shopping, please?*

shore *noun*
1 the sea-shore. 2 the land along the edge of a
lake, etc.

shorn past tense of **shear.**

short *adjective*
1 not long; occupying a small distance or time.
a short walk. 2 not tall. *a short person.* 3 not
sufficient; scarce. *Water is short.* 4 bad-
tempered. *He was rather short with me.* 5 rich
and crumbly; containing a lot of fat. *short
pastry.* **6 for short,** as a shorter form of something. *Raymond is called Ray for short.* **7 short
circuit,** a fault in an electrical circuit when
current flows along a shorter route than the
normal one. **8 short cut,** a route or method that
is quicker than the usual one. **9 short for,** a
shorter form of something. *Ray is short for
Raymond.* **10 short wave,** a radio wave with a
wavelength between 10 and 100 metres.
shortish *adjective,* **shortness** *noun*

short *adverb*
suddenly. *She stopped short.*

shortage *noun*
the situation when something is scarce or insufficient.

shortbread *noun*
a rich, sweet kind of biscuit.

shortcake *noun*
1 shortbread. 2 a light cake usually served
with fruit.

shortcoming *noun*
a fault or failure. *He has many shortcomings.*

shorten *verb*
to make or become shorter.

shorthand *noun*
1 a set of special signs for writing words down
as quickly as people say them. **2 shorthand-
typist,** someone who can write shorthand and
also do typing.

shortly *adverb*
1 soon. 2 briefly.

shorts *plural noun*
trousers with legs that do not go below the
knee.

short-sighted *adjective*
unable to see distant things clearly.

shot *noun*
1 the firing of a gun. 2 something fired from a
gun. 3 lead pellets fired from small guns. 4 a
person judged by his skill in shooting. *He is a
good shot.* 5 a heavy metal ball thrown as a
sport. 6 a stroke in tennis, cricket, etc. 7 a
photograph or filmed sequence. 8 an attempt.
Have a shot at this crossword.

shot past tense and past participle of **shoot** *verb.*

should *verb*
to have a duty or wish to; ought to. *You should
come. I should like to come.*

shoulder *noun*
1 the part of the body between the neck and the arm. 2 **shoulder-blade,** one of the two large flat bones near the top of your back.

shoulder *verb*
1 to put or rest something on your shoulder or shoulders. 2 to accept responsibility or blame.

shout *verb*
to speak or call very loudly.

shout *noun*
a shouting cry or call.

shove *verb* **(shoved, shoving)**
1 to push hard. 2 **shove off,** (*informal*) to go away.

shovel *noun*
a curved spade for lifting and moving coal, earth, sand, snow, etc.

shovel *verb* **(shovelled, shovelling)**
to move or clear with a shovel.

show *noun*
1 a display or exhibition. *a flower show.* 2 an entertainment. 3 (*informal*) something that happens or is done. *Good show!*

show *verb* (*past tense* **showed;** *past participle* **shown;** *present participle* **showing**)
1 to let something be seen. *She showed me her new bike.* 2 to make something clear to somebody. *He has shown me how to do it.* 3 to guide or lead somebody. *Show him in.* 4 to be visible. *That scratch won't show.* 5 **show off,** to try to impress people.

shower *noun*
1 a brief fall of rain or snow. 2 a lot of small things coming or falling like rain. *a shower of stones.* 3 a device to spray water on a person; a bath or wash using this device.
showery *adjective.*

shower *verb*
1 to fall or send in a shower. 2 to wash under a shower.

show-jumping *noun*
a competition in which riders make horses jump over fences and other obstacles.
show-jumper *noun*

showman *noun* **(showmen)**
someone who presents entertainments; someone who is good at attracting attention.
showmanship *noun*

showy *adjective* **(showier, showiest)**
likely to attract attention; bright or highly decorated.
showily *adverb,* **showiness** *noun*

shrank past tense of **shrink.**

shrapnel *noun*
pieces of metal scattered from an exploding shell.

shred *noun*
a tiny strip or piece torn or cut off something.

shred *verb* **(shredded, shredding)**
to tear or cut something into shreds.
shredder *noun*

shrew *noun*
1 a small animal rather like a mouse. 2 a bad-tempered woman.

shrewd *adjective*
having common sense and good judgement.
shrewdly *adverb,* **shrewdness** *noun*

shriek *noun*
a shrill scream.

shrill *adjective*
sounding very high and piercing.
shrillness *noun,* **shrilly** *adverb*

shrimp *noun*
a small shellfish.

shrine *noun*
a sacred place.

shrink *verb* (*past tense* **shrank;** *past participle* **shrunk;** *present participle* **shrinking**)
1 to become smaller. *This dress has shrunk.* 2 to make something smaller, usually by soaking it. *Their jeans have been shrunk.* 3 to move back or avoid something because of fear, embarrassment, etc. *He shrank from meeting strangers.*
shrinkage *noun*

shrivel *verb* **(shrivelled, shrivelling)**
to make or become wrinkled and dry.

shroud *noun*
1 a sheet in which a corpse is wrapped. 2 one of the ropes that supports a ship's mast.

shroud *verb*
1 to wrap in a shroud. 2 to cover or conceal.

Shrove Tuesday *noun*
the day before Ash Wednesday. *People often eat pancakes on Shrove Tuesday.*

shrub *noun*
a bush.

shrubbery *noun* **(shrubberies)**
an area full of shrubs.

shrug *verb* **(shrugged, shrugging)**
to raise your shoulders slightly as a sign that you do not care, do not know, etc.

shrunk past participle of **shrink.**

shrunken *adjective*
that has shrunk. *a shrunken head.*

shudder *verb*
to shake because you are cold or frightened.

shuffle *verb* **(shuffled, shuffling)**
1 to drag your feet along the ground as you walk. 2 to mix up playing-cards before you deal them.

shunt *verb*
to move a railway train or wagons from one line to another.
shunter *noun*

shut *verb* **(shut, shutting)**
1 to move a door, lid, cover, etc. in order to block up an opening; to close something. *She shut the door and drove off.* 2 to become closed. *The door shut suddenly.* 3 **shut down,** to stop work or business. 4 **shut up,** to shut securely; (*informal*) to stop talking.

shutter *noun*
1 a cover or screen that can be closed over a window. 2 the device in a camera that opens and closes to let light fall on the film.

shy *adjective*
afraid to meet or talk to other people; timid.
shyly *adverb,* **shyness** *noun*

Siamese *adjective*
1 of Siam (now called Thailand). **2 Siamese cat,** a cat with blue eyes and short fur. **3 Siamese twins,** twins whose bodies are joined together.

sick *adjective*
1 ill. **2** vomiting or likely to vomit. *I feel sick.* **3 sick of,** tired of; fed up with.
sickness *noun*

sicken *verb*
1 to start feeling ill. **2** to disgust; to annoy somebody very much.

sickly *adjective* **(sicklier, sickliest)**
1 unhealthy; looking weak or pale. *a sickly child.* **2** that makes you feel sick. *a sickly taste.*

side *noun*
1 a flat surface. *A cube has six sides.* **2** an edge; the area near an edge. *A triangle has three sides.* **3** the outer part of something that is not the front or the back. *Paint the side of the shed.* **4** a group of people playing, arguing, or fighting against another group. *She is on my side.*

sideboard *noun*
a long, heavy piece of furniture with drawers and cupboards, and a flat top where things can be put.

side-car *noun*
a small vehicle attached to the side of a motor cycle.

sideline *noun*
something that you do in addition to your normal work or activity.

side-show *noun*
an entertainment forming part of a large show, especially at a fair.

sideways *adverb* and *adjective*
1 to or from the side. *Crabs walk sideways.* **2** with one side facing forward. *We sat sideways in the bus.*

siding *noun*
a short length of railway line leading off the main line.

siege *noun*
(*say* seej)
the action of besieging a place or being besieged.

sieve *noun*
(*say* siv)
a device made of perforated metal, plastic, etc., used to separate the smaller parts of a substance from the larger parts.

sift *verb*
1 to put something through a sieve. **2** to examine or select facts, evidence, etc.

sigh *noun*
a sound made by breathing out heavily when you are sad, tired, relieved, etc.

sigh *verb*
to make a sigh.

sight *noun*
1 the ability to see. *She is losing her sight.* **2** something that you see. *I laughed at the sight of him in that hat.* **3** something worth seeing. *See the sights of Paris.* **4** a device that helps you to aim a gun. **5 at sight** or **on sight,** as soon as you see someone or something.

sight *verb*
to see or observe something.

sightseer *noun*
someone who goes round looking at interesting places; a tourist.
sightseeing *noun*

sign *noun*
1 a board, notice, etc. that tells or shows people something. *a road sign.* **2** something that conveys a meaning, significance, etc. *There are signs of rust.* **3** a gesture or signal. *She made a sign to them to be quiet.*

sign *verb*
1 to write your signature on something. **2** to make a sign or signal. **3** to employ somebody; to be employed.

signal *noun*
a device, gesture, sound, etc. that tells people something. *a railway signal.*

signal *verb* **(signalled, signalling)**
to make a signal to somebody.
signaller *noun*

signal-box *noun* **(signal-boxes)**
a building from which railway signals are controlled.

signalman *noun* **(signalmen)**
a man who controls railway signals.

signature *noun*
1 your name written by yourself. **2 signature tune,** a special tune used to introduce a particular programme, performer, etc.

significance *noun*
importance; what something means or implies.
significant *adjective,* **significantly** *adverb*

signify *verb* **(signified, signifying)**
to mean; to have significance.

signpost *noun*
a sign at a road junction showing the names and distances of the places that are down each road.

Sikh *noun*
(*say* seek)
someone who believes in Sikhism, one of the religions of India.

silence *noun*
absence of sound or talk; lack of noise.

silence *verb* **(silenced, silencing)**
to make a person or thing silent.

silencer *noun*
a device to make an engine or gun quieter.

silent *adjective*
without any sound; not talking.
silently *adverb*

silhouette *noun*
(*say* sil-oo-et)
a dark outline seen against a light background.

silicon *noun*
1 an element found in many rocks. **2 silicon chip,** a tiny electronic component made of a small piece of silicon.

silk *noun*
1 fine thread made by silkworms. **2** smooth, shiny cloth made from this thread.
silken *adjective,* **silky** *adjective*

silkworm *noun*
a kind of caterpillar that spins itself a cocoon.

sill *noun*
a ledge underneath a window or door.

silly *adjective* **(sillier, silliest)**
stupid.
silliness *noun*

silver *noun*
1 a precious shiny white metal. **2** coins made of silver or silver-coloured metal. **3** the colour of silver. **4 silver birch**, a birch with silvery bark. **5 silver medal**, a medal made of silver, awarded as the second prize. **6 silver wedding**, the 25th anniversary of a wedding.
silvery *adjective*

similar *adjective*
of the same kind; nearly the same as another person or thing. *Your dress is similar to mine.*
similarity *noun*, **similarly** *adverb*

simile *noun*
(*say* **sim**-i-li)
saying that one thing is like another. *'He is as brave as a lion' is a simile.*

simmer *verb*
1 to boil very gently. **2 simmer down**, to calm down.

simple *adjective* **(simpler, simplest)**
1 easy. *a simple question.* **2** not complicated. *a simple sentence.* **3** plain. *a simple dress.* **4** stupid. *I'm not so simple.*
simplicity *noun*

simplify *verb* **(simplified, simplifying)**
to make something simple or easy to understand.
simplification *noun*

simply *adverb*
1 in a simple way. *She dresses simply.* **2** completely. *She looks simply lovely.* **3** only; merely. *It is simply a question of money.*

simulate *verb* **(simulated, simulating)**
1 to reproduce the conditions for something. *a simulated flight.* **2** to pretend.
simulation *noun*, **simulator** *noun*

simultaneous *adjective*
(*say* sim-ŭl-**tay**-ni-ŭs)
happening at the same time.
simultaneously *adverb*

sin *noun*
the breaking of a religious or moral law; a very bad action.

sin *verb* **(sinned, sinning)**
to commit a sin.
sinner *noun*

since *conjunction*
1 from the time when. *Where have you been since I last saw you?* **2** because; as. *Since you have been naughty, you must stay indoors.*

since *preposition*
from the time when. *I have been here since Christmas.*

since *adverb*
from that time; before now. *He has not been seen since.*

sincere *adjective* **(sincerer, sincerest)**
truly felt or meant; genuine. *sincere good wishes.*
sincerely *adverb*, **sincerity** *noun*

sinew *noun*
1 strong tissue that joins a muscle to a bone. **2 sinews**, strength; muscles.
sinewy *adjective*

sinful *adjective*
wicked; very bad.
sinfully *adverb*, **sinfulness** *noun*

sing *verb* **(past tense sang; past participle sung; present participle singing)**
1 to make music with your voice. **2** to make a humming or whistling sound.
singer *noun*

singe *verb* **(singed, singeing)**
(*say* sinj)
to burn something slightly; to burn the edge of something.

single *adjective*
1 only one; separate. **2** designed for one person. *a single bed.* **3** not married. **4** for the journey to a place but not back again. *a single ticket.* **5 single file**, a line of people one behind the other.
singly *adverb*

single *noun*
1 a single person or thing. **2** a single ticket. **3** a record played at 45 revolutions per minute, usually with one tune on each side. **4 singles**, a game with one player on each side.

single *verb* **(singled, singling)**
single out, to pick out or distinguish from other people or things.

singular *noun*
the form of a word that refers to only one person or thing. *The singular of 'children' is 'child'.*

singular *adjective*
1 of the singular; referring to only one. **2** extraordinary. *a woman of singular courage.*
singularly *adverb*

sinister *adjective*
that looks or seems evil; wicked.

sink *noun*
a large basin with taps where you do the washing-up.

sink *verb* **(past tense sank or sunk; past participle sunk; present participle sinking)**
1 to go under water. *The liner has sunk.* **2** to make something go under water. *They sank the ship.* **3** to go or fall down. *He sank to his knees.* **4 sink in**, to penetrate; to become understood.

sinus *noun* **(sinuses)**
(*say* **sy**-nŭs)
a hollow in the bones of the skull, connected with the nose. *My sinuses are blocked.*

sip *verb* **(sipped, sipping)**
to drink a very small amount at a time.

sir *noun*
1 a word sometimes used when speaking or writing politely to a man. *Please may I leave, sir?* **2 Sir**, the title given to a knight. *Sir Francis Bacon.*

siren *noun*
a device that makes a loud hooting or screaming sound, usually to warn people about something.

sister *noun*
1 a woman or girl who has the same parents as another person. 2 a senior nurse in a hospital.
sisterly *adjective*

sit *verb* (**sat, sitting**)
1 to rest on your buttocks, as you do when you are on a chair. 2 to seat; to put somebody in a sitting position. 3 to be a candidate for an examination, etc. 4 to be situated; to stay. 5 to act as a baby-sitter.
sitter *noun*

site *noun*
1 the place where something has been built or will be built. *a building site.* 2 the place where something happens or happened. *a camping site.*

sit-in *noun*
a protest in which people stay in a building.

sitting-room *noun*
a room with comfortable chairs for sitting in.

situated *adjective*
in a particular place or situation. *The town is situated in a valley.*

situation *noun*
1 a place or position; where something is. 2 the conditions affecting a person or thing. 3 a job; employment.

six *noun* (**sixes**)
the number 6, one more than five.
sixth *adjective* and *noun*

sixpence *noun*
a British coin that used to be worth half a shilling.
sixpenny *adjective*

sixteen *noun*
the number 16, one more than fifteen.
sixteenth *adjective* and *noun*

sixty *noun* (**sixties**)
the number 60, six times ten.
sixtieth *adjective* and *noun*

size *noun*
1 how big a person or thing is. 2 the measurement something is made in. *a size eight shoe.*

size *verb* (**sized, sizing**)
1 to sort things according to their size. 2 **size up,** (*informal*) to form an opinion or judgement about something.

sizeable *adjective*
large; fairly large.

sizzle *verb* (**sizzled, sizzling**)
to make a crackling and hissing sound. *The sausages sizzled in the frying-pan.*

skate *noun*[1]
1 a boot with a steel blade attached to the sole, used for sliding smoothly over ice. 2 a roller-skate.

skate *noun*[2] (**skate**)
a large, flat, edible fish.

skate *verb* (**skated, skating**)
to move with skates on your feet.
skater *noun*

skateboard *noun*
a small board with wheels, on which you balance with both feet while it moves quickly over the ground.

skeleton *noun*
the framework of bones that is or was inside a person's or animal's body.
skeletal *adjective*

sketch *noun* (**sketches**)
1 a quick or rough drawing. 2 a short amusing play.

sketch *verb*
to draw a sketch.

skewer *noun*
a pointed piece of metal or wood, used to hold meat together for cooking or used as a tent-peg.

ski *noun*
(*say* skee)
a long piece of wood, plastic, etc. fastened to the foot for moving quickly over snow.

ski *verb* (**skied** or **ski'd, skiing**)
(*say* skee)
to move on skis.
skier *noun*

skid *verb* (**skidded, skidding**)
to slide accidentally.

skilful *adjective*
clever; having or needing skill.
skilfully *adverb*

skill *noun*
the ability to do something very well.
skilled *adjective*

skim *verb* (**skimmed, skimming**)
1 to move quickly over a surface. 2 to remove something from the surface of a liquid, especially to take the cream off milk.

skin *noun*
1 the outer covering of a person's or animal's body. 2 the outer covering of a fruit or vegetable. 3 a film that has formed on the surface of a liquid.

skin *verb* (**skinned, skinning**)
to take the skin off something.

skin-diver *noun*
someone who swims under water without a diving-suit.
skin-diving *noun*

skinny *adjective* (**skinnier, skinniest**)
very thin.

skip *verb* (**skipped, skipping**)
1 to jump or move along by hopping from one foot to the other. 2 to jump over a skipping-rope. 3 to miss out something; to ignore.

skipper *noun*
the captain of a ship, team, etc.

skipping-rope *noun*
a piece of rope, usually with a handle at each end, that is turned over your head and under your feet as you jump.

skirt *noun*
a woman's or girl's garment that hangs down from the waist.

skirt *verb*
to go round the edge of something.

skirting or **skirting-board** *noun*
a board round the bottom of the wall of a room.

skit *noun*
a parody. *He wrote a skit on 'Hamlet'.*

skittle *noun*
a piece of wood or plastic shaped like a bottle, that people try to knock down with a ball.

skull *noun*
the framework of bones in a person's head.

skunk *noun*
a black, furry, American animal that can make an unpleasant smell.

sky *noun* **(skies)**
the area above our heads when we are out of doors; the space containing the sun, moon, and stars.

skylark *noun*
a small brown bird that sings as it hovers high in the air.

skylight *noun*
a window in a roof.

skyscraper *noun*
a very tall building.

slab *noun*
1 a thick, flat piece of something. 2 (*in Australia and New Zealand*) a roughly-cut plank.

slack *adjective*
1 not pulled tight. *The rope was slack.* 2 lazy; not busy or working hard.
slackly *adverb*, **slackness** *noun*

slacken *verb*
1 to make or become slack. 2 to make or become slower. *Their speed slackened.*

slacks *plural noun*
trousers for informal occasions.

slag-heap *noun*
a heap of waste material from a coal-mine, etc.

slain past participle of **slay**.

slam *verb* **(slammed, slamming)**
1 to shut something loudly. 2 to hit violently.

slang *noun*
a kind of language used in everyday speech but not in formal writing or speaking.
slangy *adjective*

slant *verb*
1 to slope; to lean. 2 to present news, information, etc. from a particular point of view.

slap *noun*
a hit with the palm of the hand or with something flat.

slap *verb* **(slapped, slapping)**
1 to give someone a slap. 2 to put forcefully or carelessly. *We slapped paint on the walls.*

slapstick *noun*
boisterous comedy, with people hitting each other, falling over, etc.

slash *verb*
to make large cuts in something.

slat *noun*
a thin strip of wood, plastic, etc.

slate *noun*
1 a kind of grey rock that is easily split into flat plates. 2 a piece of this rock used as part of a roof.
slaty *adjective*

slaughter *verb*
1 to kill an animal for food. 2 to kill many people or animals.
slaughter *noun*

slaughterhouse *noun*
a place where animals are killed for food.

slave *noun*
a person who has to work for someone else without being paid.
slavery *noun*

slave *verb* **(slaved, slaving)**
to work very hard.

slay *verb* (*past tense* **slew**; *past participle* **slain**; *present participle* **slaying**)
(*old-fashioned or poetical use*) to kill.

sled or **sledge** *noun*
a vehicle for travelling over snow, running on strips of metal or wood instead of wheels.

sledge-hammer *noun*
a very large, heavy hammer.

sleek *adjective*
smooth and shiny. *sleek hair.*

sleep *noun*
1 the condition in which the eyes are closed, the body is relaxed, and the mind is unconscious. *You need some sleep.* 2 a time when you are in this condition. *Have a sleep.*
sleepless *adjective*

sleep *verb* **(slept, sleeping)**
to have a sleep.

sleeper *noun*
1 someone who is asleep. 2 one of the wooden or concrete beams on which a railway-line rests. 3 a sleeping-car.

sleeping-bag *noun*
a warm padded bag for sleeping in, especially when you are camping.

sleeping-car *noun*
a railway carriage fitted with beds or berths where passengers can sleep.

sleep-walker *noun*
someone who walks around while he is asleep.
sleep-walking *noun*

sleepy *adjective* **(sleepier, sleepiest)**
feeling like sleeping; wanting to sleep.
sleepily *adverb*, **sleepiness** *noun*

sleet *noun*
a mixture of rain and snow or hail.

sleeve *noun*
1 the part of a garment that covers the arm. 2 the cardboard cover for a gramophone record.
sleeveless *adjective*

sleigh *noun*
(*say* slay)
a sledge, especially a large one pulled by horses.

slender *adjective*
slim.

slept past tense and past participle of **sleep** *verb*.

slew past tense of **slay**.

slice *noun*
a thin piece cut off something.

slice *verb* **(sliced, slicing)**
to cut something into slices.

slick *adjective*
quick and clever or cunning.

slick *noun*
a large patch of oil floating on water.

slide *verb* **(slid, sliding)**
1 to move smoothly over a surface. 2 to move quickly or secretly. *The thief slid behind the curtains.*

slide *noun*
1 a sliding movement. 2 a smooth slope or a slippery surface where children can slide for fun. 3 a photograph that can be projected on a screen. 4 a small glass plate on which things are examined under a microscope. 5 a device for keeping your hair tidy.

slight *adjective*
very small; not serious or important.
slightly *adverb*

slim *adjective* **(slimmer, slimmest)**
1 thin and graceful. 2 small; scanty. *a slim chance.*

slim *verb* **(slimmed, slimming)**
to try to make yourself thinner.
slimmer *noun*

slime *noun*
unpleasant, wet, slippery stuff. *There was slime on the pond.*
slimy *adjective*

sling *verb* **(slung, slinging)**
1 to throw something, especially violently or carelessly. *They slung stones at us.* 2 to hang something up; to support something so that it hangs loosely. *He had slung the bag round his neck.*

sling *noun*
1 a piece of cloth tied round the neck to support an injured arm. 2 a device for throwing stones.

slink *verb* **(slunk, slinking)**
to move in a stealthy or guilty way. *He slunk off to bed.*

slip *verb* **(slipped, slipping)**
1 to slide without meaning to; to fall over. 2 to move quickly and quietly. 3 to escape. 4 **slipped disc,** part of the spine that causes pain because it is out of place. 5 **slip up,** to make a mistake.

slip *noun*
1 an accidental slide or fall. 2 a mistake. 3 a small piece of paper. 4 a petticoat. 5 a pillowcase.

slipper *noun*
a soft, comfortable shoe to wear indoors.

slippery *adjective*
smooth, wet, etc. so that it is difficult to stand on, hold, etc.

slit *noun*
a long cut or narrow opening in something.

slit *verb* **(slit, slitting)**
to make a slit in something.

slither *verb*
to slide; to slip as you move along.

sliver *noun*
a thin strip of wood, glass, etc.

slog *verb* **(slogged, slogging)**
1 to hit hard or wildly. 2 to work hard; to walk with effort.

slogan *noun*
a phrase used to advertise something or to sum up the aims of an organization, campaign, etc. *Their slogan was 'Ban the bomb!'*

slop *verb* **(slopped, slopping)**
to spill liquid over the edge of a container.

slope *verb* **(sloped, sloping)**
to go gradually downwards or upwards; not to be horizontal or vertical.

slope *noun*
1 a sloping surface. 2 the amount that something slopes.

sloppy *adjective* **(sloppier, sloppiest)**
1 careless. *sloppy work.* 2 runny. *This porridge is sloppy.* 3 sentimental. *a sloppy story.*
sloppily *adverb*, **sloppiness** *noun*

slosh *verb*
1 to splash or slop; to pour liquid carelessly. 2 (*slang*) to hit hard.

slot *noun*
a narrow opening to put things in.

sloth *noun*
(rhymes with *both*)
1 laziness. 2 a long-haired South American animal that lives in trees and moves slowly.

slot-machine *noun*
a machine worked by putting a coin in a slot.

slouch *verb*
to move, stand, or sit in a lazy way, especially with your head and shoulders bent forwards.

slovenly *adjective*
(*say* **sluv-ĕn-li**)
careless; untidy.

slow *adjective*
1 not quick; taking more time than usual. 2 showing a time earlier than the correct time. *That clock is slow.*
slowly *adverb*, **slowness** *noun*

slow *verb*
to go slower.

sludge *noun*
thick sticky mud, oil, etc.

slug *noun*
1 a small animal like a snail without its shell. 2 a pellet for firing from a gun.

slum *noun*
an area of old, dirty, crowded houses.

slumber *noun*
sleep.

slump *verb*
to fall heavily or suddenly.

slump *noun*
a sudden fall in prices, trade, etc.

slung past tense and past participle of **sling** *verb.*

slunk past tense and past participle of **slink.**

slush *noun*
snow that is melting.
slushy *adjective*

sly *adjective*
cunning; mischievous.
slyly *adverb,* **slyness** *noun*

smack *verb*
to slap someone, especially as a punishment.

smack *noun*
a slap, especially as a punishment.

small *adjective*
not big; less than the normal size.

smallpox *noun*
a contagious disease that produces spots on
the skin.

smart *adjective*
1 neat; dressed well. **2** clever. **3** fast. *She ran at
a smart pace.*
smarten *verb,* **smartly** *adverb,* **smartness** *noun*

smart *verb*
to feel a stinging pain.

smash *verb*
1 to break into pieces noisily and violently; to
crash. **2** to hit or move with great force.

smash *noun* **(smashes)**
1 the act or sound of smashing; a collision.
2 smash-and-grab, describing a robbery done
by smashing a window and taking something.
3 smash hit, *(informal)* something extremely
successful or popular.

smashing *adjective*
(informal) excellent.

smear *verb*
1 to rub something dirty or greasy on a surface.
2 to try to damage somebody's reputation.
smear *noun*

smell *verb* **(smelt, smelling)**
1 to use your nose to recognize or find out
about something. *I bent down and smelt the
rose.* **2** to give out a smell. *This cheese smells.*

smell *noun*
1 something that you can smell, especially
something unpleasant. **2** the ability to smell
things. *the sense of smell.*
smelly *adjective*

smelt *verb*
to melt ore so as to get metal from it.
smelter *noun*

smile *noun*
a pleased or amused expression on your face.

smile *verb* **(smiled, smiling)**
to give a smile.

smith *noun*
someone who makes things out of metal. *a
silversmith.*

smithereens *plural noun*
small fragments. *Smash it to smithereens.*

smock *noun*
a loose garment like a very long shirt.

smog *noun*
a mixture of smoke and fog.

smoke *noun*
1 the grey or blue gas that rises from a fire. **2** a
period of smoking tobacco. *He wants a smoke.*
smokeless *adjective,* **smoky** *adjective*

smoke *verb* **(smoked, smoking)**
1 to give out smoke. *The fire is smoking.* **2** to
have a lighted cigarette, cigar, or pipe between
your lips and breathe its smoke in and out.
smoker *noun*

smooth *adjective*
1 having a surface without any lumps, marks,
roughness, etc. **2** moving without bumps or
jolts. **3** not harsh; flowing easily.
smoothly *adverb,* **smoothness** *noun*

smooth *verb*
to make something smooth.

smother *verb*
1 to suffocate somebody. **2** to cover something
thickly. *a cake smothered in icing.* **3** to put out
a fire by covering it.

smoulder *verb*
to burn slowly without a flame.

smudge *noun*
a dirty mark made by rubbing something.

smuggle *verb* **(smuggled, smuggling)**
to bring something into a country secretly and
illegally.
smuggler *noun*

smut *noun*
1 a small piece of soot or dirt. **2** obscene things.
smutty *adjective*

snack *noun*
a small meal.

snag *noun*
an unexpected difficulty; an obstacle.

snail *noun*
a small soft animal with a shell. *Snails move
very slowly.*

snake *noun*
a long reptile without legs. *Some snakes give
poisonous bites.*
snaky *adjective*

snap *verb* **(snapped, snapping)**
1 to break suddenly with a sharp noise. **2** to
bite suddenly or quickly. **3** to say something
quickly and angrily. **4** to move or do something
quickly. **5** to take a snapshot of something.

snap *noun*
1 the act or sound of snapping. **2** a snapshot.
3 a card-game in which players shout 'Snap!'
when they see two similar cards.

snapshot *noun*
a photograph taken with a simple camera.

snare *noun*
a trap for catching animals.

snarl *verb*¹
to growl; to make an angry sound.

snarl *verb*²
to make or become tangled or jammed. *The
traffic was snarled up.*

snatch *verb*
to grab. *He snatched the bag from me.*

sneak *verb*
1 to move quietly and secretly. 2 (*informal*) to tell somebody that someone else has misbehaved.

sneak *noun*
(*informal*) a person who reports someone else's misbehaviour.
sneakily *adverb*, **sneaky** *adjective*

sneer *verb*
to speak or behave in a scornful way.

sneeze *verb* (**sneezed, sneezing**)
1 to push air through your nose suddenly and uncontrollably. *She often sneezed because of her cold.* 2 **not to be sneezed at**, (*informal*) valuable; important.

sneeze *noun*
the action or sound of sneezing.

sniff *verb*
1 to make a noise by drawing air in through your nose. 2 to smell something.

sniff *noun*
the action or sound of sniffing.

snigger *verb*
to laugh quietly or secretively.

snip *verb* (**snipped, snipping**)
to cut a small piece or pieces off something.

snipe *verb* (**sniped, sniping**)
to shoot at people from a hiding place.
sniper *noun*

snivel *verb* (**snivelled, snivelling**)
to cry or complain in a whining way.

snob *noun*
someone who despises people who have not got wealth, power, or particular tastes or interests.
snobbery *noun*, **snobbish** *adjective*

snooker *noun*
a game played with cues and 21 balls on a special cloth-covered table.

snoop *verb*
to pry into someone else's business.
snooper *noun*

snore *verb* (**snored, snoring**)
to breathe very noisily while sleeping.

snorkel *noun*
a tube that supplies air to someone swimming under water.

snort *verb*
to make a loud noise by forcing air out of your nose.

snout *noun*
an animal's projecting nose, or nose and jaws. *The pig raised its snout.*

snow *noun*
frozen drops of water falling from the sky as small white flakes.
snowflake *noun*

snow *verb*
it is snowing, snow is falling.

snowball *noun*
snow pressed into the shape of a ball for throwing at somebody.

snowdrop *noun*
a small white flower that comes up in winter.

snowman *noun* (**snowmen**)
a figure made of snow.

snow-plough *noun*
a vehicle or device for clearing snow from a road, railway, etc.

snow-shoe *noun*
a device attached to the foot to help you walk on deep snow without sinking in.

snowstorm *noun*
a storm with snow falling.

snowy *adjective* (**snowier, snowiest**)
1 with snow falling. *snowy weather.* 2 covered with snow. *snowy roofs.* 3 brilliantly white. *snowy sheets.*

snub *verb* (**snubbed, snubbing**)
to treat somebody in a scornful or unfriendly way.

snub-nosed *adjective*
with a short, thick nose.

snuff *noun*
powdered tobacco that you take into your nose by sniffing.

snug *adjective* (**snugger, snuggest**)
cosy.
snugly *adverb*

snuggle *verb* (**snuggled, snuggling**)
to curl up in a warm, comfortable place. *She snuggled down in bed.*

so *adverb*
1 in this or that way; in such a way; to such an extent. *Why are you so cross?* 2 very. *Cricket is so boring.* 3 also. *I was wrong but so were you.* 4 **and so on**, et cetera. 5 **or so**, or about that number. 6 **so as to**, in such a way as to; for the purpose of. 7 **so far**, up to now. 8 **so far, so good**, everything has gone well up to now. 9 **so long!**, (*informal*) goodbye. 10 **so what?**, (*informal*) what does that matter?; I don't care.

so *conjunction*
therefore; for that reason. *They threw me out, so I came here.*

soak *verb*
1 to make somebody or something very wet. 2 **soak up**, to take in a liquid in the way that a sponge does.

so-and-so *noun* (**so-and-so's**)
(*informal*) 1 a person or thing that need not be named. *Old so-and-so told me.* 2 an unpleasant person. *He's a real so-and-so.*

soap *noun*
a substance used with water for washing and cleaning things.
soapy *adjective*

soar *verb*
1 to rise or fly high in the air. 2 to rise very high. *Prices were soaring.*

sob *verb* (**sobbed, sobbing**)
to make gasping noises as you cry.

sober *adjective*
1 not intoxicated. 2 calm and serious. *a sober expression.* 3 not bright or gaudy. *sober colours.*
soberly *adverb*, **sobriety** *noun*

so-called *adjective*
named in what may be the wrong way. *This so-called gentleman slammed the door.*

soccer *noun*
(*informal*) Association football.

sociable *adjective*
(*say* **soh**-shă-bŭl)
liking to be with other people; friendly.
sociability *noun*, **sociably** *adverb*

social *adjective*
(*say* **soh**-shăl)
1 living in a community. 2 of or connected with
society. *social science.* 3 helping the people in a
community. *social worker.* 4 helping people to
meet one another. *a social club.*
socially *adverb*

socialist *noun*
someone who believes that wealth should be
equally shared and that the main industries
and resources should be controlled by the
government.
socialism *noun*, **socialist** *adjective*

society *noun* (**societies**)
1 a community; people living together in a
group or nation. 2 a group of people organized
for a particular purpose. *a philatelic society.*
3 company; companionship. *We enjoy the society of our friends.* 4 people of the higher
classes and their way of life. *That is how things
are done in society.*

sociology *noun*
(*say* soh-si-**ol**-ŏ-ji)
the study of society or societies.
sociological *adjective*, **sociologist** *noun*

sock *noun*
1 a small, soft garment that covers the foot and
the lower half of the leg. 2 **pull your socks up,**
(*informal*) to try to do better.

sock *verb*
(*informal*) to hit forcefully; to punch. *He socked
me on the jaw.*

socket *noun*
a device or hole into which something fits,
especially the place where an electric plug or
bulb is put to make a connection.

soda *noun*
1 a compound of sodium used in cleaning
(*washing-soda*), cooking (*baking-soda*), etc.
2 soda-water. 3 **soda-water,** fizzy water used in
drinks.

sodium *noun*
(*say* **soh**-di-ŭm)
a soft, silvery-white, metallic element.

sofa *noun*
a long soft seat with sides and a back.

soft *adjective*
1 not hard or firm; easily pressed or cut into a
new shape. 2 smooth; not rough or stiff.
3 gentle; not loud. 4 **soft drink,** a drink that is
not alcoholic.
softly *adverb*, **softness** *noun*

soften *verb*
to make or become softer.
softener *noun*

software *noun*
written or printed material, especially for use
with a computer.

soggy *adjective* (**soggier, soggiest**)
very wet and heavy.

soil *noun*
the earth that plants grow in.

soil *verb*
to make something dirty; to stain.

solar *adjective*
1 of or from the sun. *solar heating.* 2 **solar
system,** the sun and the planets that revolve
round it.

sold past tense and past participle of **sell.**

solder *noun*
a soft alloy that is melted to join pieces of metal
together.
solder *verb*

soldier *noun*
a member of an army.

sole *noun*
1 the bottom part of a shoe or foot. 2 an edible
flat fish.

sole *adjective*
single; only. *She was the sole survivor.*
solely *adverb*

solemn *adjective*
serious; dignified. *a solemn face.*
solemnity *noun*, **solemnly** *adverb*

solicitor *noun*
a kind of lawyer who advises clients, prepares
legal documents, etc.

solid *adjective*
1 not hollow; with no space inside. 2 that keeps
its shape; not a liquid or gas.
solidity *noun*, **solidly** *adverb*

solid *noun*
a solid thing.

solidify *verb* (**solidified, solidifying**)
to make or become solid.

soliloquy *noun*
(*say* sŏl-**il**-ŏ-kwi)
a speech in which an actor speaks his thoughts
aloud when he is alone.

solitary *adjective*
1 alone; on your own. *He lived a solitary life.*
2 single. *A solitary bird sang.*

solitude *noun*
being on your own.

solo *noun*
something sung, played, danced, or done by
one person. *She sang a solo.*
soloist *noun*

soluble *adjective*
1 that can be dissolved. 2 that can be solved.
solubility *noun*

solution *noun*
1 the answer to a problem or puzzle. 2 something dissolved in a liquid.

solve *verb* (**solved, solving**)
to find the answer to a problem or puzzle.

sombre *adjective*
gloomy; dark.

some *adjective*
1 a few. *some sweets.* 2 a certain amount of.
some cake. 3 a; an unknown. *Some fool left a
toffee on this chair!*

south

some *pronoun*
a certain or unknown number or amount. *Some of them were late.*

somebody *pronoun*
someone.

somehow *adverb*
in some way. *We must find money somehow.*

someone *pronoun*
a person.

somersault *noun*
(*say* **sum**-er-solt)
a jump in which you turn head over heels before landing on your feet.

something *pronoun*
a certain or unknown thing.

sometime *adverb*
at some time. *I saw her sometime last year.*

sometimes *adverb*
at some times. *Sometimes we walk to school.*

somewhat *adverb*
to some extent; to a certain amount. *He was somewhat annoyed.*

somewhere *adverb*
in or to some place.

son *noun*
a boy or man who is someone's child.

song *noun*
1 a tune for singing. **2** singing. *the song of the birds.* **3 a song and dance,** (*informal*) a great fuss. **4 song-bird,** a bird that sings sweetly.

sonic *adjective*
1 of sound or sound-waves. **2 sonic boom,** a bang caused by an aircraft flying at supersonic speed.

sonnet *noun*
a kind of poem with 14 lines.

soon *adverb*
1 in a short time from now. **2** not long after. **3** early; quickly. *You spoke too soon.* **4** willingly. *I'd just as soon stay at home.* **5 sooner or later,** at some time in the future.

soot *noun*
the black powder left by smoke in a chimney, on a building, etc.
sooty *adjective*

soothe *verb* (**soothed, soothing**)
1 to make somebody calm. **2** to ease a pain, ache, etc.

sophisticated *adjective*
(*say* sôf-**ist**-i-kay-tid)
1 not simple or innocent; cultured; civilized. *sophisticated people.* **2** complicated. *a sophisticated machine.*
sophistication *noun*

sopping *adjective*
very wet; soaked.

soppy *adjective* (**soppier, soppiest**)
(*informal*) sentimental; silly.

soprano *noun*
(*say* sô-**prah**-noh)
a woman or boy with a high singing-voice.

sorcerer *noun*
a wizard.
sorceress *noun,* **sorcery** *noun*

sore *adjective* (**sorer, sorest**)
1 painful; smarting. **2** annoyed.
sorely *adverb,* **soreness** *noun*

sore *noun*
a sore place on the body.

sorrow *noun*
sadness; regret
sorrowful *adjective,* **sorrowfully** *adverb*

sorry *adjective* (**sorrier, sorriest**)
feeling sorrow or pity.

sort *noun*
1 a group of things or people that are similar; a kind. *What sort of fruit do you like?* **2 sort of,** (*informal*) rather; to some extent. *I sort of expected a present.*

sort *verb*
to arrange things into groups, kinds, etc. *I must sort these books into piles.*

SOS *noun*
an urgent appeal for help. *The sinking ship sent out an SOS.*

sought past tense and past participle of **seek.**

soul *noun*
the invisible part of a person that is believed to go on living after he dies.

sound *noun*
1 something that can be heard. **2 sound-barrier,** the resistance of the air to objects moving at nearly supersonic speeds. **3 sound-effect,** a sound made artificially for use in a play, film, broadcast, etc.

sound *verb*[1]
1 to make a sound. **2** to give an impression when heard. *He sounds angry.*

sound *verb*[2]
1 to test the depth of water beneath a ship. **2 sound out,** to try to find out what somebody thinks or feels.

sound *adjective*
1 not damaged; in good condition. **2** healthy. **3** reasonable; correct. *His ideas are sound.* **4** reliable; secure. *a sound investment.* **5** thorough; deep. *a sound sleep.*
soundly *adverb,* **soundness** *noun*

sound-track *noun*
the sound that goes with a cinema film.

soup *noun*
a liquid food made from vegetables, meat, etc.

sour *adjective*
having a sharp taste like vinegar or lemons.
sourly *adverb,* **sourness** *noun*

source *noun*
the place where something comes from.

south *noun*
the direction to the right of a person facing east.

south *adjective*
1 coming from the south. **2** situated in the south.
southerly *adjective,* **southern** *adjective,* **southerner** *noun*

south *adverb*
towards the south.
southward *adjective* and *adverb,* **southwards** *adverb*

souvenir *noun*
(*say* soo-věn-**eer**)
something that you keep because it reminds you of a person, place, or event.

sou'wester *noun*
a waterproof hat with a wide flap at the back.

sovereign *noun*
1 a king or a queen. 2 an old British gold coin that used to be worth £1.

Soviet *adjective*
(*say* **soh**-vi-ět or **sov**-i-ět)
of Russia.

sow *verb* (*past tense* **sowed**; *past participle* **sown** or **sowed**; *present participle* **sowing**)
(rhymes with *go*)
to put seeds into the ground so that they will grow into plants. *Have you sown those beans? I sowed them yesterday.*
sower *noun*

sow *noun*
(rhymes with *cow*)
a female pig.

soya bean *noun*
a kind of bean from which edible oil and flour are made.

space *noun*
1 the whole area outside the earth, where the stars and planets are. 2 the distance between things. 3 an empty area; a gap. 4 a period of time.

space *verb* (**spaced, spacing**)
to arrange things with spaces between them.

spacecraft *noun* (**spacecraft**)
a vehicle for travelling in space.

spaceman *noun* (**spacemen**)
an astronaut.

spaceship *noun*
a spacecraft.

spacious *adjective*
roomy.
spaciously *adverb*, **spaciousness** *noun*

spade *noun*
1 a tool with a long handle and a wide blade for digging. 2 a playing-card with a black shape like an inverted heart printed on it.

spaghetti *noun*
(*say* spă-**get**-i)
a kind of thin macaroni. *Spaghetti looks like long pieces of string when it is cooked.*

span *noun*
1 the length from one end of something to the other, especially the distance between the tips of your thumb and little finger when your hand is spread out. 2 a part of a bridge between supports. 3 a period of time.

span *verb* (**spanned, spanning**)
to reach from one side or end of something to the other. *A bridge spanned the river.*

span past tense of **spin.**

Spaniard *noun*
a Spanish person.

spaniel *noun*
a kind of dog with long ears and silky fur.

Spanish *adjective*
of Spain.

spank *verb*
to smack somebody on the bottom as a punishment.

spanner *noun*
a tool for tightening or loosening a nut.

spar *noun*
a strong pole.

spar *verb* (**sparred, sparring**)
to practise boxing. *He was my sparring partner.*

spare *verb* (**spared, sparing**)
1 to afford; to give somebody something. *Can you spare a penny?* 2 to be merciful towards somebody; not to harm a person or thing. *Spare my feelings.* 3 to use or treat economically. *No expense will be spared.*

spare *adjective*
1 not used but kept ready in case it is needed; extra. *a spare tyre.* 2 thin; lean. 3 **go spare**, (*slang*) to get very annoyed; to go mad. 4 **spare time,** time not needed for work or other important purposes.

spare *noun*
a spare thing or part. *This garage sells spares.*

spark *noun*
1 a tiny flash. 2 a glowing speck of something hot.

sparking-plug *noun*
a device that makes a spark to ignite the fuel in an engine.

sparkle *verb* (**sparkled, sparkling**)
to shine with a lot of tiny flashes of bright light.

sparkler *noun*
a firework that sparkles.

spark-plug *noun*
a sparking-plug.

sparrow *noun*
a small brown bird. *You often see sparrows in the garden.*

sparse *adjective* (**sparser, sparsest**)
not crowded or numerous. *a sparse population.*
sparsely *adverb*, **sparseness** *noun*

spastic *noun*
someone who has a disability that makes it difficult for him to control his body.

spat past tense and past participle of **spit** *verb*.

spatter *verb*
to splash; to scatter in small drops.

spawn *noun*
the eggs of frogs, fish, and other water-animals.

speak *verb* (*past tense* **spoke;** *past participle* **spoken;** *present participle* **speaking**)
1 to say something. *Have you spoken to him? I spoke to him this morning.* 2 to be able to talk in a particular language. *Do you speak German?* 3 **speak up**, to speak more clearly or loudly.

speaker *noun*
1 a person who is speaking; someone who makes a speech. 2 a loudspeaker. 3 **the Speaker,** the person who presides over the House of Commons or similar assemblies.

spinach

spear *noun*
a long pole with a sharp point, used as a weapon.

special *adjective*
1 different from other people or things; unusual. 2 for a particular person or purpose.

specialist *noun*
an expert in a particular subject.

speciality *noun* **(specialities)**
something special that you do or have; something that you specialize in.

specialize *verb* **(specialized, specializing)**
to give particular attention to one subject or thing. *She is specializing in biology.*
specialization *noun*

specially *adverb*
especially. *I came specially to see you.*

species *noun* **(species)**
(*say* **spee**-shiz)
a group of animals or plants that are very similar. *Men and women belong to the same species.*

specific *adjective*
1 definite; precise; referring to a particular thing. 2 **specific gravity,** the weight of something compared with the same volume of water or air.
specifically *adverb*

specify *verb* **(specified, specifying)**
to name or list things precisely. *The contract specified brick walls, not wooden partitions.*
specification *noun*

specimen *noun*
1 a small amount of something that shows what the rest is like. *This painting is a specimen of her work.* 2 an example of one kind of plant, animal, or thing. *a fine specimen of an oak.*

speck *noun*
1 a tiny piece of something. 2 a tiny mark or spot.

speckled *adjective*
covered with small spots.

spectacle *noun*
1 an impressive or exciting sight or display. 2 something that you see, especially something ridiculous. 3 **spectacles,** a pair of lenses in a frame to help somebody see.

spectacular *adjective*
impressive to see.

spectator *noun*
a person who watches a game, show, incident, etc.

spectre *noun*
(*say* **spek**-ter)
a ghost.

spectrum *noun* **(spectra)**
1 the bands of colours like those you see in a rainbow. 2 a wide range of things, ideas, etc.

speech *noun* **(speeches)**
1 the action or power of speaking. 2 a talk given to a group of people.

speechless *adjective*
unable to speak.

speed *noun*
1 quickness; swiftness. 2 the rate at which something moves. 3 **at speed,** quickly.
speedily *adverb*, **speedy** *adjective*

speed *verb* **(sped** or **speeded, speeding)**
1 to go very fast or too fast. 2 **speed up,** to make or become quicker.

speedboat *noun*
a fast motor-boat.

speedometer *noun*
(*say* spee-**dom**-it-er)
a device that measures a vehicle's speed.

speedway *noun*
1 motor-cycle racing. 2 a track for motor-cycle racing.

spell *verb* **(spelt** or **spelled, spelling)**
to put letters in the right order to make a word or name. *How is your name spelt?*

spell *noun*[1]
1 a period of time. *a cold spell.* 2 a period when something is done or happens. *a spell of work.* 3 (*in Australia and New Zealand*) a period of rest from work.

spell *noun*[2]
a saying that is supposed to have magic power.

spend *verb* **(spent, spending)**
1 to use money to pay for things. 2 to pass time. *He spent a year in prison.* 3 to use up. *She spends all her energy on gardening.*

sperm *noun* **(sperms** or **sperm)**
1 the male cell that fuses with an ovum to produce offspring. 2 semen. 3 **sperm whale,** a large whale from which a waxy oil is obtained.

sphere *noun*
a globe; the shape of a ball.
spherical *adjective*

spice *noun*
a substance used to flavour food. *Spices are usually dried parts of plants like pepper and ginger.*
spicy *adjective*

spider *noun*
a small animal with eight legs that sometimes spins webs to catch insects.

spied past tense and past participle of **spy** *verb.*

spike *noun*
a pointed piece of metal; a sharp point.
spiky *adjective*

spill *verb* **(spilt** or **spilled, spilling)**
1 to let something fall out of a container. *You have spilt the milk.* 2 to fall out of a container. *The coins came spilling out.*

spill *noun*
a thin strip of wood or rolled paper used to light a fire, cigarette, etc.

spin *verb* (*past tense* **spun** or **span;** *past participle* **spun;** *present participle* **spinning**)
1 to turn round and round quickly. 2 to make pieces of wool, cotton, etc. into thread by twisting them. 3 to make a web or cocoon out of threads. *The spider spun a web.*

spinach *noun*
a dark-green vegetable.

spin-drier *noun*
a machine in which clothes are dried by spinning them round and round.

spindle *noun*
1 a thin rod on which you wind thread. 2 a pin or bar that turns round, like an axle.

spine *noun*
1 the line of bones down the middle of the back. 2 a thorn or prickle. 3 the back part of a book where the pages are joined together.
spinal *adjective*, **spiny** *adjective*

spinning-wheel *noun*
a machine for spinning thread out of wool, cotton, etc.

spin-off *noun*
something useful produced when something else is developed or done. *This chemical was a spin-off from space research.*

spinster *noun*
a woman who has not married.

spiral *adjective*
that goes round and round like the shape of a spring, the thread of a screw, or the jam in a Swiss roll.

spire *noun*
a tall, pointed part on top of a church tower.

spirit *noun*
1 the soul. 2 a ghost; a supernatural being. 3 courage; liveliness. 4 how someone feels or thinks. *She was in good spirits.* 5 an alcoholic liquid; a strong alcoholic drink.

spiritual *adjective*
of the human soul; religious.
spiritually *adverb*

spiritual *noun*
a religious song of the North American Negroes.

spiritualism *noun*
the belief that the spirits of dead people can communicate with living people.
spiritualist *noun*

spit *verb* (**spat, spitting**)
to send drops of liquid forcibly out of your mouth. *He spat into the basin.*

spit *noun*
1 a long, thin spike put through meat to hold it while it is roasted. 2 a narrow strip of land sticking out into the sea.

spite *noun*
1 a desire to hurt or annoy somebody. 2 **in spite of,** although something has happened or is happening. *They went out in spite of the rain.*
spiteful *adjective*

splash *verb*
1 to make liquid fly about, as you do when you jump into water. 2 to fly about in drops. 3 to make somebody wet by splashing. *The bus splashed us as it went past.*

splash *noun* (**splashes**)
1 the action or sound of splashing. 2 a striking display or effect.

splash-down *noun*
the landing of a spacecraft in the sea.

splendid *adjective*
magnificent; very satisfying.
splendidly *adverb*, **splendour** *noun*

splint *noun*
a straight piece of wood, metal, etc. that is tied to a broken arm or leg to hold it firm.

splinter *noun*
a small, sharp piece of wood, glass, etc. broken off a larger piece.

split *verb* (**split, splitting**)
1 to cut or break into parts; to divide. 2 (*slang*) to reveal a secret. 3 **split up,** to divide or separate.

split *noun*
1 the splitting or dividing of something; a place where something has split. 2 **the splits,** a movement where you stretch out your legs in opposite directions along the floor, at right angles to the top of your body.

splutter *verb*
to make a quick series of spitting sounds; to speak quickly but not clearly.

spoil *verb* (**spoilt** or **spoiled, spoiling**)
1 to make something less useful, pleasant, good, etc. *The rain spoilt our holiday.* 2 to make somebody selfish by always letting him have or do what he wants. *Don't spoil your child.*

spoke *noun*
one of the rods or bars that go from the centre of a wheel to the rim.

spoke past tense of **speak.**

spoken past participle of **speak.**

spokesman *noun* (**spokesmen**)
someone who speaks on behalf of a group of people.

sponge *noun*
1 a lump of soft material containing lots of tiny holes, used in washing. 2 a sea creature with a soft, porous body. 3 a soft, lightweight cake or pudding.
spongy *adjective*

sponge *verb* (**sponged, sponging**)
1 to wash something with a sponge. 2 (*informal*) to get money or help from someone without intending to return it. *He was sponging on his relatives.*
sponger *noun*

sponsor *noun*
someone who provides money, help, etc. for a person or thing, especially someone who gives money to a charity in return for something done by another person.
sponsorship *noun*

spontaneous *adjective*
(say spon-**tay**-ni-ŭs)
happening or done naturally; not forced. *A spontaneous cheer greeted the local team.*
spontaneity *noun*, **spontaneously** *adverb*

spool *noun*
a round device on which cotton, string, film, etc. is wound.

spoon *noun*
a metal or wooden device consisting of a tiny bowl with a handle, used for lifting food to your mouth or for stirring or measuring.
spoonful *noun*

squalid

sport *noun*
1 a game that exercises the body, especially a game played out of doors. *Football, netball, swimming, and tennis are all sports.* 2 games of this sort. *Are you keen on sport?* 3 (*informal*) someone who plays or behaves fairly and unselfishly. *Come on, be a sport.* 4 **sports car,** a low, fast motor car, usually with two seats. 5 **sports coat** or **sports jacket,** a man's jacket that is not part of a suit.

sporting *adjective*
1 connected with sport; interested in sport. 2 behaving fairly and unselfishly. 3 **a sporting chance,** a reasonable chance.

sportsman *noun* **(sportsmen)**
a sporting man.
sportsmanship *noun,* **sportswoman** *noun*

spot *noun*
1 a small mark that is usually round. 2 a pimple. 3 a small amount of something. 4 a place. 5 **on the spot,** immediately; in a difficult situation.
spotless *adjective,* **spotty** *adjective*

spot *verb* **(spotted, spotting)**
1 to mark with spots. 2 to notice; to watch for.
spotter *noun*

spotlight *noun*
a strong light that can shine on one small area.

spout *noun*
1 a pipe or mouth from which liquid can pour. 2 a jet of liquid.

spout *verb*
1 to come or send out in a jet of liquid. 2 (*informal*) to speak for a long time or in a pompous way.

sprain *verb*
to injure an ankle, wrist, etc. by twisting it.

sprang past tense of **spring** *verb*.

sprawl *verb*
1 to sit or lie with your arms and legs spread out. 2 to spread out loosely or untidily.

spray *verb*
to scatter tiny drops of liquid all over something.

spray *noun*[1]
1 tiny drops of liquid scattered on something. 2 a device for spraying liquid.

spray *noun*[2]
a small bunch of flowers.

spread *verb* **(spread, spreading)**
1 to lay or stretch something out to its full size. *The seagull spread its wings.* 2 to make something cover a surface. *He spread jam on his toast.* 3 to make or become widely known, felt, distributed, etc. *Spread the news.*

spread *noun*
1 the action or result of spreading. 2 the breadth or extent of something. 3 (*informal*) a huge meal.

sprightly *adjective* **(sprightlier, sprightliest)**
lively; energetic.

spring *verb* (*past tense* **sprang;** *past participle* **sprung;** *present participle* **springing**)
1 to move upwards suddenly. 2 to arise. *The trouble has sprung from carelessness.* 3 to start suddenly; to make something happen without warning. *They sprang a surprise on us.*

spring *noun*
1 a springy coil of metal. *This mattress contains springs.* 2 a springing movement. 3 a place where water rises out of the ground. 4 the season of the year when most plants start to grow.

springboard *noun*
a springy board from which people jump or dive.

spring-clean *verb*
to clean a house thoroughly in springtime.

springtime *noun*
the season of spring. *Daffodils bloom in springtime.*

springy *adjective* **(springier, springiest)**
that can bend and spring back.

sprinkle *verb* **(sprinkled, sprinkling)**
to make tiny drops or pieces fall on something.
sprinkler *noun*

sprint *verb*
to run very fast for a short distance.
sprinter *noun*

sprout *verb*
to start to grow; to produce leaves.

sprout *noun*
a Brussels sprout.

spruce *noun*
a kind of fir-tree.

spruce *adjective* **(sprucer, sprucest)**
neat; smart.

sprung past participle of **spring** *verb*.

spud *noun*
(*informal*) a potato.

spun past tense and past participle of **spin.**

spur *noun*
1 a sharp device worn on the heel of a rider's boot to urge a horse to go faster. 2 **on the spur of the moment,** without planning.

spur *verb* **(spurred, spurring)**
to urge on; to encourage.

spurt *verb*
1 to gush out or up. *Blood spurted from the cut.* 2 to speed up suddenly. *He spurted to catch the leader.*

spy *noun* **(spies)**
someone who works secretly to find out things about another country, person, etc.

spy *verb* **(spied, spying)**
1 to be a spy; to watch secretly. *He was spying on us.* 2 to see; to notice. *She spied a house in the distance.*

squabble *verb* **(squabbled, squabbling)**
to quarrel about something unimportant.

squad *noun*
a small group of people working or being trained together.

squadron *noun*
part of an air force, army, or navy.

squalid *adjective*
dirty and unpleasant. *squalid houses.*
squalidly *adverb,* **squalor** *noun*

squall *noun*
a sudden strong wind.
squally *adjective*

squander *verb*
to waste money, time, etc.

square *adjective* **(squarer, squarest)**
1 with four straight equal sides and four right angles; forming a right angle; having right angles. *a square piece of paper.* 2 of or using units that describe the size of an area. *A square metre is the size of a square with each side one metre long.* 3 equal; even; settled. 4 honest; fair. 5 **square meal,** a good, satisfying meal. 6 **square root,** the number that gives a particular number if it is multiplied by itself. *The square root of 64 is 8.*
squarely *adverb*, **squareness** *noun*

square *noun*
1 a square shape or object. 2 an area surrounded by buildings. *Leicester Square.* 3 the result of multiplying a number by itself. *9 is the square of 3.*

square *verb* **(squared, squaring)**
1 to make something square. 2 to multiply a number by itself. *5 squared is 25.* 3 to match; to be consistent. *His story doesn't square with yours.* 4 (*informal*) to bribe somebody.

squash *verb*
to press something so that it loses its shape; to crush.

squash *noun* **(squashes)**
1 a crowd; a crowded situation. 2 a fruit-flavoured drink. 3 a game played with rackets and a small ball in a special indoor court.

squat *verb* **(squatted, squatting)**
1 to sit on your heels. 2 to live in an unoccupied house without permission.
squatter *noun*

squat *adjective*
short and fat. *a squat man.*

squaw *noun*
an American Indian woman or wife.

squawk *verb*
to make a loud, harsh cry.

squeak *noun*
a tiny, shrill sound such as a mouse makes.
squeakily *adverb*, **squeaky** *adjective*

squeal *noun*
a long, shrill sound.

squeeze *verb* **(squeezed, squeezing)**
1 to press something from opposite sides, especially so as to get liquid out of it. 2 to force into or through a place, gap, etc. *We squeezed into the car.*
squeezer *noun*

squeeze *noun*
1 the action of squeezing. 2 a hug. 3 a time when money is difficult to get, borrow, etc.

squid *noun*
a sea-animal with eight short arms and two very long ones.

squint *verb*
1 to be cross eyed. 2 to peer; to look with half-shut eyes at something.

squire *noun*
the man who owns most of the land in a country district.

squirm *verb*
to wriggle; to twist your body about.

squirrel *noun*
a small animal that lives in trees. *Squirrels have very thick tails.*

squirt *verb*
to send or come out in a violent jet of liquid. *The grapefruit juice squirted in his eye.*

St. short for *Saint* or *Street.*

stab *verb* **(stabbed, stabbing)**
to pierce or wound with something sharp. *She stabbed him with a knife.*

stabilize *verb* **(stabilized, stabilizing)**
to make or become stable. *Prices have stabilized.*

stable *adjective* **(stabler, stablest)**
steady; firmly fixed.
stability *noun*, **stably** *adverb*

stable *noun*
a building where horses are kept.

stack *noun*
1 a neat pile. 2 a haystack. 3 a large amount of something.

stack *verb*
to pile things up.

stadium *noun*
a sports ground surrounded by seats for spectators.

staff *noun*
1 the people who work in an office, shop, etc. 2 the teachers in a school, college, etc. 3 a thick stick for walking with.

stag *noun*
a male deer.

stage *noun*
1 a platform for performances in a theatre or hall. 2 the point that someone or something has reached.

stage *verb* **(staged, staging)**
1 to present a performance on a stage. 2 to organize. *They staged a show for charity.*

stage-coach *noun* **(stage-coaches)**
a horse-drawn coach of a kind that used to travel regularly along the same route.

stagger *verb*
1 to walk unsteadily. 2 to amaze or confuse somebody. *I was staggered at the price.*

stagnant *adjective*
not flowing or fresh. *a stagnant pond.*

stain *noun*
a dirty mark on something, often caused by liquid.

stain *verb*
1 to make a stain on something. 2 to colour something. *stained glass.*

stainless *adjective*
1 without stains. 2 **stainless steel,** steel that does not rust easily.

startle

stair *noun*
a flat place to put your foot when walking up or down to a different level inside a building.

staircase *noun*
a series of stairs.

stake *noun*
1 a thick pointed stick to be driven into the ground. **2** the thick post to which people used to be tied to execute them by burning. **3** an amount of money bet on something.

stalactite *noun*
a stony spike hanging from the roof of a cave. *Stalactites look like icicles.*

stalagmite *noun*
a stony spike rising from the floor of a cave.

stale *adjective* **(staler, stalest)**
not fresh; musty. *stale bread.*

stalk *noun*
1 the main part of a plant above the ground. **2** a thin branch that holds a leaf, fruit, or flower.

stalk *verb*
1 to hunt stealthily. **2** to walk in a stiff or dignified way.

stall *noun*
1 a table or small open-fronted shop where things are sold, usually in the open air. **2** a place for one animal in a stable or shed. **3** one of the seats on the ground floor of a theatre or cinema.

stall *verb*
to stop suddenly. *The car engine stalled.*

stallion *noun*
a male horse.

stamen *noun*
(*say* **stay**-měn)
the part of a flower that bears pollen.

stamina *noun*
(*say* **stam**-in-ă)
the ability to endure; vigour.

stammer *verb*
to keep repeating the sounds at the beginning of words when you speak.

stamp *noun*
1 a postage stamp. **2** the act of stamping. **3** a small device for printing words or marks on something; the words or marks printed with this.

stamp *verb*
1 to bang your foot heavily on the ground. **2** to put a stamp on something. **3 stamped addressed envelope,** an envelope with an unused stamp and your own address on it.

stampede *noun*
a sudden rush by animals or people.

stand *verb* **(stood, standing)**
1 to be on your feet without moving. *She stood there like a statue.* **2** to get or put upright; to place. *Stand the vase on the table.* **3** to stay; to remain unchanged. *My offer still stands.* **4** to tolerate or endure something. *I can't stand the heat.* **5 it stands to reason,** it is reasonable or obvious. **6 stand by,** to be ready for action. **7 stand for,** to represent; to tolerate. **8 stand in,** to act as a deputy for somebody. **9 stand out,** to stick out. **10 stand up for,** to support or defend.

stand *noun*
1 something made for putting things on. *a music-stand.* **2** a stall where things are sold or displayed. **3** a grandstand. **4** a position that you stay in.

standard *noun*
1 how good something is. *a high standard of work.* **2** a thing used to measure or judge something else. *The metre is the standard for length.* **3** a flag. **4** an upright pole. **5 standard lamp,** a lamp on a pole that stands on the floor. **6 standard of living,** the sort of things that you can afford.

standard *adjective*
of the usual or average quality or kind. *standard English.*
standardize *verb*

standstill *noun*
a stop; an end to activity.

stank past tense of **stink** *verb*.

stanza *noun*
a group of lines in a poem.

staple *noun*
1 a tiny piece of metal used to fix pieces of paper together. **2** a U-shaped nail.
stapler *noun*

staple *adjective*
main; normal. *Rice is their staple food.*

star *noun*
1 one of the heavenly bodies that you see at night as specks of light. **2** one of the main performers in a film, show, etc.; a famous entertainer. **3** a shape with five or six points.
starry *adjective*

star *verb* **(starred, starring)**
to be or make a star in a film, show, etc.

starboard *noun*
the right-hand side of a ship or aircraft when you are facing forward.

starch *noun* **(starches)**
1 a white carbohydrate in bread, potatoes, etc. **2** this or a similar substance used to stiffen clothes.
starchy *adjective*

stare *verb* **(stared, staring)**
to look continuously at someone or something without moving your eyes.

starfish *noun* **(starfish** or **starfishes)**
a sea animal shaped like a star with five points.

starling *noun*
a noisy black or brown speckled bird.

start *verb*
1 to take the first steps in doing something. **2** to make something happen; to set something going. **3** to make a sudden movement. *He started at the sound of rattling chains.*
starter *noun*

start *noun*
1 the act of starting; the beginning. **2** an advantage that someone starts with. *We gave the young ones 10 minutes' start.*

starting-pistol *noun*
a pistol fired to signal the start of a race.

startle *verb* **(startled, startling)**
to surprise or alarm a person or animal.

starve *verb* **(starved, starving)**
1 to suffer or die because you have not got enough food. 2 to make somebody starve. *She was starved to death.* 3 (*informal*) to be very hungry. *Where's my dinner? I'm starving!*
starvation *noun*

state *noun*
1 the condition of a person or thing. 2 a nation. 3 a division of a country. 4 a government and its officials. 5 pomp; ceremony. 6 (*informal*) an excited or upset condition. *Don't get in a state about the robbery.*

state *verb* **(stated, stating)**
to say something clearly or formally.

stately *adjective* **(statelier, stateliest)**
majestic; dignified.
stateliness *noun*

statement *noun*
words that say something important. *The witness made a statement in court.*

statesman *noun* **(statesmen)**
someone who is important or skilled in governing a state.
statesmanship *noun*

static *adjective*
not moving; not changing.

station *noun*
1 a set of buildings where people get on or off trains or buses. 2 a building for police, firemen, or other workers who serve the public. 3 a place from which radio or television broadcasts are made.

station *verb*
to put a person somewhere for a particular purpose. *He was stationed to guard the ship.*

stationary *adjective*
not moving. *The car was stationary.*

stationery *noun*
paper, envelopes, and other things used for writing, typing, etc.

station-master *noun*
the person in charge of a railway station.

statistic *noun*
1 a piece of information expressed as a number. *The statistics show that the population has doubled.* 2 **statistics**, the science or study of information that is expressed as numbers.
statistical *adjective*, **statistically** *adverb*, **statistician** *noun*

statue *noun*
a model made of stone, metal, etc. to look like a person, animal, etc.

status *noun* **(statuses)**
1 a person's position or rank in relation to other people. 2 a good position in society; prestige.

stave *noun*
a set of five parallel lines on which music is written.

stave *verb* **(staved** or **stove, staving)**
1 to make a hole or dent in something. *The collision stove in the front of the ship.* 2 **stave off**, to keep something away. *They staved off hunger by drinking a lot of water.*

stay *verb*
1 to remain. 2 to spend time in a place as a visitor.

steady *adjective* **(steadier, steadiest)**
1 not shaking or moving; firm. 2 regular; continuous. *a steady pace.*
steadily *adverb*, **steadiness** *noun*

steady *verb* **(steadied, steadying)**
to make something steady.

steak *noun*
a thick slice of meat or fish.

steal *verb* (*past tense* **stole**; *past participle* **stolen**; *present participle* **stealing**)
1 to take and keep something that does not belong to you. *The money was stolen.* 2 to move stealthily. *He stole out of the room.*

stealthy *adjective* **(stealthier, stealthiest)**
secret and quiet. *stealthy movements.*
stealth *noun*, **stealthily** *adverb*, **stealthiness** *noun*

steam *noun*
1 the vapour that comes from boiling water. 2 energy; power. *He ran out of steam.*
steamy *adjective*

steam *verb*
1 to give out steam. 2 to move using the power of steam. *The boat steamed down the river.* 3 to cook with steam. *a steamed pudding.* 4 to cover or be covered with mist or condensation. *The windows steamed up.* 5 **steamed up**, (*slang*) excited; angry.

steam-engine *noun*
an engine driven by steam.

steamer *noun*
a steamship.

steamroller *noun*
a heavy vehicle used to flatten surfaces when making roads.

steamship *noun*
a ship driven by steam.

steed *noun*
(*old-fashioned* or *poetical use*) a horse.

steel *noun*
a strong metal made from iron.
steely *adjective*

steep *adjective*
rising or sloping sharply.
steeply *adverb*, **steepness** *noun*

steeple *noun*
a church tower with a spire.

steeplechase *noun*
a race across country or over hedges and fences.

steeplejack *noun*
someone who works on very high buildings, chimneys, etc.

steer *verb*
to make a car, ship, bicycle, etc. go in the direction you want.

steer *noun*
a young bull kept for its beef.

steering-wheel *noun*
a wheel for steering a car, boat, etc.

stem *noun*
1 a stalk. 2 the thin part of a wine-glass. 3 the main part of a verb or other word, to which different endings are attached.

stench *noun* **(stenches)**
a very unpleasant smell.

stencil *noun*
a piece of card, metal, etc. with pieces cut out of it, used to produce a picture, design, etc.

step *noun*
1 a movement made by the foot when walking, running, or dancing. 2 the sound of a person putting down his foot when walking. 3 a stair, usually out of doors. 4 one of a series of actions. 5 **steps,** a step-ladder. 6 **watch your step,** be careful.

step *verb* **(stepped, stepping)**
1 to tread or walk. 2 **step on it,** (*slang*) to hurry. 3 **step up,** to increase something.

stepchild *noun* **(stepchildren)**
a child that your husband or wife has from an earlier marriage.
stepbrother *noun,* **stepdaughter** *noun,* **stepsister** *noun,* **stepson** *noun*

stepfather *noun*
a man who is married to your mother but is not your real father.

step-ladder *noun*
a folding ladder with flat treads.

stepmother *noun*
a woman who is married to your father but is not your real mother.

steppe *noun*
a grassy plain with few trees, especially in Russia.

stepping-stone *noun*
one of a line of stones put in a river or stream to help people walk across.

stereo *adjective*
stereophonic.

stereo *noun*
1 stereophonic sound or recording. 2 (*informal*), a stereophonic record-player or radio.

stereophonic *adjective*
(*say* ste-ri-ŏ-**fon**-ik)
of sound that comes from two different directions at the same time.

sterile *adjective*
1 not fertile. 2 free from germs.
sterility *noun,* **sterilize** *verb*

sterling *noun*
British money. *Tourists paid for their meals in sterling.*

stern *noun*
the back part of a ship.

stern *adjective*
severe; strict; grim.
sternly *adverb,* **sternness** *noun*

stethoscope *noun*
(*say* steth-ŏ-skohp)
a device used by doctors for listening to patients' heart-beats, breathing, etc.

stew *verb*
to cook slowly in liquid.

stew *noun*
1 meat stewed with vegetables. 2 **in a stew,** (*informal*) very worried or agitated.

steward *noun*
1 someone whose job is to look after the passengers of a ship or aircraft. 2 an official who looks after something.
stewardess *noun*

stick *noun*
1 a long, thin piece of wood. 2 a walking-stick. 3 the implement used to hit the ball in hockey, polo, etc. 4 a long, thin piece of something. *a stick of rock.*

stick *verb* **(stuck, sticking)**
1 to push a thing into something; to put carelessly. *She stuck a pin in her finger.* 2 to fasten or join; to glue. 3 to become fixed or jammed; not to be able to move. *The door is stuck.* 4 (*informal*) to stay. *We must stick together.* 5 **stick out,** to come or push out from a surface; to be higher than the surrounding area; to be very noticeable. 6 **stick up for,** (*informal*) to stand up for. 7 **stuck with,** (*informal*) unable to avoid a person, job, etc.

sticker *noun*
a label or sign that you can stick on something.

sticking-plaster *noun*
a strip of adhesive material for covering a wound.

stick-insect *noun*
an insect whose body looks like a twig.

stickleback *noun*
a small freshwater fish with sharp spines on its back.

sticky *adjective* **(stickier, stickiest)**
1 able or likely to stick to things. 2 (*informal*) unpleasant; nasty. *He came to a sticky end.*
stickily *adverb,* **stickiness** *noun*

stiff *adjective*
1 difficult to bend or move. 2 difficult. *a stiff examination.* 3 formal; not friendly. 4 strong. *a stiff drink.*
stiffly *adverb,* **stiffness** *noun*

stiffen *verb*
to make or become stiff.

stifle *verb* **(stifled, stifling)**
1 to suffocate. 2 to suppress. *She stifled a yawn.*

stile *noun*
an arrangement of steps for people to climb over a fence.

still *adjective*
1 not moving. 2 silent. 3 not fizzy.
stillness *noun*

still *adverb*
1 up to this or that time; even now. *Are you still there? He was still there.* 2 even; yet. *He wanted still more food.*

still *conjunction*
however. *He has been unfair; still, he is your father.*

stilts *plural noun*
a pair of poles on which you can walk high above the ground.

stimulate *verb* (**stimulated, stimulating**)
to excite or interest; to make more lively or active.
stimulant *noun*, **stimulation** *noun*

stimulus *noun* (**stimuli**)
something that stimulates or produces a re-action.

sting *noun*
1 the part of an animal or plant that can cause a wound. **2** a painful wound caused by an animal or plant.

sting *verb* (**stung, stinging**)
1 to hurt somebody with a sting. *She was stung by a bee.* **2** to feel a sharp or throbbing pain. *My back is stinging from sunburn.* **3** (*slang*) to charge somebody an excessive price; to swindle. *They stung him for £10.*
stinging-nettle *noun*

stingy *adjective* (**stingier, stingiest**)
(*say* **stin**-ji)
mean; not generous.

stink *noun*
1 a stench. **2** (*informal*) a fuss.

stink *verb* (*past tense* **stank** or **stunk**; *past participle* **stunk**; *present participle* **stinking**)
to have a very unpleasant smell.

stir *verb* (**stirred, stirring**)
1 to move a liquid or soft mixture round and round, especially with a spoon. **2** to move slightly; to start to move. **3** to excite or arouse. *They stirred up trouble.*

stir *noun*
1 an act of stirring. **2** a fuss or disturbance. *The news caused a stir.*

stirrup *noun*
a metal part that hangs down from each side of a horse's saddle, for the rider to put his foot into.

stitch *noun* (**stitches**)
1 a loop of thread made in sewing or knitting. **2** a sudden pain in your side caused by running.

stoat *noun*
an animal rather like a weasel; an ermine.

stock *noun*
1 a number of things kept ready to be sold or used. **2** livestock. **3** a line of ancestors. **4** liquid made by stewing meat, vegetables, etc. **5** a garden flower with a sweet smell. **6** a kind of share in a company's capital. **7 Stock Exchange**, a place where stocks and shares are bought and sold.

stock *verb*
1 to keep a stock of something. **2** to provide a place with a stock of something.

stockade *noun*
a fence made of large upright stakes.

stock-car *noun*
an ordinary car strengthened for use in races in which bumping is allowed.

stocking *noun*
a garment that covers the whole of someone's leg and foot.

stockpile *noun*
a large stock of things kept in reserve.

stocks *plural noun*
a wooden framework in which people's legs used to be locked as a punishment.

stocky *adjective* (**stockier, stockiest**)
short and solid or strong. *a stocky man.*

stodgy *adjective* (**stodgier, stodgiest**)
1 thick and heavy; not easy to digest. *a stodgy pudding.* **2** boring. *a stodgy book.*

stoke *verb* (**stoked, stoking**)
to put fuel in a furnace or on a fire.

stole *noun*
a wide piece of material worn round the shoulders.

stole past tense of **steal**.

stolen past participle of **steal**.

stomach *noun*
1 the part of the body where food starts to be digested. **2** the abdomen.

stone *noun*
1 a hard, solid mineral which is not metal. **2** a piece of this mineral. **3** a jewel. **4** the hard seed in the middle of a cherry, plum, peach, etc. **5** a unit of weight equal to 14 pounds. *She weighs 6 stone.*

stone *verb* (**stoned, stoning**)
1 to throw stones at somebody. **2** to take the stones out of fruit. **3 stoned,** (*slang*) intoxicated by drink or drugs.

stone-deaf *adjective*
completely deaf.

stony *adjective* (**stonier, stoniest**)
1 full of stones. **2** like stone. **3** not answering or sympathizing. *a stony silence.* **4 stony** or **stony-broke,** (*slang*) having no money.

stood past tense and past participle of **stand** *verb*.

stool *noun*
a small seat without a back.

stoop *verb*
to bend your body forwards.

stop *verb* (**stopped, stopping**)
1 to finish. **2** to cease moving or working; to stay. **3** to prevent; to obstruct. **4** to fill a hole, especially in a tooth.
stoppage *noun*

stop *noun*
1 stopping; an end. **2** a place where a bus, train, etc. stops regularly.

stopper *noun*
something that fits into the top of a bottle, jar, etc. to close it.

stop-press *noun*
late news printed in a newspaper after printing has started.

stop-watch *noun* (**stop-watches**)
a watch that can be started or stopped as you wish, used for timing races, etc.

storage *noun*
1 the storing of things. **2 storage heater,** an electric heater that gives out heat which it has stored.

store *verb* (**stored, storing**)
to keep things until they are needed.

store *noun*
1 a place where things are stored. 2 things kept for future use. 3 a shop, especially a large one. 4 **in store,** that is going to happen. *There is a treat in store for you.*

storey *noun*
one whole floor of a building; all the rooms on the same level.

stork *noun*
a large bird with very long legs and a long beak.

storm *noun*
1 a very strong wind with much rain, snow, etc. 2 a violent attack or outburst. *a storm of protest.* 3 **storm in a teacup,** a great fuss over something trivial.
stormy *adjective*

storm *verb*
1 to move or behave violently or angrily. *He stormed out of the room.* 2 to attack suddenly. *They stormed the castle.*

story *noun* **(stories)**
1 words that tell of real or imaginary events. 2 (*informal*) a lie. *Don't tell stories!*

stout *adjective*
1 rather fat. 2 thick and strong. 3 brave.
stoutly *adverb*, **stoutness** *noun*.

stove *noun*
a device that produces heat for warming a room or cooking.

stow *verb*
1 to pack or store something away. 2 **stow away,** to hide on a ship or aircraft so as to travel without paying.

stowaway *noun*
someone who stows away on a ship or aircraft.

straggle *verb* **(straggled, straggling)**
1 to grow or move in an untidy way. 2 to lag behind; to wander on your own.
straggler *noun*, **straggly** *adjective*

straight *adjective*
1 going continuously in one direction; not curving or bending. 2 tidy; in proper order. 3 honest; frank. *Give me a straight answer.*

straighten *verb*
to make or become straight.

straightforward *adjective*
1 easy to understand or do; not complicated. 2 honest; frank.

strain *verb*
1 to stretch, push, or pull hard or too hard. 2 to make a great effort. 3 to put something through a sieve to separate liquid from the lumps or other things in it. *Strain the tea to get rid of the tea-leaves.*

strain *noun*
1 straining; the force of straining. 2 an injury caused by straining. 3 something that uses up your strength, patience, etc.; exhaustion.

strainer *noun*
a sieve, especially a small one for straining tea.

strait *noun*
a narrow stretch of water connecting two seas. *The Straits of Dover.*

strand *noun*
1 one of the threads or wires twisted together to make a rope, cable, etc. 2 a lock of hair.

stranded *adjective*
1 that has run on to the sand or rocks in shallow water. *the stranded ship.* 2 left in a difficult or lonely position. *They were stranded in the desert.*

strange *adjective* **(stranger, strangest)**
unusual; not known or experienced before.
strangely *adverb*, **strangeness** *noun*

stranger *noun*
1 a person that you do not know. 2 a person who is in a place he does not know.

strangle *verb* **(strangled, strangling)**
to kill someone by pressing his throat so that he cannot breathe.
strangler *noun*, **strangulation** *noun*

strap *noun*
a flat strip of leather, cloth, etc. for fastening things together or holding them in place.

strap *verb* **(strapped, strapping)**
to fasten with a strap or straps.

strategy *noun* **(strategies)**
1 a plan or policy to achieve something. 2 planning a war, campaign, etc.
strategic *adjective*, **strategist** *noun*

stratum *noun* **(strata)**
(*say* **strah**-tŭm)
one of a series of layers or levels. *You can see several strata in the cliffs.*

straw *noun*
1 dry cut stalks of corn. 2 a narrow tube for drinking through.

strawberry *noun* **(strawberries)**
a small, red, juicy fruit.

stray *verb*
to wander; to get lost.

stray *adjective*
that has strayed. *a stray cat.*

streak *noun*
a long thin line or mark.
streaky *adjective*

streak *verb*
1 to mark with streaks. 2 to move very quickly. 3 to run naked through a public place.
streaker *noun*

stream *noun*
1 a narrow river; a brook. 2 liquid flowing in one direction. 3 a number of things moving in the same direction. 4 a group in a school containing children of similar ability.

stream *verb*
1 to move in or like a stream. 2 to produce a stream of liquid. 3 to arrange schoolchildren in streams according to their ability.

streamer *noun*
a long strip of paper; a long narrow ribbon.

streamline *verb* **(streamlined, streamlining)**
to give something a smooth shape that helps it to move easily through air or water.

street *noun*
a road in a city or town.

strength *noun*
how strong a person or thing is; being strong.

strengthen *verb*
to make or become strong or stronger.

strenuous

strenuous *adjective*
needing or using great effort.
strenuously *adverb*

stress *noun* **(stresses)**
1 strain. 2 emphasis, especially the extra force with which you pronounce part of a word or phrase.

stress *verb*
to put a stress on something; to emphasize.

stretch *verb*
1 to pull something so that it becomes longer, wider, or tighter. 2 to become longer or wider when pulled. 3 to extend. 4 **stretch out**, to lie at full length.

stretch *noun* **(stretches)**
1 the action of stretching. 2 a continuous period of time or area of land.

stretcher *noun*
a framework with handles at each end, on which a sick or injured person is carried.

strew *verb (past tense* **strewed**; *past participle* **strewn** *or* **strewed**; *present participle* **strewing)**
to scatter something. *Flowers were strewn over the path.*

stricken *adjective*
overcome; strongly affected by something. *stricken with fear.*

strict *adjective*
1 demanding obedience or good behaviour. *a strict teacher.* 2 complete; exact. *the strict truth.*
strictly *adverb*, **strictness** *noun*

stride *verb (past tense* **strode**; *past participle* **stridden**; *present participle* **striding)**
to walk with long steps.

stride *noun*
1 a long step when walking or running. 2 a steady way of working. *Get into your stride.*

strife *noun*
conflict; fighting or quarrelling.

strike *verb* **(struck, striking)**
1 to hit. *The school was struck by lightning.* 2 to attack suddenly. 3 to light a match by rubbing it against something rough. 4 to sound. *The clock struck 12.* 5 to stop working until the people in charge agree to improve wages, conditions, etc. 6 to find oil, gold, etc. by drilling, mining, etc. 7 to have an impression on somebody. *The film struck me as truthful.*
striker *noun*

strike *noun*
1 a hit. 2 refusing to work, as a way of making a protest. 3 a find of oil, gold, etc. underground.

striking *adjective*
impressive; very interesting.

string *noun*
1 thin rope; a piece of thin rope. 2 a piece of stretched wire, nylon, etc. used in a musical instrument to make sounds. 3 a line or series of things. *a string of buses.* 4 **strings**, the stringed instruments in an orchestra.

string *verb* **(strung, stringing)**
1 to fasten with string. 2 to thread on a string. 3 to remove the tough fibre from beans. 4 **string out**, to spread out in a line; to extend.

stringed *adjective*
having strings. *The violin and cello are stringed instruments.*

stringy *adjective* **(stringier, stringiest)**
1 like string. 2 containing tough fibres.

strip *verb* **(stripped, stripping)**
1 to take a covering off something. 2 to undress. 3 to deprive somebody of something.

strip *noun*
1 a long, narrow piece of something. 2 **strip cartoon**, a comic strip.

stripe *noun*
1 a long, narrow band of colour. *Tigers have stripes; leopards have spots.* 2 something worn on the sleeve of a uniform to show your rank.
striped *adjective*, **stripy** *adjective*

strip-tease *noun*
an entertainment in which someone slowly undresses.

strive *verb (past tense* **strove**; *past participle* **striven**; *present participle* **striving)**
to try hard; to struggle.

strobe *noun*
a light that flashes on and off continuously.

strode past tense of **stride** *verb*.

stroke *noun*
1 a hit; a movement or action. 2 a sudden illness that often causes paralysis.

stroke *verb* **(stroked, stroking)**
to move your hand gently along something.

stroll *verb*
to walk slowly.

strong *adjective*
1 having great power, energy, or effect. *a strong horse.* 2 not easily broken or damaged. *a strong chain.* 3 with a lot of flavour or smell. *strong tea.* 4 having a particular number or size. *a crowd 20,000 strong.*
strongly *adverb*

stronghold *noun*
a fortress.

strove past tense of **strive**.

struck past tense and past participle of **strike** *verb*.

structure *noun*
1 something that has been built or put together. 2 the way that something is built or made.
structural *adjective*, **structurally** *adverb*

struggle *verb* **(struggled, struggling)**
1 to move your arms, legs, etc. in fighting or trying to get free. 2 to make strong efforts to do something.

struggle *noun*
an action or time of struggling.

strum *verb* **(strummed, strumming)**
1 to sound a guitar by running your finger across its strings. 2 to play a musical instrument carelessly or badly.

strung past tense and past participle of **string** *verb*.

strut *verb* **(strutted, strutting)**
to walk proudly or stiffly.

strut *noun*
a bar of wood or metal that strengthens a framework.

stub *verb* **(stubbed, stubbing)**
1 to knock your toe against something hard. 2 to put out a cigarette, cigar, etc. by pressing it against something hard.

stub *noun*
a short piece of something left after the rest has been used up or worn down. *a cigar stub.*

stubble *noun*
1 the short stalks of corn left in the ground after a harvest. 2 short, stiff hairs on a man's chin.

stubborn *adjective*
obstinate. *as stubborn as a mule.*
stubbornly *adverb*, **stubbornness** *noun*

stuck past tense and past participle of **stick** *verb.*

stuck-up *adjective*
(*informal*) conceited; snobbish.

stud *noun*
1 a small curved lump or knob; a short nail with a thick head. *Football boots have studs on the bottom.* 2 a device for fastening a detachable collar to a shirt.

student *noun*
someone who studies, especially at college or university.

studio *noun*
1 a place where radio or television broadcasts are made. 2 a place where cinema or television films are made. 3 the room where a painter, photographer, etc. works. 4 **studio couch,** a long couch that can be converted into a bed.

studious *adjective*
keen on studying.
studiously *adverb*

study *verb* **(studied, studying)**
1 to spend time learning about something. 2 to look at something very carefully.

study *noun* **(studies)**
1 studying a subject. 2 a room where someone studies.

stuff *noun*
a substance or material; things.

stuff *verb*
1 to fill something tightly, especially with stuffing. *She stuffed the turkey.* 2 to push something inside another thing. *He stuffed the paper into his pocket.*

stuffing *noun*
1 material used to fill the inside of something. 2 a flavoured mixture put inside poultry, etc. before cooking.

stuffy *adjective* **(stuffier, stuffiest)**
1 badly ventilated; without fresh air. 2 prim; boring.
stuffily *adverb*, **stuffiness** *noun*

stumble *verb* **(stumbled, stumbling)**
1 to lose your balance; to fall over something. 2 to speak or act hesitantly or uncertainly. 3 **stumble across** or **stumble on,** to find something accidentally.

stump *noun*
1 the bottom of a tree-trunk left in the ground when the tree is cut down. 2 one of the three upright sticks put at each end of a cricket-pitch.

stump *verb*
1 (*in cricket*) to get a batsman out by touching the stumps with the ball when he is out of his crease. 2 to be too difficult for somebody. *The question stumped him.*

stun *verb* **(stunned, stunning)**
1 to knock somebody unconscious. 2 to shock or confuse somebody. *She was stunned by the news.*

stung past tense and past participle of **sting** *verb.*

stunk past tense and past participle of **stink** *verb.*

stunt *noun*
1 something done to attract attention. *a publicity stunt.* 2 a dangerous feat, especially one performed in making a film.

stupendous *adjective*
amazing; tremendous.

stupid *adjective*
without reason or common sense; not clever or thoughtful.
stupidity *noun*, **stupidly** *adverb*

sturdy *adjective* **(sturdier, sturdiest)**
strong and vigorous or solid.
sturdily *adverb*, **sturdiness** *noun*

stutter *verb*
to stammer.

sty *noun* **(sties)**
1 a pigsty. 2 a sore swelling on an eyelid.

style *noun*
the way that something is done, made, said, or written.

stylish *adjective*
fashionable; smart.
stylishly *adverb*

stylus *noun* **(styluses)**
the device like a needle that travels in the grooves of a gramophone record to reproduce the sound.

sub *noun*
(*informal*) 1 a submarine. 2 a subscription. 3 a substitute.

subdue *verb* **(subdued, subduing)**
1 to bring under control; to overcome. 2 to make quieter or gentler.

subject *noun*
(*say* **sub**-jikt)
1 the person or thing that is being talked or written about. 2 something that is being studied. 3 (*in grammar*) the person or thing that is doing the action stated by the verb in a sentence. *In 'she hit him', the subject is 'she'.* 4 someone who is ruled by a particular king, government, etc.

subject *adjective*
(*say* **sub**-jikt)
1 ruled by a king, government, etc.; not independent. 2 **subject to,** having to obey; liable to; depending upon.

subject *verb*
(*say* sŭb-**jekt**)
1 to make a person or thing undergo something. *They subjected him to torture.* **2** to bring a country under your control.

submarine *noun*
a ship that can travel under water.

submerge *verb* **(submerged, submerging)**
to go or put under water.
submergence *noun*, **submersion** *noun*

submit *verb* **(submitted, submitting)**
1 to surrender; to let somebody rule or control you. **2** to give something to somebody for their opinion, decision, etc.
submission *noun*, **submissive** *adjective*

subordinate *adjective*
(*say* sŭb-**or**-din-ăt)
less important; lower in rank.

subordinate *verb* **(subordinated, subordinating)**
(*say* sŭb-**or**-din-ayt)
to treat something as less important than another thing.
subordination *noun*

subscribe *verb* **(subscribed, subscribing)**
to pay money, especially to pay regularly so as to be a member of a society, get a periodical, or have the use of a telephone.
subscriber *noun*, **subscription** *noun*

subsequent *adjective*
following; later. *Subsequent events proved that she was right.*
subsequently *adverb*

subside *verb* **(subsided, subsiding)**
1 to sink. **2** to become quiet or normal.
subsidence *noun*

subsidy *noun* **(subsidies)**
money paid to keep prices low, to help an industry, etc.
subsidize *verb*

substance *noun*
1 something that you can touch or see; something used for making things. **2** the essential part of something.

substantial *adjective*
1 large; considerable. **2** strong; solid.
substantially *adverb*

substitute *verb* **(substituted, substituting)**
to use somebody or something instead of another person or thing.
substitution *noun*

substitute *noun*
a person or thing substituted for another.

subtle *adjective* **(subtler, subtlest)**
(*say* sut-ĕl)
1 slight or faint but pleasant; delicate. *a subtle perfume.* **2** clever; ingenious. *a subtle joke.*
subtlely *adverb*, **subtlety** *noun*

subtract *verb*
to take one amount from another. *If you subtract 2 from 7, you get 5.*
subtraction *noun*

suburb *noun*
an area of houses on the edge of a city or large town.
suburban *adjective*, **suburbia** *noun*

subway *noun*
an underground passage for pedestrians.

succeed *verb*
1 to be successful. **2** to come after another person or thing, especially to become king or queen after another king or queen. *She succeeded to the throne.*

success *noun* **(successes)**
1 doing or getting what you wanted or intended. **2** a person or thing that does well. *The plan was a great success.*

successful *adjective*
having success.
successfully *adverb*

succession *noun*
1 a series of people or things. **2** the act of following other people or things; succeeding to a throne.

successive *adjective*
following one after another.
successively *adverb*

successor *noun*
a person or thing that succeeds another.

such *adjective*
1 of the same kind. *sweets such as these.* **2** so great; so much of. *It gave me such a fright!* **3** **such-and-such,** particular but not named. *It was at such-and-such a time.*

suck *verb*
1 to take in liquid or air through your mouth while you breathe in through your lips. *I sucked milk through a straw.* **2** to move something around inside your mouth. *She sucked a sweet.* **3** to draw in; to absorb. *Blotting-paper sucks up ink.*

suction *noun*
producing a vacuum so that liquid, air, etc. is drawn in or something sticks to the surface. *Vacuum-cleaners work by suction.*

sudden *adjective*
happening or done quickly and unexpectedly.
suddenly *adverb*, **suddenness** *noun*

suds *plural noun*
froth on soapy water.

sue *verb* **(sued, suing)**
to start a lawsuit to claim money from somebody. *I sued him for damages.*

suede *noun*
(*say* swayd)
soft velvety leather.

suet *noun*
hard fat from cattle and sheep, used in cooking.

suffer *verb*
to feel pain or sadness; to have to put up with something unpleasant.

sufficient *adjective*
enough. *Have we sufficient food?*
sufficiency *noun*, **sufficiently** *adverb*

suffix *noun* **(suffixes)**
a word or syllable joined to the end of a word to change or add to its meaning, as in forget*ful*, lion*ess*, and rust*y*.

suffocate *verb* **(suffocated, suffocating)**
1 to make it impossible or difficult for somebody to breathe. 2 to have difficulty in breathing.
suffocation *noun*

sugar *noun*
a sweet food obtained from various plants.
sugary *adjective*

suggest *verb*
1 to give somebody an idea that you think is useful. 2 to give an idea or impression of something.
suggestion *noun*

suicide *noun*
killing yourself. *He committed suicide.*
suicidal *adjective*

suit *noun*
1 a jacket and pair of trousers or skirt, sometimes with a waistcoat, that are meant to be worn together. 2 a set of clothes for a particular purpose. *a space suit.* 3 one of the four sets in a pack of playing cards. *The four suits are spades, hearts, diamonds, and clubs.* 4 a lawsuit.

suit *verb*
to be suitable or convenient for somebody or something.

suitable *adjective*
satisfactory or right for a particular person, purpose, or occasion.
suitability *noun*, **suitably** *adverb*

suitcase *noun*
a box with a lid and a handle, for carrying clothes and other things on journeys, holidays, etc.

suite *noun*
(*say* sweet)
1 a set of furniture. 2 a set of rooms. 3 a set of short musical pieces or dances.

suitor *noun*
a man who is courting a woman.

sulk *verb*
to be silent and bad-tempered.
sulkily *adverb*, **sulkiness** *noun*, **sulky** *adjective*

sullen *adjective*
sulking; bad-tempered; gloomy.
sullenly *adverb*, **sullenness** *noun*

sulphur *noun*
a yellow chemical used in industry and medicine.

sulphuric *adjective*
1 containing sulphur. 2 **sulphuric acid,** a strong, colourless acid.

sultan *noun*
the ruler of a Muslim country.

sultana *noun*
a raisin without seeds.

sum *noun*
1 the amount you get when you add numbers together. 2 a problem in arithmetic. 3 an amount of money.

sum *verb* **(summed, summing)**
sum up, to summarize, especially at the end of a discussion or talk.

summarize *verb* **(summarized, summarizing)**
to make or give a summary of something.

summary *noun* **(summaries)**
a statement of the main points of something said or written.

summer *noun*
1 the warm season between spring and autumn. 2 **summer time** or **British summer time,** the time shown by clocks that are put forward one hour for the summer. 3 **summertime,** the season of summer.

summit *noun*
1 the top of a mountain or hill. 2 a meeting between the most important people from various governments, organizations, etc.

summon *verb*
1 to order somebody to come or appear. 2 **summon up,** to get or prepare something. *He could not summon up the energy to get out of bed.*

summons *noun* **(summonses)**
a command to appear in a lawcourt.

sun *noun*
1 the star from which the earth gets warmth and light. 2 warmth and light from the sun.

sunburn *noun*
redness of the skin caused by the sun.
sunburned *adjective,* **sunburnt** *adjective*

sundae *noun*
(*say* sun-day)
a mixture of ice-cream with fruit, nuts, cream, etc.

Sunday *noun*
1 the first day of the week. 2 **Sunday school,** a place where children go for religious teaching on Sundays.

sundial *noun*
a device that shows the time by a shadow made by the sun.

sunflower *noun*
a very tall flower with a large round head.

sung past participle of **sing.**

sun-glasses *plural noun*
dark glasses to protect your eyes from the sun.

sunk past tense and past participle of **sink** *verb.*

sunlight *noun*
light from the sun.
sunlit *adjective*

sunny *adjective* **(sunnier, sunniest)**
with the sun shining; full of sunshine.

sunrise *noun*
dawn. *They left at sunrise.*

sunset *noun*
the time when the sun sets.

sunshade *noun*
a device to protect people from the sun; a parasol.

sunshine *noun*
warmth and light that come from the sun.
sunshiny *adjective*

sunspot *noun*
1 a dark patch on the sun's surface. 2 (*informal*) a sunny place.

sun-tan *noun*
a brown colour of the skin caused by the sun.
sun-tanned *adjective*

super *adjective*
(*informal*) excellent.

superb *adjective*
magnificent; excellent.
superbly *adverb*

superficial *adjective*
not deep or thorough; on the surface.
superficiality *noun*, **superficially** *adverb*

superintend *verb*
to supervise.
superintendent *noun*

superior *adjective*
1 higher or more important than someone else.
2 better than another person or thing. 3 conceited; proud.
superiority *noun*

superior *noun*
someone of higher rank or position than another person.

superlative *noun*
the form of an adjective or adverb that expresses the greatest degree of something.
Superlatives are words like 'best', 'highest', 'soonest', and 'worst'.

supermarket *noun*
a large self-service shop that sells food and other goods.

supernatural *adjective*
that cannot be explained by the normal physical laws; connected with ghosts, angels, etc.

supersonic *adjective*
faster than the speed of sound.

superstition *noun*
a belief or action that is not based on reason or evidence. *It is a superstition that it is unlucky to walk under a ladder.*
superstitious *adjective*

supervise *verb* (**supervised, supervising**)
to be in charge of something and look after it.
He supervised the building of the dam.
supervision *noun*, **supervisor** *noun*

supper *noun*
a meal or snack eaten in the evening.

supple *adjective* (**suppler, supplest**)
bending easily; flexible, not stiff.
supplely *adverb*, **suppleness** *noun*

supplement *noun*
1 a part added to a book, etc. to improve it or bring it up to date. 2 a magazine, usually in colour, sold as part of a newspaper. *the colour supplement.*
supplementary *adjective*

supply *verb* (**supplied, supplying**)
to give or sell somebody what he needs or wants.
supplier *noun*

supply *noun* (**supplies**)
1 a stock of something; things kept ready to be used when needed. 2 the action of supplying something; something supplied.

support *verb*
1 to hold something so that it does not fall down. 2 to give help, strength, or encouragement to somebody or something.
supporter *noun*

support *noun*
1 the action of supporting. 2 a person or thing that supports.

suppose *verb* (**supposed, supposing**)
1 to think; to guess that something is true.
2 **supposed to,** expected or forced to do something.
supposedly *adverb*, **supposition** *noun*

suppress *verb*
1 to stop something happening. 2 to keep something secret.
suppression *noun*, **suppressor** *noun*

supreme *adjective*
highest; greatest; most important.
supremacy *noun*, **supremely** *adverb*

sure *adjective* (**surer, surest**)
1 confident about something; convinced. 2 that will definitely happen; that is completely true.
3 safe. 4 **make sure,** to find something out or make something happen.

sure *adverb*
1 (*informal*) surely. 2 **for sure,** definitely. 3 **sure enough,** certainly; in fact.

surely *adverb*
1 certainly; definitely. 2 it must be true; I believe. *Surely I met you last year.*

surf *noun*
1 waves breaking on the shore. 2 **surf-board,** a board used in surf-riding. 3 **surf-riding,** balancing yourself on a board that is carried to the shore on the waves.

surface *noun*
1 the outside of something. 2 one of the sides of something, especially the top part.

surface *verb* (**surfaced, surfacing**)
1 to give a surface to a road, path, etc. 2 to come up to the surface of the sea, etc.

surfing *noun*
surf-riding.
surfer *noun*

surge *verb* (**surged, surging**)
to move forwards or upwards like waves.

surgeon *noun*
a doctor who deals with disease or injury by cutting the affected parts of the body.

surgery *noun* (**surgeries**)
1 the place where a doctor, dentist, etc. sees his patients. 2 the time when this place is open.
3 the work of a surgeon.
surgical *adjective*, **surgically** *adverb*

surname *noun*
your last name that is the same as your family's name.

surpass *verb*
to do or be better than others.

surplice *noun*
a loose white garment sometimes worn by clergymen, choirboys, etc.

surplus *noun* (**surpluses**)
an amount left over after you have spent or used what you need.

surprise *noun*
1 something that you did not expect. 2 the feeling you have when something happens that you did not expect.

surprise *verb* (**surprised, surprising**)
1 to be a surprise to somebody. 2 to catch or attack somebody unexpectedly.
surprisingly *adverb*

surrender *verb*
1 to stop fighting somebody and agree to obey him. 2 to give up something to somebody.

surround *verb*
to be or come all round a person or thing.

surroundings *plural noun*
the things or conditions around a person or place.

survey *noun*
(*say* **ser**-vay)
a general look at something; an inspection or examination of an area, building, etc.

survey *verb*
(*say* ser-**vay**)
to make a survey of something.
surveyor *noun*

survive *verb* (**survived, surviving**)
to stay alive; to live after somebody else dies or after a disaster.
survival *noun,* **survivor** *noun*

suspect *verb*
(*say* sŭ-**spekt**)
1 to think that somebody is not to be trusted or has done a crime. 2 to think that something unpleasant is happening or will happen.

suspect *noun*
(*say* **sus**-pekt)
somebody who is suspected.

suspend *verb*
1 to postpone. 2 to deprive somebody for a time of his job or position. *He was suspended from the team.* 3 to hang something up.

suspense *noun*
an anxious or uncertain feeling while waiting for an event, information, etc.

suspension *noun*
1 suspending; being suspended. 2 **suspension bridge,** a bridge supported by cables.

suspicion *noun*
1 suspecting; being suspected. 2 a feeling that is not definite or certain.

suspicious *adjective*
1 that makes you suspect somebody or something. *suspicious footprints.* 2 that suspects somebody or something. *a suspicious policeman.*
suspiciously *adverb*

sustain *verb*
to support; to keep somebody alive; to keep something happening.

swagger *verb*
to walk or behave in a conceited way.

swallow *verb*
1 to make something go down your throat. 2 **swallow up,** to cover or hide something.

swallow *noun*
a small bird with a forked tail and pointed wings.

swam past tense of **swim** *verb.*

swamp *verb*
1 to flood. 2 to overwhelm.

swamp *noun*
a marsh.
swampy *adjective*

swan *noun*
a large white bird with a long neck. *Swans live on or near water.*

swank *verb*
(*informal*) to swagger or boast.
swank *noun*

swap *verb* (**swapped, swapping**)
(*informal*) to swop.

swarm *noun*
a large number of bees, birds, etc. clustering or moving about together.

swarm *verb*
1 to move in a swarm. 2 to be crowded with people, insects, etc.

swastika *noun*
(*say* **swos**-tik-ă)
a sign formed by a cross with its ends bent at right angles. *The swastika was the symbol of the Nazis.*

swat *verb* (**swatted, swatting**)
(*say* swot)
to hit or crush a fly or other insect.
swatter *noun*

sway *verb*
to move from side to side.

swear *verb* (*past tense* **swore;** *past participle* **sworn;** *present participle* **swearing**)
1 to make a solemn promise. *She swore to tell the truth.* 2 to make somebody take an oath. *He was sworn to secrecy.* 3 to use curses or rude words.
swear-word *noun*

sweat *verb*
(*say* swet)
to perspire.

sweat *noun*
(*say* swet)
perspiration.
sweaty *adjective*

sweater *noun*
(*say* **swet**-er)
a jersey or pullover.

swede *noun*
a kind of turnip.

Swede *noun*
a Swedish person.

Swedish *adjective*
Of Sweden.

sweep *verb* (**swept, sweeping**)
1 to clean or clear with a broom, brush, etc. *He swept the floor.* 2 to move, remove, or change something quickly. *The flood has swept away the bridge.* 3 to move along quickly, smoothly, or proudly. *She swept out of the room.*
sweeper *noun*

sweep *noun*
1 a sweeping action or movement. *Give this room a sweep.* 2 a chimney-sweep.

sweet *adjective*
1 tasting of sugar or honey. 2 very pleasant. *a sweet smell.*
sweetly *adverb,* **sweetness** *noun*

sweet *noun*
1 a small shaped piece of sweet food made of sugar, chocolate, etc. *a bag of sweets.* 2 a pudding; the sweet course in a meal. *There is apple pie for sweet.* 3 **sweet corn,** the seeds of maize.

sweeten *verb*
to make something sweet.
sweetener *noun*

sweetheart *noun*
the person that you love very much.

sweet pea *noun*
a climbing plant with fragrant flowers.

swell *verb (past tense* **swelled;** *past participle* **swollen** or **swelled;** *present participle* **swelling)**
to get bigger or louder. *My ankle has swollen.*

swell *noun*
the rise and fall of the sea's surface.

swell *adjective*
(*informal*) excellent; very good.

swelling *noun*
a swollen place on the body.

swelter *verb*
to be uncomfortably hot.

swept
1 past tense and past participle of **sweep** *verb.* 2 **swept-back,** (*of an aircraft wing*) slanting backwards from the direction in which the aircraft flies.

swerve *verb* **(swerved, swerving)**
to move suddenly to one side. *The car swerved to avoid the cyclist.*

swift *adjective*
quick; moving quickly and easily.
swiftly *adverb,* **swiftness** *noun*

swift *noun*
a small bird that looks like a swallow.

swill *verb*
to rinse or flush something.

swill *noun*
the food and liquid given to pigs.

swim *verb (past tense* **swam;** *past participle* **swum;** *present participle* **swimming)**
1 to move yourself through the water; to be in the water for pleasure. *I swam in the sea yesterday.* 2 to cross something by swimming. *She has swum the Channel.* 3 to be covered with or full of liquid. *Her eyes were swimming with tears.* 4 to feel dizzy. *His head swam.* 5 **swimming-bath** or **swimming-pool,** an area of water designed for people to swim in.
swimmer *noun,* **swim-suit** *noun*

swim *noun*
a time spent swimming. *Let's go for a swim.*

swindle *verb* **(swindled, swindling)**
to get money or goods from somebody dishonestly; to trick or cheat.
swindler *noun*

swindle *noun*
a piece of swindling.

swine *noun*
1 a pig. 2 a person or thing that you hate.

swing *verb* **(swung, swinging)**
1 to move to and fro; to move in a curve. *The door swung open.* 2 to turn quickly or suddenly. *He had swung the car round to avoid the bus.*

swing *noun*
1 a swinging movement. 2 a seat hung on chains, ropes, etc. so that it can move backwards and forwards. 3 the amount that votes, opinions, etc. change from one side to the other. 4 **in full swing,** full of activity; working fully.

swipe *verb* **(swiped, swiping)**
1 to hit hard. 2 (*informal*) to steal something.

swirl *verb*
to move around quickly in circles; to whirl.

swish *verb*
to make a hissing or rustling sound.

Swiss *adjective*
1 of Switzerland. 2 **Swiss roll,** a thin sponge-cake spread with jam or cream and rolled up.

switch *noun* **(switches)**
1 a device that you press or turn to start or stop something working, especially something that works by electricity. 2 a sudden change of policy, methods, etc.

switch *verb*
1 to turn an electric current on or off. 2 to change something suddenly.

switchboard *noun*
a panel with switches for connecting telephone lines.

swivel *verb* **(swivelled, swivelling)**
to turn round.

swollen past participle of **swell** *verb.*

swoon *verb*
to faint. *She swooned with terror.*

swoop *verb*
to dive or come down suddenly; to make a sudden attack.

swop *verb* **(swopped, swopping)**
(*informal*) to exchange. *I swopped my comic for his sweets.*

sword *noun*
(*say* sord)
a weapon like a knife with a very long blade.

swore past tense of **swear.**

sworn past participle of **swear.**

swot *verb* **(swotted, swotting)**
(*informal*) to study hard.

swot *noun*
(*informal*) someone who swots.

swum past participle of **swim** *verb.*

swung past tense and past participle of **swing** *verb.*

sycamore *noun*
a kind of maple tree. *Sycamore seeds have wings, so they can be carried a long way by the wind.*

syllable *noun*
a word or part of a word that has one separate sound when you say it. *'El-e-phant' has three syllables; 'cat' has one syllable.*
syllabic *adjective*

syllabus *noun* **(syllabuses)**
(*say* **sil**-å-bùs)
a summary of things to be studied by a class, for an examination, etc.

symbol *noun*
a thing that represents or suggests something. *The cross is a symbol of Christianity.*
symbolic *adjective*, **symbolical** *adjective*, **symbolically** *adverb*, **symbolism** *noun*

symbolize *verb* **(symbolized, symbolizing)**
to be a symbol of something. *Red symbolizes danger.*

symmetrical *adjective*
(*say* sim-**et**-rik-ål)
that you can divide into two halves which are exactly the same but the opposite way round. *Wheels and butterflies are symmetrical.*
symmetrically *adverb*, **symmetry** *noun*

sympathize *verb* **(sympathized, sympathizing)**
to show or feel sympathy with others. *I sympathized with her ideas.*
sympathizer *noun*

sympathy *noun* **(sympathies)**
the sharing or understanding of other people's feelings, opinions, etc.
sympathetic *adjective*, **sympathetically** *adverb*

symphony *noun* **(symphonies)**
1 a long piece of music for an orchestra. **2 symphony orchestra,** a large orchestra.
symphonic *adjective*

symptom *noun*
one of the things that shows that someone is ill. *Red spots are a symptom of measles.*
symptomatic *adjective*, **symptomatically** *adverb*

synagogue *noun*
(*say* **sin**-å-gog)
a place where Jews meet for worship.

synchronize *verb*
(synchronized, synchronizing)
(*say* **sink**-rö-nyz)
1 to make things happen at the same time. **2** to make watches or clocks show the same time.
synchronization *noun*

syncopate *verb* **(syncopated, syncopating)**
(*say* **sink**-ö-payt)
to change the strength of beats in a piece of music.
syncopation *noun*

synonym *noun*
(*say* **sin**-ö-nim)
a word that means the same or almost the same as another word. *'Devilish' and 'diabolical' are synonyms.*
synonymous *adjective*

synthesis *noun* **(syntheses)**
combining parts, substances, etc. into a whole thing or system.

synthesize *verb* **(synthesized, synthesizing)**
to make a whole thing out of parts.

synthesizer *noun*
an electronic musical instrument that can make a large variety of sounds.

synthetic *adjective*
artificially made; not natural.
synthetically *adverb*

syringe *noun*
a device for sucking in and squirting out a liquid.

syrup *noun*
a thick, sticky, sweet liquid.
syrupy *adjective*

system *noun*
a set of parts, things, or ideas that work together; a way of doing something.
systematic *adjective*, **systematically** *adverb*

T

tabby *noun* **(tabbies)**
a cat with grey or brown streaks in its fur.

table *noun*
1 a piece of furniture with a flat top supported by legs. **2** a list of facts arranged in order, especially a list of the results of multiplying a number by other numbers. *multiplication tables.*

table-cloth *noun*
a cloth spread over a table.

table d'hôte *noun* **(tables d'hôte)**
(*say* tah-bül-**doht**)
a meal ordered at an inclusive price in a restaurant, etc.

tablespoon *noun*
a large spoon used for serving food.
tablespoonful *noun*

tablet *noun*
1 a pill. **2** a lump of soap. **3** a flat piece of stone, wood, etc. with words carved or written on it.

table-tennis *noun*
a game played on a table divided by a net, over which a small ball is hit with bats.

tack *noun*
1 a short nail with a flat top. *Nail down that carpet with tacks.* **2** the action of tacking in sailing; the direction you take.

tack *verb*
1 to fix something with tacks. 2 to sew something quickly with long stitches. 3 to sail a zigzag course against the wind. 4 **tack on,** to add something extra.

tackle *verb* (**tackled, tackling**)
1 to try to do something that needs doing. 2 to try to get the ball from someone else in a football game.

tackle *noun*
equipment, especially for fishing.

tacky *adjective* (**tackier, tackiest**)
sticky; not quite dry. *The paint is still tacky.*

tact *noun*
skill in not offending people.
tactful *adjective,* **tactfully** *adverb,* **tactless** *adjective,* **tactlessly** *adverb*

tactics *plural noun*
organizing people or things to do something, especially organizing troops in a battle.
tactical *adjective,* **tactically** *adverb*

tadpole *noun*
a tiny creature that lives in water and turns into a frog or toad.

tag *verb* (**tagged, tagging**)
1 to fix a label on something. 2 to follow somebody closely. 3 **tag along,** to go along with other people.

tag *noun*[1]
1 a label. 2 the metal or plastic part at the end of a shoelace, etc.

tag *noun*[2]
a game in which one child chases others.

tail *noun*
1 the part that sticks out from the rear end of the body of an animal or bird. 2 the part at the end or rear of something. *The aircraft's tail fell off.* 3 the side of a coin opposite the head.

tail *verb*
1 to remove the stalks from fruit. 2 to follow a person or thing. 3 **tail off,** to become fewer, smaller, less successful, etc.

tailor *noun*
someone whose job is to make clothes.
tailoring *noun*

take *verb* (*past tense* **took;** *past participle* **taken;** *present participle* **taking**)
1 to get hold of something. *He took a bun.* 2 to carry away; to remove. *The money was taken yesterday.* 3 to guide; to accompany. *Are you taking us to the zoo?* 4 to capture. *They took many prisoners.* 5 to have; to use. *Do you take sugar?* 6 to occupy. *Take a seat.* 7 to need; to require. *It takes two to make a quarrel.* 8 to understand; to believe. *I take it that you wish to leave.* 9 to find out; to make a note of. *Take his name.* 10 to subtract. *Take two from ten.* 11 to accept; to endure. *Can't you take a joke?* 12 to make; to get. *She took a photograph.* 13 **take in,** to deceive or swindle somebody. 14 **take off,** to remove; to begin a flight. 15 **take over,** to take control of something. 16 **take part,** to share in doing something. 17 **take place,** to happen. 18 **take up,** to start something, to occupy a place, time, etc.

take-away *noun*
a place where you can buy cooked food to take away with you.

takings *plural noun*
money that you have received.

talcum or **talcum powder** *noun*
a perfumed powder put on the skin to dry it or make it smell pleasant.

tale *noun*
a story.

talent *noun*
a natural ability to do something well. *She has a talent for singing.*
talented *adjective*

talk *verb*
to speak; to have a conversation.
talker *noun*

talk *noun*
1 a conversation or discussion. 2 a lecture.

talkative *adjective*
that talks a lot. *a talkative boy.*

tall *adjective*
1 higher than the average. *a tall pine tree.* 2 measured from the bottom to the top. *The bookcase is six feet tall.* 3 **tall story,** a story that is hard to believe.

tally *verb* (**tallied, tallying**)
to correspond or agree with something else. *Does your list tally with mine?*

talon *noun*
the claw of a bird of prey.

tambourine *noun*
a round musical instrument that you shake or hit so that it jingles.

tame *adjective* (**tamer, tamest**)
1 not wild or dangerous. *The deer are very tame.* 2 dull; uninteresting. *The football match was very tame.*
tamely *adverb,* **tameness** *noun*

tame *verb* (**tamed, taming**)
to make an animal tame.
tamer *noun*

tamper *verb*
to interfere with something; to change something so that it will not work properly.

tan *noun*
1 sun-tan. 2 a yellowish brown colour.

tan *verb* (**tanned, tanning**)
1 to make your skin brown with sun-tan. 2 to make the skin of a dead animal into leather.

tandem *noun*
a bicycle for two riders, one behind the other.

tangent *noun*
(*say* tan-jĕnt)
a straight line that touches the outside of a curve or circle.

tangerine *noun*
(*say* tan-jer-**een**)
a kind of small orange.

tangle *verb* (**tangled, tangling**)
to make or become twisted or muddled. *This string is tangled.*

tank *noun*
1 a large container for a liquid or gas. 2 a heavy armoured vehicle used in war.

tankard *noun*
a large, heavy mug for drinking from.

tanker *noun*
1 a large ship for carrying oil. 2 a large lorry for carrying a liquid.

tantalize *verb* **(tantalized, tantalizing)**
to torment somebody by showing him something that he cannot have.

tantrum *noun*
an outburst of bad temper.

tap *noun*[1]
a device for controlling the flow of a liquid or gas.

tap *noun*[2]
1 a quick, light hit. *I gave him a tap on the shoulder.* 2 tap-dancing.

tap *verb*[1] **(tapped, tapping)**
1 to take liquid out of something. 2 to fix a device to a telephone wire, etc. so that you can hear someone else's conversation.

tap *verb*[2] **(tapped, tapping)**
to hit a person or thing quickly and lightly.

tap-dancing *noun*
dancing in which you wear hard shoes that make tapping sounds on the floor.
tap-dance *noun*, **tap-dancer** *noun*

tape *noun*
1 a narrow strip of cloth, paper, plastic, etc. 2 a narrow plastic strip coated with a magnetic substance and used for making recordings.

tape *verb* **(taped, taping)**
1 to fix, cover, or surround something with tape. 2 to record sound on magnetic tape. 3 **get** or **have something taped,** to know, understand, or be able to deal with it.

tape-measure *noun*
a long strip marked in inches or centimetres for measuring lengths.

taper *verb*
to get narrower towards one end.

taper *noun*
a piece of string thinly coated with wax. *Light the gas with a taper.*

tape-recorder *noun*
a device for recording sound on magnetic tape and playing it back.
tape-recording *noun*

tapestry *noun* **(tapestries)**
(*say* **tap**-i-stri)
a piece of strong cloth with pictures or patterns woven on it.

tapioca *noun*
a starchy substance consisting of white grains used for making milk puddings.

tar *noun*
a thick, black, sticky liquid made from coal or wood and used in making roads.
tarry *adjective*

tar *verb* **(tarred, tarring)**
to coat with tar.

tarantula *noun*
(*say* tă-**ran**-tew-lă)
a large hairy spider. *A tarantula bite is painful but not poisonous.*

target *noun*
something that you aim at and try to hit or reach.

Tarmac *noun*
a mixture of tar and broken stone, used for surfacing roads, paths, playgrounds, etc.

tarnish *verb*
to lose or cause to lose brightness; to make or become stained. *Dampness tarnishes some metals.*

tarpaulin *noun*
a large piece of waterproof canvas.

tart *noun*
1 a pie containing fruit or jam. 2 (*slang*) a girl or woman, especially one with a bad reputation.

tart *adjective*
sour. *The apples are tart.*

tart *verb*
tart up, (*informal*) to dress up smartly or gaudily; to smarten something up.

tartan *noun*
Scottish woollen cloth with a criss-cross pattern. *Each clan has its own design of tartan.*

task *noun*
1 a piece of work to be done. 2 **take somebody to task,** to tell somebody off for doing wrong.

tassel *noun*
a bundle of threads tied together at the top and used to decorate something. *Dressing-gown cords often have tassels at each end.*

taste *verb* **(tasted, tasting)**
1 to eat a little bit of food or sip a drink to see what it is like. 2 to have a particular flavour.

taste *noun*
1 the flavour something has when you taste it. *This milk has a strange taste.* 2 the ability to taste things. 3 the ability to appreciate beautiful things. *Her choice of clothes shows her good taste.* 4 a tiny amount of food.
tasteful *adjective*, **tastefully** *adverb*, **tasteless** *adjective*, **tastelessly** *adverb*

tasty *adjective* **(tastier, tastiest)**
having a taste that you like.

tattered *adjective*
badly torn; in rags.

tatters *plural noun*
rags; badly torn pieces. *My coat was in tatters.*

tattoo *verb*
to make a picture or pattern on someone's skin using a needle and some dye.

tattoo *noun*[1]
a tattooed picture or pattern.

tattoo *noun*[2]
1 a drumming sound. 2 an entertainment consisting of military music, marching, etc.

tatty *adjective* **(tattier, tattiest)**
ragged or shabby; untidy.

taught past tense and past participle of **teach.**

taunt *verb*
to jeer at somebody; to insult.

taut *adjective*
stretched tightly.
tautly *adverb,* **tautness** *noun*

tavern *noun*
(*old-fashioned use*) a public house; an inn.

tawny *adjective* **(tawnier, tawniest)**
brownish yellow.

tax *noun* **(taxes)**
money that people have to pay to the government.
taxpayer *noun*

tax *verb*
1 to charge somebody a tax; to put a tax on something. 2 to pay the tax on something. *The car is taxed until June.*
taxable *adjective,* **taxation** *noun*

taxi *noun*
a car with a driver which you can hire for journeys. *Most taxis have meters to record the fare.*
taxi-cab *noun*

taxi *verb*
to move along the ground or on the water before or after flying. *The plane taxied towards the hangar.*

tea *noun*
1 a drink made by pouring hot water on the dried leaves of an evergreen shrub. 2 the dried leaves of this shrub. 3 a meal eaten in the afternoon.
teacup *noun,* **tea-leaf** *noun,* **tea-table** *noun,* **teatime** *noun*

teach *verb* **(taught, teaching)**
1 to educate. 2 to give lessons in a particular subject. *She taught history last year.*

teacher *noun*
someone who teaches others, especially in a school.

tea-cloth *noun*
1 a tea-towel 2 a cloth for a tea-table.

teak *noun*
a hard, strong wood from Asia.

team *noun*
1 a group of people who play on the same side in a game. 2 a group of people who work together.

teapot *noun*
a pot in which tea is made.

tear *verb* (*past tense* **tore**; *past participle* **torn**; *present participle* **tearing**)
(*say* tair)
1 to pull something apart, away, or into pieces. 2 to become torn. *Tissue paper tears easily.* 3 to move very quickly. *He tore down the street.*

tear *noun*[1]
(*say* teer)
1 a drop of water that comes from your eye when you cry. 2 **in tears,** crying. 3 **tear-gas,** a gas that makes your eyes water painfully.
tearful *adjective,* **tearfully** *adverb*

tear *noun*[2]
(*say* tair)
a hole or split made by tearing.

tease *verb* **(teased, teasing)**
to amuse yourself by annoying somebody or saying humorous things about him.

teaspoon *noun*
1 a small spoon. 2 the amount that this spoon holds.
teaspoonful *noun*

teat *noun*
1 a nipple through which a baby sucks milk. 2 the cap of a baby's feeding-bottle.

tea-towel *noun*
a cloth used for drying washed dishes, cutlery, etc.

Tech *noun*
(*informal*) a technical college.

technical *adjective*
1 concerned with machinery or the way that things work. 2 **technical college,** a college where technical subjects are taught.
technically *adverb,* **technician** *noun*

technique *noun*
(*say* tek-**neek**)
the method of doing something skilfully.

technology *noun* **(technologies)**
technical subjects; the study or use of technical methods.
technological *adjective,* **technologically** *adverb,* **technologist** *noun*

teddy-bear *noun*
a soft, furry, toy bear.

tedious *adjective*
(*say* **tee**-di-ŭs)
boring; annoyingly slow or long.
tediously *adverb,* **tediousness** *noun,* **tedium** *noun*

teem *verb*
1 to be full of something. *The river was teeming with fish.* 2 to rain very hard.

teenage *adjective*
of teenagers.
teenaged *adjective*

teenager *noun*
a person between 13 and 19 years old.

teens *plural noun*
the time of your life between the ages of 13 and 19. *He started playing chess in his teens.*

teeth plural of **tooth.**

teetotal *adjective*
that never drinks alcoholic drink.
teetotaller *noun*

telecommunications *plural noun*
communications by telephone, telegraph, television, etc.

telegram *noun*
a message sent by telegraph.

telegraph *noun*
1 a way of sending messages by using electric current along wires or by radio. 2 **telegraph pole,** a pole that supports telephone wires.
telegraphic *adjective,* **telegraphy** *noun*

telepathy *noun*
(*say* til-**ep**-ă thi)
communication from one person's mind to another without speaking, writing, or gestures.
telepathic *adjective*

telephone *noun*
1 a device using electric wires, radio, etc. to enable someone to speak to another person who is some distance away. **2 on the telephone,** using a telephone to speak to somebody; having a telephone in your house, office, etc. **3 telephone book,** a telephone directory. **4 telephone box,** a small enclosure containing a telephone for the public to use. **5 telephone directory,** a book containing the telephone numbers of all the people in a district. **6 telephone number,** a number given to a particular telephone and used in making connections to it.

telephone *verb* **(telephoned, telephoning)**
to speak or try to speak to someone on the telephone.

telephonist *noun*
(*say* til-**ef**-ŏn-ist)
someone who operates a telephone switchboard.

telescope *noun*
a tube with lenses at each end, through which you can see distant things more clearly. *Portable telescopes have sections that slide inside one another.*
telescopic *adjective*

televise *verb* **(televised, televising)**
to send out a programme by television.

television *noun*
1 a system using radio waves to reproduce a picture on a screen. 2 an apparatus for receiving these pictures. 3 televised programmes.

tell *verb* **(told, telling)**
1 to pass on a story, news, instructions, etc. to someone by speaking. *He told us a joke.* 2 to reveal a secret. *Promise you won't tell.* 3 to decide. *Can you tell the difference between butter and margarine?* 4 to count. *There are ten of them all told.* **5 tell off,** to speak severely to somebody who has done wrong. **6 tell tales,** to report that somebody else has done wrong.

telling *adjective*
effective; impressive. *It was a telling reply.*

telltale *noun*
a sneak.

telltale *adjective*
that reveals or indicates something. *He had a telltale spot of jam on his chin.*

telly *noun* **(tellies)**
(*informal*) 1 television. 2 a television set.

temper *noun*
1 the mood you are in. *She is in a good temper but he is in a bad temper.* 2 an angry mood. *Now she's in a temper.* **3 lose your temper,** to become very angry.

temperate *adjective*
neither extremely hot nor extremely cold; mild; moderate. *Britain has a temperate climate.*

temperature *noun*
1 how hot or cold someone or something is. 2 an unusually high body-temperature.

tempest *noun*
(*old-fashioned use*) a violent storm.
tempestuous *adjective*

temple *noun*[1]
a building where a god is worshipped.

temple *noun*[2]
part of the head between the forehead and the ear.

tempo *noun*
the speed or rhythm of something, especially of a piece of music.

temporary *adjective*
lasting, or intended to last, for only a short time.
temporarily *adverb*

tempt *verb*
to try to make somebody do wrong or do something he would not normally do; to attract somebody to do something.
temptation *noun*, **tempter** *noun*, **temptress** *noun*

ten *noun*
the number 10, one more than nine.
tenth *adjective* and *noun*

tenant *noun*
someone who rents a house, building, piece of land, etc.
tenancy *noun*

tend *verb*[1]
to be inclined or likely to do something. *Prices are tending to rise.*

tend *verb*[2]
to look after something. *The shepherds were tending their sheep.*

tendency *noun* **(tendencies)**
wanting or being likely to do something; a habit. *She has a tendency to be lazy.*

tender *adjective*
1 not tough or hard; easy to chew. *tender meat.* 2 delicate; sensitive. *tender plants.* 3 gentle; loving. *a tender smile.*
tenderly *adverb*, **tenderness** *noun*

tender *noun*
a truck attached to a steam locomotive to carry its coal and water.

tender *verb*
to give; to offer. *She tendered her resignation.*

tendon *noun*
a strong cord that joins muscle to bone.

tendril *noun*
the part of a climbing plant that twists round something to support itself.

tennis *noun*
a game played with rackets and a ball on a court with a net across the middle.

tenor *noun*
a male singer with a high voice.

tense *adjective* **(tenser, tensest)**
1 tightly stretched. 2 nervous; excited or exciting.
tensely *adverb*, **tension** *noun*

tense *noun*
a form of a verb that shows when something happens. *The past tense of 'come' is 'came'.*

tent *noun*
a kind of shelter made of canvas supported by a pole or poles.

tentacle *noun*
a long, snake-like part of an animal's body. *An octopus has eight tentacles.*

tepid *adjective*
only just warm. *tepid water.*

term *noun*
1 the period of weeks when a school or college is open. 2 a definite period. *a term of imprisonment.* 3 a word or expression. *technical terms.* 4 a condition offered or agreed. *terms of surrender.* 5 **terms,** a relationship with somebody. *They are on good terms.*

terminal *noun*
1 the place where something ends; a terminus. 2 a building where air passengers arrive or depart. 3 a place where a wire is connected to a battery, etc. 4 a device by which you can make contact with a computer.

terminate *verb* (**terminated, terminating**)
to end; to stop.
termination *noun*

terminus *noun* (**termini**)
the station at the end of a railway or bus route.

terrace *noun*
1 a row of houses joined together. 2 a level area on a slope or hillside. 3 a raised flat place next to a house or in a garden.

terrapin *noun*
a kind of tortoise that lives in water.

terrible *adjective*
awful.
terribly *adverb*

terrier *noun*
a kind of small, lively dog.

terrific *adjective*
1 very great. *a terrific speed.* 2 very good; excellent. *a terrific idea.*
terrifically *adverb*

terrify *verb* (**terrified, terrifying**)
to make a person or animal very frightened.

territory *noun* (**territories**)
an area of land, especially an area that belongs to a country or person.
territorial *adjective*

terror *noun*
great fear.

terrorist *noun*
someone who uses violence for a political cause.
terrorism *noun*

terrorize *verb* (**terrorized, terrorizing**)
to fill somebody with terror.

test *noun*
1 an examination; a series of questions, experiments, etc. to find out how good someone or something is. 2 a test-match.

test *verb*
to make a test on a person or thing.

testament *noun*
1 a written statement. 2 one of the two main parts of the Bible, the Old Testament or the New Testament.

testicle *noun*
one of the two glands in the scrotum where semen is produced.

testify *verb* (**testified, testifying**)
to give evidence; to swear that something is true.

testimonial *noun*
a letter describing someone's abilities, character, etc. *Send two testimonials when you apply for the job.*

testimony *noun* (**testimonies**)
evidence; what someone testifies.

test-match *noun* (**test-matches**)
a match between teams from different countries in cricket or some other sport.

test-tube *noun*
a glass tube, closed at one end, used for experiments in chemistry.

tether *verb*
to tie an animal so that it cannot move far.

tether *noun*
1 a rope for tethering an animal. 2 **at the end of your tether,** unable to endure something any more.

text *noun*
1 the words of a book, speech, etc. 2 a short extract from the Bible.

textbook *noun*
a book that teaches you about a subject.

textiles *plural noun*
kinds of cloth; fabrics.

texture *noun*
the way that the surface of something feels. *Silk has a smooth texture.*

than *conjunction*
compared with another person or thing. *Fred is taller than Jim.*

thank *verb*
1 to tell somebody you are pleased about something he has given you or done for you. 2 **thank you,** a way of thanking somebody.

thankful *adjective*
grateful.
thankfully *adverb*

thanks *plural noun*
1 gratitude. 2 **thanks to,** because of. *Thanks to you, we succeeded.*

that *adjective* and *pronoun*
the one there. *Whose is that book? That is mine.*

that *conjunction*
1 which; who. *This is the record that I wanted.* 2 with the result. *He was such a liar that nobody believed him.* 3 used to introduce a wish, reason, etc. *I hope that you are well.*

thatch *noun*
straw or reeds used to make a roof.

thatch *verb*
to make a roof with thatch.
thatcher *noun*

thaw *verb*
to melt; to stop being frozen.

the *adjective* (called the *definite article*)
a particular one; that or those.

theatre *noun*
1 a place where people go to see plays or shows. 2 a special room where surgical operations are done.

theatrical *adjective*
of plays or acting.
theatrically *adverb*

thee *pronoun*
(*old-fashioned use*) you. *I gave thee my commands.*

theft *noun*
stealing. *the theft of the jewels.*

their *adjective*
belonging to them. *Their coats are over there.*

theirs *pronoun*
belonging to them. *Those cakes are theirs, not ours.*

them *pronoun*
those people or things. *Give them some sweets. We can hand them round.*

theme *noun*
1 a subject. 2 a short melody.

themselves *plural noun*
1 they and nobody else. 2 **by themselves,** on their own; alone.

then *adverb*
1 after that; next. *Then there were nine.* 2 at that time. *She was happy then.* 3 in that case; therefore. *It isn't here. It must be lost, then.*

then *noun*
that time. *Have you seen him since then?*

theology *noun*
the study of religion.
theologian *noun*, **theological** *adjective*

theorem *noun*
a statement that can be proved or needs to be proved.

theory *noun* **(theories)**
1 an idea or set of ideas suggested to explain something. 2 the principles of a subject.
theoretical *adjective*, **theoretically** *adverb*

there *adverb*
1 in or to that place. 2 used to call attention to someone or something. *There's a good boy!*

therefore *adverb*
for that reason; and so.

thermometer *noun*
a device for measuring temperature.

Thermos *noun* **(Thermoses)**
a kind of vacuum flask.

thermostat *noun*
a device that automatically keeps temperature steady.
thermostatic *adjective*, **thermostatically** *adverb*

these *adjective* and *pronoun*
the people or things here.

they *pronoun*
the people or things that someone is talking about.

they're short for *they are.*

thick *adjective*
1 measuring a lot from one side to the other. *a thick book.* 2 measured from one side to the other. *a wall ten centimetres thick.* 3 crowded; dense. *thick fog.* 4 *(informal)* stupid. *Don't be so thick.*
thickly *adverb*, **thickness** *noun*

thicken *verb*
to make or become thicker.

thicket *noun*
a group of trees and shrubs growing close together.

thief *noun* **(thieves)**
someone who steals things.

thigh *noun*
the part of the leg above the knee.

thimble *noun*
a metal or plastic cover to protect the end of your finger when you are sewing.

thin *adjective* **(thinner, thinnest)**
not fat; not thick.
thinly *adverb*, **thinness** *noun*

thin *verb* **(thinned, thinning)**
to make or become thin.

thing *noun*
an object; anything that can be touched, seen, thought about, etc.

think *verb* **(thought, thinking)**
1 to use your mind. 2 to have an idea or opinion.
thinker *noun*

third *adjective*
1 next after the second. 2 **Third World,** the countries that are not politically connected with either Communist or Western countries.
thirdly *adverb*

third *noun*
one of three equal parts into which something is divided or could be divided.

thirst *noun*
the feeling that you want to drink.
thirsty *adjective*

thirteen *noun*
the number 13, one more than twelve.
thirteenth *adjective* and *noun*

thirty *noun* **(thirties)**
the number 30, three times ten.
thirtieth *adjective* and *noun*

this *adjective* and *pronoun*
the one here. *Is this the man? This is the one.*

thistle *noun*
a wild plant with prickly leaves and purple flowers.

thorn *noun*
a small pointed growth on the stem of a plant. *Roses have thorns.*

thorny *adjective* **(thornier, thorniest)**
1 full of thorns; prickly. 2 difficult; causing argument or disagreement. *a thorny problem.*

thorough *adjective*
1 done properly and carefully. *thorough work.* 2 absolute; complete. *a thorough mess.*
thoroughly *adverb*, **thoroughness** *noun*

those *adjective* and *pronoun*
the ones there. *Where are those cards? Those are the ones I want.*

thou *pronoun*
(old-fashioned use) you.

though *conjunction*
and yet; in spite of the fact that. *It is not true, though he believes it.*

though *adverb*
however; all the same. *She said she would come; she didn't, though.*

thought *noun*
1 something that you think; an idea or opinion.
2 thinking. *Give the problem some thought.*

thought past tense and past participle of **think.**

thoughtful *adjective*
1 thinking a lot. 2 thinking of other people and what they would like.
thoughtfully *adverb,* **thoughtfulness** *noun*

thoughtless *adjective*
not thinking of other people and what they would like; reckless.
thoughtlessly *adverb,* **thoughtlessness** *noun*

thousand *noun*
the number 1,000; ten hundreds.
thousandth *adjective* and *noun*

thrash *verb*
1 to keep hitting someone or something; to hit very hard. 2 to defeat a person, team, etc. 3 to move your arms and legs wildly.

thread *noun*
1 a long piece of cotton, wool, nylon, etc. used for sewing, weaving, etc. 2 a long, thin piece of something. 3 the spiral ridge round a screw or bolt.

thread *verb*
1 to put thread through the eye of a needle. 2 to put beads, pearls, etc. on a thread.

threat *noun*
1 a warning that you will punish or harm somebody if he does not do what you want. 2 a danger.

threaten *verb*
1 to make threats to somebody. 2 to be a danger to somebody or something.

three *noun*
the number 3, one more than two.

three-dimensional *adjective*
that has depth as well as height and width.

thresh *verb*
to beat corn so as to get the grain out of it.

threshold *noun*
1 the stone, board, etc. under the doorway of a house, building, etc.; the entrance. 2 the beginning of something.

threw past tense of **throw** *verb.*

thrift *noun*
being careful with money.
thriftily *adverb,* **thrifty** *adjective*

thrill *verb*
to give somebody a sudden excited feeling.

thrill *noun*
1 a thrilling feeling. 2 something that thrills you.

thriller *noun*
an exciting story, usually about crime.

thrive *verb (past tense* **throve;** *past participle* **thrived;** *present participle* **thriving)**
to prosper; to grow strongly.

throat *noun*
1 the front of the neck. 2 the tube in the neck that takes food and air into the body.

throb *verb* **(throbbed, throbbing)**
to beat or vibrate with a strong rhythm.

throne *noun*
a special chair for a king or queen.

throng *noun*
a crowd of people.

throttle *verb* **(throttled, throttling)**
1 to strangle somebody. 2 **throttle back** or **throttle down,** to reduce speed while driving a car, motor cycle, etc.

throttle *noun*
a device to control the flow of fuel to an engine; an accelerator.

through *preposition*
1 from one end or side to the other. *Climb through the window.* 2 because of; by means of. *We sold our car through an advertisement.*

through *adverb*
1 from one end or side to the other. *Can we get through?* 2 finished. *I'm through with this job.*

through *adjective*
that goes to the destination without passengers having to make a change. *a through train.*

throughout *preposition* and *adverb*
all the way through.

throve past tense of **thrive.**

throw *verb (past tense* **threw;** *past participle* **thrown;** *present participle* **throwing)**
1 to make a person or thing move through the air; to put something somewhere casually or carelessly. *Who has thrown that stick into the water? He threw it.* 2 to move your body about wildly. 3 to shape a pot on a potter's wheel. 4 **throw away,** to get rid of something.

throw *noun*
a throwing action or movement.

thrush *noun* **(thrushes)**
a bird that has a white front with brown spots on it.

thrust *verb* **(thrust, thrusting)**
to push hard. *He thrust his hands into his pockets.*

thud *noun*
the dull sound of something heavy falling on to something softer.

thumb *noun*
1 the short, thick finger at the side of each hand. 2 **under someone's thumb,** controlled or ruled by him.

thump *verb*
1 to hit something heavily. 2 to punch somebody. 3 to make a thud.

thunder *noun*
1 the loud noise that follows lightning. 2 a loud, heavy noise.
thunderous *adjective,* **thunderstorm** *noun*

Thursday *noun*
the fifth day of the week.

thus *adverb*
in this way. *She did it thus.*

thy *adjective*
(*old-fashioned use*) your.

tick *noun*
1 a small mark, usually √, made next to something when checking it. 2 the clicking sound that a clock or watch makes when it is working.

tick *verb*
1 to mark something with a tick. *She ticked the correct answers.* 2 to make the sound of a tick. *His watch was still ticking.* 3 **tick off**, (*informal*) to tell somebody off.

ticket *noun*
a piece of paper or card that allows you to see a show, travel on a bus or train, etc.

tickle *verb* (**tickled, tickling**)
1 to keep touching someone's skin lightly so as to make him laugh or feel irritated. 2 to have a tickling or itching feeling. 3 to please or amuse somebody.

ticklish *adjective*
1 likely to laugh or wriggle when tickled. *Are you ticklish?* 2 awkward; difficult. *a ticklish situation.*

tidal *adjective*
1 of the tide or tides. 2 **tidal wave**, an unusually large sea-wave.

tiddler *noun*
(*informal*) a tiny fish, child, etc.

tiddly-wink *noun*
a small counter flipped by another counter into a cup, etc. in the game of *tiddly-winks.*

tide *noun*
the rising or falling of the sea which usually happens twice a day.

tidy *adjective* (**tidier, tidiest**)
1 looking clean and orderly. *a tidy room.* 2 fairly large; considerable. *a tidy sum of money.*
tidily *adverb,* **tidiness** *noun*

tie *verb* (**tied, tying**)
1 to fasten something with string, ribbon, etc. 2 to make a knot or bow in something. 3 to finish a game or competition with an equal score or position.

tie *noun*
1 a necktie. 2 a tied result in a game or competition.

tiger *noun*
a large wild animal of the cat family, with yellow fur and black stripes.
tigress *noun*

tight *adjective*
1 fitting very closely; firmly fastened. 2 fully stretched. 3 (*informal*) drunk; intoxicated.
tightly *adverb,* **tightness** *noun*

tighten *verb*
to make or become tighter.

tightrope *noun*
a tightly stretched rope above the ground, for acrobats to perform on.

tights *plural noun*
a garment that fits tightly over the parts of the body below the waist.

tile *noun*
a thin piece of baked clay or other hard material used to cover roofs, walls, or floors.
tiled *adjective*

till *preposition* and *conjunction*
until.

till *noun*
a drawer or box for money in a shop; a cash register.

till *verb*
to cultivate land.

tiller *noun*
a long handle used to turn a boat's rudder.

tilt *verb*
1 to slope or lean. 2 to make something slope; to tip.

timber *noun*
1 wood for building or making things. 2 a beam of wood.

time *noun*
1 years, months, weeks, days, hours, minutes, and seconds; the way that these pass by. 2 a particular moment or period; an occasion. 3 a period suitable or available for something. *Is there time for another cup of tea?* 4 the rhythm and speed of a piece of music. 5 **times**, multiplied by. *5 times 3 is 15 (5 × 3 = 15).* 6 **at times** or **from time to time**, occasionally. 7 **in time**, not late; eventually. 8 **on time**, not late. 9 **time after time** or **time and again**, often; on many occasions. 10 **time-limit**, a limited amount of time for doing something; the time by which something must be done.

time *verb* (**timed, timing**)
1 to measure how long something takes. 2 to note the time when something happens or starts. 3 to arrange the time when something happens.
timer *noun*

timetable *noun*
1 a list of the times when buses, trains, etc. depart and arrive. 2 a list showing the time of school lessons in each subject.

timid *adjective*
fearful; easily frightened.
timidity *noun,* **timidly** *adverb*

timpani *plural noun*
(*say* **timp-ăn-ee**)
kettledrums.

tin *noun*
1 a soft, white metal. 2 a metal container for food.

tin *verb* (**tinned, tinning**)
to put something into tins.

tingle *verb* (**tingled, tingling**)
to have a slight stinging or tickling feeling. *Her ears were tingling with the cold.*

tinker *verb*
to try to mend or improve something unskilfully.

tinker *noun*
(*old-fashioned use*) someone who travels around mending pots and pans.

tinkle *verb* (**tinkled, tinkling**)
to make a gentle ringing sound.

tinsel *noun*
strips of glittering material used for decorations.

tint *noun*
a shade of colour, especially a pale one.
tinted *adjective*

tiny *adjective* (**tinier, tiniest**)
very small.

tip *noun*
1 the part right at the end of something. 2 a small present of money given to someone who has helped you. 3 a piece of advice. 4 a place where rubbish is left.

tip *verb* **(tipped, tipping)**
1 to turn upside down; to move on to one edge. 2 to leave rubbish somewhere. 3 to give somebody a tip.
tipper *noun*

tiptoe *verb* **(tiptoed, tiptoeing)**
to walk on your toes very quietly or carefully.

tire *verb* **(tired, tiring)**
to make or become tired.

tired *adjective*
1 feeling that you need to sleep or rest. 2 **tired of,** bored with. *I am tired of doing the housework.*

tiresome *adjective*
annoying; boring.

tissue *noun*
1 very thin, soft paper; a piece of this. 2 the substance of which an animal or plant is made.
tissue-paper *noun*

tit *noun*
a kind of small bird.

title *noun*
1 the name of a book, film, piece of music, etc. 2 a word that shows a person's position or profession, such as *Sir, Lady, Dr.,* and *Mrs.*

titter *verb*
to laugh in a silly way.

to *preposition*
1 towards. *They set off to London.* 2 as far as; so as to reach. *I am wet to the skin.* 3 compared with; rather than. *She prefers cats to dogs.* 4 used before a verb to show that it is the infinitive. *To be or not to be, that is the question.*

to *adverb*
1 to or in the proper or closed position or situation. *Push the door to.* 2 **to and fro,** backwards and forwards.

toad *noun*
an animal like a big frog. *Toads usually live on land.*

toad-in-the-hole *noun*
sausages baked in batter.

toadstool *noun*
a fungus that looks like a mushroom. *Most toadstools are poisonous.*

toast *verb*
1 to cook something by heating it under a grill, in front of a fire, etc. 2 to have a drink as a way of honouring a person or thing.
toaster *noun*

toast *noun*
1 toasted bread. 2 drinking to honour a person or thing; the person or thing honoured in this way.

tobacco *noun*
the dried leaves of certain plants prepared for smoking in cigarettes, cigars, or pipes.

tobacconist *noun*
someone who keeps a shop that sells tobacco and other things for smoking.

toboggan *noun*
a small sledge.
tobogganing *noun*

today *noun*
this day; the present time. *Today is Monday.*

today *adverb*
on this day; now. *I saw him today.*

toddler *noun*
a young child just learning to walk.

toe *noun*
1 one of the five separate parts at the end of each foot. 2 the part of a shoe or sock that covers the toes.

toffee *noun*
1 a sticky sweet made from butter and sugar. 2 **toffee-apple,** an apple coated with toffee and fixed on a small stick. 3 **toffee-nosed,** (*informal*) proud; snobbish.

together *adverb*
1 with another person or thing; with each other. *They went to school together.* 2 so as to join with one another. *Tie the ends together.*

toil *verb*
1 to work hard. 2 to move slowly and with difficulty.

toilet *noun*
1 a lavatory. 2 **toilet-paper,** paper for use in a lavatory. 3 **toilet-roll,** a roll of toilet-paper.

token *noun*
1 a card, piece of plastic, etc. used instead of money to pay for something. *a record token.* 2 a sign or signal of something. *A white flag is a token of surrender.*

told past tense and past participle of **tell.**

tolerant *adjective*
that tolerates things, especially other people's beliefs, behaviour, etc.
tolerance *noun,* **tolerantly** *adverb*

tolerate *verb* **(tolerated, tolerating)**
to allow something; not to oppose something.
tolerable *adjective,* **tolerably** *adverb,* **toleration** *noun*

toll *noun*
a payment charged for using a bridge, road, etc.

toll *verb*
to ring a bell slowly.

tom *noun*
a male cat.
tomcat *noun*

tomahawk *noun*
an axe used by American Indians.

tomato *noun* **(tomatoes)**
a soft, round, red fruit with seeds inside it. *Tomatoes are eaten raw in salads.*

tomb *noun*
(*say* toom)
a place where a corpse is buried; a grave.
tombstone *noun*

tomboy *noun*
a girl who likes doing things that boys usually do.

tommy-gun *noun*
a small machine-gun.

totalitarian

tomorrow *noun*
the day after today.

tom-tom *noun*
a drum with a low sound.

ton *noun*
1 a unit of weight equal to 2,240 pounds or about 1,016 kilograms. **2** (*informal*) a large amount. *tons of money.* **3** (*slang*) a speed of 100 miles per hour. *This motor bike can do a ton.*

tone *noun*
1 a sound, especially in music. **2** one of the five larger intervals between two notes in a musical scale. **3** a shade of a colour. **4** the quality or character of something.
tonal *adjective*, **tonally** *adverb*

tongs *plural noun*
a tool that looks rather like a pair of scissors and is used for picking up things. *sugar tongs.*

tongue *noun*
1 the long, soft part that moves about inside the mouth. **2** a language. **3** the strip of material under the laces of a shoe. **4** the clapper of a bell. **5 tongue-tied**, too shy to speak. **6 tongue-twister**, something that is very difficult to say.

tonic *noun*
something that makes a person healthier or stronger.

tonight *adverb* and *noun*
this evening or night.

tonne *noun*
a unit of weight equal to 1,000 kilograms.

tonsillitis *noun*
a disease that makes your tonsils sore.

tonsils *plural noun*
two masses of soft tissue inside your throat.

too *adverb*
1 also. *I know the answer too.* **2** more than is wanted, allowed, etc. *Don't drive too fast.*

took past tense of **take.**

tool *noun*
a device that you use to help you do a particular job. *Hammers and saws are tools.*

tooth *noun* (**teeth**)
1 one of the hard, white, bony parts that grow in your gums, used for biting and chewing. **2** one of a row of sharp parts. *the teeth of a saw.* **3 fight tooth and nail**, to fight very fiercely.
toothache *noun*, **toothbrush** *noun*, **toothed** *adjective*

toothpaste *noun*
a creamy paste for cleaning your teeth.

top *noun*¹
1 the highest part of something. **2** the upper surface of something. **3** the covering or stopper of a jar, bottle, etc.

top *noun*²
a toy that spins round and round.

top *adjective*
highest; most important.

top *verb* (**topped, topping**)
1 to put a top on something. **2** to be at the top of something. **3 top up**, to fill a container to the top.

top hat *noun*
a tall, stiff, black or grey hat worn with formal clothes.

topic *noun*
a subject to write, talk, or learn about.

topical *adjective*
connected with things that are happening now. *a topical film.*
topicality *noun*, **topically** *adverb*

topless *adjective*
not wearing any clothes over the top half of the body.

topple *verb* (**toppled, toppling**)
to overturn; to fall over.

topsy-turvy *adverb* and *adjective*
upside-down; muddled.

torch *noun* (**torches**)
a small portable lamp or light. *Torches used to be burning sticks; modern torches are worked by batteries.*

tore past tense of **tear** *verb.*

toreador *noun*
a bullfighter.

torment *verb*
1 to torture. **2** to keep annoying somebody deliberately.
tormentor *noun*

torn past participle of **tear** *verb.*

tornado *noun* (**tornadoes**)
(*say* tor-**nay**-doh)
a violent storm or whirlwind.

torpedo *noun* (**torpedoes**)
a long, tubular bomb sent under water to destroy ships and submarines.

torrent *noun*
a very strong stream or fall of water.
torrential *adjective*

tortoise *noun*
(*say* **tor**-tŭs)
a slow-moving animal with a shell over its body.

torture *verb* (**tortured, torturing**)
to make somebody feel great pain.
torture *noun*, **torturer** *noun*

Tory *noun* (**Tories**)
a Conservative.

toss *verb*
1 to throw, especially up into the air. **2** to spin a coin so as to decide something from the way it lies after falling. **3** to move about restlessly in bed.

total *noun*
the amount you get by adding everything together.

total *verb* (**totalled, totalling**)
to make a total; to add up.

total *adjective*
complete; including everything.
totally *adverb*

totalitarian *adjective*
(*say* toh-tal-i-**tair**-i-ăn)
of or like a government with only one political party.

totem-pole *noun*
a large pole carved or painted by American Indians.

totter *verb*
to walk unsteadily; to wobble.

touch *verb*
1 to feel something with your hand or fingers. 2 to come into contact with something; to hit something gently. 3 to be next to something so that there is no space in between. 4 to interfere with something. 5 to reach. *His temperature touched 104 degrees.* 6 to affect someone's emotions. *We were touched by his sad story.* 7 **touch down**, to land. *The aircraft touched down.* 8 **touch up**, to improve something by making small changes or additions.

touch *noun* **(touches)**
1 the action of touching. 2 the ability to feel things by touching them. 3 a small amount of something; a small action or piece of work. *the finishing touches.* 4 communication with somebody. *We have lost touch with them.* 5 the part of a football-field outside the playing area. 6 **touch-and-go**, uncertain; risky.

touchy *adjective* **(touchier, touchiest)**
easily or quickly offended.

tough *adjective*
1 strong; hard to break or damage. *tough shoes.* 2 hard to chew. *tough meat.* 3 firm; stubborn; rough or violent. *tough criminals.* 4 difficult. *a tough job.*
toughly *adverb*, **toughness** *noun*

toughen *verb*
to make or become tough or tougher.

tour *noun*
a journey visiting several places.

tourist *noun*
someone making a tour or visit for pleasure.
tourism *noun*

tournament *noun*
a series of contests. *a chess tournament.*

tow *verb*
(rhymes with *go*)
to pull a vehicle, boat, etc. along behind you. *They towed our car to a garage.*

toward or **towards** *preposition*
1 in the direction of. *She walked towards the sea.* 2 in relation to; regarding. *He behaved badly towards his children.* 3 as a contribution to. *Put the money towards a new bicycle.*

towel *noun*
a piece of soft cloth used for drying things.
towelling *noun*

tower *noun*
1 a tall, narrow building. *Blackpool Tower.* 2 a tall, flat-topped part of a building. *the church tower.*

tower *verb*
to be very high. *The skyscrapers towered above the city.*

town *noun*
a place where there are many houses near to each other, with shops, schools, offices, factories, etc.

town hall *noun*
a building with offices for the local council and usually a hall for public events.

towpath *noun*
a path beside a canal or river.

toy *noun*
something to play with.
toyshop *noun*

trace *noun*
1 a mark left by a person or thing; a sign. *There was no trace of the thief.* 2 a very small amount of something. *They found traces of poison in his stomach.*

trace *verb* **(traced, tracing)**
1 to copy a picture by drawing over it on transparent paper. 2 to follow the traces of a person or thing; to find.

tracing-paper *noun*
transparent paper used for tracing.

track *noun*
1 a path made by people or animals. 2 the trace of a person or thing. 3 a set of rails for trains, trams, etc. 4 a road or area of ground prepared for racing. 5 a metal belt used instead of wheels on a tank, tractor, etc. 6 **keep track of**, to know where something is, what somebody is doing, etc.

track *verb*
1 to follow the marks left by a person or animal. 2 to follow or observe something as it moves.
tracker *noun*

track suit *noun*
a warm, loose suit of a kind worn by athletes.

tract *noun*[1]
1 an area of land. 2 a series of connected parts in the body. *the digestive tract.*

tract *noun*[2]
a short pamphlet or essay, often about religion.

traction *noun*
1 pulling a load. 2 **traction-engine**, a steam or diesel engine for pulling a heavy load.

tractor *noun*
a motor vehicle used on farms for pulling heavy machines or loads.

trade *noun*
1 buying, selling, or exchanging things. 2 a job; an occupation, especially a craft. 3 **trade-mark**, a sign or name used by only one manufacturer. 4 **trade-name**, a name used by only one manufacturer. 5 **trade wind**, one of the winds that blow continually towards the Equator from the Tropics.

trade *verb* **(traded, trading)**
1 to buy, sell, or exchange things. 2 **trade in**, to give a thing to pay part of the cost of something new. *He traded in his motor cycle for a car.*
trader *noun*, **tradesman** *noun*

trade union *noun*
an organized group of workers.
trade unionism *noun*, **trade unionist** *noun*

tradition *noun*
1 the passing down of beliefs, customs, habits, etc. from one generation to another. 2 something passed on in this way.
traditional *adjective*, **traditionally** *adverb*

traffic *noun*
1 cars, buses, lorries, bicycles, etc. travelling on the road. 2 trade. *the drug traffic.* 3 **traffic-light,** a light that controls traffic. 4 **traffic warden,** someone whose job is to control the movement and parking of vehicles.

tragedy *noun* **(tragedies)**
1 a serious play about sad events. *Shakespeare's 'Hamlet' is a tragedy.* 2 a very sad event. *Her death was a tragedy.*
tragic *adjective,* **tragically** *adverb*

trail *noun*
1 a track or trace. 2 the scent and marks left behind an animal as it moves.

trail *verb*
1 to follow the trail of a person or animal. 2 to drag or be dragged along behind you; to lag behind. 3 to hang down or float loosely.

trailer *noun*
1 a vehicle that is pulled along by a car or lorry. 2 a short film advertising a film or television programme that will soon be shown.

train *noun*
1 a group of railway coaches or trucks joined together and pulled by an engine. 2 a number of people or animals making a journey together. *a camel train.* 3 a series. *a train of events.* 4 a long part of a dress that trails on the ground.

train *verb*
1 to give somebody skill or practice in something. 2 to practise. *She was training for the race.* 3 to make something grow in a particular direction. *Roses can be trained on trellises.* 4 to aim a gun. *He trained his rifle on the bridge.*
trainer *noun*

traitor *noun*
someone who betrays his country or his friends.
traitorous *adjective*

tram *noun*
a bus that runs along rails set in the road.

tramp *noun*
1 someone without a home or job who walks from place to place. 2 a long walk. 3 the sound of heavy footsteps. 4 a steam-ship carrying cargo. *a tramp steamer.*

tramp *verb*
1 to walk with heavy footsteps. 2 to walk for a long distance.

trample *verb* **(trampled, trampling)**
to tread heavily on something; to crush something with your feet.

trampoline *noun*
(*say* **tramp**-ō-leen)
a large piece of canvas joined to a frame by springs, used for bouncing up and down on.

trance *noun*
an unconscious condition like sleep.

tranny *noun* **(trannies)**
(*informal*) a transistor radio.

tranquil *adjective*
peaceful; quiet; calm.
tranquillity *noun,* **tranquilly** *adverb*

tranquillizer *noun*
a drug used to make somebody feel calm.

transaction *noun*
a piece of business.
transact *verb*

transatlantic *adjective*
across the Atlantic Ocean; American.

transfer *verb* **(transferred, transferring)**
(*say* trans-**fer**)
to move a person or thing to another place.
transference *noun*

transfer *noun*
(*say* **trans**-fer)
1 the transferring of a person or thing. 2 a picture or design that can be transferred on to a surface.

transform *verb*
to make a great change in a person or thing. *The caterpillar is transformed into a butterfly.*
transformation *noun*

transformer *noun*
a device to change the voltage of electric current.

transfusion *noun*
putting blood from one person into another person's body.

transistor *noun*
1 a tiny device that controls a flow of electricity. 2 **transistor** or **transistor radio,** a portable radio made with transistors.
transistorized *adjective*

transition *noun*
a change from one thing to another.
transitional *adjective*

transitive *adjective*
used with a direct object. *'To damage' and 'to torture' are transitive verbs.*

translate *verb* **(translated, translating)**
to put something into another language. *This German book has been translated into English.*
translation *noun,* **translator** *noun*

translucent *adjective*
that allows light to shine through. *Frosted glass is translucent but not transparent.*

transmission *noun*
1 the transmitting of something. 2 the gears that transmit power from the engine to the wheels of a vehicle.

transmit *verb* **(transmitted, transmitting)**
1 to send or pass from one person or place to another. 2 to broadcast something.
transmitter *noun*

transparency *noun* **(transparencies)**
a transparent photograph that can be projected on a screen.

transparent *adjective*
that you can see through.

transplant *verb*
to move a plant, part of a human body, etc. from one place to another.
transplant *noun,* **transplantation** *noun*

transport *verb*
(*say* trans-**port**)
to take people, animals, or things from one place to another.
transportation *noun,* **transporter** *noun*

transport *noun*
(*say* **trans**-port)
1 the action of transporting. 2 vehicles, ships, or planes.

trap *noun*
1 something designed to catch animals or people. 2 a plan to capture, detect, or cheat somebody. 3 a two-wheeled carriage pulled by a horse. 4 (*slang*) a person's mouth. *Shut your trap!*

trap *verb* (**trapped, trapping**)
1 to catch in a trap. 2 to capture, detect, or cheat somebody.
trapper *noun*

trapdoor *noun*
a door in a floor, ceiling, or roof.

trapeze *noun*
a bar hanging from two ropes, used by acrobats.

trash *noun*
rubbish; nonsense.
trashy *adjective*

travel *verb* (**travelled, travelling**)
to move from place to place.
traveller *noun*

travel *noun*
1 the action of travelling. 2 **travel agent**, someone whose job is to arrange travel and holidays for people.

trawler *noun*
a fishing-boat that pulls a large net behind it.

tray *noun*
a flat piece of wood, metal, or plastic, usually with raised edges, used for carrying food, cups, plates, etc.

treacherous *adjective*
not to be trusted; not loyal.
treacherously *adverb*, **treachery** *noun*

treacle *noun*
a thick, sweet, sticky liquid.

tread *verb* (*past tense* **trod**; *past participle* **trodden**; *present participle* **treading**)
to walk or put your foot on something. *Who has trodden on the flowers? He trod on them.*

tread *noun*
1 a sound or way of walking. 2 the part of a staircase or ladder that you put your foot on. 3 the part of a tyre that touches the ground.

treason *noun*
the action of betraying your own country.

treasure *noun*
1 valuable things, like jewels or money. 2 a precious thing. 3 **treasure-hunt**, a game in which you try to find something that is hidden.

treasure *verb* (**treasured, treasuring**)
to think that something is very precious.

treasurer *noun*
the person in charge of the money of a club, society, etc.

treasury *noun* (**treasuries**)
1 a place where treasure is stored. 2 **the Treasury**, the government department in charge of a country's money.

treat *verb*
1 to behave towards somebody or something in a certain way; to deal with. *She treats her dog badly.* 2 to give medical treatment to a person or animal. *He was treated for rheumatism.* 3 to pay for somebody else's food, drink, or entertainment. *I'll treat you to an ice-cream.*
treatment *noun*

treat *noun*
1 something special that gives somebody pleasure. 2 the action of paying for somebody else's food, drink, or entertainment.

treaty *noun* (**treaties**)
an agreement between two or more countries.

treble *adjective*
three times as many; three times as much.

treble *noun*
1 a treble amount. 2 a boy with a high singing voice.

tree *noun*
a tall plant with leaves, branches, and a thick wooden stem.

trellis *noun* (**trellises**)
a framework of crossing wooden or metal bars, used to support climbing plants.

tremble *verb* (**trembled, trembling**)
to shake gently, especially with fear.

tremendous *adjective*
1 very large. 2 excellent.
tremendously *adverb*

tremor *noun*
a shaking or trembling.

trench *noun* (**trenches**)
a long hole dug in the ground; a ditch.

trend *noun*
the general direction in which something is going; a tendency.

trendy *adjective* (**trendier, trendiest**)
(*informal*) fashionable; trying to be up to date.
trendily *adverb*, **trendiness** *noun*

trespass *verb*
to go on someone's land or property without permission.
trespasser *noun*

trestle *noun*
1 one of a set of supports on which you place a board to make a table. 2 **trestle-table**, a table made in this way.

trial *noun*
1 trying something to see how well it works. 2 trying a person in a lawcourt. 3 **on trial**, being tried.

triangle *noun*
1 a flat shape with three straight sides and three corners. 2 a percussion instrument made from a metal rod bent into a triangle.
triangular *adjective*

tribe *noun*
a group of families living together, ruled by a chief.
tribal *adjective*, **tribesman** *noun*

tributary *noun* (**tributaries**)
a river or stream that flows into a larger one or a lake.

tribute *noun*
a speech, gift, etc. to show that you like or respect somebody.

trick *noun*
1 something done to deceive or fool somebody. 2 a clever action. 3 the winning of one round of a card-game like whist.

trick *verb*
to deceive or fool somebody.
trickery *noun*, **trickster** *noun*

trickle *verb* (**trickled, trickling**)
to flow slowly. *Tears trickled down her face.*

tricky *adjective* (**trickier, trickiest**)
1 difficult; that needs skill. *a tricky job.* 2 deceitful; cunning. *a tricky salesman.*

tricycle *noun*
a vehicle like a bicycle with three wheels.

tried past tense and past participle of **try** *verb.*

trifle *noun*
1 a pudding made of sponge-cake covered with custard, fruit, cream, etc. 2 a very small amount of something. 3 something that has little importance or value.

trigger *noun*
the lever that you pull to fire a gun.

trillion *noun*
a million billions.

trim *adjective* (**trimmer, trimmest**)
neat; tidy.

trim *verb* (**trimmed, trimming**)
1 to cut the edges or unwanted parts off something. 2 to decorate a piece of clothing. 3 to arrange sails to suit the wind. 4 to balance a boat or aircraft by arranging its cargo or passengers.

Trinity *noun*
the Trinity, God regarded as Father, Son, and Holy Spirit.

trio *noun*
1 three people or things. 2 a group of three musicians. 3 a piece of music for three musicians.

trip *verb* (**tripped, tripping**)
1 to fall over something. 2 to make somebody fall over. 3 to move with quick, gentle steps.

trip *noun*
1 a journey, usually a short one. 2 the action of tripping.

tripe *noun*
1 part of the stomach of an ox used as food. 2 (*informal*) nonsense.

triple *adjective*
consisting of three parts.

triplet *noun*
one of three children or animals born at the same time from the same mother.

tripod *noun*
(*say* try-pod)
a support with three legs. *Fix the camera on a tripod.*

triumph *noun*
1 a great success; a victory. 2 a celebration of a victory.
triumphal *adjective*, **triumphant** *adjective*, **triumphantly** *adverb*

trivial *adjective*
not important; not valuable.
triviality *noun*, **trivially** *adverb*

trod, trodden, see **tread** *verb.*

trolley *noun*
1 a small table on wheels. 2 a small cart or truck. 3 a kind of large basket on wheels, used in supermarkets.

trombone *noun*
a large brass musical instrument with a sliding tube.

troop *noun*
1 an organized group of soldiers, Scouts, etc. 2 **troops,** soldiers.

troop *verb*
to move along in large numbers.

trophy *noun* (**trophies**)
a prize or souvenir for a victory or success. *Silver cups were given to the winners as trophies.*

tropic *noun*
1 a line of latitude about 23½° north of the equator (*Tropic of Cancer*) or about 23½° south of the equator (*Tropic of Capricorn*). 2 **tropics,** the hot regions between these two latitudes.
tropical *adjective*

trot *verb* (**trotted, trotting**)
to run but not to canter or gallop. *The horse trotted along.*

trot *noun*
1 a trotting run. 2 **on the trot,** (*informal*) one after another; continually busy. *He worked ten days on the trot.*

trouble *noun*
1 something that upsets, worries, or bothers you; something difficult or unpleasant. 2 **take trouble,** to take great care in doing something.

trouble *verb* (**troubled, troubling**)
1 to cause trouble to somebody. 2 to take trouble.

troublesome *adjective*
that causes trouble.

trough *noun*
(*say* trof)
1 a long, narrow box for cattle, horses, etc. to eat or drink from. 2 an area of low pressure between two areas of high pressure.

trousers *plural noun*
a garment worn over the lower half of the body, with two parts to cover the legs.

trout *noun* (**trout**)
a freshwater fish.

trowel *noun*
1 a tool for digging small holes, lifting plants, etc. 2 a tool with a flat blade for spreading cement, mortar, etc.

truant *noun*
1 a child who stays away from school without permission. 2 **play truant,** to be a truant.
truancy *noun*

truce *noun*
an agreement to stop fighting for a while.

truck *noun*
1 a railway wagon for carrying goods. 2 a lorry. 3 a cart.

trudge *verb* **(trudged, trudging)**
to walk slowly and heavily.

true *adjective* **(truer, truest)**
1 real; correct; factual. *a true story.* **2** loyal; faithful. *a true friend.*
truly *adverb*

trump *noun*
a playing-card that is of higher value than cards in other suits. *For this game of whist, hearts are trumps.*

trumpet *noun*
a brass wind-instrument.
trumpeter *noun*

truncheon *noun*
a short, thick stick carried by a policeman.

trundle *verb* **(trundled, trundling)**
to move along noisily or awkwardly.

trunk *noun*
1 the main stem of a tree. **2** an elephant's long nose. **3** a large box for carrying or storing clothes, etc. **4** the human body except for the head, legs, and arms. **5 trunk-call,** a long-distance telephone-call. **6 trunk-road,** a main road. **7 trunks,** shorts worn for swimming, athletics, etc.

trust *verb*
1 to believe that a person or thing is good, truthful, or strong. **2** to hope. *I trust that you are well.* **3 trust somebody with something,** to let him use it or look after it.

trust *noun*
1 the feeling that a person or thing can be trusted. **2** responsibility; being trusted.
trustful *adjective,* **trustfully** *adverb*

trustworthy *adjective*
that can be trusted; reliable.

truth *noun*
something that is true; the quality of being true.
truthful *adjective,* **truthfully** *adverb,* **truthfulness** *noun*

try *verb* **(tried, trying)**
1 to attempt. **2** to try out something. *Try sleeping on your back.* **3** to examine the charges against someone in a lawcourt. **4** to annoy somebody. *You are very trying.* **5 try on,** to put on clothes to see if they fit. **6 try out,** to use or do something to see if it works.

try *noun* **(tries)**
1 an attempt. **2** in Rugby football, putting the ball down on the ground behind your opponents' goal so as to score points.

T-shirt *noun*
a shirt or vest with short sleeves.

tub *noun*
a round container. *a tub of ice-cream.*

tuba *noun*
(*say* **tew**-bă)
a large brass wind-instrument with a deep sound.

tube *noun*
1 a long, thin, hollow piece of metal, plastic, rubber, glass, etc. **2** a long, hollow container. *a tube of toothpaste.* **3** the underground railway in London. *She goes to work by tube.*
tubing *noun*

tubular *adjective*
shaped like a tube.

tuck *verb*
1 to push the loose end of something into a tidy place. **2 tuck in,** (*informal*) to eat vigorously. **3 tuck up,** to put the bedclothes snugly round somebody.

tuck *noun*
1 a flat fold stitched in a garment. **2** (*slang*) food, especially what children enjoy eating. **3 tuck-shop,** a shop that sells tuck to children.

Tuesday *noun*
the third day of the week.

tuft *noun*
a bunch of threads, grass, hair, feathers, etc. held or growing together.

tug *noun*
1 a hard or sudden pull. **2** a powerful boat used for towing ships. **3 tug of war,** a contest between two teams pulling a rope from opposite ends.

tug *verb* **(tugged, tugging)**
to pull hard.

tulip *noun*
a brightly-coloured flower that grows from a bulb in springtime.

tumble *verb* **(tumbled, tumbling)**
to fall over or down.

tumbler *noun*
1 a drinking-glass with no stem or handle. **2** an acrobat.

tummy *noun* **(tummies)**
(*informal*) the stomach.

tumour *noun*
(*say* **tew**-mer)
a diseased growth on or in the body.

tumult *noun*
(*say* **tew**-mult)
an uproar.
tumultuous *adjective*

tuna *noun* **(tuna or tunas)**
(*say* **tew**-nă)
a large sea-fish used as food.

tune *noun*
1 a short piece of music; a pleasant series of musical notes. **2 in tune,** at the correct musical pitch.
tuneful *adjective,* **tuneless** *adjective*

tune *verb* **(tuned, tuning)**
1 to put a musical instrument in tune. **2** to adjust a radio or television set so as to receive a particular programme. **3** to adjust an engine so that it works smoothly.
tuner *noun*

tunic *noun*
(*say* **tew**-nik)
a long or close-fitting jacket.

tunnel *noun*
a long hole made under the ground or through a hill, especially for a railway.

tunnel *verb* **(tunnelled, tunnelling)**
to make a tunnel.

turban *noun*
a covering for the head made by wrapping a long strip of cloth round it.

turbine *noun*
a motor that is driven by a flow of water or gas.

turbulent *adjective*
violent; not controlled. *turbulent waves.*
turbulence *noun*

turf *noun* **(turfs** or **turves)**
1 short grass and the soil it is growing on. **2** a piece of grass and soil cut out of the ground.

Turk *noun*
a Turkish person.

turkey *noun*
a large bird used for its meat.

Turkish *adjective*
1 of Turkey. **2 Turkish bath,** a bath in steam or hot air. **3 Turkish delight,** a sweet consisting of lumps like jelly covered in powdered sugar.

turmoil *noun*
a disturbance; confusion.

turn *verb*
1 to move round; to move to a new direction. **2** to become. *He turned pale.* **3** to change. *The frog turned into a prince.* **4** to make something change. *She turned the milk into cheese.* **5** to move a switch, tap, etc. to control something. *Turn on the radio.* **6 turn down,** to reduce the volume, flow, etc.; to reject something. **7 turn out,** to happen; to expel; to empty a place or thing so as to clean or search it. **8 turn up,** to appear or arrive; to increase the volume, flow, etc.

turn *noun*
1 the action of turning. **2** a place where a road bends; a junction. **3** the proper time for something to happen. *It's your turn to wash up.* **4** a short performance in a show. **5** (*informal*) an attack of illness; a nervous shock. *It gave me a nasty turn.* **6 good turn,** a helpful action. **7 in turn,** first one and then the other; following one after another.

turnip *noun*
a plant with a large, round, white root used as a vegetable.

turnover *noun*
a small pie made of pastry folded over fruit, jam, etc.

turnstile *noun*
a revolving gate that admits one person at a time.

turntable *noun*
the revolving part of a record-player that you put the record on.

turpentine *noun*
(*say* ter-pĕn-tyn)
an oil used to make paint thinner and to clean paint-brushes.

turquoise *noun*
(*say* ter-kwoiz)
1 sky-blue or greenish blue. **2** a blue jewel.

turret *noun*
1 a small tower in a castle. **2** a revolving structure containing a gun.

turtle *noun*
1 a sea-animal that looks like a tortoise. **2 turn turtle,** to capsize.

tusk *noun*
a long pointed tooth that sticks out of the mouth of an elephant, walrus, or boar.

tutor *noun*
a teacher, especially one who teaches one person at a time.

TV short for **television.**

tweed *noun*
a thick woollen cloth.

tweezers *plural noun*
a small tool for gripping or picking up small things like stamps and hairs.

twelve *noun*
the number 12, one more than eleven.
twelfth *adjective* and *noun*

twenty *noun* **(twenties)**
the number 20, one more than nineteen.
twentieth *adjective* and *noun*

twice *adverb*
two times; with double the amount.

twiddle *verb* **(twiddled, twiddling)**
to turn something round or over and over in an idle way. *He just twiddled his thumbs.*

twig *noun*
a short, thin branch.

twilight *noun*
the time just before sunrise or just after sunset; the dim light at these times.

twin *noun*
1 one of two children or animals born at the same time from one mother. **2** one of two things that are exactly alike.

twine *noun*
strong, thin string.

twinkle *verb* **(twinkled, twinkling)**
to sparkle.

twirl *verb*
to turn round and round quickly.

twist *verb*
1 to turn something round. *He twisted my arm.* **2** to turn round or from side to side. *The river twisted along the valley.* **3** to bend out of its proper shape. *My wheel is twisted.* **4** (*informal*) to swindle somebody.
twister *noun*

twist *noun*
1 a twisting movement or action. **2 round the twist,** (*slang*) mad.

twitch *verb*
to jerk; to move suddenly and quickly. *The rabbit was twitching its nose.*

twitter *verb*
to make quick chirping sounds. *The sparrows twittered.*

two *noun*
1 the number 2, one more than one. **2 in two minds,** undecided. **3 two-piece,** consisting of two separate parts.

tying present participle of **tie** *verb.*

type *noun*
1 a group or class of similar people or things; a kind or sort of something. **2** letters, figures, etc. designed for use in printing.

type *verb* **(typed, typing)**
to write something with a typewriter.
typist *noun*

typewriter *noun*
a machine with keys that you press to print letters or figures on a sheet of paper.
typewritten *adjective*

typhoon *noun*
a violent windy storm.

typical *adjective*
1 belonging to a particular type. 2 normal; usual.
typically *adverb*

tyranny *noun* **(tyrannies)**
(*say* ti-ră-ni)
the way that a tyrant rules people.
tyrannical *adjective*, **tyrannous** *adjective*

tyrant *noun*
(*say* ty-rănt)
someone who rules people cruelly or unjustly.

tyre *noun*
a circle of rubber round the rim of a wheel.
Tyres are usually hollow tubes filled with air.

U

udder *noun*
the part of a cow, goat, etc. from which milk is taken.

ugly *adjective* **(uglier, ugliest)**
1 not beautiful; unpleasant to look at. 2 threatening; dangerous.
ugliness *noun*

ulcer *noun*
a sore on the surface of part of the body.

ultimate *adjective*
1 last; final. 2 basic. *the ultimate cause.*
ultimately *adverb*

umbilical cord *noun*
the tube connecting the bodies of a mother and her baby until the baby is born.

umbrella *noun*
a round piece of cloth stretched over a folding frame, used to protect yourself from rain or snow.

umpire *noun*
a referee in cricket, tennis, and some other games.

unable *adjective*
not able. *She was unable to hear.*

unanimous *adjective*
(*say* yoo-**nan**-im-ŭs)
that everyone agrees to. *a unanimous decision.*
unanimity *noun*, **unanimously** *adverb*

unavoidable *adjective*
that you cannot avoid; bound to happen.
unavoidably *adverb*

unbearable *adjective*
that you cannot bear or endure.
unbearably *adverb*

unbelievable *adjective*
that you cannot believe; amazing.
unbelievably *adverb*

uncertain *adjective*
not certain; not reliable.
uncertainly *adverb*, **uncertainty** *noun*

uncle *noun*
the brother of your father or mother; your aunt's husband.

uncomfortable *adjective*
not comfortable.
uncomfortably *adverb*

unconscious *adjective*
not conscious; not aware.
unconsciously *adverb*, **unconsciousness** *noun*

uncontrollable *adjective*
that you cannot control or stop.
uncontrollably *adverb*

uncover *verb*
to take the cover or top off something; to reveal something.

undecided *adjective*
not decided; uncertain.

under *preposition*
1 lower than; below. *under the desk.* 2 less than. *under 5 years old.* 3 ruled or controlled by. *under his command.* 4 in the process of; undergoing. *The road is under repair.* 5 using; moving by means of. *under its own steam.*

under *adverb*
in or to a lower place. *The diver went under.*

underclothes *plural noun*
underwear.
underclothing *noun*

underdeveloped *adjective*
not fully developed; not as rich as it might be. *an underdeveloped country.*

underfoot *adverb*
under your feet; on the ground.

undergo *verb* (*past tense* **underwent**; *past participle* **undergone**; *present participle* **undergoing**)
to experience or suffer something; to pass through something.

undergraduate *noun*
a student at a university who has not yet taken a degree.

underground *noun*
a railway that runs through tunnels under the ground.

underground *adverb and adjective*
1 under the ground. 2 done or working in secret.

undergrowth noun
bushes and other plants growing under tall trees.

underhand adjective
secret; deceitful.

underlie verb (past tense **underlay**; past participle **underlain**; present participle **underlying**)
1 to be or lie under something. 2 to be the basis or explanation for something.

underline verb (**underlined, underlining**)
1 to draw a line under a word. 2 to emphasize something.

undermine verb (**undermined, undermining**)
1 to make a hollow or tunnel beneath something. 2 to weaken something gradually.

underneath preposition and adverb
below; under.

underpants plural noun
a piece of underwear worn between the waist and thighs.

underpass noun (**underpasses**)
a place where one road goes under another.

understand verb (**understood, understanding**)
1 to know what something means, what it is, or how it works. *She understood what the Frenchman said.* 2 to learn; to have heard. *I understand he has measles.* 3 to be sympathetic or tolerant. *He is very understanding.*
understandable adjective, **understandably** adverb

understanding noun
1 the power to understand or think; intelligence. 2 agreement; harmony. 3 sympathy; tolerance.

undertake verb (past tense **undertook**; past participle **undertaken**; present participle **undertaking**)
to agree or promise to do something; to start doing something.

undertaker noun
someone whose job is to arrange funerals.

underwater adjective
placed, used, or done under water.

underwear noun
clothes worn next to the skin, under other clothes.

underworld noun
1 in legends, the place for the spirits of the dead; hell. 2 criminals.

undesirable adjective
not wanted; not liked.

undeveloped adjective
not developed; underdeveloped.

undo verb (past tense **undid**; past participle **undone**; present participle **undoing**)
1 to unfasten something. *I undid the knot. Your shoe is undone.* 2 to destroy the effect of something. *He has undone our good work.*

undoubted adjective
definite; certain.
undoubtedly adverb

undress verb
to take clothes off.

unearth verb
1 to dig up something. 2 to find something by searching.

unearthly adjective
supernatural; strange and frightening.

uneasy adjective
uncomfortable; worried.
uneasily adverb, **uneasiness** noun

unemployed adjective
without a job.
unemployment noun

uneven adjective
not level; not regular.
unevenly adverb, **unevenness** noun

unexpected adjective
not expected; surprising.
unexpectedly adverb, **unexpectedness** noun

unfair adjective
not fair; unjust.
unfairly adverb, **unfairness** noun

unfamiliar adjective
not familiar.

unfasten verb
to open something that has been fastened.

unfavourable adjective
not favourable.
unfavourably adverb

unfinished adjective
not finished.

unfold verb
1 to open or spread out. 2 to make or become known slowly. *as the story unfolds.*

unforgettable adjective
that you cannot forget.

unforgivable adjective
that you cannot forgive.

unfortunate adjective
1 unlucky. 2 that you regret. *an unfortunate argument.*
unfortunately adverb

unfreeze verb (past tense **unfroze**; past participle **unfrozen**; present participle **unfreezing**)
to thaw; to change back into a normal condition after being frozen.

unfriendly adjective
not friendly.
unfriendliness noun

ungrateful adjective
not grateful.
ungratefully adverb

unhappy adjective (**unhappier, unhappiest**)
not happy; unfortunate.
unhappily adverb, **unhappiness** noun

unhealthy adjective (**unhealthier, unhealthiest**)
not healthy.

unheard adjective
1 not heard. 2 **unheard-of,** never known or done before; extraordinary.

unicorn noun
(say **yoo**-nik-orn)
an imaginary animal like a horse with a long, straight horn growing out of the front of its head.

uniform *noun*
the special clothes worn by members of an army, organization, school, etc.
uniformed *adjective*

uniform *adjective*
always the same; not changing.
uniformity *noun*, **uniformly** *adverb*

unify *verb* **(unified, unifying)**
to make into one thing; to unite.
unification *noun*

unimportant *adjective*
not important.
unimportance *noun*

uninhabited *adjective*
not inhabited.

unintentional *adjective*
not intentional.
unintentionally *adverb*

uninterested *adjective*
not interested.

uninteresting *adjective*
not interesting.

union *noun*
1 the joining of things together; a united thing. 2 a trade union. 3 **Union Jack,** the British Flag.

unique *adjective*
(*say* yoo-**neek**)
that is the only one of its kind; very unusual. *This jewel is unique.*
uniquely *adverb*, **uniqueness** *noun*

unison *noun*
(*say* **yoo**-nis-ŏn)
in unison, making the same sound together; agreeing.

unit *noun*
1 an amount used in measuring or counting. *Centimetres are units of length, and pence are units of money.* 2 a single person or thing. 3 a group of people or things that belong together.

unite *verb* **(united, uniting)**
to form into one thing; to join together.

unity *noun* **(unities)**
1 being united; agreement. 2 a complete thing.

universal *adjective*
concerning or including everyone and everything.
universally *adverb*

universe *noun*
everything that exists.

university *noun* **(universities)**
a place where people go to study for degrees after they have left school.

unjust *adjective*
not fair; not just.
unjustly *adverb*

unkind *adjective*
not kind. *an unkind remark.*
unkindly *adverb*, **unkindness** *noun*

unknown *adjective*
not known. *He is unknown to me.*

unless *conjunction*
if not; except when. *We shall not go unless we have to.*

unlike *preposition*
differently from. *Unlike me, she enjoys sport.*

unlike *adjective*
not similar; different. *The two children are unlike.*

unlikely *adjective* **(unlikelier, unlikeliest)**
not likely to happen or be true.

unload *verb*
to take off the things carried by a car, lorry, boat, etc.

unlock *verb*
to open a door, box, etc. with a key.

unlucky *adjective* **(unluckier, unluckiest)**
not lucky.
unluckily *adverb*

unmistakable *adjective*
obvious; definite.
unmistakably *adverb*

unnecessary *adjective*
not necessary.
unnecessarily *adverb*

unoccupied *adjective*
not occupied; empty.

unpack *verb*
to take things out of a suitcase, box, etc.

unpleasant *adjective*
not pleasant.
unpleasantly *adverb*, **unpleasantness** *noun*

unpopular *adjective*
not popular.
unpopularity *noun*

unravel *verb* **(unravelled, unravelling)**
to undo something that is knitted or tangled.

unrest *noun*
disturbance; a discontented feeling.

unroll *verb*
to open something that has been rolled up.

unruly *adjective* **(unrulier, unruliest)**
(*say* un-**roo**-li)
difficult to control; behaving badly.
unruliness *noun*

unscrew *verb*
to undo something that has been screwed up.

unseen *adjective*
not seen; invisible; that you have not seen before.

unselfish *adjective*
not selfish.
unselfishly *adverb*, **unselfishness** *noun*

unsteady *adjective* **(unsteadier, unsteadiest)**
not steady.
unsteadily *adverb*, **unsteadiness** *noun*

unsuccessful *adjective*
not successful.
unsuccessfully *adverb*

unsuitable *adjective*
not suitable.
unsuitably *adverb*

untidy *adjective* **(untidier, untidiest)**
not tidy.
untidily *adverb*, **untidiness** *noun*

usable

untie *verb* (untied, untying)
to undo something that has been tied.

until *preposition* and *conjunction*
up to a particular time; up to the time when.

unto *preposition*
(old-fashioned use) to.

untold *adjective*
not able to be counted or measured. *untold wealth*.

untrue *adjective*
not true.

untruth *noun*
a lie.
untruthful *adjective*, **untruthfully** *adverb*

unused *adjective*
1 (*say* un-**ewzd**) not used. *an unused stamp*. 2 (*say* un-**ewst**) not familiar with something. *He is unused to eating meat*.

unusual *adjective*
not usual; strange or rare.
unusually *adverb*

unwanted *adjective*
not wanted.

unwell *adjective*
not well; ill.

unwilling *adjective*
not willing.
unwillingly *adverb*, **unwillingness** *noun*

unwind *verb* (unwound, unwinding)
(rhymes with *find*)
1 to unroll or become unrolled. 2 to relax.

unwrap *verb* (unwrapped, unwrapping)
to take something out of what it is wrapped in.

unzip *verb* (unzipped, unzipping)
to undo a zip-fastener.

up *adverb*
1 in or to a standing or upright position. 2 in or to a high or higher place. 3 completely. *Eat up your carrots*. 4 out of bed. *It's time to get up*. 5 finished. *Your time is up*. 6 (*informal*) happening. *Something is up*. 7 **up against**, faced with difficulties, dangers, etc. 8 **up and down**, backwards and forwards; to and fro. 9 **up to**, until; busy with; capable of; needed from. 10 **up to date**, suiting what is now needed, known, or fashionable; modern.

up *preposition*
in or to a higher position on something. *Climb up the mountain*.

upheaval *noun*
a sudden or violent change or disturbance.

uphill *adjective*
1 sloping upwards. 2 difficult. *an uphill job*.

uphold *verb* (upheld, upholding)
to support; to agree with something.

upholster *verb*
to provide furniture with covers, padding, springs, etc.
upholstery *noun*

upkeep *noun*
the cost of looking after something and keeping it in good condition.

upland *noun*
a high district.

upon *preposition*
on.

upper *adjective*
1 higher. 2 **upper class,** the people in society who are the richest, most influential, etc.

upright *adjective*
1 erect; vertical. 2 honest.

uprising *noun*
a rebellion; a revolt.

uproar *noun*
a loud noise or disturbance.
uproarious *adjective*

upset *verb* (upset, upsetting)
1 to make somebody unhappy. 2 to knock over; to overturn.

upside-down *adverb* and *adjective*
1 turned over so that the top is at the bottom. 2 very untidy; in disorder.

upstairs *adverb* and *adjective*
to or on a higher floor.

uptight *adjective*
(*informal*) upset; annoyed; nervous.

upward *adjective*
moving or directed upwards. *an upward glance*.

upward or **upwards** *adverb*
towards a higher place; up.

uranium *noun*
(*say* yoor-**ay**-ni-ŭm)
a valuable metal used as a source of atomic energy.

urban *adjective*
of, in, or like a town or city.

urchin *noun*
a poor or mischievous boy.

urge *verb* (urged, urging)
1 to try to make somebody do something. 2 to drive people or animals forward.

urge *noun*
a sudden strong desire or wish.

urgent *adjective*
that must be done or dealt with immediately.
urgency *noun*, **urgently** *adverb*

urinate *verb* (urinated, urinating)
(*say* **yoor**-in-ayt)
to pass urine out of your body.
urinal *noun*, **urination** *noun*

urine *noun*
(*say* **yoor**-in)
waste liquid that collects in the bladder and is passed out of the body.
urinary *adjective*

urn *noun*
1 a large metal container in which water is heated. 2 a kind of vase.

us *pronoun*
a word used for *we*, usually when it is the object of a sentence. *We thanked him and he thanked us*.

U.S. or **U.S.A.** short for *United States of America*.

usable *adjective*
that you can use.

usage *noun*
(*say* **yoo**-sij)
the way that something is used, especially the way that a language is used.

use *verb* **(used, using)**
(*say* yooz)
1 to do a job with something. *Have you used my pen? I am using it now.* **2 used to** (*say* yoost-too), did in the past; having the habit of. *I used to like her. He's not used to hard work.* **3 use up,** to use all of something; to consume.
user *noun*

use *noun*
(*say* yooss)
1 the action of using something; being used. **2** the purpose or value of something. *That money is no use to us.*

used *adjective*
(*say* yoozd)
second-hand. *a used car.*

useful *adjective*
1 that can be used a lot; helpful. **2** (*informal*) talented; capable. *a useful cricketer.*
usefully *adverb*, **usefulness** *noun*

useless *adjective*
not useful.
uselessly *adverb*, **uselessness** *noun*

usher *noun*
someone who shows people to their seats in a theatre, church, etc.

usherette *noun*
a female usher, especially in a cinema.

usual *adjective*
such as happens often or all the time; expected.
usually *adverb*

utensil *noun*
(*say* yoo-**ten**-sil)
a device used in the house, especially in the kitchen.

utilize *verb* **(utilized, utilizing)**
to use something.
utilization *noun*

utmost *adjective*
farthest; greatest. *Change the fuse with the utmost care.*

utter *verb*
to say; to make a sound with your mouth. *She uttered a scream.*
utterance *noun*

utter *adjective*
complete; absolute. *He is an utter fool.*
utterly *adverb*

U-turn *noun*
turning a vehicle round in one movement so that it faces in the opposite direction.

V

vacant *adjective*
1 empty; available. **2** not thoughtful; not intelligent. *a vacant stare.*
vacancy *noun*, **vacantly** *adverb*

vacation *noun*
(*say* vă-**kay**-shŏn)
a holiday, especially between the terms at a university.

vaccinate *verb* **(vaccinated, vaccinating)**
(*say* **vak**-sin-ayt)
to immunize somebody, especially against smallpox.
vaccination *noun*

vaccine *noun*
(*say* **vak**-seen)
a substance used for inoculating people.

vacuum *noun*
1 a completely empty space; a space without any air in it. **2** (*informal*) a vacuum cleaner. **3 vacuum cleaner,** a device that sucks up dust and dirt. **4 vacuum flask,** a container with a vacuum between its two walls, to keep the contents at an unchanging temperature.

vagina *noun*
(*say* vă-**jy**-nă)
the passage in the female body between the vulva and the womb.

vague *adjective* **(vaguer, vaguest)**
not definite; not clear.
vaguely *adverb*, **vagueness** *noun*

vain *adjective*
1 too proud of yourself, especially of how you look. **2** useless. *They made vain attempts to save her.* **3 in vain,** with no result; uselessly.
vainly *adverb*

valentine *noun*
1 a card sent on St. Valentine's Day (14 February) to somebody you love. **2** the person you send a valentine to.

valiant *adjective*
brave; courageous.
valiantly *adverb*

valid *adjective*
that can be accepted or used; legal. *This passport is not valid.*
validity *noun*

valley *noun*
an area of low land between hills.

valuable *adjective*
worth a lot of money; of great value.

valuables *plural noun*
valuable things.

vent

value *noun*
1 the amount of money that something could be sold for. 2 how useful or important something is. 3 **value-added tax,** a tax on the value of goods or services.
valueless *adjective*

value *verb* **(valued, valuing)**
1 to think that something is valuable. 2 to estimate the value of a thing.
valuation *noun*, **valuer** *noun*

valve *noun*
1 a device used to control the flow of gas or liquid. 2 a device that controls the flow of electricity.

vampire *noun*
a mythical creature that sucks people's blood.

van *noun*
a small lorry.

vandal *noun*
someone who deliberately breaks or spoils things. *Vandals broke the seats in the park.*
vandalism *noun*

vane *noun*
1 a pointer that shows which way the wind is blowing. 2 a blade or surface that acts on, or is moved by, air or water. *Windmills and propellers have vanes.*

vanilla *noun*
the flavouring used for white ice-cream.

vanish *verb*
to disappear.

vanity *noun*
being too proud of yourself.

vanquish *verb*
to conquer; to overcome.

vapour *noun*
a visible gas produced by heat; steam or mist.

variable *adjective*
that varies or changes.

variation *noun*
1 varying; alteration. 2 something that has changed or been changed.

varied *adjective*
of various kinds.

variety *noun* **(varieties)**
1 a number of different kinds of things. *There was a variety of sweets.* 2 a particular kind of something. *rare varieties of butterflies.* 3 change; a situation where things are not always the same. *a life full of variety.* 4 an entertainment including items of various kinds. *a variety show.*

various *adjective*
1 of different kinds. *for various reasons.* 2 several. *He uses various names.*

varnish *noun* **(varnishes)**
a transparent paint that gives a hard, shiny surface.

vary *verb* **(varied, varying)**
to change; to keep changing; to be different.

vase *noun*
(*say* vahz)
a jar used for holding flowers or as an ornament.

vast *adjective*
very large; very wide.
vastly *adverb*, **vastness** *noun*

vat *noun*
a very large container for liquid.

V.A.T. short for *value-added tax.*

vault *verb*
to jump over something, especially with the help of your hands or a pole.

vault *noun*
1 a vaulting jump. 2 an arched roof. 3 an underground room.

veal *noun*
calf's flesh used as food.

vector *noun*
(*in Mathematics*) a quantity that has size and direction.

veer *verb*
to swerve; to change direction.

vegetable *noun*
a plant that can be used as food.

vegetarian *noun*
(*say* vej-I-**tair**-ree-ån)
someone who does not eat meat.

vegetation *noun*
plants that are growing.

— **vehicle** *noun*
a device for carrying people or things on land or in space. *Cars, lorries, buses, and carts are all vehicles.*

veil *noun*
a piece of thin material to cover the face or head.

vein *noun*
1 one of the tubes in the body through which blood flows. 2 a line or streak on a leaf, rock, insect's wing, etc. 3 a long deposit of a mineral in the middle of rock.

velocity *noun* **(velocities)**
(*say* vil-**os**-I-ti)
speed. *It reached the velocity of sound.*

velvet *noun*
a kind of thick, soft material. *She wore a velvet skirt.*
velvety *adjective*

venereal *adjective*
(*say* vin-**eer**-i-ål)
caused by sexual intercourse. *a venereal disease.*

vengeance *noun*
1 revenge. 2 **with a vengeance,** very strongly or effectively.

venison *noun*
deer's flesh used as food.

venom *noun*
1 the poison of snakes. 2 hatred; a very bitter feeling towards somebody.
venomous *adjective*

vent *noun*
1 an opening in something, especially to let out smoke, gas, etc. 2 **give vent to,** to express your feelings openly. *He gave vent to his anger.*

ventilate

ventilate *verb* **(ventilated, ventilating)**
to let air move freely in and out of a place.
ventilation *noun,* **ventilator** *noun*

ventriloquist *noun*
(*say* ven-**tril**-ŏ-kwist)
an entertainer who makes his voice seem to
come from something away from himself.
ventriloquism *noun*

venture *noun*
something you decide to do that is dangerous
or adventurous.

veranda *noun*
(*say* vĕ-**ran**-dă)
a long, open place with a roof and floor along
the outside of a house.

verb *noun*
a word that says what someone or something is
doing, feeling, etc. *Verbs are words like 'bring',
'eat', 'sit', and 'suffer'.*

verdict *noun*
the decision made by a judge or jury.

verge *noun*
a strip of grass beside a road or path.

verify *verb* **(verified, verifying)**
to find or show the truth of something.
verification *noun*

verruca *noun*
(*say* ver-**oo**-kă)
a wart on the sole of your foot.

versatile *adjective*
(*say* **ver**-să-tyl)
able to do or be used for many different things.
versatility *noun*

verse *noun*
1 poetry. **2** a group of lines in a poem or song.
3 one of the numbered parts of a chapter in the
Bible.

version *noun*
1 someone's account of something that has
happened. *His version of the accident is different from mine.* **2** something translated or rewritten. *a new version of the Bible.* **3** a particular form of a thing. *a new version of this car.*

versus *preposition*
against; competing with. *Arsenal versus Aston
Villa.*

vertebra *noun* **(vertebrae)**
(*say* **ver**-tib-ră)
one of the bones that form the backbone.

vertebrate *noun*
(*say* **vert**-i-brăt)
an animal with a backbone.

vertex *noun* **(vertices)**
1 one of the points of a triangle, square, etc.
2 the highest point of something.

vertical *adjective*
at a right angle to a flat surface; directed or
moving straight up; upright.
vertically *adverb*

very *adverb*
extremely; most. *Ice is very cold.*

very *adjective*
exact; actual. *That's the very thing we need!*

vessel *noun*
1 a boat; a ship. **2** a container. **3** a tube inside
an animal or plant, carrying blood or some
other liquid.

vest *noun*
a piece of underwear worn on the top half of the
body.

vestry *noun* **(vestries)**
a room in a church where the clergyman or
choir get ready for a service.

vet *noun*
a veterinary surgeon.

veteran *noun*
1 a person with long experience, especially as a
soldier. **2** **veteran car,** a very old car.

veterinary *adjective*
(*say* **vet**-rin-ri)
1 concerned with the diseases of animals.
2 **veterinary surgeon,** a person trained to heal
sick animals.

veto *noun* **(vetoes)**
(*say* **veet**-oh)
a refusal to let something happen; the right to
prohibit something.

vex *verb*
to annoy; to cause somebody worry.
vexation *noun,* **vexatious** *adjective*

V.H.F. short for *very high frequency.*

via *preposition*
(*say* **vy**-ă)
going through; stopping at. *This train goes to
London via Leeds.*

viaduct *noun*
(*say* **vy**-ă-dukt)
a long bridge with many arches.

vibraphone *noun*
(*say* **vy**-bră-fohn)
a musical instrument like a xylophone with
metal bars under which there are tiny electric
fans making a vibrating effect.

vibrate *verb* **(vibrated, vibrating)**
to move quickly to and fro; to make a quivering
sound.
vibration *noun*

vicar *noun*
a clergyman who is in charge of a parish.

vicarage *noun*
the house of a vicar.

vice *noun*[1]
1 evil; wickedness. **2** an evil or bad habit or
characteristic.

vice *noun*[2]
a device for holding something in place while
you work on it.

vice-captain *noun*
a deputy for a captain.

vice-president *noun*
a deputy for a president.

vice versa *adverb*
(*say* vy-si-**ver**-să)
the other way round. *'We talk about them and
vice versa' means 'We talk about them and they
talk about us'.*

vicinity *noun* (vicinities)
the neighbourhood; the surrounding district. *There are shops in the vicinity of their house.*

vicious *adjective*
(*say* **vish**-ŭs)
cruel; dangerously wicked or strong.
viciously *adverb*, **viciousness** *noun*

victim *noun*
a person who suffers from something; someone who is killed, injured, robbed, etc.

victor *noun*
the winner of a battle or contest.

Victorian *adjective*
of the time when Queen Victoria reigned (1837–1901).

victory *noun* (victories)
success in a battle, contest, or game.
victorious *adjective*

video *noun*
(*say* **vid**-i-oh)
the recording on tape of pictures and sound.
video-cassette *noun*, **video-recorder** *noun*

videotape *noun*
magnetic tape suitable for video recording.

view *noun*
1 what you can see from one place. *What a lovely view!* 2 someone's opinion. *She has strong views about teaching.* 3 **in view** or **on view,** that you can see. 4 **in view of,** because of. 5 **with a view to,** with the intention of.

view *verb*
to look at something; to consider.
viewer *noun*

vigilant *adjective*
(*say* **vij**-i-lănt)
watchful:
vigilance *noun*, **vigilantly** *adverb*

vigorous *adjective*
full of vigour.
vigorously *adverb*

vigour *noun*
energy; liveliness; strength.

Viking *noun*
(*say* **vy**-king)
one of the Scandinavian pirates or traders that sailed to various parts of Europe between the 8th and 10th centuries.

vile *adjective* (viler, vilest)
disgusting. *a vile smell.*
vilely *adverb*, **vileness** *noun*

village *noun*
a group of houses and other buildings in the country. *Villages are smaller than towns.*
villager *noun*

villain *noun*
a wicked person.
villainous *adjective*, **villainy** *noun*

vine *noun*
a plant on which grapes grow.

vinegar *noun*
a sour liquid used to flavour food. *Do you want vinegar on your fish and chips?*

vineyard *noun*
(*say* **vin**-yard)
an area of land where vines are grown to produce grapes.

vinyl *noun*
(*say* **vy**-nil)
a kind of plastic.

viola *noun*
(*say* vee-**oh**-lă)
a stringed instrument rather like a violin but slightly larger and with a lower pitch.

violate *verb* (violated, violating)
1 to break a promise or law. 2 to disturb; to treat a person or place without respect.
violation *noun*, **violator** *noun*

violence *noun*
force that does harm or damage.
violent *adjective*, **violently** *adverb*

violet *noun*
1 purple. 2 a small plant that usually has purple flowers.

violin *noun*
a musical instrument with four strings played by a bow.
violinist *noun*

V.I.P. short for *very important person.*

viper *noun*
a small poisonous snake; an adder.

virgin *noun*
a person, especially a girl or woman, who has not yet had sexual intercourse.
virginity *noun*

virtual *adjective*
actual; as good as the real thing. *His silence was a virtual admission that he was guilty.*
virtually *adverb*

virtue *noun*
1 goodness; excellence. 2 a particular kind of goodness. *Honesty is a virtue.*
virtuous *adjective*, **virtuously** *adverb*

virus *noun* (viruses)
(*say* **vy**-rŭs)
a microscopic creature that can cause disease.

visible *adjective*
that you can see. *The ship was visible on the horizon.*
visibility *noun*, **visibly** *adverb*

vision *noun*
1 the power to see. 2 something that you see or imagine, especially in a dream. 3 imagination; understanding.

visit *verb*
1 to go to see a person or place; to stay somewhere for a while. 2 **visiting-card,** a card with your name and address printed on it.
visit *noun*, **visitor** *noun*

visor *noun*
(*say* **vy**-zer)
1 the part of a helmet that closes over the face. 2 a shield to protect the eyes from bright light or sunshine.

visual *adjective*
1 of or used in seeing. 2 **visual aids,** pictures, films, etc. used by teachers.
visually *adverb*

visualize *verb* **(visualized, visualizing)**
to imagine something.

vital *adjective*
1 that you need so that you can live; connected with living. 2 extremely important; essential.
vitally *adverb*

vitality *noun*
liveliness; energy.

vitamin *noun*
(*say* vit-ă-min or **vyt**-ă-min)
a substance in food that you need to stay healthy.

vivid *adjective*
bright; clear; lively. *She gave a vivid description of the storm.*
vividly *adverb*, **vividness** *noun*

vivisection *noun*
doing surgical experiments on live animals. *Do you agree with vivisection?*

vixen *noun*
a female fox.

vocabulary *noun* **(vocabularies)**
(*say* vŏ-**kab**-yoo-lă-ri)
1 a list of words used in a particular book, language, etc. 2 the words that a person knows and uses.

vocal *adjective*
of or using the voice.
vocally *adverb*

vocalist *noun*
a singer.

vodka *noun*
a strong alcoholic drink especially popular in Russia.

voice *noun*
1 the sound of speaking or singing. 2 the power to speak or sing. *She lost her voice.*

voice *verb* **(voiced, voicing)**
to say something. *He voiced their objections to the plan.*

volcano *noun* **(volcanoes)**
a mountain with a hole at the top from which molten lava sometimes flows.
volcanic *adjective*

vole *noun*
a small animal rather like a rat.

volley *noun*
1 a number of bullets or shells fired at the same time. 2 in tennis and some other games, hitting back the ball before it bounces. 3 **volley-ball**, a game in which two teams hit a large ball to and fro over a net with their hands.

volt *noun*
a unit for measuring electric current.
voltage *noun*

volume *noun*
1 the amount of space filled by something. 2 an amount. *The volume of work has increased.* 3 the power of sound; how loud something is. *Turn down the volume!* 4 a book, especially one of a set. *Shakespeare's plays in 3 volumes.*

voluntary *adjective*
done or working willingly or without getting paid.
voluntarily *adverb*

volunteer *verb*
1 to offer to do something that you do not have to do. 2 to give something willingly or freely.

volunteer *noun*
someone who volunteers to do something.

vomit *verb*
to bring food back from the stomach through the mouth.

vote *verb* **(voted, voting)**
to show which person or thing you prefer by putting up your hand, making a mark on paper, etc.
voter *noun*

vote *noun*
1 the act of voting. 2 the power to vote.

voucher *noun*
a piece of paper showing that you have paid something or that you can receive something. *This gift voucher can be exchanged for groceries.*

vow *noun*
a solemn promise.

vow *verb*
to make a vow.

vowel *noun*
any of the letters a, e, i, o, u, and sometimes y.

voyage *noun*
a journey by ship, especially a long journey.
voyager *noun*

vulgar *adjective*
1 rude; without good manners. 2 **vulgar fraction**, a fraction shown by numbers above and below a line, not a decimal fraction. $\frac{3}{10}$ *is a vulgar fraction.*
vulgarity *noun*, **vulgarly** *adverb*

vulture *noun*
a large bird that eats dead animals.

vulva *noun*
the outer parts of the female genitals.

W

wad *noun*
a pad or bundle of soft material, pieces of paper, etc.

waddle *verb* **(waddled, waddling)**
to walk like a duck, with short steps, rocking from side to side.

wade *verb* (**waded, wading**)
to walk through water.

wafer *noun*
a very thin kind of biscuit, often eaten with ice-cream.

wag *verb* (**wagged, wagging**)
to move quickly to and fro; to shake. *The dog wagged its tail.*

wage *noun* or **wages** *plural noun*
the money paid to someone for the job he does.

wage *verb* (**waged, waging**)
to carry on a war or campaign.

wager *noun*
(*say* **way**-jer)
a bet.

waggle *verb* (**waggled, waggling**)
to wag. *He waggled his finger.*

wagon *noun*
1 a cart with four wheels, pulled by a horse or ox. **2** an open railway-truck.

wagtail *noun*
a kind of bird with a long tail.

wail *verb*
to make a long, sad cry; to moan or howl.

waist *noun*
the narrow part in the middle of the body.

waistcoat *noun*
a close-fitting jacket without sleeves, usually worn under a loose jacket.

wait *verb*
1 to remain in a place or situation until something happens. **2** to be a waiter. **3 waiting-list,** a list of people waiting for something to become available.

waiter *noun*
someone whose job is to serve people with food in a restaurant or hotel.
waitress *noun*

wake *verb* (*past tense* **woke;** *past participle* **woken;** *present participle* **waking**)
1 to stop sleeping. *Wake up! I woke when I heard the bell. Has he woken up yet?* **2** to make somebody stop sleeping. *You have woken the baby.*

wake *noun*
1 the track left on the water by a ship. **2 in the wake of,** following.

waken *verb*
to wake.

walk *verb*
to move along on your feet at an ordinary speed.
walker *noun*

walk *noun*
1 a journey on foot. **2** the way that someone walks. *He has a funny walk.* **3** a path or route for walking. *There are some lovely walks near here.* **4 walk of life,** your job or occupation. **5 walk-over,** an easy victory.

walkie-talkie *noun*
a small portable radio transmitter and receiver.

walking-stick *noun*
a stick carried or used as a support when you walk.

wall *noun*
1 one of the sides of a building or room. **2** a barrier of bricks or stone surrounding a garden, field, etc. **3 up the wall,** (*informal*) mad. **4 wall-to-wall,** of a carpet that covers the whole floor of a room.
walled *adjective*

wallaby *noun* (**wallabies**)
(*say* **wol**-ă-bi)
a kind of small kangaroo.

wallet *noun*
a small, flat, folding case for holding banknotes, documents, etc.

wallflower *noun*
a sweet-smelling garden plant.

wallop *verb*
(*informal*) to hit hard; to thrash or beat.

wallow *verb*
1 to roll about in water, mud, etc. **2** to get great pleasure from something.

wallpaper *noun*
paper used to cover the walls of rooms.

walnut *noun*
a kind of nut with a wrinkled surface.

walrus *noun* (**walruses**)
a large arctic sea-animal with two long tusks.

waltz *noun* (**waltzes**)
a dance with three beats to a bar.

wand *noun*
a short, thin stick, especially used by a conjurer.

wander *verb*
1 to go about without trying to reach a particular place. **2** to stray.
wanderer *noun*

wane *verb* (**waned, waning**)
to become less or smaller. *His popularity was waning.*

wangle *verb* (**wangled, wangling**)
(*informal*) to get or arrange something by trickery or persuasion.

want *verb*
1 to feel that you would like to have something. **2** to need something. **3** to be without something; to lack. **4** to be poor. *Waste not, want not.*

want *noun*
1 a desire or need. **2** a lack of something.

wanted *adjective*
that the police wish to find or arrest. *He was a wanted man.*

war *noun*
1 fighting between nations or armies; a long period of such fighting. **2** a serious struggle or effort. *the war on poverty.*

warble *verb* (**warbled, warbling**)
to sing gently, like some birds.

warbler *noun*
a kind of small bird.

ward *noun*
1 a room for patients in a hospital. **2** a child looked after by a guardian. **3** an area of a town or city represented by a councillor.

ward *verb*
ward off, to keep something away.

warden *noun*
1 the person in charge of a hostel, college, etc.; a supervisor. 2 a traffic warden.

warder *noun*
someone in charge of prisoners in a prison.

wardrobe *noun*
1 a cupboard to hang clothes in. 2 a stock of clothes or costumes.

ware *noun*
1 manufactured goods, especially pottery. 2 **wares**, goods offered for sale.

warehouse *noun*
a large building where goods are stored.

warfare *noun*
making war; fighting.

warhead *noun*
the explosive head of a missile.

warlike *adjective*
that likes fighting; ready for war.

warm *adjective*
1 fairly hot; not cold. 2 enthusiastic; kind. *a warm welcome.* 3 near something that you are looking for in a game. *You're getting warm!* **warmly** *adverb*, **warmth** *noun*

warm *verb*
to make or become warm.

warn *verb*
to tell somebody about a danger or future event.
warning *noun*

warp *verb*
(*say* worp)
1 to bend or twist because of dampness, heat, etc. *The rain warped the boards.* 2 to distort; to make something unnatural. *Her ideas are warped.*

warrant *noun*
a document that entitles you to do something, especially to arrest somebody or search a place.

warren *noun*
a piece of ground where there are many rabbit burrows.

warrior *noun*
someone who fights in battles; a soldier.

warship *noun*
a ship designed for use in war.

wart *noun*
a small, hard lump on the skin.

wary *adjective* (**warier, wariest**)
(*say* wair-i)
cautious; careful.
warily *adverb*, **wariness** *noun*

was first and third person singular past tense of **be.**

wash *verb*
1 to clean something with water. 2 to flow. *Waves washed over the deck.* 3 to carry along by means of moving liquid. *The sailor was washed overboard.* 4 to be accepted or believed. *That story won't wash.* 5 **wash up,** to wash dishes and cutlery after a meal.
washable *adjective*

wash *noun* (**washes**)
1 the action of washing. 2 the disturbed water or air behind a moving ship or aircraft.

washer *noun*
1 a small ring of metal, rubber, etc. placed between two surfaces, especially under a bolt or screw. 2 a washing-machine.

washing *noun*
clothes that need washing, are being washed, or have been washed.

washing-machine *noun*
a machine for washing clothes, etc.

wash-out *noun*
(*slang*) a complete failure.

wasn't short for *was not.*

wasp *noun*
a flying insect that can sting.

waste *verb* (**wasted, wasting**)
1 to use more of something than you need to; to use something without getting enough results. 2 to make no use of something. 3 to make or become weak or useless.
wastage *noun*

waste *adjective*
1 not wanted; thrown away. *waste paper.* 2 not used or usable; not cultivated. *waste land.* 3 **waste-paper basket,** a container for waste paper.

waste *noun*
1 the action of wasting something. *It's a waste of time.* 2 things that are not wanted or used; rubbish. 3 an area of waste land. *the wastes of Alaska.*
wasteful *adjective*, **wastefully** *adverb*, **wastefulness** *noun*

watch *verb*
1 to look at a person or thing for some while. 2 to be on guard or ready for something to happen. 3 to take care of something.
watcher *noun*

watch *noun* (**watches**)
1 a device like a small clock, usually worn on the wrist. 2 the action of watching. 3 a period of duty on a ship.

watchful *adjective*
watching; alert; careful.
watchfully *adverb*, **watchfulness** *noun*

watchman *noun* (**watchmen**)
someone whose job is to guard a building or other place, especially at night.

water *noun*
1 a transparent, colourless liquid that is a compound of hydrogen and oxygen. 2 the tide. *at high water.* 3 urine.

water *verb*
1 to sprinkle something with water. *Have you watered the plants?* 2 to give water to an animal. 3 to produce water, tears, or saliva. *The smell of bacon makes my mouth water.* 4 **water down,** to dilute.

water-closet *noun*
a lavatory with a pan that is flushed by water.

water-colour *noun*
1 a paint that can be mixed with water. 2 a painting done with this kind of paint.

watercress *noun*
a kind of cress that grows in water.

waterfall *noun*
a place where a river or stream flows over a cliff or large rock.

watering-can *noun*
a container with a long spout, for watering plants.

waterlogged *adjective*
completely soaked or filled with water.

water polo *noun*
a game played by swimmers with a ball like a football.

waterproof *adjective*
that keeps water out. *a waterproof coat.*

water-ski *noun*
one of a pair of skis on which someone stands for *water-skiing*, skimming over the surface of water while being towed by a motor boat.

watertight *adjective*
1 that water cannot get into. *watertight boots.* **2** that cannot be changed or questioned. *a watertight agreement.*

waterway *noun*
a route that ships can travel on.

waterworks *noun*
the place from which water is supplied to a district.

watery *adjective*
1 of or like water. **2** full of water.

watt *noun*
a unit of electric power.

wave *verb* (**waved, waving**)
1 to move your hand to and fro, usually to say hello or goodbye to someone. **2** to move to and fro or up and down. **3** to make hair into waves or curls.

wave *noun*
1 a ridge on the surface of water, especially on the sea. **2** a curving piece of hair; a curl. **3** a period or surge of something strong. *a wave of anger.* **4** one of the wave-like movements in which sound, heat, light, etc. travel. **5** the action of waving.

wavelength *noun*
the size of a radio wave or electric wave.

waver *verb*
to be unsteady or uncertain; to move unsteadily.
waverer *noun*

wavy *adjective* (**wavier, waviest**)
full of waves or curves.

wax *noun* (**waxes**)
a slippery substance that melts easily. *Wax is used for making candles, crayons, and polish.*
waxy *adjective*

wax *verb*
to grow bigger.

waxwork *noun*
a model of a person, etc. made of wax.

way *noun*
1 a road or path. **2** a route; the direction or distance to a place. **3** how something is done; a method. **4** a respect. *It's a good idea in some ways.* **5** a condition or state. *Things are in a bad way.* **6** no way, (*informal*) that is impossible; that is not true.

W.C. short for **water-closet.**

we *pronoun*
a word used by someone to refer to himself and other people who are doing, thinking, etc. the same as himself.

weak *adjective*
not strong; easy to break, bend, defeat, etc.
weakly *adverb*, **weakness** *noun*

weaken *verb*
to make or become weak or weaker.

weakling *noun*
a weak person.

wealth *noun*
1 riches; much money or property. **2** a large quantity. *This book has a wealth of illustrations.*

wealthy *adjective* (**wealthier, wealthiest**)
rich.

weapon *noun*
something used to hurt other people in a battle or fight.

wear *verb* (*past tense* **wore**; *past participle* **worn**; *present participle* **wearing**)
1 to be dressed in something. *I wore that dress last night.* **2** to have something attached to your clothes. *He often wears that badge.* **3** to damage something by rubbing or using it; to become damaged like this. *Your sleeve has worn thin.* **4** to last. *This cloth wears well.* **5 wear off,** to become less; to disappear. **6 wear out,** to make or become weak or useless.
wearer *noun*

wear *noun*
1 clothes. *men's wear.* **2** gradual damage done by rubbing or using something.

weary *adjective* (**wearier, weariest**)
tired.
wearily *adverb*, **weariness** *noun*

weasel *noun*
a small, fierce animal with a slender body.

weather *noun*
1 the rain, snow, wind, sunshine, etc. at a particular time or place. **2 under the weather,** feeling ill or depressed.

weather *verb*
1 to expose something to the rain, sun, etc. *This timber is weathered.* **2** to come through something successfully. *They weathered the storm.*

weave *verb* (*past tense* **wove**; *past participle* **woven**; *present participle* **weaving**)
1 to make something by passing threads or strips over and under other threads or strips. *This basket was woven from straw.* **2** to twist and turn. *He wove through the traffic.*
weaver *noun*

web *noun*
1 a cobweb. **2** a network.

webbed or **web-footed** *adjective*
with toes joined by pieces of skin. *Ducks have webbed feet. They are web-footed.*

wed *verb* (*past tense* **wedded**; *past participle* **wedded** or **wed**; *present participle* **wedding**)
1 to marry. **2** to unite; to join.

we'd short for *we had, we should,* or *we would.*

wedding *noun*
the ceremony when a man and woman get married.

wedge *noun*
a piece of wood, metal, etc. that is thick at one end and thin at the other.

wedge *verb* **(wedged, wedging)**
to put or keep something firmly in place, especially with a wedge.

Wednesday *noun*
the fourth day of the week.

weed *noun*
a wild plant that grows where it is not wanted.

weed *verb*
to remove weeds from the ground.

weedy *adjective* **(weedier, weediest)**
1 full of weeds. 2 weak; thin.

week *noun*
a period of seven days, especially from Sunday to the following Saturday.

weekday *noun*
any day except Sunday.

weekend *noun*
Saturday and Sunday.

weekly *adjective* and *adverb*
happening once a week; for a week.

weep *verb* **(wept, weeping)**
1 to cry; to shed tears. 2 **weeping,** that has drooping branches. *a weeping willow.*

weigh *verb*
1 to find out how heavy something is. 2 to have a certain weight. 3 **weigh anchor,** to raise the anchor and start a voyage. 4 **weigh down,** to hold something down; to depress or trouble somebody. 5 **weigh up,** to estimate; to consider.

weighing-machine *noun*
a device for weighing people or things.

weight *noun*
1 how heavy something is. 2 a piece of metal of known weight, used on scales to weigh things. 3 a heavy object.
weightless *adjective*

weighty *adjective* **(weightier, weightiest)**
1 heavy. 2 important.

weir *noun*
(*say* weer)
a small dam across a river or canal to control the flow of water.

weird *adjective*
(*say* weerd)
very strange; not natural.
weirdly *adverb,* **weirdness** *noun*

welcome *adjective*
1 that you are glad to get or see. *a welcome gift.* 2 allowed or free to do or take something. *You are welcome to use my bicycle.*

welcome *verb* **(welcomed, welcoming)**
to show that you are pleased when a person or thing arrives.

weld *verb*
to join two pieces of metal together by heat or pressure.
welder *noun*

welfare *noun*
people's health, happiness, or comfort.

well *noun*
a deep hole dug or drilled to get water or oil out of the ground.

well *adverb* **(better, best)**
1 in a good or right way. *He swims well.* 2 actually; probably. *It may well be our last chance.* 3 **well off,** fairly rich; lucky.

well *adjective*
1 in good health. *She is not well.* 2 good; satisfactory. *All is well.*

we'll short for *we shall* or *we will.*

well-being *noun*
health or happiness.

wellingtons or **wellington boots** *plural noun*
rubber or plastic boots that reach up to the knee.

well-known *adjective*
known by many people.

well-mannered *adjective*
with good manners.

Welsh *adjective*
1 of Wales. 2 **Welsh rabbit,** melted cheese on a piece of toast.
Welshman *noun*

went past tense of **go** *verb.*

wept past tense and past participle of **weep.**

were plural and 2nd person singular past tense of **be.**

we're short for *we are.*

west *noun*
1 the direction in which the sun sets. 2 **the West,** Europe; the countries of Europe and America that are not Communist.

west *adjective*
1 coming from the west. *a west wind.* 2 situated in the west. *the west coast.*
westerly *adjective*

west *adverb*
towards the west.
westward *adjective* and *adverb,* **westwards** *adverb*

western *adjective*
of or in the west.

western *noun*
a film or story about cowboys, American Indians, etc.

wet *adjective* **(wetter, wettest)**
1 covered or soaked in water or other liquid. 2 not dry. *wet paint.* 3 rainy. *wet weather.*
wetly *adverb,* **wetness** *noun*

wet *verb* **(wetted, wetting)**
to make something wet.

whack *verb*
to hit hard, especially with a stick.

whale *noun*
1 a very large sea-animal. **2 a whale of a,** (*informal*) a very great or good. *We had a whale of a time.*

whaler *noun*
a person or ship that hunts whales.
whaling *noun*

wharf *noun*
(*say* worf)
a quay where ships are loaded or unloaded.

what *adjective*
1 used to ask the amount or kind of something. *What food have you got?* **2** used to say how strange or great a person or thing is. *What a fool you are!*

what *pronoun*
1 the thing that; what thing or things. *What did you say? This is what I said.* **2 what's what,** (*informal*) what is important or useful. *She knows what's what.*

whatever *pronoun*
no matter what; anything or everything that. *Whatever happens, do whatever you like.*

whatever *adjective*
of any kind or amount. *Get whatever help you can.*

wheat *noun*
a cereal from which flour is made.

wheel *noun*
1 a round device that turns on an axle. **2** a horizontal revolving disc on which clay is made into a pot.

wheel *verb*
1 to push along a bicycle, cart, etc. **2** to move in a curve or circle.

wheelbarrow *noun*
a small cart with one wheel at the front and two handles at the back.

wheelchair *noun*
a chair on wheels for an invalid.

wheeze *verb* (**wheezed, wheezing**)
to make a whistling or gasping noise as you breathe.

whelk *noun*
a shellfish that looks like a snail.

when *adverb*
at what time. *When can you come to tea?*

when *conjunction*
1 at the time that. *The bird flew away when I moved.* **2** because; considering that. *Why do you smoke when you know it is dangerous?*

whenever *adverb* and *conjunction*
at any time; every time. *Whenever I see him, he's asleep.*

where *adverb* and *conjunction*
in or to what place; in or to that place.

whereas *conjunction*
but. *Some people like sailing whereas others hate it.*

whereupon *adverb*
after that; and then.

wherever *adverb*
in or to whatever place; no matter where.

whether *conjunction*
if. *I don't know whether she is here or not.*

whey *noun*
(*say* way)
the watery liquid left when milk forms curds.

which *adjective*
what particular. *Which way did he go?*

which *pronoun*
what person or thing. *Which is your teacher?*

whichever *pronoun* and *adjective*
that or those which; any which. *Take whichever you like.*

whiff *noun*
a puff or slight smell of smoke, gas, etc.

while *conjunction*
1 during the time that; as long as. *Whistle while you work.* **2** but; although. *She was dressed in black, while I was in white.*

while *noun*
a period of time. *We have waited all this while.*

while *verb* (**whiled, whiling**)
while away, to pass time. *We whiled away the time on the river.*

whilst *conjunction*
while.

whimper *verb*
to make feeble crying sounds. *The dog whimpered while I bathed its leg.*

whine *verb* (**whined, whining**)
to make a long, high, miserable or piercing sound. *Stop that child whining!*

whinny *verb* (**whinnied, whinnying**)
to neigh gently or happily.

whip *noun*
a cord or strip of leather fixed to a handle and used for hitting people or animals.

whip *verb* (**whipped, whipping**)
1 to hit a person or animal with a whip. **2** to beat cream, eggs, etc. into a froth. **3** to move or take suddenly. *He whipped out a gun.* **4** (*informal*) to steal something.

whirl *verb*
to turn or spin very quickly.

whirlpool *noun*
a stong whirling current of water.

whirlwind *noun*
a very strong wind that whirls around or blows in a spiral.

whirr *verb*
to make a continuous buzzing sound.

whisk *verb*
1 to move something very quickly. **2** to stir something briskly.

whisk *noun*
1 a device for whisking eggs, cream, etc. **2** a whisking movement.

whisker *noun*
a hair growing on the face of a person or animal.

whisky *noun* (**whiskies**)
a very strong alcoholic drink.

whisper

whisper *verb*
to speak very softly; to talk secretly.

whisper *noun*
a whispering voice or sound.

whist *noun*
a card-game usually for four people.

whistle *verb* (**whistled, whistling**)
to make a shrill or musical sound by blowing through your lips.
whistler *noun*

whistle *noun*
1 a whistling sound. 2 a device that makes a shrill sound when you blow into it.

Whit *noun*
1 Whitsun. 2 **Whit Sunday,** the 7th Sunday after Easter.

white *adjective* (**whiter, whitest**)
1 of the very lightest colour, like snow or milk. 2 **white coffee,** coffee with milk or cream. 3 **white elephant,** something useless. 4 **white-hot,** extremely hot.
whiteness *noun*, **whitish** *adjective*

white *noun*
1 white colour. 2 a white person.

whiten *verb*
to make or become white.

whitewash *noun*
a liquid painted on walls and ceilings to make them white.

Whitsun *noun*
Whit Sunday, or the period around it.

whiz *verb* (**whizzed, whizzing**)
1 to move very quickly. 2 to sound like something rushing through the air.

who *pronoun*
which person; which people. *Who threw that?*

whole *adjective*
1 complete; not broken or damaged. 2 **whole number,** a number without any fractions.

whole *noun*
1 a complete thing. 2 **on the whole,** considering everything; mainly.

wholemeal *adjective*
made from the whole grain of wheat, etc. *wholemeal bread.*

wholesale *adjective and adverb*
1 sold in large quantities, usually to shopkeepers. 2 on a large scale; including everybody or everything. *wholesale destruction.*

wholesome *adjective*
good for health; healthy. *wholesome food.*

wholly *adverb*
completely; entirely.

whom *pronoun*
a word used instead of *who* when it is the object of a sentence or preceded by *to, of, by,* etc. *To whom did you give the parcel?*

whoop *noun*
(*say* woop)
a loud excited cry.

whoopee *interjection*
(*say* wuup-ee)
a joyful exclamation. *It's a holiday! Whoopee!*

whooping-cough *noun*
(*say* hoop-ing-kof)
an illness that makes you cough and gasp.

who's short for *who has* or *who is. Who's coming for a swim?*

whose *pronoun*
belonging to what person; of whom; of which. *Whose bike is that?*

why *adverb*
for what reason or purpose.

wick *noun*
1 the string that goes through the middle of a candle. 2 the strip of material that you light in a lamp or heater that uses oil.

wicked *adjective*
very bad or cruel; doing things that are wrong or spiteful.
wickedly *adverb*, **wickedness** *noun*

wicker or **wickerwork** *noun*
things made of reeds or canes woven together.

wicket *noun*
1 the set of three stumps with two bails on top of them in cricket. 2 the part of a cricket ground between or near the wickets. 3 **wicket-keeper,** the fielder in cricket who stands behind the batsman's wicket.

wide *adjective* (**wider, widest**)
1 measuring a lot from one side to the other. *a wide river.* 2 from one side to the other. *The room is 4 metres wide.* 3 covering a great area. *wide knowledge.*
widely *adverb*, **wideness** *noun*

wide *adverb* (**wider, widest**)
1 completely; fully. *wide awake.* 2 far from the target. *His shot went wide.* 3 over a large area. *She travelled far and wide.*

widen *verb*
to make or become wider.

widespread *adjective*
existing in many places; common.

widow *noun*
a woman whose husband has died.

widower *noun*
a man whose wife has died.

width *noun*
how wide something is.

wield *verb*
(*say* weeld)
to hold something and use it. *He wielded a sword.*

wife *noun* (**wives**)
a woman who is married to a particular man. *Henry VIII had six wives.*

wig *noun*
a covering of false hair worn on the head.

wiggle *verb* (**wiggled, wiggling**)
to move from side to side; to wriggle.
wiggly *adjective*

wigwam *noun*
the tent of an American Indian.

wild *adjective*
1 not tame; not looked after by people. *a wild dog.* 2 not grown by people; not cultivated. *a wild flower.* 3 not civilized. *wild tribes.* 4 not controlled; violent. *wild behaviour.*
wildly *adverb,* **wildness** *noun*

wilderness *noun* (**wildernesses**)
an area of wild country; a desert.

wildlife *noun*
wild animals.

wilful *adjective*
1 obstinate. *a wilful child.* 2 deliberate. *wilful disobedience.*
wilfully *adverb,* **wilfulness** *noun*

will *verb* (*past tense* **would**)
shall; is or are going to. *She will like this.*

willing *adjective*
ready and happy to do what is wanted.
willingly *adverb,* **willingness** *noun*

willow *noun*
a tree with thin, flexible branches. *Willows often grow near water.*

wilt *verb*
to lose freshness or strength; to droop.

wily *adjective* (**wilier, wiliest**)
crafty; cunning.

win *verb* (**won, winning**)
1 to do best in a contest, game, batttle, etc. 2 to get something by using effort, skill, etc. *She won the prize.*

wince *verb* (**winced, wincing**)
to make a slight movement because you are in pain, unhappy, etc.

winch *noun* (**winches**)
a device for lifting or pulling things, using a rope or cable that goes round a wheel.

wind *noun*
(rhymes with *tinned*)
1 a current of air. 2 gas in the stomach that makes you uncomfortable. 3 breath used for a purpose. 4 the wind instruments of an orchestra. 5 **get** or **have the wind up,** (*slang*) to be scared. 6 **wind instrument,** a musical instrument that you blow into.

wind *verb* (**wound, winding**)
(rhymes with *find*)
1 to turn or go in twists, curves, or circles. 2 to wind up a watch or clock. 3 **wind up,** to make a watch, clock, etc. work by turning a key; to close a business; (*informal*) to end in a place or condition. *I have wound up my watch. He wound up in gaol.*

windfall *noun*
1 a fruit blown down from a tree. 2 a piece of unexpected good luck, especially getting a sum of money.

windmill *noun*
a mill worked by the wind that turns four projecting parts called 'sails' shaped like a cross.

window *noun*
an opening in a wall, roof, etc. to let in light and air, usually filled with glass; this piece of glass.

windpipe *noun*
the tube through which air reaches the lungs.

windscreen *noun*
the window at the front of a motor vehicle.

windward *adjective*
that faces the wind. *the windward side of the ship.*

windy *adjective* (**windier, windiest**)
with much wind. *a windy night.*

wine *noun*
1 an alcoholic drink made from grapes or other plants. 2 a dark red colour.

wing *noun*
1 one of the parts of a bird or insect that it uses for flying. 2 one of the long, flat projections that support an aircraft in the air. 3 part of a building that extends from the main part. 4 the part of a motor vehicle's body above a wheel. 5 one of the players in football, hockey, etc. whose place is at the side of the pitch. 6 **on the wing,** flying. 7 **take wing,** to fly away. 8 **wings,** the sides of a theatre stage.
winged *adjective,* **wingless** *adjective*

wink *verb*
1 to close and open your eye quickly. 2 to flicker or twinkle.

wink *noun*
1 the action of winking. 2 a short period of sleep. *I didn't sleep a wink.*

winkle *noun*
an edible shellfish.

winner *noun*
1 a person who wins something. 2 something very successful. *Her book is a winner.*

winnings *plural noun*
money won by betting, in a game, etc.

winter *noun*
the coldest season of the year, between autumn and spring.
wintry *adjective*

wipe *verb* (**wiped, wiping**)
1 to dry or clean something by rubbing it. 2 **wipe out,** to destroy; to remove.
wiper *noun*

wire *noun*
1 a long thin strip of metal, especially used to carry electric current. 2 (*informal*) a telegram.

wire *verb* (**wired, wiring**)
1 to provide something with wires. 2 to fix with wire.

wireless *noun* (**wirelesses**)
1 radio. 2 a radio set.

wiry *adjective* (**wirier, wiriest**)
1 like wire. 2 lean and strong.

wisdom *noun*
1 being wise. 2 wise sayings or writings. 3 **wisdom tooth,** a molar that may grow at the back of your jaw much later than the other teeth.

wise *adjective* (**wiser, wisest**)
knowing or understanding many things.
wisely *adverb*

wish *verb*
1 to think or say that you would like something. 2 to say that you hope someone will get something. *We wish you a merry Christmas.*

wish *noun* **(wishes)**
1 something you want. 2 the action of wishing.

wishbone *noun*
a forked bone from a bird like a chicken. *Two people break the wishbone and the person who gets the bigger piece can make a wish.*

wisp *noun*
a thin piece of hair, straw, smoke, etc.
wispy *adjective*

wistful *adjective*
sadly longing for something.
wistfully *adverb*, **wistfulness** *noun*

wit *noun*
1 intelligence; cleverness. 2 a clever kind of humour; the ability to be cleverly humorous. 3 a witty person.

witch *noun* **(witches)**
1 a woman who uses magic to do evil things. 2 **witch-doctor**, a magician in a primitive tribe.

witchcraft *noun*
using magic to do evil things.

with *preposition*
1 having. *a man with a wooden leg.* 2 in the company of; accompanied by. *I came with a friend.* 3 using. *Hit it with a hammer.* 4 against. *They fought with each other.* 5 because of. *He shook with laughter.* 6 towards; concerning. *Be patient with me.*

withdraw *verb* (*past tense* **withdrew**; *past participle* **withdrawn**; *present participle* **withdrawing**)
1 to take away or back; to remove. *She withdrew money from the bank.* 2 to retreat; to leave. *They have withdrawn from the frontier.*
withdrawal *noun*

wither *verb*
to shrivel; to wilt.

withhold *verb* **(withheld, withholding)**
to refuse to give something to somebody. *He withheld his permission.*

within *preposition* and *adverb*
inside; not beyond something.

without *preposition*
not having; free from. *They were without food.*

withstand *verb* **(withstood, withstanding)**
to resist; to endure successfully.

witness *noun* **(witnesses)**
1 a person who sees something happen. *There were no witnesses of the accident.* 2 someone who gives evidence in a lawcourt.

witty *adjective* **(wittier, wittiest)**
clever and amusing.
wittily *adverb*, **wittiness** *noun*

wizard *noun*
a man who can do magic things; an amazing person.
wizardry *noun*

wobble *verb* **(wobbled, wobbling)**
to move unsteadily from side to side; to shake. *The jelly was wobbling.*
wobbly *adjective*

woe *noun*
sorrow; misfortune.
woeful *adjective*, **woefully** *adverb*

woke, woken, see **wake** *verb*.

wolf *noun* **(wolves)**
a wild animal like a large, fierce dog.

woman *noun* **(women)**
a grown-up female human being.

womb *noun*
(*say* woom)
the part of a female's body where babies develop before they are born.

won past tense and past participle of **win**.

wonder *noun*
1 a feeling of surprise and admiration. 2 something that makes you feel surprised and admiring; a marvel. 3 **no wonder**, it is not surprising.

wonder *verb*
1 to feel that you want to know or decide about something. 2 to feel wonder at something.

wonderful *adjective*
1 astonishing. 2 excellent.
wonderfully *adverb*

won't short for *will not*.

wood *noun*
1 the substance of which trees are made. 2 a lot of trees growing together.

wooded *adjective*
covered with growing trees.

wooden *adjective*
1 made of wood. *a wooden leg.* 2 stiff; awkward. *His movements were wooden.*

woodland *noun*
wooded country.

woodpecker *noun*
a bird that makes holes in trees with its beak, to find insects to eat.

woodwind *noun*
wind instruments that are usually made of wood, such as the clarinet and oboe.

woodwork *noun*
1 making things with wood. 2 things made out of wood.

woodworm *noun* **(woodworm** or **woodworms)**
the larva of a beetle that bores into wood.

woody *adjective* **(woodier, woodiest)**
1 like wood. 2 full of trees.

wool *noun*
1 the thick, soft hair of sheep, goats, etc. 2 thread or cloth made from this hair.

woollen *adjective*
made of wool.

woollens *plural noun*
clothes made of wool.

woolly *adjective* **(woollier, woolliest)**
1 covered with wool. 2 of or like wool. 3 not clear; vague. *He had woolly ideas.*
woolliness *noun*

word *noun*
1 a letter or group of letters that means something when you write it. 2 a sound or group of sounds that means something when you say it. 3 a promise. *He cannot keep his word.* 4 a command; an order. *Run when I give the word.* 5 a message; information. *We sent word that we had arrived safely.*

word-blindness *noun*
difficulty in reading and spelling, caused by a brain condition.

wordy *adjective* **(wordier, wordiest)**
using too many words. *a wordy speech.*

wore past tense of **wear** *verb.*

work *noun*
1 something that you have to do that needs effort or energy. *Weeding is hard work.* 2 a person's job. *Has Dad gone to work yet?* 3 something produced by work. *The teacher marked our work.* 4 **at work,** working; functioning. 5 **work of art,** a painting, sculpture, etc. 6 **works,** a factory; the moving parts of a machine.

work *verb*
1 to do work. 2 to have a job; to be employed. *She works in a bank.* 3 to act or operate correctly or successfully. *Is the lift working?* 4 to make something act or operate. *Can you work the lift?* 5 to become gradually. *The screw had worked loose.* 6 **work out,** to find an answer by working or calculating; to have a particular result. 7 **work to rule,** to make a protest or delay by following strictly the rules of your work.

workable *adjective*
usable; practicable.

worker *noun*
1 someone who works. 2 a member of the working class. 3 a bee, ant, etc. that does the work in a hive or colony.

working *noun*
1 a mine or quarry. 2 **working** or **workings,** the way that something works.

working class *noun* **(working classes)**
those who work for wages, especially in industry; the poorest group of people.

workman *noun* **(workmen)**
a man who does a job, especially for pay.

workmanship *noun*
skill in working, or the result of such skill.

workshop *noun*
a place where things are made or mended.

world *noun*
1 the planet that we live on, with all its peoples; the earth. 2 the universe. 3 a place or area; a particular activity. *the world of sport.*

worldly *adjective* **(worldlier, worldliest)**
of or interested in money, possessions, etc. **worldliness** *noun*

worm *noun*
1 a small, thin, wriggling animal without legs, especially an earthworm. 2 an unimportant or disliked person.

worm *verb*
to move by wriggling or crawling.

worn past participle of **wear** *verb.*

worry *verb* **(worried, worrying)**
1 to trouble somebody; to make somebody think of something bad that may happen. 2 to be worried. 3 to hold something in your teeth and shake it. *The dog was worrying the rat.* **worrier** *noun*

worry *noun* **(worries)**
1 being worried. 2 something that worries you.

worse *adjective* and *adverb*
more bad or more badly; less good or less well.

worsen *verb*
to make or become worse.

worship *verb* **(worshipped, worshipping)**
to give praise or respect to God or a god. **worshipper** *noun*

worship *noun*
worshipping; religious ceremonies or services.

worst *adjective* and *adverb*
most bad or most badly; least good or least well.

worth *adjective*
1 having a certain value. *This stamp is worth £100.* 2 that deserves; good enough for. *That book is worth reading.*

worth *noun*
value. *a book of little worth.*

worthless *adjective*
with no value; useless.

worthwhile *adjective*
important or good enough to do; useful.

worthy *adjective* **(worthier, worthiest)**
1 that deserves respect or support; good. *a worthy cause.* 2 **worthy of,** that deserves; good enough for. *This charity is worthy of support.* **worthily** *adverb,* **worthiness** *noun*

would *verb*
1 past tense of **will** *verb.* 2 to wish or agree to do something. *He would come if he could.*

wound *noun*
(*say* woond)
an injury done to the body or the feelings.

wound *verb*
(*say* woond)
to give somebody a wound.

wound past tense and past participle of **wind** *verb.*
(*say* wownd)

wove, woven, see **weave.**

wrap *verb* **(wrapped, wrapping)**
to put paper, cloth, etc. round something.

wrapper *noun*
a piece of paper or cloth wrapped round something.

wrath *noun*
(rhymes with *cloth*)
(*old-fashioned use*) anger.
wrathful *adjective,* **wrathfully** *adverb*

wreath *noun*
(*say* reeth)
flowers, branches, etc. bound together to make a circle. *wreaths of holly.*

wreathe *verb* **(wreathed, wreathing)**
(*say* reeth)
1 to surround or decorate something with a wreath. 2 to cover. *Her face was wreathed in smiles.*

wreck *verb*
to damage something, especially a ship, so badly that it cannot be used again.
wrecker *noun*

wreck *noun*
1 a wrecked ship, car, building, etc. 2 the wrecking of something.

wreckage *noun*
the pieces of a wreck.

wren *noun*
a very small, brown bird.

wrench *verb*
to pull or twist something suddenly or violently. *He wrenched the door open.*

wrench *noun* (wrenches)
1 a wrenching movement. 2 a tool for gripping and turning bolts, nuts, etc.

wrestle *verb* (wrestled, wrestling)
1 to struggle with somebody and try to throw him to the ground. 2 to struggle with a difficulty, problem, etc.
wrestler *noun*

wretch *noun* (wretches)
someone who is unhappy, poor, or disliked.

wretched *adjective*
(*say* **rech**-id)
1 unhappy; miserable; poor. *a wretched beggar.* 2 not satisfactory or pleasant. *This wretched car won't start.*

wriggle *verb* (wriggled, wriggling)
to twist and turn your body around.
wriggler *noun*, **wriggly** *adjective*

wring *verb* (wrung, wringing)
1 to squeeze or twist a wet thing to get the water out of it. *Have you wrung out your swimsuit?* 2 to squeeze or twist something. *I'll wring your neck!* 3 **wringing wet**, very wet; soaked.

wringer *noun*
a device for squeezing water out of clothes.

wrinkle *noun*
a small crease or line in the skin or on a surface.

wrinkle *verb* (wrinkled, wrinkling)
to make wrinkles.

wrist *noun*
1 the thin part of your arm where it joins your hand. 2 **wrist-watch**, a watch that you wear on your wrist.

write *verb* (*past tense* **wrote**; *past participle* **written**; *present participle* **writing**)
1 to put words or signs on paper or some other surface so that people can read them. *Who wrote these words on the wall?* 2 to be the author or composer of something. *'Hamlet' was written by Shakespeare.* 3 to send a letter to somebody.
writer *noun*, **writing** *noun*

writhe *verb* (writhed, writhing)
(*say* ryth)
to twist your body about because you are in pain or discomfort.

wrong *adjective*
1 not fair; not moral. *Is it wrong to swear?* 2 incorrect. *Your answer is wrong.* 3 not working properly. *There's something wrong with the engine.*
wrongly *adverb*, **wrongness** *noun*

wrong *noun*
1 something that is wrong. 2 **in the wrong**, having done or said something wrong.

wrote past tense of **write**.

wrung past tense and past participle of **wring**.

wry *adjective* (wrier, wriest)
twisted; showing disgust or disappointment. *a wry smile.*

X

Xmas *noun* (Xmases)
Christmas.

X-ray *noun*
1 a ray that can penetrate something solid. 2 a photograph of the inside of something, especially part of the body, made by means of X-rays.

X-ray *verb*
to make an X-ray photograph of something.

xylophone *noun*
(*say* **zy**-lŏ-fohn)
a musical instrument made of wooden bars that you hit with small hammers.

Y

yacht *noun*
(*say* yot)
1 a sailing boat used for racing or cruising. **2** a private ship.
yachting *noun*, **yachtsman** *noun*

yank *verb*
to pull something strongly and suddenly.

yap *verb* (**yapped, yapping**)
to make a shrill barking sound. *a yapping dog.*

yard *noun*[1]
a measure of length, 36 inches or about 91 centimetres.

yard *noun*[2]
a piece of ground surrounded by or next to walls or buildings.

yarn *noun*
1 thread. **2** (*informal*) a story.

yawn *verb*
1 to open your mouth wide and breathe in deeply when you are tired or bored. **2** to form a wide opening. *The chasm yawned beneath them.*

yawn *noun*
the action of yawning.

ye *pronoun*
(*old-fashioned use*) you.

year *noun*
the time that the earth takes to go right round the sun; twelve months.
yearly *adjective and adverb*

yearn *verb*
to long for something.

yeast *noun*
a substance used in making bread, beer, wine, etc.

yell *noun*
a loud cry; a shout.

yellow *noun*
the colour of lemons or buttercups.

yellow *adjective*
1 yellow in colour. **2** (*informal*) cowardly. **3 yellow fever,** a tropical disease that makes your skin yellow.
yellowish *adjective*

yelp *verb*
to make a shrill bark or cry.

yeoman *noun* (**yeomen**)
(*say* **yoh**-măn)
1 (*old-fashioned use*) a man who runs a small farm. **2 Yeoman of the Guard,** a guard at the Tower of London; a beefeater.

yes *interjection*
a word used for agreeing to something.

yesterday *noun and adverb*
the day before today.

yet *adverb*
1 up to now; by this time. *Has the postman called yet?* **2** eventually. *I'll get even with him yet.* **3** in addition; even; still. *She became yet more excited.*

yet *conjunction*
nevertheless. *It is strange, yet it is true.*

yeti *noun*
(*say* **yet**-i)
a monstrous animal thought to live in the Himalayas.

yew *noun*
an evergreen tree with dark leaves like needles.

yield *verb*
1 to surrender; to give in. *He yielded to persuasion.* **2** to produce a crop, profit, etc. *These trees yield good apples.*

yield *noun*
an amount produced by something. *What is the yield of wheat per acre?*

yodel *verb* (**yodelled, yodelling**)
to sing or shout with your voice often going from low to high notes. *The Swiss mountaineer was yodelling.*
yodeller *noun*

yoga *noun*
(*say* **yoh**-gă)
a method of meditation and self-control.

yoghurt *noun*
(*say* **yog**-ert)
sour fermented milk. *Yoghurt is often flavoured with fruit.*

yoke *noun*
1 a curved piece of wood put across the necks of animals pulling a cart. **2** a curved piece of wood put across somebody's shoulders to carry a load on either side.

yolk *noun*
(rhymes with *coke*)
the yellow part of an egg.

Yom Kippur *noun*
an important religious day for Jews.

yonder *adverb and adjective*
(*old-fashioned use*) that is over there. *Yonder peasant, who is he?*

Yorkshire pudding *noun*
a pudding made of batter and usually eaten with roast beef.

you *pronoun*
1 the person or people someone is speaking to. *Who are you?* **2** people; everyone; anyone. *You can never be too sure.*

young *adjective*
born not long ago; that has existed for a short time; not old.

young *noun*
children or young animals. *The hen defended its young.*

youngster *noun*
a young person.

your or **yours** *adjective*
belonging to you; of you.

yours *pronoun*
1 the things belonging to you. *I've found this pen of yours.* **2 yours faithfully, yours sincerely, yours truly,** ways of ending a letter before you sign it.

yourself *pronoun* **(yourselves)**
1 you and no one else. **2 by yourself,** on your own.

youth *noun*
1 being young; the period when you are young. *She was a swimmer in her youth.* **2** a young person, especially a young man. *a youth of 16.* **3** young people. *a youth club.*
youthful *adjective*

Z

zeal *noun*
enthusiasm; keenness.
zealous *adjective,* **zealously** *adverb*

zebra *noun*
(*say* **zeb**-ră)
1 an animal like a horse with black and white stripes. *Zebras are found in Africa.* **2 zebra-crossing,** part of a road marked with broad white stripes for pedestrians to cross.

zero *noun*
1 nought; the figure 0; nothing. **2 zero hour,** the time when something is planned to start.

zest *noun*
zeal; great enjoyment or interest.

zigzag *noun*
a line or route full of sharp turns from one side to the other.

zigzag *verb* **(zigzagged, zigzagging)**
to move in a zigzag.

zinc *noun*
a white metal.

zip *noun*
1 a zip-fastener. **2** a sharp sound like a bullet going through the air. **3** liveliness; energy.

zip *verb* **(zipped, zipping)**
1 to fasten something with a zip-fastener. **2** to move quickly with a sharp sound.

zip-fastener or **zipper** *noun*
a device with two rows of small teeth for joining two pieces of material together.

zodiac *noun*
(*say* **zoh**-di-ak)
an area of the sky divided into twelve equal parts in astrology.

zone *noun*
a district; an area. *a parking zone.*

zoo *noun*
a place where wild animals are kept so that people can look at them.

zoology *noun*
(*say* zoo-**ol**-ŏ-ji or zoh-**ol**-ŏ-ji)
the scientific study of animals.
zoological *adjective,* **zoologist** *noun*

zoom *verb*
to move very quickly, especially upwards.

Countries of the World

Country	People	Adjective
Afghanistan (af-**gan**-i-stahn)	Afghans	Afghan
Albania (al-**bay**-ni-ă)	Albanians	Albanian
Algeria (al-**jeer**-i-ă)	Algerians	Algerian
America (see United States of America)		
Andorra (and-**o**-ră)	Andorrans	Andorran
Angola (an-**goh**-lă)	Angolans	Angolan
Antigua (an-**tee**-gă)	Antiguans	Antiguan
Argentina (ar-jĕn-**teen**-ă)	Argentinians	Argentinian or Argentine
Australia (oss-**tray**-li-ă)	Australians	Australian
Austria (**oss**-stri-ă)	Austrians	Austrian
the Bahamas (bă-**hah**-măz)	Bahamians	Bahamian
Bahrain (bah-**rayn**)	Bahrainis	Bahraini
Bangladesh (bang-lă-**desh**)	Bangladeshis	Bangladeshi
Barbados (bar-**bay**-dŏs)	Barbadians	Barbadian
Belgium	Belgians	Belgian
Belize (bĕl-**eez**)	Belizians	Belizian
Benin (ben-**een**)	Beninese	Beninese
Bermuda (ber-**mew**-dă)	Bermudians	Bermudian
Bhutan (boo-**tahn**)	Bhutanese	Bhutanese
Bolivia (bŏ-**liv**-i-ă)	Bolivians	Bolivian
Botswana (bot-**swah**-nă)		
Brazil	Brazilians	Brazilian
Britain	British	British
Brunei (**broon**- i)		
Bulgaria (bul-**gair**-i-ă)	Bulgarians	Bulgarian
Burma	Burmese	Burmese
Burundi (bŭ-**run**-di)	Burundians	Burundian
Cameroon (kam-er-**oon**)	Cameroonians	Cameroonian
Canada	Canadians	Canadian
Cape Verde Islands (kayp **verd**)	Cape Verdeans	Cape Verdean
Cayman Islands	Cayman Islanders	
Central African Republic		
Chad	Chadians	Chadian
Chile (**chil**-i)	Chileans	Chilean
China	Chinese	Chinese
Colombia (kŏ-**lom**-bi-ă)	Colombians	Colombian
Comoros (kŏm-**or**-ohz)	Comorans	Comoran
Congo	Congolese	Congolese
Costa Rica (kos-tă **ree**-ka)	Costa Ricans	Costa Rican
Cuba	Cubans	Cuban
Cyprus	Cypriots	Cypriot
Czechoslovakia (chek-oh-slŏ-**vak**-i-ă)	Czechs or Czechoslovaks	Czech or Czechoslovak
Denmark	Danes	Danish
Djibouti (ji-**boo**-ti)	Djiboutians	Djiboutian
Dominica (dom-in-**ee**-kă)	Dominicans	Dominican
Dominican Republic (dŏm-**in**-i-kăn)	Dominicans	Dominican

Country	People	Adjective
Ecuador (**ek**-wă-dor)	Ecuadoreans	Ecuadorean
Egypt	Egyptians	Egyptian
El Salvador (el **sal**-vă-dor)	Salvadoreans	Salvadorean
England	English	English
Equatorial Guinea (**gi**-ni)	Equatorial Guineans	
Ethiopia (eeth-i-**oh**-pi-ă)	Ethiopians	Ethiopian
Falkland Islands	Falkland Islanders	
Fiji (**fee**-jee)	Fijians	Fijian
Finland	Finns	Finnish
France	French	French
Gabon (gab-**on**)	Gabonese	Gabonese
Gambia (**gam**-bi-ă)	Gambians	Gambian
German Democratic Republic (East Germany)	East Germans	East German
Germany, Federal Republic of (West Germany)	West Germans	West German
Ghana (**gah**-nă)	Ghanaians	Ghanaian
Gibraltar	Gibraltarians	Gibraltarian
Great Britain (see Britain)		
Greece	Greeks	Greek
Grenada (grĕn-**ay**-dă)	Grenadians	Grenadian
Guatemala (gwat-i-**mah**-lă)	Guatemalans	Guatemalan
Guinea (**gi**-ni)	Guineans	Guinean
Guinea-Bissau (gi-ni **bis**-ow)		
Guyana (gy-**an**-ă)	Guyanese	Guyanese
Haiti (**hy**-ti)	Haitians	Haitian
Holland (see Netherlands)		
Honduras (hon-**dewr**-ăs)	Hondurans	Honduran
Hong Kong		
Hungary	Hungarians	Hungarian
Iceland	Icelanders	Icelandic
India	Indians	Indian
Indonesia (in-dŏ-**nee**-zhă)	Indonesians	Indonesian
Iran (i-**rahn**)	Iranians	Iranian
Iraq (i-**rahk**)	Iraqis	Iraqi
Ireland, Republic of	Irish	Irish
Israel (**iz**-rayl)	Israelis	Israeli
Italy	Italians	Italian
Ivory Coast		
Jamaica	Jamaicans	Jamaican
Japan	Japanese	Japanese
Jordan	Jordanians	Jordanian
Kampuchea (kam-puu-**chee**-á)	Kampucheans	Kampuchean
Kenya (**ken**-yă)	Kenyans	Kenyan
Kiribati (ki-ri-**bas**)		Kiribati
Korea (kŏ-**ree**-ă)	Koreans	Korean
Kuwait (koo-**wayt**)	Kuwaitis	Kuwaiti
Laos (**lah**-oss)	Laotians	Laotian
Lebanon (**leb**-ă-nŏn)	Lebanese	Lebanese

Country	People	Adjective
Lesotho (lĕ-**soo**-too)	Basotho	
Liberia (ly-**beer**-i-ă)	Liberians	Liberian
Libya	Libyans	Libyan
Liechtenstein (**lik**-tĕn-styn)	Liechtensteiners	
Luxemburg	Luxemburgers	
Madagascar	Malagasies	Malagasy
Malawi (mă-**lah**-wi)	Malawians	Malawian
Malaysia (mă-**lay**-zhă)	Malaysians	Malaysian
Maldives, the (**mawl**-divz)	Maldivians	Maldivian
Mali (**mah**-li)	Malians	Malian
Malta	Maltese	Maltese
Mauritania (mo-ri-**tay**-ni-ă)	Mauritanians	Mauritanian
Mauritius (mă-**rish**-ŭs)	Mauritians	Mauritian
Mexico	Mexicans	Mexican
Monaco (**mon**-ă-koh)	Monegasques	Monegasque
Mongolia (mong-**oh**-li-ă)	Mongolians	Mongolian
Montserrat (mont-se-**rat**)		
Morocco (mŏ-**rok**-oh)	Moroccans	Moroccan
Mozambique (moh-zam-**beek**)	Mozambicans	Mozambican
Nauru (now-**roo**)	Nauruans	Nauruan
Nepal (nĕ-**pawl**)	Nepalese	Nepalese
Netherlands (**ne**th-er-lăndz)	Dutch	Dutch
New Zealand	New Zealanders	
Nicaragua (nik-er-**ag**-yoo-ă)	Nicaraguans	Nicaraguan
Niger (nee-zhair)		
Nigeria (ny-**jeer**-i-ă)	Nigerians	Nigerian
Northern Ireland	Northern Irish	Northern Irish
Norway	Norwegians	Norwegian
Oman (oh-**mahn**)	Omanis	Omani
Pakistan (pah-kis-**tahn**)	Pakistanis	Pakistani
Panama (pan-ă-**mah**)	Panamanians	Panamanian
Papua New Guinea (**pap**-oo-ă)	Papua New Guineans	Papua New Guinean
Paraguay (**pa**-ră-gwy)	Paraguayans	Paraguayan
Peru (per-**oo**)	Peruvians	Peruvian
Philipines (**fil**-i-peenz)	Filipinos	Filipino or Philippine
Pitcairn Islands	Pitcairn Islanders	
Poland	Poles	Polish
Portugal	Portuguese	Portuguese
Puerto Rico (pwer-toh **ree**-koh)	Puerto Ricans	Puerto Rican
Qatar (**kat**-ar)	Qataris	Qatari
Romania (roo-**may**-ni-ă)	Romanians	Romanian
Russia (see Union of Soviet Socialist Republics)		
Rwanda (roo-**an**-dă)	Rwandans	Rwandan
St. Helena	St. Helenians	St. Helenian
St. Kitts-Nevis-Anguilla		
St. Lucia	St. Lucians	St. Lucian
St. Vincent	Vincentians	Vincentian
San Marino (san mă-**ree**-noh)		

Country	People	Adjective
São Tomé and Principe (sah-oo tŏm-**ay** and **prin**-si-pi)		
Saudi Arabia (**sow**-di ă-**ray**-bi-ă)	Saudi Arabians	Saudi Arabian
Scotland	Scots	Scots or Scottish
Senegal (sen-i-**gawl**)	Senegalese	Senegalese
Seychelles (say-**shelz**)	Seychellois	Seychellois
Sierra Leone (si-**e**-ră li-**ohn**)	Sierra Leoneans	Sierra Leonean
Singapore	Singaporeans	Singaporean
Solomon Islands	Solomon Islanders	
Somalia (sŏm-**ah**-li-ă)	Somalis	Somali
South Africa	South Africans	South African
Soviet Union (see Union of Soviet Socialist Republics)		
Spain	Spaniards	Spanish
Sri Lanka (sri **lank**-ă)	Sri Lankans	Sri Lankan
Sudan (sŭ-**dahn**)	Sudanese	Sudanese
Surinam (soor-i-**nam**)	Surinamers or Surinamese	Surinamese
Swaziland (**swah**-zi-land)	Swazis	Swazi
Sweden	Swedes	Swedish
Switzerland	Swiss	Swiss
Syria (**si**-ri-ă)	Syrians	Syrian
Taiwan (ty-**wann**)	Taiwanese	Taiwanese
Tanzania (tan-ză-**nee**-ă)	Tanzanians	Tanzanian
Thailand (**ty**-land)	Thais	Thai
Togo (**toh**-goh)	Togolese	Togolese
Tonga	Tongans	Tongan
Trinidad and Tobago (tŏ-**bay**-goh)	Trinidadians or Tobagans	Trinidadian or Tobagan
Tunisia (tew-**niz**-i-ă)	Tunisians	Tunisian
Turkey	Turks	Turkish
Tuvalu (too-**vah**-loo)	Tuvaluans	Tuvaluan
Uganda (yoo-**gan**-dă)	Ugandans	Ugandan
Union of Soviet Socialist Republics	Russians	Russian or Soviet
United Arab Emirates		
United Kingdom	British	British
United States of America	Americans	American
Upper Volta	Upper Voltans	Upper Voltan
Uruguay (**yoor**-ŭ-gwy)	Uruguayans	Uruguayan
Vanuatu (van-wah-**too**)		
Vatican City		Vatican
Venezuela (ven-ez-**way**-lă)	Venezuelans	Venezuelan
Vietnam	Vietnamese	Vietnamese
Virgin Islands	Virgin Islanders	
Wales	Welsh	Welsh
Western Samoa (să-**moh**-ă)	Western Samoans	Western Samoan
Yemen Arab Republic	Yemenis	Yemeni
Yemen, People's Democratic Republic of	South Yemenis	South Yemeni
Yugoslavia (yoo-goh-**slah**-vi-ă)	Yugoslavs	Yugoslav
Zaire (zah-**eer**)	Zaireans	Zairean
Zambia (**zam**-bi-ă)	Zambians	Zambian
Zimbabwe (zim-**bahb**-wi)	Zimbabweans	Zimbabwean

Punctuation

Punctuation marks are used in writing as signs to the reader to help him understand the structure of what he is reading, and, if he is reading aloud, to tell him when to pause, and when and how to inflect his voice. We could probably manage without punctuation altogether, but it would make reading much more difficult. On the other hand, too much punctuation is both distracting and unnecessary, so it is important to know what each mark stands for and how it is used.

. full stop

a A full stop is used to mark the end of a sentence.

My name is Peter Brown. I live in Birmingham.

b A full stop is sometimes used to mark an abbreviation.

Mr. J. R. Smith   i.e.   B.B.C.

, comma

a A comma is used to separate items in lists of words, phrases, or clauses.

The vase contained red, pink, yellow, and white roses.

If you take your time, stay calm, think hard, and write clearly, you will pass your exam.

b A comma is often used after a clause or phrase which comes before the main clause, especially when this helps to make the sense of the sentence clearer.

When the sun is shining, everyone feels happier.

To get there on time, she left half an hour early.

c A comma is used before and after any word or group of words, such as a clause or comment, which interrupts the sentence, and before any such group which is added on to the sentence.

The fire, although it had been lit several hours before, was still blazing fiercely.

You should, indeed you must, report this to the police.

I think it's time for tea, don't you?

d A comma is sometimes used to separate clauses linked by a conjunction (such as *and, as, but, for, or*), especially when the first clause is long.

We had been hoping to go to the seaside for a holiday, but had to change our plans at the last minute.

; semicolon

A semicolon marks a longer pause than a comma. It is used to separate two or more clauses which are of more or less equal importance in a sentence, but are not (usually) joined by a conjunction.

The sun was getting low; the shadows were growing longer; it was time to go home.

: colon

a A colon is used before a list of things or examples, and is often preceded by phrases like *such as, for example, as follows*.

Please bring the following things to school tomorrow: pencils, paper, a rubber, and a ruler.

b A colon is often used in place of a semicolon when the clause which follows it explains or develops the idea in the first clause.

The garden had been neglected for a long time: it was overgrown and full of weeds.

? question mark

A question mark is used at the end of a *direct* question:

What is your name? Where do you live?

but not in an *indirect* question:

He asked me what my name was and where I lived.

! exclamation mark

An exclamation mark is used at the end of a sentence or a remark which expresses great surprise, anger, or some other strong feeling.

'What a wonderful surprise!' she cried.

Go away and never come back!

() brackets

Brackets are used to separate extra information or some additional comment from the rest of the sentence.

Schooldays (so we are told) are the happiest days of our lives.

Note: brackets are also called **parentheses** (*say* pă-**ren**-thi-seez).

— dash

a A dash is used instead of a colon or a semicolon to make the writing more vivid or dramatic. It is longer than a hyphen.

So you have been lying to me all along—how can I ever trust you again?

b One dash or two can be used in place of brackets.

Schooldays—so we are told—are the happiest days of our lives.

Schooldays are the happiest days of our lives—or so we are told.

' ' or " " quotation marks or inverted commas

a Quotation marks are used to enclose all words and punctuation in direct speech. When direct speech is quoted within direct speech, double quotation marks are used within single quotation marks (or sometimes *vice versa*).

'Can you tell me the way to the station?' I asked.

'Did you say "Which way is the station?" or something else?' asked the judge.

b Quotation marks are used when you want to draw special attention to a word or phrase that is unusual in some way.

Next, the clay pot has to be 'fired'.

'Giggle' and 'tingle' are intransitive verbs.

' apostrophe

a An apostrophe is used to show a shortened form, when one or more letters or numbers have been left out.

I'm (= I am)   *we're* (= we are)   *it's* (= it is *or* it has)
can't (= cannot)   *haven't* (= have not)
The Beatles became famous in '62 or '63 (= 1962 or 1963).

b An apostrophe is used with *s* to show who owns something.

the dog's bone   = the bone of the dog
the dog's bones   = the bones of the dog
the dogs' bones   = the bones of the dogs
(*but* The dog is eating its (*not* it's) bone.)

one woman's coat   *two women's coats*

c An apostrophe is used to show the plural of letters in the alphabet.

There are three l's in syllable.